Elements of
Language

INTRODUCTORY COURSE

Judith L. Irvin

Lee Odell

Richard Vacca

Renée Hobbs

Grammar, Usage, and Mechanics
Instructional Framework by

John E. Warriner

HOLT, RINEHART AND WINSTON

A Harcourt Education Company

Orlando • **Austin** • New York • San Diego • London

JUDITH L. IRVIN helped establish the conceptual basis for the reading strand of *Elements of Language*. Dr. Irvin taught middle school for several years before entering her career as a university professor. She now teaches courses in curriculum and instructional leadership and literacy at Florida State University. Her many publications include *Reading and the High School Student: Strategies to Enhance Literacy* (2nd edition with Buehl and Klemp) and *Integrating Literacy and Learning in the Content Area Classroom* (3rd edition with Buehl and Radcliffe). Her latest book (with Meltzer and Dukes) is the result of a Carnegie-funded project and is titled *Taking Action: A Leadership Model for Improving Adolescent Literacy*, published by the Association for Supervision and Curriculum Development (2007).

LEE ODELL helped establish the pedagogical framework for the composition strand of *Elements of Language*. In addition, he guided the development of the scope and sequence and pedagogical design of the Writing Workshops. Dr. Odell is Professor of Composition Theory and Research and has served as Director of the Writing Program at Rensselaer Polytechnic Institute. He began his career teaching English in middle and high schools. More recently he has worked with teachers in grades K–12 to establish a program that involves students from all disciplines in writing across the curriculum and for communities outside their classrooms. Dr. Odell's most recent book (with Susan Katz) is *Writing in a Visual Age* (2005). He is Past Chair of the Conference on College Composition and Communication and of NCTE's Assembly for Research.

RICHARD VACCA helped establish the conceptual basis for the reading strand of *Elements of Language*. In addition, he guided the development of the pedagogical design and the scope and sequence of skills in the Reading Workshops. Dr. Vacca is Professor Emeritus of Literacy Education at Kent State University and is a past President of the International Reading Association. Originally a middle school and high school teacher, Dr. Vacca served as project director of the Cleveland Writing Project for several years. He is the co-author of *Content Area Reading; Reading and Learning to Read;* and articles and chapters related to adolescents'

literacy development. In 1989, Dr. Vacca received the College Reading Association's A.B. Herr Award for Outstanding Contributions to Reading Education.

RENÉE HOBBS helped develop the theoretical framework for the viewing and representing strand of *Elements of Language*. She guided the development of the scope and sequence and served as the authority on terminology, definitions, and pedagogy. Dr. Hobbs is a Professor in the School of Communication and Theater and Director of the Media Education Lab at Temple University. Active in the field of media education for more than twenty years, Dr. Hobbs created the Harvard Institute in Media Education at the Harvard Graduate School of Education. She created Assignment: Media Literacy for the Maryland State Department of Education and Viewing and Representing: Media Literacy in Texas for the Texas Education Agency. She works actively in staff development in school districts nationwide and conducts research to explore the relationship between media literacy and the development of print literacy skills. Dr. Hobbs has contributed articles and chapters on media, technology, and education to many publications. Her latest book, *Reading the Media: Media Literacy in High School English* (Teachers College Press, 2007), documents the impact of a longstanding media literacy program on the development of adolescents' reading comprehension skills.

JOHN E. WARRINER was a high school English teacher when he developed the original organizational structure for his classic *English Grammar and Composition* series. The approach pioneered by Mr. Warriner was distinctive, and the editorial staff of Holt, Rinehart and Winston have worked diligently to retain the unique qualities of his pedagogy. For the same reason, HRW continues to credit Mr. Warriner as an author of *Elements of Language* in recognition of his groundbreaking work. John Warriner also co-authored the *English Workshop* series and was editor of *Short Stories: Characters in Conflict*. Throughout his long career, however, teaching remained Mr. Warriner's major interest, and he taught for thirty-two years in junior and senior high schools and in college.

The following teachers and students worked with HRW's editorial staff to provide models of student writing for the book.

Teachers

Jane Anderson
Garfield Elementary School
Sand Springs, Oklahoma

Peter J. Caron
Cumberland Middle School
Cumberland, Rhode Island

Dorothy Harrington
Marshall Middle School
Beaumont, Texas

Debra Hester
Richbourg Middle School
Crestview, Florida

Dana Humphrey
North Middle School
O'Fallon, Missouri

Students

Natalie Banta and Amy Tidwell
Olympus Junior High School
Salt Lake City, Utah

Diana DeGarmo
Garfield Elementary School
Sand Springs, Oklahoma

Tyler Duckworth
Liberty Middle School
Morganton, North Carolina

Matthew Hester
Richbourg Middle School
Crestview, Florida

Genna Offerman
Marshall Middle School
Beaumont, Texas

Anthony C. Rodrigues
Cumberland Middle School
Cumberland, Rhode Island

Stephanie Thompson
North Middle School
O'Fallon, Missouri

The following teachers participated in the pre-publication field test or review of prototype materials for the *Elements of Language* series.

Nadene Adams
Robert Gray Middle School
Portland, Oregon

Carol Alves
Apopka High School
Apopka, Florida

Susan Atkinson
O. P. Norman Junior High School
Kaufman, Texas

Sheryl L. Babione
Fremont Ross High School
Fremont, Ohio

Jane Baker
Elkins High School
Missouri City, Texas

Martha Barnard
Scarborough High School
Houston, Texas

Jennifer S. Barr
James Bowie High School
Austin, Texas

Leslie Benefield
Reed Middle School
Duncanville, Texas

Gina Birdsall
Irving High School
Irving, Texas

Sara J. Brennan
Murchison Middle School
Austin, Texas

Janelle Brinck
Leander Middle School
Leander, Texas

Geraldine K. Brooks
William B. Travis High School
Austin, Texas

Peter J. Caron
Cumberland Middle School
Cumberland, Rhode Island

Patty Cave
O. P. Norman Junior High School
Kaufman, Texas

Mary Cathyrne Coe
Pocatello High School
Pocatello, Idaho

Continued

Geri-Lee DeGennaro
Tarpon Springs High School
Tarpon Springs, Florida

Karen Dendy
Stephen F. Austin Middle School
Irving, Texas

Dianne Franz
Tarpon Springs Middle School
Tarpon Springs, Florida

Doris F. Frazier
East Millbrook Magnet Middle
  School
Raleigh, North Carolina

Shayne G. Goodrum
C. E. Jordan High School
Durham, North Carolina

Bonnie L. Hall
St. Ann School
Lansing, Illinois

Doris Ann Hall
Forest Meadow Junior High
  School
Dallas, Texas

James M. Harris
Mayfield High School
Mayfield Village, Ohio

Lynne Hoover
Fremont Ross High School
Fremont, Ohio

Patricia A. Humphreys
James Bowie High School
Austin, Texas

Jennifer L. Jones
Oliver Wendell Holmes Middle
  School
Dallas, Texas

Kathryn R. Jones
Murchison Middle School
Austin, Texas

Bonnie Just
Narbonne High School
Harbor City, California

Vincent Kimball
Patterson High School #405
Baltimore, Maryland

Nancy C. Long
MacArthur High School
Houston, Texas

Carol M. Mackey
Ft. Lauderdale Christian School
Ft. Lauderdale, Florida

Jan Jennings McCown
Johnston High School
Austin, Texas

Alice Kelly McCurdy
Rusk Middle School
Dallas, Texas

Elizabeth Morris
Northshore High School
Slidell, Louisiana

Victoria Reis
Western High School
Ft. Lauderdale, Florida

Dean Richardson
Scarborough High School
Houston, Texas

Susan M. Rogers
Freedom High School
Morganton, North Carolina

Sammy Rusk
North Mesquite High School
Mesquite, Texas

Carole B. San Miguel
James Bowie High School
Austin, Texas

Jane Saunders
William B. Travis High School
Austin, Texas

Gina Sawyer
Reed Middle School
Duncanville, Texas

Laura R. Schauermann
MacArthur High School
Houston, Texas

Stephen Shearer
MacArthur High School
Houston, Texas

Elizabeth Curry Smith
Tarpon Springs High School
Tarpon Springs, Florida

Jeannette M. Spain
Stephen F. Austin High School
Sugar Land, Texas

Carrie Speer
Northshore High School
Slidell, Louisiana

Trina Steffes
MacArthur High School
Houston, Texas

Andrea G. Freirich Stewart
Freedom High School
Morganton, North Carolina

Diana O. Torres
Johnston High School
Austin, Texas

Jan Voorhees
Whitesboro High School
Marcy, New York

Ann E. Walsh
Bedichek Middle School
Austin, Texas

Mary Jane Warden
Onahan School
Chicago, Illinois

Beth Westbrook
Covington Middle School
Austin, Texas

Char-Lene Wilkins
Morenci Area High School
Morenci, Michigan

CONTENTS IN BRIEF

CONTENTS

The Sentence

CHAPTER 1

Subject and Predicate, Kinds of Sentences **48**

Parts of Speech Overview

CHAPTER 2

Noun, Pronoun, Adjective **70**

Parts of Speech Overview
Verb, Adverb, Preposition, Conjunction,

CHAPTER

3

Contents   **ix**

The Phrase and the Clause

CHAPTER

4

Prepositional Phrases, Independent and Subordinate Clauses, Sentence Structure **120**

Using Verbs Correctly
Principal Parts, Regular and Irregular

CHAPTER

7

Using Pronouns Correctly
Subject and Object Forms **222**

CHAPTER

8

Using Modifiers Correctly
Comparison and Placement **242**

CHAPTER
9

Punctuation
Underlining (Italics), Quotation Marks,
Apostrophes, Hyphens **334**

Spelling

Correcting Common Errors

CHAPTER 22

Responding to a Novel **604**

Informational Text

Exposition

Sharing Your Research 638

Informational Text

Exposition

Informational Text

Persuasion

Making a Difference 678

MODELS

STUDENT'S OVERVIEW

Elements of Language is divided into four major parts.

PART 1 Grammar, Usage, and Mechanics

These are the basics that will help you make your writing correct and polished—the structure of language, the rules that govern how language is used, and the nuts and bolts of correct written English. Each chapter includes

- a Diagnostic Preview to measure your understanding of chapter content

- instruction and practice exercises that introduce and build on grammar, usage, and mechanics concepts

- marginal Help, Tips & Tricks, and Think as a Reader/Writer features to offer useful information in a condensed format

- a Chapter Review to reinforce your mastery of concepts

- a Writing Application that guides you to use acquired language skills in your own writing

PART 2 Sentences and Paragraphs

Learn to construct clear and effective sentences and paragraphs—what parts to include, how to organize ideas, and how to write these essential parts of compositions with style.

PART 3 Communications

This section ties together the essential skills and strategies you use in all types of communication—reading, writing, listening, speaking, viewing, and representing.

Reading Workshops In these workshops, you read an article, a story, an editorial—a real-life example of a type of writing you will later compose on your own. In addition, these workshops help you practice the reading process through

- a Reading Skill and Reading Focus specific to each type of writing

- Vocabulary Mini-Lessons to help you understand unfamiliar words, and

- Test-Taking Mini-Lessons targeting common reading objectives

Writing Workshops In these workshops, you brainstorm ideas and use the writing process to produce your own article, story, editorial—and more. These workshops also include

- Writing and Critical-Thinking Mini-Lessons to help you master important aspects of each type of writing

- an organizational framework and models to guide your writing

- evaluation charts with concrete steps for revising

- Connections to Literature and Connections to Life, activities that extend writing workshop skills and concepts to other areas of your life

- Test-Taking Mini-Lessons to help you respond to writing prompts for tests

Focus on Speaking and Listening
Focus on Viewing and Representing

This is your chance to sharpen your skills in presenting your ideas visually and orally and to learn how to take a more critical view of what you hear and see.

PART 4 **Quick Reference Handbook**

Use this handy guide any time you need concise tips to help you communicate more effectively—whether you need to find information in a variety of media, make sense of what you read, prepare for tests, or present your ideas in a published document, a speech, or a visual.

Elements of Language on the Internet

Put the communication strategies in *Elements of Language* to work by logging on to the Internet. At the *Elements of Language* Internet site, you can dissect the prose of professional writers, crack the codes of the advertising industry, and find out how your communication skills can help you in the real world.

As you move through *Elements of Language*, you will find the best online resources at **go.hrw.com.**

Taking Tests: Strategies and Practice

Taking Reading Tests

In the years ahead, you'll probably take many **standardized tests**. A standardized reading test contains **reading passages** followed by **multiple-choice questions**. Some tests also have an open-ended **essay question**. The following strategies and practice will help you with the reading sections of Tennessee's achievement test and with other tests.

THINKING IT THROUGH

Reading Test Strategies

▶ **STEP 1** **Watch your time.** Divide the test time by the number of questions to estimate how much time you can spend on each question. Check as you work to see if you need to speed up.

▶ **STEP 2** **Concentrate.** Carefully read the directions and any introduction to the reading passage. As you read the passage, don't let your attention wander. If you're allowed to mark the test booklet, underline or circle key words.

▶ **STEP 3** **Understand the question.** Look for tricky words like *not* and *except;* they require you to choose an answer that is false or opposite in some way. Don't fall for answers that make true statements but don't answer the question that's being asked. Never choose an answer until you've read *all* of the choices.

▶ **STEP 4** **Make educated guesses.** You may recognize the correct answer easily. If not, first get rid of the one or two answers you know are wrong. Then, from the remaining answers, choose the one you think is most likely to be right.

▶ **STEP 5** **Keep going.** Don't get stuck. Skip difficult questions, and go back to them later if you have time at the end.

▶ **STEP 6** **Don't lose your place.** Match each question to the number on the answer sheet. If you skip a question, be sure to skip that number on the answer sheet.

▶ **STEP 7** **Take another look.** Before time runs out, try answering questions you skipped the first time round. Be sure to check your answer sheet carefully, and erase any stray pencil marks.

TIP Before the test, ask about how the test is scored. If no points are taken off for wrong answers, plan to answer every question. If wrong answers count against you, answer questions you know and those you can answer with an educated guess.

Read the following passages carefully. Then, choose the **best** answer to each question.

Do Animals Think?

by Ellen Lambeth

This panther looks deep in thought. But don't let that pose fool you. Animals often do things that may make you think they're thinking.

Thinking about thinking is tricky, because thinking isn't something you can see. It goes on inside the brain. We know when we're doing it. But who can tell if an animal is thinking? It's not easy.

For example, check out the animal actions below. Do they show that the animals are thinking—or not thinking? What do you think? (We'll tell you later what scientists think.)

- A bird builds a nest that's just right for its eggs and babies.

- An octopus uses its arms to open a jar with food inside.

- A lion sneaks around behind its prey and then chases it toward another lion that's hiding and waiting.

- A salmon returns from the ocean to the same stream where it hatched.

"Do Animals Think?" by Ellen Lambeth from *Ranger Rick,* vol. 31, issue 3, March 1997. Copyright © 1997 by **National Wildlife Federation.** Reproduced by permission of the publisher.

What Is Thinking?

It may be easier to first explain what thinking isn't. For example, it isn't needed for things animals do automatically—like when a beaver dams a stream with sticks, mud, and grasses.

The beaver is making a pond, but it didn't learn how to do that. It doesn't think about doing it, either. Some animals just do what they do—kind of like robots—and they do it the same way every time. Scientists call this kind of behavior instinct.

But what about when an animal does learn to do something? Is that thinking? For example, you can teach a dog to give you its paw and "shake hands" for a treat. Even a worm can learn to follow a maze! But most scientists don't believe that the worm—or even the dog—is thinking when it learns such tricks.

A sheepdog at work, though, is a different story. One of the dog's jobs is to single out one sheep from a flock. The dog knows how to do that because it was trained.

But say the sheep doesn't want to leave the flock. It moves this way or that, or tries to duck behind another sheep. The dog must figure out a plan and keep changing that plan until it "outsmarts" the sheep, cutting it away from the others. Many people would agree that the sheepdog must be thinking about what it's doing.

Thinking Tests

For a long time, scientists didn't study animal thinking. Most of them didn't believe that animals could think. They thought humans were the only thinking animals.

Now more scientists are studying this subject. But it's very hard to prove things that no one can see or measure. So some scientists decided to take a look at brains.

Is bigger better? No. Cow brains are bigger than dog brains, but that doesn't make cows smarter than dogs. And squirrels have some of the biggest brains of all for their body size. But squirrels aren't even close to being the smartest animals in the world. So the size of a brain may give some clues about brain power, but it doesn't prove anything.

Other scientists study thinking by watching how animals solve problems. They watch animals in the wild. Or they set up thinking tests in a lab.

For example, a scientist might put some food just out of an animal's reach. One kind of animal may grab a stick and use it to slide the food over. Another kind might not be able to figure out a way to get the food. Some scientists think animals that have lots of problems to solve must be smarter than animals with simple lives.

Scientists also study certain kinds of behavior for clues about thinking. They watch for three things: whether animals use tools, how they act with each other, and how they communicate. . . .

So, Think About It

What did you decide about the animals in the beginning of this story? Well, the bird and salmon are using instinct. Their behaviors are amazing, but they stay the same, no matter what. The lion and octopus are most likely thinking. Why? Because each is carrying out some kind of plan to solve a problem. And if things were different, they could change their plans and solve their problems in different ways.

Many people think certain animals—such as whales and dolphins, monkeys and apes, wolves and dogs, crows and jays—are especially smart. But each might be smart at some things and not at others. It all depends on the lives they lead.

More and more scientists are coming up with new ways to study animal brain power. They often disagree. But many are sure that we humans aren't the only thinkers. And that leaves us with plenty to think about!

1. What is the main idea of this passage?
   A. There is evidence that some animals can think.
   B. Smarter animals have bigger brains than less intelligent animals.
   C. Nearly all animals have the ability to solve problems.
   D. Some animals can use man-made tools.

2. Which of the following actions shows that the animal might be thinking?
   F. A bird living in the north migrates to a warm climate in the fall.
   G. A bird speaks in return for a treat from its owner.
   H. A bird soaks dog food in water to soften it.
   J. A baby bird flies for the first time.

3. Which experiment might a scientist use to determine whether an animal is thinking?
   A. putting food for it in a maze
   B. teaching it to perform a trick
   C. setting up a problem and giving it a tool
   D. watching it raise its young in the wild

4. *Instinct* is repeated behavior that
   F. parents must teach their young
   G. requires thinking and problem solving
   H. imitates what everyone else is doing
   J. is not learned and does not change

5. According to the passage, how do the beaver and the sheepdog differ?
   A. Both animals think, but the sheepdog's actions prove it is smarter.
   B. The sheepdog thinks while herding, but the beaver uses instinct to build a dam.
   C. Scientists believe that the sheepdog is working and the beaver is not.
   D. The beaver is less intelligent than the sheepdog because its brain is smaller.

6. What does *cutting* mean in the following sentence?
   The dog must . . . keep changing that plan until it 'outsmarts' the sheep, cutting it away from the others.
   F. piercing with a sharp object
   G. separating something from a group
   H. pretending not to see someone
   J. shortening or making less

7. Why does the writer include the bulleted (•) items on the first page of the passage?
   A. to prepare readers by making them think about specific animal behaviors
   B. to show readers how the rest of the passage will be organized
   C. to give readers examples of experiments scientists have done
   D. to test whether readers are paying attention to the topic

8. From studying animals' brains, scientists have concluded that
   F. bigger brains indicate higher intelligence
   G. smaller brains indicate higher intelligence
   H. smaller brains indicate less intelligence
   J. brain size is not directly related to intelligence

Write several paragraphs in response to *one* of the following questions:

9. The passage talks about three kinds of animal behavior: instinct, trained behavior, and thought. Explain the differences among these behaviors, and give an example of each kind.

10. So, what is your answer—*do* animals think? State your opinion and support it with your own observations and with details from the article.

CRITTER CREW

by Anna Mearns

When Hurricane Andrew hit South Florida, it wiped out the homes, food, and water supplies of thousands of people.

That was bad enough. But just imagine what a hurricane can do to the cage of a wild animal. R-i-p! Many cages were torn open by the storm. And out dashed the animals!

"It was like a nightmare," says Todd Hardwick. Todd runs a business in Miami, Florida, called Pesky Critters. He and his helpers recapture escaped animals. They also take away wild animals that have gotten into people's homes.

"In the first few days after the hurricane," Todd says, "we saw thousands of monkeys running loose. One day we saw 400 of them up in the trees! And we saw strange animals that looked like tiny reindeer.

"They were running and jumping over fences in backyards." Todd also found boa constrictors, parrots, lizards—and one very hungry cougar (mountain lion).

Cougar Capture

Just after the hurricane, Todd got a call from a man looking for his lost female cougar. Todd looked for the cougar for almost a month, but couldn't find her.

Finally, Todd explains, he got a call from the mother of a three-year-old girl. The girl had found a huge, wild cat under her house! The frightened mother called Todd for help.

Todd and his assistant, Jill Voight, came right away. Just as they suspected, it was the missing cougar.

The only way to get close to the animal was to crawl under the house. So Todd went in on his hands and knees and shot the cougar with a tranquilizer (TRANK-weh-lie-zer) dart. The dart contained medicine to put her to sleep.

The cougar dashed out as soon as she was shot. Then the medicine started to work. When the cougar became very sleepy, Todd put on special long gloves and caught her.

Finally, with Jill's help, he put her in a cage. When he delivered the cougar to her owner, the man started to cry for joy. He was so happy to see her alive!

Python Under the House

Recapturing escaped cougars is all in a day's work for Todd. He's used to it—there are lots of weird animals where he lives. That's because lots of people bring wild animals into Miami by plane and by boat. And it's easy to keep animals there because the climate is warm year round.

But sometimes the new owners get tired of caring for wild pets and let them go. Todd thinks that's what may have happened to the huge python he found hiding under a house in the suburbs. The snake's owners had let it go in a local state park, where it lived for eight years.

Then one night, a family that lived next to the park heard an animal scream. When they looked out, they saw a huge snake with its mouth around a full-grown raccoon. After it finished eating, the snake went into a burrow it had dug under their house.

Todd and three friends spent two whole days digging out the snake. They widened the snake's burrow, which ran from the front of the house to the back. Then Todd put two friends on one side of the house. He put himself and a friend on the other.

Todd lowered himself toward the snake while his friend hung onto his legs. Todd was carrying a stick with a loop of rope at the end. When the snake started to strike at his face, Todd quickly flipped the rope over its head.

He and his friends then pulled the snake out. It was huge—22 feet (7 m) long and 250 pounds (113 kg). Finally, Todd took the snake home. He kept it there until he found someone who could care for it.

Alligators at Home

The python fit right into Todd's zoo-like home. He has permits to keep many different kinds of animals. He has four monitor lizards there. (He found one of the lizards stuck in a car engine.) He has nine iguana lizards. He has an ostrich-like bird from South America called a rhea (REE-uh)—which he named "Pizza Rhea." Then there are the two alligators, the tortoise, the flamingo, the Asian deer, and the 50 parrots.

Todd likes animals.

When he was 12, Todd found an orphaned mockingbird and helped raise it. That's when he got really interested in animals. "I used to track animals in my area. I'd catch live raccoons and opossums just to look at them," he says. "But I always put them right back in the wild."

People got to know about Todd and his love for wild animals. "They'd call me and say, hey, we have a raccoon in our attic, or a snake in our pool—could you come get it out?" he says.

Todd got very good at live-trapping animals. When he was 18, he became an official "nuisance wildlife trapper." That means the state of Florida gave him a license to start a business helping people get rid of pesky wildlife.

11. Which sentence gives the **best** description of Todd Hardwick's job?
    A. He rescues pets separated from their owners during hurricanes.
    B. He uses tranquilizer darts to rescue lost pets.
    C. He finds and rescues escaped pets and wild animals.
    D. He traps wild animals and sells them to zoos.

12. What is the difference between how Todd caught the cougar and the python?
    F. He had to crawl under a house to get the cougar, but the python was in a cage.
    G. He used a steak to tempt the cougar and a raccoon to tempt the python.
    H. He used his assistant to catch the cougar but caught the python himself.
    J. He used a tranquilizer dart for the cougar and a roped stick for the snake.

13. Unlike some pest-control companies, Todd's company, Pesky Critters,
    A. does all of its work after hurricanes
    B. works only with rescuing lost pets
    C. traps wild animals and pets alive
    D. exterminates pests

14. Why did the owner of the cougar cry?
    F. The cougar died during a hurricane.
    G. Todd sold the cougar for a lot of money.
    H. The cougar had been shot and was badly wounded.
    J. Todd rescued the cougar and returned it to its owner.

continued

15. From the types of animals Todd traps in Miami, we can predict that his business would probably be

   A. more successful in a northern city

   B. less successful in a northern city

   C. successful anywhere in the country

   D. more successful in a rural area

16. We can infer that Todd is good at

   F. solving problems

   G. organizing large groups of people

   H. treating sick animals

   J. attracting new customers

17. What conclusion can you make based on this passage?

   A. People should learn how to protect themselves from wild animals.

   B. A person's childhood interest may lead to a career.

   C. No one should have a wild animal as a pet.

   D. A pet that is well cared for will never leave its owner.

Comparing the Passages

18. How are the topics of these two passages similar?

   F. Both discuss the behavior of animals.

   G. Both ask whether animals think.

   H. Both tell about animal rescues.

   J. Both show that animals have feelings.

Write several paragraphs in response to *one* of the following questions:

19. Different types of articles appear in different types of magazines. Explain why the first passage might be published as an article in a science magazine. Then, explain why the second one might be published in a more general magazine. Use details from the passages to explain your ideas.

20. Both the scientists in the first passage and Todd Hardwick in the second passage are interested in animals, but in different ways. Use details and information from the passages to contrast their interests (explain the differences between them).

Taking Writing Tests

Standardized tests measure your writing skills in two ways:

- An **on-demand writing prompt,** such as the kind you'll see on Tennessee's writing test, gives you a situation and asks you to write an organized, well-developed **essay** in a limited time. A prompt may ask you to write a narrative, expository, or persuasive essay.
- **Multiple-choice questions** test your knowledge of sentence construction and revision and of paragraph content and organization.

Use the following strategies to write any type of essay. You'll recognize these steps—you know them already as the steps in the writing process.

THINKING IT THROUGH   Writing Test Strategies

▶ **STEP 1   Read the writing prompt carefully.** Underline key verbs (such as *analyze, argue, explain, discuss*) that tell you what to do. (Before the test, review the chart of **key verbs that appear in essay questions, page 772.**) A prompt may ask you to do more than one thing. Cover all parts of the prompt—including addressing the correct audience— or you'll lose points.

▶ **STEP 2   Think before you write.** If you have forty-five minutes to write an essay, take ten minutes or so for prewriting. Use scratch paper to brainstorm ideas, make a cluster diagram or a rough outline, and gather details. Plan how to organize and support ideas.

▶ **STEP 3   Draft your essay.** Spend about two thirds of your time drafting your essay. Express your ideas as clearly as you can. Write a strong opening paragraph and a definite closing, and add many specific details to support and elaborate your main points.

▶ **STEP 4   Edit and revise as you write.** Leave enough time at the end to re-read your draft and make your ideas easier to follow. To add a word or a sentence, mark a caret (∧) and insert it neatly.

▶ **STEP 5   Proofread your essay.** Find and correct all errors in grammar, punctuation, capitalization, and spelling.

TIP   Don't skip this prewriting step. Using prewriting strategies will result in a stronger, more interesting essay.

Reference Note

For more on writing an **autobiographical incident,** see pages 479–492.

Narrative Writing

Sample Writing Prompt *Describe an experience you had that changed your perspective—that made you see the world or yourself differently. As you retell your experience, add details that make clear where the story takes place and who the characters are. Be sure to tell how the incident changed you or what you learned.*

A story map like the one below can help you plan to write about an autobiographical incident. Be sure to do what the prompt asks you to do—add details of setting and characters.

Setting: *Central City homeless shelter, Thanksgiving last year; icy winds; people waiting outside for hours; long, quiet lines*

Characters: *Me; my mom; Mike, a homeless guy in his 60s*

What happened: *I didn't want to volunteer to serve food, but Mom made me. I felt really uncomfortable at first, dishing up mashed potatoes and gravy. But I got to talking to people, especially afterwards to a guy named Mike, who told me about his growing up and how he got to be homeless.*

How the experience changed me: *Now I see homeless people as individuals with a whole history, with hopes and fears. I realize how easy it is to become homeless, and I'm much more grateful for what I have.*

Expository Writing

Sample Writing Prompt *A time capsule is being buried in the cornerstone of the new city hall, and it won't be opened for one hundred years. Describe three objects you would place in the time capsule that will tell people of the future what life is like where you live at the beginning of the twenty-first century. Tell why you've chosen each object.*

One writer gathered his ideas by using a chart:

Object	Why I Chose It
cell phone	Instant phone contact; can stay in touch with family and friends anywhere you go; can play music, movies, and video games

portable music player and four favorite songs	Your own personal great music wherever you go. This will give an idea of the many kinds of music we have.
laptop computer	The Internet is the biggest thing of the early 21st century. People use it for fun, for e-mail, and for research.

An expository writing prompt may ask you to explain parts of a topic, as in the example above, or to explain a process, causes and effects, or problems and solutions. To make your ideas clear to readers, always include plenty of facts, examples, and other kinds of details as support.

Persuasive Writing

Sample Writing Prompt   *A neighbor has asked your advice about what kind of pet to adopt. Should she have a cat, a dog, or another kind of pet? State your opinion, and give at least two reasons to support your view.*

You probably already know what kind of pet you'll recommend. (With some issues, you need to carefully consider both sides—the pros and cons—before you decide what you think.) Here's a cluster diagram by a student who thinks her neighbor should adopt a cat and who is trying to think of reasons and evidence to support her opinion.

Reference Note

For more on **persuasive writing,** see pages 689–704.

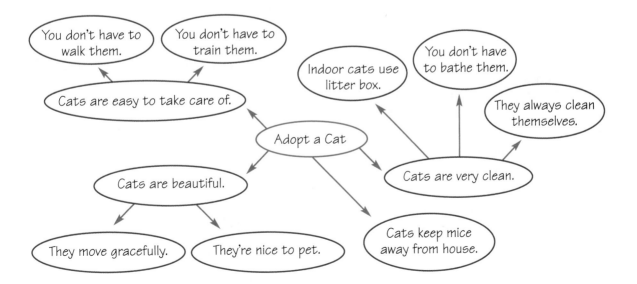

TIP Review the strategies on page 1, which also apply to multiple-choice writing questions.

Multiple-Choice Writing Questions

Multiple-choice writing questions like the ones below are another way to test your understanding of sentence and paragraph structure and of the conventions of standard English (grammar, usage, punctuation, capitalization, and spelling).

Read the following paragraph. Then, choose the best answer for each question.

(1) For most living things, danger is all around. (2) Often it strikes suddenly when a predator launches a surprise attack. (3) In other cases it develops slowly—the onset of disease or threat of starvation, for example. (4) Living things defend themselves from danger in countless ways. (5) Many animals have sharp senses and take emergency action at the first sign of trouble. (6) Most try to escape, but some have special protection that allows them to withstand an attack. (7) Plants also need defenses, particularly against hungry animals. (8) However, they are rooted to the ground and cannot run away as animals can. (9) Instead, they use spines, thorns, and special chemicals to make themselves unpleasant or dangerous to eat.

1. The **best** topic sentence for this paragraph is
  A. sentence 2
  B. sentence 3
  C. sentence 4
  D. sentence 9

2. Where is the **best** place to add this sentence?

  A porcupine, for instance, is covered with sharp spines that discourage predators.

  F. after sentence 4
  G. after sentence 5
  H. after sentence 6
  J. Nowhere; it destroys unity.

3. A *predator* (sentence 2) is
  A. a natural disaster
  B. any plant or animal
  C. a disease or injury to an animal
  D. an animal that kills another animal

4. Sentences 5 and 6 elaborate (by giving examples) the statement made in
  F. sentence 1
  G. sentence 3
  H. sentence 4
  J. sentence 7

5. In sentence 2, the word *Often* is
  A. a noun
  B. a pronoun
  C. an adjective
  D. an adverb

6. What is the direct object in sentence 7?

   F. plants

   G. defenses

   H. against

   J. animals

7. What is the **best** way to combine these two sentences?

> Turtles protect themselves. They withdraw their heads and limbs under a tough shell.

   A. Turtles protect themselves; and they withdraw their heads and limbs under a tough shell.

   B. Turtles protect themselves, they withdraw their heads and limbs under a tough shell.

   C. Turtles protect themselves by withdrawing their heads and limbs under a tough shell.

   D. Turtles protect themselves in order to withdraw their heads and limbs under a tough shell.

8. How should the following sentence be corrected?

> A ladybug uses it's bright colors and pattern to warn predators that it tastes terrible.

   F. Change *it's* to *its.*

   G. Add a comma after *colors.*

   H. Change *it tastes* to *they taste.*

   J. Make no change; the sentence is correct.

9. Which word is misspelled?

> Some <u>butterflies</u> and moths <u>wear</u> colors
>   **A**   **B**
> and patterns that mimic <u>there</u> poisonous,
>   **C**
> bad-tasting relatives. NO ERROR
>   **D**

10. Andre has found a book about insects. Which of the following would **most** quickly show him where the book discusses how insects use camouflage as a defense?

   F. the table of contents

   G. the index

   H. the introduction

   J. the glossary

Reference Note

For more on preparing for reading and writing tests, see the **Test-Taking Mini-Lesson** in each Part 3 chapter and **Studying and Test Taking** on pages 767–776.

A STUDENT'S GUIDE FOR LANGUAGE ARTS SKILLS AND STRATEGIES AND COUNTDOWN TO TESTING

Language Arts Skills and Strategies

Throughout your school career, you've become familiar with the language arts skills and strategies that help you read, write, and create and analyze presentations or media messages. These skills not only help you do well in your classes and on state tests, but also help you communicate effectively with others.

For a list of the most common language arts skills and strategies, take a look at the chart on the next seven pages. This chart provides definitions with specific examples from *Elements of Language* for each skill and strategy. Use this list as a quick reference to the skills and strategies you will practice this year.

Countdown to Testing

One way to show that you know language arts skills and strategies is to take a test. In fact, many states require that students take standardized tests to show mastery of these language arts skills. To help you prepare for such a test, use the weekly Countdown to Testing activities that appear on pages 22–45.

The Countdown to Testing section consists of 20 weeks of questions. During each week, you will answer one multiple-choice question each day. Here are a few important points to remember about the questions.

▹ Some of the questions refer to a passage, and if they do, the directions at the top of each page will direct you to the passage.

▹ Some of the questions include sentences or graphics you must analyze in order to answer the question.

▹ All of the questions have a page reference showing you where to go in your textbook to find more information about the skill or strategy the question covers.

By answering these questions in Countdown to Testing, you'll have more practice using language arts skills and strategies, and you'll be better prepared for standardized tests.

LANGUAGE ARTS SKILLS AND STRATEGIES

The following chart lists the four strands of language arts, plus the skills and strategies within these strands that are commonly addressed in language arts classrooms. Each skill or strategy appears in a yellow-tint box. To the right of each skill or strategy you'll find a specific example from your textbook.

READING

Comprehension

▶ **Identifying Main Idea and Details:** identifying the most important point or focus of a passage and the details that support or explain that focus	The **Reading Skill** on pages 505–506 gives instruction, examples, and practice on identifying a main idea. The **Test-Taking Mini-Lessons** on pages 509 and 579 give instruction on and examples of identifying main idea and details on reading tests.
▶ **Forming Generalizations:** creating a statement based on specific situations or people that applies to many individuals or situations	The **Reading Skill** on pages 473–475 gives instruction, examples, and practice on forming generalizations. For additional instruction and examples, see pages 739–740.
▶ **Summarizing:** noting the most important ideas of a text	For instruction on and examples of summarizing, see pages 743 and 770.
▶ **Drawing Conclusions:** adding information you already know to information in a text in order to make a judgment	The **Reading Skill** on pages 644–645 gives instruction, examples, and practice on drawing conclusions. For additional instruction and examples, see page 739.
▶ **Determining Author's Purpose:** noting the author's reason for writing—to inform, persuade, entertain, or express oneself	The **Reading Focus** on pages 646–647 gives instruction, examples, and practice on determining author's purpose.
▶ **Distinguishing Fact and Opinion:** being able to tell the difference between information that can be proved (facts) and personal beliefs (opinions)	The **Reading Focus** on pages 683–684 gives instruction, examples, and practice on identifying facts and opinions. The **Test-Taking Mini-Lesson** on page 688 gives instruction on and examples of identifying fact and opinion on reading tests.
▶ **Making Predictions:** the act of deciding what you think will happen next in a text	The **Reading Skill** on pages 539–540 gives instruction on and examples of making predictions. The **Test-Taking Mini-Lesson** on page 545 gives instruction on and examples of making predictions on reading tests.

▶ **Identifying Causes and Effects:** noting the difference between causes (what makes something happen) and effects (what happens as a result of a cause)

The **Critical-Thinking Mini-Lesson** on page 517 gives instruction, examples, and practice on analyzing cause-and-effect.

▶ **Identifying Point of View:** determining an author's attitude about a subject

The **Reading Skill** on pages 609–610 gives instruction, examples, and practice on determining point of view.

▶ **Analyzing Text Structures:** recognizing the organizational patterns authors use

To help you analyze text structures, see pages 743–744.

▶ **Making Inferences:** making educated guesses about ideas and details not directly stated in a text

The **Reading Skills** on pages 473–475 and 644–645 give instruction, examples, and practice on inferring. The **Test-Taking Mini-Lesson** on page 478 gives instruction on and examples of inferring on reading tests.

▶ **Paraphrasing:** restating in your own words ideas you have read

The **Writing Mini-Lesson** on page 658 gives instruction, examples, and practice on paraphrasing. See 740 for additional instruction and examples.

▶ **Analyzing Persuasive Techniques:** understanding how authors persuade

See page 741 for instruction and examples on analyzing persuasive techniques.

▶ **Taking Reading Tests:** answering reading questions on standardized tests

For strategies and practice on answering multiple-choice questions and extended response questions, see pages 1–8 and 767–776. The **Test-Taking Mini-Lessons** on pages 478, 509, 545, 579, 612, 649, and 688 give instruction on and examples of how to answer reading test questions.

Vocabulary

▶ **Using Context Clues:** determining the meanings of words through surrounding text

The **Vocabulary Mini-Lesson** on page 477 gives step-by-step instruction, examples, and practice on using context clues.

▶ **Analyzing Word Structure:** looking at a word's root, prefix, or suffix to help figure out its meaning

The **Vocabulary Mini-Lessons** on pages 578 and 648 give instruction, examples, and practice on analyzing word structure. See pages 749–750 for additional instruction and examples.

▶ **Using Multiple-Meaning Words:** identifying a word's meaning in context

The **Vocabulary Mini-Lesson** on page 508 gives step-by-step instruction, examples, and practice on multiple-meaning words.

▶ **Understanding the Origins of English Words:** studying how words came into the English language

To understand and study the history of English, see pages 724–727.

▶ **Understanding Connotation and Denotation:** understanding the difference between word associations and word definitions

To understand and study connotations and denotations of words, see page 748.

WRITING

Writing Strategies

▶ **Progressing through the Writing Process:** using the four stages of writing to create texts

See pages 466–467 for an explanation of each stage of the writing process.

▶ **Considering Audience and Purpose:** choosing words and sentences to address the reason for writing a text and the people you are writing for

The prewriting stage of each of the **Writing Workshops** on pages 479, 510, 546, 580, 613, 650, and 689 gives instruction and examples on how to consider audience and purpose.

▶ **Evaluating and Revising for Coherence and Unity:** assessing connections between details

See pages 449–455 for instruction, examples and practice on unity and coherence.

▶ **Evaluating and Revising for Content and Organization:** assessing writing to improve the development and order of the ideas in a text

The evaluating and revising stage of each of the **Writing Workshops** on pages 488, 521, 555, 591, 623, 666, and 700 gives instruction, examples, and practice on revising content and organization. See pages 455–456 for instruction, examples, and practice on how to elaborate in a text.

▶ **Evaluating and Revising for Conciseness and Clarity:** assessing writing to improve the precision of word choice and sentences in a text

The **Focus On** features on pages 490, 523, 557, 593, 625, 668, and 702 give instruction, examples, and practice on revising word choice or sentences. **Chapter 16** on pages 428–442 gives instruction, examples, and practice on improving sentence style.

Writing Applications

▶ **Writing Narrative Texts:** producing texts that tell a story

The **Connections to Literature** on pages 628–629 gives instruction, examples, and practice on writing a short story.

▶ **Writing Expository Texts:** producing texts that explore or explain

The **Writing Workshops** on pages 510–527, 546–563, 580–598, and 650–673 give instruction, examples, and practice on writing a newspaper article, a "how-to" paper, a comparison-contrast essay, and a research report, respectively.

▶ **Writing Persuasive Texts:** producing texts to influence readers

The **Writing Workshop** on pages 689–707 gives instruction, examples, and practice on the process of writing a persuasive letter.

▷ **Writing Expressive Texts:** producing texts to share feelings and thoughts

The **Writing Workshop** on pages 479–493 gives instruction, examples, and practice on the process of writing an autobiographical incident.

▷ **Writing Responses to Literature:** producing texts that respond to a piece of literature

The **Writing Workshop** on pages 613–627 gives instruction, examples, and practice on the process of writing a book review. The **Connections to Literature** on pages 630–632 gives instruction, examples, and practice on the process of writing an interpretation of a poem.

▷ **Writing Creative Texts:** producing texts that use language in an original and imaginative way

The **Connections to Literature** features on pages 494–496 and 628–629 give instruction, examples, and practice on the process of writing a poem and a short story, respectively. The **Critical-Thinking Mini-Lesson** on page 617 gives instruction, examples, and practice on the elements of a plot.

▷ **Writing Descriptive Texts:** using sensory details to create a dominant impression of a subject

The **Connections to Life** on pages 561–562 gives instruction and practice on creating a descriptive paragraph.

▷ **Writing Correspondence:** using the correct format to write business and personal communications

For instruction and examples on writing letters, e-mails, and memos, see pages 791–795.

▷ **Taking Writing Tests:** answering multiple-choice writing questions and responding to on-demand writing prompts

For strategies and practice on responding to writing tests, see pages 9–13 and 771. The **Test-Taking Mini-Lessons** on pages 493, 560, 597, 671, and 705 give instruction in and examples of strategies for answering on-demand writing prompts.

Written Language Conventions

▷ **Proofreading for Correct Modifier Usage:** reading a final text to identify and correct errors in comparison and placement

Chapter 9, pages 242–265, gives instruction, examples, and practice on using modifiers correctly. The **Grammar Link** on page 594 gives instruction, examples, and practice on using comparatives correctly.

▷ **Proofreading for Correct Verb Usage:** reading a final text to identify and correct errors in tense shift, subject-verb agreement, and irregular verbs

Chapter 6, pages 168–191, and **Chapter 7,** pages 192–221, give instruction, examples, and practice on using verbs correctly.

▷ **Proofreading for Correct Pronoun Usage:** reading a final text to identify and correct errors in case and pronoun-antecedent agreement

Chapter 6, pages 183–190, and **Chapter 8,** pages 222–241, give instruction, examples, and practice on using pronouns correctly.

▶ **Proofreading for Fragments and Run-On Sentences:** reading a final text to identify and correct errors in sentence structure	**Chapter 16,** pages 428–434, gives instruction, examples, and practice on correcting fragments and run-on sentences. The **Grammar Link** on page 524 gives instruction, examples, and practice on correcting run-on sentences.
▶ **Proofreading for Correct Spelling:** reading a final text to identify and correct errors in spelling	**Chapter 14,** pages 360–388, gives instruction, examples, and practice on spelling correctly.
▶ **Proofreading for Correct Punctuation:** reading a final text to identify and correct errors in punctuation	**Chapters 12** and **13,** on pages 308–359, give instruction, examples, and practice on punctuating text correctly. The **Grammar Links** on pages 558, 669, and 703 give instruction, examples, and practice on using commas in a series, punctuating titles, and punctuating possessives, respectively.
▶ **Proofreading for Correct Capitalization:** reading a final text to correct errors in capitalization	**Chapter 11,** pages 284–307, gives instruction, examples, and practice on using capital letters correctly.
▶ **Proofreading for Correct Manuscript Style:** reading a final text to correct errors in indentation and spacing	For instruction and examples on guidelines for manuscript style, see page 716.

Grammar

▶ **Understanding and Identifying the Parts of Speech:** recognizing the eight parts of speech	**Chapters 2** and **3** on pages 70–119 give instruction, examples, and practice on identifying and using the eight parts of speech.
▶ **Understanding and Identifying the Parts of a Sentence:** recognizing subject, predicate, and complements of a sentence	**Chapter 1** on pages 48–69 and **Chapter 5** on pages 150–166 give instruction, examples, and practice on identifying and using the subject, predicate, and complements of a sentence.
▶ **Understanding and Identifying Phrases and Clauses:** recognizing phrases and clauses	**Chapter 4** on pages 120–149 gives instruction, examples, and practice on identifying and using phrases and clauses.
▶ **Understanding and Identifying Sentence Structure:** recognizing kinds of sentences and the four basic sentence structures	**Chapter 4** on pages 142–147 gives instruction, examples, and practice on the classification of sentences and the four basic sentence structures.

SPEAKING AND LISTENING

Speaking and Listening Strategies

▶ **Understanding the Techniques of Clear and Distinct Speech:** studying the strategies of an effective speaker

For instruction and strategies for effective speaking, see 755–756.

▶ **Analyzing Oral Texts:** listening to an oral presentation in order to understand its message and purpose

For instruction and strategies for analyzing oral texts, see pages 764–765.

▶ **Understanding the Listening Process:** studying the skills involved in an effective listening process

For instruction and strategies for the listening process, see pages 761–766.

Speaking and Listening Applications

▶ **Giving and Listening to an Informative Speech:** presenting and listening to a speech that explains

The **Focus on Speaking and Listening** on pages 674–676 gives instruction, examples and practice on giving and listening to a research presentation.

▶ **Giving and Listening to a Persuasive Speech:** presenting and listening to a speech that presents a position

The **Focus on Speaking and Listening** on pages 708–710 gives instruction, examples and practice on presenting and evaluating a persuasive speech.

▶ **Giving and Listening to a Narrative Speech:** presenting and listening to a story

The **Focus on Speaking and Listening** on pages 497–498 gives instruction, examples and practice on presenting a story.

▶ **Giving and Listening to an Oral Interpretation:** presenting and listening to a reading of written material

For instruction and strategies for oral interpretation, see pages 759–760.

▶ **Participating in an Oral Discussion:** presenting and listening to discussions

For instruction and strategies for a group discussion, see page 757–758.

▶ **Presenting and Listening to a Poetry Reading:** presenting and listening to a presentation of a poem

For instruction and strategies for oral interpretation of a poem, see pages 759–760.

VIEWING AND REPRESENTING

Viewing and Representing Strategies

▷ **Understanding Electronic Media Terms:** studying terms used by the electronic media

See pages 777–785 for instruction on and examples of electronic media terms.

▷ **Understanding Print Media Terms:** studying terms used by the print media

See pages 785–788 for instruction on and examples of print media terms.

▷ **Understanding Text Features:** studying the tools writers use in their texts to make their ideas stand out

The **Designing Your Writing** features on pages 57, 565, and 638 give instruction, examples, and practice on using drop letters, text design, and titles and subheads, respectively.

▷ **Understanding Visuals and Graphics:** studying how writers use illustrations, graphics, charts, drawings and other elements to enhance their text message

The **Designing Your Writing** features on pages 486, 553, and 595 give instruction, examples, and practice for using graphics and illustrations.

▷ **Understanding Layout Features:** studying the elements writers use for the presentation of their message

The **Designing Your Writing** features on pages 529–530, 618, and 661 give instruction, examples, and practice on using layout features. For additional instruction and examples, see pages 717–719.

▷ **Analyzing Print and Electronic Media:** looking at print and electronic media in order to figure out the message and purpose

The **Connections to Life** on page 598 gives instruction, examples, and practice on comparing documentaries. The **Focus on Viewing and Representing** features on pages 599–602 and 633–636 give instruction, examples, and practice on analyzing media coverage.

Viewing and Representing Applications

▷ **Creating Print Media:** producing print media texts

The **Connections to Life** features on pages 526 and 706 give instruction, examples, and practice on writing a newspaper column and a humorous advertisement, respectively. The **Designing Your Writing** features on pages 486, 529, 553, 595, and 661 give instruction on and examples of using graphic elements.

▷ **Creating Electronic Media:** producing electronic media texts

The **Focus on Viewing and Representing** on page 531–534 gives instruction, examples, and practice on producing a TV news segment.

WEEK 1

DIRECTIONS **Answer each question below on the day of the week assigned to it.**

MONDAY

Study the graphic to the right. Then answer the question that follows.

What is the probable purpose of this graphic?

A to show where the mountains are
B to show the San Andreas fault in California
C to predict the next earthquake
D to show where and how plates collide

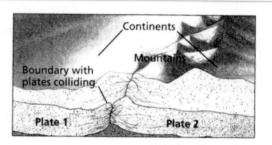

Quick Reference Handbook, page 745

TUESDAY

There may be a problem in the structure of the word group below. Choose the best revision, or select D.

Joe is my friend we are in the same class.

A Joe is my friend. And in the same class.
B Joe is my friend, and we are in the same class.
C In the same class, Joe is my friend.
D correct as is

Chapter 16, page 431

WEDNESDAY

Choose the word in the group that means the same, or about the same, as the underlined word.

During the dry season, water conservation was on everyone's mind.

A saving
B usage
C cost
D availability

Vocabulary Mini-Lesson, page 611

THURSDAY

Read the following sentence. Choose the response that fixes the underlined error. If there is no error, choose D.

The Jones twins and my cousin is going to spend the night next Friday.

A Jones twins and my cousin are going
B Jones twins and my cousin will be going
C Jones twins and my cousin gone
D correct as is

Chapter 6, page 177

FRIDAY

Read the following sentence. Choose the response that fixes the underlined error. If there is no error, choose D.

"Please take this note to the office, Mrs. Ruiz said."

A office," Mrs. Ruiz said.
B office, Mrs. Ruiz said.
C office, "Mrs. Ruiz said."
D correct as is

Chapter 13, page 338

DIRECTIONS **Read the following poem.**

from *Casey at the Bat*

Ernest Lawrence Thayer

The outlook wasn't brilliant for the Mudville nine that day:
The score stood four to two, with but one inning more to play;
And so, when Cooney died at first, and Barrows did the same,
A sickly silence fell upon the patrons of the game.

5 A straggling few got up to go in deep despair. The rest
Clung to that hope which springs eternal in the human breast;
They thought, if only Casey could but get a whack at that,
They'd put up even money now, with Casey at the bat.

But Flynn preceded Casey, as did also Jimmy Blake,
10 And the former was a pudding, and the latter was a fake;
So upon that <u>stricken</u> multitude grim melancholy sat,
For there seemed but little chance of Casey's getting to the bat.

But Flynn let drive a single, to the wonderment of all,
And Blake, the much-despised, tore the cover off the ball;
15 And when the dust had lifted, and they saw what had occurred,
There was Jimmy safe on second, and Flynn a-hugging third.

Then from the gladdened multitude went up a joyous yell;
It bounded from the mountaintop, and rattled in the dell;
It struck upon the hillside, and recoiled upon the flat,
20 For Casey, mighty Casey, was advancing to the bat.

There was ease in Casey's manner as he stepped into his place;
There was pride in Casey's bearing and a smile on Casey's face.
And when, responding to the cheers, he lightly doffed his hat,
No stranger in the crowd could doubt 'twas Casey at the bat.

25 Ten thousand eyes were on him as he rubbed his hands with dirt;
Five thousand tongues applauded when he wiped them on his shirt;
Then while the <u>writhing</u> pitcher ground the ball into his hip,
Defiance flashed in Casey's eye, a sneer curled Casey's lip. . . .

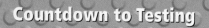

WEEK 2

DIRECTIONS The questions below refer to the poem "Casey at the Bat" on page 23. Answer each question below on the day of the week assigned to it.

MONDAY

Which of the following words or phrases <u>best</u> describes the rhythm of the poem?

A complex
B like natural speech
C regular
D stressed

Connections to Literature, page 630

TUESDAY

The phrase "deep despair" in line 5 is an example of

A personification.
B metaphor.
C simile.
D alliteration.

Connections to Literature, page 494

WEDNESDAY

If you were to present on oral interpretation of this poem, what would be the <u>best</u> tone of voice to use?

A mock-serious
B neutral
C joyous
D enthusiastic

Quick Reference Handbook, page 759

THURSDAY

What is the meaning of <u>stricken</u> in line 11?

A hit by a baseball
B having struck out
C unfaithful to the team
D overwhelmed by misfortune

Test-Taking Mini-Lesson, page 612

FRIDAY

In each group of four lines in this poem,

A even-numbered lines rhyme.
B odd-numbered lines rhyme.
C the first two lines rhyme, and the last two lines rhyme.
D the first and last lines rhyme, and the second and third lines rhyme.

Connections to Literature, page 630

WEEK 3

DIRECTIONS **The questions below refer to the poem "Casey at the Bat" on page 23. Answer each question below on the day of the week assigned to it.**

MONDAY

In lines 20–22, the speaker <u>most</u> likely repeats *Casey* five times in order to

A avoid having to find words that rhyme with Casey.
B make the audience feel tired of Casey.
C focus attention on Casey and build suspense.
D break up the rhythm of the poem.

Connections to Literature, page 630

TUESDAY

You can tell this excerpt is from a narrative poem because it

A focuses on a single image.
B tells a story.
C has one character.
D includes figurative language.

Connections to Literature, page 494

WEDNESDAY

In line 17, "went up a joyous yell" is an example of inverted word order, in which

A the verb comes before the subject.
B the noun comes before the verb.
C there is no direct object.
D there is no verb at all.

Chapter 6, page 180

THURSDAY

What is the meaning of <u>writhing</u> in line 27?

A twisting and turning
B cowardly
C standing as still as a statue
D bursting with energy

Test-Taking Mini-Lesson, page 612

FRIDAY

If a movie actor were portraying Casey as he appears in lines 21–28, how would the director tell him to act?

A extremely generous
B very humble
C highly confident
D dazed and confused

Focus on Viewing and Representing, page 634

WEEK 4

DIRECTIONS Answer each question below on the day of the week assigned to it.

MONDAY

Roger burned a pan of macaroni. All of the following are possible causes, except for one, which is a possible effect. Identify the possible effect.

A The burner was set too high.
B The pan took a long time to clean.
C He forgot to stir the macaroni.
D He cooked the macaroni for too long.

Critical-Thinking Mini-Lesson, page 517

TUESDAY

There may be a structure problem in the sentence below. Choose the <u>best</u> revision, or select *D*.

Tim does not play soccer, and Juan does not play soccer.

A Tim and Juan neither one plays soccer.
B Neither Tim nor Juan plays soccer.
C Neither Tim nor Juan play soccer.
D correct as is

Chapter 16, page 438; Chapter 3, page 113

WEDNESDAY

Read the following sentence. Choose the response that fixes the underlined error. If there is no error, choose *D*.

<u>Japan's mount Fuji</u> was the subject of the painting.

A Japan's mount fuji
B Japan's Mount fuji
C Japan's Mount Fuji
D correct as is

Chapter 11, page 288

THURSDAY

Decide which of the underlined words in the set below is misspelled. If all are correct, choose *D*.

A <u>You're</u> the first person to arrive.
B <u>Their</u> going to meet us at the party.
C <u>Who's</u> going to bring the sandwiches?
D no mistake

Chapter 14, page 380

FRIDAY

For his science class, Laine is preparing to write an essay about butterflies and moths. Which of these would <u>most</u> help Laine to organize his information?

A a list of the types of butterflies in Laine's area
B a chart comparing and contrasting butterflies and moths
C a color photograph of a butterfly
D a list describing all the features of a moth

Writing Workshop, page 584

WEEK 5

DIRECTIONS **Answer each question below on the day of the week assigned to it.**

MONDAY

Read the first sentence below. Choose the response that uses the underlined word in the same way as it is used in the first sentence.

We made a <u>film</u> about science experiments to show at open house.

A The soapy water left a <u>film</u> on the floor.

B The audience watched the <u>film</u> with great interest.

C Who will <u>film</u> the football game on Friday?

D The <u>film</u> over the lens gave the picture a dreamy quality.

Vocabulary Mini-Lesson, page 508

TUESDAY

There may be a problem in the structure of the sentence below. Choose the <u>best</u> revision, or select *D*.

My science teacher is Mr. Snow and he is taking us on a field trip.

A My science teacher is Mr. Snow and is taking us on a field trip.

B Mr. Snow is my science teacher, taking us on a field trip.

C My science teacher, Mr. Snow, is taking us on a field trip.

D correct as is

Chapter 16, page 435

WEDNESDAY

Read the following sentence. Choose the response that fixes the underlined error. If there is no error, choose *D*.

<u>Two streetcars and a bus goes</u> by my house each morning.

A Two streetcars and a bus is going

B Two streetcars and a bus go

C Two streetcars and a bus gone

D correct as is

Chapter 6, page 177

THURSDAY

Read the following sentence. Choose the response that fixes the underlined error. If there is no error, choose *D*.

The sun rose at <u>6.30</u> this morning.

A 6,30

B 6 30

C 6:30

D correct as is

Chapter 12, page 327

FRIDAY

Which of the following is an opinion?

A "The Star-Spangled Banner" is our national anthem.

B The first words of our national anthem are, "O, say can you see."

C Francis Scott Key wrote "The Star-Spangled Banner."

D Our national anthem is difficult to sing.

Test-Taking Mini-Lesson, page 688

WEEK 6

DIRECTIONS Answer each question below on the day of the week assigned to it.

MONDAY

Decide which of the underlined words in the set below is misspelled. If all are correct, choose _D_.

A Jake's blue-and-yellow jacket is <u>reversible</u>.
B How many tickets are <u>available</u> for the play?
C My next class is held in a <u>portable</u> building.
D no mistake

Chapter 14, page 361

TUESDAY

Read the following sentence. Choose the response that fixes the underlined error. If there is no error, choose _D_.

The other team gave a party for <u>they and us</u>.

A them and us
B they and we
C them and we
D correct as is

Chapter 8, page 233

WEDNESDAY

There may be a problem in the structure of the word group below. Select the <u>best</u> revision, or choose _D_.

Went to basketball practice after school.

A Went to basketball practice, after school.
B Mario after school to basketball practice.
C Mario went to basketball practice after school.
D correct as is

Chapter 16, page 428

THURSDAY

Read the following sentence. Choose the response that fixes the underlined error. If there is no error, choose _D_.

The band played <u>better</u> at last week's competition than ever before.

A gooder
B more better
C best
D correct as is

Chapter 9, page 249

FRIDAY

Which of the following clue words are <u>most</u> likely to be found in an essay comparing and contrasting cats and dogs?

A on the other hand
B as a result
C most important
D if . . . then

Quick Reference Handbook, page 739

WEEK 7

DIRECTIONS **Answer each question below on the day of the week assigned to it.**

MONDAY

Read the following sentence. Choose the response that fixes the underlined error. If there is no error, choose D.

Have you read the poem <u>"The Raven," by Edgar Allan Poe?</u>

A "The Raven, by Edgar Allan Poe?"

B The Raven, by Edgar Allan Poe?

C The Raven, by "Edgar Allan Poe?"

D correct as is

Chapter 13, page 343

TUESDAY

There may be a problem in the structure of the word group below. Select the <u>best</u> revision, or choose D.

I read about a missing dog that was found in the park in the newspaper yesterday.

A Yesterday, I read about a missing dog that was found in the park in the newspaper.

B I read about a missing dog that was found yesterday in the park in the newspaper.

C In the newspaper yesterday, I read about a missing dog that was found in the park.

D correct as is

Chapter 9, page 257

WEDNESDAY

There may be a problem in the structure of the sentence below. Select the <u>best</u> revision, or choose D.

Judy wants to learn to surf, she does not live near the ocean.

A Judy wants to learn to surf, and she does not live near the ocean.

B Judy wants to learn to surf, but she does not live near the ocean.

C Judy wants to learn to surf, because she does not live near the ocean.

D correct as is

Chapter 16, page 431

THURSDAY

Choose the word or phrase that means the same, or about the same, as the underlined word.

They planned to travel from California to Colorado <u>via</u> Arizona.

A as well as

B instead of

C by way of

D along with

Vocabulary Mini-Lesson, page 611

FRIDAY

Read the following sentence. Choose the response that fixes the underlined error. If there is no error, choose D.

By next Sunday, I <u>had been</u> away from home for ten days.

A will be

B have been

C will have been

D correct as is

Chapter 7, page 206

WEEK 8

DIRECTIONS **Answer each question below on the day of the week assigned to it.**

MONDAY

Read the following sentence. Choose the response that fixes the underlined error. If there is no error, choose D.

Marty and Seth <u>has been playing</u> on the same team for three years.

A will playing
B have been playing
C is playing
D correct as is

Chapter 6, page 177

TUESDAY

Decide which of the underlined words in the set below is misspelled. If all are correct, choose D.

A Something is <u>causing</u> the boat to rock.
B That is an <u>adorible</u> kitten.
C The <u>stranger</u> rode into town on a white horse.
D no mistake

Chapter 14, page 361

WEDNESDAY

Maya is preparing to write a personal narrative. Maya could best organize ideas for her essay using a

A chart comparing and contrasting types of vacations.
B list of events, in order, from Maya's vacation.
C list of questions about the beach.
D chart showing how to pack for vacation.

Critical-Thinking Mini-Lesson, page 483

THURSDAY

There may be a grammar problem in the sentence below. Select the <u>best</u> revision, or choose D.

Vincent doesn't have no more time to practice.

A Vincent doesn't hardly have more time to practice.
B Vincent does not have no more time to practice.
C Vincent doesn't have any more time to practice.
D correct as is

Chapter 9, page 255

FRIDAY

Which of the following is a statement of fact?

A The emu is a funny-looking fellow.
B It is a large, flightless bird.
C Emu eggs are beautiful and valuable.
D It is better to breed emus than ostriches.

Test-Taking Mini-Lesson, page 688

DIRECTIONS **Read the following article.**

Cold or Flu?

1   Sometimes, especially during the winter months, you might notice increased numbers of people coughing, sneezing, or complaining about aches and pains. You might be a victim of a cold, the flu, or some other similar illness yourself. Many people use words such as *cold* or *flu*, but they may not have a clear understanding that even though these maladies are similar, there are differences as well. A patient with the flu, for example, will show symptoms different from those of a patient with a cold.

2   A cold is a minor viral infection that generally involves a runny or stuffy nose, a sore throat, and some discomfort. There may be a moderate amount of coughing. Fevers are sometimes associated with the common cold. The patient usually suffers for five to seven days. Treating a cold's symptoms will make a patient feel better, but nothing can cure a cold. Treatment includes rest, plenty of fluids, and decongestants.

3   Sometimes colds can develop into more serious respiratory infections, such as bronchitis and pneumonia. Bronchitis is an inflammation of the bronchial tubes in the lungs. It can make breathing difficult. Pneumonia is an even more dangerous pulmonary condition. Both of these are serious infections that are usually related to bacteria; but in some cases, such as viral pneumonia, they can also be caused by viruses. Bacterial throat and lung infections are usually treated with antibiotic medicines that a doctor would prescribe. Viral cases, including colds, do not respond to antibiotics.

4   Unlike a cold, the flu is a more serious virus that can last longer and cause more suffering. A flu sufferer may have a severe cough. A case of the flu is often accompanied by a fever that might range from 101° to 104° and last for three to four days. The patient often suffers severe discomfort including headaches and body aches. Patients may feel weak and exhausted for several weeks.

5   The treatment for the flu is much the same as the treatments for other viral infections—rest, fluids, and over-the-counter medicines that relieve the sniffling, coughing, and fever. The flu, like other viral infections, does not respond to antibiotic medicines. Sufferers just have to wait out the discomfort. In fact, no matter which of these conditions you may eventually come down with, you are going to feel miserable for a while.

WEEK 9

DIRECTIONS The questions below refer to the article "Cold or Flu?" on page 31. Answer each question below on the day of the week assigned to it.

MONDAY

What does the word <u>maladies</u> in Paragraph 1 mean?

A aches

B symptoms

C patients

D illnesses

Test-Taking Mini-Lesson, page 612

TUESDAY

What usually accompanies a cold?

A a severe cough

B runny nose

C a high fever

D serious body aches

Test-Taking Mini Lesson, page 579

WEDNESDAY

What is the fourth paragraph <u>mostly</u> about?

A flu

B colds

C sore throats

D pneumonia

Reading Workshop, page 505

THURSDAY

What is bronchitis <u>usually</u> caused by?

A taking antibiotics

B a virus

C bacteria

D the flu

Chapter 17, page 459

FRIDAY

Reading this passage would probably be <u>most</u> useful for

A doctors.

B nurses.

C public health officials.

D the general public.

Writing Workshop, page 582

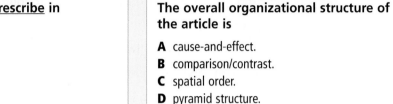

WEEK 10

DIRECTIONS The questions below refer to the article "Cold or Flu?" on page 31.
Answer each question below on the day of the week assigned to it.

MONDAY

What does the word <u>prescribe</u> in Paragraph 3 mean?

A order
B want
C make
D take

Test-Taking Mini-Lesson, page 612

TUESDAY

The overall organizational structure of the article is

A cause-and-effect.
B comparison/contrast.
C spatial order.
D pyramid structure.

Reading Workshop, page 576

WEDNESDAY

Which is an opinion expressed in the passage?

A A cold is a minor viral infection.
B The patient usually suffers for five to seven days.
C The flu does not respond to antibiotic medicines.
D You are going to feel miserable for a while.

Test-Taking Mini-Lesson, page 688

THURSDAY

One thing that the cold and the flu have in common is that both

A are severe infections.
B are caused by bacteria.
C are caused by a virus.
D result in bronchitis.

Reading Workshop, page 575

FRIDAY

The author's purpose in this article is to

A persuade the public to get flu shots.
B provide medical information.
C express feelings about illness.
D entertain future nurses.

Reading Workshop, page 646

DIRECTIONS **Read the following student draft of a book review.**

Treasure from the Sea?

1   Would you return a precious stone if it meant finding inner peace? Kino must make this difficult decision in John Steinbeck's <u>novella</u> *The Pearl*.

2   Kino is a pearl diver who lives on the Gulf of California. When his infant son is stung by a scorpion, Kino does not have the funds to pay for a doctor. His luck changes when he finds a large pearl. He believes the pearl is the key to happiness and wealth.

3   As news spreads about Kino's treasure, greed and envy take over. Everyone wants the pearl. And the money it will bring for them. As others try to <u>secure</u> the pearl, Kino and his wife Juana encounter disaster and tragedy. The pearl brings out the worst in people, including Kino. To free her family from its misfortune, Juana wants to throw away the pearl. Greed overcomes Kino, who reacts violently toward Juana.

4   The ultimate sacrifice occurs when Kino and Juana flee from their town. Trackers pursue the pearl, and Kino defends what is his. A fatal shot is fired, and the pearl must be returned to the ocean.

5   *The Pearl* is plausible and powerful, and the characters are ordinary people, and they have realistic feelings about wealth. This short novel offers readers a lesson but does not end like a fairy tale.

WEEK 11

DIRECTIONS The questions below refer to the student draft "Treasure from the Sea?" on page 34. Answer each question below on the day of the week assigned to it.

MONDAY

According to the book review, what is the conflict in *The Pearl*?

A Kino's son fights stormy seas in order to find a pearl.

B Kino and his son fight over a pearl.

C Kino must choose between wealth and inner peace.

D Kino gets stung by a scorpion.

Reading Workshop, page 608

TUESDAY

According to the review, the book's setting is

A the Gulf of California.

B a jewelry store.

C a fishing boat.

D the present day.

Reading Workshop, page 608

WEDNESDAY

According to the review, the main character of *The Pearl* is

A Kino's son.

B Juana.

C Kino.

D Steinbeck.

Reading Workshop, page 608

THURSDAY

The reviewer's point of view on *The Pearl* is

A mostly positive.

B mostly negative.

C thoroughly negative.

D thoroughly positive.

Reading Workshop, page 609

FRIDAY

You can tell from the passage that a <u>novella</u> is a

A long novel.

B short story.

C small book.

D short novel.

Vocabulary Mini-Lesson, page 611

WEEK 12

DIRECTIONS The questions below refer to the student draft "Treasure from the Sea?" on page 34. Answer each question below on the day of the week assigned to it.

MONDAY

Which of the following is the book reviewer's opinion?

A "*The Pearl* is plausible and powerful . . ."
B "Trackers pursue the pearl, and Kino defends what is his."
C "Would you return a precious stone. . . .?"
D "A fatal shot is fired. . . ."

Test-Taking Mini-Lesson, page 688

TUESDAY

The word <u>secure</u> in Paragraph 3 means

A be safe.
B get.
C insure.
D own.

Vocabulary Mini-Lesson, page 611

WEDNESDAY

The "ultimate sacrifice" in Paragraph 5 probably refers to

A the last chapter of the book.
B someone losing his or her life.
C Juana's divorcing Kino.
D Kino's being arrested and sent to jail.

Reading Workshop, page 644

THURSDAY

Read the two word groups. Choose the response that fixes the underlined error.

Everyone wants the <u>pearl. And the money</u> it will bring them.

A pearl and the money
B pearl; and the money
C pearl; because of the money
D correct as is

Chapter 16, page 428

FRIDAY

Read the following sentence. Then select the choice that represents the <u>best</u> revision.

"*The Pearl* is plausible and powerful, and the characters are ordinary people, and they have realistic feelings about wealth."

A *The Pearl* is plausible and powerful; and the characters are ordinary people; and they have realistic feelings about wealth.
B Because *The Pearl* is plausible and powerful, the characters are ordinary people, and they have realistic feelings about wealth.
C *The Pearl* is plausible and powerful because the characters are ordinary people who have realistic feelings about wealth.
D no revision necessary

Chapter 16, page 432

WEEK 13

DIRECTIONS Answer each question below on the day of the week assigned to it.

MONDAY

Look at the following graphic organizer. For which type of writing is it <u>most</u> useful?

A autobiographical incident
B persuasive essay
C comparison/contrast essay
D newspaper article

Writing Workshop, page 584

TUESDAY

Read the following sentence. Choose the response that fixes the underlined error. If there is no error, choose *D*.

Josh enjoyed the <u>book, he</u> wants to read more by the author.

A book; he
B book he
C book he,
D Correct as is

Chapter 12, page 325

WEDNESDAY

Read the sentence below. Choose the response in which the underlined word is used in the same way as it is used in the first sentence.

We heard the coach <u>boom</u> the instructions loudly through the microphone.

A The business <u>boom</u> caused many new people to move to town.
B The sailor tied the <u>boom</u> to the bottom of the sail.
C Attendance will surely <u>boom</u> when we add two performances.
D That actor can really <u>boom</u> out the lines!

Vocabulary Mini-Lesson, page 508

THURSDAY

There may be a problem in the structure of the word group below. Select the <u>best</u> revision, or choose *D*.

Marco, along with his brother.

A Marco, who is going with his brother.
B Marco is going, along with his brother.
C Along with his brother is going.
D correct as is

Chapter 16, page 428

FRIDAY

There may be a problem in the sentence structure of the words below. Select the <u>best</u> revision, or choose *D*.

I found a dog in the park without a name tag.

A Without a name tag, I found a dog in the park.
B In the park, I found a dog without a name tag.
C In the park without a name tag, I found a dog.
D correct as is

Chapter 9, page 257

WEEK 14

DIRECTIONS Answer each question below on the day of the week assigned to it.

MONDAY

Decide which of the underlined words in the set below is misspelled. If all are correct, choose *D*.

A Joan's cat is the <u>laziest</u> animal I've ever seen.
B Mr. Garza has the <u>prettiest</u> garden on our block.
C the baby's <u>crying</u> woke up the other children.
D no mistake

Chapter 14, page 366

TUESDAY

Read the following sentence. Choose the response that fixes the underlined error. If there is no error, choose *D*.

<u>Him and me</u> went to the ballgame last night.

A He and me
B Him and I
C He and I
D correct as is

Chapter 8, page 225

WEDNESDAY

Read the following sentence. Choose the response that fixes the underlined error. If there is no error, choose *D*.

Shondra was elected <u>President of Mrs. Lee's class.</u>

A president of Mrs. Lee's Class.
B president of Mrs. Lee's class.
C President of mrs. Lee's class.
D correct as is

Chapter 11, page 299

THURSDAY

Traditional newspaper articles have an inverted pyramid structure, which means that the article's

A middle part contains the climax, or most exciting information.
B conclusion summarizes the most important information.
C beginning summarizes the most important information.
D organization is chronological, or time-ordered.

Reading Workshop, page 506

FRIDAY

There may be a grammar problem in the sentence below. Select the <u>best</u> revision, or choose *D*.

Jim and Juan have went to the store to buy milk.

A Jim and Juan have gone to the store to buy milk.
B Jim and Juan has went to the store to buy milk.
C Jim and Juan has gone to the store to buy milk.
D correct as is

Chapter 7, page 196

WEEK 15

DIRECTIONS Answer each question below on the day of the week assigned to it.

MONDAY

Choose the word or phrase that means the same, or about the same, as the underlined word.

The runner flew like a <u>meteor</u> across the finish line.

A cannon ball
B shooting star
C winged horse
D speeding bird

Vocabulary Mini-Lesson, page 477

TUESDAY

Which of the following is an opinion?

A Dinosaurs became extinct about 65 million years ago.
B Tyrannosaurus rex lived in the Cretaceous era.
C T. rex was the fiercest dinosaur of all.
D Scientists have decided that the brontosaurus was misnamed.

Test-Taking Mini-Lesson, page 688

WEDNESDAY

Lia's teacher asked the class to write a comparison-contrast essay. First Lia made a list of possible topics for her essay. Each of these would be a good choice for a topic <u>except</u>

A plums and peaches.
B our solar system.
C birds and bats.
D soccer and basketball.

Writing Workshop, page 580

THURSDAY

Read the following sentence. Choose the response that fixes the underlined error. If there is no error, choose *D*.

Kim found a lost <u>kitten, so</u> she took it to the animal shelter.

A kitten so
B kitten; so
C kitten so,
D correct as is

Chapter 12, page 316

FRIDAY

Read the following sentence. Choose the response that fixes the underlined error. If there is no error, choose *D*.

The bell <u>rung</u> before I finished the game.

A ringed
B rang
C was rang
D correct as is

Chapter 7, page 196

WEEK 16

DIRECTIONS **Answer each question below on the day of the week assigned to it.**

MONDAY

There may be a problem in the sentence structure of the words below. Select the <u>best</u> revision, or choose D.

Wearing a raincoat and carrying an umbrella, stepped into the pouring rain.

A Wore a raincoat, carried an umbrella, and stepped into the pouring rain.
B Stepping into the pouring rain wearing a raincoat and carrying an umbrella.
C Wearing a raincoat and carrying an umbrella, she stepped into the pouring rain.
D correct as is

Chapter 16, page 428

TUESDAY

Select the choice that correctly combines the sentences below.

Sam watched the artist. The artist made a sketch.

A While Sam watching, the artist made a sketch.
B Sam watched the artist how he made a sketch.
C Sam watched the artist make a sketch.
D Sam watched the artist, make a sketch.

Chapter 16, page 440

WEDNESDAY

Decide which of the underlined words in the set below is misspelled. If all are correct, choose D.

A It is important to pay attention to water <u>conservation</u> rules.
B The <u>decoration</u> on the cake makes it special.
C The contest judges gave <u>considerasion</u> to the age of the skaters.
D no mistake

Chapter 14, page 361

THURSDAY

Read the following sentence. Choose the response that fixes the underlined error. If there is no error, choose D.

Jamaica is an <u>island in the caribbean sea.</u>

A Island in the Caribbean sea.
B Island in the Caribbean Sea.
C island in the Caribbean Sea.
D correct as is

Chapter 11, page 288

FRIDAY

There may be a grammar problem in the sentence below. Select the <u>best</u> revision, or choose D.

The rose is the prettier of the two flowers.

A The rose is the most pretty of the two flowers.
B The rose is the more prettier of the two flowers.
C The rose is the prettiest of the two flowers.
D correct as is

Chapter 9, page 245

WEEK 17

DIRECTIONS **Answer each question below on the day of the week assigned to it.**

MONDAY

Read the following sentence. Choose the response that fixes the underlined error. If there is no error, choose _D_.

<u>There's</u> lots of new books in the library.

A they're

B Their's

C There are

D correct as is

Chapter 6, page 180

TUESDAY

Select the choice that correctly combines the following two sentences.

Mika likes baseball. Jenna prefers soccer.

A Mika likes baseball. But Jenna soccer.

B Mika likes baseball; but Jenna prefers soccer.

C Mika likes baseball, but Jenn prefers soccer.

D Mika likes baseball but Jenna prefers soccer.

Chapter 16, page 438

WEDNESDAY

Read the sentence below. Choose the response that uses the underlined word in the same way as it is used in the first sentence.

She threw the <u>core</u> of the pear into the trash can.

A the speaker went right to the <u>core</u> of the problem.

B You need to <u>core</u> those apples before you bake them.

C The fruit <u>core</u> usually holds the seeds.

D The scientists studied the <u>core</u> of the earth.

Vocabulary Mini-Lesson, page 508

THURSDAY

Read the following sentence. Choose the response that fixes the underlined error. If there is no error, choose _D_.

Jeff sent <u>she and me</u> a postcard from the beach.

A her and me

B she and I

C me and she

D correct as is

Chapter 8, page 229

FRIDAY

Sana is preparing to write a research report about the emu, a large Australian bird. She found a library book called _Australia's Animal Life_. Where should she look in the book to see if it includes information about emus?

A the index   **C** the copyright page

B the title page   **D** the bibliography

Quick Reference Handbook, page 729

DIRECTIONS **Read the following article.**

The Smelly Skunks

"How do you keep a skunk from smelling?"—the old joke goes—"Put a clothespin on its nose." No bigger than a housecat, the skunk is avoided by much larger animals, such as bears, wolves, mountain lions, and humans. Animals avoid skunks because skunks have the ability to produce and spray a foul-smelling liquid—the worst-smelling liquid produced by any animal. No wonder the skunk has few natural enemies—except for the occasional bobcat and great horned owl, which seem to be <u>immune</u> to the skunk's odor.

Skunks belong to the family of mammals know as mustelids, which includes weasels, ferrets, minks, wolverines, badgers, and otters. Skunks are small, furry animals that have distinctive black-and-white markings. A fully grown skunk weighs about eight pounds. It has short legs and a long, flexible backbone. Skunks move with a characteristic waddle.

Skunks are peaceful creatures who use their foul-smelling spray only when threatened. Before a skunk releases the yellowish, oily liquid, it will issue a series of warnings. First, it will stamp with its front feet; next, it will rake the ground with its claws. If these early-warning signals don't work, the skunk will arch its back, hiss, and raise its tail.

A skunk's defensive spray is stored in two glandular pouches beneath its tail. When it sprays, the skunk tightens the muscles around each pouch to force the liquid through the openings, which resemble the nozzles of small water hoses. Skunks can spray accurately as far a fifteen feet, and, if necessary, they can spray several times in a row.

40 An animal or human who has been unlucky enough to come within spraying range of a skunk that considers itself in jeopardy may wear a distinctive odor for days or even weeks. Household bleach can be effective in removing the musky odor from clothes. Vinegar or tomato juice helps remove the odor from hair or skin.

There are three main types of skunks: striped, hog-nosed, and spotted. The striped 50 skunk, whose scientific name is *Mephitis mephitis,* is the most common species in the United States. *Mephitis* means "evil smelling," and *Mephitis mephitis* means "double the stink."

Skunks tend to live underground in dens lined with dry leaves. They are <u>nocturnal</u> animals, preferring to sleep during the day. Female skunks usually give birth to four or five young in a litter. Skunks are solitary, self-sufficient, and independent.

Skunks eat caterpillars, insects such as beetles and crickets, and small rodents. They will also eat snakes. Frequently, skunks will prowl highways, feeding on insects, snakes, turtles, and other creatures killed by passing cars. Other skunks are killed by cars too. Thus, the automobile is one of the skunk's deadliest enemies.

WEEK 18

DIRECTIONS The questions below refer to the article "The Smelly Skunks" on page 42. Answer each question below on the day of the week assigned to it.

MONDAY

What causes large animals to avoid skunks?

A Skunks are fierce fighters.
B Skunks produce a foul-smelling spray.
C Skunks put on a frightening display.
D Skunks produce a powerful poison.

Quick Reference Handbook, 738

TUESDAY

In this article, <u>immune</u> (line 13) means

A lacking the ability to smell.
B having the ability to resist.
C having the power to attract.
D having the power to defeat.

Test-Taking Mini-Lesson, page 612

WEDNESDAY

Which sentence supports the author's statement that skunks are peaceful creatures who spray only when threatened?

A No bigger than a housecat, the skunk is avoided by much larger animals.
B Skunks can spray accurately as far a fifteen feet.
C Before a skunk releases the yellowish, oily liquid, it will issue a series of warnings.
D They are nocturnal animals, preferring to sleep during the day.

Test-Taking Mini-Lesson, page 579

THURSDAY

Which of these is the <u>most</u> common skunk in the United States?

A the long-tailed skunk
B the hog-nosed skunk
C the striped skunk
D the spotted skunk

Test-Taking Mini-Lesson, page 579

FRIDAY

If you wanted to learn more about skunks, you should

A read a book about mustelids.
B visit a botanical garden.
C read a book about badgers.
D look in an encyclopedia under "Insects."

Writing Workshop, page 654

WEEK **19**

DIRECTIONS **The questions below refer to the article "The Smelly Skunks" on page 42. Answer each question below on the day of the week assigned to it.**

MONDAY

Which of these statements from the article is an opinion?

A Skunks have few natural enemies.
B Skunks spray only when threatened.
C Skunks have the worst smell of any animal.
D Skunks are solitary animals.

Test-Taking Mini-Lesson, page 688

TUESDAY

Fully grown skunks are about the same size as

A bears.
B wolves.
C mountain lions.
D housecats.

Test-Taking Mini-Lesson, page 579

WEDNESDAY

Which of these is a clue to the meaning of the word nocturnal **(line 56)?**

A "give birth to four or five young"
B "live underground"
C "solitary, self-sufficient, and independent"
D "preferring to sleep during the day"

Vocabulary Mini-Lesson, page 611

THURSDAY

Most skunks live

A under low bushes.
B in nests in the tops of trees.
C in holes in dead trees.
D in underground dens.

Test-Taking Mini-Lesson, page 579

FRIDAY

This article is mainly about

A why skunks smell.
B skunks and their relatives.
C the striped skunk.
D facts about skunks.

Reading Workshop, page 505

WEEK 20

DIRECTIONS **Answer each question below on the day of the week assigned to it.**

MONDAY

Decide which of the underlined words in the set below is misspelled. If all are correct, choose D.

A Mr. and Mrs. Lee are in town, and <u>their</u> coming for dinner tonight.

B Put your things over <u>there</u> by the bookshelf.

C All students should bring <u>their</u> papers to the front of the room.

D no mistake

Chapter 14, page 380

TUESDAY

Read the following sentence. Choose the response that fixes the underlined error. If there is no error, choose D.

The White House is located on <u>Pennsylvania avenue in Washington, d.c.</u>

A pennsylvania avenue in Washington, D.C.

B Pennsylvania Avenue in Washington, D.C.

C Pennsylvania avenue in Washington, d.c.

D correct as is

Chapter 11, page 288

WEDNESDAY

Select the choice that shows the <u>best</u> way to combine the following two sentences.

We practiced our lines. The band members went over the music.

A We practiced our lines and the band members went over the music.

B We practiced our lines while the band members went over the music.

C We practiced our lines And the band members went over the music.

D We practiced our lines; and the band members went over the music.

Chapter 16, page 440

THURSDAY

Meena left her house late for school. Three items below are effects of her lateness. One is a cause. Identify the cause.

A She was marked down as tardy.

B She could not find her shoes.

C She missed the bus.

D She missed the morning assembly.

Critical-Thinking Mini-Lesson, page 517

FRIDAY

Choose the word in the group that means the same, or about the same, as the underlined word.

The <u>gallant</u> knight made way for the lady by throwing his cape over the muddy puddle.

A courteous

B handsome

C messy

D thoughtless

Vocabulary Mini-Lesson, page 477

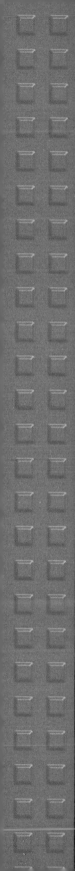

Grammar, Usage, and Mechanics

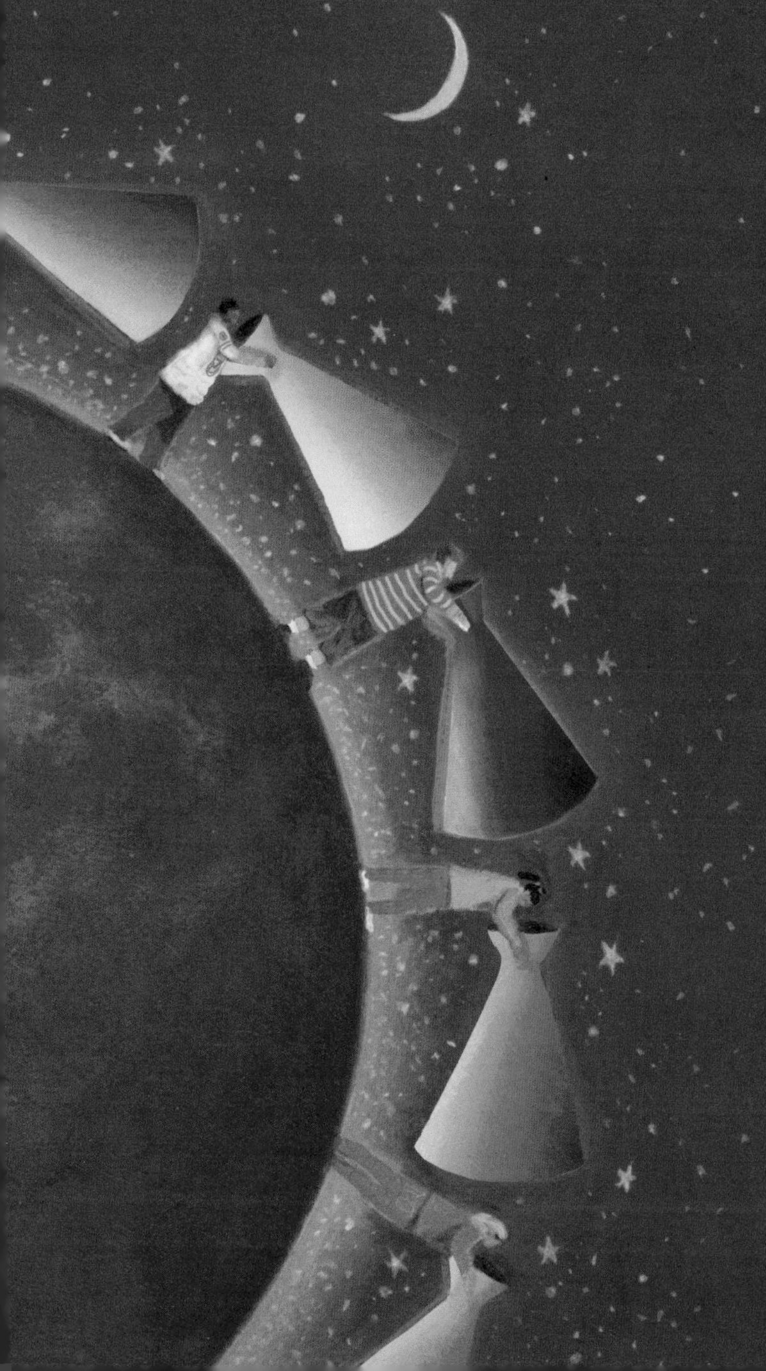

Grammar

Usage

Mechanics

internet connect

go.hrw.com

GO TO: go.hrw.com
KEYWORD: EOLang

The Sentence
Subject and Predicate, Kinds of Sentences

Diagnostic Preview

A. Identifying Sentences

If a word group is a sentence, add a capital letter at the beginning and punctuate the sentence with an appropriate end mark. If a word group is not a sentence, write *sentence fragment*.

EXAMPLES   **1.** followed the trail on the map
        1. sentence fragment

        2. the López twins come from Nuevo Laredo, Mexico
        2. The López twins come from Nuevo Laredo, Mexico.

1. we read the postcards from our Asian pen pals
2. our school has a homework hot line
3. definitely mailed the invitations yesterday
4. Will you practice guitar before dinner
5. going to the Washington Monument

B. Identifying Simple Subjects and Simple Predicates

Identify the simple subject and the simple predicate in each of the following sentences.

EXAMPLES **1.** Last year my family traveled to Mecca, Saudi Arabia.

     1. family—simple subject; traveled—simple predicate

    2. The crowded corner market is having a sale.

     2. market—simple subject; is having—simple predicate

┌HELP┐

A subject or a predicate in Part B may be compound.

6. My grandmother plays mah-jongg with my friends and me every Saturday.

7. The farmers have plowed the fields and will plant potatoes.

8. At night you can rent roller skates for half price at the rink near my house.

9. On the sand lay a beautiful seashell.

10. On Saturday, Amy, Theo, and I walked through Chinatown and took pictures.

11. Many students in our class have volunteered for the charity softball game.

12. Where did you put Isabella's fuzzy, green wool sweater?

13. *Island of the Blue Dolphins* by Scott O'Dell is one of my favorite books.

14. Beyond the large rocks at the far end of the beach is a small cave.

15. During the last week of vacation, my brother, sister and I hiked through the rain forest.

C. Punctuating and Classifying Sentences by Purpose

For each of the following sentences, add the appropriate end mark. Then, classify each sentence as *declarative, interrogative, imperative,* or *exclamatory.*

EXAMPLES **1.** Have you read this poem by José Garcia Villa

     1. Have you read this poem by José Garcia Villa?— interrogative

    2. We sampled a Cuban dish at the international fair.

     2. We sampled a Cuban dish at the international fair.—declarative

16. Please answer the phone

17. What a good time we had

18. Has anyone seen the cat

19. They sat on a bench and played checkers

20. Whose book is this

21. Hang that jacket in the hall closet
22. How we laughed
23. Water is composed of oxygen and hydrogen
24. Call this number in case of an emergency
25. Did you say to turn left here

Sentence or Sentence Fragment?

1a. A *sentence* is a word group that contains a subject and a verb and that expresses a complete thought.

A sentence begins with a capital letter and ends with a period, a question mark, or an exclamation point.

EXAMPLES **O**ctavio Paz won a Nobel Prize in literature**.** [The subject is *Octavio Paz,* and the verb is *won.*]

Stop**.** [The understood subject is *you,* and the verb is *Stop.*]

Do you collect coins**?** [The subject is *you,* and the verb is *Do collect.*]

I actually rode on an elephant**!** [The subject is *I,* and the verb is *rode.*]

A *sentence fragment* is a word group that looks like a sentence but either does not contain both a subject and a verb or does not express a complete thought.

SENTENCE FRAGMENT	Visited an old Spanish mission in San Diego. [The subject is missing. Who visited the mission?]
SENTENCE	My family visited an old Spanish mission in San Diego.
SENTENCE FRAGMENT	Alonzo's sisters and brothers. [The verb is missing. What did Alonzo's sisters and brothers do?]
SENTENCE	Alonzo's sisters and brothers planned a surprise party for his birthday.

Reference Note

For information on the **understood subject,** see page 64.

TIPS & TRICKS

To tell whether a group of words is a sentence or a sentence fragment, ask yourself these three questions:

1. What is the subject?
2. What is the verb?
3. What is the complete thought the word group expresses?

If you cannot answer any one of these questions, the word group may not be a sentence.

SKILLS FOCUS

Identify and use complete sentences. Identify and correct sentence fragments.

SENTENCE FRAGMENT	As I walked to school yesterday. [This thought is not complete. What happened as I walked to school yesterday?]
SENTENCE	As I walked to school yesterday, I saw Mr. Saunders walking his dog.

NOTE A word group that has a subject and a verb and that expresses a complete thought is called an **independent clause.** An independent clause can stand alone as a sentence. A word group that has a subject and a verb but does not express a complete thought (such as *As I walked to school yesterday*) is called a **subordinate clause.**

Reference Note
For more about **independent and subordinate clauses,** see page 135.

Exercise 1 Identifying Sentences

Identify each of the following word groups as a *sentence* or a *sentence fragment.* If a word group is a sentence, rewrite the sentence, using a capital letter at the beginning and adding an end mark.

EXAMPLE 1. my aunt and uncle raise shar-peis
          1. *sentence—My aunt and uncle raise shar-peis.*

1. my aunt, my uncle, and my cousins at their house in the country last weekend
2. after dinner, Aunt Marie told me about the history of the shar-pei breed
3. bred these dogs in China
4. just look at all that loose, wrinkled skin
5. protected them from injury during a fight
6. gentle and a lot of fun with children
7. playing catch with Queenie
8. the little balls of fur were Queenie's new puppies
9. have you ever seen such a sight as these puppies
10. what a good time we had

Think as a Reader/Writer

In speech, people often use sentence fragments. Such fragments usually are not confusing because the context and the speaker's tone of voice and expressions help to complete the meaning.

Professional writers, too, may use sentence fragments to create specific effects in their writing. However, in your writing at school, you should use complete sentences.

Reference Note
For more information on **revising sentence fragments,** see page 430.

Exercise 2 Identifying and Revising Sentences and Sentence Fragments

Some of the following word groups are sentences, and others are sentence fragments. If a word group is a sentence, write *sentence.* If a word group is not a sentence, add words to make the word group a sentence.

EXAMPLE **1.** A common custom worldwide.

1. *Weddings are a common custom worldwide.*

1. Having been introduced to the guest of honor.
2. Hold your horses there, young fellow.
3. Dancing in the air around the garden.
4. It will be on your right.
5. Just how does a fire extinguisher work?
6. One of the only examples of this type of Aztec art in this area.
7. Three pennies, a quarter, a bus token, and four acorns.
8. He called Sunday night.
9. An instrument popular in Africa, the kalimba.
10. How we laughed at that movie!

Review A Writing Complete Sentences

Some of the following word groups are sentences. If a word group is a sentence, rewrite it, adding a capital letter and end punctuation. If a word group is not a sentence, rewrite it, adding a subject or a verb, a capital letter, and end punctuation to make it a sentence.

EXAMPLE **1.** wrote a play

1. *Our language arts class wrote a play.*

1. sent us a postcard from the Philippines
2. it was cold at the skating rink
3. helped me with my science project
4. a surfer on a huge wave
5. was hungry at lunchtime
6. it is too late for a game of checkers
7. is that the American Falls or the Horseshoe Falls
8. the Cuban family next door
9. what time is your mom picking us up
10. the governor of my state

Subject and Predicate

Sentences consist of two basic parts: *subjects* and *predicates*.

The Subject

1b. The **subject** tells *whom* or *what* the sentence is about.

EXAMPLES **Lois Lenski** wrote *Strawberry Girl.*

The tooth with a point is called a canine.

To find the subject, ask yourself *who* or *what* is doing something or *about whom* or *what* something is being said.

EXAMPLES **My best friend** sits next to me in science class. [*Who* sits? My best friend sits.]

Science class is very interesting this year. [*What* is interesting? Science class is.]

The Position of the Subject

The subject may come at the beginning, in the middle, or even at the end of a sentence.

EXAMPLES After school, **Theresa** went to band practice.

Under our house was **a tiny kitten.**

Exercise 3 Identifying Subjects

Identify the subject in each of these sentences.

EXAMPLE **1.** The final score was tied.

1. The final score

1. Many games use rackets or paddles.
2. Tennis can be an exhausting sport.
3. Badminton rackets don't weigh very much.
4. Table-tennis paddles are covered with rubber.
5. Racquetball uses special rackets.
6. In Florida, citrus trees grow an important crop.
7. After three to five years, fruit grows on the new trees.
8. Does Florida grow all of the citrus fruit in the nation?
9. California also grows oranges and other citrus fruit.
10. From Texas comes the Star Ruby grapefruit.

SKILLS FOCUS

Identify the subject of a sentence.

Complete Subject and Simple Subject

The **complete subject** consists of all the words needed to tell *whom* or *what* the sentence is about. The **simple subject** is part of the complete subject.

1c. The **simple subject** is the main word or word group that tells *whom* or *what* the sentence is about.

EXAMPLES   **The Korean market** is closed today.

      complete subject   The Korean market
      simple subject   market

      A brightly colored blue jay sat on the windowsill.

      complete subject   A brightly colored blue jay
      simple subject   blue jay

Sometimes the same word or words make up both the simple subject and the complete subject.

EXAMPLES   In the canyon, **we** saw hawks. [*We* is both the complete subject and the simple subject.]

      Little Rascal is the story of a boy and his pet raccoon. [The title *Little Rascal* is both the complete subject and the simple subject.]

NOTE   In this book, the term *subject* generally refers to the simple subject unless otherwise indicated.

Exercise 4 **Identifying Complete Subjects and Simple Subjects**

Identify the complete subject of each of the following sentences. Then, underline the simple subject.

EXAMPLE   1. From the chimney came a thick cloud of smoke.

      1. a thick <u>cloud</u> of smoke

1. Several tents were set up in the park.
2. Have you heard the new song by Cara Marie?
3. News travels fast in our town.
4. Above the fort, the flag was still flying.
5. Beyond those distant mountains lies an ancient American Indian village.

6. Those newspaper reporters have been interviewing the mayor all morning.
7. On the shelf was a beautiful blue bowl.
8. According to folklore, Pecos Bill made the Grand Canyon.
9. The blue candles burned all night long.
10. In the drawer were some chopsticks.

The Predicate

1d. The *predicate* of a sentence tells something about the subject.

EXAMPLES   Lois Lenski **wrote *Strawberry Girl.***

The tooth with a point **is called a canine.**

Exercise 5 **Identifying Predicates**

Identify the predicate in each of the following sentences.

EXAMPLE   **1.** Many people would like to have a robot.

    1. would like to have a robot

1. Robots are machines with "brains."
2. The robot's brain is a computer.
3. Not all robots look like humans.
4. Some robots look like toy cars.
5. One robot explored some of the surface of Mars.
6. Many companies use robots.
7. Cars of the future may be guided by robots.
8. Some household jobs can be done by robots.
9. A robot could clean your room.
10. You might like to have a robot to help with your daily chores.

The Position of the Predicate

The predicate usually comes after the subject. Sometimes, however, part or all of the predicate comes before the subject.

EXAMPLES   **Quickly** we **learned the layout of the small Hopi village.**

At the entrance to the science fair were maps of the exhibits.

SKILLS FOCUS

Identify the predicate of a sentence.

Exercise 6 Identifying Predicates

Write each of the following sentences. Then, underline the predicate.

EXAMPLE   1. At noon we went to a Mexican restaurant.

1. *At noon* we *went to a Mexican restaurant.*

1. Our family likes different kinds of food.
2. Last night Dad prepared spaghetti and a salad for supper.
3. Sometimes Mom makes chow mein.
4. With chow mein she serves egg rolls.
5. At the Greek bakery we buy fresh pita bread.
6. Tomorrow Erica will make German potato salad.
7. Lately, tacos have become my favorite food.
8. Carefully, I spoon grated lettuce and cheese into a tortilla.
9. After that come the other ingredients.
10. In the United States, people enjoy a wide variety of foods.

HELP

Although the example in Exercise 7 shows two possible answers, you need to give only one answer for each item.

Exercise 7 Writing Predicates

Make a sentence out of each of the following words or word groups by adding a predicate to fill the blank or blanks.

EXAMPLE   1. ____ everyone ____

1. *With a shout of joy, everyone took a paddle and began to row.*

or

As the waves crashed against the raft, everyone grabbed for the sides.

1. Foamy white water ____.
2. The hot summer air ____.
3. A strong current ____.
4. ____ the eyes of every person on board ____.
5. The lightweight paddles ____.
6. ____ dangerous rocks and swirls ____.
7. Quick action by everyone ____.
8. A sleek, blue rubber raft ____.
9. The man in the white helmet and blue life jacket ____.
10. ____ the people in this photograph ____.

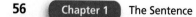

Complete Predicate and Simple Predicate

The *complete predicate* consists of a verb and all the words that describe the verb and complete its meaning.

1e. The *simple predicate,* or *verb,* is the main word or word group in the complete predicate.

EXAMPLES   The nurse **lifted the patient carefully.**

complete predicate   lifted the patient carefully
simple predicate (verb)   lifted

I **saw a picture of a Siberian tiger.**

complete predicate   saw a picture of a Siberian tiger
simple predicate (verb)   saw

Exercise 8   Identifying Complete Predicates and Verbs

Identify the complete predicate of each of the following sentences. Then, underline the verb.

EXAMPLE   1. For several reasons, space travel fascinates me.
         1. *For several reasons fascinates me*

1. My class traveled by train to Houston, Texas.
2. In Houston my classmates and I visited the Lyndon B. Johnson Space Center.
3. The center displays moon rocks.
4. At the center, astronauts train for their flights.
5. In one room we saw several unusual computers.
6. On the way home, we stopped at the Astrodome for a tour.
7. The stadium covers nine-and-a-half acres of land.
8. Several teams play there.
9. Every year the Astrodome attracts thousands of tourists.
10. Actually, I had more fun at the space center.

The simple predicate may be a single verb or a *verb phrase* (a verb with one or more helping verbs).

EXAMPLES   Yoshi **went** to Japan last summer. [single verb]

The park **is located** near a lake. [verb phrase]

We **should have planned** a picnic. [verb phrase]

Reference Note

For information on **helping verbs,** see page 95.

SKILLS FOCUS

Identify the simple predicate of a sentence. Identify the complete predicate of a sentence.

NOTE The words *not* and *never* and the contraction *–n't* are not verbs. They are never part of a verb or verb phrase.

EXAMPLE Kendra **should**n't **have added** another hot pepper to the sauce.

Exercise 9 Identifying Complete Predicates and Verbs

Identify the complete predicate in each of the following sentences. Then, underline the verb.

EXAMPLE 1. The Liberty Bell was made in England.

1. *was made* in England

1. I am writing a report on the Liberty Bell.
2. The Pennsylvania Assembly ordered the Liberty Bell.
3. Thomas Lester had made the bell in London.
4. In 1752, the bell was cracked by its own clapper.
5. American patriots hid the bell from the British army.
6. The bell was not brought back to Philadelphia until 1778.
7. The Liberty Bell cracked again in 1835.
8. This bell has been rung on many historic occasions.
9. The bell is exhibited in the Liberty Bell Pavilion.
10. We will be seeing it on our field trip to Philadelphia.

Finding the Subject

Sometimes it may be difficult to find the subject of a sentence. In such cases, find the verb first. Then, ask yourself *Who?* or *What?* before the verb.

EXAMPLES Next semester you may take art or music. [The verb is *may take*. *Who* may take? *You* may take. *You* is the subject of the sentence.]

Can your sister drive us to the park? [The verb is *Can drive*. *Who* can drive? *Sister* can drive. *Sister* is the subject of the sentence.]

Please read the first chapter. [The verb is *read. Who* should read? *You* should read. *You* is the understood subject of the sentence.]

Reference Note

For more information on **understood subjects,** see page 64.

Compound Subject and Compound Verb

Compound Subject

1f. A *compound subject* consists of two or more subjects that are joined by a conjunction and that have the same verb.

The parts of a compound subject are most often connected by *and* or *or.*

EXAMPLES   **Minneapolis** and **St. Paul** are called the "Twin Cities." [The two parts of the compound subject have the same verb, *are called.*]

Will **Mrs. Jones** or **Ms. Lopez** chaperone our field trip? [The two parts of the compound subject have the same verb, *Will chaperone.*]

Flutes, clarinets, and **oboes** are all woodwind instruments. [The three parts of the compound subject have the same verb, *are.*]

Reference Note

Notice that **commas** are **used to separate three or more parts of a compound subject.** For more about this use of commas, see page 314.

Exercise 10   **Identifying Compound Subjects**

Identify the compound subjects in each of the following sentences.

EXAMPLE   **1.** October and June are my favorite months.

        1. October, June

1. Wild ducks and geese migrate south each year.
2. Stars and planets form a galaxy.
3. Someday dolphins and people may be able to communicate with each other.
4. Baseball and soccer are the two most popular sports at my sister's school.
5. Eggs and flour are two ingredients in pancakes.
6. Every year bugs and rabbits raid our vegetable garden.
7. Pizza or ravioli will be served.
8. At a party, balloons or horns make the best noisemakers.
9. Dachshunds, Chihuahuas, Lhasa apsos, and Pekingese ran around in the yard.
10. In the Tower of London are famous jewels and crowns.

Identify the subject of a sentence. Identify the compound subject of a sentence.

Compound Verb

1g. A *compound verb* consists of two or more verbs that are joined by a conjunction and that have the same subject.

A connecting word such as *and* or *but* is used to join the parts of a compound verb.

EXAMPLES   Ben **overslept** but **caught** his bus anyway.

Conchita **hums, sings,** or **listens** to the radio all day.

My father **bought** a Chinese wok and **cooked** vegetables in it.

Exercise 11   **Identifying Compound Verbs**

Identify the compound verbs in the following sentences.

EXAMPLE   1.   I have proofread my paper and made a final copy.
           1.   *have proofread, made*

1. Mai and her parents left Vietnam and arrived in California in 2004.
2. Julie received good grades and made the honor roll.
3. Every week, our band practices together and writes songs.
4. Before supper I usually set the table or peel the vegetables.
5. Floyd asked for a watch but received a bike instead.
6. We gathered firewood and headed back to camp.
7. Last week everyone gave a speech or recited a poem.
8. The referee will call a rain delay or postpone the game.
9. I remembered the bread but forgot the milk.
10. The Greek restaurant has closed but will reopen soon.

Exercise 12   **Writing Compound Subjects and Compound Verbs**

Make sentences by adding compound subjects or compound verbs to fill in the blanks in the following word groups.

EXAMPLES   1.   _____ are coming to the party.
           1.   *Fran and Terry are coming to the party.*

              2.   At the mall, we _____.
              2.   *At the mall, we ate lunch and went to a movie.*

1. _____ are beginning a stamp collection.

HELP

Remember to include helping verbs when you are identifying verbs in Exercise 11.

SKILLS FOCUS

Identify compound verbs in a sentence.

---

2. _____ were my favorite teachers last year.
3. The creature from outer space _____.
4. At the end of the play, the cast _____.
5. Last week _____ were interviewed on a talk show.
6. In the garage are _____.
7. During the storm, we _____.
8. At the front door were _____.
9. After school, my friends _____.
10. He _____ before the birthday party.

Review B Identifying Subjects and Verbs

Identify the subjects and verbs in each of the following sentences.

EXAMPLE
  1. In the history of African American music are many unforgettable names.

  1. names—subject; are—verb

┌HELP┐
Some of the subjects and verbs in Review B are compound.

1. You may recognize the man in the picture on this page.
2. Most people immediately think of his deep, raspy voice.
3. Ray Charles is called the father of soul music.
4. He lost his sight at the age of seven and became an orphan at fifteen.
5. However, misfortune and trouble did not stop Ray Charles.
6. His musical genius turned his troubles into songs.
7. Today, the songs of Ray Charles are heard all over the world.
8. Do his songs contain different musical styles?
9. Gospel, jazz, blues, and even pop are all part of his sound.
10. His special style and powerful performances have long drawn fans to Ray Charles's music.

A sentence may have both a compound subject and a compound verb.

```
             S      S    V          V
EXAMPLES   Zina and I bought corn and fed the ducks.

             S          S    V          V
           Carrots and celery are crunchy and satisfy your
           appetite.
```

SKILLS FOCUS

Identify the compound subject of a sentence.
Identify compound verbs in a sentence.

NOTE Sometimes a sentence will contain more than one subject and verb, but neither the subject nor verb will be compound.

EXAMPLES

    S V   S   V

I like apples, but my **sister prefers** oranges.
[compound sentence]

                      S   V

In San Antonio, **we toured** the Alamo, while our

     S   V

friends visited the Riverwalk.
[complex sentence]

     S   V   S   V

David wipes the table, and **Cindy dries** the dishes

         S   V

that **Dad has washed.**
[compound-complex sentence]

Reference Note

For more information about **compound, complex,** and **compound-complex sentences,** see page 143.

Think as a *Reader/Writer*

In your own writing, you can combine ideas by creating compound subjects and verbs. Combining sentences in this way will help make your writing smoother and easier to read. Compare the examples below.

CHOPPY
Susan went hiking in the mountains. Mark went hiking, too. Aunt Connie went with them.

REVISED
Susan, Mark, and Aunt Connie went hiking in the mountains.

Reference Note

For more information on **combining sentences,** see page 435.

Exercise 13 **Identifying Compound Subjects and Compound Verbs**

Identify the compound subject and the compound verb in each of the following sentences.

EXAMPLE   **1.** Tina and Julia washed the dog and dried it.

           1. Tina, Julia—subject; washed, dried—verb

1. Alice and Reiko sang and played the piano.
2. Either Dwayne or I will find the coach and ask his advice.
3. Patrick and she read the same biography of Dr. Martin Luther King, Jr., and reported on it.
4. Roses and lilacs look pretty and smell good.
5. The dentist or her assistant cleans and polishes my teeth.
6. In many traditional Japanese homes, doors or partitions are framed in wood, left open in the middle, and then covered with rice paper.
7. Larry and she washed the dishes but did not dry them.
8. The lamb and its mother had leapt the fence but were still inside the yard.
9. Fish, rays, turtles, and dolphins live in the Gulf of Mexico and often swim near the shore.
10. Did Uncle Ted or his children call or visit you on their way through town?

Review C Identifying Subjects and Predicates

Identify the complete subject and the complete predicate in each of the following sentences. Then, underline the simple subject and the verb.

┌HELP┐
Some of the subjects and verbs in Review C are compound.

EXAMPLE   **1.** Reports and legends of huge apelike creatures fascinate many people.

       1. subject—*Reports* and *legends* of huge apelike creatures; predicate—*fascinate* many people

1. These creatures are known as *Yeti* in the Himalayas and as *Rakshas* in Katmandu.
2. American Indians of the Northwest call them *Mammoth.*
3. *Sasquatch* and *Bigfoot* are other common names for these mysterious creatures.
4. Since 1818, they have been seen and described by people in the United States and Canada.
5. According to most accounts, Bigfoot adults are very strong and large and smell very bad.
6. Their huge footprints have been measured and cast in plaster by eager searchers.
7. However, these reports and bits of evidence generally do not convince scientists.
8. Not one live Bigfoot has ever been captured by either scientists or the general public.
9. As a result, the Bigfoot is simply a fantasy to most people.
10. Still, in pockets of deep wilderness across the country might live whole families of these shy creatures.

Review D Writing Sentences

Tell whether each of the following sentence parts can be used as a *subject* or a *predicate.* Then, use each sentence part in a sentence. Begin each sentence with a capital letter, and end it with the correct mark of punctuation. Use a variety of subjects and verbs in your sentences.

EXAMPLE   **1.** will drive us home

       1. predicate—*Will your mother drive us home?*

1. my favorite book
2. watched a good mystery

3. the flying saucer

3. the flying saucer
4. the oldest house in town
5. prepares delicious Korean food
6. growled and bared its teeth
7. the shiny red car and the bicycle
8. caught a huge fish
9. can borrow your skates
10. the best tacos and enchiladas in town

Kinds of Sentences

Sentences may be classified according to purpose.

Sentences may be classified according to purpose.

1h. A *declarative sentence* makes a statement and ends with a period.

EXAMPLES   Our media center has several computers**.**

Patrick Henry lived in Virginia**.**

1i. An *imperative sentence* gives a command or makes a request. Most imperative sentences end with a period. A strong command ends with an exclamation point.

EXAMPLES   Please pass the potatoes**.** [request]

Sit down**.** [command]

Stop shouting**!** [strong command]

The subject of a command or a request is always *you*, even if the word *you* never appears in the sentence. In such cases, *you* is called the **understood subject.**

EXAMPLES   [**You**] Please pass the potatoes**.**

[**You**] Stop shouting**!**

1j. An *interrogative sentence* asks a question and ends with a question mark.

EXAMPLES   Did the Apollo 13 spacecraft reach the moon**?**

How old are you**?**

Reference Note

For information on **how sentences can be classified according to structure,** see page 142.

SKILLS FOCUS

Classify sentences by purpose. Identify and use declarative sentences. Identify and use imperative sentences. Identify and use interrogative sentences.

1k. An *exclamatory sentence* shows excitement or expresses strong feeling and ends with an exclamation point.

EXAMPLES   What a difficult assignment that was**!**

I got her autograph**!**

Exercise 14 Classifying Sentences by Purpose

Write each of the following sentences, and add an appropriate end mark. Identify the sentence as *declarative, interrogative, imperative,* or *exclamatory.*

EXAMPLE   **1.** What a funny show that was

   1. What a funny show that was!—exclamatory

1. Please help me find my umbrella
2. How happy I am
3. Have you and your sister been to the new video store on Congress Avenue
4. Go east for three blocks, and look for a yellow mailbox next to a red door
5. My father and I are cleaning the attic together later this afternoon
6. What a delicious salad this is
7. During our last summer vacation, we toured the garment district in New York City
8. Do you like barbecued chicken
9. My surprise visit last month pleased both my grandmother and Aunt Gabriela
10. When is your next piano lesson

Review E Classifying Sentences by Purpose

For each of the sentences on the following page, add an appropriate end mark. Then, identify each sentence as *declarative, imperative, interrogative,* or *exclamatory.*

EXAMPLE   **1.** Have you ever seen the Grand Canyon

   1. Have you ever seen the Grand Canyon?
   —interrogative

Think as a
Reader/Writer

Be careful not to overuse exclamation points in your writing. Save them for sentences that really do show strong emotion. When used too much, exclamation points lose their effect.

OVERUSED
For her birthday, Katy's parents threw her a bowling party! About twenty friends and family members attended, and we all had a great time! I had two strikes in one game!

IMPROVED
For her birthday, Katy's parents threw her a bowling party. About twenty friends and family members attended, and we all had a great time. I had two strikes in one game!

GRAMMAR

Identify and use exclamatory sentences.

Think as a
Reader/Writer

In any kind of writing, correct end punctuation is important. However, it is especially important in written conversations. The punctuation helps a reader know how a speaker says something. A sentence can mean very different things when its end punctuation is changed. Try reading the following sentences aloud to hear the difference.

DECLARATIVE
   He's my hero.

INTERROGATIVE
   He's my hero?

EXCLAMATORY
   He's my hero!

1. We enjoyed our vacation in the Southwest
2. Dad took these photographs when our family visited the Grand Canyon
3. Our guide spoke both Spanish and English
4. How pretty the sunset is
5. Don't stand so close to the edge
6. Did you buy any turquoise-and-silver jewelry
7. It was quite chilly at night
8. What a great movie we saw about the canyon
9. Did you take the short hike or the long one
10. Look at us riding on mules in this canyon

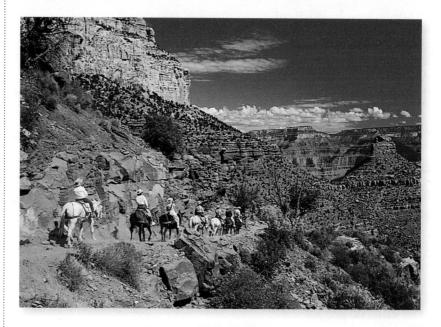

Chapter Review

A. Identifying Sentences

For each of the following word groups that is a sentence, add a capital letter at the beginning and punctuate the sentence with an appropriate end mark. If a group is not a sentence, write *sentence fragment.*

1. burned brightly throughout the night
2. he studies computer programming after school
3. the band sounds so wonderful tonight
4. whenever the mountains are covered with fog
5. over the past two thousand years
6. be seated
7. behind us barked the dogs
8. just as I neared the castle's drawbridge
9. should we sand the wood now
10. the artist carving the totem pole

B. Identifying the Complete Subject and the Complete Predicate

Write each of the following sentences. Then, underline the complete subject once and the complete predicate twice.

11. *Black Beauty* is a story about a horse.
12. Sometimes bats fly into our chimney.
13. A wonderful smell of baking bread came from the kitchen and filled the house.
14. The chief will speak to you now.
15. Milk and cheese can help you develop strong bones.
16. Two eagles and a hawk live near our house.
17. Adele peeled and ate the orange.
18. Several knights guarded the castle and drove off the dragon.
19. Under the lettuce was my tomato.
20. Will Ahmad and Nadim set the table before lunch?

C. Identifying Simple Subjects and Simple Predicates

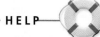

HELP

Sentences in Part C may contain compound subjects and compound verbs.

For each of the following sentences, write the simple subject and the simple predicate.

21. The winner is Mr. Otis Kwan!

22. Suddenly, the clock stopped.

23. Many cactuses have grown in the garden.

24. Have you ever eaten yakitori?

25. Yancy and Rollo will meet us at the shopping mall.

26. When did they reach the summit of Mount Fairweather?

27. Yellow, orange, and red have always been my favorite colors.

28. Prince and Princess jumped the fence and barked at my brother's friend.

29. The sports banquet will be held on April 4.

30. We bought milk and bread but forgot the eggs.

D. Punctuating and Classifying Sentences by Purpose

Write each sentence, adding an appropriate end mark. Then, classify each sentence as *declarative, imperative, interrogative,* or *exclamatory.*

31. Listen to them

32. What music they make

33. My name is Lucy

34. Tell me more about your trip to Romania

35. How long has Marlon played the zither

36. I will ask her to come over for dinner

37. Who is the star of the film

38. Stop it now

39. I'm so happy to see you

40. Which pair of shoes did you decide to buy

Writing Application

Using Sentence Variety

Sentences Classified by Purpose   As a special project, your social studies class is creating a comic book. Each class member will contribute a comic strip about a particular historical event or historical person. In your comic strip, include at least one of each of the four kinds of sentences—declarative, imperative, interrogative, and exclamatory.

Prewriting   First, jot down some ideas for the characters and story line of your comic strip. You may want to look through your social studies book for ideas. Then, plan the frames of your comic strip. Think about how you could include the four types of sentences in your characters' dialogue. For example, what request or command could a character make?

Writing   Use your prewriting notes to help you make a draft of your comic strip. Use word balloons to add the dialogue to the pictures. As you write, you may decide to add details. Keep in mind that you will be able to add details in the pictures that go with the words.

Revising   Ask a friend to read your cartoon. Are your characters' conversations clear? Can your friend follow the story line? If not, you may need to add, revise, or rearrange sentences.

Publishing   Check your comic strip for errors in grammar, spelling, and punctuation. Make sure that you have used all four kinds of sentences and that you have used periods, question marks, and exclamation points correctly for each kind of sentence. You and your classmates may want to photocopy all the comic strips and gather them in a folder for each member of the class.

SKILLS FOCUS

Identify and use declarative sentences. Identify and use imperative sentences. Identify and use interrogative sentences. Identify and use exclamatory sentences.

LUANN reprinted by permission of United Feature Syndicate, Inc.

Parts of Speech Overview

Noun, Pronoun, Adjective

Diagnostic Preview

Identifying Nouns, Pronouns, and Adjectives

Identify each of the italicized words in the following sentences as a *noun*, a *pronoun*, or an *adjective*.

EXAMPLE   1. Her older *brother* has an *important* test today.

        1. brother—noun; important—adjective

1. The *Romans* built a huge system of roads, *some* of which are still used.
2. Last summer we visited *Alaska,* which is our *largest* state.
3. *Which* of the projects does *that* illustrate?
4. The *Hawaiian* dancers wore *colorful* costumes.
5. *The* bubbling volcano, *inactive* for years, is now a popular tourist attraction.
6. The campers enjoyed *themselves* as they watched the sun set behind the *mountains.*
7. "*That* notebook is *mine,*" Angela said.
8. *They* made a touchdown just before the final *whistle.*
9. *Colombo* is the capital *city* of Sri Lanka.
10. The pen with the *blue* ink is *hers.*

The Noun

2a. A *noun* is a word or word group that is used to name a person, place, thing, or idea.

Persons	parents, Scott, teacher, Ms. Theresa Vargas, sister, linebackers, baby sitter
Places	White House, states, Nairobi, school
Things	rocket, desks, ocean, hamster, computer, Newbery Medal, Golden Gate Bridge
Ideas	danger, freedom, kindness, fears, dream

Notice that some nouns are made up of more than one word. A *compound noun* is a single noun made up of two or more words used together. The compound noun may be written as one word, as a hyphenated word, or as two or more words.

One Word	daydream, Iceland
Hyphenated Word	self-esteem, sister-in-law
Two Words	Rita Rodriguez, family room

Exercise 1 Identifying Nouns

Identify the nouns in the following sentences.

EXAMPLE   **1.** Clara Barton was the founder of the American Red Cross.

1. Clara Barton, founder, American Red Cross

1. Clara Barton was born in Massachusetts.
2. She was educated in a rural school and grew up with a love of books.
3. She began her career as a teacher.
4. During the Civil War, however, she distributed medicine and other supplies.
5. Later she helped find soldiers who were missing in action.

SKILLS FOCUS

Identify and use nouns. Identify and use compound nouns.

6. She organized the American Red Cross and was its president for many years.

7. She raised money for the Red Cross and worked with victims of floods and other disasters.

8. Her kindness touched the lives of countless men, women and children.

9. Her life has been an inspiration to many people who have followed in her footsteps.

10. What a remarkable career and legacy she left the people of the world!

Proper Nouns and Common Nouns

Reference Note

For information about **capitalizing proper nouns,** see page 287.

A *proper noun* names a particular person, place, thing, or idea and begins with a capital letter. A *common noun* names any one of a group of persons, places, things, or ideas. It is usually not capitalized.

Common Nouns	Proper Nouns
woman	Aunt Josie
teacher	Jaime Escalante
city	Los Angeles
country	Germany
continent	Asia
monument	Lincoln Memorial
team	Karr Cougars
book	*Barrio Boy*
holiday	Chinese New Year
religion	Judaism
language	Swahili

Exercise 2 **Identifying Common and Proper Nouns**

Identify the nouns in the following sentences, and label them *common* or *proper*.

SKILLS FOCUS

Identify and use common nouns. Identify and use proper nouns.

EXAMPLE   1. The people of Japan celebrate many holidays.

1. *people—common; Japan—proper; holidays—common*

1. The picture below is of the Snow Festival in Sapporo.
2. Many groups work together to build these giant sculptures of snow.
3. Do you recognize any of the statues or buildings?
4. Is that the Statue of Liberty made out of snow?

5. In the historic city of Kyoto each June, you can see a parade of spears.
6. A popular fair in Tokyo offers pickled radishes.
7. Many villages are colorfully decorated for the Feast of the Lanterns.
8. Toshiro said that his town enjoys the Star Festival every summer.
9. Several flowers, among them the iris and the lily, have their own special days.
10. The birthday of Buddha is observed in April.

Exercise 3 **Substituting Proper Nouns for Common Nouns**

In the sentences on the next page, substitute a proper noun for each italicized common noun. You may need to change or leave out some other words in each sentence. You may also make up proper names to use.

EXAMPLE   1. The *principal* awarded the *student* the prize for the best creative essay.

1. *Ms. Chen awarded Paula Perez the prize for the best creative essay.*

1. The *student* is from a *city.*
2. Usually, my *uncle* looks through the *newspaper* after we finish dinner.
3. The *child* watched a *movie.*
4. A *teacher* asked a *student* to talk about growing up in Mexico.
5. My *cousin* read that *book.*
6. Surrounded by newspaper reporters, the *mayor* stood outside the *building.*
7. Does the *girl* go to this *school?*
8. That *singer* wrote the *song.*
9. My *neighbor* bought her husband a new *car* for his birthday last Saturday.
10. When he was a college student, the *coach* played for that *team.*
11. The *painting* is in a *museum.*
12. The *officer* directed us to the *bridge.*
13. My relatives, who are originally from a *town,* now live in a *city.*
14. The librarian asked my *classmate* to return the *book* as soon as possible.
15. That *newspaper* is published daily; this *magazine* is published weekly.
16. Ted read a *poem* for the *teacher.*
17. That *state* borders the *ocean.*
18. The owner of that store visited a *country* during a *month.*
19. A *man* flew to a *city* one day.
20. Last week the *president* talked about the history of our *nation.*

Exercise 4 Using Proper Nouns

Developers are planning to build a new shopping mall in your neighborhood. They are trying to find out what kinds of stores and other attractions the community would like at the mall. The developers have prepared the following survey.

Answer each question with a complete sentence. Underline each proper noun that you use.

EXAMPLE   1. When would you be most likely to go to the mall?

　　　　　　1. *I would be most likely to visit the mall on <u>Saturdays</u>, especially in <u>August</u> and <u>November</u>.*

New Mall Questionnaire

1. What stores would you most like to see at the mall?
2. What would you be most likely to buy at the mall?
3. What types of movies would you prefer to see at the mall theater?
4. What restaurants would you like to have in the mall's food court?
5. Would you go to the mall arcade? If so, what games would you play?
6. What brands of clothes do you prefer?
7. Would you purchase books or magazines at the mall? If so, what books or magazines interest you?
8. To what clubs, organizations, or associations do you belong?
9. What special or seasonal events would attract you to the mall?
10. At what nearby malls do you sometimes shop?

Review A　**Identifying and Classifying Nouns**

Identify the nouns in the following sentences, and label them *common* or *proper*.

EXAMPLE   1. In 1989, President George H.W. Bush gave General Colin Powell a big job.

　　　　　　1. *1989—common; President George H.W. Bush—proper; General Colin Powell—proper; job—common*

1. He appointed Powell leader of the Joint Chiefs of Staff.
2. Powell became one of the top military officers in the United States.
3. In the photo here, he is shown talking with soldiers during the Persian Gulf War.
4. Do you think the troops were excited to meet the general?
5. Powell grew up in the Bronx, a neighborhood in New York City.
6. His parents came to the United States from Jamaica.
7. Powell graduated from the City College of New York.
8. There he joined the Reserve Officers' Training Corps.
9. Did you know that Powell was awarded the Purple Heart during the Vietnam War?
10. In his speeches, he often encourages students to graduate from high school.

The Pronoun

2b. A *pronoun* is a word that is used in place of one or more nouns or pronouns.

In each of the following examples, an arrow is drawn from a pronoun to the noun or nouns it stands for in the sentence.

Reference Note

For information about choosing **pronouns that agree with their antecedents,** see page 183.

EXAMPLES   When Cindy Davis came to the bus stop, **she** was wearing a cast.

The trees and bushes are dry; **they** should be watered.

This stable is large. **It** has stalls for thirty horses.

The word or word group that a pronoun stands for is called its *antecedent.*

EXAMPLES   My **aunt** sold her car. [*Aunt* is the antecedent of *her.*]

Anthony, call your mother. [*Anthony* is the antecedent of *your.*]

Identify and use pronouns.

Sometimes the antecedent is not stated because the reader can understand the meaning of the sentence without it.

EXAMPLES   Call **your** mother. [The antecedent of *your* is clearly the person to whom the sentence is directed.]

They beat **us** fair and square. [The antecedent of *They* is clearly the team that the speaker played against. The antecedent of *us* is clearly the team of which the speaker is a member.]

> **Exercise 5** **Substituting Pronouns for Nouns**

In each of the following sentences, replace the repeated nouns with pronouns.

EXAMPLE   1. Viviana set up Viviana's game on the table.
   1. *Viviana set up her game on the table.*

1. The passengers on the departing ocean liner waved to the passengers' friends on shore.
2. The test was so long that I almost didn't finish the test.
3. Rachel's neighbors asked Rachel to baby-sit.
4. Carlos said that Carlos had already cleaned Carlos's room.
5. The directions were long, but the directions were clear.
6. Mom was born in Nigeria, and Mom speaks French, English, Spanish, and Italian.
7. Ask those police officers if the police officers know the way to Alhambra Avenue.
8. The twins saved the twins' money; now, that new bicycle built for two is the twins'.
9. Did Warren's aunt fix some tacos for Warren?
10. Our whole family spent the weekend at home, but our whole family had the best time ever.

Personal Pronouns

A *personal pronoun* refers to the one speaking (*first person*), the one spoken to (*second person*), or the one spoken about (*third person*). Personal pronouns have both singular and plural forms.

EXAMPLE   **I** am sure **he** told **you** about **their** plans.

┌HELP─

When you use a pronoun, be sure that its antecedent is clear. If two or more nouns in the sentence could be the antecedent, the reader may not be able to tell what the sentence means. Rewording the sentence to change the position of the pronoun can make the meaning clearer.

EXAMPLES
Janet talked to Caroline after she saw the movie. [Who saw the movie, Janet or Caroline?]

After Janet saw the movie, **she** talked to Caroline. [The pronoun *she* now clearly refers to the antecedent *Janet.*]

After Caroline saw the movie, Janet talked to **her.** [The pronoun *her* now clearly refers to the antecedent *Caroline.*]

SKILLS FOCUS

Identify and use personal pronouns.

Personal Pronouns		
	Singular	**Plural**
First person	I, me, my, mine	we, us, our, ours
Second person	you, your, yours	you, your, yours
Third person	he, him, his, she, her, hers, it, its	they, them, their, theirs

The ***possessive pronouns***—*my, mine, our, ours, your, yours, her, hers, his, its, their,* and *theirs*—are personal pronouns that are used to show ownership or possession.

EXAMPLES   Nina stored **her** suitcase under **her** bed.

Is that paper **yours** or **mine**?

NOTE   Some teachers prefer to call some possessive forms of pronouns (such as *my, your,* and *our*) adjectives. Follow your teacher's instructions regarding possessive forms.

Reflexive and Intensive Pronouns

A ***reflexive pronoun*** refers to the subject and is necessary to the basic meaning of the sentence. An ***intensive pronoun*** emphasizes its antecedent and is unnecessary to the basic meaning of the sentence.

Reflexive and Intensive Pronouns	
First person	myself, ourselves
Second person	yourself, yourselves
Third person	himself, herself, itself, themselves

REFLEXIVE   We enjoyed **ourselves** at the party.

She bought **herself** a new set of Spanish lesson tapes.

INTENSIVE   David **himself** bought a sandwich.

The award will be presented by the principal **herself**.

Exercise 6 Identifying Pronouns

Identify all of the pronouns in each of the following sentences.

EXAMPLE   **1.** I lent her my camera.

   1. I, her, my

1. The dentist asked me several questions before examining my teeth.
2. Dad asked the mechanics working on his car to call him about his bill.
3. Our cousins have decided they will visit Peru.
4. She asked herself where she could have put her book.
5. He washed the mats thoroughly and put them out in the sun to dry.
6. Here is a postcard from Egypt for you and me.
7. We helped ourselves to tacos and refried beans.
8. You gave us your support when we needed it.
9. He had to do his social studies homework before playing soccer with us.
10. I found the weak battery and replaced it myself.

Exercise 7 Identifying Types of Pronouns

In each of the following sentences, identify the italicized pronoun as *personal*, *reflexive*, or *intensive*.

EXAMPLE   **1.** Eric gave *her* a flower.

   1. personal

1. Darren *himself* did not know where the gifts were hidden.
2. Did Teri offer *them* directions to the community center?
3. Elena is a very good actress, and *she* always learns her lines very quickly.
4. Kara treated *herself* to a short nap after a long day.
5. Although *it* fell from the top branches of the elm tree, the chipmunk was not injured.
6. Have *you* told Dennis about the new sports complex?
7. Tracy and Ed carried the aquarium to the car *themselves*.
8. Brian and Erin just arrived home, so *they* have not started their homework assignment yet.
9. Rosalia congratulated *herself* on meeting her goal.
10. The dog made *itself* dizzy by chasing its own tail.

TIPS & TRICKS

If you are not sure whether a pronoun is reflexive or intensive, use this test: Read the sentence aloud, omitting the pronoun. If the meaning of the sentence stays the same, the pronoun is intensive. If the meaning changes, the pronoun is reflexive.

EXAMPLES
Jeremy repaired the tire **himself.** [Without *himself,* the meaning stays the same. The pronoun is intensive.]

The children enjoyed **themselves** at the park. [Without *themselves,* the sentence doesn't make sense. The pronoun is reflexive.]

Demonstrative Pronouns

A *demonstrative pronoun* points out a specific person, place, thing, or idea.

Demonstrative Pronouns			
this	that	these	those

EXAMPLES   What is **that**?

This is the uniform once worn by Satchel Paige.

These are the shoes he used to wear.

Are **those** really his autographs?

NOTE   *This, that, these,* and *those* can also be used as adjectives. When these words are used to modify a noun or pronoun, they are called *demonstrative adjectives.*

PRONOUN   **This** is a delicious papaya. [*This* refers to *papaya.*]

ADJECTIVE   **This** papaya is delicious. [*This* modifies *papaya.*]

PRONOUN   **That** is the stamp my cousin sent from Sweden. [*That* refers to *stamp.*]

ADJECTIVE   **That** stamp was the first in my collection. [*That* modifies *stamp.*]

Reference Note

For information on **adjectives,** see page 84.

Indefinite Pronouns

An *indefinite pronoun* refers to a person, a place, a thing, or an idea that may or may not be specifically named.

Reference Note

For more information on **indefinite pronouns,** see page 175.

Common Indefinite Pronouns			
all	each	more	one
any	either	much	other
anybody	everybody	neither	several
anyone	everyone	nobody	some
anything	few	none	somebody
both	many	no one	something

SKILLS FOCUS

Identify and use demonstrative pronouns. Identify and use indefinite pronouns.

EXAMPLES   **Everyone** in the class was invited to the party.

None of the boys knew **much** about camping.

NOTE   Most words that can be used as indefinite pronouns can also be used as adjectives.

PRONOUN   **Some** are bored by this movie.

ADJECTIVE   **Some** people are bored by this movie.

Exercise 8   **Identifying Pronouns**

Identify the italicized pronoun in each of the following sentences as *indefinite* or *demonstrative*.

EXAMPLE   1. *Someone* has been sitting in my chair.

1. *indefinite*

1. Are you asking *anyone* to the dance this weekend?
2. *This* is my jacket; that one must be yours.
3. *Something* is different about your hair.
4. *That* was the funniest thing I have ever seen a kitten do!
5. *This* is good, but Chrissy's report is better.
6. The armadillo paused at the puddle and drank *some* of the water.
7. Are *those* the socks you are wearing with those shoes?
8. We have to choose between *these* and the ones we looked at yesterday.
9. Linda did more sit-ups than *several* who tried before her.
10. *Nobody* knows the answer to that.

Review B   **Identifying Pronouns**

Identify the pronoun or pronouns in each of the following sentences.

EXAMPLE   1. Everyone in my class likes going on field trips.

1. *Everyone; my*

1. Last week, we really enjoyed ourselves at the National Museum of African Art.
2. It has been part of the Smithsonian Institution in Washington, D.C., since 1979.

3. In 1987, the museum's collection was moved to its present underground facility.
4. Our teacher, Ms. Martinez, told us about the museum before we went there.
5. She said the entrance is made of pink granite.
6. I was surprised by the six domes on top.
7. Everyone had at least one question to ask our museum guide.
8. We enjoyed hearing her lively explanations of the artwork.
9. This is a photograph of one of my favorite objects at the museum.
10. Do you like it?

Mask, Bassa Peoples, Liberia. Wood, pigment, bone or ivory, iron ($9\frac{1}{2}$" X $5\frac{3}{4}$" X $4\frac{1}{2}$"). National Museum of African Art, Eliot Elisofon Archives, Smithsonian Institution, #88-5-1. Photo Credit: Franko Khoury.

Interrogative Pronouns

An *interrogative pronoun* introduces a question.

Interrogative Pronouns				
what	which	who	whom	whose

EXAMPLES   **What** is the first event in the contest?

Who is going to represent our team?

To **whom** is the e-mail addressed?

Which of the books are you reading?

Whose is the car in the driveway?

SKILLS FOCUS

Identify and use interrogative pronouns.

Relative Pronouns

A *relative pronoun* introduces a subordinate clause.

Reference Note

For information on **subordinate clauses,** see page 136.

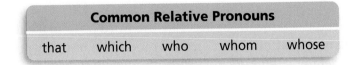

Common Relative Pronouns

that	which	who	whom	whose

EXAMPLES   Harry S. Truman, **who** became president when Franklin D. Roosevelt died, surprised many people with his victory over Thomas Dewey in 1948.

Robins are among the birds **that** migrate south for the winter.

Exercise 9 **Identifying Relative and Interrogative Pronouns**

Identify the italicized pronouns in each of the following sentences as *relative* or *interrogative*.

EXAMPLE   **1.** *Which* of those snow sculptures do you think will win the prize?

   1. interrogative

1. The only student *that* could complete the obstacle course was Sophia.
2. *What* was the name of the volcano that erupted in Washington?
3. *What* was causing that sound outside your room at night?
4. "*Who* left all of those markers on the floor yesterday?" asked Ms. Jackson.
5. Lilacs, *which* are known throughout the world for their fragrant flowers, grow best in northern climates.
6. The new teacher, *whom* we have not yet met, will start Monday.
7. *Which* of you remembers the name of the author of "The Celebrated Jumping Frog of Calaveras County"?
8. *Whose* turn is it to take out the trash?
9. The light bulb, *which* had been flickering for a few days, finally burned out.
10. To *whom* did you lend your textbook?

GRAMMAR

SKILLS FOCUS

Identify and use relative pronouns.

Think as a
Reader/Writer

Some adjectives are more specific and vivid than others. You can make your writing more interesting by replacing dull adjectives with more vivid ones.

ORIGINAL
Mr. Sato is a **nice** man. [The adjective *nice* is dull and doesn't really say much about Mr. Sato.]

REVISED
Mr. Sato is a **generous** man. [The adjective *generous* is more specific about Mr. Sato.]

Reference Note
For information on using *a* and *an,* see page 268.

SKILLS FOCUS

Identify and use adjectives. Identify and use articles.

The Adjective

2c. An *adjective* is a word that is used to modify a noun or a pronoun.

To *modify* a word means to describe the word or to make its meaning more definite. An adjective modifies a noun or pronoun by telling *what kind, which one, how many,* or *how much.*

What Kind?	Which One or Ones?	How Many or How Much?
gentle dog	**sixth** grade	**two** tickets
Irish town	**these** books	**full** pitcher
scary movie	**other** people	**most** players
purple shoes	**any** song	**no** work

Adjectives usually come before the words they modify. Sometimes, however, an adjective comes after the word it modifies.

EXAMPLES   The dog is **gentle.** [The predicate adjective *gentle* modifies *dog.*]

The sea, **blue** and **sparkling,** stretched out before us invitingly. [The adjectives *blue* and *sparkling* modify the noun *sea.*]

NOTE   The adjectives *a, an,* and *the* are called **articles.**

Exercise 10   Identifying Adjectives

Identify each adjective in the following sentences. Do not include *a, an,* or *the.*

EXAMPLE   **1.** The sky was clear, and the night was cold.

1. clear, cold

1. A silvery moon rode down the western sky.
2. It shed a pale light on the quiet countryside.
3. Long meadows spread out between two hills.
4. The smell of the wild grass was strong.
5. The only sound we heard was the sharp crackle of the fire.

6. Suddenly, several stars came out.

7. I watched until the entire sky glowed with bright stars.

8. I was lonely and happy at the same time.

9. I finally became sleepy and longed for my warm bed.

10. Soon I went indoors and fell into a deep sleep.

2
c

Exercise 11 **Identifying Adjectives and the Words They Modify**

Identify the adjectives and the words they modify in the following sentences. Do not include *a, an,* or *the.*

EXAMPLE   **1.** It costs five dollars to go to that movie.

  1. five—dollars; that—movie

1. I have a free ticket for the last game.

2. We ate spicy crawfish, and they were delicious.

3. The new neighbor is helpful and nice.

4. The bear, angry and hungry, surprised the campers.

5. Many students compete in the regional events.

6. Will country musicians play at the county fair?

7. Despite the long delay, we remained cheerful.

8. A shiny coin stared up at me from the the icy sidewalk.

9. Take one booklet and pass the rest to the next row.

10. A few colorful birds perched in the tall, green trees on the bank of the river.

> **COMPUTER TIP**
>
> You can use the computer's thesaurus to find synonyms to replace dull or overused adjectives in your writing. Always check the meaning of an unfamiliar adjective in a dictionary, though, to make sure it is just the right word.

Exercise 12 **Writing Adjectives for a Story**

The following story is about a cave exploration. Copy the sentences, adding an appropriate adjective for each blank. Underline the adjectives you add.

EXAMPLE   **1.** Exploring caves is ____ on ____ days.

  1. Exploring caves is <u>fun</u> on <u>hot</u> days.

1. Have you ever been in a ____ cave like the one shown at right?

2. Would you say it looks ____ and ____?

3. My father and I explored this ____ cave once.

4. It was ____ but ____, too.

5. We found some ____ rock formations.

6. We also heard ____ sounds.

7. My father took some ___ photographs.

8. We looked up and saw ___ bats flying above our heads.

9. After exploring for about ___ hours, we were ready to see the sky again.

10. Spelunking, as cave exploring is called, can be a very ___ experience, if you have a ___ guide.

Proper Adjectives

A ***proper adjective*** is formed from a proper noun and begins with a capital letter.

Reference Note

For information on **capitalizing proper adjectives,** see page 296.

HELP

Some proper nouns, such as *Easter* and *Sioux*, do not change spelling when they are used as proper adjectives.

Proper Nouns	Proper Adjectives
Japan	**Japanese** islands
Easter	**Easter** Sunday
Queen Victoria	**Victorian** drama
Sioux	**Sioux** customs

Exercise 13 Identifying Adjectives

Identify all of the adjectives in the following sentences. Then, underline each proper adjective. Do not include the articles *a*, *an*, or *the*.

EXAMPLE
1. The Navajo weaver made a blanket on a wooden loom.

1. *Navajo, wooden*

1. Music can express sad or happy feelings.

2. The quartet sang several Irish songs.

3. The gold watch with the fancy chain was made by a famous Swiss watchmaker.

4. She is a Balinese dancer.

5. On vacation, Mom enjoys long, quiet breakfasts.

6. Many Australian people are of British origin.

7. The Egyptian mummies are on display on the first floor.

8. We are proud of Joshua.

9. The movie is based on a popular Russian novel.

10. In Canadian football, a team has twelve players on the field at one time.

SKILLS FOCUS

Identify and use proper adjectives.

Exercise 14 · Writing Proper Adjectives

Change the following proper nouns into proper adjectives. Then, use each proper adjective in a sentence.

EXAMPLE   **1.** France

         1. French—We bought French bread at the bakery.

1. England   **6.** Thanksgiving
2. Inca   **7.** Shakespeare
3. Hinduism   **8.** Korea
4. Celt   **9.** Navajo
5. Alaska   **10.** Boston

> **HELP**
>
> You may want to use a dictionary to help you spell the adjectives in Exercise 14.

Demonstrative Adjectives

This, that, these, and *those* can be used both as adjectives and as pronouns. When they modify nouns or pronouns, they are called ***demonstrative adjectives.*** When they are used alone, they are called ***demonstrative pronouns.***

ADJECTIVE   What are **these** skates doing in the living room?
PRONOUN   What are **these** doing in the living room?

ADJECTIVE   I prefer **that** brand of frozen yogurt.
PRONOUN   I prefer **that.**

> **Reference Note**
>
> For more information on **demonstrative pronouns,** see page 80.

Exercise 15 · Identifying Demonstrative Pronouns and Demonstrative Adjectives

In each of the following sentences, identify the italicized word as a *demonstrative pronoun* or a *demonstrative adjective.*

EXAMPLE   **1.** Who gave you *those* beautiful flowers?

         1. demonstrative adjective

1. *That* is the strangest hot-air balloon I have ever seen!
2. Will *those* squirrels find enough to eat during the winter?
3. My dog, Manda, has been chewing on *this* piece of rawhide for three weeks.
4. *These* are the only shoes I can find that will fit you.
5. According to the guidebook, *those* are the largest trees in North America.

> **SKILLS FOCUS**
>
> Identify and use demonstrative adjectives.

6. Is *that* your final offer?
7. The geese always return to *these* same lakes.
8. What do you plan to do with *that* lump of clay?
9. I'm afraid she's gone too far *this* time.
10. Can *this* be the same person I knew back in third grade?

Review C **Identifying Adjectives**

Identify the adjectives in the following sentences. Do not include *a, an,* or *the.*

EXAMPLE   1. I enjoy visiting the large railroad museum in our city.

     1. *large, railroad*

1. Museums can be interesting.
2. Large cities have different kinds of museums.
3. Some museums display sculpture and paintings.
4. These museums may focus on one special kind of art.
5. For example, they might specialize in Chinese art or Mexican art.
6. Other museums feature birds, sea creatures, dinosaurs, and other animals.
7. A curator holds an important job in a museum.
8. A curator needs to know many facts about a particular display.
9. Some valuable objects must be displayed in a stable environment.
10. Some people prefer displays of modern art, while others enjoy exhibits of folk art.

Review D **Identifying Nouns, Pronouns, and Adjectives**

Identify all of the nouns, pronouns, and adjectives in each of the following sentences. Do not include *a, an,* or *the.*

EXAMPLE   1. I think models make a great hobby.

     1. *I—pronoun; models—noun; great—adjective; hobby—noun*

1. Do you have a favorite hobby?
2. Models are enjoyable and educational.

3. They require little space.
4. I keep mine on a bookshelf my dad and I built ourselves.
5. Models are packaged in kits.
6. My favorite models are historic ships and antique planes.
7. On my last birthday, my parents gave me two model kits of biplanes.
8. They came with directions in several languages.
9. Many of the tiny parts are designed for an exact fit.
10. Do you think the bright decals add a realistic look?

Review E Identifying Nouns, Pronouns, and Adjectives

Identify all of the nouns, pronouns, and adjectives in each of the following sentences. Do not include *a*, *an*, or *the*.

EXAMPLE   1. Pueblos are practical housing for people in hot, dry regions.

1. *Pueblos—noun; practical—adjective; housing—noun; people—noun; hot—adjective; dry—adjective; regions—noun*

1. The brown building in the photograph contains several individual homes.
2. *Pueblo* is a Spanish word for a structure like this and for a town.
3. This building is located at the Taos Pueblo in New Mexico.

4. Can you tell how pueblos are made?

5. They are built of adobe.

6. People make adobe by mixing mud with grass or straw.

7. They shape the mixture into bricks and let them bake in the sun.

8. Buildings made with this material stay cool during the summer months.

9. Anyone on a visit to the Southwest can find other pueblos like this one.

10. Old pueblos built by the Hopi and the Zuni fascinate me.

Review F **Writing Sentences Using Nouns, Pronouns, and Adjectives**

Write ten original sentences using the parts of speech given below. In each sentence, underline the word that is the listed part of speech.

EXAMPLE **1.** an adjective that comes after the word it describes
   1. Our guide was very helpful.

1. a proper noun
2. a possessive pronoun
3. an adjective that tells *how many*
4. a reflexive pronoun
5. a proper adjective
6. an article
7. a third-person pronoun
8. a demonstrative adjective
9. an indefinite pronoun
10. a noun that names an idea

Chapter Review

A. Identifying Nouns, Pronouns, and Adjectives

Identify each italicized word or word group in the following sentences as a *noun*, a *pronoun*, or an *adjective*.

1. My *best* friend plays *soccer*.
2. *We* went to *Boston* last summer.
3. Help *yourself* to some *Chinese* food.
4. What a *beautiful* garden *Mrs. Murakami* has!
5. *These* directions were *accurate*.
6. *That* is a fast *merry-go-round*.
7. Juana invited *us* to *her* fiesta.
8. A *sharp* knife is *necessary* for making a wood carving.
9. Almost *everyone* in the band takes private music *lessons*.
10. *This* story is my *favorite* one.

B. Identifying Common and Proper Nouns

Identify the nouns in the following sentences, and label each *common* or *proper*.

11. The religion our family practices is Islam.
12. Was Spanish the first language your mother spoke?
13. The musicians in the band play guitars, keyboards, and drums.
14. My favorite movie is *Charlie and the Chocolate Factory*.
15. Many American tourists visit London in the summer.

C. Identifying Pronouns

Identify all of the pronouns in each of the following sentences.

16. My cat ate all of its food this morning.
17. Each of the girls said someone had already told her about the band concert.
18. I brought a casserole to the potluck dinner and put it in the oven.

19. The doctor herself removed his bandages.

20. Did anyone notice the person who delivered the package?

21. "I think this winter is going to be long and cold," he said to himself.

22. Didn't you ask him not to do that?

23. That book is not the one that I wanted to read.

24. We asked ourselves if he really intended to come to our party.

25. Which of the sweaters is yours?

D. Identifying Proper and Demonstrative Adjectives

Identify the adjectives in the following sentences. Do not include the articles *a, an,* or *the.* Then, label each *proper adjective* and each *demonstrative adjective.*

26. The Easter holiday lasted for one short week.

27. The apple, glossy and red, rolled out of the bag and across the smooth table.

28. The rain was steady throughout that gloomy afternoon.

29. Would you like these French pastries, or would you rather have those?

30. The Siamese cat is playful, but that old tabby is aloof.

E. Identifying Nouns, Pronouns, and Adjectives

Identify each *noun, pronoun,* and *adjective* in the following sentences. Do not include the articles *a, an,* and *the.*

31. Someone told me about the movie.

32. We are moving to Belgium, a European country.

33. J. S. Bach, a German composer, wrote many pieces for the harpsichord.

34. "Is this the tape you wanted?" asked Mr. Imagi.

35 Ted talked himself into the purchase of a new computer.

36. Some of the old songs are lovely.

37. These colors are brighter than those.

38. Professor Auerbach herself will present the award to us.

39. The Swedish car in the driveway is ours.

40. Does anybody know when the city of San Antonio was founded?

Writing Application
Using Pronouns in a Plot Summary

Pronouns and Antecedents   You are in a filmmaking class at the community center and need ideas for a project. The theme of the project is science fiction movie spoofs. Write a plot summary for a short movie. Explain the plot of the movie, and describe the characters. Be sure that the pronouns you use refer clearly to their antecedents.

Prewriting   In a spoof, a writer imitates and makes fun of another work. Imagine several science fiction movie spoofs— for example, *There's an Alien in My Soup* or *Nerds from Neptune*. Choose the idea that you like the best. Then, brainstorm some ideas for a simple plot. Jot down brief descriptions of the setting and the characters in the movie.

Writing   Use your notes to help you write your first draft. Summarize what happens in the movie from beginning to end. Describe each character as you introduce him or her. Keep the props and costumes simple—you are working on a low budget.

Revising   Ask a friend to read your movie idea. Is the plot interesting? Is it funny? Can your friend tell which character is performing each action? If not, you may need to revise some details. Check to make sure each pronoun refers clearly to its antecedent.

Publishing   Read your summary one more time to catch other errors in spelling, grammar, and punctuation. You may want to develop one scene from your plot summary. With the help of several classmates, dramatize this scene in front of the class. Use simple masks and props to create the effect of science fiction.

Reference Note

For more about **developing plots,** see Chapter 22.

SKILLS FOCUS

Write a summary. Demonstrate understanding of correct pronoun and antecedent agreement.

Parts of Speech Overview

Verb, Adverb, Preposition, Conjunction, Interjection

Diagnostic Preview

Identifying Verbs, Adverbs, Prepositions, Conjunctions, and Interjections

Identify each of the italicized words or word groups in the following sentences as a *verb*, an *adverb*, a *preposition*, a *conjunction*, or an *interjection*.

EXAMPLE **1.** A tornado *is* a terrible *and* violent storm.

  1. is—verb; and—conjunction

1. The tornado *struck* our neighborhood *without* warning.
2. We do *not* have a basement in our house.
3. I grabbed my dog Muffin *and* ran *into* the bathroom, the safest room in the house.
4. Muffin and I were *tightly* wedged *between* the sink and the bathtub.
5. *Either* the house was shaking *or* I was, and the air *became* very cold.
6. *Suddenly,* a siren went *off.*

7. A tornado *had been sighted* right *in* the area.
8. Then everything suddenly *grew* calm—it seemed almost *too* calm.
9. I *was* ready for the worst, *but* the tornado did not touch my house *or* any other home in the area.
10. *Well,* I was frightened, *but* I was not hurt.

The Verb

3a. A *verb* is a word that expresses action or a state of being.

EXAMPLES   We **went** to Boston last April.

Is a firefly a kind of beetle?

Every complete sentence has a verb. The verb says something about the subject.

In this book, verbs are classified in three ways — (1) as *main* or *helping* verbs, (2) as *action* or *linking* verbs, and (3) as *transitive* or *intransitive* verbs.

Main Verbs and Helping Verbs

In many sentences, a single word is all that is needed to express the action or the state of being.

EXAMPLES   The dog **barked** all night.

Brett **throws** the ball a long way.

Mr. Rivera **is** the new English teacher.

In other sentences, the verb consists of a main verb and one or more helping verbs.

A ***helping verb*** (also called an *auxiliary* verb) helps the ***main verb*** to express action or a state of being.

EXAMPLES   **can** speak

will learn

should have been fed

Reference Note

For more information about **verbs,** see page 192.

TIPS & TRICKS

Remember, a verb cannot be a helping verb unless there is another verb for it to help. If a verb such as *was* or *had* is the only verb in a sentence, it is not a helping verb.

EXAMPLES

I **had** called my grandmother already. [*Had* is helping the main verb, *called.*]

They **had** a good time at the nature center. [*Had* is the only verb; there is no other verb for it to help.]

SKILLS FOCUS

Identify and use verbs. Identify and use helping verbs.

Together, the main verb and its helping verb or verbs are called a ***verb phrase.***

EXAMPLES   Many students **can speak** Spanish.

I **will be learning** all the state capitals tonight.

The dog **should have been fed** by now.

Commonly Used Helping Verbs					
am	being	do	have	must	were
are	can	does	is	shall	will
be	could	had	may	should	would
been	did	has	might	was	

NOTE   Some words can be used as both helping verbs and main verbs.

HELPING VERB   I **do** wash the dishes.

MAIN VERB   I will **do** the dishes.

Sometimes a verb phrase is interrupted by another part of speech.

EXAMPLES   Suzanne **should** not **call** so late at night. [The verb phrase *should call* is interrupted by the adverb *not.*]

The scientists **did**n't **think** the asteroid would hit the earth. [The verb phrase *did think* is interrupted by –*n't,* the contraction for *not.*]

Did you **watch** Shania Twain's new video? [The verb phrase *Did watch* is interrupted by the subject *you.*]

---HELP---

The word *not* and its contraction, –*n't,* are adverbs telling *to what extent;* neither is part of a verb phrase.

Exercise 1   **Identifying Verb Phrases and Helping Verbs**

Identify the verb phrase in each of the following sentences. Then, underline the helping verb or verbs.

EXAMPLE   1. We are going to Arizona this summer.
1. <u>are</u> going

1. The Petrified Forest has long attracted many tourists.

SKILLS FOCUS

Identify and use verb phrases.

2. Its spectacular beauty has captured their imaginations.
3. Visitors can see the Painted Desert at the same time.
4. The colors of the desert do not remain the same for long.
5. Specimens of petrified wood are exhibited at the tourist information center.
6. Have you ever seen a piece of petrified wood?
7. A guide will gladly explain the process of petrification.
8. Visitors can purchase the fossilized wood as a souvenir.
9. Tours of the Petrified Forest are not recommended for amateur hikers.
10. Hikes must be arranged with park rangers.

Exercise 2 Using Verb Phrases in Original Sentences

Use each of the following word groups as the subject of a sentence with a verb phrase. Make some of your sentences questions. Underline each helping verb and the main verb in each sentence.

EXAMPLE   **1.** your neighbor's dog
                 1. *Can your neighbor's dog <u>do</u> tricks?*

1. my bicycle
2. the astronauts
3. a tiny kitten
4. the hard assignment
5. a famous singer
6. some strange footprints
7. my grandmother
8. the subway
9. a funny costume
10. the refreshments
11. the Los Angeles Dodgers
12. his favorite movie
13. the bird watchers' club
14. the new computer chip
15. Queen Elizabeth
16. her school picture
17. today's newspaper
18. a slice of bread
19. the pencil sharpener
20. my calendar

Review A Identifying Verbs

Identify the verbs in each of the following sentences. Be sure to include helping verbs.

EXAMPLE   **1.** Fairy tales are sometimes called folk tales.
                 1. *are called*

1. Long ago, many people could not read.

2. Instead, they would memorize stories.

3. Then they would tell the stories to their family members and friends.

4. In this way, the people, or folk, passed the tales on from generation to generation.

5. Finally, some people wrote the collected stories.

6. Two German brothers, Jakob and Wilhelm Grimm, published a famous collection of German folk tales.

7. The brothers had heard many of the tales from their older relatives.

8. Their collection of stories became extremely popular all over the world.

9. "Sleeping Beauty," "Cinderella," and "Rumpelstiltskin" were all preserved by the brothers Grimm.

10. In your library, you can probably find these tales and many others, too.

Action Verbs

An **action verb** expresses either physical or mental activity.

PHYSICAL ACTIVITY   I **have used** a computer in math class.

Please **cook** dinner, Jerome.

MENTAL ACTIVITY   Fran **understands** the science assignment better than anyone else does.

The magician **is thinking** of a number.

Exercise 3   **Identifying Action Verbs**

Identify the action verb in each of the following sentences.

EXAMPLE   **1.** The Maricopa people live in Arizona.

1. live

1. The Maricopa make unusual pottery.

2. For this pottery they use two kinds of clay.

3. One kind of clay forms the bowl or platter itself.

4. The other kind of clay colors the pottery.

5. First, the potters mold the clay by hand.

6. Then, they shape it into beautiful bowls and vases.

7. With the second type of clay, the potters create designs.

8. They often etch designs on the pottery with a toothpick.

9. Each family of potters has its own special designs.

10. These designs preserve Maricopa traditions from generation to generation.

Linking Verbs

A *linking verb* connects, or links, the subject to a word or word group that identifies or describes the subject.

EXAMPLES Sandra Cisneros **is** a writer. [The verb *is* connects *writer* with the subject *Sandra Cisneros*.]

The firefighters **had appeared** victorious. [The verb phrase *had appeared* connects *victorious* with the subject *firefighters*.]

The new superintendent **was** she. [The verb *was* connects *she* with the subject *superintendent*.]

Some Linking Verbs Formed from the Verb *Be*		
am	has been	may be
is	have been	might be
are	had been	can be
was	will be	should be
were	shall be	would have been

Other Linking Verbs			
appear	grow	seem	stay
become	look	smell	taste
feel	remain	sound	turn

Some verbs may be either action verbs or linking verbs, depending on how they are used.

ACTION   They **sounded** the bell for a fire drill.

LINKING Mom **sounded** happy about her new job. [The verb *sounded* links *happy* with the subject *Mom*.]

Think as a *Reader/Writer*

In the sentence *The new superintendent was she,* the pronoun *she* after the linking verb may sound strange. Many people would use *her* in informal speech. However, in formal, standard English, *she* is the correct form in this sentence.

Reference Note

For more about **pronouns following linking verbs,** see page 159. For information on **formal and informal language,** see page 267.

SKILLS FOCUS

Identify and use linking verbs.
(page 98): Identify and use action verbs.

TIPS & TRICKS

If you are not sure if a verb is being used as a linking verb or an action verb, try substituting *is* or *are* for the verb. If the sentence still makes sense, the verb is probably a linking verb. If the sentence does not make sense, the verb is probably an action verb.

EXAMPLES
James **looks** taller. [*James is taller* makes sense; here, *looks* is a linking verb.]

James **looks** out the window. [*James is out the window* does not make sense; here, *looks* is an action verb.]

ACTION   The judge **will look** at my science project.

LINKING   Ann **will look** funny in her gorilla costume. [The verb phrase *will look* links *funny* with the subject *Ann*.]

Exercise 4 **Identifying Linking Verbs**

Identify the linking verbs or verb phrases in the following sentences.

EXAMPLE   **1.** Peanut soup made from fresh roasted peanuts tastes good.

    1. tastes

1. Peanuts remain an important crop around the world.
2. The peanut, which is high in protein, is native to South America.
3. Peanuts grow ripe underground.
4. The seeds are the edible part of the plant.
5. The peanut has become an important ingredient in more than three hundred common products, such as wood stains, shampoo, printer's ink, and soap.
6. Of course, roasting peanuts smell wonderful.
7. Peanut butter was the invention of a St. Louis doctor in 1890.
8. Before then, thanks to George Washington Carver, the peanut had become one of the major crops of the South.
9. Carver, a scientist who experimented with peanuts and other plants, had been a slave.
10. It may seem strange, but Carver once prepared an entire dinner out of peanuts.

HELP

Remember to include helping verbs in your answers to Exercise 5.

Exercise 5 **Identifying Action Verbs and Linking Verbs**

Identify the verb in each of the following sentences as an *action verb* or a *linking verb*.

EXAMPLES   **1.** John Johnson was one of the most successful business leaders in the United States.

    1. was—linking verb

    2. Johnson published many popular magazines.

    2. published—action verb

1. The photograph at right shows John Johnson as a success.
2. Johnson's life was not always easy.
3. The small Arkansas town of his childhood had no high school.
4. Therefore, Johnson's mother moved to Chicago.
5. In Chicago, Johnson attended high school with classmates Redd Foxx and Nat "King" Cole.
6. During the Great Depression of the 1930s, Johnson's family grew very poor.
7. However, Johnson studied hard.
8. He became an honor student, the class president, and the editor of the high school newspaper.
9. Johnson started his first magazine with a loan.
10. He later owned a group of companies worth $200 million per year.

Transitive and Intransitive Verbs

A *transitive verb* is a verb that expresses an action directed toward a person, place, thing, or idea. With transitive verbs, the action passes from the doer—the subject—to the receiver of the action. Words that receive the action of a transitive verb are called *objects.*

EXAMPLES Tamisha **entertained** the child. [The object *child* receives the action of the verb *entertained.*]

Felipe **visited** San Juan. [The object *San Juan* receives the action of the verb *visited.*]

An *intransitive verb* tells something about the subject or expresses action without the action passing to a receiver, or object.

EXAMPLES The children **smiled.**

The horses **galloped** across the prairie.

I **am** here.

Reference Note

For more about **objects in sentences,** see page 153.

SKILLS FOCUS

Identify and use transitive verbs. Identify and use intransitive verbs.

> **NOTE** Not everything that follows a verb is an object. Many words or word groups that come after the verb give more information without receiving the action of the verb.
>
> EXAMPLES   Tameka writes **poetry.** [The object *poetry* receives the action of the transitive verb *writes.*]
>
> Tameka writes **daily.** [The word *daily* tells when she performs the action of the intransitive verb *writes,* but *daily* does not receive the action and is not an object.]
>
> Tameka writes **in the morning.** [The word group *in the morning* tells when she performs the action of the verb *writes,* but *in the morning* does not receive the action and is not an object.]

Some action verbs may be either transitive or intransitive, depending on how they are used in a sentence.

EXAMPLES   My cousin Julio **plays** baseball on a Caribbean League team. [transitive]

My cousin Julio **plays** every week. [intransitive]

Kanani **studies** Chinese each day after school. [transitive]

Kanani **studies** hard. [intransitive]

> **NOTE** Linking verbs are intransitive.
>
> EXAMPLES   This soup **tastes** too salty. [The linking verb *tastes* does not express any action for an object to receive. When used as a linking verb, *tastes* is intransitive.]
>
> **Does** the box **seem** heavier than it should be? [The linking verb *Does seem* does not express any action for an object to receive. *Does seem* is intransitive.]

Exercise 6   **Identifying Transitive and Intransitive Verbs**

For each of the following sentences, identify the italicized verb as *transitive* or *intransitive.*

EXAMPLE   **1.** Computers *affect* our lives every day.

        1. transitive

1. Computers *make* calculations incredibly quickly.
2. They *perform* many tasks that people often find boring and difficult.
3. Many businesses *benefit* from these machines.
4. Some people *work* at home using computers.
5. Computers *do* word processing, a very useful operation for writers.
6. They also *run* programs that allow you to make your own music and movies.
7. Hand-held computers *fit* easily into a purse, bag, or backpack.
8. My mother *bought* a laptop that weighs only two and a half pounds.
9. Because of high-speed Internet, Web sites *appear* almost instantly.
10. A computer's ability to store mass amounts of information *helps* my mother organize her work.

Exercise 7 Using Transitive and Intransitive Verbs

Write an appropriate verb for each of the following sentences. Then, identify the verb as *transitive* or *intransitive*.

HELP

Although the example in Exercise 7 gives two possible answers, you need to write only one answer for each item.

EXAMPLE   **1.** He _____ my older brother's best friend.

        1. is—intransitive

             or

       knows—transitive

1. Aunt Teresa _____ us about some of the traditions of the Cherokee.
2. Our experiment with plants and photosynthesis _____.
3. Billy and I _____ green beans and carrots.
4. By noon, the hot sun _____ the ice.
5. Everything _____ fine to me.
6. In the twilight, a shrimp boat _____ into the bay.
7. _____ these hurdles, Jason.
8. _____ Bogotá the capital of Colombia?
9. Wow! What a crazy tie that _____!
10. Several African nations _____ elections this year.

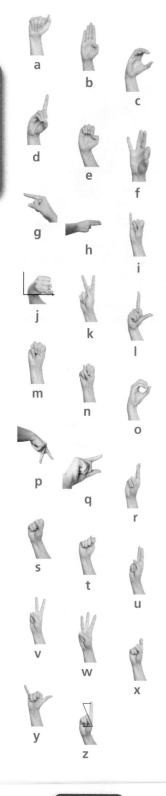

a

b

c

d

e

f

g

h

i

j

k

l

m

n

o

p

q

r

s

t

u

v

w

x

y

z

Review B Identifying Verbs

Identify the verb in each of the following sentences. Be sure to include helping verbs. Then, tell whether the verb is used as an *action* or *linking verb*. Then, tell whether it is *transitive* or *intransitive*.

EXAMPLE
1. Can you form the letters of the sign language alphabet?

1. *Can form—action, transitive*

1. The alphabet chart at left is helpful.
2. Perhaps you and a friend could practice together.
3. At first, it may be a challenge.
4. Many people communicate with these letters as well as thousands of other signs.
5. Many people use forms of sign language.
6. For example, referees, coaches, and football players sometimes give signals in sign language.
7. Some stroke victims must learn sign language during their recovery period.
8. Scientists have taught hundreds of signs to gorillas and chimpanzees.
9. These animals have been talking to people and to each other in sign language.
10. In the picture below, the gorilla on the left and the woman are having a conversation in sign language.

The Adverb

3b. An *adverb* is a word that modifies a verb, an adjective, or another adverb.

Just as an adjective makes the meaning of a noun or a pronoun more definite, an adverb makes the meaning of a verb, an adjective, or another adverb more definite.

EXAMPLES   Reporters **quickly** gather the news. [The adverb *quickly* modifies the verb *gather*.]

The route is **too** long. [The adverb *too* modifies the adjective *long*.]

Our newspaper carrier delivers the paper **very early.** [The adverb *very* modifies another adverb, *early*. The adverb *early* modifies the verb *delivers*.]

Adverbs answer the following questions:

Where?	How often?	To what extent?
When?	*or*	*or*
How?	How long?	How much?

EXAMPLES   Please put the package **there.** [*There* modifies the verb *put* and tells *where*.]

I will call you **later.** [*Later* modifies the verb phrase *will call* and tells *when*.]

Softly, I shut my door. [*Softly* modifies the verb *shut* and tells *how*.]

Alannah **always** reads science fiction novels. [*Always* modifies the verb *reads* and tells *how often*.]

Would you please **briefly** explain what you mean? [*Briefly* modifies the verb phrase *Would explain* and tells *how long*.]

An owl hooted **very** late last night. [The adverb *very* modifies the adverb *late* and tells *to what extent*.]

The lemonade was **too** sour. [*Too* modifies the adjective *sour* and tells *how much*.]

─HELP─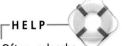

Often, adverbs can be recognized by the suffix *–ly*. Remember, however, that not all adverbs end in *–ly* and not all words that end in *–ly* are adverbs.

ADVERBS
swam	**quickly**
left	**later**

ADJECTIVES
only	friend
early	flight

SKILLS FOCUS

Identify and use adverbs.

Words Often Used as Adverbs	
Where?	here, there, away, up, outside
When?	now, then, later, soon, ago
How?	clearly, easily, quietly, slowly
How often? *or* How long?	never, always, often, seldom frequently, usually, forever
To what extent? *or* How much?	very, hardly, almost, so, really most, nearly, quite, less, only

The Position of Adverbs

Adverbs may come before, after, or between the words they
modify.

EXAMPLES **Quietly,** she will tiptoe from the stage. [*Quietly* comes
          before *will tiptoe,* the verb phrase it modifies.]

          She will **quietly** tiptoe from the stage. [*Quietly* comes
          between *will* and *tiptoe,* the verb phrase it modifies.]

          She will tiptoe **quietly** from the stage. [*Quietly* comes
          after *will tiptoe,* the verb phrase it modifies.]

Exercise 8 **Identifying Adverbs**

Identify the adverb in each of the following sentences. Then,
give the word or words each adverb modifies.

EXAMPLE   1. Williamsburg is a very interesting place.
           1. *very—interesting*

1. Visitors to Williamsburg can truly imagine what life
    must have been like in the 1700s.
2. As you can see in the photo on the opposite page, Williams-
    burg was carefully built to resemble a small town of the past.
3. On one street a wigmaker slowly makes old-fashioned
    powdered wigs.
4. Nearby, a silversmith designs beautiful candlesticks,
    platters, and jewelry.

5. Down the block the bookbinder skillfully crafts book covers out of leather.
6. His neighbor, the blacksmith, is certainly important because he makes shoes for horses.
7. In colonial times people could seldom afford new shoes for themselves.
8. Nowadays, many curious tourists visit the bootmaker's shop.
9. Another very popular craftsman makes lovely musical instruments.
10. Williamsburg definitely gives tourists the feeling that they have visited the past.

Exercise 9 **Identifying Adverbs and the Words They Modify**

Each of the following sentences contains at least one adverb. Identify each adverb. Then, give the word each adverb modifies. Be prepared to tell whether the word modified is a verb, an adjective, or an adverb.

EXAMPLE   1. If you look closely at a world map, you can quite easily find Brazil.
           1. *closely—look; quite—easily; easily—can find*

1. The nation of Brazil actually covers almost half of the continent of South America.
2. A large portion of the Amazon rain forest grows there.
3. Many people have become more active in the preservation of the rain forest.
4. The loss of the rain forest may seriously affect the planet's climate.
5. Very early in the sixteenth century, Brazil was colonized by the Portuguese.
6. The country later became an independent republic.
7. Brazilians often say *Bom día*, which means "good day" in Portuguese.
8. In Brazil, sports fans can almost always find a soccer game in progress.
9. Brasília, the capital of Brazil, is an extremely modern city.
10. My aunt travels frequently, but she hasn't been to Brasília.

HELP

In the example sentence in Exercise 9, *look* is a verb, *easily* is an adverb, and *can find* is a verb.

Exercise 10 Writing Appropriate Adverbs

Write the following sentences. Then, fill in each blank with an appropriate adverb. Use a different adverb in each sentence.

EXAMPLE   1. ____ I learned some Spanish words.

1. *Quickly, I learned some Spanish words.*

1. I ____ watch TV after school.
2. You will ____ bait a hook yourself.
3. My little sister crept down the stairs ____.
4. Do you think that you can ____ find the answer to the math problem?
5. She is ____ eager for lunch.
6. In the evening, the African drums beat ____.
7. People in the highest balcony could ____ hear the speakers onstage.
8. Does thunder ____ follow lightning?
9. Would you dim the light ____ for me?
10. The sky over Honolulu was ____ clear that I could see for miles.

The Preposition

3c. A *preposition* is a word that shows the relationship between a noun or a pronoun and another word in the sentence.

EXAMPLES   Your math book is **underneath** your coat, Allen. [The preposition *underneath* shows the relationship of *coat* to *book.*]

The one **behind** us honked his horn. [The preposition *behind* shows the relationship of *us* to *one.*]

Notice how changing the preposition in the following sentences changes the relationship between *hit* and *net.*

I hit the ball **over** the net.

I hit the ball **into** the net.

I hit the ball **under** the net.

I hit the ball **against** the net.

I hit the ball **across** the net.

Commonly Used Prepositions		
aboard	between	past
about	beyond	since
above	by	through
across	down	throughout
after	during	till
against	except	to
along	for	toward
among	from	under
around	in	underneath
at	into	until
before	like	up
behind	of	upon
below	off	with
beneath	on	within
beside	over	without

Some prepositions are made up of more than one word. These are called *compound prepositions.*

Some Compound Prepositions		
according to	in addition to	next to
aside from	in place of	on account of
because of	in spite of	out of

The Prepositional Phrase

A preposition always has at least one noun or pronoun as an object. This noun or pronoun is called the ***object of the preposition.*** The preposition, its object, and any modifiers of the object make up a ***prepositional phrase.*** Generally, the object of the preposition follows the preposition.

EXAMPLES   The pile **of dry leaves** had grown much larger. [The preposition *of* relates its object, *leaves,* to *pile.* The adjective *dry* modifies *leaves.*]

Reference Note

For more information about **prepositional phrases,** see Chapter 4.

SKILLS FOCUS

Identify and use prepositional phrases correctly.

He poured sauce **over the pizza.** [The preposition *over* relates its object, *pizza,* to *poured.* The article *the* modifies *pizza.*]

A preposition may have more than one object.

EXAMPLES   This flea collar is **for cats** and **dogs.** [The preposition *for* has the two objects *cats* and *dogs.*]

My big sister had to decide **between the University of Wisconsin** and **Carroll College.** [The preposition *between* has the two objects *the University of Wisconsin* and *Carroll College.*]

Exercise 11 Identifying Prepositions and Their Objects

Identify the prepositional phrase in each of the following sentences. Underline the preposition, and circle its object.

EXAMPLE   1. Otters are related to weasels and minks.
1. <u>to</u> (weasels) and (minks)

1. Yesterday afternoon, we planted a sapling behind the garage.
2. I bought a pattern for a sari.
3. They live near the airport.
4. For his birthday, my brother wants a guitar.
5. The pictures won't be developed until Friday or Monday.
6. I received a letter from my aunt and uncle.
7. The largest of all falcons is the arctic falcon.
8. What are the answers to the third and fourth questions?
9. There are many uses for peanuts.
10. I think that you might need a graphing calculator for that problem.

Exercise 12 Using Prepositions

Using the treasure map on the next page, give an appropriate preposition for each of the following sentences. Be sure to use a variety of prepositions.

EXAMPLE   1. Can you find the *X* ____ this map?
1. on

1. Our rowboat rests ____ Mournful Beach.
2. Follow the path ____ the treasure.

TIPS & TRICKS

When you are looking for the object of a preposition, be careful. Sometimes the object comes before, not after, the preposition.

EXAMPLES
This is the movie that I told you about on Tuesday. [*That* is the object of the preposition *about.*]

TIPS & TRICKS

Ending a sentence with a preposition is becoming more accepted in casual speech and informal writing. However, in formal writing it is generally best to avoid doing so.

3. Notice that Skull Rock lies ____ the cliff.

4. A sandy path leads ____ the stone ruins.

5. Did you jump ____ the fallen tree along the cliff?

6. Don't slip ____ the path up Lookout Hill!

7. Walk ____ the river.

8. Go ____ the waterfall!

9. You need not walk ____ the woods.

10. The treasure is ____ the open field and the gnarled oak tree.

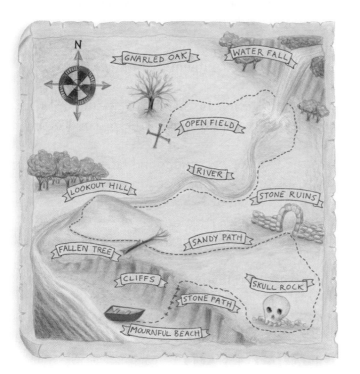

Preposition or Adverb?

Some words may be used as both prepositions and adverbs. Remember that a preposition always has at least one noun or pronoun as an object. An adverb never does. If you can't tell whether a word is used as an adverb or a preposition, look for an object.

PREPOSITION   Clouds gathered **above** us. [*Us* is the object of the preposition *above*.]

ADVERB   Clouds gathered **above**. [no object]

SKILLS FOCUS

Identify and use adverbs.
Identify and use prepositions.

PREPOSITION	Meet me **outside** the gym tomorrow morning.
	[*Gym* is the object of the preposition *outside*.]
ADVERB	Meet me **outside** tomorrow morning. [no object]

Exercise 13 Identifying Adverbs and Prepositions

Identify the italicized word in each of the following sentences as either an *adverb* or a *preposition*.

EXAMPLE   **1.** *Above* us, wispy clouds filled the sky.

          1. preposition

1. Before it rains, bring your bike *in.*
2. Had you ever seen an authentic Chinese New Year Parade *before*?
3. Bright red and green lights sparkled *down* the street.
4. Smoke from the campfire quickly disappeared *in* the heavy fog.
5. Andy turned the log *over* and found fat, squirming worms.
6. A submarine surfaced *next to* an aircraft carrier.
7. Will we read a poem by Nikki Giovanni *next*?
8. Turn that stereo *down* right now!
9. Millicent, did you remember to send a thank-you note *to* Mr. Bernstein?
10. What kind *of* dog is that?

The Conjunction

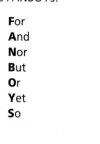

3d. A *conjunction* is a word that joins words or groups of words.

A ***coordinating conjunction*** joins words or word groups that are used in the same way.

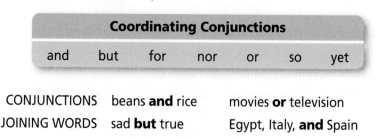

Coordinating Conjunctions
and   but   for   nor   or   so   yet

| CONJUNCTIONS | beans **and** rice | movies **or** television |
| JOINING WORDS | sad **but** true | Egypt, Italy, **and** Spain |

CONJUNCTIONS	go for a walk **or** read a book
JOINING PHRASES	after breakfast **but** before lunch
	cooking dinner **and** fixing breakfast

CONJUNCTIONS	I wanted to call, **but** it was late.
JOINING CLAUSES	The deer ran, **for** they smelled smoke.
	We knocked on the door, **and** they answered.

Reference Note
For information on using **commas to join words, phrases, or clauses,** see page 314.

NOTE The word *for* can be used either as a conjunction or as a preposition.

CONJUNCTION	The zebra turned toward the watering hole, **for** it was getting thirsty. [*For* joins the two sentences.]
PREPOSITION	The zebra lay down in the shade **for** a nap. [*For* shows the relationship between the object *nap* and the verb *lay.*]

Reference Note
For more information on using **prepositions,** see page 108.

Correlative conjunctions are pairs of conjunctions that join words or word groups that are used in the same way.

Correlative Conjunctions

both . . . . and	not only . . . but also
either . . . . or	whether . . . or
neither . . . . nor	

EXAMPLES **Both** Michael Jordan **and** David Robinson planned to play in the charity softball game. [two nouns]

Chris turned **neither** to the west **nor** to the east. [two prepositional phrases]

Not only did Babe Didrikson Zaharias set world records in track and field, **but** she **also** won more than fifty golf tournaments. [two independent clauses]

Exercise 14 Identifying Conjunctions

Identify the conjunction in each of the following sentences.

EXAMPLE 1. Lena or I will pitch at batting practice.
1. *or*

SKILLS FOCUS
Identify and use conjunctions. Identify and use coordinating conjunctions. Identify and use correlative conjunctions.

1. Julio and Roger joined the soccer team.
2. Whether it rains or not, we will be there.
3. Many Chinese plays include dancing and acrobatics.
4. The squirrels are burying nuts, for the long, cold winter will be here soon.
5. Did Nancy finish her final book report, or is she still working on it?
6. Not only strong but also graceful, the eagle is a beautiful bird.
7. He is not here, nor has he called.
8. The Boys Choir of Harlem will be singing tonight, so we bought tickets.
9. I already addressed the envelope but have not taken it to the post office yet.
10. I have enough money for either popcorn or juice.

The Interjection

3e. An *interjection* is a word that expresses emotion.

An interjection has no grammatical relation to the rest of the sentence.

Often, an interjection is followed by an exclamation point.

EXAMPLES   **Aha!** I knew you were hiding there.

Oops! I punched in the wrong numbers.

Is that a wasp? **Ouch!**

Sometimes an interjection is set off by a comma or a pair of commas.

EXAMPLES   **Well,** what do you think?

The fish weighed, **oh,** about three pounds.

It's time to go, **alas.**

Common Interjections			
aha	hey	ouch	whew
alas	hooray	ow	wow
aw	oh	ugh	yikes
goodness	oops	well	yippee

Exercise 15 Writing Interjections

Have you ever heard the expression "an accident waiting to happen"? How many accidents are waiting to happen in the picture below? Write appropriate interjections to complete the following sentences that the people in the picture might say.

EXAMPLE   1. _____, Vince, have you seen my other roller skate anywhere?

1. *Oh, Vince, have you seen my other roller skate anywhere?*

1. _____! I almost sat on the cat.
2. _____! Watch out for that book!
3. _____! Something on the stove is burning.
4. _____, Lila! Be careful with that milk!
5. _____, we will have to get a new cord for our lamp.
6. Something smells bad, _____.
7. Down the stairs comes Dad with, _____, the biggest present I've ever seen!
8. At last the party is over, _____.
9. _____! Look out for the roller skate.
10. The party was, _____, interesting to say the least.

┌─HELP─┐

In Exercise 15, use a variety of interjections from the list on the previous page.

Determining Parts of Speech

3f. The way a word is used in a sentence determines what part of speech it is.

Remember that you cannot tell what part of speech a word is until you know how it is used in a particular sentence. The same word may be used as different parts of speech.

| VERB | Do you **like** guacamole? |
| PREPOSITION | That looks **like** guacamole. |

| ADVERB | The cat climbed **up.** |
| PREPOSITION | The cat climbed **up** the tree. |

NOUN	We threw pennies into the wishing **well.**
ADJECTIVE	Janice isn't feeling **well.**
ADVERB	Did you do **well** on the test?
INTERJECTION	**Well,** what did he say?

Review C Identifying Parts of Speech

Identify the italicized word or words in each of the following sentences as a *noun*, a *pronoun*, an *adjective*, a *verb*, an *adverb*, a *preposition*, a *conjunction*, or an *interjection*.

EXAMPLE   1. Some scientists *study* bones.

1. *study—verb*

1. The fans lined up *outside* the stadium.
2. *She* always drives to work.
3. Those *plants* grow best in sandy soil.
4. *Either* Rhea *or* Susan bought paper cups for the party.
5. Their parents *own* a card store.
6. N. Scott Momaday has written several books, *but* I have read only one of them.
7. *Oops*! I dropped my backpack.
8. We play *outdoors* every day until dinner time.
9. This video looks *new*.
10. You don't sound *too* happy.

┌HELP┐
You may want
to review Chapter 2
before completing Review C.

SKILLS FOCUS

Identify parts of speech.

Chapter Review

A. Identifying Verb Phrases and Helping Verbs

Identify the verb phrase in each of the following sentences. Then, underline each helping verb.

1. Tolbert could not see his brother in the fog.
2. Does Nguyen know the words to the song?
3. Dana might come to the party after all.
4. You should have brought your friend home for our special Chinese dinner last night.
5. Will you join the dance?

B. Identifying Action and Linking Verbs

Identify the verb in each of the following sentences as an *action verb* or a *linking verb*.

6. Ivan will be a superb guitar player someday.
7. Our dog Tadger brought an old bone home yesterday.
8. The whole-wheat bread smelled delicious.
9. Jacqui smelled the exhaust of the huge truck in the next lane of the freeway.
10. Will you look for me in the parade tomorrow?

C. Identifying Transitive and Intransitive Verbs

For each of the following sentences, identify the italicized verb as *transitive* or *intransitive*.

11. Francisco *opened* the door to the cellar.
12. Even the judge *seemed* uncertain about the answer.
13. The piano player *performs* twice each night.
14. We *performed* the play three times that weekend.
15. We *dine* every night at seven.

D. Identifying Adverbs and the Words They Modify

Identify the adverb or adverbs in each of the following sentences. Then, give the word each adverb modifies.

16. Mr. Chavez never watches television, but he listens to the radio often.

17. Carefully open the dryer, and check to see whether the clothes are too wet.

18. Did you awake very early?

19. Our old cat creeps gingerly from room to room.

20. Recently, I received an extremely interesting letter from my pen pal in Italy.

E. Identifying Prepositions and Their Objects

Identify the prepositional phrase in each of the following sentences. Underline the preposition once and its object twice.

21. Tanya's pet hamster likes sleeping behind the computer.

22. Has your house ever lost power during a thunderstorm?

23. Some animals hunt only between dusk and dawn.

24. Bring me the largest head of lettuce, please.

25. According to my father, my uncle was a carpenter.

F. Identifying Verbs, Adverbs, Prepositions, Conjunctions, and Interjections

Identify each italicized word or word group in the following sentences as a *verb*, an *adverb*, a *preposition*, a *conjunction*, or an *interjection*.

26. I always have fun *at* a water park.

27. You *can slide* as fast as a sled down the huge water slide.

28. *Wow!* What a truly exciting ride that is!

29. Some parks *rent* inner tubes *inexpensively*.

30. You *may become* tired, *but* you won't be bored.

G. Determining Parts of Speech

Identify the italicized word in each of the following sentences as a *verb*, an *adjective*, an *adverb*, a *preposition*, or an *interjection*.

31. *Well*, I suppose you know what you are doing.

32. Ms. Jefferson will not be back in school until she is *well*.

33. When I sat down on the couch, my sister moved *over*.

34. The bowls are in the cupboard *over* the sink.

35. Did you *test* the batteries before you installed them?

Writing Application
Using Verbs in a List

Helping Verbs and Linking Verbs   You and your classmates have decided to list some goals for the coming year. The theme for your lists is "How I Can Make the World a Better Place." Write a list of ten or more goals or resolutions for yourself. Make each of your resolutions a complete sentence. In your list, use the verb form *be* at least two times as a helping verb and three times as a linking verb.

Prewriting   First, think of some realistic goals you can set for yourself. List as many goals as you can.

Writing   From your list, choose the resolutions that seem the most important and the most manageable. Write each of them as a complete sentence.

Revising   Read through your list. Are your resolutions clear and specific? Will you really be able to keep them? If not, revise or replace some of the resolutions.

Publishing   Be sure that you've used a form of the verb *be* as a helping verb twice and as a linking verb three times. Make sure that all of your sentences are complete. Identify each helping verb and linking verb. Do a final check for errors in grammar, spelling, and punctuation. You and your classmates may want to have everyone in the class submit one or two of their favorite resolutions and compile a list of resolutions for the entire class. Post the list on the bulletin board.

Reference Note

For information on **complete sentences,** see page 428.

SKILLS FOCUS

Identify and use helping verbs. Identify and use linking verbs.

The Phrase and the Clause

Prepositional Phrases, Independent and Subordinate Clauses, Sentence Structure

Diagnostic Preview

A. Identifying Adjective Phrases and Adverb Phrases

Identify the prepositional phrase in each of the following sentences, and tell whether the phrase is used as an *adjective phrase* or an *adverb phrase*. Then, give the word or words that the phrase modifies.

EXAMPLE   1. This newspaper article on weather patterns is interesting.
            1. *on weather patterns; adjective phrase—article*

1. The hikers are ready for a break.
2. Yesterday we rode our bikes through the park.
3. That store has something for everyone.
4. The Reverend Jesse Jackson spoke at the convention.
5. Most children like books with colorful pictures.
6. Students from both South America and North America attended the meet.

7. I wear heavy wool socks under my hiking boots.
8. Joel and Tina are participating in the Special Olympics.
9. The door to the secret room is locked.
10. According to the map, Tony's farm is just ahead.

B. Identifying Independent Clauses and Subordinate Clauses

For each of the following items, identify the italicized word group as either an *independent clause* or a *subordinate clause.*

EXAMPLE   1. Marco got the tables ready *while Nestor set up the chairs.*

          1. *subordinate clause*

11. *When school is out,* these halls seem quite lonely.
12. As far as I can tell, the red piece goes right here, and *the green piece goes under there.*
13. *If you exercise regularly,* your endurance will increase.
14. Just before the train sped across the road, *the bell rang,* and the gate went down.
15. *Geronimo,* who was a leader of the Apache, *died in the early part of the twentieth century.*

C. Identifying Types of Sentences

Identify each of the following sentences as *simple, compound, complex,* or *compound-complex.*

EXAMPLE   1. Mom is late, but she will be here soon.

          1. *compound*

16. Jaleel learned several African folk tales and recited them.
17. Raccoons and opossums steal our garbage as the dogs bark at them from inside the house.
18. The school bus stopped suddenly, but no one was hurt.
19. The dance committee has chosen a Hawaiian theme, so the volunteers will decorate the gym with flowers and greenery while Todd finds the right music.
20. Luis Gonzalez stepped up to the plate, and the crowd roared enthusiastically.

The Phrase

4a. A *phrase* is a group of related words that is used as a single part of speech and that does not contain both a verb and its subject.

EXAMPLES   could have been looking [no subject]

in the backyard [no subject or verb]

Reference Note

For more about **clauses,** see page 135.

NOTE   If a word group has both a subject and a verb, it is called a *clause.*

EXAMPLES   The coyote howled. [*Coyote* is the subject of the verb *howled.*]

when the Peytons left [*Peytons* is the subject of the verb *left.*]

Phrases cannot stand alone as sentences. They must be used with other words to make a complete sentence.

PHRASE   **in the box**
SENTENCE   We put the tapes **in the box.**

Exercise 1   Identifying Phrases and Sentences

Identify each of the following word groups as *a phrase* or *not a phrase.*

EXAMPLE   1. some people enjoy skiing
1. *not a phrase*

1. ski lifts are used for Alpine skiing
2. down the snowy hills
3. slalom skiers race through gates
4. during the race
5. before the other skiers
6. skiers love the Colorado slopes
7. with tiny snowflakes on my face
8. for a hot cup of soup
9. we sat beside the cozy fire
10. maybe I can go again next year

SKILLS FOCUS

Use phrases correctly.

Prepositional Phrases

4b. A *prepositional phrase* includes a preposition, the object of the preposition, and any modifiers of that object.

Reference Note

For more about **objects of prepositions,** see page 109.

Prepositions show the relationship of a noun or pronoun to another word in the sentence. The noun or pronoun that follows a preposition is called the ***object of the preposition.*** A preposition, its object, and any modifiers of the object are all part of the prepositional phrase.

EXAMPLES   The man **from Singapore** was giving a speech. [The preposition *from* shows the relationship between the object *Singapore* and the noun *man.*]

The tree **in front of the window** blocks our view. [The compound preposition *in front of* shows the relationship between the object *window* and the noun *tree. The* modifies *window.*]

Please hand me the book **on the long, green table.** [The preposition *on* shows the relationship between the object *table* and the noun *book. The* adjectives *the, long,* and *green* modify *table.*]

A preposition may have more than one object.

EXAMPLES   Aaron showed his arrowhead collection to **Tranh** and **her.** [The preposition *to* has two objects.]

The dinner of **baked chicken, salad,** and **two vegetables** also came with dessert. [The preposition *of* has three objects.]

Exercise 2   **Identifying Prepositional Phrases and Their Objects**

For each of the following sentences, identify the prepositional phrase and circle the object or objects of the preposition.

EXAMPLE   **1.** Dinosaurs and other giant reptiles roamed across the earth sixty-five million years ago.

1. across the (earth)

1. Although some of the dinosaurs were enormous, others were quite small.

SKILLS FOCUS

Identify and use prepositional phrases correctly.

2. The drawing on this page includes a stegosaurus, thirty feet long, and a saltopus, not quite three feet long.
3. Many dinosaurs fed on plants and vegetables.
4. Dinosaurs with sharp teeth ate flesh.
5. Can you imagine seeing this flying reptile, the pterodactyl, above you?
6. It once lived in Europe and Africa.
7. Until a few years ago, scientists believed that all dinosaurs were coldblooded.
8. According to recent studies, however, some dinosaurs may have been warmblooded.
9. Many scientists say that birds and crocodiles may be related to dinosaurs.
10. Some people in science even claim that birds are living dinosaurs.

Exercise 3 Identifying Prepositional Phrases and Their Objects

Identify the prepositional phrase in each of the following sentences. Underline each preposition, and circle its object or objects.

EXAMPLE 1. The package was for my brother and me.
         1. for my (brother) and (me)

1. The Sahara is a huge desert that lies south of the Mediterranean.

2. We waited until lunchtime.
3. The house across the street has green shutters.
4. Do not make repairs on the brakes yourself.
5. Maura said that the word *lasso* comes from a Spanish word that means "snare."
6. May I sit between you and him?
7. The woman in the blue uniform is my aunt.
8. The *Cherokee Phoenix* was the first newspaper printed in an American Indian language.
9. He is saving money for a stereo and a guitar.
10. The messenger slipped the note under the door.

Exercise 4 **Writing Appropriate Prepositional Phrases**

Write the following sentences, filling in each blank with an appropriate prepositional phrase.

EXAMPLE   **1.** We saw Jason _____.
            1. We saw Jason at the mall.

1. My favorite comedian will appear _____.
2. That bus always arrives _____.
3. The fans _____ cheered every score.
4. The children tumbled _____.
5. The light _____ is broken.
6. Our car waited _____.
7. _____ sat a bald eagle.
8. A rich vein of gold ran _____.
9. _____ dashed a frightened squirrel.
10. His grandmother told us a story _____.

Adjective Phrases

4c. A prepositional phrase that modifies a noun or pronoun is called an *adjective phrase*.

In other words, an adjective phrase is a prepositional phrase that is used as an adjective.

            ADJECTIVE   **Icy** chunks fell from the skyscraper.
ADJECTIVE PHRASE   Chunks **of ice** fell from the skyscraper.

Reference Note

For more information about **adjectives,** see page 84.

SKILLS FOCUS

Identify and use adjective phrases correctly.

Adjective phrases answer the same questions that single-word adjectives answer.

What kind?	Which one?
How many?	How much?

EXAMPLES   Mr. Arnaud ordered a dinner **of boiled crawfish.**
   [The adjective phrase modifies the noun *dinner.* The
   phrase answers the question *What kind?*]

   The one **with the big pockets** costs a little more.
   [The adjective phrase modifies the pronoun *one.* The
   phrase answers the question *Which one?*]

   There was enough room **for only three people.** [The
   adjective phrase modifies the noun *room.* The phrase
   answers the question *How much?*]

Notice in these examples that an adjective phrase generally
follows the word it modifies.

Exercise 5   Identifying Adjective Phrases

Identify the adjective phrase in each of the following
sentences. Then, give the word that the phrase modifies.

EXAMPLE   1. Diego Rivera was a famous painter from Mexico.
   1. *from Mexico—painter*

1. People throughout the world enjoy Rivera's art.
2. One photograph on the next page shows an indoor mural
   that he painted.
3. Rivera often painted the walls of buildings.
4. His murals are beautiful examples of popular twentieth-
   century art.
5. Rivera's artworks often include symbols of Mexican
   culture.
6. His work with other Mexican artists was also very important.
7. Rivera was a major influence on the mural artist Juan
   O'Gorman.

8. O'Gorman's mural on the left beautifies a university library.
9. O'Gorman does not paint his murals; instead, he uses tiny pieces of colored tile.
10. The complicated pattern upon the library walls fascinates everyone who sees it.

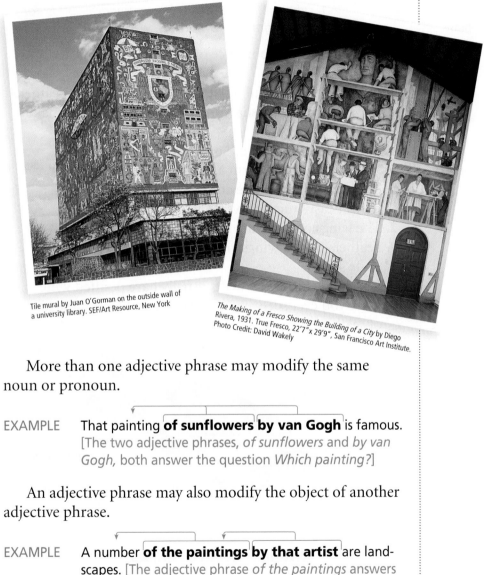

Tile mural by Juan O'Gorman on the outside wall of a university library. SEF/Art Resource, New York

The Making of a Fresco Showing the Building of a City by Diego Rivera, 1931. True Fresco, 22'7"x 29'9", San Francisco Art Institute. Photo Credit: David Wakely

More than one adjective phrase may modify the same noun or pronoun.

EXAMPLE   That painting **of sunflowers by van Gogh** is famous.
[The two adjective phrases, *of sunflowers* and *by van Gogh,* both answer the question *Which painting?*]

An adjective phrase may also modify the object of another adjective phrase.

EXAMPLE   A number **of the paintings by that artist** are land-scapes. [The adjective phrase *of the paintings* answers the question *What kind of number?* The adjective phrase *by that artist* answers the question *Which paintings?*]

SKILLS FOCUS

Identify and use adjective phrases correctly.

Exercise 6 Identifying Adjective Phrases

Identify each adjective phrase in the following sentences. Then, give the noun or pronoun the phrase modifies.

EXAMPLE   1. This book about birds of North America has won many awards for photography.

         1. *about birds—book; of North America—birds; for photography—awards*

1. It explains the importance of flight in the survival of the bird population.
2. The key to successful flight is the structure of the feather.
3. As you can see, the shaft and the vane are the two main parts of a feather.
4. The area inside the quill of a feather is hollow.
5. Barbs on the shaft form a feather's vane.
6. The curves in the vane and the notches of the feather permit easy, quick movement.
7. The wings of airplanes resemble birds' wings.
8. Feathers on the wings and tails of birds often are quite showy.
9. Fast-flying birds like swifts usually have pointed wings.
10. Have you ever seen any of the birds that have these kinds of feathers?

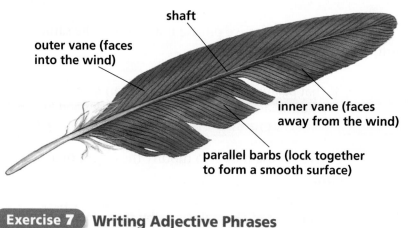

shaft

outer vane (faces into the wind)

inner vane (faces away from the wind)

parallel barbs (lock together to form a smooth surface)

Exercise 7 Writing Adjective Phrases

Fill in the blank in each of the following sentences with an appropriate adjective phrase.

EXAMPLE   1. That storm _____ might be dangerous.

         1. *That storm from the east might be dangerous.*

1. The shelf ____ is too high to reach.
2. I certainly hope that my gorilla costume wins a prize ____.
3. The girl ____ is one of my best friends.
4. The argument ____ really wasn't very important.
5. My favorite birthday present was the one ____.
6. Give your ticket to the man ____.
7. Did you see a bear on your trip ____?
8. Put the groceries ____ away, please.
9. My sister is the girl ____.
10. As I looked around the house, I noticed that an African design decorated the wall ____.

Adverb Phrases

4d. A prepositional phrase that is used to modify a verb, an adjective, or an adverb is called an *adverb phrase.*

In other words, an adverb phrase is a prepositional phrase that is used as an adverb.

ADVERB	We walk **there** every Saturday.
ADVERB PHRASE	We walk **along the lake** every Saturday.

Adverb phrases answer the same questions that single-word adverbs answer.

When?	Where?	Why?
How?	How often?	How long?

EXAMPLES   The statue stands **next to a large oak tree.** [The adverb phrase modifies the verb *stands* and answers the question *Where?*]

Ready **by dawn,** the travelers set out early to reach the capital. [The adverb phrase modifies the adjective *Ready* and answers the question *When?*]

Are these jeans long enough **for you**? [The adverb phrase modifies the adverb *enough* and answers the question *How?*]

Reference Note

For more about **adverbs,** see page 105.

SKILLS FOCUS

Identify and use adverb phrases correctly.

HELP

Be sure to ask yourself what question the phrase answers. Often, a phrase that comes right after a noun looks as though it is modifying that noun, but it is actually answering the question *When?*, *Where?*, or *How long?* about the verb. In the last example to the right, *over the bridge* does not tell us *which* bikes, but *where* we rode them.

HELP

Remember, an adverb phrase modifies a verb, an adjective, or an adverb.

NOTE Adverb phrases may appear anywhere in a sentence. They may come before or after the words they modify. Also, other words may come between an adverb phrase and the word or words it modifies.

EXAMPLES **After swimming lessons,** Aunt Helen drove us home.

Dad has been afraid **of snakes** since he was a boy.

We rode our bikes **over the bridge.**

Exercise 8   Identifying Adverb Phrases

Identify the adverb phrase used in each of the following sentences. Then, write the word or words the phrase modifies.

EXAMPLE   1. My hamster disappeared for three days.
1. *for three days—disappeared*

1. That mirror hung in the front hall.
2. The cat is afraid of thunderstorms.
3. The normally graceful acrobat plunged into the net but did not hurt herself.
4. Mayor Hernandez will speak at our school.
5. Mom discovered several field mice in the cellar.
6. With great courage, Rosa Parks disobeyed the bus driver.
7. She jogs around the reservoir every morning.
8. For a beginner, he plays well.
9. Soon, my shoes were full of sand.
10. We have planted several new varieties of day lilies along the fence.

As with adjective phrases, more than one adverb phrase can modify the same word.

EXAMPLE   Cesar Chavez worked **with the United Farm Workers for many years.** [Both adverb phrases, *with the United Farm Workers* and *for many years,* modify the verb *worked.*]

SKILLS FOCUS

Identify and use adverb phrases correctly.

An adverb phrase may be followed by an adjective phrase that modifies the object of the preposition in the adverb phrase.

EXAMPLE   Yesterday we went **to an exhibit of rare coins.** [The adverb phrase *to an exhibit* modifies the verb *went.* The adjective phrase *of rare coins* modifies *exhibit,* the object of the preposition in the adverb phrase.]

Exercise 9 Identifying Adverb Phrases

Identify the adverb phrase used in each of the following sentences. After each phrase, give the word or words the phrase modifies.

EXAMPLES   **1.** On Passover evening, we prepare a Seder, which is a Jewish holiday meal and ceremony.

    1. On Passover evening—prepare

    2. Passover celebrates a time long ago when Jewish slaves freed themselves from their masters.

    2. from their masters—freed

1. On Passover, many of our relatives visit our home.
2. We always invite them for the Seder.
3. Our whole family helps with the preparations.
4. Soon, everything is ready for this special meal.
5. In this photograph you can see how beautiful our holiday table is.
6. Holding all the special Passover foods, the Seder plate is displayed in the center of the table.

7. On the plate is a roasted egg representing new life.
8. Horseradish, which represents slavery's bitterness, is placed near the egg.
9. The other carefully arranged foods are also used during the Passover feast.
10. Throughout the entire meal, everyone enjoys a variety of delicious foods.

Writing Sentences with Adverb Phrases

Write ten sentences using the following word groups as adverb phrases. Underline each phrase. Then, draw an arrow from the phrase to the word or words it modifies.

EXAMPLE   1. for the airport

             1. *My grandparents left for the airport.*

1. down the hall
2. by them
3. in the mall
4. under the car
5. onto the diving board
6. over our heads
7. by a Navajo woman
8. through the sky
9. at five o'clock sharp
10. from Egypt

Review A   **Identifying Adjective and Adverb Phrases**

Each of the following sentences contains a prepositional phrase. Identify each phrase, and label it *adjective phrase* or *adverb phrase*.

EXAMPLES   1. Wilma Rudolph won three gold medals in the 1960 Olympic games.

             1. *in the 1960 Olympic games—adverb phrase*

            2. Rudolph overcame many obstacles in her life.

             2. *in her life—adjective phrase*

1. Wilma Rudolph did not have the childhood you might expect of a future Olympic athlete.
2. She and her twenty-one sisters and brothers were raised in a needy family.
3. Rudolph suffered from polio and scarlet fever when she was four years old.
4. Illnesses like these were often deadly.
5. For many years afterward, Rudolph used a leg brace when she walked.
6. Still, she never lost sight of her dreams.
7. She battled the odds against her.
8. With her family's help, she exercised hard every day.
9. All of her hard work made her strong.
10. Years later, she gained fame as a world-class athlete.

Review B **Identifying Adjective and Adverb Phrases**

Each of the following sentences contains at least one prepositional phrase. Identify each prepositional phrase, and label
each one *adjective phrase* or *adverb phrase.*

EXAMPLES
1. In China, farmers are considered the backbone of the country.
   1. *In China—adverb phrase; of the country—adjective phrase*

2. With over one billion people to feed, China asks much from its farmers.
   2. *With over one billion people to feed—adjective phrase; from its farmers—adverb phrase*

1. Many of the Chinese people are farmers.
2. They generally work their farms by hand.
3. Chinese farmers usually use hand tools instead of large machines.
4. Farmland throughout China is carefully prepared, planted, and weeded.
5. Farmers also harvest their crops with great care.
6. In the hills, the Chinese make flat terraces.
7. As you can see, water from high terraces can flow to lower terraces.
8. Farmers build ridges around the terraces so that the terraces can be flooded during the growing season.
9. In flat areas, water is pumped out of the ground.
10. Another Chinese method of irrigation is shown in the lower picture.

HELP

Although two possible answers are shown in the example, you need to write only one sentence for each item in Review C.

Review C **Using Prepositional Phrases in Sentences**

Use each of the following prepositional phrases in a sentence. Then, underline the word or word group that the prepositional phrase modifies.

EXAMPLE **1.** across the street

1. They <u>live</u> across the street.

or

The <u>store</u> across the street is open.

1. among the papers
2. over the fence
3. for your sister
4. toward him
5. about the schedule
6. before class
7. along the wall
8. through the door
9. under the table
10. in the evening
11. across the narrow bridge
12. near you and Anna Maria
13. aboard the sailboat
14. to the Grand Canyon
15. beneath the handmade quilt
16. according to the scientist
17. beyond the farthest planet
18. next to the blue helmet
19. upon the highest tree branch
20. from my brother and me

Review D **Writing Sentences with Adjective Phrases and Adverb Phrases**

Use each of the following phrases in two separate sentences. In the first sentence, use the phrase as an adjective. In the second sentence, use the phrase as an adverb.

EXAMPLE **1.** in Indiana

1. The people in Indiana are called "Hoosiers."
We once lived in Indiana.

1. from California
2. in my class
3. along the path
4. under the bridge
5. behind you
6. throughout the summer
7. at the beginning
8. around the corner
9. during dinner
10. on the patio

The Clause

4e. A *clause* is a word group that contains a verb and its subject and that is used as a sentence or as part of a sentence.

Every clause contains a subject and a verb. However, not all clauses express complete thoughts. Clauses that express complete thoughts are called ***independent clauses.*** Clauses that do not express complete thoughts are called ***subordinate clauses.***

Independent Clauses

4f. An ***independent*** (or ***main***) ***clause*** expresses a complete thought and can stand by itself as a sentence.

EXAMPLES
$$\overset{\text{S}}{\text{Gertie}} \overset{\text{V}}{\text{practices}} \text{ soccer every day.}$$

$$\overset{\text{S}}{\text{She}} \overset{\text{V}}{\text{has improved}} \text{ a great deal.}$$

$$\text{Her } \overset{\text{S}}{\text{team}} \overset{\text{V}}{\text{won}} \text{ yesterday's game.}$$

When an independent clause stands alone, it is called a sentence. Usually, the term *independent clause* is used only when such a clause is joined with another clause.

SENTENCE **He worked on the jigsaw puzzle.**

INDEPENDENT CLAUSE After Kevin had fed the cats, **he worked on the jigsaw puzzle.**

SKILLS FOCUS

Use clauses correctly. Identify and use independent clauses.

GRAMMAR

┌─ **HELP** ─

A subordinate clause that is capitalized and punctuated as if it were a sentence is a **sentence fragment.** Avoid using sentence fragments in your writing.

Reference Note

For more on **correcting sentence fragments,** see page 428.

Subordinate Clauses

4g. A *subordinate* (or *dependent*) *clause* does not express a complete thought and cannot stand by itself as a complete sentence.

EXAMPLES $\overset{\text{S}}{}\ \overset{\text{V}}{}$ if you finish on time

$\overset{\text{S}}{}\ \overset{\text{V}}{}$ which we found on the sidewalk

Subordinate means "lesser in rank or importance." A subordinate clause must be joined with at least one independent clause to make a sentence and express a complete thought.

SUBORDINATE CLAUSES

that Dad cooked for us

if you set realistic goals

before the sun sets

SENTENCES

We all enjoyed the dinner **that Dad cooked for us.**

If you set realistic goals, you are more likely to succeed.

Before the sun sets, I need to mow the lawn.

Notice the words that begin the subordinate clauses: *that, if,* and *before.* The chart below lists some other words that can signal the beginning of a subordinate clause.

Words Often Used to Begin Subordinate Clauses			
after	because	that	wherever
although	before	though	whether
as	how	unless	which
as if	if	until	while
as long as	since	when	who
as much as	so that	whenever	whom
as though	than	where	whose

SKILLS FOCUS

Identify and use subordinate clauses.

Identifying Independent and Subordinate Clauses

For each of the following items, identify the italicized word group as either an *independent clause* or a *subordinate clause.*

EXAMPLES   **1.** I'll do the experiment *if you will record the results.*

      1. subordinate clause

     2. *Ignacio,* who is an artist, *painted the banner.*

     2. *independent clause*

1. *While Dad was sleeping,* we decorated the house for his birthday party.
2. Just as Terri came in the door, *the phone rang.*
3. Somalis, *who traditionally raise and export livestock,* are nomadic.
4. Before you accept the invitation, *ask your mother.*
5. Do you know *when the train should arrive*?
6. *Although he was better at social studies,* he loved art.
7. Two uniformed soldiers guarded the entrance *where an iron gate stood.*
8. When the snows melt, *these streams will fill and rush down to the valley.*
9. That art paper *that you are using* really soaks up ink.
10. *Toni Morrison,* whose parents were once sharecroppers, *won the Pulitzer Prize.*

Adjective Clauses

4h. An *adjective clause* is a subordinate clause that modifies a noun or pronoun.

Like an adjective or an adjective phrase, an adjective clause may modify a noun or a pronoun. Unlike an adjective phrase, an adjective clause contains both a subject and verb.

ADJECTIVE   a **white** cat

ADJECTIVE PHRASE   a cat **with white fur** [*With white fur* does not have a subject and verb.]

ADJECTIVE CLAUSE   a cat **that has white fur** [*That has white fur* has a subject, *that,* and a verb, *has.*]

Reference Note

For information about **nouns,** see page 71. For information about **pronouns,** see page 76.

SKILLS FOCUS

Identify and use adjective clauses.

An adjective clause usually follows the noun or pronoun it modifies and tells *Which one?* or *What kind?*

EXAMPLES   The runner **who came in second** was Tina. [The adjective clause modifies the noun *runner* and answers the question *Which one?*]

I would like a dog **that I could take for long walks.** [The adjective clause modifies the noun *dog* and answers the question *What kind?*]

Exercise 12 Identifying Adjective Clauses

Identify each adjective clause in the following sentences.

EXAMPLE   1. Her coat was lined with fleece that kept her warm.
   1. *that kept her warm*

1. Jordan, whose aunt once rode on the space shuttle, is visiting her this summer.
2. Grandfather gave me that arrowhead, which has been in our family for generations.
3. The doctor looked at the notes that the nurse had written.
4. What was the name of the man who helped us?
5. Panama hats, which are prized far and wide, are woven of jipijapa leaves.
6. We could not have done it without Harry, whose skill saved the day.
7. Have you heard of Sister Juana Ines de la Cruz, the Mexican nun who championed women's rights in 1691?
8. Argentina's pampas, where fine herds of cattle graze, offer ranchers rich and vast grasslands.
9. Since ancient times, Asian ginger has been prized for the tang that it gives many dishes.
10. Ric, whom Doris calls "The Prince," is always a good sport.

Exercise 13 Using Adjective Clauses in Sentences

Write ten sentences using the following word groups as adjective clauses.

EXAMPLE   1. where I grew up
   1. *This is the street where I grew up.*

1. which had been imported from Japan
2. who is always on time
3. that live in this ecosystem
4. where the roses grow
5. whose short stories appear in your text
6. whom you talked about yesterday
7. that was having a sale
8. which may or may not be true
9. for whom our school is named
10. whose hard work made this event possible

Adverb Clauses

4i. An *adverb clause* is a subordinate clause that modifies a verb, an adjective, or an adverb.

Like an adverb or an adverb phrase, an adverb clause may modify a verb, an adjective, or another adverb. Unlike an adverb phrase, an adverb clause contains a subject and verb.

ADVERB	**Shyly,** the toddler hid behind her mother.
ADVERB PHRASE	**With a shy smile,** the toddler hid behind her mother. [*With a shy smile* does not have a subject and verb.]
ADVERB CLAUSE	**Since the toddler was shy,** she hid behind her mother. [*Since the toddler was shy* has a subject, *toddler,* and a verb, *was.*]

An adverb clause answers the following questions: *How? When? Where? Why? To what extent? How much? How long?* or *Under what conditions?*

EXAMPLES   **After he had moved the books,** Marvin dusted the shelves. [The adverb clause tells *when* Marvin dusted the shelves.]

Then he put the books back **where they belonged.** [The adverb clause tells *where* he put the books.]

He cleaned his room **because it was very messy.** [The adverb clause tells *why* he cleaned his room.]

HELP

Introductory adverb clauses are usually set off by commas.

EXAMPLES

After we built the camp-fire, we roasted hot dogs.

Although the song is good, it is not one of their best.

Reference Note

For more information on **using commas to set off introductory elements,** see page 320.

SKILLS FOCUS

Identify and use adverb clauses.

Exercise 14 Identifying Adverb Clauses

Identify each adverb clause in the following sentences.

EXAMPLE   1. Call when you can.

       1. *when you can*

1. Tiny wildflowers sprang up wherever they could.
2. Unless you want to sink, do not pull that large plug at the bottom of the boat.
3. Wind blew softly across the sand dunes while the caravan made its way home.
4. As soon as the cows come in, they must be fed.
5. To our surprise, when we entered the woods, a dozen armadillos were foraging right in front of us.
6. Although the piano had not been used for some time, it was still in tune.
7. Unless the shipment arrives today, the order will not be ready on time.
8. Because the airplane had been painted yellow, it was easily seen from the ground.
9. I'm not going if you're not going.
10. I had never heard anyone sing as he did.

Think as a *Reader/Writer*

In most cases, deciding where to place an adverb clause is a matter of style, not correctness.

As he leapt across the gorge, Rex glanced back at his alien pursuers.

Rex glanced back at his alien pursuers as he leapt across the gorge.

Which sentence might you use in a science fiction story? The sentence to choose would be the one that looks and sounds better in the context—the rest of the paragraph to which the sentence belongs.

Exercise 15 Writing Sentences with Adverb Clauses

Write twenty sentences using the following word groups as adverb clauses.

EXAMPLE   1. as soon as he can

       1. *He will be here as soon as he can.*

1. when I save enough money
2. if things go according to the schedule
3. since we have lived here
4. after the assembly was over
5. before school starts
6. although we couldn't speak Japanese
7. than she is
8. because they were going to the rink
9. until the sun set
10. while the lions are drinking from the river

11. as long as the band plays
12. whenever the train arrives at the station
13. unless the dog is on a leash
14. wherever you see grasshoppers
15. although the trail was steep
16. when Alexa won the marathon
17. so that we could use the computer
18. while the storm was raging
19. than you are
20. as though they had run ten miles

Review E **Identifying Clauses**

For each of the following sentences, identify the italicized clause as an *independent clause* or a *subordinate clause*. Then, identify each subordinate clause as an *adjective clause* or an *adverb clause*.

EXAMPLE   1. Those Japanese sandals *that you are wearing* are zoris.

  1. *subordinate clause—adjective clause*

  1. *Camels stamped and bellowed in annoyance* when packs were put on them.
  2. Aloe plants, *which originated in Africa,* are now widely available in the United States.
  3. As far as scientists can tell, *there is no connection between these two events.*
  4. *If you adjust the blinds,* you won't have that glare on your monitor.
  5. The castanets, *which were quite old,* had been Melanie's grandmother's.
  6. *You were always singing* when you were little.
  7. Three Indian elephants patiently towed the logs *that had just been cut.*
  8. Stay with us *as long as you want.*
  9. *Southeast Asia depends heavily on the seasonal rain* that the monsoons bring.
  10. The Forbidden City, *where China's emperors lived,* is enclosed by walls.

HELP

Although two possible answers are shown in the example, you need to write only one sentence for each item in Review F.

Review F **Writing Sentences with Clauses and Prepositional Phrases**

Use each of the following phrases and clauses in a sentence. Then, underline the word that the phrase or clause modifies.

EXAMPLE   1. under the flat rock
                   1. *Under the flat rock <u>lived</u> many odd insects.*

                                    or

                   The <u>insects</u> under the flat rock wriggled.

1. with a cowboy hat
2. who told us about computers
3. under the surface
4. since the club meets in the afternoon
5. for yourself
6. through the puddles
7. over the treetops
8. before we ate dinner
9. that grow along the fence
10. toward us

Sentence Structure

Simple Sentences

Reference Note

For information about **independent clauses** and **subordinate clauses,** see page 135.

4j. A *simple sentence* has one independent clause and no subordinate clauses.

A simple sentence may have a compound subject, a compound verb, or both. Although a compound subject has two or more parts, it is still considered a single subject. In the same way, a compound verb or verb phrase is considered one verb.

SKILLS FOCUS

Classify sentences by structure. Identify and use simple sentences. *(page 143):* Identify and use compound sentences.

                         S   V
EXAMPLES   My **mother belongs** to the Friends of the Library.
             [single subject and single verb]

                    S   S   V
             Argentina and **Chile are** in South America.
             [compound subject]

S   V   V
Jeannette read *Stuart Little* and **reported** on it.
[compound verb]

S   S   V
The **acrobats** and **jugglers did** amazing tricks and

V
were rewarded with a standing ovation. [compound
subject and compound verb]

Compound Sentences

4k. A *compound sentence* consists of two or more
independent clauses, usually joined by a comma and a
connecting word.

In a compound sentence, a coordinating conjunction (*and, but,
for, nor, or, so,* or *yet*) generally connects the independent clauses.
A comma usually comes before the conjunction in a compound
sentence.

EXAMPLES   I forgot my lunch, **but** Dad ran to the bus with it.

She likes sweets, **yet** she seldom buys them.

Notice in the second example above that, usually, a sentence is
compound if the subject is repeated.
     Sometimes the independent clauses in a compound
sentence are joined by a semicolon.

EXAMPLES   The blue one is mine; it has my initials on it.

The spider is not an insect; it is an arachnid.

Exercise 16   **Identifying Simple Sentences and
Compound Sentences**

Identify each of the following sentences as *simple* or *compound.*

EXAMPLE   **1.** That story by Lensey Namioka is good, and you
should read it.

1. *compound*

1. My dad and I like tacos, and we're making them for dinner.
2. Some trees and shrubs live thousands of years.
3. It rained, but we marched in the parade anyway.
4. Mr. Edwards will lead the singing, for Ms. Cruz is ill.

Reference Note

For more information
about **using commas
with conjunctions,** see
page 316. For more about
using **semicolons,** see
page 325.

Think as a
Reader/Writer

Sometimes you can com-
bine two simple sentences
to make one compound
sentence. Just connect the
two simple sentences by
using a comma and *and,
but, for, nor, or, so,* or *yet.*

ORIGINAL
   The rain has stopped. The
   sky is still dreary and gray.

COMBINED
   The rain has stopped, **but**
   the sky is still dreary and
   gray.

Combining sentences this
way can help make your
writing smoother and more
interesting.

5. My aunts, uncles, and cousins from Costa Rica visited us last summer.

6. I had worked hard all morning, and I still had not finished the job by lunchtime.

7. Abe peeled and chopped all of the onions and dumped them into a huge pot.

8. All ravens are crows, but not all crows are ravens.

9. Chippewa and Ojibwa are two names for the same American Indian people.

10. I liked this movie best; it was the most exciting one.

Review G **Identifying Simple Sentences and Compound Sentences**

Identify each of the following sentences as *simple* or *compound*.

EXAMPLE
    1. Have you or Sandy ever seen the movie *The Bridge on the River Kwai*?

    1. *simple*

1. My stepbrother is only eight years old, and he is fascinated by bridges.

2. We buy postcards with pictures of bridges, for he likes to collect them.

3. He has several cards of stone bridges.

4. Stone bridges are strong but are costly to build.
5. Many bridges are quite beautiful.
6. The Central American rope bridge shown here is one kind of suspension bridge.
7. The modern bridge on the previous page is another kind of suspension bridge.
8. Suspension bridges may look dangerous, yet most are safe.
9. Bridges must be inspected regularly.
10. My stepbrother collects postcards of bridges, and I collect postcards of towers.

Complex Sentences

4I. A *complex sentence* contains one independent clause and at least one subordinate clause.

Subordinate clauses usually begin with a word such as *who, whose, which, that, after, as, if, since,* and *when.* A subordinate clause can appear at the beginning, in the middle, or at the end of a complex sentence.

EXAMPLES   Before Chen planted his garden, he made a sketch of the layout.

                                     S   V
independent clause   he made a sketch of the layout

                                            S   V
subordinate clause   Before Chen planted his garden

When bees collect pollen, they fertilize the plants that they visit.

                                     S   V
independent clause   they fertilize the plants

                                     S   V
subordinate clause   When bees collect pollen

                                   S   V
subordinate clause   that they visit

SKILLS FOCUS

Identify and use complex sentences.

Sentence Structure   **145**

Compound-Complex Sentences

4m. A sentence with two or more independent clauses and at least one subordinate clause is a *compound-complex sentence.*

EXAMPLE   I picked up the branches that had fallen during the storm, and Rosa mowed the grass.

	S V
independent clause	I picked up the branches
	S V
independent clause	Rosa mowed the grass
	S V
subordinate clause	that had fallen during the storm

Exercise 17 **Classifying Sentences by Structure**

Identify each of the following sentences as *simple, compound, complex,* or *compound-complex.*

EXAMPLE   **1.** It was raining, but the sun was shining when we looked out the window.

    1. compound-complex

1. Cuba's capital is Havana, and this beautiful city has been the center of Cuban culture since 1552.
2. The heavy branches of an oak tree hung over our table and shaded us from the sun.
3. When you are looking at a work by Monet, stand back at least fifteen or twenty feet.
4. As it happens, you're right and I'm wrong.
5. Seashells filled Liz's suitcase and spilled onto the floor.
6. According to our records, your next appointment isn't until next month, but we do thank you for your call.
7. The Internet and other forms of electronic communication are shaping the world's future.
8. Because opinions are still divided, further discussion will be necessary.
9. The clock's minute hand is moving, but the second hand has stopped.
10. Between Asia and Africa lies a land bridge that is known as the Sinai Peninsula.

SKILLS FOCUS

Identify and use compound-complex sentences.

Chapter Review

A. Identifying Adjective and Adverb Phrases

Identify the prepositional phrase in each of the following sentences, and tell whether the phrase is used as an *adjective phrase* or an *adverb phrase*. Then, give the word or words that the phrase modifies.

1. The crowd waved banners during the game.
2. That book about the Underground Railroad is interesting.
3. Have you seen the pictures of the Wongs' new house?
4. The water in my glass was cold.
5. Uncle Eduardo carefully knocked the snow off his boots.
6. You should travel to Utah if you have never seen a beautiful desert.
7. Do you have any old CD's by the Three Tenors?
8. The swings in the park are a bit rusty.
9. A clown handed balloons to the children.
10. The mail carrier left a package on the front porch.

B. Identifying Independent and Subordinate Clauses

For each of the following items, identify the italicized word group as either an *independent clause* or a *subordinate clause*.

11. Yamile and her family enjoyed their vacation in Indonesia, *which is a country made up of thousands of islands.*
12. *Whenever he pressed the button,* another buzzer sounded.
13. After Luis worked out on the weight machines and swam ten laps in the pool, *he took a shower.*
14. Bring an extra sweatshirt with you *if you have one.*
15. *Martin enjoys speaking Japanese* when he visits the Nakamuras.
16. Before you leave for school, *do you always remember to brush your teeth*?
17. Is Rena the one *who went to New Zealand*?
18. *Did our grandmother ever tell you* how she came to this country from Latvia?

19. *Unless you don't like getting wet and working outside all day,* we could use your help at the Spanish club car wash on Saturday.

20. *Mr. Boylan,* whom we met several times at school events, *is the author of a novel.*

C. Identifying Clauses

For each of the following sentences, identify each italicized clause as an *adjective clause* or an *adverb clause*.

21. *When you have a chance,* send me an e-mail.

22. Anyone *who knows Vita* can tell you how smart she is.

23. *When the Castillo family arrived at the ski lodge that evening,* they went right to bed.

24. The theater company, *which had come to town only that afternoon,* put on a spectacular show.

25. Sherlock Holmes, *whose creator was Sir Arthur Conan Doyle,* is probably the most famous fictional detective in literature.

D. Identifying Types of Sentences

Identify each of the following sentences as *simple, compound, complex,* or *compound-complex.*

26. Sir Ernest Shackleton was an Antarctic explorer.

27. He wanted to be the first man to reach the South Pole, and in 1908, he led a party that came within ninety-seven miles of the pole.

28. In 1914, he led the British Imperial Trans-Antarctic Expedition to Antarctica.

29. Shackleton intended to cross Antarctica, which no one else had ever crossed before.

30. Before the expedition could land, Shackleton's ship, the *Endurance,* was trapped in the ice of the Weddell Sea for ten months.

31. Finally, the ice crushed the ship, and Shackleton and his men were stranded on the ice for five more months.

32. The men escaped the ice in small boats, and they landed on Elephant Island, where they lived in a makeshift camp.

33. Shackleton and five other men sailed to South Georgia Island, where they sought help from Norwegian whalers.

34. Shackleton's first attempts to return to Elephant Island did not succeed, but he finally rescued his crew on August 30, 1916.

35. Shackleton's expedition failed to cross Antarctica, but he brought all of his men home safely.

Writing Application

Using Prepositional Phrases in a Story

Using Prepositional Phrases to Add Detail The Friends of Animals Society is having a contest for the best true-life pet story. The winner of the contest will have his or her story published in the local newspaper. Write a brief story to enter in the contest. In your story, tell about an unusual pet that you have heard about or known. Use at least five adjective phrases and five adverb phrases in your story.

Prewriting First, you will need to choose a pet about which to write. Then, jot down details about how the animal looks and how it acts. In your notes, focus on a specific time when the animal did something funny or amazing.

Writing Begin your draft with an attention-grabbing paragraph. Introduce and describe your main character. Be sure that you have included any human characters that play a part in the story. Also, describe the story's setting—for example, your kitchen, your neighbor's backyard, or the woods.

Revising Ask a friend to read your draft. Depending on what your friend tells you, you may need to add, cut, or rearrange details. Make sure you have used at least five adjective phrases and five adverb phrases.

Publishing Check your story carefully for errors in grammar, spelling, and punctuation. You and your classmates may want to collect your stories into a booklet. Along with your stories, you might include pictures or drawings of the pets you have written about.

SKILLS FOCUS

Write autobiographical narratives. Identify and use prepositional phrases correctly. Identify and use adjective phrases correctly. Identify and use adverb phrases correctly.

CHAPTER

5

Complements
Direct and Indirect Objects, Subject Complements

Diagnostic Preview

Identifying Complements

Identify each complement in the following sentences as a *direct object,* an *indirect object,* a *predicate nominative,* or a *predicate adjective.*

HELP

Some sentences in the Diagnostic Preview have more than one complement.

EXAMPLE 1. Many forests are cold and snowy.

1. *cold—predicate adjective; snowy—predicate adjective*

1. We made our parents a family tree for their anniversary.
2. The sun disappeared, and the wind suddenly grew cold.
3. The home of the former president is now a library and museum.
4. The newspaper published an article and an editorial about ex-Mayor Sharon Pratt Dixon.
5. My uncle gave my sister and brother ice skates.
6. After the long hike, all of the Scouts felt sore and sleepy.
7. Leaders of the Ojibwa people held a meeting last summer.
8. I wrote my name and address in my book.
9. Your dog certainly appears healthy to me.
10. They always send us grapefruit and oranges from Florida.
11. Most stars in our galaxy are invisible to the human eye.

12. Did the workers capture an alligator in the sewer system?
13. Our trip on the Staten Island ferry became an adventure.
14. The air show featured balloons and parachutes.
15. The maples are becoming gold and red early this year.
16. My parents bought themselves several Beatles albums.
17. Aunt Kathleen gave Ricardo and me tickets for the show.
18. The two most popular sports at my school are football and volleyball.
19. The water in the pool looked clean and fresh.
20. My mother's homemade Sabbath bread tastes delicious.

Recognizing Complements

5a. A *complement* is a word or word group that completes the meaning of a verb.

Every sentence has a subject and a verb. Sometimes the subject and the verb can express a complete thought all by themselves.

> S V
> EXAMPLES Adriana swam.
>
> S   V
> The puppy was sleeping.

Often, however, a verb needs a complement to complete its meaning.

> S   V
> INCOMPLETE My aunt found [*what?*]
>
> S   V   C
> COMPLETE My aunt found a **wallet.** [The noun *wallet* completes the meaning of the verb *found.*]
>
> S   V
> INCOMPLETE Sarah bought [*what?*]
>
> S   V   C   C
> COMPLETE Sarah bought **herself** a new **jacket.** [The pronoun *herself* and the noun *jacket* complete the meaning of the verb *bought.*]

┌ TIPS & TRICKS ┐

You can remember the difference in spelling between *complement* (the grammar term) and *compliment* (an expression of affection or respect) by remembering that a compl**e**ment compl**e**tes a sentence.

SKILLS FOCUS

Identify complements in sentences.

To find the complement in a sentence, try this trick. Cross out all the prepositional phrases first. Then, look for the subject, verb, and any complements that are in the rest of the sentence.

EXAMPLE

James threw the ball ~~over the defender~~ and ~~into the receiver's arms~~. [The subject is *James*. The verb is *threw*. *Defender* and *arms* cannot be complements because they are both in prepositional phrases. The complement is *ball*.]

Reference Note

For more about **adverbs,** see page 105. For more about **prepositions** and **prepositional phrases,** see pages 108 and 109.

	S	V	
INCOMPLETE	The longcase clock was [*what?*]		

	S	V	C
COMPLETE	The longcase clock was an **antique.** [The noun *antique* completes the meaning of the verb *was.*]		

	S	V	
INCOMPLETE	The elephant seemed [*what?*]		

	S	V	C
COMPLETE	The elephant seemed **tired.** [The adjective *tired* completes the meaning of the verb *seemed.*]		

An adverb is never a complement.

ADVERB   The koala chews slowly. [The adverb *slowly* modifies the verb by telling *how* the koala chews.]

COMPLEMENT   The koala chews eucalyptus **leaves.** [The noun *leaves* completes the meaning of the verb *chews* by telling *what* the koala chews.]

A complement is never a part of a prepositional phrase.

OBJECT OF PREPOSITION   Hannah is riding to her friend's house. [The noun *house* is the object of the preposition *to.*]

COMPLEMENT   Hannah is riding her **bicycle.** [The noun *bicycle* completes the meaning of the verb phrase *is riding* by telling *what* Hannah is riding.]

Exercise 1   Writing Complements

Write an appropriate complement to complete each of the following sentences.

EXAMPLE   **1.** The class seemed ____ to go on the field trip.

 1. *happy*

1. Yesterday, Uncle Joe sent me a ____ in the mail.
2. Did you lend ____ your calculator?
3. After college, she became a ____ in Chicago.
4. This puppy looks ____ to me, Doctor.
5. Is your brother still a ____ in Montana?
6. The sky was ____ and ____ that winter night.
7. Give ____ a hand, please.

8. Was that _____ in the dinosaur costume?
9. My little brother ran into the house and showed us a _____.
10. Next on the program for the recital, the middle school chorus will sing _____.

Objects of Verbs

Direct objects and *indirect objects* complete the meaning of transitive verbs.

Direct Objects

The direct object is one type of complement. It completes the meaning of a transitive verb.

5b. A *direct object* is a noun, pronoun, or word group that tells *who* or *what* receives the action of the verb.

A direct object answers the question *Whom?* or *What?* after a transitive verb.

EXAMPLES   My brother bought a **model.** [My brother bought *what?* Bought a *model.* The noun *model* receives the action of the verb *bought.*]

Jan called **somebody** for the assignment. [Jan called *whom?* Called *somebody.* The pronoun *somebody* receives the action of the verb *called.*]

Corey studied **Mother Teresa** in his history class. [Corey studied *whom?* Studied *Mother Teresa.* The compound noun *Mother Teresa* receives the action of the verb *studied.*]

A direct object may be a compound of two or more objects.

EXAMPLES   Did the car have spoked **wheels** and a **spoiler**? [The compound direct object of the verb *Did have* is *wheels* and *spoiler.*]

She needed **glue, paint,** and **decals** for her model. [The compound direct object of the verb *needed* is *glue, paint,* and *decals.*]

Reference Note

For more information about **transitive verbs,** see page 101.

SKILLS FOCUS

Identify direct objects in sentences.

Reference Note

For more about **linking verbs,** see page 99.

Link to Literature

A direct object can never follow a linking verb because a linking verb does not express action.

LINKING VERB   Julia Morgan **was** an architect. [The verb *was* does not express action; therefore, *architect* is not a direct object.]

Exercise 2   Identifying Direct Objects

Identify each direct object in the following sentences. Remember that a direct object may be compound.

EXAMPLE   **1.** Do you enjoy books and movies about horses?

        1. books, movies

1. If so, then you probably know some stories by Marguerite Henry.

2. Her books about horses have thrilled readers for more than forty years.

3. Henry wrote many popular books, such as *Misty of Chincoteague* and *King of the Wind.*

4. Her book *King of the Wind* won the Newbery Medal in 1949.

Wesley Dennis, illustration from *King of the Wind* by Marguerite Henry. Illustration © 1947; copyright renewed 1976 by Morgan and Charles Reid Dennis.

5. The book tells the adventures of the boy Agba and his beautiful Arabian horse.
6. Agba fed milk and honey to the newborn colt.
7. Sometimes the playful colt bit Agba's fingers.
8. The head of the stables often mistreated Agba and the young colt.
9. Later, the boy and the horse left their home and traveled to England.
10. Read *King of the Wind*, and learn more about the adventures of Agba and his horse.

Wesley Dennis, illustration from *King of the Wind* by Marguerite Henry. Illustration © 1947; copyright renewed 1976 by Morgan and Charles Reid Dennis.

Indirect Objects

The indirect object is another type of complement. Like the direct object, the indirect object helps complete the meaning of a transitive verb. If a sentence has an indirect object, it must also have a direct object.

5c. An *indirect object* is a noun, pronoun, or word group that usually comes between the verb and the direct object. An indirect object tells *to whom* or *to what* or *for whom* or *for what* the action of the verb is done.

EXAMPLES   I gave that **problem** some thought. [The noun *problem* is the indirect object of the verb *gave* and answers the question "*To what* did I give some thought?"]

Dad bought **himself** some peanuts. [The pronoun *himself* is the indirect object of the verb *bought* and answers the question "*For whom* did Dad buy peanuts?"]

Luke sent **David Robinson** a fan letter. [The compound noun *David Robinson* is the indirect object of the verb *sent* and answers the question "*To whom* did Luke send a fan letter?"]

TIPS & TRICKS

Here is a trick you can use to see whether a word is an indirect object. Move the word from before the direct object to after it, and add either *to* or *for*. If the sentence still makes sense, you know the word is an indirect object in the original sentence.

EXAMPLE
Carol sold Steve her old television.

Carol sold her old television **to** Steve. [The sentence means the same thing either way.]

 SKILLS FOCUS

Identify indirect objects in sentences.

If the word *to* or *for* is used, the noun, pronoun, or word group following it is part of a prepositional phrase and cannot be an indirect object.

Reference Note

For more information about **prepositional phrases** and **objects of prepositions,** see page 123.

OBJECTS OF PREPOSITIONS	The ship's captain gave orders to the **crew.**
	Vinnie made some lasagna for **us.**
INDIRECT OBJECTS	The ship's captain gave the **crew** orders.
	Vinnie made **us** some lasagna.

Like a direct object, an indirect object can be compound.

EXAMPLES   She gave **Ed** and **me** the list of summer activities. [*Ed* and *me* are indirect objects of the verb *gave.* They answer the question "*To whom* did she give the list?"]

Did the peacock show **you** and your **sister** its tail feathers? [*You* and *sister* are indirect objects of the verb *Did show.* They answer the question "*To whom* did the peacock show its tail feathers?"]

HELP

Some sentences in Exercise 3 do not have indirect objects.

Exercise 3 Identifying Direct and Indirect Objects

Identify the direct objects and indirect objects in the following sentences. Remember not to confuse objects of prepositions with direct objects and indirect objects.

EXAMPLE   **1.** Gabriel sent me a postcard from Ecuador.

    1. me—indirect object; postcard—direct object

   1. In Ecuador, Gabriel visited many of his relatives.
   2. His aunt Luz and uncle Rodrigo showed him the railroad in San Lorenzo.
   3. They also visited the port in Esmeraldas.
   4. Ecuador exports bananas and coffee.
   5. Gabriel's cousin showed him some other sights.
   6. She told Gabriel stories about Ecuadoran heroes.
   7. Gabriel and his relatives rode a train high into the Andes Mountains.
   8. They took photos from the train.
   9. Gabriel enjoyed his visit to Ecuador.
   10. He brought us some unusual souvenirs.

Exercise 4 Writing Direct and Indirect Objects

Write an appropriate direct or indirect object to complete each of the following sentences.

EXAMPLE   **1.** This weekend we are painting the ____.

       1. kitchen

1. The President made a ____ on television last night.

2. Did your dad teach ____ those magic tricks?

3. Wow! The governor wrote ____ a letter!

4. Then Marianne asked ____ the question in all our minds.

5. A mechanic replaced the truck's ____.

6. Save ____ a place at your table.

7. Are you still studying ____?

8. Okay, I'll owe ____ two hours' use of my skateboard.

9. Have you taken ____ for a walk?

10. Sam made ____ a table in shop class.

Review A Identifying Direct and Indirect Objects

Identify the direct objects and indirect objects in the following sentences.

EXAMPLE   **1.** Have you ever given board games much thought?

       1. board games—indirect object; thought—direct object

1. For centuries, people have enjoyed games of strategy.

2. Interest in strategy games has given us chess and checkers.

3. My brother showed me a book about different kinds of board games.

4. Board games reflect many different interests and appeal to all kinds of people.

5. Some games teach players lessons useful in careers and sports.

6. Of course, word games can give people hours of fun.

7. During the more difficult word games, Mrs. Hampton sometimes helps Chen and me.

8. Do you like trivia games?

9. Sharon's uncle bought Ronnie and her one of the new quiz games.

10. A popular television show inspired the game.

HELP

Some sentences in Review A do not have indirect objects.

Subject Complements

5d. A *subject complement* is a word or word group that is in the predicate and that identifies or describes the subject.

A linking verb connects a subject complement to the subject.

EXAMPLES   Mrs. Suarez is a helpful **neighbor.** [The subject complement *neighbor* identifies the subject *Mrs. Suarez.* The linking verb *is* connects *Mrs. Suarez* and *neighbor.*]

The airport appears very **busy.** [The subject complement *busy* describes the subject *airport.* The linking verb *appears* connects *airport* and *busy.*]

What smells so **good**? [The subject complement *good* describes the subject *What.* The linking verb *smells* connects *What* and *good.*]

He was the **one** in the middle of the line, in fact. [The subject complement *one* identifies the subject *He.* The linking verb *was* connects *He* and *one.*]

The author of that story is **Anne McCaffrey.** [The subject complement *Anne McCaffrey* identifies the subject *author.* The linking verb *is* connects *author* and *Anne McCaffrey.*]

Subject complements always complete the meaning of linking verbs, not action verbs.

Common Linking Verbs					
appear	become	grow	remain	smell	stay
be	feel	look	seem	sound	taste

The two kinds of subject complements are the *predicate nominative* and the *predicate adjective.*

Predicate Nominatives

5e. A *predicate nominative* is a word or word group that is in the predicate and that identifies the subject or refers to it.

A predicate nominative may be a noun, a pronoun, or a word group that functions as a noun. A predicate nominative is connected to the subject by a linking verb.

EXAMPLES Seaweed is **algae,** as I remember. [The noun *algae* is a predicate nominative following the linking verb *is*. *Algae* identifies the subject *Seaweed*.]

Was the first runner-up really **he**? [The pronoun *he* is a predicate nominative completing the meaning of the linking verb *Was*. *He* identifies the subject *runner-up*.]

NOTE Expressions such as *It's I* and *That was she* may sound awkward even though they are correct. In informal situations, many people use *It's me* and *That was her*. Such expressions may one day become acceptable in formal situations as well. For now, however, it is best to follow the rules of standard, formal English in all formal speaking and writing.

Reference Note

For more about **formal and informal English,** see page 267.

Be careful not to mistake a direct object for a predicate nominative. A predicate nominative always completes the meaning of a linking verb.

DIRECT OBJECT My brother admired the **acrobat.** [*Acrobat* is the direct object of the action verb *admired*.]

PREDICATE NOMINATIVE My brother became an **acrobat.** [*Acrobat* is the predicate nominative completing the meaning of the linking verb *became*.]

A predicate nominative may be compound.

EXAMPLES Maya Angelou is a great **poet** and **storyteller.** [*Poet* and *storyteller* are predicate nominatives. They identify the subject *Maya Angelou* and complete the meaning of the linking verb *is*.]

Is the shark a **fish** or a **mammal**? [*Fish* and *mammal* are predicate nominatives. They refer to the subject *shark* and complete the meaning of the linking verb *Is*.]

Yesterday was my **birthday, Labor Day,** and the first **day** of the week! [*Birthday, Labor Day*, and *day* are predicate nominatives. They identify the subject *Yesterday* and complete the meaning of the linking verb *was*.]

SKILLS FOCUS

Identify predicate nominatives in sentences.

┌HELP┐

Some sentences
in Exercise 5 have a
compound predicate
nominative.

Think as a
Reader/Writer

Be careful not to overuse
the linking verb *be* in your
writing. Read your writing.
Do you get the feeling that
nothing is happening, that
nobody is doing anything?
If so, you may have used
too many *be* verbs. When
possible, replace a dull *be*
verb with a verb that
expresses action.

BE VERB
  My father **is** a cabinet
  maker.

ACTION VERB
  My father **makes** cabinets.

SKILLS FOCUS

Identify predicate adjec-
tives in sentences.

Exercise 5 **Identifying Predicate Nominatives**

Identify the predicate nominative in each of the following
sentences.

EXAMPLES
  1. Mount Rushmore is a national memorial.
  1. memorial

  2. Is that bird a finch or a sparrow?
  2. finch, sparrow

1. San Juan is the capital of Puerto Rico.
2. Her mother will remain president of the P.T.A.
3. Athens, Greece, has long been a center of art and drama.
4. The platypus and the spiny anteater are mammals.
5. The object of Juan Ponce de León's quest was the Fountain of Youth.
6. The peace pipe, or calumet, is a symbol of honor and power among American Indians.
7. Quebec is the largest province in Canada.
8. In 1959, Hawaii became our fiftieth state.
9. That bird must be an eagle.
10. The fourth planet from the sun is Mars.
11. Didn't she eventually become a senator?
12. He remained an umpire for over thirty years.
13. You are not the only one in the room.
14. Hiawatha was a real person.
15. Aren't you the oldest daughter in your family?
16. Could the problem with the engine be an empty gas tank?
17. Lucy Craft Laney was the founder of the Haines Normal and Industrial Institute.
18. For more information about Sadaharu Oh, Japan's great baseball star, a good source is "Move Over for Oh-San" in *Sports Illustrated*.
19. Was the author Chaim Potok or Amy Tan?
20. Be an example for others.

Predicate Adjectives

5f. A *predicate adjective* is an adjective that is in the predicate and that describes the subject.

A predicate adjective is connected to the subject by a linking verb.

EXAMPLES　By 9:30 P.M., I was very **tired.** [The adjective *tired* describes the subject *I*.]

I believe that Jacob is **Nigerian.** [The adjective *Nigerian* describes the subject *Jacob*.]

Like a predicate nominative, a predicate adjective may be compound.

EXAMPLES　The blanket felt **soft** and **fuzzy.** [Both *soft* and *fuzzy* describe the subject *blanket*.]

The cave looked **cold, damp,** and **uncomfortable.** [*Cold, damp,* and *uncomfortable* all describe the subject *cave*.]

Exercise 6　Identifying Predicate Adjectives

Identify the predicate adjective in each of the following sentences.

EXAMPLES　**1.** The porpoise seemed friendly.
　　　　　1. friendly

　　　　　2. Does that alligator look hungry?
　　　　　2. hungry

1. Everyone felt ready for the test.
2. Those fresh strawberries smell delicious.
3. The front tire looks flat to me.
4. Everyone appeared interested in the debate.
5. That scratch may become worse.
6. She is talented in music.
7. During the movie, I became restless and bored.
8. Van looks upset about his grades.
9. Queen Liliuokalani was quite popular with the Hawaiian people.
10. The computer program does not seem difficult to Dana.
11. After a two-hour nap, the baby was still sleepy.
12. These ants are quick and industrious.
13. Even in winter, pine trees stay green.
14. Remain calm in an emergency, and do not panic.
15. This machine has always been inexpensive but efficient.

COMPUTER TIP

If you do overuse *be* verbs in your writing, a computer can help you fix the problem. Use the computer's search function to find each occurrence of *am, are, is, was, were, be, been,* and *being* in a piece of your writing. For each case, decide whether you need to use the *be* verb. If possible, replace it with an action verb, or revise the sentence some other way to add variety.

┌HELP─

Some sentences in Exercise 6 have a compound predicate adjective.

16. A giraffe's legs are very skinny.
17. The hikers were hot and thirsty after the long trek.
18. Isn't that statue African?
19. Don't be jealous of Tiger, the new kitten.
20. Is that myth Greek or Roman?

Review B Identifying Subject Complements

Identify each subject complement in the following sentences, and label it a *predicate nominative* or a *predicate adjective*.

EXAMPLE   1. The character Jahdu is a magical trickster.
         1. *trickster—predicate nominative*

1. A trickster is a character who plays tricks on others.
2. Tricksters have been popular in many folk tales throughout the world.
3. Jahdu, however, is the creation of Virginia Hamilton.
4. Her collections of folk tales, such as *The Dark Way* and *In the Beginning*, are very enjoyable.
5. Jahdu may be her most unusual hero.
6. He certainly seems clever and playful.
7. Even Jahdu's home, a forest on the Mountain of Paths, sounds mysterious.
8. Jahdu can stay invisible by using special dust.
9. He can become any object, from a boy to a taxicab.
10. Why are tricksters like Jahdu always such entertaining characters?

Review C Identifying Complements

Identify each complement in the following sentences, and label it a *direct object,* an *indirect object,* a *predicate nominative,* or a *predicate adjective.*

EXAMPLE   1. One pet of President Theodore Roosevelt's family was Algonquin, a pony.
         1. *Algonquin—predicate nominative*

1. Some presidents' pets have become famous.
2. Someone may have shown you the book by President George H.W. Bush's pet, Millie.
3. Millie, a spaniel, became an author.

┌─HELP─────
A sentence in Review B may have a compound subject complement.

│ Link to │ Literature │

┌─HELP─────
Some sentences in Review C have more than one complement or a compound complement.

4. With the help of Mrs. Bush, Millie told a great deal about her days at the White House.
5. President Richard Nixon's best-known pet was Checkers, a cocker spaniel.
6. President Bill Clinton had both a cat named Socks and a dog named Buddy.
7. President William Howard Taft kept a pet cow.
8. Some presidential pets looked quite strange at the White House.
9. A pet mockingbird was a favorite companion of Thomas Jefferson.
10. Calvin Coolidge's raccoon, Rebecca, appeared comfortable at the White House.

GRAMMAR

Review D **Identifying Complements**

Identify each complement in the following sentences as a *direct object*, an *indirect object*, a *predicate nominative*, or a *predicate adjective*.

EXAMPLE   **1.** Have you ever seen a sari or a bindi?
     1. sari; bindi—direct object

┌─HELP─┐

Some sentences in Review D have more than one complement or a compound complement.

1. Many women from India wear these items.
2. A sari is a traditional Indian garment of cotton or silk.
3. Women wrap the sari's long, brightly printed cloth around their bodies.
4. As you can see, the softly draped sari is both graceful and charming.
5. Some women buy themselves cloth woven with golden threads for an elegant look.
6. As you might imagine, sari wearers can become quite chilled in the winter.
7. In cold climates, Indian women wear their beautiful, lightweight garments under sturdy winter coats.
8. Another traditional ornament for many Indian women is the colored dot in the middle of their foreheads.
9. The word for the dot is *bindi.*
10. The bindi gives the wearer a look of beauty and refinement.

Subject Complements   **163**

Write a sentence using each of the following kinds of complements. Underline the complement or complements in each
sentence. Use a variety of subjects and verbs in your sentences.

EXAMPLES   **1.** a compound predicate nominative
1. My aunt is a <u>swimmer</u> and a <u>jogger</u>.

2. a direct object
2. Lindsey tossed Sabra the <u>softball</u>.

3. a pronoun used as a predicate nominative
3. The winner of the science fair is <u>she</u>.

1. a predicate adjective
2. an indirect object
3. a direct object
4. a predicate nominative
5. a compound predicate adjective
6. a compound predicate nominative
7. a compound direct object
8. a compound indirect object
9. a pronoun used as an indirect object
10. a pronoun used as a direct object

Chapter Review

A. Identifying Direct and Indirect Objects

Identify the *direct objects* and *indirect objects* in the following sentences.

┌HELP┐

Not all sentences in Part A have indirect objects.

1. James Baldwin wrote stories, novels, and essays.
2. Vita made her mother a scarf for her birthday.
3. He handed Amy and me an ad for the concert.
4. A park ranger told Mike the story of Forest Park.
5. Tropical forests give us many helpful plants.
6. Did she tell you about the bear?
7. The senator read the crowd a rousing speech.
8. The tourist gave the pigeons in Trafalgar Square some of his sandwich.
9. On the ferry to Ireland, Mr. McCourt told us the history of Dublin.
10. Bring me the wrench from the workbench, please.

B. Identifying Subject Complements

Identify the subject complements in the following sentences, and label each a *predicate nominative* or a *predicate adjective*.

11. Tuesday is the last day for soccer tryouts.
12. These peaches taste sweet and juicy.
13. Two common desert creatures are the lizard and the snake.
14. My cousin Tena has become an excellent weaver of Navajo blankets.
15. The soil in that pot feels dry to me.
16. The hero of the movie was a songwriter and a singer.
17. Why is Bill Gates so famous and so successful?
18. The three Brontë sisters were Charlotte, Emily, and Anne.
19. *The Adventures of Huckleberry Finn* is probably Mark Twain's best-known book.
20. The movie is shallow, silly, and boring.

C. Identifying Complements

Identify the complements in the following sentences, and label each a *direct object*, an *indirect object*, a *predicate nominative*, or a *predicate adjective*.

21. Madrid is the capital of Spain.

22. Did you give me your new address?

23. These sketches of yours are wonderful!

24. Dr. Jonas Salk developed a vaccine to prevent polio.

25. Pam Adams is my best friend.

26. My father sent his mother and father two tickets to Mexico.

27. Your handwriting is neat and readable.

28. The longest play by Shakespeare is *Hamlet.*

29. Hugo handed his teacher the papers.

30. My father tossed the dog an old bone.

31. Jamie Wiseman is my favorite rugby player.

32. Thunder sometimes gives me a headache.

33. Are these toys safe for children?

34. My dad is buying my mother a bicycle.

35. Light reflectors for a bike are a good idea.

36. The wizard granted them three wishes.

37. Our trip to Villahermosa was short but exciting.

38. Angelo painted a beautiful picture of his mother.

39. Have you eaten lunch yet?

40. Miki is one of the best spellers in the class.

Writing Application
Using Complements in a Paragraph

Direct Objects and Indirect Objects   For National Hobby Month, students in your class are making posters about their hobbies. Each poster will include drawings or pictures and a written description of the hobby. Write a paragraph about your hobby to go on your poster. Use at least three direct objects and two indirect objects in your paragraph.

Identify direct objects in sentences. Identify indirect objects in sentences.

Prewriting Choose a topic for your poster project. You could write about any collection, sport, craft, or activity that you enjoy in your free time. You could also write about a hobby that you are interested in starting. Freewrite about the hobby. Be sure to tell why you enjoy it or why you think you would enjoy it. If the hobby is new to you, find out more about it from another hobbyist or from the library.

Writing Begin your paragraph with a main-idea sentence that clearly identifies the hobby or special interest. Check your prewriting notes often to find details you can use in describing the hobby.

Revising Read your paragraph aloud. Does it give enough information about your hobby? Would someone unfamiliar with the hobby find it interesting? Add, cut, or rearrange details to make your paragraph easier to understand. Identify the transitive verbs in your paragraph. Have you used at least three direct objects and two indirect objects? You may need to revise some sentences.

Publishing Read over your paragraph for spelling, grammar, and punctuation errors, and correct any you find. You and your classmates may want to make posters using your paragraphs and some pictures. Cut pictures out of magazines and brochures, or draw your own. Then, attach your writing and art to pieces of poster board and display the posters in the classroom.

Reference Note

For information about **main idea sentences,** see page 445.

Agreement
Subject and Verb, Pronoun and Antecedent

Diagnostic Preview

A. Choosing Verbs That Agree in Number with Their Subjects

Find the subject of each of the following sentences. Then, choose the form of the verb in parentheses that agrees with the subject.

EXAMPLE　**1.** Janelle and Brad (*are, is*) in the drama club.

　　　　1. Janelle, Brad—are

1. Neither the passengers nor the pilot (*was, were*) injured.
2. There (*are, is*) two exciting new rides at the amusement park.
3. That book of Spanish folk tales (*is, are*) selling out.
4. (*Here are, Here's*) some books about Hawaii.
5. Shel Silverstein and Ogden Nash (*appeal, appeals*) to both children and grown-ups.
6. Velma and her little sister (*was, were*) reading a story by Gyo Fujikawa.
7. (*Was, Were*) your parents happy with the results?
8. Why (*doesn't, don't*) she and Megan bring the lemonade with them to the picnic?
9. The dishes on that shelf (*look, looks*) clean.

10. Either the cats or the dog (*has, have*) upset the plants.
11. There (*go, goes*) two more deer!
12. I (*am, is*) crocheting an afghan.
13. Why (*wasn't, weren't*) you at the scout meeting yesterday?
14. Several paintings by that artist (*are, is*) now on exhibit at the mall.
15. They (*doesn't, don't*) know how to find their way to the family reunion.

B. Choosing Pronouns That Agree with Their Antecedents

For each of the following sentences, identify the pronoun that agrees with its antecedent.

EXAMPLES   **1.** Either Eileen or Barbara will bring (*her, their*) notes.
   1. her

   2. When Dennis and Aaron were younger, (*he, they*) rode the same bus to school.
   2. they

16. A student should proofread (*his or her, their*) work carefully before turning in the final copy.
17. Carlos and Andrew finally watched the videos (*he, they*) had borrowed.
18. Everyone on the girls' volleyball team has picked up (*her, their*) equipment.
19. The cat had batted its toy under the sofa and couldn't reach (*it, them*).
20. Jennifer or Sharon will leave early so that (*she, they*) can prepare the display.
21. Most of the trees in the park had lost (*its, their*) leaves.
22. If you aren't going to finish those crossword puzzles, may I do (*it, them*)?
23. Each of the drawings was hung on the wall in (*its, their*) frame.
24. When Martin and Stephanie were not rehearsing onstage, (*he or she, they*) studied their lines in the hall.
25. Did one of the chickens lose (*its, their*) feathers?

Number

Number is the form a word takes to show whether the word is singular or plural.

6a. Words that refer to one person, place, thing, or idea are generally *singular* in number. Words that refer to more than one person, place, thing, or idea are generally *plural* in number.

Singular	tepee	I	baby	mouse
Plural	tepees	we	babies	mice

Exercise 1 **Identifying Singular and Plural Words**

Identify each of the following words as *singular* or *plural*.

EXAMPLE   **1.** activities

    1. plural

1. peach	**11.** dirt
2. libraries	**12.** dress
3. highway	**13.** someone
4. knife	**14.** feet
5. shelves	**15.** fantasy
6. children	**16.** society
7. they	**17.** potatoes
8. enchiladas	**18.** people
9. women	**19.** several
10. America	**20.** fathers-in-law

Agreement of Subject and Verb

6b. A verb should agree in number with its subject.

A subject and verb *agree* when they have the same number.

(1) Singular subjects take singular verbs.

EXAMPLES   The **ocean roars** in the distance. [The singular verb *roars* agrees with the singular subject *ocean*.]

    She plays the violin well. [The singular verb *plays* agrees with the singular subject *She*.]

HELP

Most nouns that end in *–s* are plural (*igloos, sisters*). Most verbs that end in *–s* are singular (*sings, tries*).

EXAMPLES
  My **sisters sing.**
  My **sister sings.**

    However, verbs used with the singular pronouns *I* and *you* do not end in *–s*.

EXAMPLES
  I sing.
  You sing.

Reference Note

The plurals of some nouns do not end in *–s* (*mice, Chinese, aircraft*). For more about **spelling the plural forms of nouns,** see page 369.

SKILLS FOCUS

Understand agreement. Demonstrate understanding of correct subject-verb agreement. Use verbs that agree with singular subjects.

USAGE

(2) Plural subjects take plural verbs.

EXAMPLES **Squirrels eat** the seeds from the bird feeder. [The plural verb *eat* agrees with the plural subject *Squirrels*.]

They practice after school. [The plural verb *practice* agrees with the plural subject *They*.]

When a sentence contains a verb phrase, the first helping verb in the phrase agrees with the subject.

EXAMPLES **Latrice has** been studying Arabic.
They have been studying Arabic.

Reference Note

For information on **verb phrases,** see page 96.

Exercise 2 **Identifying the Number of Subjects and Verbs**

Identify each of the following subjects and verbs as either *singular* or *plural*.

EXAMPLE 1. flag waves
        1. *singular*

┌**HELP**─────

All verbs in Exercise 2 agree with their subjects.

1. socks match
2. lightning crackles
3. leaves rustle
4. mosquitoes buzz
5. Lyle baby-sits
6. bands march
7. Richelle knits
8. they listen
9. singer practices
10. horses whinny
11. crows fly
12. Shannon chooses
13. boat floats
14. we learn
15. leg aches
16. Roger guesses
17. poets write
18. cells divide
19. he knows
20. ice cube melts

Exercise 3 **Changing the Number of Subjects and Verbs**

All of the subjects and verbs in the following sentences agree in number. Rewrite each sentence, changing the subject and verb from singular to plural or from plural to singular.

EXAMPLE 1. Lions roar on the plains of Kenya.
        1. *A lion roars on the plains of Kenya.*

1. Maps show the shape of a country.

SKILLS FOCUS

Use verbs that agree with plural subjects.

USAGE

2. What countries are highlighted on the map below?
3. Does an ocean form Kenya's eastern border?
4. Visitors enjoy Kenya's beautiful scenery.
5. Mount Kenya's peaks are covered with snow.
6. Wildlife parks have been created in Kenya.
7. In the picture below, rangers patrol a park to protect the animals.
8. They certainly have unusual transportation.
9. Many industries are located in Kenya's capital, Nairobi.
10. Kenyan farmers grow such crops as wheat, corn, and rice.

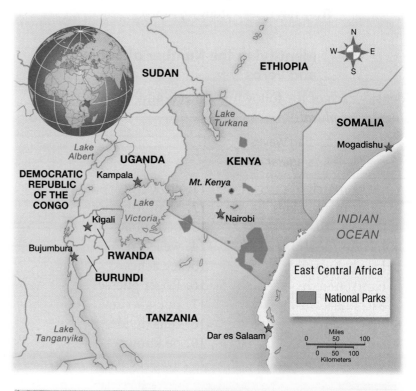

Exercise 4 Choosing Verbs That Agree in Number with Their Subjects

For each of the following sentences, choose the form of the verb in parentheses that agrees with the subject.

EXAMPLE   1. The kitten (*pounces, pounce*) on the ball.
             1. *pounces*

1. Firefighters (*risks, risk*) their lives to save others.
2. The snowplow (*clears, clear*) the road quickly.
3. Some dancers (*like, likes*) reggae music best.
4. St. Augustine, Florida, (*has, have*) many old buildings.
5. Some students (*chooses, choose*) to play volleyball.
6. At the science fair, the winner always (*receives, receive*) a savings bond.
7. Strong winds (*whistles, whistle*) through the old house.
8. Each Saturday, club members (*picks, pick*) up the litter in the park.
9. The principal (*makes, make*) announcements over the loudspeaker each day.
10. Doctors (*says, say*) that listening to loud music can harm people's hearing.

Problems in Agreement
Phrases Between Subject and Verb

6c. The number of a subject is not changed by a phrase following the subject.

EXAMPLES   These **shades** of blue **are** my favorite colors.

The **ballerina** with long black braids **has** been my sister's ballet teacher for two years.

However, if the subject is the indefinite pronoun *all, any, more, most, none,* or *some,* its number may be determined by the object of a prepositional phrase that follows it.

EXAMPLES   **Some** of the oranges **are** gone. [*Some* refers to the plural noun *oranges.*]

Some of the fruit **is** gone. [*Some* refers to the singular noun *fruit.*]

USAGE

Reference Note

For information on **phrases,** see Chapter 4.

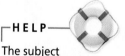

┌HELP┐

The subject of a sentence is never in a prepositional phrase.

EXAMPLE

The **apples** in the refrigerator are not cold yet. [*Apples* is the subject. *Refrigerator* cannot be the subject because it is part of the prepositional phrase *in the refrigerator.*]

NOTE *As well as, along with, together with,* and *in addition to* are compound prepositions. Phrases beginning with compound prepositions do not affect the number of a subject or verb.

EXAMPLE   **Myra,** along with her brothers, **helps** with household chores each evening. [The prepositional phrase *along with her brothers* does not affect the number of the subject *Myra. Myra* is singular and takes a singular verb, *helps.*]

Exercise 5 **Choosing Verbs That Agree in Number with Their Subjects**

In each of the following sentences, choose the form of the verb in parentheses that agrees with the subject.

EXAMPLE   **1.** Islands off the coast (*has, have*) a life of their own.
    1. have

1. The second-largest island of the United States (*is, are*) located in the Gulf of Alaska.
2. The thirteen thousand people on Kodiak Island (*is, are*) mostly of Scandinavian, Russian, or Native Arctic descent.
3. The citizens of Kodiak (*calls, call*) Alaska the mainland.
4. Sacks of mail (*is, are*) flown there from the mainland.
5. Industries in the community, originally known as Kikhtak, (*includes, include*) farming, fishing, and mining.
6. One cannery on the island (*cans, can*) salmon eggs, or roe.
7. Many residents on the mainland (*considers, consider*) roe a delicacy.
8. Bears like this one (*catch, catches*) fresh salmon.
9. However, their search for leftovers often (*create, creates*) problems for Kodiak.
10. The officials of one town (*has, have*) had to put a special bear-proof fence around the garbage dump.

Indefinite Pronouns

Personal pronouns refer to specific people, places, things, or ideas. A pronoun that does not refer to a definite person, place, thing, or idea is called an *indefinite pronoun.*

Personal Pronouns	she	you	we	them
Indefinite Pronouns	each	many	anyone	all

6d. The following indefinite pronouns are singular: *anybody, anyone, anything, each, either, everybody, everyone, everything, neither, nobody, no one, nothing, one, somebody, someone,* and *something.*

EXAMPLES   **One** of the stars **is** from my home town.

Each of the tourists **was** given a souvenir.

Does everybody in the restaurant like pita bread?

6
d

Exercise 6 **Choosing Verbs That Agree in Number with Their Subjects**

In the following sentences, choose the form of the verb in parentheses that agrees with the subject.

EXAMPLE   1. Neither of the teams (*is, are*) on the field.
             1. *is*

1. Nearly everybody in Ruby Lee's family (*enjoy, enjoys*) tomato soup.
2. Neither of them (*was, were*) wearing a helmet.
3. Somebody in the class (*speaks, speak*) French.
4. Nobody in the first two rows (*want, wants*) to volunteer to be the magician's assistant.
5. Each of these songs (*is, are*) by Josephine Marie.
6. Someone in the crowd (*is, are*) waving a pennant, but I can't tell whether it's Nick.
7. Everyone in those exercise classes (*has, have*) lost weight.
8. One of the band members (*play, plays*) lead guitar and sings backup vocals.
9. No one (*was, were*) listening to the speaker.
10. (*Do, Does*) either of them know how?

USAGE

HELP

The pronouns listed in Rule 6f aren't always followed by prepositional phrases.

EXAMPLES

All are here.

Some has spilled.

In such cases you should look at the **context**—the sentences before and after the pronoun—to see if the pronoun refers to a singular or a plural word.

6e. The following indefinite pronouns are plural: *both, few, many, several.*

EXAMPLES   **Both overflow** occasionally.

Few of the guests **are** wearing formal clothes.

Many of the newer houses **have** built-in smoke detectors.

Several in the group **say** yes.

6f. The indefinite pronouns *all, any, more, most, none,* and *some* may be singular or plural, depending on their meaning in a sentence.

Often, the object of a preposition that follows the pronoun indicates whether the pronoun is singular or plural. If the object of the preposition is singular, the pronoun usually is singular. If the object is plural, the pronoun usually is plural.

EXAMPLES   **All** of the snow **has** melted. [*All* is singular because *snow* is singular. The helping verb *has* is singular to agree with *All.*]

All of the snowflakes **have** melted. [*All* is plural because *snowflakes* is plural. The helping verb *have* is plural to agree with *All.*]

Some of the birdseed **is** left in the feeder. [*Some* is singular because *birdseed* is singular. The helping verb *is* is singular to agree with *Some.*]

Some of the sunflower seeds **are** left in the feeder. [*Some* is plural because *seeds* is plural. The helping verb *are* is plural to agree with *Some.*]

Exercise 7   **Choosing Verbs That Agree in Number with Their Subjects**

Choose the correct form of the verb in parentheses in each of the following sentences.

EXAMPLE   **1.** Many of these puppies (*needs, need*) a good home.

1. need

1. Most of the balloons (*has, have*) long strings.

2. All of the girls wearing purple uniforms (*plays, play*) on the softball team.

3. Both of the sneakers (*gives, give*) me blisters.
4. Most of these recipes (*requires, require*) ricotta cheese.
5. Some of the artists (*paint, paints*) landscapes.
6. Few of those songs (*was, were*) composed by Duke Ellington.
7. None of the apartments (*has, have*) been painted.
8. All of the jewels (*is, are*) in the safe.
9. Many in the crowd (*waves, wave*) signs.
10. All of the writing (*is, are*) upside down.

Compound Subjects

A compound subject is made up of two or more subjects that are connected by the conjunction *and, or,* or *nor.* These connected subjects share the same verb.

6g. Subjects joined by *and* generally take a plural verb.

EXAMPLES **Red** and **blue are** the school's colors.

New **uniforms** and **instruments were ordered** for the marching band.

Mr. Lewis, Mrs. Kirk, and **Ms. Jefferson have applied** for new jobs.

Exercise 8 **Choosing Verbs That Agree in Number with Their Subjects**

Identify the compound subject in each of the following sentences. Then, choose the form of the verb in parentheses that agrees with the compound subject.

EXAMPLE **1.** Volcanoes and earthquakes (*is, are*) common in that area.
         1. Volcanoes, earthquakes—are

1. The blanket and the robe (*has, have*) Navajo designs.
2. Wind, hail, and freezing rain (*is, are*) predicted for Thursday.
3. A desk and a bookcase (*were, was*) moved into Ella's room.
4. Savannas and velds (*is, are*) two kinds of grasslands found in Africa.

┌─HELP─┐

Some indefinite pronouns, such as *both, each,* and *some,* can also be used as adjectives. When an indefinite adjective comes before the subject of a sentence, the verb agrees with the subject as it normally would.

EXAMPLES
   Children love playing in the park.

   Both children love playing in the park.

   The **child loves** playing in the park.

   Each child loves playing in the park.

USAGE

Reference Note

For information on **conjunctions,** see page 112.

SKILLS FOCUS

Use verbs that agree with compound subjects.

5. A delivery truck and a car with a trailer (*were, was*) stalled on the highway.
6. A raccoon and a possum (*raid, raids*) our vegetable garden every night.
7. Mandy and her aunt (*goes, go*) to the Chinese market every Saturday.
8. Eric and Jarvis (*were, was*) asked to introduce the speaker.
9. Mosquitoes and earwigs (*has, have*) invaded our backyard.
10. Ketchup, onions, and mustard (*goes, go*) well on many sandwiches.

6h. Singular subjects that are joined by *or* or *nor* take a singular verb.

EXAMPLES
A new marble **statue** or a **fountain has been planned** for the park.

On Mondays, either **Manuel** or **Stephie baby-sits** the children.

6i. Plural subjects joined by *or* or *nor* take a plural verb.

EXAMPLES
Either **potatoes** or **beans are served** with the baked chicken.

Tulips or **pansies make** a lovely border for a sidewalk.

6j. When a singular subject and a plural subject are joined by *or* or *nor*, the verb agrees with the subject nearer the verb.

EXAMPLES
Either the **engineers** or their **boss has made** this mistake. [The singular helping verb *has* agrees with the nearer subject, *boss.*]

Either the **boss** or the **engineers have made** this mistake. [The plural helping verb *have* agrees with the nearer subject, *engineers.*]

A soft **blanket** or some warm **booties make** a baby comfortable. [The plural helping verb *make* agrees with the nearer subject, *booties.*]

Some warm **booties** or a soft **blanket makes** a baby comfortable. [The singular verb *makes* agrees with the nearer subject, *blanket.*]

SKILLS FOCUS

Use verbs that agree with compound subjects.

Oral Practice 1 **Using Correct Verbs with Compound Subjects Joined by *Or* or *Nor***

Read each of the following sentences aloud, stressing the words in italics.

1. A *desert* or a *jungle is* the setting for the play.
2. The *table* or the *bookshelves need* dusting first.
3. Neither the *bus* nor the *train stops* in our town.
4. Neither *jokes* nor funny *stories make* Gordon laugh.
5. *Flowers* or a colorful *picture makes* a room brighter and more cheerful.
6. Either the *story* or the *poems are* by Langston Hughes.
7. At this restaurant, *rice* or *potatoes come* with the tandoori chicken dinner.
8. Neither the *Carolinas* nor *Illinois borders* Texas.

Review A **Choosing Verbs That Agree in Number with Their Subjects**

For each of the following sentences, choose the form of the verb in parentheses that agrees with the subject.

EXAMPLE   1. Tara and Chen (*are, is*) reading the same book.
           1. *are*

1. Many vegetables (*grow, grows*) quite large during Alaska's long summer days.
2. His mother (*teach, teaches*) math.
3. All of the boats in the harbor (*belong, belongs*) to the village.
4. You and your cousins (*are, is*) invited to the party.
5. Either the wall clock or our wristwatches (*tell, tells*) the correct time.
6. The new magazines on the kitchen table (*are, is*) for the hospital waiting room.
7. My list of favorite paintings (*include, includes*) *Starry Night* and the *Mona Lisa*.
8. Both my big brother and my sister (*deliver, delivers*) the morning newspaper.
9. Neither pencils nor an eraser (*are, is*) permitted.
10. The clowns and jugglers (*has, have*) always been my favorite circus performers.

Think as a *Reader/Writer*

Compound subjects that have both singular and plural parts can sound awkward even though they are correct. Try to avoid such constructions by revising the sentence.

AWKWARD
Jewelry or flowers make a nice Mother's Day gift.

REVISED
Jewelry makes a nice Mother's Day gift, and **flowers do,** too.

USAGE

Proofreading a Paragraph for Errors in Subject-Verb Agreement

Most sentences in the following paragraph contain a verb that does not agree in number with its subject. If a sentence is incorrect, give the correct verb form. If a sentence is already correct, write *C*.

EXAMPLE   **[1]** Holiday customs throughout the world is fun to study.

1. *are*

[1] In Sweden, adults and children celebrates St. Lucia's Day. [2] Everyone there know St. Lucia as the Queen of Light. [3] Many people eagerly look forward to the December 13 holiday. [4] Girls especially enjoys the day. [5] By tradition, the oldest girl in the family dress as St. Lucia. [6] The girl in the picture above is ready to play her part. [7] You surely has noticed the girl's headdress. [8] A crown of lighted candles are hard to miss! [9] Each of the young Lucias also wear a white robe. [10] Early in the morning, the costumed girls bring breakfast to the adults of the household.

Subject After the Verb

6k. When the subject follows the verb, find the subject and make sure that the verb agrees with it.

The subject usually follows the verb in questions and in sentences that begin with *there* and *here*.

EXAMPLES   **Are** the **birds** in the nest?

Is the **nest** on a high branch?

There **go** the **dragons**.

There **goes** the **dragon**.

NOTE The contractions *there's* and *here's* contain the verb *is*. These contractions are singular and should be used only with singular subjects.

EXAMPLES   There**'s Uncle Max**.

Here**'s** your **allowance**.

┌ TIPS **&** TRICKS ┐

When the subject of a sentence comes after the verb, the word order is said to be *inverted*. To find the subject of a sentence with inverted order, restate the sentence in normal subject-verb word order.

INVERTED
How much time **has he spent** at the lake?

NORMAL
He has spent how much time at the lake?

INVERTED
Here **are** the **toys**.

NORMAL
The **toys are** here.

Exercise 9 Choosing Verbs That Agree in Number with Their Subjects

Identify the subject of each sentence. Then, choose the form of the verb in parentheses that agrees with the subject.

EXAMPLE **1.** There (*was, were*) a baby rabbit hiding in the grass.

    1. rabbit—was

1. There (*are, is*) a new foreign-exchange student at my brother's high school.
2. (*Was, Were*) the fans cheering for the other team?
3. (*Has, Have*) the Washingtons moved into their new home?
4. Here (*stand, stands*) one brave, young woman and her only son, Dale.
5. (*Has, Have*) the bees left the hive?
6. (*There's, There are*) several correct answers to that tough question.
7. How long (*has, have*) the Huang family owned this tai chi studio?
8. (*Here are, Here's*) the shells that we collected from Driftwood Beach.
9. (*There's, There are*) a pint of fresh strawberries on the kitchen table.
10. There (*were, was*) Amy and Wanda in the doorway.

The Contractions *Don't* and *Doesn't*

6l. The word *don't* is the contraction of *do not.* Use *don't* with all plural subjects and with the pronouns *I* and *you.*

EXAMPLES **I don't** have my keys.   **Dogs don't** meow.

            You don't care.   **Don't they** know?

            We don't agree.   The **boots don't** fit.

6m. The word *doesn't* is the contraction of *does not.* Use *doesn't* with all singular subjects except the pronouns *I* and *you.*

EXAMPLES **He doesn't** know you.   **Don doesn't** like thunder.

            She doesn't see it.   **Doesn't** the **car** run?

            It doesn't work.   A **penguin doesn't** fly.

USAGE

Reference Note

For more information on **contractions,** see page 350.

SKILLS FOCUS

Demonstrate understanding of correct subject-verb agreement.

Oral Practice 2   Using *Don't* and *Doesn't* Correctly

Read each of the following sentences aloud, stressing the words in italics.

1. *He doesn't* want us to give him a party.
2. *Margo* and *Jim don't* have any money left.
3. *Lynna doesn't* remember the punchline.
4. The *bus doesn't* stop here.
5. *They don't* believe that old story.
6. *It doesn't* snow here in October.
7. *You don't* sing the blues anymore.
8. That Zuni *vase doesn't* look very old.

Exercise 10   Writing *Don't* and *Doesn't* with Subjects

Identify the subject in each of the following sentences. Then, choose the contraction, either *don't* or *doesn't*, that agrees with the subject.

EXAMPLE   **1.** Our cats _____ like catnip.
　　　　　 1. cats—don't

1. My parents _____ listen to rap music.
2. I _____ have much homework tonight.
3. Jerome _____ play the guitar as well as Angela does.
4. The pizza _____ have enough onions, mushrooms, green peppers, or cheese.
5. They _____ permit diving into the pool.
6. This bedroom _____ look very neat.
7. My ski boots _____ fit me this year.
8. Matthew enjoys playing lacrosse, but he _____ like to play soccer.
9. You _____ live on this street anymore.
10. It _____ seem possible that Leon grew an inch in one month.

Review C   Proofreading for Errors in Subject-Verb Agreement

Most of the following sentences contain a verb that does not agree in number with its subject. Correct each incorrect verb. If a sentence is already correct, write *C*.

EXAMPLE   **1.** Is the people in the picture worried?

       1. Are

1. There is sharks swimming all around them.

2. However, the people doesn't seem to care.

3. Has they lost their senses?

4. No, there aren't anything for them to worry about in this shark exhibit.

5. There's a transparent tunnel right through the shark pool.

6. Everyone who visits the exhibit ride a moving walkway through the tunnel.

7. The sharks don't seem to mind the people.

8. Actually, sharks in the wild doesn't attack people very often.

9. Of course, sharks does eat almost anything.

10. Caution and respect, therefore, is necessary in shark-inhabited waters.

Agreement of Pronoun and Antecedent

A pronoun usually refers to a noun or another pronoun called its ***antecedent.*** When you use a pronoun, make sure that it agrees with its antecedent.

6n. A pronoun should agree in gender with its antecedent.

Some singular personal pronouns have forms that indicate gender. Feminine pronouns refer to females. Masculine pronouns refer to males. Neuter pronouns refer to things (neither male nor female) and sometimes to animals.

Feminine	she	her	hers
Masculine	he	him	his
Neuter	it	it	its

Reference Note

For more information on **antecedents,** see page 76.

SKILLS FOCUS

Understand agreement. Demonstrate understanding of correct pronoun and antecedent agreement. Use pronouns that agree in number and gender with singular antecedents.

EXAMPLES **Rosa** said **she** lost **her** glasses.

Hank took **his** journal to the beach with **him.**

Manny chose that **bike** because of **its** color and styling.

The antecedent of a personal pronoun can be another kind of pronoun. In such cases, you can often look in a phrase that follows the antecedent to tell which personal pronoun to use.

EXAMPLE **One** of those **ladies** left **her** scarf in the car.

Each of the **boys** brought **his** own softball mitt.

Some singular antecedents may be either masculine or feminine. In such cases, use both the masculine and feminine forms of the pronoun.

EXAMPLE **Nobody** in the class finished **his or her** paper early.

NOTE In informal speech and writing, people often use a plural pronoun to refer to a singular antecedent that may be either feminine or masculine.

INFORMAL Every actor in the play had already memorized their lines.

Such usage is grammatically incorrect and should be avoided, especially in formal situations.

6o. A pronoun should agree with its antecedent in number.

A pronoun that refers to a singular antecedent is singular in number. A pronoun that refers to a plural antecedent is plural in number.

EXAMPLES Please put the lawn **mower** away after you have finished using **it.**

These **tools** will last longer if you take good care of **them.**

(1) Use a singular pronoun to refer to the indefinite pronouns *anybody, anyone, anything, each, either, everybody, everyone, everything, neither, nobody, no one, nothing, one, somebody, someone,* and *something.*

Think as a
Reader/Writer

To avoid the awkward use of *his or her,* try to rephrase the sentence.

AWKWARD
Each of the actors had memorized **his or her** lines.

REVISED
All of the actors had memorized **their** lines.

Reference Note

For more information about **indefinite pronouns,** see page 80.

USAGE

EXAMPLES Has **one** of the hamsters hurt **its** leg?

Someone left **his or her** jacket on the bus.

Everyone on the girls' team has **her** own locker.

(2) Use a plural pronoun to refer to the indefinite pronouns *both, few, many,* and *several.*

EXAMPLES **Both** of the birds had hidden **their** nests well.

Several of the spiders continue to live under that log; it is where **they** hatched.

On a night like this, **few** of the travelers will reach **their** destinations on schedule.

(3) The indefinite pronouns *all, any, more, most, none,* and *some* may be singular or plural, depending on their meaning in a sentence.

EXAMPLES **None** of the cereal has lost **its** crunch. [*None* is singular because it refers to the singular noun *cereal.*]
None of the cereal flakes have lost **their** crunch. [*None* is plural because it refers to the plural noun *flakes.*]

(4) Use a singular pronoun to refer to two or more singular antecedents joined by *or* or *nor.*

EXAMPLES Either **Miguel or Randall** has **his** paintings on display.

Neither **Karli nor Marta** will lend you **her** book.

Using a pronoun to refer to antecedents of different numbers may create an unclear or awkward sentence.

UNCLEAR Neither the kittens nor their mother liked her new food. [*Her* agrees with the nearest antecedent, *mother.* However, it is unclear if the kittens disliked their own new food or if they disliked their mother's new food.]

UNCLEAR Neither the kittens' mother nor the kittens liked their new food. [*Their* agrees with the nearest antecedent, *kittens.* However, it is unclear if the mother disliked her own new food or if she disliked her kittens' new food.]

AWKWARD Neither the kittens nor their mother liked their or her new food.

Think as a *Reader/Writer*

Sentences with singular antecedents joined by *or* can sound awkward if the antecedents are of different genders. If a sentence sounds awkward, revise it to avoid the problem.

AWKWARD
Mark or Sherrie will bring his or her flashlight.

REVISED
Either **Mark** will bring **his** flashlight, or **Sherrie** will bring **hers.**

SKILLS FOCUS

Demonstrate understanding of correct pronoun and antecedent agreement. Use pronouns that agree in number and gender with singular antecedents. Use pronouns that agree with plural antecedents.

It is best to revise sentences to avoid unclear and awkward constructions like the ones on the previous page.

REVISED   Neither the kittens nor their mother liked **the** new food.

        None of the cats liked **their** new food.

(5) Use a plural pronoun to refer to two or more antecedents joined by *and*.

EXAMPLES   When **Tyrell and Davis** get home, **they** will be surprised.

        Have **Chelsea and Susan** tried on **their** new outfits?

Exercise 11 **Proofreading for Pronoun-Antecedent Agreement**

Most of the following sentences contain errors in pronoun-antecedent agreement. Identify the incorrect pronoun, and write the correct pronoun. If a sentence is already correct, write *C.*

EXAMPLE   1. Colby and everybody else brought his or her calculators.

        1. *his or her—their*

1. Neither Chile nor Argentina has given their consent to the project.
2. These knives are sharp; be careful with it!
3. Of course, Mrs. Chin and her daughters will give us her assistance.
4. Everyone needs to take their project home by Friday.
5. Many of the houses were decorated with ribbons on its doors for the holidays.
6. Neither Frank nor Paul has had their hair cut recently.
7. Every one of the dogs is required to have a numbered tag attached to their collar.
8. That song on the radio sounds familiar, but I can't remember its title.
9. Roseanne and Kimberly, I believe, recently lost her glasses.
10. Have any of the horses escaped its corral?

Exercise 12 Proofreading for Pronoun-Antecedent Agreement

Most of the following sentences contain pronouns that do not agree with their antecedents. Identify each incorrect pronoun, and write the correct pronoun. If a sentence is already correct, write *C*.

EXAMPLE   1. On the first day, no one knew their partner.

　　　　　1. *their—his or her*

1. Somebody in the back row left their umbrella behind.
2. At last, all of the kittens were having their nap.
3. Several of the students had large scholarships given to him or her by local businesses.
4. Anybody in the sixth grade should know their phone number.
5. Neither of the antique cars had their original paint job.
6. Did many of the apprentices later change his or her trade?
7. Yes, anyone can enter their pet in the contest.
8. Few of the boys know the procedure, but he will learn it quickly.
9. None of the girls brought their books.
10. Both of the packages had been opened, and it sat forgotten on the floor.

Exercise 13 Proofreading for Pronoun-Antecedent Agreement

Most of the following sentences contain a pronoun that does not agree in number or gender with its antecedent or antecedents. Identify each incorrect pronoun, and write the correct pronoun. If a sentence is already correct, write *C*.

EXAMPLE   1. Either Abe or Brian will give their speech first.

　　　　　1. *their—his*

1. Gold and silver gain worth from its rarity.
2. Ask Mr. Reed or Mr. Steinhauer if they will lend you a pen or a pencil.
3. The house at the corner and the house next door have flowers growing in front of it.

4. The birds and the butterflies have flown south to their winter homes.

5. Can even a princess or a queen have their every wish?

6. Pepper tastes good in a recipe, but not all by themselves.

7. A single red rose or a lily does not cost much, and it will look nice on the table.

8. Each of the grocery stores advertises their sales in the Sunday paper.

9. Neither Dan nor Bob likes onions on his sandwich.

10. More of the oranges have stickers on it than I thought.

Exercise 14 **Proofreading for Pronoun-Antecedent Agreement**

Most of the following sentences contain a pronoun that does not agree in number or gender with its antecedent or antecedents. Correct each incorrect pronoun. If a sentence is already correct, write *C*.

EXAMPLE   **1.** Delia and Dawn told me about her idea for a neighborhood show.

    1. their

1. Both of my parents gave us his or her permission, so we used my front yard.

2. The name of our play, which was actually a rock opera, was *Strange Night,* and I wrote it.

3. Two trees lent us its trunks for a stage.

4. Somebody bought popcorn with their allowance and sold it to the audience.

5. Everyone in the neighborhood brought his or her own chair to the show.

6. Either Matt or Freddy practiced his dance routine.

7. Lisa and Tanya play guitar, so we asked her to be in our band.

8. Joan wore a costume with pink flowers and bluebirds on it.

9. Of course, a few dogs and one unhappy cat made its entrance at an improper moment.

10. Tickets were only fifty cents, and we sold all of it before the show began.

Chapter Review

A. Choosing Verbs That Agree in Number with Their Subjects

For each of the following sentences, identify the subject. Then, choose the form of the verb in parentheses that agrees with the subject.

1. The flowers in that garden (*need, needs*) water.
2. She and her cousin (*play, plays*) tennis every weekend except in the winter.
3. Either Paulette or Lily (*attend, attends*) all the local performances of the Alvin Ailey dancers.
4. There (*was, were*) several teachers at the game.
5. All of the corn (*has, have*) dried up.
6. (*Was, Were*) Liang and his sister born in Taiwan?
7. None of the trucks (*has, have*) arrived yet.
8. My best friend at school (*doesn't, don't*) live in our neighborhood.
9. (*Was, Were*) you heating some bean and cheese burritos in the microwave?
10. Here (*come, comes*) Elena and James.
11. Only one of my three dogs, my beagle Neptune, really (*enjoy, enjoys*) the beach.
12. Either the students or their teacher (*has, have*) decided on the color of the new bulletin board.
13. (*Doesn't, Don't*) that sweater belong to Ralph?
14. Neither the clerk nor the shoppers (*was, were*) aware of the fire down the street.
15. Where (*was, were*) you last night around supper time?
16. Several houses in our neighborhood (*is, are*) for sale.
17. My brother and I often (*play, plays*) checkers together.
18. Either he or she (*is, are*) next in line.
19. Marilu (*don't, doesn't*) know the name of the author.
20. There (*was, were*) no other people there besides us.

B. Changing the Number of Subjects and Verbs

All the subjects and verbs in the following sentences agree in number. Rewrite each sentence, changing the subject and verb from singular to plural or from plural to singular. You may have to add or delete *a, an,* or *the.*

21. Dogs bark in the middle of the night.
22. A bird sings in the distance.
23. Books have fallen off the shelf.
24. A camel passes.
25. Cars move down the highway.
26. Do elephants eat grass?
27. The man has eaten lunch.
28. Many people are at the river today.
29. She has an unusual hobby.
30. Police officers protect the people.

C. Proofreading for Errors in Pronoun-Antecedent Agreement

Most of the following sentences contain a pronoun that does not agree in number or gender with its antecedent or antecedents. Write each incorrect pronoun. Then, write the pronoun that agrees with the antecedent. If a sentence is already correct, write *C.*

31. We had to call the parking lot attendant because two cars and one truck had its lights on.
32. Each of the ducks was tagged with an electronic device around their left leg.
33. Tim and Donny promised he would bring some snacks to the party.
34. Frances or Donna will sing her favorite number.
35. I can't remember which one of my grandfathers spent their eighteenth and nineteenth years fighting in World War II.
36. Both my brother and my sister might lend me his or her favorite videos.

37. Somebody left the engine running in their car.

38. Did one of the applicants forget to sign his or her forms?

39. Most of the customers complained that his or her food was cold.

40. Neither of the robins had their winter plumage.

Writing Application

Using Agreement in Instructions

Subject-Verb Agreement   Your family is going on a weekend trip. A neighbor has agreed to look after your pets. Write a note giving your neighbor complete instructions for tending the animals. To avoid confusing your reader, make sure the subjects and verbs in your sentences agree.

Prewriting   Think about pets that you have had or that someone you know has had. If you have never cared for a pet, talk to someone who has. Take notes on caring for each pet.

Writing   Write a draft of your note. Explain the daily care of the pets step by step. The more specific your instructions are, the better. With your teacher's permission, you may use informal, standard English if you are writing to someone you know well.

Revising   Read your note aloud. Can you follow each step of the instructions? Are all the steps in order? Have you included all the necessary information? If not, revise your note to make it clear and complete.

Publishing   After you have revised your note, check each sentence for subject-verb and pronoun-antecedent agreement. Take special care with any verb that is part of a contraction. Check your note for any other errors in grammar, punctuation, and spelling. Find or make pictures that illustrate each of your steps. With your teacher's permission, mount the pictures on a storyboard and display the storyboard in your classroom.

Reference Note

For more about **informal English,** see page 267.

USAGE

SKILLS FOCUS

Write instructions. Demonstrate understanding of correct subject-verb agreement.

7

Using Verbs Correctly
Principal Parts, Regular and Irregular Verbs, Tense

Diagnostic Preview

Revising Incorrect Verb Forms in Sentences

Most of the following sentences contain an error in the use of verbs. If a verb form is incorrect, write the correct form. If the sentence is already correct, write *C*.

EXAMPLE   **1.** The last movie I seen was terrible.

           1. saw

1. My friends and I recently have set through several bad movies.

2. Has anyone ever wrote a letter to complain about how many bad movies there are?

3. Last Saturday our local theater run two bad movies!

4. My friends J. D. and Carolyn had went with me to the movie theater.

5. We had hoped that we would enjoy *Out of the Swamp*.

6. In the beginning of the movie, a huge swamp creature raised out of the muddy water.

7. It begun to crawl slowly toward a cow in a field.

8. The cow had been laying under a tree.

9. She never even seen the swamp monster.
10. I had sank back in my seat, expecting the monster to pounce.
11. Then the lights come back on.
12. What a disappointment—the film had broke!
13. It taked a long time before the machine came back on.
14. Some little children throwed popcorn up in the air.
15. Others drunk noisily through their straws.
16. I had sat my popcorn on the floor by my seat, and some-one kicked it over.
17. Finally, the theater manager choosed another movie to show us, but it was only a silly cartoon about a penguin and a polar bear.
18. The penguin wore a fur coat it had stole from a sleeping polar bear.
19. The bear awoke, become angry, and chased the penguin all over the place.
20. Finally, the penguin gave back the coat and swum to Miami Beach to get warm.

Principal Parts of Verbs

The four basic forms of a verb are called the ***principal parts*** of the verb.

7a. The four principal parts of a verb are the *base form,* the *present participle*, the *past,* and the *past participle*.

Base Form	Present Participle	Past	Past Participle
start	[is] starting	started	[have] started
wear	[is] wearing	wore	[have] worn

NOTE   The words *is* and *have* are included in this chart because present participle and past participle verb forms require helping verbs (forms of *be* and *have*) to form tenses.

┌HELP┐

Some people refer to the base form as the *infinitive.* Follow your teacher's directions when labeling this form.

Reference Note

For more information about **helping verbs,** see page 95.

SKILLS FOCUS

Identify and use the principal parts of verbs.

As you can see from their names, the principal parts of a verb are used to express time.

PRESENT TIME   She **wears** a blue uniform.

Ray **has been wearing** his baseball cap.

PAST TIME   Yesterday, we **wore** sweaters.

I **had worn** braces for three months.

FUTURE TIME   Jessica **will wear** her new dress at the party.

By next spring, Joey **will have worn** holes in those shoes.

A verb that forms its past and past participle by adding –*d* or –*ed* is called a ***regular verb.*** A verb that forms its past and past participle differently is called an ***irregular verb.***

Regular Verbs

7b. A ***regular verb*** forms its past and past participle by adding –*d* or –*ed* to the base form.

Base Form	Present Participle	Past	Past Participle
wash	[is] washing	washed	[have] washed
hop	[is] hopping	hopped	[have] hopped
use	[is] using	used	[have] used

Reference Note

For more about **spelling rules,** see Chapter 14.

NOTE   Most regular verbs that end in –*e* drop the –*e* before adding –*ing.* Some regular verbs double the final consonant before adding –*ing* or –*ed.*

EXAMPLES   cause   **caus**ing   **caus**ed
drop   **dropp**ing   **dropp**ed

Use regular verbs correctly.

One common error in forming the past or past participle of a regular verb is to leave off the –*d* or –*ed* ending.

NONSTANDARD   Josh was suppose to meet us here.

STANDARD   Josh was **supposed** to meet us here.

Oral Practice 1 **Using Regular Verbs**

Read the following sentences aloud, stressing each italicized verb.

1. We *are supposed* to practice sit-ups this morning.
2. With the help of his guide dog, the man *crossed* the street.
3. Carlos and Rita *have ordered* soup and salad.
4. Her family *had moved* from Trinidad to Brooklyn.
5. Some American Indians *used* to use shells for money.
6. Many *called* shell money "wampum."
7. Larry *has saved* most of his allowance for the past two months.
8. My grandmother *worked* at the computer store.

Exercise 1 **Forming the Principal Parts of Regular Verbs**

Write the four principal parts for each of the following verbs.

EXAMPLE 1. hope
1. *hope; [is] hoping; hoped; [have] hoped*

1. skate	8. rob	15. imagine
2. pick	9. laugh	16. question
3. live	10. love	17. ask
4. move	11. hop	18. worry
5. talk	12. snow	19. turn
6. stun	13. cook	20. experiment
7. enjoy	14. examine	

┌HELP┐

Remember that the spelling of some verbs changes when *–ing* or *–ed* is added.

USAGE

Exercise 2 **Using the Principal Parts of Regular Verbs**

Complete each of the following sentences with the correct form of the given italicized verb.

EXAMPLE 1. *paint* Henry Ossawa Tanner _____ many kinds of subjects.
1. *painted*

1. *create* Tanner _____ images showing people, nature, history, and religion.

The Banjo Lesson by Henry Ossawa Tanner, 1893. Oil on canvas. Hampton University Museum, Hampton, Virginia.

2. *learn*   What is the boy in this painting _____ to do?

3. *title*   Not surprisingly, Tanner _____ this painting *The Banjo Lesson.*

4. *live*   The artist, a native of Pittsburgh, _____ from 1859 to 1937.

5. *move*   At the age of thirty-two, Tanner _____ to Paris to study and work.

6. *visit*   Other African American artists _____ Tanner in France.

7. *admire*   For years, people have _____ Tanner's paintings.

8. *plan*   Our teacher is _____ to show us more of Tanner's work.

9. *want*   I have _____ to see Tanner's famous portrait of Booker T. Washington.

10. *praise*   In his book *Up from Slavery,* Washington _____ Tanner's talent.

Irregular Verbs

7c. An *irregular verb* forms its past and past participle in some other way than by adding *–d* or *–ed* to the base form.

An irregular verb forms its past and past participle in one of the following ways:

- changing vowels

Base Form	Past	Past Participle
win	won	[have] won
sing	sang	[have] sung
hold	held	[have] held

SKILLS FOCUS

Use irregular verbs correctly.

USAGE

- changing consonants

Base Form	Past	Past Participle
make	made	[have] made
lend	lent	[have] lent
hear	heard	[have] heard

- changing vowels *and* consonants

Base Form	Past	Past Participle
catch	caught	[have] caught
draw	drew	[have] drawn
tear	tore	[have] torn

- making no change

Base Form	Past	Past Participle
burst	burst	[have] burst
cut	cut	[have] cut
hurt	hurt	[have] hurt

NOTE   If you are not sure about the principal parts of a verb, look up the verb in a current dictionary. Entries for irregular verbs list the principal parts of the verb.

Reference Note

For more about **using a dictionary,** see "The Dictionary" in the Quick Reference Handbook.

Common Irregular Verbs			
Base Form	Present Participle	Past	Past Participle
become	[is] becoming	became	[have] become
begin	[is] beginning	began	[have] begun
blow	[is] blowing	blew	[have] blown
break	[is] breaking	broke	[have] broken

(continued)

USAGE

7
c

(continued)

Common Irregular Verbs

Base Form	Present Participle	Past	Past Participle
bring	[is] bringing	brought	[have] brought
buy	[is] buying	bought	[have] bought
choose	[is] choosing	chose	[have] chosen
come	[is] coming	came	[have] come
do	[is] doing	did	[have] done
drink	[is] drinking	drank	[have] drunk
drive	[is] driving	drove	[have] driven
eat	[is] eating	ate	[have] eaten
fall	[is] falling	fell	[have] fallen
feel	[is] feeling	felt	[have] felt
find	[is] finding	found	[have] found
freeze	[is] freezing	froze	[have] frozen
get	[is] getting	got	[have] gotten *or* got
give	[is] giving	gave	[have] given
go	[is] going	went	[have] gone
grow	[is] growing	grew	[have] grown
have	[is] having	had	[have] had
hear	[is] hearing	heard	[have] heard
hit	[is] hitting	hit	[have] hit
hold	[is] holding	held	[have] held
keep	[is] keeping	kept	[have] kept
know	[is] knowing	knew	[have] known

Oral Practice 2 **Using Irregular Verbs**

Read the following sentences aloud, stressing each italicized verb.

1. I *have begun* to learn karate.
2. We *chose* to stay indoors.
3. Earline never *had drunk* buttermilk before.
4. We *did* our homework after dinner.
5. Anna and Dee *have* almost *broken* the school record for the fifty-yard dash.

6. The wind *has blown* fiercely for three days.

7. Last Saturday, Isaac *brought* me a book about tennis.

8. The water pipes in the laundry room *have frozen* again.

Exercise 3 **Identifying the Correct Forms of Irregular Verbs**

Choose the correct verb form in parentheses in each of the following sentences.

EXAMPLE　**1.** The children have finally (*broke, broken*) the piñata.

　　　　　　1. broken

1. We had just (*began, begun*) our project when I got sick.

2. The Ruiz family (*drove, driven*) across the country.

3. Has anyone (*brung, brought*) extra batteries for the radio?

4. I have finally (*chose, chosen*) a book to borrow.

5. Last week the lake (*froze, frozen*) hard enough for skating.

6. My brother and I have (*gave, given*) away all our comic books to the children's hospital.

7. It is amazing that no one has ever (*fell, fallen*) off that old ladder.

8. Everyone (*went, gone*) back to the classroom to watch the video of the spelling bee.

9. David's aunt (*came, come*) here to attend his bar mitzvah.

10. Have you (*ate, eaten*) at the new Philippine restaurant?

11. They should not have (*drank, drunk*) so much ice water after playing tennis.

12. After our guests had (*ate, eaten*), we all toured the city.

13. We have (*came, come*) to expect great things from you.

14. By the time Jason arrived, Gina had already (*went, gone*).

15. When they left, Uncle Enrique (*gave, given*) them some Cuban bread.

16. Their team (*chose, chosen*) another topic for the debate.

17. Oh, yes, Chris and I have (*knew, known*) each other since kindergarten.

18. He (*did, done*) the experiment that very afternoon.

19. Lenny had never (*drove, driven*) a tractor before that day.

20. We must have (*blew, blown*) up a hundred balloons for my little brother's birthday party.

USAGE

Identifying the Correct Forms of Irregular Verbs

Choose the correct verb form in parentheses in each of the following sentences.

EXAMPLE **1.** Jameel has already (*drank, drunk*) a large glass of orange juice, but he is still thirsty.

1. drunk

1. The wool sweater (*felt, feeled*) scratchy, so I did not buy it.
2. Ramón (*got, gotten*) a part in the school play.
3. The new houseplant has already (*grew, grown*) several inches since we bought it.
4. Leslie (*become, became*) my best friend back in first grade.
5. I (*holded, held*) on to the dog's leash tightly.
6. Our neighbors have (*buyed, bought*) a new doghouse for their German shepherd.
7. Kani has (*kept, keeped*) a log of his study time.
8. Yesterday we finally (*finded, found*) a copy of Pat Mora's latest book.
9. In last night's ballgame, Heather (*hit, hitted*) another home run.
10. Have you ever (*hear, heard*) traditional Japanese music?

More Common Irregular Verbs			
Base Form	Present Participle	Past	Past Participle
lead	[is] leading	led	[have] led
leave	[is] leaving	left	[have] left
lose	[is] losing	lost	[have] lost
pay	[is] paying	paid	[have] paid
put	[is] putting	put	[have] put
read	[is] reading	read	[have] read
ride	[is] riding	rode	[have] ridden
ring	[is] ringing	rang	[have] rung
run	[is] running	ran	[have] run
say	[is] saying	said	[have] said

More Common Irregular Verbs			
Base Form	Present Participle	Past	Past Participle
see	[is] seeing	saw	[have] seen
send	[is] sending	sent	[have] sent
shrink	[is] shrinking	shrank *or* shrunk	[have] shrunk
sing	[is] singing	sang	[have] sung
sink	[is] sinking	sank *or* sunk	[have] sunk
speak	[is] speaking	spoke	[have] spoken
stand	[is] standing	stood	[have] stood
steal	[is] stealing	stole	[have] stolen
swim	[is] swimming	swam	[have] swum
take	[is] taking	took	[have] taken
teach	[is] teaching	taught	[have] taught
tell	[is] telling	told	[have] told
throw	[is] throwing	threw	[have] thrown
wear	[is] wearing	wore	[have] worn
write	[is] writing	wrote	[have] written

Oral Practice 3 **Using Irregular Verbs**

Read the following sentences aloud, stressing the italicized verbs.

1. Despite the blinding snowstorm, the Saint Bernard *had led* the rescue party to the stranded hikers.
2. The school bell *rang* five minutes late every afternoon this week.
3. When she visited New York City, Julia *saw* the Ellis Island Immigration Museum.
4. How many sixth-graders would you guess *have ridden* on this school bus?
5. What is the longest distance you *have swum*?
6. George *ran* to the corner to see the antique fire engine.
7. My favorite artist *sang* on the awards show.
8. *Have* you ever *written* haiku?

"*You don't say 'He taked my chair'...it's 'My chair was tooken'.*"

FAMILY CIRCUS reprinted with special permission of King Features Syndicate, Inc.

USAGE

Choose the correct verb form in parentheses in each of the following sentences.

EXAMPLE   **1.** Ms. Toyama (*took, taken*) her new kitten to the veterinarian.

     1. took

1. Who (*ran, run*) faster, Jesse or Cindy?
2. That cute little puppy has (*stole, stolen*) a biscuit.
3. The Boys Choir of Harlem has never (*sang, sung*) more beautifully.
4. Jimmy's toy sailboat had (*sank, sunk*) to the bottom of the lake.
5. Have you (*thrown, throwed*) yesterday's paper into the recycling bin?
6. Maria had (*wore, worn*) her new spring outfit to the party.
7. Until yesterday, no one had ever (*swam, swum*) across Crystal Lake.
8. Before she followed the white rabbit through the tiny door, Alice had (*shrank, shrunk*) to a very small size!
9. The students have (*written, wrote*) a letter to the mayor.
10. I have never (*spoke, spoken*) to a large audience before.
11. An open convertible (*lead, led*) the ticker tape parade.
12. Vulcan's hammer (*rang, rung*) as he worked metal for the Roman gods.
13. Why had the dog (*took, taken*) the cell phone outside?
14. We (*saw, seen*) a whole stack of petri dishes in the back of the lab closet.
15. Not only have I never (*rode, ridden*) a roller coaster, but I probably never will.
16. Have you (*spoke, spoken*) to your parents about taking those tuba lessons?
17. The children simply (*sang, sung*) "The Bear Went over the Mountain" until the baby sitter read them another story.
18. Why have all those people (*swam, swum*) across the English Channel?
19. The detective always (*wore, worn*) a porkpie hat.
20. The clever fox (*threw, throw*) the dog off the trail.

Exercise 6 Identifying the Correct Forms of Irregular Verbs

Choose the correct verb form in parentheses in each of the following sentences.

EXAMPLE   **1.** Uncle Alberto (*leaded, led*) the parade.

       1. led

1. Justin (*putted, put*) the soy sauce on the table.
2. Have Grandma and Grandpa (*left, leaved*) already?
3. The family (*said, sayed*) grace and then ate dinner.
4. The senator (*stood, standed*) up and waved to the crowd.
5. Has Leta (*readed, read*) the story "Miss Awful" yet?
6. After school Angela (*taught, teached*) me the new dance.
7. Each Christmas, Aunt Arlene has (*sended, sent*) me a classic children's book.
8. Mom (*paid, payed*) for the groceries, and we went home.
9. Ms. Cata (*telled, told*) the children a Hopi myth.
10. Lucas has (*losed, lost*) his favorite comic book.

Review A Proofreading for Errors in Irregular Verbs

Most of the following sentences contain an incorrect verb form. Identify each error, and write the correct form of the verb. If a sentence is already correct, write *C.*

EXAMPLE   **1.** Many stories have been wrote about the American athlete Jesse Owens.

      1. wrote—written

1. Owens breaked several sports records during his career.
2. At the Olympic games of 1936, he winned four gold medals.
3. A photographer took this picture of one of Owens's victories.
4. Owens's career begun in an unusual way.
5. As a little boy, Owens had been very sick, and later he run to strengthen his lungs.
6. In high school, the other boys on the track team done their practicing after school, but Owens had to work.

USAGE

7. Owens's coach encouraged him to practice an hour before school and brung him breakfast every morning.
8. The coach knowed Owens's parents couldn't afford to send their son to college.
9. The coach seen that something had to be done, and he helped Owens's father find a job.
10. Later, Owens went to Ohio State University, where he became a track star.

Review B Writing the Past and Past Participle Forms of Irregular Verbs

For each of the following sentences, write the correct past or past participle form of the italicized verb.

EXAMPLE   **1.** *take*   Gloria has ___ the last envelope.
          1. *taken*

1. *read*   Has everyone ___ the assignment for today?
2. *burst*   Suddenly, the door ___ open.
3. *drive*   We have ___ on Oklahoma's Indian Nation Turnpike.
4. *find*   Have you ___ your socks yet?
5. *speak*   Who ___ at this year's Hispanic Heritage awards ceremony?
6. *grow*   Patricia has ___ two inches in one year.
7. *hear*   One of the hikers had ___ the distant growl of a bear.
8. *give*   Mrs. Matsuo ___ me a copy of the book *Origami: Japanese Paper-Folding.*
9. *freeze*   The water in the birdbath has ___ again.
10. *choose*   Which play have they ___ to perform?
11. *wear*   The Highland School Band has always ___ Scottish kilts.
12. *know*   Noriko ___ the way to Lynn's house.
13. *teach*   Ms. Brook has ___ all of us how to work together.
14. *send*   My sweater was too small, so I ___ it to my cousin.
15. *ring*   Who ___ the doorbell a moment ago?
16. *hold*   The puppy ___ up its injured paw.

17. *hit*　　David _____ a ball past third base in the ninth inning.

18. *leave*　　Have you _____ your towel at the pool?

19. *see*　　We had never _____ a koala before.

20. *buy*　　Jerome _____ the decorations for the party.

Review C　**Proofreading for Incorrect Verb Forms**

Read each of the following sentences. If the form of a verb is wrong, write the correct past or past participle form. If the sentence is already correct, write *C*.

EXAMPLE　**1.** Dr. Seuss knowed how to please readers of all ages.

　　　　　1. knew

1. Have you ever saw the wacky characters shown here?

2. The imagination of Dr. Seuss brought both of them to life.

3. You may have bursted out laughing at the Cat in the Hat, Horton the elephant, or the Grinch.

4. In one story, the mean Grinch stoled Christmas.

5. In another, a bird gived Horton an egg to hatch.

6. The Lorax spoke out in support of the trees and the environment.

7. The Cat in the Hat has always wore his striped hat.

8. During his lifetime, Dr. Seuss must have wrote about fifty books with unusual characters.

9. Many children have began reading with his books.

10. Dr. Seuss choosed *The Lorax* as his own favorite book.

Dr. Seuss, *The Lorax*. © 1971 by Theodor S. Geisel and Audrey S. Geisel. Reprinted by permission of Random House, Inc.

Dr. Seuss, *The Cat in the Hat*. © 1957 by Dr. Seuss. Copyright renewed 1985 by Theodor S. Geisel and Audrey S. Geisel. Reprinted by permission of Random House, Inc.

USAGE

Tense

7d. The *tense* of a verb indicates the time of the action or the state of being that is expressed by the verb.

The six tenses are *present, past, future, present perfect, past perfect,* and *future perfect.* These tenses are formed from the principal parts of verbs. Each of these six tenses has its own uses. The following time line shows the relationships between tenses.

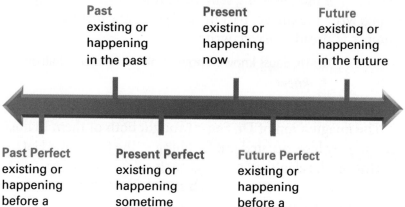

Past	Present	Future
existing or happening in the past	existing or happening now	existing or happening in the future

Past Perfect	Present Perfect	Future Perfect
existing or happening before a specific time in the past	existing or happening sometime before now; may be continuing now	existing or happening before a specific time in the future

Listing all the forms of a verb is called *conjugating* the verb.

Conjugation of the Verb *Wear*	
Present Tense	
Singular	**Plural**
I wear	we wear
you wear	you wear
he, she, *or* it wears	they wear
Past Tense	
Singular	**Plural**
I wore	we wore
you wore	you wore
he, she, *or* it wore	they wore

SKILLS FOCUS

Understand verb tenses.

Conjugation of the Verb *Wear*	
Future Tense	
Singular	**Plural**
I will (shall) wear	we will (shall) wear
you will (shall) wear	you will (shall) wear
he, she, *or* it will (shall) wear	they will (shall) wear
Present Perfect Tense	
Singular	**Plural**
I have worn	we have worn
you have worn	you have worn
he, she, *or* it has worn	they have worn
Past Perfect Tense	
Singular	**Plural**
I had worn	we had worn
you had worn	you had worn
he, she, *or* it had worn	they had worn
Future Perfect Tense	
Singular	**Plural**
I will (shall) have worn	we will (shall) have worn
you will (shall) have worn	you will (shall) have worn
he, she, *or* it will (shall) have worn	they will (shall) have worn

TIPS & TRICKS

Traditionally, the helping verb *shall* was used only in certain situations. Now, however, *shall* can be used almost any time that you would use *will*.

USAGE

Progressive Forms

Each of the six tenses also has a form called the *progressive form.* The progressive form expresses continuing action or state of being. It is made up of the appropriate tense of the verb *be* plus the present participle of a verb. The progressive is not a separate tense. It is just a different form that each tense can take.

SKILLS FOCUS

Understand the use of progressive tense.

Present Progressive	am, are, is wearing
Past Progressive	was, were wearing
Future Progressive	will (shall) be wearing
Present Perfect Progressive	has, have been wearing
Past Perfect Progressive	had been wearing
Future Perfect Progressive	will (shall) have been wearing

The Verb *Be*

The verb *be* is the most irregular of all the irregular verbs in English. Note the many different forms of *be* in the following conjugation.

Conjugation of the Verb *Be*	
Present Tense	
Singular	**Plural**
I am	we are
you are	you are
he, she, *or* it is	they are
Present Progressive: am, are, is being	
Past Tense	
Singular	**Plural**
I was	we were
you were	you were
he, she, *or* it was	they were
Past Progressive: was, were being	
Future Tense	
Singular	**Plural**
I will (shall) be	we will (shall) be
you will (shall) be	you will (shall) be
he, she, *or* it will (shall) be	they will (shall) be

┌HELP─

The present and past progressive forms of *be* are the most common. The other progressive forms of *be* are hardly ever used.

EXAMPLES
will (shall) be being
[future progressive]

has, have been being
[present perfect progressive]

Conjugation of the Verb *Be*	
Present Perfect Tense	
Singular	**Plural**
I have been	we have been
you have been	you have been
he, she, *or* it has been	they have been
Past Perfect Tense	
Singular	**Plural**
I had been	we had been
you had been	you had been
he, she, *or* it had been	they had been
Future Perfect Tense	
Singular	**Plural**
I will (shall) have been	we will (shall) have been
you will (shall) have been	you will (shall) have been
he, she, *or* it will (shall) have been	they will (shall) have been

USAGE

Exercise 7 **Identifying Tenses**

Identify the verb's tense in each of the following sentences.

EXAMPLE   **1.** A trolley noisily rolled down the track.

    1. *past*

1. Oh, no! Who fed this to the paper shredder?
2. Yes, Mom actually drinks that green stuff from the juicer.
3. Benjamin has left Des Moines.
4. Had you heard Andrés Segovia's music before then?
5. A mosaic of colorful tiles will decorate the entryway.
6. By my twenty-first birthday, I will have qualified for my pilot's license.
7. The committee will notify you of its decision.
8. Will you have saved enough money by then?
9. Evidently, I had thought of every possibility but one.
10. They are using the new modem now.

Consistency of Tense

7e. Do not change needlessly from one tense to another.

To write about events that take place at about the same time, use verbs in the same tense. To write about events that occur at different times, use verbs in different tenses.

INCONSISTENT   The cat jumped onto the counter and steals the sandwich. [The events happen at about the same time, but *jumped* is in the past tense, and *steals* is in the present tense.]

CONSISTENT   The cat **jumped** onto the counter and **stole** the sandwich. [Both verbs are in the past tense.]

CONSISTENT   The cat **jumps** onto the counter and **steals** the sandwich. [Both verbs are in the present tense.]

Exercise 8   Revising a Paragraph for Consistency of Tense

Read the following paragraph, and decide whether to rewrite it in the present or the past tense. Then, rewrite all of the sentences, changing the verb forms to correct any needless shifts in tense.

EXAMPLE   [1] Since our school has a computer network, we "chatted" with students from other schools.

     1. *Since our school has a computer network, we "chat" with students from other schools.*

             or

     Since our school had a computer network, we "chatted" with students from other schools.

[1] We trade essays with other English classes. [2] They read and commented on our essays, and we read and comment on theirs. [3] We also share reports with other classes in the school. [4] In Spanish I, we are writing letters to students in Argentina. [5] We practiced our Spanish. [6] They wrote back to us in English. [7] The computer classes sent a newsletter to all the other classes every week. [8] Every student has e-mail. [9] Students send messages to each other and to teachers. [10] E-mail made it easy to ask questions about assignments.

Six Confusing Verbs

Sit and *Set*

The verb *sit* means "to be seated" or "to rest." *Sit* seldom takes a direct object. The verb *set* means "to put (something) in a place." *Set* usually takes a direct object. Notice that *set* has the same form for the base form, past, and past participle.

Reference Note

For more about **direct objects,** see page 153.

Base Form	Present Participle	Past	Past Participle
sit	[is] sitting	sat	[have] sat
set	[is] setting	set	[have] set

EXAMPLES   I **will sit** in the easy chair. [no direct object]
I **will set** the cushion in the easy chair. [I will set what? *Cushion* is the direct object.]

The worker **has sat** there. [no direct object]
The workers **have set** their equipment there. [The workers have set what? *Equipment* is the direct object.]

TIPS & TRICKS

If you do not know whether to use *sit* or *set* in a sentence, try substituting *put.* If the sentence makes sense with *put,* use *set.* If not, use *sit.*

EXAMPLE
Jill (*set, sat*) the books on the shelf.

TEST
Jill put the books on the shelf. [The sentence makes sense with *put.*]

ANSWER
Jill **set** the books on the shelf.

Oral Practice 4 **Using the Forms of *Sit* and *Set* Correctly**

Read the following sentences aloud, stressing each italicized verb.

1. Before she left, Josie *had set* two loaves of French bread on the table.
2. The clown *sat* on the broken chair.
3. They *are sitting* down to rest awhile.
4. *Has* she *set* her bracelet on the night stand?
5. The Clarks' car *has sat* in the driveway for a week.
6. My little brother *sits* still for only a few seconds at a time.
7. The teacher *is setting* the best projects in the display case in the hall.
8. The librarian *set* the book about Michael Jordan on the large table.

SKILLS FOCUS

Use verbs correctly. Distinguish between words often confused.

USAGE

> Exercise 9 **Writing the Forms of *Sit* and *Set***

Write the correct form of *sit* or *set* to complete each of the
following sentences.

EXAMPLE   1. The girls _____ on the porch swing yesterday.
             1. *sat*

1. At the party yesterday, we _____ the birthday presents on
   the coffee table.
2. Then we _____ on the floor to play a game.
3. Alana had been _____ next to Rosa.
4. The Jiménez twins never _____ together, even though it
   was their birthday.
5. Mrs. Jiménez _____ a large cake on the table.
6. Mr. Jiménez had already _____ party hats and favors around
   the table.
7. He also _____ out the plates.
8. One of the twins _____ on a hat by mistake.
9. At every party we always _____ quietly while the birthday
   person makes a wish.
10. Yesterday, we _____ still twice as long for the Jiménez twins!

Rise and *Raise*

The verb *rise* means "to go up" or "to get up." *Rise* does not take a
direct object. The verb *raise* means "to lift (something) up" or "to
cause (something) to rise." *Raise* usually takes a direct object.

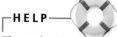

Base Form	Present Participle	Past	Past Participle
rise	[is] rising	rose	[have] risen
raise	[is] raising	raised	[have] raised

EXAMPLES   The winner **is rising** to receive his medal. [no
            direct object]

            The winner **is raising** her arms in triumph. [The
            winner is raising what? *Arms* is the direct object.]

            Taxes **rose** quickly. [no direct object]
            Congress **raised** taxes. [Congress raised what? *Taxes*
            is the direct object.]

Oral Practice 5 **Using the Forms of *Rise* and *Raise* Correctly**

Read the following sentences aloud, stressing each italicized verb.

1. The audience *had risen* from their seats to applaud Bonnie Raitt.
2. They *raised* the curtains for the play to start.
3. Dark smoke *rose* from the fire.
4. They always *rise* early on Saturday mornings.
5. The wind *had raised* the Chinese dragon kite high above the trees.
6. They *are raising* the banners.
7. The huge crane *can raise* the steel beams off the ground.
8. The temperature *was rising* quickly.

Exercise 10 **Writing the Forms of *Rise* and *Raise***

To complete each of the following sentences, supply the correct form of *rise* or *raise*.

EXAMPLE   1. We will _____ a banner.
                1. *raise*

1. Before the game the color guards _____ the flag.
2. The fans were _____ for the national anthem.
3. The pitcher _____ his arm to throw the ball.
4. The baseball seemed to _____ above the batter's head.
5. Someone in front of me was _____ a sign that blocked my view.
6. I have _____ my voice to cheer a hundred times during one game.
7. When the sun had _____ too high, the players couldn't see the high fly balls.
8. Whenever someone hits a home run, the fans _____ their mitts to catch the baseball.
9. Yesterday, everyone _____ when Marcus Jackson hit a home run.
10. As soon as the ninth inning was over, we _____ to leave.

Lie and Lay

The verb *lie* generally means "to recline," "to be in a place," or "to remain lying down." *Lie* does not take a direct object. The verb *lay* generally means "to put (something) down" or "to place (something)." *Lay* usually takes a direct object.

┌HELP───
The verb *lie* has definitions other than the ones given here. Another common definition is "to tell an untruth."

EXAMPLE
    Little Terry did not **lie** about spilling the milk.

When used this way, *lie* usually does not take a direct object. Its past and past participle forms are *lied* and [*have*] *lied*.

Base Form	Present Participle	Past	Past Participle
lie	[is] lying	lay	[have] lain
lay	[is] laying	laid	[have] laid

EXAMPLES   The beam **is lying** near the edge. [no direct object]
The workers **are laying** the beams near the edge. [The workers are laying what? *Beams* is the direct object.]

The newspaper **lay** on the kitchen table. [no direct object]
Sara **laid** the newspaper on the kitchen table. [Sara laid what? *Newspaper* is the direct object.]

The beach blanket **has lain** under the umbrella. [no direct object]
They **have laid** the beach blanket under the umbrella. [They have laid what? *Blanket* is the direct object.]

Oral Practice 6 Using the Forms of *Lie* and *Lay* Correctly

Read the following sentences aloud, stressing each italicized verb.

1. The corrected test paper *lay* on the desk.
2. My teddy bear *lies* on my bed all day.
3. Before the sale, the clerk *laid* samples on the counter.
4. *Have* those toys *lain* outside too long?
5. The Inuit hunter *was laying* his harpoon on the ice.
6. Last night, I *was lying* on the sofa reading a book when the phone rang.
7. I think the hero *has laid* a trap for the villain.
8. *Lay* the baby gently in the crib.

| COMPUTER TIP
If you have trouble using *sit, set, rise, raise, lie,* and *lay* correctly, a computer may be helpful. Use the search function to find and highlight all the uses of these confusing verbs in your writing. Then, look at each case carefully to determine whether you have used the correct form, and revise if necessary.

Exercise 11 **Writing the Forms of *Lie* and *Lay***

To complete each of the following sentences, write the correct form of *lie* or *lay*.

EXAMPLE   **1.** Children often _____ toys in the wrong places.

        1. lay

1. The remote control for the television is _____ under the rocking chair.
2. How long has it _____ there?
3. My brother Ramón probably _____ it there last night.
4. He was _____ on the floor, watching television.
5. Julia, my younger sister, is always _____ her toys in front of the television set.
6. She has _____ little parts from her board games all over the house.
7. Whenever Mom and Dad find one of these parts, they usually _____ it on the bookcase.
8. Yesterday, Dad _____ down on some hard plastic pieces on the sofa.
9. Now those broken bits of plastic _____ at the bottom of the wastebasket.
10. Today, Julia has _____ every single toy safely in the toy chest in her room.

Review D **Identifying the Correct Forms of *Sit* and *Set*, *Rise* and *Raise*, and *Lie* and *Lay***

Choose the correct verb from the pair in parentheses in each of the following sentences.

EXAMPLE   **1.** Dad (*sat, set*) the scrapbook from our visit to the Hopi reservation on the table and opened it to the picture shown on the next page.

        1. set

1. One of the first people we saw was a young Hopi mother with a small baby (*lying, laying*) in her arms.
2. Around lunchtime, I was glad I had not (*lain, laid*) aside my hat, because the sun was very hot.
3. A Hopi artist (*sat, set*) quietly in the shade, painting a beautiful design on a pot.

4. At the reservation, everyone (*sat, set*) quietly during the Hopi Snake Dance.

5. One dancer had (*risen, raised*) a snake above his head for the crowd to see.

6. The growing corn (*rises, raises*) high in the Hopi country of Arizona.

7. Hot and very tired, I (*lay, laid*) on a bench at the Hopi trading post.

8. In a moment, Dad had (*rose, raised*) his hat to shade my face from the sun.

9. When we entered the pueblo, a Hopi woman (*rose, raised*) from her chair to greet us.

10. Smiling, the woman (*sat, set*) a beautiful coiled basket on the counter.

Review E **Proofreading for Correct Verb Forms**

Identify the incorrect verb form in each of the following sentences. Then, write the correct form.

EXAMPLE   **1.** Lately, everyone in our neighborhood has did more to keep physically fit.

   1. did—done

1. No one is setting down anymore—except on stationary bicycles.
2. My mom has rode 150 miles so far.
3. In addition, I have never knew so many aerobic dancers.
4. Yesterday afternoon, I swum twelve laps in the pool.
5. Last month, a famous exercise instructor choosed our neighborhood for her new fitness center.
6. Many people seen her interviews on local talk shows.
7. All of a sudden, adults and children have began going to the center.
8. Each person is suppose to use different kinds of equipment.
9. Last night, I rose a fifty-pound weight.
10. So far, no one has broke a leg on the cross-country ski machine.
11. Mom had went to several gyms over the years.
12. After my workout, I just laid on the floor, out of breath.
13. She and I have took several classes at that gym.
14. I must have ran a thousand miles on that treadmill.
15. We never worn fancy outfits, only sweat pants and T-shirts.
16. I had chose an hour soaking in the whirlpool as my first exercise plan.
17. However, I seen the dancers and heard the music.
18. Now I have knowed many of the dancers for a long time.
19. My energy level has raised, and I'm happier.
20. Don't sit those free weights down; keep at it!

Review F Using the Correct Forms of Verbs

Write the correct past or past participle form of the verb in parentheses in each of the following sentences.

EXAMPLE **1.** I have (*grow*) tired of this TV program.
  1. grown

1. Grant (*feel*) proud and happy after winning the chess tournament.
2. Over the years, I have (*keep*) all the postcards from my grandparents.
3. Mother has (*lose*) the sash for her kimono.

4. The room quickly (*become*) crowded with curious fans.
5. Mr. Shaw (*tell*) us to read about the life of Harriet Jacobs.
6. Have you (*make*) the hat for your costume yet?
7. All night the faithful Irish setter (*stand*) watch over the homestead.
8. Has Yoshi ever (*ride*) a horse before?
9. Have you ever (*hear*) the story of Pocahontas?
10. Juanita (*say*) the biscuits would be ready soon.
11. As the sun set, the temperature (*begin*) to drop.
12. A squirrel had (*eat*) all the seed we put out for the birds.
13. Has Darius (*run*) ten laps yet?
14. All the band members (*wear*) the same color socks on Friday.
15. At halftime, our team (*lead*) by two goals.
16. The secret agent had easily (*break*) the code and deciphered the message.
17. A whippoorwill (*sing*), crickets chirped, and a breeze rustled the leaves.
18. While I washed the dishes, Diane (*take*) the trash out.
19. A baby raccoon had (*fall*) from the tree into the soft pile of pine needles.
20. Have you (*give*) Dad his Father's Day present?

FRANK & ERNEST reprinted by permission of Newspaper Enterprise Association, Inc.

Chapter Review

A. Using Correct Forms of Irregular Verbs

For each of the following sentences, write the correct past or past participle form of the verb in parentheses.

1. We had (*ride*) in the car for several hours.
2. Six inches of snow had (*fall*) the night before.
3. I never (*know*) snow was so beautiful.
4. The wind had (*blow*) some of it into high drifts.
5. As we (*go*) past them, they looked like white hills.
6. My brother Ernest had (*bring*) some comics to read.
7. I (*lie*) back and looked at the scenery.
8. Unfortunately, the car heater had (*break*).
9. We all (*wear*) our heavy coats and mittens.
10. However, my ears almost (*freeze*).
11. My favorite wool cap had (*shrink*) to a tiny size in the dryer.
12. During the long ride home, we (*sing*) some songs.
13. At noon, we (*eat*) lunch at a roadside cafeteria.
14. The clerk (*rise*) and asked if we would like some hot chocolate.
15. I (*drink*) two cups of hot cocoa.
16. Mom and I (*run*) around the parking lot to wake up.
17. After lunch, Ernie (*begin*) to feel sleepy.
18. I had never (*sit*) so long in a car before.
19. All warmed up, Ernie (*sink*) into a deep sleep.
20. We had (*come*) a long way.

B. Writing the Past and Past Participle Forms of Irregular Verbs

For each of the following sentences, write the correct past or past participle form of the verb in parentheses.

21. Have you (*hear*) the good news about Barbara?
22. The lower branches of the tree (*break*) in the storm.

USAGE

23. Our current mayor has (*lead*) three successful administrations.
24. The train was crowded, so we stood in the aisle and (*hold*) on to the luggage rack.
25. The tired dog (*lie*) down as soon as it arrived home.
26. As far as I know, they haven't (*see*) that movie.
27. She has always (*set*) the table herself, but tonight she has no time.
28. "So far, children," said Ms. Espinosa, "that robin has (*fly*) all the way from Minnesota on its way to the Gulf Coast for the winter."
29. She (*wear*) her blue parka to the parade.
30. "Time to get up, everyone!" said Mom from the base of the stairs. "The sun has already (*rise*)."

C. Proofreading for Correct Verb Forms

For each of the following sentences, identify the incorrect verb form. Then, write the correct form.

31. When Dad was a boy in Iowa, he keeped bees.
32. Before I laid down to sleep, I had packed everything I would need for today's trip.
33. Has Everett sit out the food for the picnic?
34. Nobody in our family had ever went to college before Mom did.
35. I have never rode on a camel, but I'd like to someday.
36. Yesterday's class begun with a speed drill.
37. She felt triumphant because she had never hitted a fly ball before.
38. The unit stood at attention as Corporal Martinez rose the flag.
39. The builder lay the plans on the table.
40. Both Leyla and Hussain brung some delicious falafel to the anniversary party.

Writing Application
Using Verbs in a Description

Forms and Tenses of Verbs   Many scientists and writers make predictions about the future. They base their predictions on past and present trends. Write a paragraph or two describing how one everyday item such as a car, a house, a home appliance, or a school might be different one hundred years from now. In your description, be sure to use the correct forms and tenses of verbs.

Prewriting   Choose a topic that interests you, such as video games or skyscrapers. Based on what you already know about the topic, make some predictions about the future. Write down as many details as you can.

Writing   Begin your draft by telling what time period your predictions concern. Then, use your notes to write a clear, vivid description of something in that future time.

Revising   Have a classmate read your composition. How does it sound? Do your predictions sound possible? Add, cut, or revise details to make your description clear and believable.

Publishing   Read your paragraph carefully to check for errors in grammar, spelling, and punctuation. Take special care with the forms of verbs. Use a dictionary to check the forms of any irregular verbs you are not sure about. You may want to present your final draft to the class as a multimedia computer presentation, an illustrated bulletin board, or a three-dimensional mobile.

USAGE

SKILLS FOCUS

Write descriptive essays. Use descriptive strategies. Use verb tenses appropriately and consistently.

Using Pronouns Correctly

Subject and Object Forms

Diagnostic Preview

Revising Incorrect Pronoun Forms in Sentences

Most of the following sentences contain an incorrect pronoun form. If a pronoun is used incorrectly, write the incorrect form of the pronoun and give the correct form. If a sentence is already correct, write *C*.

EXAMPLE   **1.** The police officer complimented us and they on knowing the rules of bicycle safety.

      1. they—them

1. The members of our bicycle club are Everett, Coral, Jackie, and me.
2. Us four call our club the Ramblers, named after a bicycle that was popular in the early 1900s.
3. Mrs. Wheeler gave an old three-speed bike to we four.
4. Whom explained the special bicycle safety course?
5. Our cousins gave Coral and I their old ten-speed bikes.
6. Each of we Ramblers rides after school.
7. Sometimes we ride with the members of the Derailers, a racing club.
8. On Saturday mornings, we and them meet at the school.
9. Who told us about the bike trail along the river?

10. Everett warned we three about being careful because sometimes the Derailers are reckless.
11. He saw other riders and they at an intersection.
12. A car almost ran over two of them!
13. When the Ramblers ride with the Derailers, it is us who obey all the safety rules.
14. Everett, Coral, Jackie, and I entered a safety contest.
15. Other clubs and us competed for a tandem bike.
16. Everett and her taught Jackie how to ride it and shift gears.
17. One by one, us contestants went through the course.
18. Of all of we riders, the most careless were the Derailers.
19. Jackie and me were nervous as the judges were deciding.
20. Finally, the judges announced that the winners of the contest were us Ramblers.

The Forms of Personal Pronouns

The form of a personal pronoun shows how it can be used in a sentence. Pronouns used as subjects and predicate nominatives are in the **subject form.**

EXAMPLES   **He** and **I** went to the post office. [subject]

           The winner of the marathon is **she.** [predicate nominative]

Pronouns used as direct objects and indirect objects of verbs and as objects of prepositions are in the **object form.**

EXAMPLES   Mr. García helped **him** and **me** with yesterday's homework. [direct objects]

           The clerk gave **us** the package. [indirect object]

           When is Theo going to give the flowers to **her**? [object of a preposition]

Possessive forms (*my, mine, your, yours, his, her, hers, its, their, theirs, our, ours*) are used to show ownership or possession.

EXAMPLES   **My** sister had to turn the box on **its** end to get it through the door.

           A mother bear is very protective of **her** cubs.

┌HELP─

The subject form of pronouns is also sometimes known as the **nominative case.** The object form of pronouns is sometimes known as the **objective case.**

SKILLS FOCUS

Use pronouns correctly. Use case forms of personal pronouns correctly. Identify and use nominative-case pronouns correctly. Identify and use objective-case pronouns correctly. Identify and use possessive-case pronouns correctly.

The Forms of Personal Pronouns   **223**

USAGE

Personal Pronouns		
	Singular	**Plural**
Subject Form	I you he, she, it	we you they
Object Form	me you him, her, it	us you them
Possessive Form	my, mine your, yours his, her, hers, its	our, ours your, yours their, theirs

Notice that the pronouns *you* and *it* are the same in the subject form and object form.

NOTE Some authorities prefer to call possessive forms such as *our, your,* and *their* possessive adjectives. Follow your teacher's instructions regarding possessive forms.

Exercise 1 Identifying Pronouns

Identify each of the following pronouns as a *subject form,* an *object form,* or a *possessive form.* If the pronoun can be used as either the subject form or the object form, write *subject or object.*

EXAMPLE 1. they
1. *subject form*

1. him   3. it   5. our   7. you   9. he
2. me   4. we   6. them   8. their   10. your

Exercise 2 Identifying Pronouns in Sentences

For each of the following sentences, identify the pronoun in italics as a *subject form,* an *object form,* or a *possessive form.*

EXAMPLE 1. Ever since *he* could remember, Edward Bannister had wanted to be an artist.
1. *subject form*

1. He had to work hard to reach *his* goal.
2. Although Bannister was born in Canada, many consider *him* an American artist.
3. Bannister's parents died when *he* was young.
4. The little money they had was left to *their* son.
5. The young Bannister couldn't afford paper, so *he* drew on barn doors and fences.
6. Later, Bannister met Christiana Carteaux and married *her*.
7. She was from Rhode Island, where *her* people, the Narragansett, lived.
8. In 1876, a Philadelphia artistic society recognized Bannister by awarding *him* a gold medal for the painting shown here.
9. Bannister treasured his prize and regarded *it* as a great honor.
10. What do *you* think of the painting?

Edward Bannister, *Under the Oaks* (1876). Oil on canvas. National Museum of American Art, Washington DC/Art Resource, New York.

The Subject Form

Pronoun as Subject

The *subject* tells whom or what the sentence is about.

8a. Use the subject form for a pronoun that is the subject of a verb.

SKILLS FOCUS

Identify and use nominative-case pronouns correctly.

TIPS & TRICKS

To test whether a pronoun is used correctly in a compound subject, try each form of the pronoun separately.

EXAMPLE
(*She, Her*) and (*I, me*) practiced hard. [*She practiced* or *Her practiced*? *I practiced* or *me practiced*?]

ANSWER
She and **I** practiced hard.

EXAMPLES   **I** walked to school. [*I* is the subject of the verb *walked*.]

Did **they** get to the theater on time? [*They* is the subject of the verb *Did get*.]

Dan said that **he** and **she** live on the Tigua reservation near El Paso, Texas. [*He* and *she* are the compound subject of the verb *live*.]

Oral Practice 1 Using Pronouns as Subjects

Read the following sentences aloud, stressing the italicized pronouns.

1. *She* and Ahmed solve crossword puzzles.
2. Are *they* very hard puzzles to solve?
3. Dad and *I* finished putting together a jigsaw puzzle last night.
4. *We* worked for three hours!
5. Finally, *you* and *he* found the missing pieces.
6. *He* and *I* liked the completed picture of flamenco dancers.
7. *They* are from Spain.
8. *We* agreed that *we* would like to see them dance.

Exercise 3 Identifying Correct Pronoun Forms

Choose the correct form of the pronoun in parentheses in each of the following sentences.

EXAMPLE   **1.** Brad and (*me, I*) wrote a skit based on the myth about Pygmalion.

1. *I*

1. (*Him, He*) and I thought the myth was funny.
2. (*We, Us*) asked Angela to play a part in the skit.
3. Neither (*she, her*) nor Doreen wanted to play a statue that came to life.
4. Finally Brad and (*me, I*) convinced Doreen that it would be a funny version of the myth.
5. (*Him, He*) and I flipped a coin to see who would play the part of Pygmalion.
6. The next day (*we, us*) were ready to perform.
7. Doreen and (*me, I*) began giggling when Brad pretended to be the beautiful statue.

8. In the skit, when Pygmalion returned from the festival of Venus, (*him, he*) and the statue were supposed to hug.
9. Instead of hugging, (*they, them*) laughed too hard to say the lines correctly.
10. Doreen, Brad, and (*I, me*) finally took a bow, and the class applauded.

Pronoun as Predicate Nominative

A *predicate nominative* completes the meaning of a linking verb and identifies or refers to the subject of the sentence.

8b. Use the subject form for a pronoun that is a predicate nominative.

A pronoun used as a predicate nominative usually follows a form of the verb *be* (such as *am, are, is, was, were, be, been,* or *being*).

EXAMPLES   The next singer is **she.** [*She* completes the meaning of the linking verb *is* and identifies the subject *singer.*]

The first two speakers might be **he** and **I.** [*He* and *I* complete the meaning of the linking verb *might be* and identify the subject *speakers.*]

Was the winner really **she**? [*She* completes the meaning of the linking verb *Was* and identifies the subject *winner.*]

(Oral Practice 2) **Using Pronouns as Predicate Nominatives**

Read the following sentences aloud, stressing the italicized pronouns.

1. The stars of that movie were *he* and *she.*
2. The actors from Australia must be *they.*
3. Of course, the mountain man is *he.*
4. Was the actress really *she,* Jeremy?
5. The director could have been *he.*
6. The villains are *he* and *they.*
7. The movie's biggest fans may be *you* and *I.*
8. The next ones to rent the film will be *we,* I think.

Reference Note

For more information on **predicate nominatives,** see page 158.

TIPS & TRICKS

To help you identify the predicate nominative in a question, try rearranging the words to make a statement.

QUESTION
Was the winner really she?

STATEMENT
The winner was really she.

As you can see in the statement form, the subject is *winner,* the verb is *was,* and the predicate nominative is *she.*

SKILLS FOCUS

Identify and use nominative-case pronouns correctly.

8
b

USAGE

Expressions such as *It's me* and *That's him* are common in everyday speech. However, these expressions contain the object forms *me* and *him* used incorrectly as predicate nominatives.

Such expressions should be avoided in formal writing and speaking. If the subject form of the pronoun sounds awkward as the predicate nominative, revise the sentence.

AWKWARD
The next speakers will be **he** and **I.**

REVISED
He and **I** will be the next speakers.

HELP

Although most of the sentences in Exercise 5 have more than one possible correct answer, you need to give only one for each sentence.

Exercise 4 Identifying Pronouns Used as Predicate Nominatives

Choose the correct form of the pronoun in parentheses in each of the following sentences.

EXAMPLE   **1.** The man behind the curtain is *(him, he)*.
         1. he

1. The winners are you and (*me, I*).
2. It might have been (*he, him*).
3. The cooks for the traditional Vietnamese meal were (*them, they*).
4. Could it have been (*we, us*)?
5. Every year the speaker has been (*her, she*).
6. That was Carl and (*they, them*) in the swimming pool.
7. The volleyball fans in our family are Dad and (*she, her*).
8. First on the Black History Month program will be (*us, we*).
9. Was that (*he, him*) at the door?
10. Last year, the class treasurer was (*he, him*).

Exercise 5 Writing Sentences with Pronouns Used as Predicate Nominatives

Supply pronouns to complete the following sentences correctly. Use a variety of pronouns, but do not use *you* or *it*.

EXAMPLE   **1.** The man in the silliest costume was _____.
         1. he

1. The person in the gorilla suit must be _____.
2. The next contestants will be _____ and _____.
3. The winners should have been _____.
4. Can that singer be _____, Samuel?
5. The one sitting in the back row was _____.
6. The first ones in line were my friends and _____.
7. "Excellent interpreters of Shakespeare's characters were _____ and _____," said Mr. Simmons.
8. Are the next entrants on stage _____?
9. The leader of that dragon team is probably _____.
10. Finalists in the contest will be Ted, Lisa, or _____.

Review A **Identifying Correct Pronoun Forms**

Choose the correct form of the pronoun in parentheses in each of the following sentences.

EXAMPLE   **1.** Last summer Carl, Felicia, and (*us, we*) went to Felicia San Antonio, Texas.

          1. we

1. Carl and (*she, her*) took these photographs.

2. Early one morning (*him, he*) and (*she, her*) visited the Alamo.

3. That could be (*him, he*) in the crowd outside the Alamo.

4. Felicia and (*I, me*) listened to a mariachi band on the Riverwalk.

5. Of course, the musicians in the picture at right are (*they, them*).

6. Don't (*they, them*) look as though they're having a good time?

7. Carl and (*I, me*) enjoyed visiting the Spanish Governor's Palace in the afternoon.

8. Felicia, Carl, and (*us, we*) particularly liked the palace.

9. In fact, the first guests there that morning were (*us, we*).

10. Maybe you and (*they, them*) will get a chance to visit San Antonio someday.

The Object Form

Pronoun as Direct Object

A ***direct object*** completes the meaning of an action verb and tells *who* or *what* receives the action of the verb.

Reference Note

For more about **direct objects,** see page 153.

The Forms of Personal Pronouns   **229**

Just as there are good manners in behavior, there are also good manners in language. In English, it is polite to put first-person pronouns (*I, me, mine, we, us, ours*) last in compound constructions.

EXAMPLES
Veronica showed **Roberto and me** how to use the software program.

She and I arrived early for softball practice.

TIPS & TRICKS

To help you choose the correct pronoun in a compound object, try each pronoun separately in the sentence.

EXAMPLE
Ms. Stone praised Alonzo and (*we, us*). [*Ms. Stone praised we* or *Ms. Stone praised us*?]

ANSWER
Ms. Stone praised Alonzo and **us**.

USAGE

8c. Use the object form for a pronoun that is the direct object of a verb.

EXAMPLES   The teacher thanked **me** for cleaning the chalkboard. [*Teacher* is the subject of the verb *thanked*. The teacher thanked whom? The direct object is *me*.]

The answer surprised **us**. [*Answer* is the subject of the verb *surprised*. The answer surprised whom? The direct object is *us*.]

Have you told **him** about the change in plans? [*You* is the subject of the verb *Have told*. You have told whom? The direct object is *him*.]

Fred saw **them** and **me** last night. [*Fred* is the subject of the verb *saw*. Fred saw whom? The compound direct object is *them* and *me*.]

Oral Practice 3   **Using Pronouns as Direct Objects**

Read the following sentences aloud, stressing the italicized pronouns.

1. Kathy found *them* and *me* by the fountain.
2. Mr. Winters took *us* to the rodeo.
3. Did you see *her* and *him* at the Cajun restaurant?
4. Tyrone frightened *us* with his rubber spider.
5. Ellis invited Luis, Jared, and *me* to his party.
6. The mayor met *them* at Howard University.
7. Uncle Ken thanked *her* for the gift.
8. The fans cheered Anthony and *her*.

Exercise 6   **Identifying Pronouns Used as Direct Objects**

Choose the correct form of the pronoun in parentheses in each of the following sentences.

EXAMPLE   1. Marcus met Howard and (*I, me*) at the game.
1. *me*

1. Mrs. Freeman invited Leroy and (*I, me*) to a Kwanzaa party.
2. The spectators watched (*we, us*) and (*they, them*).
3. The shoes don't fit (*her, she*) or (*I, me*).

4. Sean called Marco and (*he, him*) on the telephone.
5. Our new neighbors asked (*we, us*) for directions to the synagogue.
6. They hired Tía and (*us, we*) to rake their yard.
7. The puppy followed Louis and (*he, him*) all the way home.
8. Last week, friends from Panama visited (*us, we*).
9. Odessa thanked (*her, she*) and (*me, I*) for helping.
10. The usher showed Greg and (*them, they*) to their seats.

Pronoun as Indirect Object

An ***indirect object*** may come between an action verb and a direct object. An indirect object tells *to whom* or *to what* or *for whom* or *for what* something is done.

8d. Use the object form for a pronoun that is the indirect object of a verb.

EXAMPLES   Scott handed **me** a note. [Scott handed what? *Note* is the direct object. To whom did he hand a note? The indirect object is *me*.]

Coretta baked **them** some muffins. [Coretta baked what? *Muffins* is the direct object. For whom did Coretta bake muffins? The indirect object is *them*.]

Elizabeth sent **him** and **me** some oranges from Florida. [Elizabeth sent what? *Oranges* is the direct object. To whom did Elizabeth send oranges? The compound indirect object is *him* and *me*.]

Oral Practice 4 **Using Pronouns as Indirect Objects**

Read the following sentences aloud, stressing the italicized pronouns.

1. Mr. Krebs showed Bill and *them* the rock collection.
2. Paco told *me* the answer to the riddle.
3. Mr. Thibaut gives *us* lacrosse lessons.
4. We bought *her* and *him* a present.
5. The artists drew *us* and *them* some pictures.
6. The server brought *me* a bagel with cream cheese.
7. A pen pal in Hawaii sent *her* some shells.
8. My uncle Shannon told *us* a funny story about leprechauns.

Reference Note
For more about **indirect objects,** see page 155.

USAGE

┌─**HELP**─
Indirect objects do not follow prepositions. If *to* or *for* precedes a pronoun, the pronoun is the object of a preposition, not an indirect object.

Reference Note
For more information about **prepositions and their objects,** see page 109.

SKILLS FOCUS

Identify and use objective-case pronouns correctly.

Choose the correct form of the pronoun in parentheses in each of the following sentences.

EXAMPLE **1.** At the start of class, Mr. Chou assigned (*we, us*) new seats.

1. *us*

1. The store clerk gave (*they, them*) a discount.
2. For lunch, Anthony fixed (*he, him*) and (*she, her*) bean burritos with salsa.
3. Would you please show (*her, she*) and (*me, I*) that Navajo dream catcher?
4. Those green apples gave both Christopher and (*he, him*) stomachaches.
5. The waiter brought (*us, we*) some ice water.
6. Why don't you sing (*she, her*) a lullaby?
7. Have they made (*we, us*) the costumes for the play?
8. An usher handed (*me, I*) a program of the recital.
9. The Red Cross volunteers showed (*we, us*) and (*they, them*) a movie about first aid.
10. Please send (*me, I*) your new address.

Review B Revising Incorrect Pronoun Forms in Paragraphs

In most of the sentences in the following paragraphs, at least one pronoun has been used incorrectly. Identify each incorrect pronoun, and give the correct form. If all of the pronouns in a sentence are already correct, write *C*.

EXAMPLE **[1]** Ms. Fisher took several of my friends and I to the museum.

1. *I—me*

[1] At the Museum of Natural History, Luisa and me wanted to see the American Indian exhibit. [2] The museum guide showed she and I the displays of Hopi pottery and baskets. [3] Both she and I were especially interested in the kachina dolls. [4] After half an hour, Ms. Fisher found us.

USAGE

[5] Then Luisa, her, and I joined the rest of the group. [6] Another guide had been giving Ms. Fisher and they information about the Masai people in Africa. [7] Them and us decided to see the exhibit about ancient Egypt next.

[8] A group of little children passed Ms. Fisher and we on the stairway as we were going to the exhibit. [9] The ones who reached the exhibit first were them. [10] Jeff, the jokester, said that they wanted to find their "mummies." [11] Ms. Fisher and us laughed at the terrible pun. [12] She gave him a pat on the back. [13] We asked her not to encourage him. [14] The museum guide led the children and we to the back of the room. [15] There, he showed us and they a model of a pyramid. [16] Then Ms. Fisher and him explained how the Egyptians prepared mummies. [17] Was it her who asked about King Tutankhamen? [18] Of course, Luisa and me recognized this golden mask right away. [19] As we were leaving, the guide gave the children and we some booklets about King Tut and other famous ancient Egyptians. [20] He handed Luisa and I booklets about the builders of the pyramids.

The golden funerary mask of Egyptian King Tutankhamen. Egyptian National Museum, Cairo, Egypt/SuperStock.

Pronoun as Object of a Preposition

The *object of a preposition* is a noun or a pronoun that follows a preposition. Together, the preposition, its object, and any modifiers of that object make a *prepositional phrase.*

8e. Use the object form for a pronoun that is the object of a preposition.

EXAMPLES   above **me**   beside **us**   with **them**

           for **him**   toward **you**   next to **her**

Reference Note

For more information about **prepositions,** see page 108.

> **Oral Practice 5**   **Using Pronouns as Objects of Prepositions**

Read the sentences on the following page aloud, stressing the italicized pronouns.

SKILLS FOCUS

Identify and use objective-case pronouns correctly.

1. The lemonade stand was built by Chuck and *me*.
2. The younger children rode in front of *us*.
3. Just between *you* and *me*, that game wasn't much fun.
4. Everyone has gone except the Taylors and *them*.
5. Give the message to *him* or *her*.
6. Why don't you sit here beside *me*, Ben?
7. Were those pictures of Amish families taken by *him*?
8. Donna went to the Cinco de Mayo parade with *them*.

Exercise 8 **Identifying Pronouns Used as Objects of Prepositions**

Choose the correct form of the pronoun in parentheses in each of the following sentences.

EXAMPLE   1. Someone else should have sent an invitation to (*they, them*).

  1. *them*

1. In the first round, Michael Chang played against (*he, him*).
2. Did you sit with Martha or (*her, she*) at the game?
3. Peggy sent homemade birthday cards to Josh, you, and (*them, they*).
4. There is a bee flying around (*he, him*) and you.
5. If you have a complaint, tell it to Mr. Ramis or (*she, her*).
6. Ms. Young divided the projects among (*us, we*).
7. This secret is strictly between you and (*me, I*).
8. Can you believe the weather balloon dropped right in front of (*we, us*)?
9. Please don't ride the Alaskan ferry without Jim and (*me, I*).
10. One of the clowns threw confetti at us and (*they, them*).

Special Pronoun Problems
Who and Whom

The pronoun *who* has two different forms. *Who* is the subject form. *Whom* is the object form.

When you are choosing between *who* and *whom* in a question, follow these steps:

STEP 1	Rephrase the question as a statement.
STEP 2	Identify how the pronoun is used in the statement—as a subject, a predicate nominative, a direct object, an indirect object, or an object of a preposition.
STEP 3	Determine whether the subject form or the object form is correct according to the rules of standard English.
STEP 4	Select the correct form—*who* or *whom*.

EXAMPLE	(*Who, Whom*) rang the bell?
STEP 1	The statement is (*Who, Whom*) *rang the bell*.
STEP 2	The pronoun is the subject of the verb *rang*.
STEP 3	As the subject, the pronoun should be in the subject form.
STEP 4	The subject form is *who*.
ANSWER	**Who** rang the bell?

EXAMPLE	(*Who, Whom*) does Lindsay see?
STEP 1	The statement is *Lindsay does see (who, whom)*.
STEP 2	The pronoun is the direct object of the verb *does see*.
STEP 3	A direct object should be in the object form.
STEP 4	The object form is *whom*.
ANSWER	**Whom** does Lindsay see?

EXAMPLE	To (*who, whom*) did Jo give the gift?
STEP 1	The statement is *Jo did give the gift to (who, whom)*.
STEP 2	The pronoun is the object of the preposition *to*.
STEP 3	The object of a preposition should be in the object form.
STEP 4	The object form is *whom*.
ANSWER	To **whom** did Jo give the gift?

Think as a
Reader/Writer

The use of *whom* is becoming less common in informal English. Informally, you may begin any question with *who*. In formal written and spoken English, however, you should distinguish between *who* and *whom*. *Who* is used as a subject or a predicate nominative, and *whom* is used as an object.

USAGE

Oral Practice 6 **Using Pronouns Correctly in Sentences**

Read the following sentences aloud, stressing the italicized pronouns.

1. *Who* owns the sailboat over there?
2. To *whom* did you throw the ball?
3. *Whom* did Miguel marry?

4. *Who* was the stranger with the ten-gallon hat?

5. For *whom* did you knit that sweater?

6. *Who* is the author of that book about Jackie Robinson?

7. *Whom* did Josh choose as his subject?

8. By *whom* was this work painted?

Pronouns with Appositives

Reference Note

For more information about **appositives,** see page 318.

Sometimes a pronoun is followed directly by a noun that identifies the pronoun. Such a noun is called an ***appositive.*** To help you choose which pronoun to use before an appositive, omit the appositive and try each form of the pronoun separately.

EXAMPLE   **(*We, Us*) Girl Scouts swam laps.** [*Girl Scouts* is the appositive identifying the pronoun. *We swam laps* or *Us swam laps?*]

ANSWER   **We** Girl Scouts swam laps.

EXAMPLE   **The director gave an award to (*we, us*) actors.** [*Actors* is the appositive identifying the pronoun. *The director gave an award to we* or *The director gave an award to us?*]

ANSWER   The director gave an award to **us** actors.

Exercise 9 **Identifying the Correct Forms of Pronouns in Sentences**

Choose the correct form of the pronoun in parentheses in each of the following sentences.

EXAMPLE   **1. (*Who, Whom*) can do the most jumping jacks?**

           1. Who

1. (*We, Us*) baseball players always warm up before practice.

2. (*Who, Whom*) knows how to stretch properly?

3. Coach Anderson has special exercises for (*we, us*) pitchers.

4. To (*who, whom*) did the coach assign thirty sit-ups?

5. (*Who, Whom*) do you favor for tomorrow's game?

6. Would you teach (*we, us*) girls that new batting stance?

7. Please take (*we, us*) fans with you to the next game.

8. The ones with the new gloves and jerseys should have been (*we, us*) fielders.
9. (*Who, Whom*) should start the lineup?
10. With (*who, whom*) do you practice after school?

Review C **Revising Incorrect Pronoun Forms in Sentences**

Identify each incorrect pronoun in the following sentences. Then, write the correct pronoun. If a sentence is already correct, write *C*.

EXAMPLE   1. At first Karen and me thought that Lucy was imagining things.
         1. me—*I*

1. Lucy told Karen and I that creatures from outer space had just landed.
2. She was certain it was them at the park.
3. Whom would believe such a ridiculous story?
4. Us girls laughed and laughed.
5. Lucy looked at we two with tears in her eyes.
6. Karen and I agreed to go to the park to look around.
7. Lucy walked between Karen and me, showing the way.
8. In the park she and us hid behind some tall bushes.
9. Suddenly a strong wind almost blew we three down.
10. A green light shone on Karen and I, and a red one shone on Lucy.
11. Whom could it be?
12. One of the creatures spoke to us girls.
13. Very slowly, Karen, Lucy, and me stepped out from behind the bushes.
14. "You almost scared they and me silly!" shouted a creature, pointing at the others.
15. Neither Karen nor her could speak, and I could make only a squeaking noise.
16. Then the man inside the costume explained to we three girls that a movie company was filming in the park.
17. They and we could have been in an accident.
18. The fireworks hidden in the bushes might have hurt one of we girls.

19. Lucy told the director and he about being afraid of the space creatures in the park.

20. If you see the movie, the short purple creatures under the spaceship are us three girls.

Review D **Replacing Nouns with Pronouns**

Revise each of the following sentences, substituting pronouns for the words in italics.

EXAMPLE   **1.** The bird hopped lightly into the *bird's* nest.
             1. The bird hopped lightly into its nest.

1. David, I have already asked *David* several times to clean your room.

2. The raccoon reached into the water, caught a fish, and ate *the fish.*

3. *Anne and Paula* should be here in a few minutes.

4. *Sandra* will be reading my report to the class tomorrow.

5. Don't forget to return Reginald's book to *Reginald.*

6. As soon as Willis finishes dinner, *Willis* must leave for play practice.

7. Diane, did you turn in *Diane's* permission slip yet?

8. Mario and I have decided to do *Mario's and my* project as a musical skit.

9. In his locker, Felipe has a photograph of his favorite WNBA star with *Felipe.*

10. The dogs came running in as soon as they knew *the dogs'* food dish was filled.

Chapter Review

A. Identifying Correct Pronoun Forms

For each of the following sentences, write the correct form of the pronoun in parentheses.

1. Could that be (*she, her*) at the bus stop?
2. The guest speakers were Dr. Lucia Sanchez and (*he, him*).
3. Are you and (*they, them*) going to the basketball game?
4. You and (*I, me*) have been friends for a long time.
5. Sometimes, even our parents cannot tell (*we, us*) apart.
6. (*We, Us*) players surprised the coach with a victory party.
7. (*Who, Whom*) is bringing the holiday turkey?
8. Laura lent my sister and (*I, me*) her new bicycle.
9. Mr. Lee will divide the money between you and (*I, me*).
10. To (*who, whom*) is the envelope addressed?
11. Please keep this information between you and (*she, her*).
12. Did Maria or (*she, her*) call Grandmother Lopez?
13. Mom and (*they, them*) have gone shopping.
14. Can you show Charlie and (*she, her*) how to fish?
15. Danny and (*I, me*) are practicing woodcraft for camp.
16. Why didn't you tell me about (*he, him*)?
17. Eldon and (*we, us*) were tired of playing checkers.
18. Mom and Dad promised Keith and (*they, them*) a puppy.
19. Was (*he, him*) the only one in the theater?
20. Would you lend your notes to (*we, us*)?

B. Identifying Pronouns Used as Predicate Nominatives

For each of the following sentences, write the correct form of the pronoun in parentheses.

21. The bus driver was (*he, him*).
22. That was Mr. San Miguel and (*they, them*) at the stadium last night.

23. The most devoted animal-lovers I know are Melanie and (*her, she*).

24. The junior racquetball champion last year was (*her, she*).

25. Once or twice a month the lifeguard at the local pool is (*he, him*).

26. Was that (*they, them*) in the parking lot?

27. Second on the program at the concert was (*he, him*).

28. It could have been (*her, she*), but I doubt it.

29. The devoted Rangers fans in our class are Gregorio and (*he, him*).

30. The visitors from Taiwan must be (*they, them*).

C. Identifying the Correct Forms of Pronouns Used as Subjects, Direct Objects, Indirect Objects, and Objects of Prepositions

For each of the following sentences, choose the correct form of the pronoun in parentheses and tell whether it is used as a *subject*, a *direct object*, an *indirect object*, or an *object of a preposition*.

31. The one who cheered loudest was the girl behind (*I, me*).

32. Did Isabel travel to Santa Fe with John and (*her, she*)?

33. (*We, Us*) baseball fans welcomed the decision not to move the team.

34. Peter called (*her, she*) and (*I, me*) last night.

35. (*We, Us*) cousins had a yard sale.

36. Tomas and José gave (*we, us*) their addresses in Mexico.

37. Her grandmother in Oregon sent (*her, she*) some apples.

38. On the hike, Christie and Maggie walked ahead of (*I, me*).

39. The teacher scolded us and (*he, him*) for being late.

40. I bought (*they, them*) an anniversary present.

Writing Application
Using Correct Pronoun Forms in Writing

Using Pronouns   Health Awareness Week is coming up soon. Your class has been chosen to perform a skit on a health-related topic for the rest of the school. Your teacher has asked each class member to write down an idea for an entertaining, informative skit. Write a paragraph or two describing a skit that your class could perform. Be sure to use correct pronoun forms in your description.

Prewriting   First, you will need to decide on a topic for the skit. Think about the health concerns of people your age. For example, you might plan a skit about the dangers of smoking or the importance of regular dental check-ups. After you choose a topic, brainstorm some ideas for a simple, entertaining skit. Be sure to list any props or costumes your class will need.

Writing   Use your notes to help you write your draft. First, tell what the skit is about and why it is appropriate for Health Awareness Week. Then, explain what happens in the skit from beginning to end. Be sure to tell in a general way what each character does and says. Describe the props and costumes that your class can make or bring from home.

SKILLS FOCUS

Write to entertain. Use pronouns correctly.

Revising   Ask a classmate to read your paragraph. Is the information given in the skit correct? Does the skit sound entertaining? Is it clear which character does and says what? If not, revise your paragraph. Add details that will make the skit more fun and interesting.

Publishing   Check your sentences to be sure you have used pronouns correctly and clearly. Read through your description carefully to check for errors in grammar, spelling, and punctuation. Use this chapter to help you check for errors in pronoun forms.

Your class may want to hold a contest for the best skit idea. Using the best idea, work together to develop the skit in more detail. Then, with your teacher's permission, give a performance of the skit for other classes.

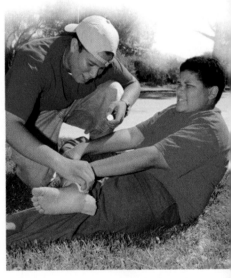

USAGE

Using Modifiers Correctly
Comparison and Placement

Diagnostic Preview

Correcting Errors in the Form, Use, and Placement of Modifiers

Most of the following sentences contain an error in the use of modifiers or negative words. If a sentence has an error, rewrite the sentence correctly. If a sentence is already correct, write *C*.

EXAMPLE   **1.** The weather looks more worse today.

       1. The weather looks worse today.

1. Of the students in class, Odelle writes better.

2. Can you throw farthest with a softball or with a baseball?

3. Juan seemed very happy that we had visited him.

4. No one knew nothing about the tornado.

5. The vegetables were eaten by rabbits that we had planted.

6. Throughout history, many people have written regular in their diaries.

7. The people who moved in next door are the most friendliest neighbors who have ever lived there.

8. The bread smelled wonderfully.

9. Did that armadillo make it across the road with a limp?

10. Wynton Marsalis plays the trumpet good.
11. If you don't feel well today, you shouldn't go out.
12. We read a story written by Mark Twain yesterday.
13. Mai is one of the most persistent people I know.
14. I felt sadly at the end of *Old Yeller.*
15. The boy ordered a sandwich that was hungry.
16. The team usually wins the game that has the better defense.
17. Tanya is the youngest of my brothers and sisters.
18. It doesn't make no difference to Brian.
19. I'm not sure which I like best, horror movies or comedies.
20. Arthurine's piano playing sounds very nicely to me.
21. The storm came up so sudden that it surprised us.
22. The house looks differently to me.
23. Lena and Ivan are twins, and Lena is the oldest one.
24. We couldn't hardly believe the news!
25. Miyoko looks well in her new school uniform.

What Is a Modifier?

A *modifier* is a word, a phrase, or a clause that makes the meaning of a word or word group more specific. The two kinds of modifiers are *adjectives* and *adverbs*.

One-Word Modifiers

Adjectives

9a. *Adjectives* make the meanings of nouns and pronouns more specific.

EXAMPLES   **That** one is my favorite. [The adjective *That* tells which one.]

Does Stephen know the **secret** combination? [The adjective *secret* tells what kind of combination.]

Estéban has saved **more** money than I have. [The adjective *more* tells how much money.]

Four horses grazed peacefully at the foot of the hill. [The adjective *Four* tells how many horses.]

Reference Note

For more about **adjectives,** see page 84. For more about **adverbs,** see page 105.

SKILLS FOCUS

Use modifiers correctly. Identify and use adjectives.

USAGE

Reference Note

For more about **phrases**, see page 122.

Reference Note

For more about **clauses**, see page 135.

SKILLS FOCUS

Identify and use adverbs. Identify and use adjective phrases correctly. Identify and use adverb phrases correctly. Identify and use adjective clauses. Identify and use adverb clauses.

Adverbs

9b. *Adverbs* make the meanings of verbs, adjectives, and other adverbs more specific.

EXAMPLES   The car backfired **loudly.** [The adverb *loudly* makes the meaning of the verb *backfired* more specific.]

The painting is **quite** old. [The adverb *quite* makes the meaning of the adjective *old* more specific.]

The bear traveled **surprisingly** quickly. [The adverb *surprisingly* makes the meaning of the adverb *quickly* more specific.]

Phrases Used as Modifiers

Like one-word modifiers, phrases can also be used as adjectives and adverbs.

EXAMPLES   The cat **with the short tail** is my favorite. [The prepositional phrase *with the short tail* acts as an adjective that modifies the noun *cat*.]

Mr. Rodriguez planted the new bushes **along the fence.** [The prepositional phrase *along the fence* acts as an adverb that modifies the verb *planted*.]

Clauses Used as Modifiers

Like words and phrases, clauses can also be used as modifiers.

EXAMPLES   Spaghetti is the food **that I like best.** [The adjective clause *that I like best* modifies the noun *food*.]

Before Mario went downstairs, he washed his face and hands. [The adverb clause *Before Mario went downstairs* modifies the verb *washed*.]

Exercise 1 **Identifying Modifiers as Adjectives or Adverbs**

Tell whether the italicized word or word group in each of the following sentences is used as an *adjective* or an *adverb*. Then, identify the word that it modifies.

EXAMPLE   **1.** Ms. Olivarez is the woman *on the left*.

  1. adjective—woman

1. The squirrel darted *quickly* up the tree trunk and hid among the leaves.
2. Wang Wei was a talented painter *of landscapes.*
3. Gabriela can ski faster *than I can.*
4. Is *this* poem the one that you wrote?
5. The man *who has curly hair* is my Uncle Thaddeus.
6. *Soon* you will need to put the bread in the oven.
7. *Before the performance* the actors practiced their lines and gestures.
8. Mountain biking is the sport *that I enjoy most.*
9. Tasmania is an island *off the coast of Australia.*
10. *Because the weather was hot,* we sat with our feet in the stream.

Comparison of Adjectives and Adverbs

When adjectives and adverbs are used in comparisons, they take different forms. The specific form they take depends upon how many things are being compared. The different forms of comparison are called *degrees of comparison.*

9c. The three degrees of comparison of modifiers are the *positive,* the *comparative,* and the *superlative.*

(1) The *positive degree* is used when only one thing is being modified and no comparison is being made.

EXAMPLES   *Felita* is a **good** book.

Shawn runs **quickly.**

The horse jumped **gracefully.**

(2) The *comparative degree* is used when two things are being compared.

EXAMPLES   In my opinion, *Nilda* is a **better** book than *Felita.*

Juanita runs **more quickly** than Shawn.

Which of the two horses jumped **more gracefully**?

TIPS & TRICKS

Here is a way to remember which form of a modifier to use. When comparing two things, use *–er* (the two-letter ending). When comparing three or more things, use *–est* (the three-letter ending).

SKILLS FOCUS

Use the comparative forms of modifiers correctly. Use the superlative forms of modifiers correctly.

(3) The *superlative degree* is used when three or more things are being compared.

EXAMPLES *Nilda* is one of the **best** books I've read.

Which member of the team runs **most quickly**?

Regular Comparison

Most one-syllable modifiers form the comparative degree by adding –*er* and the superlative degree by adding –*est*.

Positive	Comparative	Superlative
near	near**er**	near**est**
sad	sadd**er**	sadd**est**
cute	cut**er**	cut**est**
bright	bright**er**	bright**est**

Two-syllable modifiers can form the comparative degree by adding –*er* or by using *more*. They can form the superlative degree by adding –*est* or by using *most*.

Positive	Comparative	Superlative
fancy	fanci**er**	fanci**est**
lonely	loneli**er**	loneli**est**
cheerful	**more** cheerful	**most** cheerful
quickly	**more** quickly	**most** quickly

NOTE When you add –*er* or –*est* to some modifiers, you may also need to change the spelling of the base word.

EXAMPLES sad   **sadd**er   **sadd**est
[The final *d* is doubled.]

cute   **cut**er   **cut**est
[The final *e* is dropped.]

fancy   **fanci**er   **fanci**est
[The final *y* is changed to *i*.]

Modifiers that have three or more syllables form the comparative degree by using *more* and the superlative degree by using *most.*

Positive	Comparative	Superlative
difficult	**more** difficult	**most** difficult
interesting	**more** interesting	**most** interesting
skillfully	**more** skillfully	**most** skillfully

Decreasing Comparison

To show a decrease in the qualities they express, modifiers form the comparative degree by using *less* and the superlative degree by using *least.*

Positive	Comparative	Superlative
clean	**less** clean	**least** clean
humorous	**less** humorous	**least** humorous
carefully	**less** carefully	**least** carefully

Exercise 2 **Writing Comparative and Superlative Forms**

Give the comparative forms and the superlative forms for each of the following modifiers.

EXAMPLES **1.** calm
    1. calmer, calmest; less calm, least calm

    2. happy
    2. happier, happiest; less happy, least happy

1. nervous
2. great
3. hot
4. funny
5. noisy
6. easily
7. poor
8. young
9. swiftly
10. intelligent
11. politely
12. efficient
13. old
14. thoughtfully
15. sweet
16. angrily
17. ancient
18. neatly
19. lovely
20. long

─HELP─
A dictionary will tell you when a word forms its comparative or superlative form in some way other than just by adding *–er* or *–est* or *more* or *most.*

   Be sure to look in a dictionary if you are not sure whether a word has irregular comparative or superlative forms.

   A dictionary will also tell you if you need to double a final consonant (or otherwise change the spelling of a word) before adding *–er* or *–est.*

USAGE

Reference Note

For more about **how to spell words when adding *–er* or *–est,*** see page 367.

─HELP─
Some words in Exercise 2 may have more than one acceptable comparative and superlative form. You need to give only one comparative and one superlative form for each item.

HELP

In Exercise 3, do not use decreasing comparisons.

Exercise 3   Using Comparative and Superlative Forms Correctly in Sentences

Give the correct form of the italicized modifier for each blank in the following sentences.

EXAMPLE   **1.** *large*   As the illustration below shows, the moon appears ____ during the full-moon phase.

     1. *largest*

1. *near*   The moon is the earth's ____ neighbor in space.

2. *close*   At its ____ point to the earth, the moon is 221,456 miles away.

3. *bright*   Seen from the earth, the full moon is ____ than the new moon.

4. *small*   The moon appears ____ during the crescent phase than at other times.

5. *difficult*   It is ____ to see the new moon than the crescent moon.

6. *common*   The word *crescent* is ____ than the word *gibbous*, which means "partly rounded."

7. *frequently*   We notice the moon ____ when it is full than when it is new.

8. *big*   Do you know why the moon appears ____ on some nights than on others?

9. *quickly*   The changes in the moon's appearance take place because the moon travels ____ around the earth than the earth travels around the sun.

10. *slowly*   The moons of some other planets move ____ than our moon.

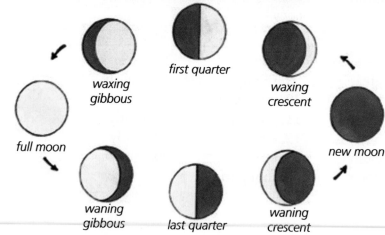

waxing gibbous

first quarter

waxing crescent

full moon

new moon

waning gibbous

last quarter

waning crescent

Irregular Comparison

Some modifiers do not form their comparative and superlative degrees by using the regular methods.

Positive	Comparative	Superlative
good	better	best
well	better	best
bad	worse	worst
many	more	most
much	more	most

NOTE You do not need to add *–er/–est, more/most,* or *less/least* to an irregular comparison. For example, *worse,* all by itself, is the comparative form of *bad. Worser* and *more worse* are non-standard forms.

Exercise 4 Using Irregular Comparative and Superlative Forms

Give the correct form of the italicized modifier for each blank in the following sentences.

EXAMPLE   **1.** *many*   Let's see which of the two teams can wash _____ cars.

　　　　　1. more

1. *bad*   This is the _____ cold I have ever had.
2. *much*   We have _____ homework now than we had last year.
3. *well*   Derrick feels _____ today than he did last night.
4. *good*   This peach has a _____ flavor than that one.
5. *well*   Of all the instruments he can play, Shen Li plays the banjo _____.
6. *much*   Catherine ate _____ enchilada casserole on Monday than she had eaten on Sunday.
7. *many*   Of all the volunteers, Doreen has collected the _____ donations for the animal shelter.
8. *bad*   Our team played the _____ game in history.
9. *good*   The judges will now award the prize for the _____ essay.

COMPUTER TIP

A computer can help you find and correct problems with modifiers. A spell-checker will highlight nonstandard forms such as *worser, bestest,* and *gracefuller.*

However, the computer cannot tell you that you have used the superlative form where you should have used the comparative. You will have to look carefully for such errors when you proofread your writing.

USAGE

SKILLS FOCUS

Use the comparative forms of modifiers correctly. Use the superlative forms of modifiers correctly.

10. *many*   I have ____ baseball cards than John does.
11. *good*   Who is the ____ Japanese chef in town?
12. *much*   Of all the ranchers, she knows the ____ about lambs and sheep.
13. *bad*   Wow! That was the ____ storm I have ever seen.
14. *well*   I think that another variety of blackberry might grow ____ than these do.
15. *many*   Who got the ____ signatures for the petition?
16. *well*   In my opinion, out of all the artists in the world, these Chinese masters paint landscapes ____.
17. *bad*   Traffic is always ____ at this time of day than at any other time.
18. *many*   This year, ____ people attended the ceremony at the reservation than last year.
19. *good*   Of the book, the movie, and the play, which was ____?
20. *much*   Of these two containers, which holds ____ juice?

Special Problems in Using Modifiers

9d. The modifiers *good* and *well* have different uses.

(1) Use *good* to modify a noun or a pronoun.

EXAMPLES   The farmers had a **good** crop this year. [The adjective *good* modifies the noun *crop*.]

The book was **better** than the movie. [The adjective *better* modifies the noun *book*.]

Of all the players, she is the **best** one. [The adjective *best* modifies the pronoun *one*.]

Good should not be used to modify a verb.

NONSTANDARD   N. Scott Momaday writes good.

STANDARD   N. Scott Momaday writes **well.**

(2) Use *well* to modify a verb.

EXAMPLES   The day started **well.** [The adverb *well* modifies the verb *started*.]

The team played **better** in the second half. [The adverb *better* modifies the verb *played*.]

Tina Thompson played **best** in the final game. [The adverb *best* modifies the verb *played*.]

Well can also mean "in good health." When *well* has this meaning, it acts as an adjective.

EXAMPLE   Does Sherry feel **well** today? [The adjective *well* modifies the noun *Sherry*.]

9e. Use adjectives, not adverbs, after linking verbs.

Linking verbs, such as *look, feel, seem,* and *become,* are often followed by predicate adjectives. These adjectives describe, or modify, the subject.

EXAMPLES   Mayor Rodríguez should feel **confident** [not *confidently*] about this election. [The predicate adjective *confident* modifies the subject *Mayor Rodríguez*.]

Did Chris seem **sad** [not *sadly*] to you? [The predicate adjective *sad* modifies the subject *Chris*.]

Exercise 5 **Choosing Correct Modifiers After Linking Verbs and Action Verbs**

Choose the correct modifier of the two in parentheses in each of the following sentences.

EXAMPLE   **1.** Ellen said that Murray's matzo ball soup tasted (*delicious, deliciously*).

1. *delicious*

1. The band became (*nervous, nervously*) before the show.
2. You may get a higher score if you remain (*calm, calmly*) while taking the test.
3. We (*eager, eagerly*) tasted the potato pancakes.
4. Cheryl sews (*good, well*), so she made all the puppets for the show.
5. The mariachi band appeared (*sudden, suddenly*) at our table.
6. Ooh, these wild strawberries taste (*good, well*).
7. The plums tasted (*sour, sourly*).
8. Mr. Duncan was looking (*close, closely*) at my essay.

─HELP─

Some linking verbs can also be used as action verbs. As action verbs, they may be modified by adverbs.

LINKING VERB
   Jeanette looked **alert** [not *alertly*] during the game. [*Alert* modifies the subject *Jeanette*.]

ACTION VERB
   Jeanette looked **alertly** around the gym. [*Alertly* modifies the verb *looked*.]

Reference Note

For more about **linking verbs,** see page 99.

USAGE

9. Those trophies certainly look (*good, well*) up there, Piper.
10. The bicyclist looked (*cautious, cautiously*) both ways before crossing the street.
11. Adobe, dried mud brick, stands up (*good, well*) under the hot Southwestern sun.
12. Peg looked at her broken skate (*anxious, anxiously*).
13. Don't you think vanilla smells as (*good, well*) as or better than those expensive perfumes?
14. Akira Kurosawa was (*good, well*) at making Shakespeare's plays into movies.
15. Sylvia certainly looked (*pretty, prettily*) in her new outfit.
16. Even for beginners, green beans grow (*good, well*), and quickly, too.
17. We didn't know that you could vault so (*good, well*).
18. Erica was (*happy, happily*) to help us.
19. Oh, you are too (*good, well*) at chess for me.
20. Some tropical fish don't get along very (*good, well*) with each other.

9f. Avoid using double comparisons.

A **double comparison** is the use of both *–er* and *more* (or *less*) or both *–est* and *most* (or *least*) to form a single comparison. When you make a comparison, use only one of these forms, not both.

| NONSTANDARD | That was the actor's most scariest role. |
| STANDARD | That was the actor's **scariest** role. |

| NONSTANDARD | The kitten is less livelier than the puppy. |
| STANDARD | The kitten is **less lively** than the puppy. |

NOTE Remember that irregular comparisons do not use *–er/–est, more/most* or *less/least*. Adding these to an irregular modifier is a double comparison.

| NONSTANDARD | more better |
| STANDARD | **better** |

| NONSTANDARD | worstest |
| STANDARD | **worst** |

SKILLS FOCUS

Use modifiers correctly.

Exercise 6 **Revising Double Comparisons**

Each of the following sentences contains a double compari-son. Identify the double comparison, and then write the correct form of each comparison.

EXAMPLE **1.** Are you feeling more better now?

    1. more better—better

1. That must be the bestest song you've written yet!
2. Hit the ball less harder next time.
3. Dates are one of the most popularest foods in Africa and Asia.
4. Nicki, this was the most liveliest party ever.
5. The ancient Chinese made paper more earlier than any other people.
6. Yikes, this computer game is the most hardest one I've played.
7. The least jolliest of the characters was Jo.
8. Sure, I think Spanish is more easier to learn than English.
9. Please do visit us more oftener.
10. Maybe Friday will arrive more sooner this week.

Review A **Writing Comparative and Superlative Forms in Sentences**

For each blank in the following sentences, give the correct form of comparison of the italicized word.

EXAMPLE **1.** *noisy* This is the _____ class in school.

    1. noisiest

1. *bad*   Yesterday was the _____ day of my entire life.
2. *good*   Tomorrow should be _____ than today was.
3. *old*   The _____ American Indian tepee in the world can be seen at the Smithsonian Institution.
4. *soon*   Your party ended _____ than I had hoped.
5. *funny*   That is the _____ joke I've ever heard.
6. *rapidly* Which can run _____, the cheetah or the lion?
7. *beautifully* This piñata is _____ decorated than the other one.
8. *well*   I did well on the first half of the test, but I did _____ on the second half.

9. *joyfully*   Of all the songbirds in our yard, the mocking-birds sing ____.

10. *strange*   This is the ____ book I have ever read!

Review B **Proofreading a Paragraph for Correct Forms of Modifiers**

Most of the sentences in the following paragraph have errors in English usage. If a sentence contains an error, identify the error and then write the correct usage. If a sentence is already correct, write *C*.

EXAMPLE   **[1]** You may not recognize the man in the picture on the left, but you probably know his more famous characters.

1. more famous—most famous

[1] This man, Alexandre Dumas, wrote two of the most popularest books in history—*The Three Musketeers* and *The Count of Monte Cristo*. [2] Born in France, Dumas was poor but had a good education. [3] As a young playwright, he rose quick to fame. [4] In person, Dumas always seemed cheerfully. [5] Like their author, his historical novels are colorful and full of adventure. [6] Their fame grew rapid, and the public demanded more of them. [7] In response to this demand, Dumas hired many assistants, who probably wrote most of his

Link to ▮▮ Literature

later books than he did. [8] Dumas's son, who was also named Alexandre, was a writer, too, and he became famously with the publication of *Camille*. [9] At that time, the younger Dumas was often thought of as a more better writer than his father. [10] Today, however, the friendship of the three musketeers remains aliver than ever in film, print, and even comic books.

Double Negatives

Negative words are a common part of everyday speaking and writing. These words include the modifiers *no, not, never,* and *hardly*. Notice how negative words change the meaning of the following sentences.

POSITIVE   We can count in Spanish.

NEGATIVE   We can**not** count in Spanish.

POSITIVE   They ride their bikes on the highway.

NEGATIVE   They **never** ride their bikes on the highway.

Common Negative Words			
barely	never	none	nothing
hardly	no	no one	nowhere
neither	nobody	not (–n't)	scarcely

9g. Avoid using double negatives.

A *double negative* is the use of two or more negative words to express one negative idea.

NONSTANDARD   Sheila did not tell no one her idea. [The negative words are *not* and *no one*.]

STANDARD   Sheila did **not** tell anyone her idea.

STANDARD   Sheila told **no one** her idea.

NONSTANDARD   Rodney hardly said nothing. [The negative words are *hardly* and *nothing*.]

STANDARD   Rodney **hardly** said anything.

STANDARD   Rodney said almost **nothing.**

9
g

USAGE

Think as a
Reader/Writer

Some fiction writers use double negatives in dialogue. This technique can help make certain characters sound more realistic. However, in your formal speaking and writing, you should avoid using double negatives.

SKILLS FOCUS

Use modifiers correctly.

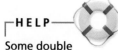
Exercise 7 Revising Sentences to Correct Double Negatives

Revise each of the following sentences to eliminate the double negative.

EXAMPLE 1. Those books don't have no pictures.
1. *Those books don't have any pictures.*
or
Those books have no pictures.

1. The Plains Indians did not waste no part of a bear, deer, or buffalo.
2. Ms. Wooster never tries nothing new to eat.
3. Movie and TV stars from Hollywood never visit nowhere near our town.
4. Until last summer, I didn't know nothing about Braille music notation.
5. By Thanksgiving, the store didn't have none of the silver jewelry left.
6. I'm so excited that I can't hardly sit still.
7. No one brought nothing to eat on the hike.
8. Strangely enough, Frieda hasn't never tasted our delicious Cuban bread.
9. There isn't no more pudding in the bowl.
10. Our dog never fights with neither one of our cats.

Review C Proofreading Sentences for Correct Use of Modifiers

Most of the following sentences contain errors in the use of modifiers. If a sentence is incorrect, write it correctly. If a sentence is already correct, write *C.*

EXAMPLE 1. Haven't you never made a paper airplane or a paper hat?
1. *Haven't you ever made a paper airplane or a paper hat?*
or
Have you never made a paper airplane or a paper hat?

USAGE

1. Making Japanese origami figures is much more easier than I thought it would be.
2. Origami, the ancient Japanese art of paper folding, wasn't hardly known in the United States before the 1960s.
3. Now, many people know how to fold the most cleverest traditional origami animals.
4. In true origami, artists do not never cut or paste the paper.
5. A beginner doesn't need nothing but a sheet of paper to create an origami figure.
6. With a bit of patience, anyone can make a folded-paper figure rather quick.
7. Even kindergartners can do a good job making the simple sailboat shown in the diagram.
8. Other origami figures require more greater time and patience than this sailboat.
9. Today, there probably isn't no one better at origami than Akira Yoshizawa.
10. Even the most difficult figure is not too hard for him, and he has invented many beautiful new figures.

Placement of Modifiers

9h. Place modifying words, phrases, and clauses as close as possible to the words they modify.

Notice how the meaning of the following sentences changes when the position of the phrase *from Brazil* changes.

The singer **from Brazil** gave a radio interview for her fans. [The phrase modifies *singer.*]

The singer gave a radio interview for her fans **from Brazil.** [The phrase modifies *fans.*]

From Brazil, the singer gave a radio interview for her fans. [The phrase modifies *gave.*]

A modifer that seems to modify the wrong word in a sentence is called a *misplaced modifier.*

SKILLS FOCUS

Place modifiers properly.

Adjectives and Adverbs

The placement of an adjective or adverb may affect the meaning of a sentence. Avoid placing an adjective or adverb so that it appears to modify a word that you didn't mean it to modify.

EXAMPLES   Jackie borrowed some camping equipment **only** for the weekend. [She borrowed the equipment for the weekend, not for any other time.]

Only Jackie borrowed some camping equipment for the weekend. [Jackie—and no one else—borrowed some equipment.]

Jackie borrowed **only** some camping equipment for the weekend. [She borrowed some camping equipment but nothing else.]

Nearly all of the skaters fell. [Most of the skaters fell.]

All of the skaters **nearly** fell. [All of the skaters came close to falling but did not fall.]

Today Randall said he would help me build a birdhouse. [Randall made the statement today.]

Randall said he would help me build a birdhouse **today**. [Randall will help with the birdhouse today.]

Prepositional Phrases

A *prepositional phrase* includes a preposition, the object of the preposition, and any modifiers of that object.

A prepositional phrase used as an adjective generally should be placed directly after the word it modifies.

MISPLACED   Ms. Ruiz got a sweater for her dog with a snowflake pattern.

CLEAR   Ms. Ruiz got a sweater **with a snowflake pattern** for her dog.

MISPLACED   This book describes Nat Turner's struggle for freedom by Judith Berry Griffin.

CLEAR   This book **by Judith Berry Griffin** describes Nat Turner's struggle for freedom.

Reference Note

For more information about **prepositions** and **prepositional phrases,** see pages 108 and 109.

USAGE

A prepositional phrase used as an adverb should be placed near the word it modifies.

MISPLACED   Roberto read that some turtles can swim quite fast in a magazine.

CLEAR   Roberto read **in a magazine** that some turtles can swim quite fast.

MISPLACED   I watched a movie that George Lucas produced on Friday.

CLEAR   **On Friday,** I watched a movie that George Lucas produced.

Avoid placing a prepositional phrase where it can modify either of two words. Place the phrase so that it clearly modifies the word you intend it to modify.

MISPLACED   Cynthia Ann said after her ballet class she would take out the trash. [Does the phrase *after her ballet class* modify *said* or *would take*?]

CLEAR   Cynthia Ann said she would take out the trash **after her ballet class.** [The phrase modifies *would take.*]

CLEAR   **After her ballet class** Cynthia Ann said she would take out the trash. [The phrase modifies *said.*]

Exercise 8   Correcting Misplaced Prepositional Phrases

Find any misplaced prepositional phrases in each of the following sentences. Then, revise the sentence, placing the phrase near the word it modifies. If a sentence is already correct, write *C.*

EXAMPLE   1. I read about the car thieves who were caught in this morning's paper.

1. *I read in this morning's paper about the car thieves who were caught.*

or

In this morning's paper, I read about the car thieves who were caught.

1. Michael went outside to trim the hedges with Bruce.
2. I saw the ants marching through my magnifying glass.

HELP

Some sentences in Exercise 8 may be corrected in more than one way. You need to give just one revision for each.

SKILLS FOCUS

Place modifiers properly.

3. Angelo borrowed a radio from Kim with a weather band.
4. That man bought the rare photograph of Geronimo with the cell phone.
5. The robin sat carefully on the eggs in its nest.
6. The frog seemed to be staring at the moon in the pond.
7. We could see the wheat growing from our back windows.
8. The sound designer told us about recording a herd of gnus in class today.
9. Many people watched the televised ballgame in Fred's living room.
10. I found the collection of records your father bought in the attic.

Adjective Clauses

An *adjective clause* modifies a noun or a pronoun. Most adjective clauses begin with a relative pronoun—*that, which, who, whom,* or *whose.*

Like adjective phrases, adjective clauses should generally be placed directly after the words they modify.

MISPLACED Mrs. Chu gives the sculptures to her friends that she carves. [Does Mrs. Chu carve her friends?]

CLEAR Mrs. Chu gives the sculptures **that she carves** to her friends.

MISPLACED The students met with a tutor who needed help in math. [Did the tutor need help in math?]

CLEAR The students **who needed help in math** met with a tutor.

Reference Note

For more about **adjective clauses,** see page 137.

COMPUTER TIP

Your computer can help you correct misplaced modifiers. You can use the cut-and-paste function to place a misplaced modifier closer to the word it modifies.

HELP

Some sentences in Exercise 9 may be revised in more than one way. You need to give just one revision for each.

SKILLS FOCUS

Place modifiers properly.

> **Exercise 9** Correcting Misplaced Adjective Clauses

Find any misplaced adjective clauses in each of the following sentences. Then, revise the sentence, placing the clause near the word it modifies. If a sentence is already correct, write *C.*

EXAMPLE 1. The students wanted to work on a project at the school that they had designed themselves.

1. *The students at the school wanted to work on a project that they had designed themselves.*

1. The girl is from my class that won the spelling bee.
2. The blue jay moved carefully through the snow with small hops, which had begun to melt.
3. I hardly recognized my uncle Ken when he came for a visit, whose beard had turned white.
4. Kwanzaa, which was first celebrated in 1966, is an African American holiday developed by Maulana Karenga.
5. The expression "that's the ticket," which means "that's the correct thing," comes from a mispronunciation of the French word *etiquette*.
6. My oldest brother just graduated from college, who lives in Rhode Island.
7. Jason's favorite shirt already has another stain on it, which was just washed.
8. That team played in front of a sellout crowd, which was having its best season ever.
9. "The Rum Tum Tugger," is a poem about a cat, which we studied in class.
10. We like to watch the many butterflies in the fields on the weekends, that are behind our house.

Review D — **Proofreading a Paragraph for Correct Placement of Modifiers**

Most of the following sentences have misplaced modifying words, phrases, or clauses. If the sentence contains an error, revise the sentence by placing the modifier in the correct place. If the sentence is already correct, write *C*.

EXAMPLE **[1]** Sometimes the person can be a hero who seems least likely.

1. *Sometimes the person who seems least likely can be a hero.*

[1] J.R.R. Tolkien's *The Hobbit* is a wonderful story that has a very complicated adventure about a simple person. [2] Hobbits are very small, quiet people, and most of the world had never heard of them until a few of them began to have adventures. [3] The hero of the story, Bilbo Baggins, is not a typical hero, who likes nothing more than chatting with his neighbors, sleeping, and eating. [4] Bilbo's quiet life is

HELP

Some sentences in Review D may be correctly revised in more than one way. You need to give just one revision for each.

Link to Literature

interrupted when the wizard Gandalf chooses him to help a band of dwarves from a dragon recover their treasure. [5] Bilbo saves the dwarves several times on their way to their old home under the Lonely Mountain, despite being small and shy. [6] Bilbo also finds a magical ring along the way that can make him invisible. [7] Bilbo gets the dwarves out of trouble with the ring and the wizard Gandalf. [8] When they finally reach the mountain, Bilbo tricks the dragon Smaug into revealing a spot in his armor that is weak. [9] The dragon is very angry and attacks a nearby town, but an archer kills Smaug, who has been told about the weak spot. [10] Bilbo goes back to his quiet life, but in *The Lord of the Rings* his nephew Frodo inherits the ring and saves the world.

Chapter Review

A. Identifying the Correct Forms of Modifiers

Choose the correct form of the modifier in parentheses in each of the following sentences.

1. Cool water tastes (*good, well*) on a hot day.
2. The wind howled (*fierce, fiercely*) last night.
3. Which twin is (*taller, tallest*), Marcus or Jim?
4. *Forever Friends* is the (*best, bestest*) book I've read this year.
5. Sergio has always played (*good, well*) during an important match.
6. The roses in the vase smelled (*sweet, sweetly*).
7. They could view the eclipse (*more clear, more clearly*) than we could.
8. Which of these two winter coats is the (*best, better*) value?
9. Of all the days in the week, Friday goes by (*more, most*) slowly for me.
10. Ernesto felt (*good, well*) about volunteering to help collect money for the homeless.
11. Is this the (*darkest, darker*) copy of the three?
12. The (*faster, fastest*) runner is the captain of the track team.
13. Mr. Chen told them to be (*better, more better*) prepared tomorrow.
14. Joni's way of solving the math puzzle was much (*more easier, easier*) than Ken's.
15. We felt (*sleepy, sleepily*) after lunch.

B. Correcting Double Negatives

┌HELP┐

In some cases, a double negative can be corrected in more than one way. However, you need to give only one revision for each sentence in Part B.

Most of the following sentences contain errors in the use of negative words. If the sentence is incorrect, write it correctly. If the sentence is already correct, write *C*.

16. None of us knows nothing about astronomy.
17. Wendell can hardly wait to see Serge Laîné in concert.
18. Kathy hasn't never heard of the Romanovs.

USAGE

19. Last night we couldn't see no stars through the telescope.

20. Whenever I want fresh strawberries, there are never none in the house.

C. Writing Comparative and Superlative Forms

Write the comparative and superlative forms for each of the following modifiers.

┌HELP┐

Remember to include forms showing decreasing comparison in your answers to Part C.

21. difficult   **26.** good

22. new   **27.** light

23. quickly   **28.** short

24. cold   **29.** clearly

25. fantastic   **30.** noisy

D. Correcting Misplaced Phrases and Clauses

Find any misplaced phrases and clauses in each of the following sentences. Then, revise each incorrect sentence, placing the phrase or clause near the word it modifies.

31. I heard about the bad weather on the radio.

32. The man drove the sports car with the beard.

33. Arthur borrowed a mountain bike from his friend with eighteen speeds.

34. Uncle Mark and Aunt Jennifer were watching the meteor shower in the backyard.

35. We saw the fog rising from our car.

36. I gave a bracelet to my friend that was made of silver.

37. Mom saw a museum exhibit of ancient pottery made in the American Southwest on Tuesday.

38. Una read about the latest political developments in the newspaper.

39. The mayor said she would lead the St. Patrick's Day parade at her press conference.

40. The woman won the rare book who had on the red hat.

USAGE

Writing Application
Using Negative Words in Description

Negative Words   Everyone has a bad day now and then. Yesterday, it was your turn. You were late for school because your alarm clock did not go off. From then on, things just got worse. Write a letter to a friend giving a funny description of your unlucky day. Make sure that you use negative words correctly.

Prewriting   Write down some notes about a real or imaginary bad day in your life. List at least five things that went wrong during the day. The events can be big or small. Tell how you felt when one thing after another went wrong.

Writing   In your letter, explain the events of your day in the order they happened. Describe each event in detail. Also describe your reactions to the events. You may want to exaggerate some details for a humorous effect.

Revising   Ask a friend to read your letter. Have you described the events clearly? Do your descriptions give a vivid, humorous picture of your day? If not, add or revise details.

Publishing   Be sure that your letter follows the correct form for a personal letter. Proofread your letter carefully for errors in grammar, spelling and punctuation. Read through each sentence one more time to check that negative words are used correctly. With your teacher's permission, you and your classmates may wish to present your descriptions in class and vote on who survived the worst day.

USAGE

Reference Note

For information on **writing a personal letter,** see "Writing" in the Quick Reference Handbook.

SKILLS FOCUS

Use descriptive strategies. Write a letter. Use appropriate word choice and precise wording.

A Glossary of Usage

Common Usage Problems

Diagnostic Preview

Correcting Errors in Usage

Each of the following sentences contains an error in the use of formal, standard English. Rewrite each sentence correctly.

EXAMPLE **1.** I knew all the answers accept the last one.

             1. I knew all the answers except the last one.

1. If you're going to the library, would you please bring these books there for me?
2. The water tasted kind of salty.
3. Has Jamila finished the assignment all ready?
4. Leon went to the doctor because he didn't feel good.
5. They should of asked for directions.
6. We found nothing but a old shoe.
7. Bao will try and fix her bike today.
8. The tuna looked all right but smelled badly.
9. Albert can't hardly wait to read that biography of the Olympic star Jesse Owens.
10. Why is this mitt more expensive then that one?
11. He knocked a bowl of plantains off of the table.
12. In rural Vietnam, children often take care of there family's water buffalo.

13. After school we use to have band practice.
14. Tanya made less mistakes after she had started practicing.
15. Do you know who's pencil this is?
16. Mr. Abeyto assigned me to this here seat.
17. A glitch is when a mistake is made by a computer.
18. Did Ann say how come she won't attend the meeting?
19. The food was shared between the families of the village.
20. At one time, Bessie Coleman was the only black woman pilot anywhere in the world.

About the Glossary

This chapter contains an alphabetical list, or **glossary**, of common problems in English usage. You will notice that some examples in this glossary are labeled *nonstandard, standard, formal,* or *informal.*

The label **nonstandard** identifies usage that is acceptable only in the most casual speaking situations and in writing that attempts to re-create casual speech. **Standard** English is language that is grammatically correct and appropriate in formal and informal situations. **Formal** identifies standard usage that is appropriate in serious speaking and writing situations (such as in speeches and in writing for school). The label **informal** indicates standard usage common in conversation and in everyday writing such as personal letters. When doing the exercises in this chapter, be sure to use only standard English.

The following are examples of formal and informal English.

Reference Note

For a list of **words often confused,** see page 373. Use the **index** at the back of the book to find discussions of other usage problems.

Formal	Informal
angry	steamed
unpleasant	yucky
agreeable	cool
very impressive	totally awesome
accelerate	step on it

SKILLS FOCUS

Demonstrate understanding of standard English usage.

USAGE

a, an Use *a* before words beginning with a consonant sound; use *an* before words beginning with a vowel sound. Keep in mind that the sound, not the actual letter, that a word begins with tells you whether *a* or *an* should be used.

EXAMPLES The airplane was parked in **a** hangar.

She lives on **a** one-way street. [*A* is used because *one* begins with a consonant sound.]

My father works in **an** office.

They arrived **an** hour early. [*An* is used because *hour* begins with a vowel sound.]

accept, except *Accept* is a verb; it means "to receive." *Except* may be used as either a verb or a preposition. When it is used as a verb, *except* means "to leave out." As a preposition, *except* means "excluding" or "but."

EXAMPLES The winners of the spelling bee proudly **accepted** their awards. [verb]

Because Josh had a sprained ankle, he was **excepted** from gym class. [verb]

All the food **except** the won-ton soup was ready. [preposition]

ain't Avoid using this word in speaking and writing; it is nonstandard English.

all right *All right* can be used as an adjective that means "satisfactory" or "unhurt." As an adverb, *all right* means "well enough." *All right* should be written as two words.

EXAMPLES This tie looks **all right** with that blue shirt. [adjective]

The baby squirrel had fallen out of its nest, but it was **all right.** [adjective]

Lorenzo and I did **all right** on the pop quiz. [adverb]

"Beats me why I ain't gettin' no better marks in English."

USAGE

a lot   *A lot* should be written as two words.

EXAMPLE   I can make **a lot** of my mom's recipes.

already, all ready   *Already* means "previously." *All ready* means "completely prepared" or "in readiness."

EXAMPLES   We looked for Jay, but he had **already** left.

I had studied for two hours on Sunday night and was **all ready** for the test on Monday.

among   See **between, among.**

anyways, anywheres, everywheres, nowheres, somewheres   These words should have no final *s*.

EXAMPLE   They looked **everywhere** [not *everywheres*] for the missing puzzle piece.

at   Do not use *at* after *where.*

NONSTANDARD   Where is the Chinese kite exhibit at?

STANDARD   Where is the Chinese kite exhibit?

bad, badly   *Bad* is an adjective. It modifies nouns and pronouns. *Badly* is an adverb. It modifies verbs, adjectives, and adverbs.

EXAMPLES   The milk smelled **bad.** [The predicate adjective *bad* modifies *milk*.]

Before I took lessons, I played the piano **badly.** [The adverb *badly* modifies the verb *played*.]

between, among   Use *between* when you are referring to two things at a time even when they are part of a group consisting of more than two.

EXAMPLES   Kim got in line **between** Lee and Rene.

Be sure to weed **between** all ten rows of carrots. [Although there are ten rows of carrots, the weeding is done *between* any two of them.]

Use *among* when you are referring to a group rather than to separate individuals.

EXAMPLE   The four winners divided the prize **among** themselves.

USAGE

For each of the following sentences, choose the word or word group in parentheses that is correct according to the rules of formal, standard usage.

EXAMPLE
1. The picture on this page is titled *After Supper, West Chester,* but the scene could be almost (*anywhere, anywheres*).

1. *anywhere*

1. This colorful work was painted by (*a, an*) artist named Horace Pippin, who lived from 1888 to 1946.
2. By the time Pippin was in elementary school, he was (*already, all ready*) a talented artist.
3. In fact, he had won a drawing contest and had eagerly (*accepted, excepted*) the prize, a box of crayons and a set of watercolor paints.
4. In World War I, Pippin was once caught (*among, between*) U.S. troops and the enemy.
5. During this battle (*somewheres, somewhere*) in France, Pippin's right arm—the arm he used when painting—was seriously wounded.
6. For a long time, Pippin felt quite (*bad, badly*) about his disability, but he was determined to paint again.
7. After Pippin recovered, he tried (*alot, a lot*) of new ways to paint; the most successful was to hold up his right hand with his left arm.

8. It (*ain't, is not*) surprising that one of his first paintings after the war portrayed a battle scene.
9. When Pippin painted *After Supper, West Chester,* in 1935, he was remembering the small town in Pennsylvania (*where he was born, where he was born at*).
10. I think that the painter of this peaceful scene must have felt (*all right, alright*) about his work and about himself.

Horace Pippin, *After Supper, West Chester* (1935). Collection Leon Hecht and Robert Pincus-Witten, New York. © 1991 Gridley/Graves.

bring, take *Bring* means "to come carrying something." *Take* means "to go carrying something." Think of *bring* as related to *come* (*to*) and *take* as related to *go* (*from*).

EXAMPLES   Make sure that you **bring** your book when you come to my house.

Always remember to **take** your coat when you go outside during the winter.

could of Do not write *of* with the helping verb *could*. Write *could have*. Also avoid *ought to of, should of, would of, might of,* and *must of.*

EXAMPLES   Yvetta wished she **could have** [not *could of*] gone to the movie Saturday night.

We **should have** [not *should of*] asked your mom for permission to go to the park.

don't, doesn't See page 181.

everywheres See **anyways,** etc.

except, accept See **accept, except.**

fewer, less *Fewer* is used with plural words. *Less* is used with singular words. *Fewer* tells "how many"; *less* tells "how much."

EXAMPLES   This road has **fewer** stoplights than any of the other roads in the county.

This road has **less** traffic than any of the other roads in the county.

good, well *Good* is an adjective. Do not use *good* to modify a verb; use *well*, which can be used as an adverb.

NONSTANDARD   Heather sings good.

STANDARD   Heather sings **well.**

Although it is usually an adverb, *well* is also used as an adjective to mean "healthy."

EXAMPLE   Keiko went home from school today because she didn't feel **well.**

┌─ **TIPS** & **TRICKS** ─┐

Could of, should of, etc., are common errors because they are mistaken for the contractions of *could have, should have,* etc. When spoken, *could've* sounds like *could of.* The difference is hardly noticeable in speech, but it is very noticeable in writing.

USAGE

┌─ **TIPS** & **TRICKS** ─┐

Use *fewer* with things that can be counted. Use *less* with things that cannot be counted.

EXAMPLE
Yolanda has (*fewer, less*) pets than Kristi does.

ASK
Can you count pets? [yes]

ANSWER
Yolanda has **fewer** pets than Kristi does.

SKILLS FOCUS

Demonstrate understanding of standard English usage. Avoid common usage problems.

NOTE *Feel good* and *feel well* mean different things. *Feel good* means "to feel happy or pleased." *Feel well* means "to feel healthy."

EXAMPLES   I feel **good** when I'm with my friends.

Rashid had a cold, and he still doesn't feel **well**.

had of   See **of**.

had ought, hadn't ought   The verb *ought* should not be used with *had*.

NONSTANDARD   They had ought to be more careful.

STANDARD   They **ought** to be more careful.

NONSTANDARD   You hadn't ought to have said that.

STANDARD   You **oughtn't** to have said that.

or

You **shouldn't** have said that.

hardly, scarcely   *Hardly* and *scarcely* are negative words. They should not be used with other negative words to express a single negative idea.

EXAMPLES   Pedro **can** [not *can't*] **hardly** wait for the fiesta.

The sun **has** [not *hasn't*] **scarcely** shone today.

hisself, theirself, theirselves   These words are nonstandard English. Use *himself* and *themselves*.

EXAMPLES   Mr. Ogata said he would do the work **himself** [not *hisself*], I believe.

They congratulated **themselves** [not *theirselves*] on their victory.

how come   In informal English, *how come* is often used instead of *why*. In formal English, *why* is preferred.

INFORMAL   How come she can leave early?

FORMAL   **Why** can she leave early?

Exercise 2 **Identifying Correct Usage**

For each of the following sentences, choose the word or word group in parentheses that is correct according to the rules of formal, standard usage.

EXAMPLE   1. There might be (*fewer, less*) accidents if people were more alert around small children.

     1. *fewer*

1. Everyone knows that children are not always as careful as they (*ought, had ought*) to be.
2. However, young children (*can hardly, can't hardly*) be blamed for being curious and adventurous.
3. Just a few days ago, I was involved in a scary situation that (*could of, could have*) led to a serious accident.
4. After I (*brought, took*) my little brother Gerald home from a walk, I called my friend Susan.
5. Gerald quickly wandered off by (*hisself, himself*).
6. I don't know (*how come, why*) he always disappears when I'm on the phone.
7. I found Gerald climbing onto the stove, and in (*fewer, less*) than a second, I lifted him down.
8. I told him that he (*could have, could of*) been burned.
9. He said he would be (*good, well*) from then on.
10. Although the experience was frightening, it turned out (*good, well*).

Review A **Proofreading a Paragraph for Correct Usage**

Each of the sentences in the following paragraph has at least one error in the use of standard, formal English. Identify each error. Then, write the correct usage.

EXAMPLE   **[1]** The game of soccer has proved to be more popular than the king of England hisself.

     1. *hisself—himself*

[1] Derby, England, may have been the town where soccer was first played at. [2] Sometime around the third century A.D., an early version of the game was played among two towns.

[3] Anywheres from fifty to several hundred people played in a match. [4] Back then, soccer had less rules than it does today and the participants probably didn't behave very good. [5] By the fifteenth century, the government had all ready outlawed the sport. [6] The king said that young people had ought to be training theirselves in archery instead of playing soccer. [7] According to the king, archery practice was alright because bows and arrows could be used against a enemy. [8] However, many people didn't hardly obey the king's rule, and soccer continued to grow in popularity. [9] Perhaps later kings felt badly about outlawing soccer. [10] Eventually the government had to except that soccer had become the most popular sport in England.

its, it's   *Its* is the possessive form of the personal pronoun *it*. *Its* is used to show ownership. *It's* is a contraction of *it is* or *it has*.

EXAMPLES   The raccoon washed **its** face in the shallows of the stream. [possessive pronoun]

My grandparents have a dog; **it's** a collie. [contraction of *it is*]

It's been sunny and warm all day. [contraction of *It has*]

kind of, sort of   In informal English, *kind of* and *sort of* are often used to mean "somewhat" or "rather." In formal English, however, it is better to use *somewhat* or *rather*.

INFORMAL   That story is kind of funny.

FORMAL   That story is **rather** funny.

learn, teach   *Learn* means "to gain knowledge." *Teach* means "to instruct" or "to show how."

EXAMPLES   The students from Vietnam are **learning** English.

Ms. Sanita is **teaching** them.

less   See **fewer, less.**

lie, lay   See page 214.

might of, must of   See **could of.**

SKILLS FOCUS

Demonstrate understanding of standard English usage. Avoid common usage problems.

nowheres   See **anyways,** etc.

of   Do not use *of* with prepositions such as *inside, off,* and *outside.*

EXAMPLES   Mrs. Cardona stood **outside** [not *outside of*] the office.

The child stepped **off** [not *off of*] the porch.

We heard a noise **inside** [not *inside of*] the engine.

Of is also unnecessary with *had.*

EXAMPLE   If we **had** [not *had of*] known you were hungry, we would have brought some food.

ought to of   See **could of.**

rise, raise   See page 212.

should of   See **could of.**

sit, set   See page 211.

somewheres   See **anyways,** etc.

sort of   See **kind of, sort of.**

suppose to, supposed to   Do not leave the *d* off *supposed* when you write *supposed to.*

EXAMPLE   They were **supposed to** [not *suppose to*] join us at the gate.

take, bring   See **bring, take.**

than, then   *Than* is a conjunction used in making comparisons. *Then* is an adverb meaning "next" or "after that."

EXAMPLES   This cheese is tastier **than** that one.

First the phone rang, and **then** someone knocked on the door.

that there   See **this here, that there.**

their, there, they're   *Their* is the possessive form of *they.* It is used to show ownership. *There* is used to mean "at that place" or to begin a sentence. *They're* is a contraction of *they are.*

Reference Note

For information on **using of with helping verbs,** see **could of,** page 271.

USAGE

TIPS & TRICKS

Than helps show a contrast between two things. *Then* tells something about time. If you have trouble choosing between *than* and *then,* ask yourself whether you want to (1) show a contrast or (2) specify a time.

EXAMPLE
I think this book is more difficult (*than, then*) the other one.

CONTRAST OR TIME?
contrast [Use *than.*]

ANSWER
I think this book is more difficult **than** the other one.

USAGE

EXAMPLES   The children played happily with **their** toys. [*Their* tells whose toys.]

We are going over **there** very soon. [*There* tells where we are going.]

There are twelve members in our club. [*There* begins the sentence but does not add to the sentence's meaning.]

They're going to have a Juneteenth picnic. [*They're* is a contraction of *They are.*]

theirself, theirselves   See **hisself,** etc.

them   *Them* should not be used as an adjective. Use *the, these,* or *those.*

EXAMPLE   How much are **those** [not *them*] baseball cards?

Exercise 3   **Identifying Correct Usage**

For each of the following sentences, choose the word or word group in parentheses that is correct according to the rules of formal, standard English.

EXAMPLE   1. For years, scientists have studied Mayan writing on temples and (*inside of, inside*) caves.

1. *inside*

1. Some scientists are (*learning, teaching*) themselves how to understand this writing.
2. The Ancient Mayas didn't use an alphabet to write (*there, their, they're*) language.
3. Instead, they drew symbols like (*them, these*) small pictures shown at left.
4. As you can see, the sign for jaguar looked (*somewhat, sort of*) like a jaguar.
5. At times, it could be difficult to tell what a picture was (*suppose, supposed*) to represent.
6. (*Its, It's*) meaning was made clear by the use of another small symbol.
7. (*There, Their, They're*) is an example of this technique in the illustration in the middle.

Jaguar

Scarf

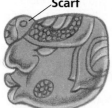

Lord

Man

8. When a scarf symbol was added to the symbol for man, (*then, than*) the picture meant "lord."

9. Mayan writing contained other symbols that stood for syllables rather (*then, than*) entire words.

10. (*Its, It's*) clear we still have a great deal to learn about this beautiful, ancient language.

Review B **Identifying Correct Usage**

Choose the correct word or words in parentheses in each of the following sentences.

EXAMPLE 1. Our club will (*accept, except*) anyone interested in computers.

1. accept

1. Well, I (*should of, should have*) seen that coming.
2. Few chiefs were more powerful (*than, then*) Sitting Bull.
3. Maybe this dog can't find (*its, it's*) way home.
4. You didn't do too (*bad, badly*) in that last race.
5. David sings pretty (*good, well*), doesn't he?
6. Thanks, you've been (*a lot, alot*) of help!
7. We (*had ought, ought*) to plant our garden next week.
8. That book has (*all ready, already*) been checked out.
9. The lenses were dirty, but (*their, there, they're*) clean now.
10. Would you (*learn, teach*) us how to use those castanets?

this here, that there Do not use *here* and *there* after *this* and *that*.

EXAMPLE Do you want **this** [not *this here*] book or **that** [not *that there*] one?

try and In informal English, *try and* is often used for *try to*. In formal English, the correct form is *try to*.

INFORMAL Pat will try and explain the problem.

FORMAL Pat will **try to** explain the problem.

use to, used to Do not leave the *d* off *used* when you write *used to*.

EXAMPLE Dr. Chang **used to** [not *use to*] live next door to us.

SKILLS FOCUS

Demonstrate understanding of standard English usage. Avoid common usage problems.

way, ways Use *way*, not *ways*, when referring to a distance.

EXAMPLE   We traveled a long **way** [not *ways*] today.

well See **good, well.**

when, where Do not use *when* or *where* incorrectly to begin a definition.

NONSTANDARD   A phrase is when a group of words is used as a part of speech.

STANDARD   A phrase is a group of words that is used as a part of speech.

Do not use *where* for *that.*

EXAMPLE   I read **that** [not *where*] the concert has been canceled.

whose, who's *Whose* is the possessive form of *who.* It shows ownership. *Who's* is a contraction of *who is* or *who has.*

EXAMPLES   **Whose** dog is that? [possessive pronoun]

Who's [*Who is*] the bravest person you know?

He's the only one **who's** [*who has*] turned in a report.

would of See **could of.**

your, you're *Your* is the possessive form of *you. You're* is the contraction of *you are.*

EXAMPLES   Do you have **your** watch with you? [possessive pronoun]

You're late today. [contraction of *you are*]

| COMPUTER TIP

A computer's spellchecker can identify words that are nonstandard, such as *ain't, hisself,* and *everywheres.* However, the spellchecker cannot tell you when you have used a correctly spelled word in the wrong way. For example, if you use *whose* where you should use *who's,* the computer probably will not find the error. Always proofread your writing carefully to correct such errors in usage.

Exercise 4 **Identifying Correct Usage**

For each of the following sentences, choose the word or word group in parentheses that is correct according to the rules of formal, standard English.

EXAMPLE   **1.** Take a map on (*your, you're*) next camping trip.
1. *your*

1. A trail map is (*when a map shows, a map that shows*) trails, campsites, and geographical features for a given area.

2. For a safe camping trip, a map like (*this here, this*) one can be very important.
3. Hikers who are not (*used to, use to*) an area often easily lose their way.
4. Every year, rangers report (*where, that*) some campers were lost for a day or more.
5. If you don't want to get lost, (*try and, try to*) get a good trail map.
6. In fact, every hiker in your group (*who's, whose*) able to read a map should have one.
7. With the map, you can choose a (*good, well*) location for your campsite.

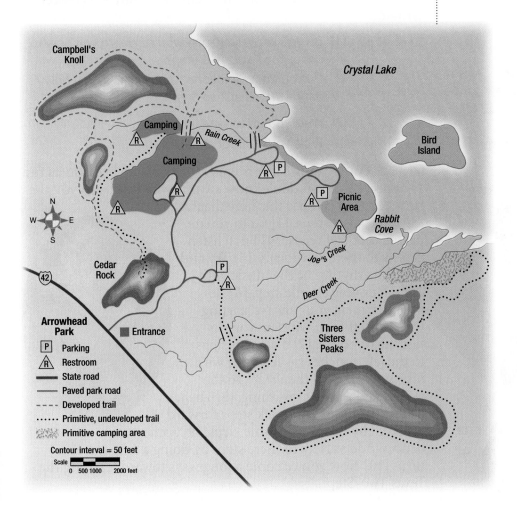

8. When you begin your hike, mark where (*your, you're*) campsite is on the map.

9. If you go quite a (*way, ways*) from your campsite, note your path on the map, too.

10. As (*your, you're*) walking, your trail map can help you figure out exactly where you are.

Review C **Proofreading a Paragraph for Correct Usage**

Most of the sentences in the following paragraph contain errors in the use of formal, standard English. If a sentence is incorrect, rewrite it correctly. If a sentence is already correct, write *C*.

EXAMPLES **[1]** Do you know someone who can learn you how to dance the Texas Two-Step?

1. *Do you know someone who can teach you how to dance the Texas Two-Step?*

[2] Well, your in for a real treat!

2. *Well, you're in for a real treat!*

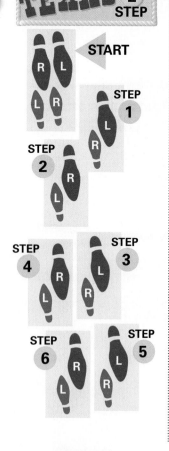

[1] Country music lovers enjoy the two-step because its fun to dance. [2] If you don't know anyone who can teach you the two-step, you can use this here diagram to learn the basic steps. [3] Grab you're partner and get ready. [4] First, listen closely to them musicians. [5] Try and catch the rhythm of the music with a small double shuffle step. [6] Remember, men, your always starting with the left foot; women, you do just the opposite. [7] The man steps to the left, touches his left shoe with his right one, and then steps to the right and does the same thing. [8] Then, he takes two kind of quick steps forward followed by two slow shuffle steps. [9] Some dancers add variety to there steps by doing a sidestep or a turn. [10] Now you've come a long ways toward learning the Texas Two-Step!

Chapter Review

A. Revising Sentences by Correcting Errors in Usage

In each of the following sets of sentences, choose the letter of the sentence that contains an error. Then, write the sentence correctly, using formal, standard English.

1. a. Everyone was at the meeting except Diego.
   b. Does you're dog bite?
   c. Andy waited outside the dentist's office.

2. a. The landfill smelled badly.
   b. No one knew whose knapsack that was.
   c. We could hardly wait for the rain to stop.

3. a. Mr. Catalano says that spiders ain't insects.
   b. I feel rather tired today.
   c. Do you accept personal checks?

4. a. Nina can run faster than he can.
   b. Anna would have finished, but she was interrupted.
   c. Be sure to bring a extra pencil with you.

5. a. The cow and its calf stood in the meadow.
   b. Less students signed up for tutoring this month.
   c. What is the difference between these brands of basketball shoes?

6. a. We did as we were told.
   b. Everyone was already to go.
   c. I used to enjoy playing tennis.

7. a. Penny, bring this book when you go home.
   b. Ms. Michaelson told us that our plan was all right.
   c. Julie said that it's already time to go.

8. a. The team had fewer fouls in the last game.
   b. They looked everywhere for him.
   c. Do you know where he is at?

USAGE

9. **a.** Water-skiing is more fun than I thought.
   b. We hiked a long way before we pitched camp.
   c. Try and get to the meeting on time, please.

10. **a.** Their team has never beaten your team.
    b. A pop fly is when a ball is batted high into the infield.
    c. I finished my homework; then I called Duane.

B. Revising Sentences by Correcting Errors in Usage

Each of the following sentences contains an error in the use of formal, standard English. Rewrite each sentence correctly.

11. They could have come if the plane had of been on time.
12. That ain't an expensive hotel.
13. We talked quietly between the three of us.
14. That parade was the noisiest I've ever heard anywheres.
15. This here beach is beautiful!
16. When the semi-trailer drove past the house, the picture fell off of Aunt Edna's wall.
17. I should of taken my camera inside the cave.
18. Its one of the nicest beaches near Port Aransas.
19. I wasn't hardly scared on the cable car.
20. You hadn't ought to miss the national park.
21. After spending most of the weekend in the library, I was already for the exam.
22. Earlier in the race, I could of caught up with her.
23. "I'm doing good. How are you doing?"
24. Every major country in Western Europe accept Switzerland and Norway belongs to the European Union.
25. Mom and Dad treated theirselves to dinner at a fine restaurant on their anniversary.
26. It hasn't hardly rained all month in west Texas.
27. The birds flew toward there nests.
28. Boston is a long ways from San Francisco.
29. When I was a baby, I use to eat dog biscuits.
30. "Your late today," said Ms. Jimenez. "Next time, remember to set your watch."

Writing Application
Using Formal English in a Letter

Formal, Standard Usage   You are an after-school helper at a day-care center. The teachers at the center plan to take the children on a field trip. One of the teachers has asked you to write a letter to send to the children's parents. The letter should tell where the children will visit and describe some of the things they will do there. The letter should also list any special items the children need to take with them.

Prewriting   First, decide where the children will go on their field trip. They might go to a library, a park, a museum, or a fire station. Then, list the kinds of activities in which the children might participate. Note how the children will travel—for example, by bus or car. Also, note any special clothing or other things they might need for the field trip. List all the details you can imagine.

Writing   Begin your draft with a polite greeting to the parents. Then, clearly explain why the children are going on the field trip. Invite the parents to call the day-care center with any questions they might have. In your letter, avoid using any informal or non-standard expressions.

Revising   Read over your work carefully, and then ask a friend to read your letter. Does your reader understand the information in the letter? Does the letter follow the guidelines for a proper business letter? Revise any information that is unclear.

Publishing   Check your letter for correct spelling, punctuation, and grammar. With your teacher's permission, you may want to discuss the planned field trip with the rest of the class. Post your letter on a class bulletin board or Web page.

HELP

Use the Glossary of Usage to help you write the letter in formal, standard English.

Reference Note

For more about **writing business letters,** see "Writing" in the Quick Reference Handbook.

SKILLS FOCUS

Write a letter. Demonstrate awareness of formal and informal English.

USAGE

Capital Letters
Rules for Capitalization

Diagnostic Preview

Correcting Sentences by Capitalizing Words

For each of the following sentences, correctly write each word that should be capitalized but is not. If a sentence is already correct, write *C*.

EXAMPLE   **1.** our guest speaker will be mayor Masella.
       1. Our, Mayor

1. Today i learned the song "simple gifts" from my friend.
2. "Hansel and Gretel" is a well-known fairy tale.
3. The kane county fall carnival will be held on saturday, october 19.
4. I believe that the recent trip to japan was organized by dr. alexander.
5. Let's ask the club treasurer, ms. lee.
6. Have you met professor martínez, rondelle?
7. Luis valdez filmed *the shepherd's tale*, a traditional mexican play, for tv.
8. The greek god of war was ares.
9. My mother wrote to senator smith about the base closing.
10. members of congress often debate issues.
11. The letter began, "dear Ms. Joy."

12. Have you seen any of Mary cassatt's paintings?
13. I didn't know that there are mummies in the american museum of natural history.
14. A venezuelan exchange student will be living with our family for eight months.
15. The graduation ceremony was held at Newberry college.
16. When is the jewish holiday yom kippur this year?
17. Grandma asked me what i want for my birthday.
18. Monique said, "that movie is about World war II."
19. Next spring uncle William is going to take me on a hiking trip to mount Elbert.
20. Darnell took a rafting trip on the Colorado river.

Using Capital Letters

11a. Capitalize the first word in every sentence.

EXAMPLE   **M**y sister has soccer practice after school. **T**hen she has to do her homework.

The first word of a directly quoted sentence should begin with a capital letter, whether or not the quotation comes at the beginning of your sentence.

EXAMPLE   Reiko asked, "**H**ave you finished your report?"

Traditionally, the first word of every line of poetry begins with a capital letter.

EXAMPLE   **L**et the rain kiss you.
Let the rain beat upon your head with silver liquid drops.
Let the rain sing you a lullaby.
The rain makes still pools on the sidewalk.
The rain makes running pools in the gutter.
The rain plays a little sleep-song on our roof at night—
And I love the rain.

Langston Hughes, "April Rain Song"

NOTE   Some poets do not follow this style. When you quote from a poem, use capital letters exactly as the poet uses them.

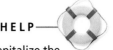

┌HELP─

Capitalize the first word of a sentence fragment used in dialogue.

EXAMPLE
Helena asked, "Have you ever read a Terry Brooks novel?"
Jenny answered, "**N**o, not yet."

MECHANICS

SKILLS FOCUS

Use capitalization correctly.

Reference Note

For information about **writing letters,** see "Writing" in the Quick Reference Handbook. For information on using **colons in letters,** see page 327. For information on using **commas in letters,** see page 322.

11b. Capitalize the first word in both the salutation and the closing of a letter.

SALUTATIONS   **D**ear Service Manager:

                    Dear Adam,

                    My dear Brenda,

CLOSINGS   **S**incerely,

                    Yours truly,

                    Very truly yours,

11c. Capitalize the pronoun *I*.

EXAMPLE   When **I** returned home, **I** walked the dog.

Exercise 1 Proofreading Sentences for Correct Capitalization

If a sentence has one or more errors in capitalization, correctly write each word that should be capitalized. If a sentence is already correct, write *C*.

EXAMPLE   **1.** What time should i call?

            1. I

1. my library report on Edwin Arlington Robinson is due at the end of next month.
2. My sister memorized the limerick that begins, "a tutor who tooted a flute."
3. Aren't you glad that tomorrow is a holiday?
4. Elizabeth said, "we need to buy some more shampoo."
5. My grandparents let me watch television only after i have finished all my chores.
6. I used "yours truly" to close my letter.
7. How many yen did you spend during your vacation in Japan, Alexander?
8. "Everything i need to make the spaghetti sauce is right here," Nanna said.
9. two groups that i like will perform in concert next month in the park.
10. Greg said, "tomorrow is a holiday, so there will be no mail delivery."

SKILLS FOCUS

Use capitalization correctly. *(page 287):* Capitalize proper nouns and adjectives correctly.

11d. Capitalize proper nouns.

A *proper noun* names a particular person, place, thing, or idea. Proper nouns are capitalized. A *common noun* names a kind or type of person, place, thing, or idea. A common noun generally is not capitalized unless it begins a sentence or is part of a title.

Reference Note

For more about **proper nouns** and **common nouns,** see page 72.

Proper Nouns	Common Nouns
Fairview **S**chool	middle school
November	month
Toni **M**orrison	writer
Red **S**ox	team
Kenya	country
Queen **E**lizabeth	queen
Motorola	company

NOTE As you may already have noticed, some proper nouns consist of more than one word. In these names, short words such as prepositions (those of fewer than five letters) and articles (*a, an,* and *the*) are not capitalized.

EXAMPLES **I**sle **o**f **W**ight   **A**ttila **t**he **H**un

(1) Capitalize the names of persons and animals.

Persons	
Kazue **S**awai	**H**arriet **T**ubman
Golda **M**eir	**E**ric the **R**ed
Heitor **V**illa-Lobos	**W. C. H**andy

Animals	
Lassie	**R**over
Shamu	**S**ocks

Think as a
Reader/Writer

Some names consist of more than one part. The different parts may begin with capital letters only or with a combination of capital and lowercase letters. If you are not sure about the spelling of a name, ask the person with that name, or check a reference source.

EXAMPLES
du **M**aurier, **D**u**P**ont,
van **G**ogh, **V**an **B**uren,
La **V**erne, **d**e **l**a **T**our

MECHANICS

(2) Capitalize geographical names.

Type of Name	Examples	
Continents	Asia	North America
	Australia	Europe
Countries	Denmark	Thailand
	Burkina Faso	Costa Rica
Cities, Towns	Minneapolis	New Delhi
	Havana	San Diego
States	Maryland	Mississippi
	West Virginia	Oregon
Islands	Hawaiian Islands	Isle of Wight
	Leyte	Key West
Bodies of Water	Yangtze River	Lake Okeechobee
	Hudson Bay	Caribbean Sea
Streets, Highways	Front Street	Sunset Boulevard
	Fifth Avenue	Interstate 55

NOTE   In a hyphenated street number, the second part of the number is not capitalized.

EXAMPLE   Forty-ninth Street

Type of Name	Examples	
Parks	San Antonio Missions	Yellowstone National Park
Mountains	Adirondacks	Mount Kilimanjaro
	Pine Mountain	Andes
Forests	Sherwood Forest	Sierra National Forest
	Black Forest	
Sections of the Country	the South	the Northwest
	Corn Belt	New England

COMPUTER TIP

You may be able to use your spellchecker to help you correctly capitalize people's names, geographical names, and other proper nouns. Each time you use a proper noun in your writing, make sure you have spelled and capitalized it correctly. Then, add the name to your computer's dictionary or spellchecker.

SKILLS FOCUS

Capitalize proper nouns and adjectives correctly.

> **NOTE** Words such as *east, west, northeast,* or *southwest* are not
> capitalized when the words indicate a direction.
>
> EXAMPLES   Turn **e**ast when you reach the river. [direction]
>
>   **M**ae goes to college in the **E**ast. [section of the country]

Exercise 2   Writing Proper Nouns

For each common noun given below, write two proper nouns
that name the same kind of person or thing. Be sure to use
capital letters correctly.

EXAMPLE   **1.** lake

   1. Lake Louise, Lake Ontario

1. river   **6.** singer   **11.** dog   **16.** explorer
2. street   **7.** island   **12.** politician **17.** mountain
3. actor   **8.** state   **13.** city   **18.** lake
4. park   **9.** country   **14.** pet   **19.** continent
5. friend   **10.** ocean   **15.** painter   **20.** athlete

┌**HELP**──
A dictionary
and an atlas can help
you correctly complete
Exercise 2.

Exercise 3   Proofreading for the Correct Use of Capital Letters

If a sentence has an error in capitalization, correctly write
the word that should be capitalized. If the sentence is already
correct, write *C.*

EXAMPLE   **1.** Huge rigs pump oil from beneath the North sea.

   1. Sea

1. María Ayala and eileen Barnes are going to Chicago.
2. Our neighbor Ken Oshige recently moved to canada.
3. Midway island is in the Pacific Ocean.
4. We could see mount Hood from the airplane window.
5. After you turn off the highway, head north for three miles.
6. During the sixteenth century, explorers from Spain
   brought horses to the west.
7. Several of us went camping near the guadalupe River.
8. My closest friend just moved to Ohio with shadow, her cat.
9. Hawaii Volcanoes National park is in Hawaii.
10. The bookstore is located on Maple street in New Orleans.

(3) Capitalize the names of organizations, teams, institutions, and government bodies.

Type of Name	Examples
Organizations	Math Club Oakdale Chamber of Commerce Boy Scouts
Teams	New York Mets Los Angeles Lakers Riverside Raiders
Institutions	University of Oklahoma Kennedy Middle School Mount Sinai Hospital
Government Bodies	League of Arab States Department of Education Federal Bureau of Investigation

TIPS & TRICKS

The names of government bodies are generally abbreviated.

EXAMPLES
FBI   IRS

Reference Note

For more information on **abbreviations,** see pages 296 and 311.

NOTE Do not capitalize words such as *hotel, theater,* and *high school* unless they are part of a proper name.

EXAMPLES	Fremont Hotel	the hotel
	Apollo Theater	a theater
	Ames High School	that high school

(4) Capitalize the names of special events, holidays, and calendar items.

Type of Name	Examples	
Special Events	World Series New York Marathon	Parade of Roses Tulip Festival
Holidays	Thanksgiving Labor Day	Martin Luther King, Jr., Day
Calendar Items	Sunday Father's Day	December April Fools' Day

SKILLS FOCUS

Capitalize proper nouns and adjectives correctly.

MECHANICS

Do not capitalize the name of a season unless it is part of a proper name.

EXAMPLES   a **w**inter storm   the **W**inter **F**estival

(5) Capitalize the names of historical events and periods.

Type of Name	Examples	
Historical Events	**B**oston **T**ea **P**arty **B**attle of **H**astings **W**ar of 1812	**N**ew **D**eal **M**arch on **W**ashington
Historical Periods	**B**ronze **A**ge **R**eformation	**G**reat **D**epression **R**enaissance

Exercise 4 **Correcting Errors in the Use of Capital Letters**

For the following sentences, identify each word that should be capitalized but is not. Then, write the word or words correctly.

EXAMPLE   **1.** Hart middle school is having a book fair.

    1. Middle School

1. Would you like to go to the movies this friday?
2. I think that the special Olympics will be held in our town this year.
3. What plans have you made for easter?
4. My sister and I were born at memorial Hospital.
5. The Rotary club donated equipment for our school's gym.
6. Did dinosaurs live during the stone Age?
7. My favorite baseball team is the Atlanta braves.
8. I always look forward to the first day of springfest.
9. The united states Congress is made up of the senate and the house of representatives.
10. Did you see any fireworks on the fourth of July?
11. Donna's youngest sister is going to join the girl scouts next Wednesday.
12. Our family has a wonderful time at the Alaska renaissance festival each year.

MECHANICS

13. The Grand hotel used to have Roman and Egyptian statues in its lobby.
14. Dave teaches at either the university of Florida or the university of Miami.
15. Why would you like to have lived during the middle ages?
16. If you like baseball games, you will enjoy watching the Texas rangers play.
17. Mrs. Nelson's class prepared the library display about civil rights day.
18. For fifteen years, spring carnival has been our school's main fund-raiser.
19. During the French revolution, people demanded their freedom and rights.
20. We'll be visiting my cousin's high school in may.

(6) Capitalize the names of nationalities, races, and peoples.

Type of Name	Examples	
Nationalities, Races, and Peoples	**M**exican	**S**wiss
	Micronesian	**C**aucasian
	Cherokee	**B**antu

(7) Capitalize the names of businesses and the brand names of business products.

Type of Name	Examples
Businesses	**J.** and **J. C**onstruction, **I**nc.
	Uptown **S**hoe **S**tore
	Grommet **M**anufacturing **C**ompany
Business Products	**G**oodyear **A**quatred
	Nikon **P**ronea
	Ford **R**anger

NOTE Names of types of products are not capitalized.

EXAMPLES Goodyear **t**ires, Nikon **c**amera, Ford **t**ruck

(8) Capitalize the names of ships, trains, aircraft, and spacecraft.

Type of Name	Examples	
Ships	**S**anta **M**aria	**M**onitor
Trains	**C**oast **S**tarlight	**C**ity of **M**iami
Aircraft	**S**pruce **G**oose	**S**pirit of **S**t. Louis
Spacecraft	**C**olumbia	**L**unar **P**rospector

Reference Note

For information on using **italics (underlining) for the names of vehicles,** see page 337.

(9) Capitalize the names of buildings and other structures.

Type of Name	Examples	
Buildings	**F**latiron **B**uilding **G**allier **H**all	**W**orld **T**rade **C**enter
Other Structures	**H**oover **D**am **A**strodome	**G**olden **G**ate **B**ridge

(10) Capitalize the names of monuments, memorials, and awards.

Statue of **L**iberty	**L**incoln **M**emorial	**P**ulitzer **P**rize

COMPUTER TIP

A computer's spellchecker or grammar checker might spot some capitalization errors for you.

However, you cannot rely on these programs to find all your mistakes. Since many words are capitalized in some situations but not in others, the computer cannot find every error. Also, the computer might mistakenly highlight a word that is already correct.

Always proofread your writing carefully to make sure you have used capital letters correctly.

(11) Capitalize the names of religions and their followers, holy days and celebrations, sacred writings, and specific deities.

Type of Name	Examples	
Religions and Followers	**B**uddhism **T**aoism	**C**hristian **J**ew
Holy Days and Celebrations	**P**urim **C**hristmas	**R**amadan **A**sh **W**ednesday
Sacred Writings	**D**ead **S**ea **S**crolls **B**ible	**K**oran **T**almud
Specific Deities	**A**llah **G**od	**V**ishnu **J**ehovah

MECHANICS

NOTE The words *god* and *goddess* are not capitalized when they refer to deities of ancient mythology. However, the names of specific mythological gods and goddesses are capitalized.

EXAMPLE   The Roman **g**od of the sea was **N**eptune.

(12) Capitalize the names of planets, stars, constellations, and other heavenly bodies.

Mars	**P**luto	**N**orth **S**tar	**B**etelgeuse
Milky **W**ay	**B**ig **D**ipper	**U**rsa **M**inor	**S**irius

NOTE The word *earth* is not capitalized unless it is used along with the names of other heavenly bodies that are capitalized. The words *sun* and *moon* generally are not capitalized.

EXAMPLES China is home to one fourth of the people on **e**arth.

How far is Saturn from **E**arth?

The **s**un rose at 7:09 this morning.

Exercise 5 **Correcting Sentences by Using Capital Letters Correctly**

For each of the following sentences, correctly write the word or words that should be capitalized.

EXAMPLE   1. We went to the leesburg library to learn more about african american history.

1. *Leesburg Library, African American*

1. The methodist quoted a verse from the bible.
2. Bob has a chevrolet truck.
3. On a clear night you can see venus from earth.
4. My teacher took a cruise on the *song of Norway.*
5. Meet me in front of the Woolworth building.
6. Pilar received the Junior Achievement award.
7. Otis made a detailed scale model of the spacecraft *nozomi.*
8. Elena wrote a poem about the Greek god zeus.
9. Some navajo make beautiful silver jewelry.
10. Who were the first europeans to settle in Mexico?

SKILLS FOCUS

Capitalize proper nouns and adjectives correctly.

Correcting Sentences by Capitalizing Proper Nouns

For each of the following sentences, correctly write the word or words that should be capitalized.

EXAMPLE   **1.** In the late nineteenth century, henry morton stanley explored an area of africa occupied by ancestors of the bambuti.

    1. Henry Morton Stanley, Africa, Bambuti

1. The bambuti people live in the ituri forest, which is located in the northeast area of the Democratic republic of the congo.

2. This forest is located almost exactly in the middle of the continent of africa.

3. It lies north of mungbere, as shown in the boxed area on the map to the right.

4. The bambuti people, also known as twides, aka, or efe, have lived there for many thousands of years.

5. The earliest record of people like the Bambuti is found in the notes of explorers from egypt about 2500 B.C.

6. Other early reports of these people are found on colorful tiles in italy and in the records of explorers from portugal.

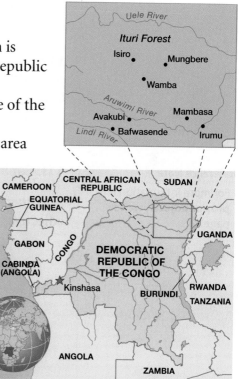

7. Stanley met some of the bambuti people, but he didn't write much about them.

8. In the 1920s, paul schebesta went to africa to learn more about the Bambuti people.

9. He learned that the bambuti are very different from the bantu and from other neighbors.

10. In fact, the bambuti were probably the first people in the rain forest that stretches across central africa from the atlantic ocean on the western coast to the eastern grasslands.

11e. Do not capitalize the names of school subjects, except course names followed by a numeral and the names of language classes.

EXAMPLES   social studies, science, health, art, Woodworking II, Consumer Education I, Spanish, English

11f. Capitalize proper adjectives.

A ***proper adjective*** is formed from a proper noun. Proper adjectives are usually capitalized.

Proper Noun	Proper Adjective
Mexico	Mexican carvings
King Arthur	Arthurian legend
Judaism	Judaic laws
Mars	Martian landscape

11g. Most abbreviations are capitalized.

Capitalize abbreviations that come before and after personal names.

EXAMPLES   Mr., Ms., Mrs., Dr., Gen., M.D., RN, Jr., Sr.

Capitalize abbreviations of the names of organizations, businesses, and government bodies.

EXAMPLES   Inc., Co., Corp., FBI, UN, NAACP, FDA

In addresses, capitalize abbreviations such as those for roads, rooms, and post office boxes.

EXAMPLES   Ave., Dr., Rd., St., Apt., Rm., P.O. Box

Reference Note
For more information on **proper adjectives,** see page 86.

Reference Note
For information on using **abbreviations,** see page 311.

SKILLS FOCUS

Use capitalization correctly. Capitalize proper nouns and adjectives correctly.

MECHANICS

Abbreviations of geographical names are capitalized.

EXAMPLES **N.Y.C.**   **S**t. Louis   **N.** America   **O**kla.

> NOTE A two-letter state abbreviation without periods is used when the abbreviation is followed by a ZIP Code. Each letter of the abbreviation is capitalized.
>
> EXAMPLES Austin, **TX** 78704-6364
>
> New Orleans, **LA** 70131-5140

Some abbreviations, especially those for measurements, are not capitalized.

EXAMPLES etc., **e.g.**, **v**ol., **c**hap., **i**n., **y**d, **l**b, **c**c, **m**l, **m**m

Exercise 6 Correcting Errors in Capitalization

For each of the following sentences, correctly write each word or abbreviation that should be capitalized.

EXAMPLE **1.** I went with mrs. McCain to visit mr. Brennan in the retirement home.

1. Mrs., Mr.

1. The address was p.o. box 32, Green Bay, Wi 54305.
2. The new student had just moved to our town from st. Petersburg, Florida.
3. Will gen. Scott Quinn be speaking tonight?
4. Mr. Lloyd Mitchell, jr., has been appointed president of Sprockets and Widgets, inc.
5. The next speaker for Career Day will be Chet Patterson, rn, who works at the local hospital.
6. Blair O'Brien, cpa, has a top-floor office in the Hanley corp. building.
7. The Fbi, the Fda, and the Un have decided to cooperate on the investigation.
8. Are you taking art II or spanish?
9. Many scottish people have celtic, scandinavian, and irish ancestors.
10. The Chisholm Trail, which stretched over one thousand miles from San Antonio, tex., to Abilene, kans., was used by cowboys to drive cattle north.

MECHANICS

Read the following letter. For each numbered word group, identify any words or abbreviations that are not capitalized correctly. Rewrite the words or abbreviations with correct capitalization. If a sentence is already correct, write *C*.

EXAMPLE   **[1]** 1066 south Norman st.

1. *South, St.*

March 14, 2008

Mr. Leonard Thornton
1234 Windswept Dr.
[1] Lancaster, Pa 17601

[2] dear Mr. Thornton:

   [3] I think that the easiest thing you could do to help make lancaster better is to make it safer to ride bicycles here. **[4]** My friend James almost got hit by a car on his way to Memorial middle school. **[5]** As a member of our city's Transportation advisory Board, you can do a lot to encourage cyclists to wear helmets.

   [6] Also, in Earth Science I class, we have learned that if more people used bicycles instead of cars, the air would be cleaner. **[7]** One company that I know of, Universal Solutions, inc., rewards people who ride bicycles to work. **[8]** Many cities, such as Boulder, colorado, are building bicycle lanes. **[9]** maybe you could help with programs like these. Thank you for your attention to this matter.

        [10] yours truly,

Tate Washington

        Tate Washington

11h. Capitalize titles.

(1) Capitalize a person's title when the title comes before the person's name.

EXAMPLES   **J**udge O'Connor   **P**rincipal Walsh

               Mrs. Santos   **D**octor Ellis

               Senator Topping   **P**resident Truman

(2) Titles used alone or following a person's name generally are not capitalized.

EXAMPLES   Judy Klein, our club **p**resident, led the meeting.

               The **s**ecretary gave a speech to Congress.

However, a title used alone in direct address usually is capitalized.

EXAMPLES   Can the cast come off today, **D**octor?

               Good morning, **M**a'am [or **m**a'am].

(3) Capitalize a word showing a family relationship when the word is used before or in place of a person's name.

EXAMPLES   Are **U**ncle Carlos and **A**unt Rosa here yet?

               Either **M**om or **D**ad will drive us to the show.

Do not capitalize a word showing a family relationship when the word follows a possessive noun or pronoun.

EXAMPLE   My **c**ousin Dena and her **n**iece Leotie made stew.

Exercise 7 **Correcting Sentences by Capitalizing Words**

For each of the following sentences, correctly write the word or words that should be capitalized. If a sentence is already correct, write *C*.

EXAMPLE   **1.** Thank you, aunt Shirley, for the pretty sweater.
             1. Aunt

1. He says that judge Johnson is very strict.
2. Reuben's mother, mrs. Santos, owns the new restaurant.

HELP

You may capitalize a title used alone or following a person's name if you want to emphasize the person's high office.

EXAMPLE
    Please come and meet Texas' native daughter and our country's **S**ecretary of **S**tate.

MECHANICS

SKILLS FOCUS

Capitalize titles correctly.

3. Will your uncle be at the party?

4. Well, doctor Sakamoto, do I need braces?

5. Did the secretary of state attend the meeting?

6. Is cousin Josie going to Israel?

7. Please accept my apologies, senator.

8. On Saturday, aunt Latisha will arrive from Savannah.

9. Does professor Jones teach American history?

10. I learned to swim at grandpa Brown's cottage on the lake last summer.

Review C Using Capital Letters Correctly in Sentences

For each of the following sentences, correctly write the word or words that should be capitalized.

EXAMPLE   **1.** The Civil war is sometimes called the war between the states.

            1. War, War Between the States

1. There is a fountain in the middle of lake Eola.

2. dr. jones teaches at York high school.

3. Some of these folk songs are mexican.

4. the atlantic borders the states from maine to florida.

5. Someday i would like to bicycle through europe.

6. all of my friends came to the party.

7. Have you visited the Washington monument?

8. Our history class wrote letters to the secretary-general of the united nations.

9. There's a long detour on highway 50 just east of brooksville, dad.

10. Our first fall camping trip will be in october.

(4) Capitalize the first and last words and all important words in titles and subtitles.

Unimportant words in a title include:

- articles (*a, an, the*)
- coordinating conjunctions (*and, but, for, nor, or, so, yet*)
- prepositions of fewer than five letters (such as *by, for, into, on, with*)

Reference Note

For a list of **prepositions,** see page 109.

MECHANICS

Type of Name	Examples	
Books	*The Horse and His Boy*	*Dust Tracks on a Road*
Magazines	*Sports Illustrated for Kids*	*Essence* *Reader's Digest*
Newspapers	*Detroit Free Press* *The Fresno Bee*	*Tulsa Tribune* *The Denver Post*
Poems	"The City Is So Big" "The Sneetches"	"For a Poet" "Steam Shovel"
Short Stories	"The Day the Sun Came Out"	"The Six Rows of Pompons"
Plays	*Once on This Island*	*A Chorus Line*
Comic Strips	*Peanuts*	*Rose Is Rose*
Movies	*Babe: Pig in the City*	*A Bug's Life* *The King and I*
Television Programs	*Touched by an Angel* *Sister, Sister*	*Star Trek: Deep Space Nine*
Videos	*The Lion King II: Simba's Pride*	*Basic Sign Language*
Video Games	*Mario Kart 64*	*Escape Velocity*
Albums and CDs	*Bringing Down the Horse* *Tiger Woods: The Makings of a Champion*	*Mi Tierra* *Ray of Light* *My Family Tree: A Recorded History*
Works of Art	*Delfina and Dimas*	*Forever Free*
Musical Works	"Oh, What a Beautiful Morning"	*Peter and the Wolf* "Angel of Mine"

Reference Note

For guidelines on using **italics (underlining)** and **quotation marks with titles,** see pages 336 and 343.

MECHANICS

SKILLS FOCUS

Capitalize titles correctly.

┌HELP┐

The official title of a book is found on the title page. The official title of a newspaper or periodical is found on the masthead, which usually appears on the editorial page or the table of contents.

NOTE An article (*a, an,* or *the*) before a title is not capitalized unless it is the first word of the official title.

EXAMPLES Do you read the *Sacramento Bee*?

Grandmother showed Nehal and me an article in *The Workbasket.*

My mother reads *The Wall Street Journal.*

Coordinating conjunctions and prepositions that begin a title or subtitle are capitalized.

EXAMPLES I have read *Through the Looking Glass* three times.

Marcia said that *But I'll Be Back Again* was very interesting.

Exercise 8 **Writing Titles for Imaginary Works**

Create a title for each item described below. Be sure each title is capitalized correctly.

EXAMPLE 1. a video about training pet birds
    1. How to Be Your Bird's Best Friend

1. a movie about an American Indian detective who solves a murder mystery
2. a magazine for people interested in video games about fly-fishing in Montana
3. a book about choosing the best breed of dog as a pet for your family
4. a song about saving the rain forests
5. a painting about life in a modern suburb somewhere in the United States
6. a poem about a new baby brother or sister coming home for the first time
7. a play about a student's first day at a new school in a South American country
8. a television show about the humorous people who visit the local library
9. a short story about students who go on a field trip to an animal park and get stuck there overnight
10. a newspaper published by the athletics department

Exercise 9 Correctly Capitalizing Titles

Correct any incorrect capital or lowercase letters in titles in the following sentences. If a sentence is already correct, write *C*.

EXAMPLE   **1.** Mom gave me an article called "the importance Of fitness."

     1. "The Importance of Fitness"

1. "Heart And Soul" is the only piano duet we can play.

2. Do you read *National geographic World*?

3. My little sister loves *the Cat in the Hat*.

4. I saw *Around the World in Eighty Days* on television.

5. We enjoy watching reruns of *The Cosby show*.

6. My mother likes to work the crossword puzzle in *the New York times*.

7. The children look forward to receiving their copies of *Ranger rick* each month.

8. Tony's short story "a few words about Aunt Frederica's dog Smitty and all his friends" certainly has the longest title of any story written by a member of the class.

9. "A Poem About A Poem" is the title of Mary Elizabeth's funny poem.

10. Jack Johnson's music is a special feature of the movie *curious george*.

Review D Proofreading a Paragraph to Correct Errors in Capitalization

Proofread the following paragraph, correcting any errors in the use of capital and lowercase letters.

EXAMPLE   **[1]** what a huge Ship the *titanic* was!

     1. What, ship, Titanic

[1] This magnificent ocean liner sank on april 15, 1912. [2] For more than seventy years, the *Titanic* lay untouched in the icy waters of the atlantic ocean. [3] Then, on September 1, 1985, Dr. Robert Ballard of the woods hole oceanographic institution and his crew found the ship. [4] To view the Ocean floor, the scientists used the remote-controlled vehicle *Argo*, shown on the next page. [5] once they discovered the ship, they attached a special underwater sled to *Argo*. [6] The sled,

with its lights and camera, provided dr. Ballard with more than twenty thousand photographs of the *Titanic*. **[7]** In 1986, Dr. Ballard and his Team returned to explore the wreck of the british ocean liner once more. **[8]** using a minisubmarine, the team was able to explore the sunken ship. **[9]** after years of wondering about the *Titanic,* underwater explorers finally found the Wreck and uncovered the truth about its fate. **[10]** In his book *The discovery of the Titanic,* Dr. Ballard tells about his underwater adventures.

Chapter Review

A. Proofreading Sentences for Correct Capitalization

For each of the following sentences, correctly write the word or words that contain an error in capitalization.

1. Sean's dog, Ransom, is a german shepherd.
2. Our Spring vacation begins on march 26.
3. Write to me at 439 Walnut street.
4. Mira asked, "do you know why the *Titanic* sank?"
5. In 2005, Mohamed ElBaradei won the Nobel peace prize.
6. As soon as i finish my English homework, i'll call you.
7. She would like to go to College someday.
8. We watched a scene from *Romeo And Juliet.*
9. Eric's orthodontist is dr. McCambridge.
10. On Saturday my aunt is taking us to jones beach.
11. Dad used the general Electric waffle iron to make breakfast.
12. have you seen my copy of *newsweek*?
13. The Peace corps volunteers helped build a bridge.
14. The capital of Peru is lima.
15. The French revolution changed european society.
16. The spacecraft *sputnik 2* carried a dog named Laika.
17. Tom's brother is a roman catholic priest.
18. Although I live in Biloxi now, I'm from the north.
19. I answered, "the gulf of Mexico, I think."
20. Are you taking spanish or art this year?

B. Correcting Sentences by Using Capital Letters Correctly

For the following sentences, correctly write each word that contains an incorrect capital or lowercase letter.

21. Malaysia is in the Southeastern part of Asia.

22. Its largest ethnic groups are malay, chinese, and indian.
23. The capital and largest city is kuala lumpur.
24. Much of the world's Rubber comes from Malaysia.
25. Other Major products are Tin and Palm Oil.
26. Most inhabitants of malaysia are muslims.
27. Malaysia is a constitutional monarchy headed by a King.
28. The Prime Minister is the Leader of the Government.
29. Many Malays wear the Sarong, a kind of skirt.
30. The Encyclopedia called *World book* can give you more information about Malaysia.

C. Correcting Errors in Capitalization

For the following sentences and word groups, correctly write each word and each abbreviation that should be capitalized.

31. Todd's new address is 1240 mud road, Setauket, Ny 11733-2851.
32. The exchange student is from San remo, Italy.
33. My parents' favorite television movie is *Lonesome dove*.
34. We went with mrs. Rigatti to see the floats in the San gennaro Festival.
35. It was a surprise to learn that uncle Elwood had been in the Cia all those years.
36. isn't your aunt Etta here?
37. Mont blanc, the highest peak in the alps, was first climbed in 1786.
38. We sent a petition to mayor Moore.
39. Millie enjoyed reading *Anne of Green gables* so much that she rented the movie.
40. yours sincerely, Beth Tewes

Writing Application
Using Capital Letters in an Essay

Proper Nouns   Your social studies teacher has asked you to write about a vacation you would like to take to a historical place. Write an essay telling where you would like to go and why you would like to go there. In your essay, use at least five proper nouns.

Prewriting   First, brainstorm a list of historical places that interest you. Which of these places would you most like to visit? Write down notes about what you would do during your visit.

Writing   Begin your rough draft by stating where you would like to go and why. Explain what historical event or events happened at that place. Then, tell what particular areas or landmarks you would visit. Be sure to use at least five proper nouns naming places, events, and people.

Revising   Ask a friend to read your draft and tell you if any parts seem unclear or uninteresting. Then, revise anything that is confusing or boring.

Publishing   Use an encyclopedia or other reference source to check the spelling of any proper nouns you have included. Proofread your essay carefully for any other errors in grammar, spelling, capitalization, and punctuation. Put your essay on poster board, along with pictures or drawings of the place you wrote about in your essay. With your teacher's permission, display your poster in the classroom.

┌─HELP────
An encyclopedia can help you learn more about historical places.

MECHANICS

SKILLS FOCUS

Write descriptive essays. Identify and use proper nouns.

Punctuation
End Marks, Commas, Semicolons, Colons

Diagnostic Preview

Using Periods, Question Marks, Exclamation Points, Commas, Semicolons, and Colons Correctly

The following sentences lack necessary periods, question marks, exclamation points, commas, semicolons, and colons. Write the letter, word, or words that should be followed by a punctuation mark. Then, add the correct punctuation mark after each word. For numerals, write the entire numeral and insert the correct punctuation mark.

EXAMPLE   1. Mr. Cotton my next-door neighbor asked me to pick up his mail while he is away
            1. *Cotton, neighbor, away.*

1. The mangos and papayas and avocados will make a good fruit salad
2. Before the slide presentation began Ms Jee gave a short clear history of Korea
3. Ray Charles a popular singer and musician became blind at the age of seven
4. I've taken classes in photography ceramics and weaving
5. When will dinner be ready
6. Here comes a tornado
7. Cheryl will take gymnastics Eddie will take piano lessons

8. Ted mowed the lawn cleaned the garage and painted the shed

9. Would 6 30 P.M be too early

10. This Zuni ring was made in Santa Fe N Mex

11. I finished the letter but I haven't proofread it yet

12. Dear Senator Hutchison

13. We will learn about the federal court system then we will visit the county courthouse.

14. Sara Eric and Manuel can speak both Spanish and English

15. Hurry, get me some ice

16. Yes I did clean my room

17. When you go cross-country skiing, bring the following items skis boots poles and ski wax

18. Shall we leave at 9 00 A.M.

19. Mr Pak when is the Chinese New Year

20. The Scouts' annual dinner will be held February 19 2001.

End Marks

An **end mark** is a punctuation mark placed at the end of a sentence. *Periods, question marks,* and *exclamation points* are end marks. Periods are also used after some abbreviations.

12a. Use a period at the end of a statement (a declarative sentence).

EXAMPLES French is the official language of Haiti, but many people there speak Haitian Creole.

I will write to you soon.

12b. Use a question mark at the end of a question (an interrogative sentence).

EXAMPLES Have you heard that rapper's new song?

Where should I meet you?

12c. Use an exclamation point at the end of an exclamation (an exclamatory sentence).

EXAMPLES What a cute puppy that is!

This egg drop soup is delicious!

┌─HELP─
Periods (decimal points) are also used to separate dollars from cents and whole numbers from fractions.

EXAMPLES
$6.57 [six dollars and fifty-seven cents]

2.7 [two and seven tenths]

In some countries a comma is used instead of a period in such cases.

MECHANICS

SKILLS FOCUS

Use end marks correctly. Use periods correctly. Use question marks correctly. Use exclamation points correctly.

Think as a Reader/Writer

In your own writing, make sure to use exclamation points only when you want to emphasize a strong feeling. Do not overuse exclamation points, or they will lose their effectiveness.

ORIGINAL
The little gray cat looked up at Judy! With one look, Judy knew this was the kitty for her! How lucky that she had visited the animal shelter today!

REVISED
The little gray cat looked up at Judy. With one look, Judy knew this was the kitty for her. How lucky that she had visited the animal shelter today!

12d. Use either a period or an exclamation point at the end of a request or a command (an imperative sentence).

Use a period after an imperative sentence that makes a request or a mild command. Use an exclamation point after a strong command.

EXAMPLES   Please sit down. [a request]

              Sit down. [a mild command]

              Sit down right now! [a strong command]

Exercise 1   Correcting Sentences by Adding End Marks

Write the last word of each sentence, and add a period, a question mark, or an exclamation point.

EXAMPLE   **1.** What time is it

            1. it?

1. When does the bus come
2. What a great game that was
3. Did you bring your lunch today
4. Hyo was born in Korea
5. I don't understand the assignment
6. Who can identify the subject of this sentence
7. Pardon me, sir
8. Imagine me at the White House
9. Get the iguana back into your room right now
10. The legend for this map is in the lower right-hand corner

Exercise 2   Correcting a Paragraph by Adding Capital Letters and End Marks

Decide where the sentences in the following paragraph begin and end. Rewrite each sentence, providing the needed capital letters and end marks.

EXAMPLE   what an ancient art weaving is
             What an ancient art weaving is!

     have you ever been to Hawaii the first Europeans who landed there found chiefs dressed in beautiful feather cloaks

---HELP---

When you finish Exercise 2, you should have ten complete sentences.

SKILLS FOCUS

Use periods correctly. Use exclamation points correctly.

feathers for cloaks like the one shown here came from thousands of birds different-colored feathers were arranged in royal designs the feathers were then attached to a base of woven fibers cloaks were worn in battle and for ceremonies most of the islanders did not wear such fine garments colorful prints are worn by all kinds of people on the islands every Friday is Aloha Friday on that day many people wear Hawaiian prints and live flowers

Robert Dampier, *Kamehameha III* (1825). Oil on canvas (24⅛" × 20⅞"). Honolulu Academy of Arts, gift of Mrs. C. Montague Cooke, Jr., Charles M. Cooke III, and Mrs. Heston Wren, in memory of Dr. C. Montague Cooke, Jr., 1951.

12e. Many abbreviations are followed by periods.

Types of Abbreviations	Examples			
Personal Names	I. M. Pei		J. C. Watts	
	Vicki L. Ruíz		M.F.K. Fisher	
Titles Used with Names	Mr.	Mrs.	Ms.	Jr.
	Dr.	Sr.	Ph.D.	D.D.S.
Organizations	Assn.	Co.	Corp.	Inc.

TIPS & TRICKS

When writing the initials of someone's name, place a space between two initials (*as in I. M. Pei*). Do not place a space between three initials (as in *M.F.K. Fisher*).

Reference Note

For more on **using capital letters for abbreviations,** see page 296.

NOTE Abbreviations for government agencies and some widely used abbreviations are written without periods. Each letter of such abbreviations (which are called *acronyms*) is capitalized.

EXAMPLES

CIA (**C**entral **I**ntelligence **A**gency)

NOS (**N**ational **O**cean **S**ervice)

PC (**p**ersonal **c**omputer)

RFD (**R**ural **F**ree **D**elivery)

TV (**tele**vision)

SKILLS FOCUS

Use abbreviations correctly.

The abbreviations *A.D.* and *B.C.* need special attention. Place *A.D.* before the year and *B.C.* after the year.

EXAMPLES

231 **B.C.**1

A.D. 590

There is one exception to this rule. For centuries expressed in words, place both *A.D.* and *B.C.* after the century.

EXAMPLES

fifth century **B.C.**

second century **A.D.**

┌**HELP**─

If you are not sure whether to use periods with an abbreviation, look up the abbreviation in a dictionary, an encyclopedia, or another reliable reference source.

┌**HELP**─

Some sentences in Review A need more than one punctuation mark.

Types of Abbreviations	Examples		
Times	A.M.	B.C.	Aug.
	P.M.	A.D.	Sat.
Addresses	Ave.	Blvd.	Ct.
	P.O. Box	Rd.	St.
Geographical Names	Ark.	Colo.	D.C.
	St. Paul	P.R.	U.S.

NOTE A two-letter state abbreviation without periods is used only when it is followed by a ZIP Code. Both letters of the abbreviation are capitalized. No mark of punctuation is used between the abbreviation and the ZIP Code.

EXAMPLES   Washington, **DC** 20013

San Juan, **PR** 00904

Abbreviations for units of measure are usually written without periods and are not capitalized.

EXAMPLES   cc, kg, ml, m, ft, lb, qt

However, you should use a period with the abbreviation *in.* (for *inch*) to prevent confusing it with the word *in.*

When an abbreviation that has a period ends a sentence, another period is not needed. However, a question mark or an exclamation point is used in such situations if it is needed.

EXAMPLES   The game lasted until 8:30 P.M.

Did it start at 5:00 P.M.?

Review A   **Correcting Sentences by Adding Punctuation**

Write the following sentences, adding periods, question marks, and exclamation points where they are needed.

EXAMPLE   1.   Some caterpillars become butterflies

1.   *Some caterpillars become butterflies.*

1. Will Mr Highwater be teaching the science course

2. Just after 3:00 PM., the sun came out
3. The letter from Ms E J Hunter was dated Fri, Nov 12
4. How heavy the traffic was on First Avenue
5. Do your measuring cups say *ml* or *oz*
6. Address comments to 7890 E Kyle Dr, Oswego, New York.
7. By 300 B.C., Chinese cooks already had a philosophy of five tastes
8. The city of St Petersburg is situated on a peninsula
9. Apply at the loading dock at H J Movers, Inc
10. On TV tonight, Dr Melba West will explain nutrition.

Review B **Using Punctuation Correctly**

For each of the following sentences, write the word or words that should be followed by a period, question mark, or exclamation point. Add the proper punctuation after each word.

EXAMPLE   **1.** My neighbor Mr Nhuong showed me this picture of people celebrating the Vietnamese holiday Tet

1. Mr., Tet.

1. Unlike New Year's Day, which is always on Jan 1, Tet can fall on any day in late January or early February
2. Moreover, Tet isn't just one single day; the celebration lasts a whole week
3. Wouldn't you like a week-long holiday
4. Even here at 8420 Beaconcrest Ave, the Nhuong family still enjoy their traditions
5. According to Mr. Nhuong, the name of the first person to visit a house can bring good or bad luck to the family
6. Since my nickname is Lucky, the Nhuongs asked me to be their first visitor and to arrive by 7:00 AM
7. I tried hard not to be late
8. One of the Nhuongs' relatives flew in from Santa Barbara, Calif, later that morning
9. Mrs Nhuong prepared a huge breakfast, and we all sat down to enjoy it
10. What a great meal that was

Commas

End marks are used to separate complete thoughts. **Commas,** however, are generally used to separate words or groups of words within a complete thought. If you fail to use necessary commas, you may confuse your reader.

CONFUSING   The members of the team are Jo Ann Jerry Lee Darrin Marcia and Jeanne. [How many members?]

CLEAR   The members of the team are Jo Ann, Jerry Lee, Darrin, Marcia, and Jeanne. [five members]

Items in a Series

12f. Use commas to separate items in a series.

A **series** is three or more items written one after the other. The items may be single words or word groups.

Words in a Series
Sugar cane, bananas, and citrus fruits are grown in Jamaica. [nouns]
Yesterday I dusted, vacuumed, and mopped. [verbs]
The day was wet, cold, and windy. [adjectives]

Word Groups in a Series
At the beach we swam, built sand castles, and played volleyball. [predicates]
I searched for the lost contact lens in the sink, on the counter, and on the floor. [prepositional phrases]
Please punch the time card when you arrive, when you take lunch, and when you leave. [clauses]

When all the items in a series are joined by *and, or,* or *nor,* do not use commas to separate them.

EXAMPLES   I've seen snakes **and** lizards **and** toads in our yard.

Shall we go bowling **or** rent a movie **or** listen to music?

Exercise 3 **Proofreading Sentences for the Correct Use of Commas**

Most of the following sentences need commas. If a sentence needs commas, write the word before each missing comma; then, add the comma. If a sentence is already correct, write *C*.

EXAMPLE   **1.** Beverley DeGale Claire Jackson and Iman won Candace Awards in 1997.

     1. DeGale, Jackson,

1. I finished my dinner brushed my teeth combed my hair and ran out the door.
2. The nurse checked the patient's pulse took his temperature and gave him a glass of water.
3. For lunch we had milk tuna sandwiches and pears.
4. Cora Jack and Tomás all entered the contest.
5. Marcus plays golf and football and volleyball.
6. The U.S. Marine Corps is prepared for battle on land on the sea and in the air.
7. For her birthday on September 27, my sister wants a dog and a cat and a hamster and a bird.
8. Jan told Raul where she had been, where she was, and where she was going.
9. This project is fun easy fast and inexpensive.
10. Balloons were floating in the living room the kitchen the bedrooms and the dining room.

12g. Use commas to separate two or more adjectives that come before a noun.

EXAMPLES   Pita is a round, flat bread of the Middle East.

         James Earl Jones certainly has a deep, strong, commanding voice.

Do not place a comma between an adjective and the noun immediately following it.

INCORRECT   Alexandra and I found an old, rusty, bicycle in the vacant lot down the street.

CORRECT   Alexandra and I found an old, rusty bicycle in the vacant lot down the street.

┌**HELP**──

Use a semicolon rather than a comma between phrases in a series when the phrases contain commas.

EXAMPLE
The three sections of this project will be due on Tuesday, March 3; on Thursday, March 19; and on Friday, April 3.

Reference Note
For more information about **semicolons,** see page 325.

SKILLS FOCUS

Use commas correctly to separate items in a series.

MECHANICS

To see whether a comma is needed between two adjectives, insert *and* between the adjectives (*tall and pine,* for example). If *and* sounds awkward there, do not use a comma.

Another test you can use is to switch the order of the adjectives. If the sentence still makes sense when you switch them, use a comma.

Sometimes the last adjective in a series is thought of as part of the noun. In that case, do not use a comma before the last adjective.

EXAMPLES The tall pine tree [not *tall, pine tree*] swayed.

Kimchi is a spicy Korean dish [not *spicy, Korean dish*] made with pickled cabbage.

(Exercise 4) **Proofreading Sentences for the Correct Use of Commas**

For each of the following sentences, write the word that should be followed by a comma; then, add the comma. If a sentence is already correct, write *C*.

EXAMPLE 1. Mrs. Hirata taught us several beautiful old Japanese folk songs.

1. *beautiful,*

1. His calm wrinkled face told a story.
2. François Toussaint L'Ouverture was a brilliant patriotic Haitian leader.
3. The huge lively wriggling kingfish dropped from the hook.
4. There's a sleek shiny bicycle in the store window.
5. The sound of the soft steady rain put me to sleep.
6. We read Chief Black Hawk's moving farewell speech.
7. I washed my hands in the cold clear spring water.
8. May I please have some of that spicy delicious soup?
9. The old diary had ragged yellowed pages.
10. The crowded dining room is filled with people celebrating my parents' anniversary.

Compound Sentences

12h. Use a comma before *and, but, for, nor, or, so,* or *yet* when it joins independent clauses in a compound sentence.

EXAMPLES Theo will bring the potato salad, and Sarah will bring the apple juice.

Congress passed the bill, but I believe the president vetoed it.

I went to bed early, for I had a big day ahead of me.

Think as a
Reader/Writer

In your reading, you may see very short compound sentences that do not use commas.

EXAMPLE
I'm tired and I'm hungry.

However, a comma before a conjunction in a compound sentence is always correct.

NOTE Do not confuse a compound sentence with a simple sentence containing a compound verb. No comma is needed between the parts of a compound verb.

| COMPOUND SENTENCE | We ran relay races first, and then we ate lunch. |
| SIMPLE SENTENCE | We ran the relay races first and then ate lunch. [The sentence contains a compound verb.] |

However, a compound verb made up of three or more verbs generally does require commas.

EXAMPLE   We **ran** the relay races**,** **ate** lunch**,** and then **prepared** for the individual races.

Reference Note

For more information on **compound sentences,** see pages 440 and 143. For more information on **compound verbs,** see page 60.

Exercise 5 **Correcting Compound Sentences by Adding Commas**

Some of the following sentences are compound and need to have commas added. If a sentence needs a comma, write the word or numeral before the missing comma; then, add the comma. If a sentence is already correct, write *C*.

EXAMPLE   **1.** The storm brought heavy rain but a tornado did the most damage.

   1. *rain,*

1. At the Native American Heritage Festival, Mary Johns wove baskets from sweet grass and Alice Billie made rings from beads.
2. The sailboat was almost hidden by the fog yet we could see part of the mast.
3. German Silva of Mexico was the fastest male runner in the 1994 and 1995 New York City Marathons and Tegla Loroupe of Kenya was the female winner in both races.
4. Would you like to play checkers or shall we go to the lake instead?
5. I called my friends and told them the news.
6. Jim practiced the piano piece all month for he wanted to do well at the recital.

SKILLS FOCUS

Use commas correctly in compound sentences.

MECHANICS

7. Many people are used to celebrating New Year's Day on January 1 but the Chinese New Year begins between January 21 and February 19.
8. The lake contains fish and is home to several alligators.
9. The old oak tree shaded the house but the shade kept the grass from growing.
10. I wanted to buy a camera so I mowed yards in the neighborhood to earn extra money.

Interrupters

12i. Use commas to set off an expression that interrupts a sentence.

Two commas are used to set off an interrupting expression—one before and one after the expression.

EXAMPLES   My favorite gospel singers, BeBe and CeCe Winans, were on TV last night.

As you leave, Jesse, please close the door quietly.

Sometimes an "interrupter" comes at the beginning or the end of the sentence. In such cases, only one comma is needed.

EXAMPLES   Yes, I'll call back later.

How did you do in karate class today, Kami?

(1) Use commas to set off appositives and appositive phrases that are not necessary to the meaning of a sentence.

An *appositive* is a noun or a pronoun that identifies or describes another noun or pronoun beside it. An *appositive phrase* is an appositive with its modifiers.

EXAMPLES   A gymnast, **Mrs. Shaw,** will coach us. [The appositive *Mrs. Shaw* identifies the gymnast.]

This book is about geology, **the science of the earth and its rocks.** [*The science of the earth and its rocks* is an appositive phrase that identifies *geology*.]

Do not use commas when an appositive is necessary to the meaning of a sentence.

EXAMPLES My cousin Roberto lives in Puerto Rico. [I have more than one cousin and am using his name to identify which cousin I mean.]

The character Alice is based on Alice Liddell. [Alice is one of several characters; the appositive tells which character is meant.]

Exercise 6 Punctuating Appositives

Most of the following sentences contain at least one error in the punctuation of appositives and appositive phrases. Write each word that should be followed by a comma, and add the comma. If a sentence is already correct, write *C*.

EXAMPLE   **1.** Two cold drinks lemonade and punch were available to the guests.

1. *Two cold drinks, lemonade and punch, were available to the guests.*

1. The park a beautiful place for a party was lit by street-lights and had a bandstand.
2. Our hosts Mr. and Mrs. Worthington greeted us at the entrance.
3. Some of the men were wearing boaters straw hats popular at the time.
4. My friend Eliza Wolcott sat in the shade at our table.
5. Do you see an empty table a quiet place for conversation?
6. Somehow a puppy the pet of one of the guests got onto the dance floor.

Pierre Auguste Renoir, *Ball at the Moulin de la Galette* (1876). Paris, Musée d'Orsay, Paris, Giraudon/Art Resource, New York.

7. Edward Finch, the best dancer has his choice of partners.
8. Music mostly waltzes filled the air.
9. A young woman in a striped dress a new bride, is remembering her wedding.
10. Listen to laughter and lively conversation, the sounds of happy people.

MECHANICS

(2) Use commas to set off words used in direct address.

EXAMPLES Ms. Jacobs, please explain the assignment.

Do you know who Santa Anna was, Beth?

You're right, Inés, to say he was a Mexican general.

In the sentences above, the words *Ms. Jacobs, Beth,* and *Inés* are **nouns of direct address.** They identify the person or persons spoken to or addressed.

┌HELP──
Some sentences
in Exercise 7 need more
than one comma.

Exercise 7 Correcting Sentences by Adding Commas

For each of the following sentences, write each word that should be followed by a comma; then, add the comma.

EXAMPLE 1. Are you sure you left your book in the room James?

      1. room,

1. Michi will you read the haiku you wrote?
2. Carla please bring me the newspaper when you finish with it.
3. Did you bring the tickets Jorge?
4. After all the work we've done Ann it would be a shame to turn it in late.
5. If you mow the lawn Kelly I'll rake the clippings.
6. Please Mom can you drive me to rehearsal?
7. Mr. Ferguson you have a telephone call.
8. You are dismissed class.
9. How long have you worked here David?
10. The problem my friends is simply lack of effort.

Introductory Words, Phrases, and Clauses

12j. Use a comma after certain introductory elements.

(1) Use a comma after *yes, no,* or any mild exclamation such as *well* or *why* at the beginning of a sentence.

SKILLS FOCUS

Use commas correctly to
set off introductory
elements.

EXAMPLES **Yes,** you may use my pencil.

Why, it's Arthur!

Well, I think you should apologize.

MECHANICS

(2) Use a comma after two or more introductory preposi-tional phrases.

EXAMPLE   **In the valley at the base of the hill,** a herd of buffalo grazes.

Also, use a comma after a single long introductory prepositional phrase.

EXAMPLE   **On the winter morning when Kenan discovered the strange visitor,** the rosebush burst into bloom.

Use a comma after a single short introductory prepositional phrase when the comma is necessary to make the sentence clear.

CONFUSING   In the evening sunlight faded in the western sky.

CLEAR   **In the evening,** sunlight faded in the western sky.
[The comma is needed so that the reader does not read "evening sunlight."]

(3) Use a comma after an introductory adverb clause.

EXAMPLE   **After the show is over,** we will go out to eat.

NOTE An adverb clause that comes at the end of a sentence usually is not preceded by a comma.

EXAMPLE   We will go out to eat **after the show is over.**

Reference Note

For more about **prepositional phrases,** see page 109. For more about **adverb clauses,** see page 139.

Exercise 8 **Using Commas with Introductory Elements**

If a comma is needed in a sentence, write the word before the missing comma and add the comma. If a sentence is already punctuated correctly, write *C*.

EXAMPLE   **1.** After he left we noticed that his hat was on the table.
        1. *left,*

1. Before eating the birds were singing noisily.
2. On the table in the kitchen dinner was getting cold.
3. Although he trained hard for a month, Juan could not break his own record.
4. Yes that is a cardinal.
5. On her way to school in the morning Roseanne was thinking about her project.

6. When I have time on the weekends I like to hook rugs.
7. Well you had better make up your mind soon.
8. With the decorations in the living room in place Julie was ready for her mother's birthday party.
9. In the corner of the room a night light showed the way to the door.
10. Because the snow cover was so thin the deer had no trouble finding food.

Conventional Uses

12k. Use commas in certain conventional situations.

(1) Use commas to separate items in dates and addresses.

EXAMPLES   Bill Cosby was born on July 12, 1937, in Philadelphia, Pennsylvania.

Saturday, May 10, will be the day of the soccer playoff.

My aunt has lived at 41 Jefferson Street, Northfield, Minnesota, since 2008.

Notice that a comma separates the last item in a date or in an address from the words that follow it. However, a comma does not separate a month from a day (*July 12*) or a house number from a street name (*41 Jefferson Street*).

NOTE   No punctuation is used between the state abbreviation and the ZIP Code.

EXAMPLE   Cerritos, **CA 90701**

(2) Use a comma after the salutation of a personal letter and after the closing of any letter.

EXAMPLES   Dear Grandma and Grandpa,   Love,

Dear Tyrone,   Sincerely,

Exercise 9   **Using Commas Correctly in Conventional Situations**

Write the following items and sentences, inserting or deleting commas as needed.

TIPS & TRICKS

Business letters use a colon, not a comma, after the salutation.

EXAMPLE
Dear Ms. Hinojosa:

SKILLS FOCUS

Use commas correctly in conventional situations.

EXAMPLE   **1.** Friday February 11 is the first day of the fair.
            1. Friday, February 11, is the first day of the fair.

1. Yours truly
2. Shirley Chisholm was born on November 30 1924, in New York City.
3. The first female principal chief of the Cherokee Nation is Wilma Mankiller, who was born near Rocky Mountain Oklahoma.
4. Write to me at 327, Adams Way Darrouzett TX 79024.
5. The Harvest Carnival is on Friday October 30 2009.
6. Dear Uncle Sig
7. Address orders to Pretty Good Camping Supplies P.O. Box 528 Southborough, MA, 01772.
8. He made his stage debut on May, 25, 1928 in London England.
9. Friday July 6 2012 will be my grandparents' golden wedding anniversary.
10. The main office in Santa Barbara California has a new fax number.

┌─**HELP**─

Commas are also used in numbers greater than and including one thousand. Use a comma before every third digit to the left of the decimal point.

EXAMPLE
7,386,149.00 [seven million three hundred eighty-six thousand one hundred forty-nine]

Unnecessary Commas

12l. Do not use unnecessary commas.

Too much punctuation can be just as confusing as not enough punctuation, especially where the use of commas is concerned.

CONFUSING   My friend, Jessica, said she would feed my cat and my dog while I'm away, but now, she tells me, she will be too busy.

CLEAR   My friend Jessica said she would feed my cat and my dog while I'm away, but now she tells me she will be too busy.

Have a reason for every comma or other mark of punctuation that you use. When there is no rule requiring punctuation and when the meaning of the sentence is clear without one, do not insert any punctuation mark.

Use commas correctly.

Proofreading a Letter for the Correct Use of Commas

The sentences in the following letter each contain an error in the use of commas. Rewrite the letter, adding or deleting commas as needed.

EXAMPLES **[1]** July, 6, 2008
          1. *July 6, 2008*

          [2] Dear Tom
          2. *Dear Tom,*

Dear Tom,

   [1] Well on July 4, 2008, Aunt Lil kept her promise and took me up in her airplane. **[2]** Wow! What a view of the canyons valleys, and plateaus we had! **[3]** We flew over a hill, and saw a small herd of mustangs. **[4]** Aunt Lil circled above the horses and the plane's shadow frightened the stallion. **[5]** The whole herd stampeded with tails, and manes and hooves flying in a storm of dust all the way down into the valley. **[6]** One black colt trailed behind but his mother quickly nudged him onward. **[7]** In a moment the swift sturdy mustangs, descendants of the fiery steeds of the Spanish conquistadors, were galloping into the woods. **[8]** I wish you could have seen them Tom! **[9]** At least I remembered my camera so here is a picture of those beautiful horses.

                    [10] Yours truly

                    Sal

MECHANICS

Semicolons

A semicolon is part period and part comma. Like a period, it can separate complete thoughts. Like a comma, it can separate items within a sentence.

12m. Use a semicolon between parts of a compound sentence if they are not joined by *and, but, for, nor, or, so,* or *yet.*

EXAMPLES   Todd's report is about Arizona; mine is about Utah.

The rain clouds are moving in quickly; let's head home.

> NOTE   Use a semicolon to join independent clauses only if the ideas in the independent clauses are closely related. Otherwise, use a period to make two separate sentences.
>
> EXAMPLES   Do not touch that tree frog; it may be poisonous.
> [The two ideas are closely related.]
>
> Do not touch that tree frog. Everyone stay together.
> [The two ideas are not closely related.]

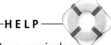

┌─HELP─

Use a semicolon rather than a comma between phrases in a series when the phrases contain commas.

EXAMPLE
The acrobats are traveling from Albuquerque, New Mexico; through Phoenix, Arizona; and finally to San Diego, California.

MECHANICS

(Exercise 10) **Proofreading Sentences for the Correct Use of Semicolons**

Most of the following sentences have commas where there should be semicolons. If a sentence needs a semicolon, write the words before and after the missing semicolon; then, insert the semicolon. If a sentence is already correct, write *C.*

EXAMPLE   **1.** Mary Vaux Walcott treasured her box of watercolor paints, she took it with her everywhere she went.

1. *paints; she*

1. As a young girl, she visited the Canadian Rockies each year, there she began to paint wildflowers.
2. She loved mountain climbing, she often crossed rugged areas to find new wildflowers.
3. She painted her flowers from life, for she did not like to rely on pencil sketches.
4. You can see five of her paintings on the next page, aren't they beautiful?

SKILLS FOCUS

Use semicolons correctly.
Use semicolons correctly in compound sentences.

5. Painting A shows a western red lily, such lilies wither quickly when picked.
6. Painting B is of a bottle gentian, a fall flower, it grows in bogs and swamps.
7. American wisteria is a climbing plant, and you can see in Painting C that it has many showy flowers.
8. Painting D shows blossoms of the American waterlily opening in early morning, their aroma draws insects.
9. Painting E is of Carolina jessamine, it spreads its fragrant flowers through treetops.
10. Mary Vaux Walcott is known as "the Audubon of North American wildflowers," for she painted more than seven hundred species.

A

B

C

D

E

Mary Vaux Walcott, *Bottle Gentian*. Watercolor. National Museum of American Art

MECHANICS

Colons

A colon usually signals that more information follows.

12n. Use a colon before a list of items, especially after expressions such as *the following* and *as follows*.

EXAMPLES   These are the winners of the poetry contest**:** Carmen Santiago, Justin Douglass, and Steven Yellowfeather.

Pack the following items for your overnight trip**:** a toothbrush, toothpaste, and your hairbrush.

The order of the colors seen through a prism is as follows**:** red, orange, yellow, green, blue, indigo, and violet.

> NOTE Do not use a colon between a preposition and its object or between a verb and its object. Either omit the colon or reword the sentence.
>
> INCORRECT   My report includes: a table of contents, three chapters, illustrations, and a list of sources.
>
> CORRECT   My report includes a table of contents, three chapters, illustrations, and a list of sources.
>
> CORRECT   My report includes **the following parts:** a table of contents, three chapters, illustrations, and a list of sources.

Colons may also be used to introduce long, formal statements and quotations.

EXAMPLE   Mark Twain had a very definite opinion on happiness**:** "The best way to cheer yourself is to try to cheer somebody else up."

12o. Use a colon between the hour and the minute when you write the time.

EXAMPLES   8**:**55 A.M.   9**:**15 P.M.   6**:**22 this morning

12p. Use a colon after the salutation of a business letter.

EXAMPLES   Dear Sir or Madam**:**   Dear Mrs. Jordan**:**

Dear Sales Manager**:**   To Whom It May Concern**:**

MECHANICS

TIPS & TRICKS

Personal letters use a comma, not a colon, after the salutation.

EXAMPLE
Dear John**,**

SKILLS FOCUS

Use colons correctly. Use colons correctly to introduce a list of items. Use colons correctly to introduce a long, formal statement. Use colons correctly to introduce a quotation. Use colons correctly in conventional situations.

Exercise 11 **Using Colons Correctly**

Most of the following items contain an error in the use of colons. Rewrite each incorrect sentence to correct the error. If a sentence is already correct, write *C*.

EXAMPLE   **1.** Bring the following items to class your notebook, a pencil, and your textbook.

       1. Bring the following items to class: your notebook, a pencil, and your textbook.

1. We visited the following cities Bayamón, Ponce, and San Juan.
2. A good baby sitter should have the following qualities promptness, reliability, an interest in children, and common sense.
3. To stay healthy, you should not smoke or chew tobacco.
4. Add these items to your shopping list tissues, toothpaste, and shampoo.
5. A good friend should be: loving, loyal, and honest.
6. The first bell rings at 8 10 A.M., and the second bell rings twenty minutes later.
7. Your homework includes: your spelling worksheet, one chapter of reading, and a rough draft of your English composition for Monday.
8. The recipe for Brunswick stew called for these ingredients lamb, carrots, potatoes, and onions.
9. Every time we see her, Grandmother likes to remind us of her favorite Ben Franklin saying "Whatever is begun in anger ends in shame."
10. Dear Sir or Madam

┌HELP─

Some of the sentences in Review D contain more than one punctuation error.

Review D **Proofreading a Letter for the Correct Use of Punctuation**

Proofread the following letter for errors in punctuation. Then, rewrite the letter, adding the necessary periods, question marks, commas, semicolons, and colons.

EXAMPLE   **[1]** 1200 E Halifax Avenue

       1. 1200 E. Halifax Avenue

[1]   January 11 2009

Superintendent of Schools
Baltimore City Board of Education
200 E. North Avenue
Baltimore, MD 21202

[2] Dear Superintendent

   [3] Would your students be interested in visiting an African American wax museum   **[4]** The only one of its kind is right here in Baltimore **[5]** The Great Blacks in Wax Museum features life-size wax models of famous African Americans **[6]** These wax images include leaders in education, civil rights and science **[7]** The museum displays statues of the following people Rosa Parks, Phillis Wheatley, Crispus Attucks, Carter G Woodson, Dred Scott, Harriet Tubman, Booker T. Washington, Frederick Douglass, and many others.

   [8] Our company offers students and teachers discount tours of the museum during Black History Month discount tours of other historic attractions are also available then **[9]** For more information, please call me between 8 30 A.M. and 5 30 P.M.

   [10]   Yours truly,

   Jane Lee Harper

   Jane Lee Harper
   President
   Uhuru Guided Tours

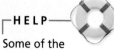

HELP

Some of the sentences in Review E contain more than one punctuation error.

Review E Using End Marks, Commas, Semicolons, and Colons Correctly

Each of the following items contains at least one error in the use of end marks, commas, semicolons, or colons. Rewrite the items, adding or changing punctuation to correct each error.

EXAMPLE
1. Mrs. Hunter how long will the leaves remain that color.

1. *Mrs. Hunter, how long will the leaves remain that color?*

1. Liechtenstein a country not quite as large as Washington, D.C. is one of the smallest countries in Europe
2. The students gathered signatures on a petition and a spokesperson presented their argument for better sidewalks.
3. That must be the biggest fish in the whole lake?
4. Did you find out which president created the Peace Corps in 1961.
5. Dear Sir
6. No I haven't seen that new movie but I've heard it's absolutely terrific.
7. Fort Sumter; the site of the first shots fired in the Civil War; is located in Charleston South Carolina.
8. After the sparrows finished in the birdbath they flew up to the feeder!
9. A long white shiny limousine pulled into the parking lot, after that came a bus and a police officer on a motorcycle.
10. Before you may read your mystery novel you must finish your homework clean your room and walk the dog.

Chapter Review

A. Using Punctuation Correctly

Periods, question marks, exclamation points, commas, semi-colons, and colons are missing in the following items. Write the word or numeral before each missing punctuation mark, and add the correct mark.

1. Flora please pass the pepper
2. Did Fred once work for Interactive Corp
3. We are learning about meteorology the study of weather
4. The shirts come in the following four colors blue green brown and red
5. Yasunari Kawabata won the 1968 Nobel Prize in literature he was the first Japanese writer to win the prize
6. Watch out
7. I wish I could go to camp this summer but I have to stay home because I caught chickenpox.
8. Dear Mom and Dad
9. I taught Zachary how to swim
10. While Dr Sanchez is on jury duty Dr Kelley is seeing his patients
11. My youngest sister was born on April 12 2007
12. She is a bright lively child
13. His address is 2330 River Rd Sterling VA 22170-2322
14. The Mandan and Hidatsa peoples in North Dakota harvested wild rice and they traded it for buffalo hides and dried meat
15. Have you ever been to Austin Texas
16. Well Eric my favorite actor is Denzel Washington
17. Tom Brokaw a former national newscaster was born in South Dakota
18. I get up at 6 00 A M. on school days
19. Yes a taco is a fried filled tortilla
20. The meeting will be held Sunday February 23 at 2 00 P M

B. Using Punctuation Correctly

Periods, question marks, exclamation points, commas, semicolons, and colons are missing in the following items. Write the word or numeral before each missing punctuation mark, and add the correct mark.

21. Wow Thanks for the new bike Grandpa.
22. What a friendly obedient dog you have
23. Dawn finished her report read the paper cooked dinner and set the table.
24. Can you tell me his address or should I ask someone else
25. Write to 637 West Elk Ave, Washington DC 20015-2602.
26. Our mechanic could not find anything wrong with the water pump the problem must be somewhere else.
27. Answer the following questions
    (1) Was Lincoln a successful leader
    (2) Could the Civil War have ended sooner
    (3) How important was the naval blockade
28. One of our troop leaders Ms. Wells is teaching us photography.
29. We'll need some minnows worms aren't good bait in salt water.
30. Ned the oldest in my family has many responsibilities.
31. Aren't you going to Glasgow Scotland this summer
32. She hid the lantern the keys two maps and the gold.
33. Before June 1 2008 I had never heard of Christine then she was on the front page of every paper.
34. Get those filthy muddy cowboy boots of yours out of this house now
35. Chiles rellenos are very spicy you'll like them.
36. Go to the cave build a fire and wait for Sabrina.
37. No Teresa there was no TV in those days.
38. Color this one yellow Mr Papastratos won't mind.
39. Let's finish this we'll see about starting something new tomorrow.
40. Dear Mr President

Writing Application
Using End Marks in a Screenplay

Kinds of Sentences   You are a scriptwriter for a popular TV show. You are writing a scene in which one of the characters wins one million dollars in a sweepstakes. Write down the character's response to the good news. Use a variety of end marks to help express the character's feelings.

Prewriting   First, you will need to make up a character or use one from a TV show you have seen. How would that person feel if he or she won a million dollars? Write down some notes on how you think your character would react.

Writing   Using your prewriting notes, write a draft of what your character will say. Make your draft at least one paragraph long. Use end punctuation to help express the character's emotions.

Revising   Read your character's response aloud. Does it sound realistic? Check to make sure you have used a variety of end marks to express your character's feelings.

Publishing   Check your writing for any errors in grammar, spelling, and punctuation. In small groups, exchange papers with another student. Take turns reading the papers to the group as if you each were one of the characters. Use the punctuation as a guide to what the character is feeling and to how you should read the response.

SKILLS FOCUS

Develop characters. Use end marks correctly.

MECHANICS

Million Dollar Sweepstakes

Date *September 10, 2009*

$ *1,000,000.00*

Pay to the order of *Winner*

One Million dollars and *00*/*100* ——— Dollars

Administrator

Punctuation

Underlining (Italics), Quotation Marks, Apostrophes, Hyphens

Diagnostic Preview

A. Proofreading Sentences for the Correct Use of Underlining (Italics) and Quotation Marks

Each of the following sentences contains at least one error in the use of underlining (italics) or quotation marks. Rewrite each sentence correctly.

EXAMPLE　**1.** The recent movie of Shakespeare's "Hamlet" is true to the original play.

　　　　　1. The recent movie of Shakespeare's <u>Hamlet</u> is true to the original play.

1. "The next short story we will be reading is called *All Summer in a Day*," Mr. Willis told us.
2. My younger brother learned how to play the song Yesterday on the piano.
3. Isn't your favorite poem The Unicorn?
4. "Wasn't that a song? asked Carrie."
5. I think a folk singer wrote it, answered Tony.

6. Juanita said that "she would hum a bit of it."
7. Brad commented, "I think my parents have a copy of it".
8. "Can you bring it to class"? Elena asked.
9. "Who said, Time is money"? Gerald asked.
10. "Benjamin Franklin wrote it," answered Karen, "in a book called Advice to a Young Tradesman."
11. "I think, said Theo, that you're right."
12. "Into the Woods" is a musical comedy in which characters from several different fairy tales meet in the same forest.
13. Kelly's favorite episode of *The Simpsons* is titled Bart of Darkness.
14. Sean often wonders what makes van Gogh's painting "Twelve Sunflowers in a Vase" so interesting.
15. Melba built a model of the Merrimack for extra credit in social studies.

B. Proofreading Sentences for the Correct Use of Apostrophes and Hyphens

Each of the following sentences contains at least one error in the use of apostrophes or hyphens. Rewrite each sentence correctly.

EXAMPLE   1. We havent finished dinner yet.
          1. *We haven't finished dinner yet.*

16. My teachers house is being painted.
17. Each classroom has thirty four desks.
18. This recipe I'm trying calls for fresh greens, potatoes, car rots, and onions.
19. The assembly then featured a speech by the new president elect of the student council.
20. Whos going to sample this dish?
21. Dont forget the soy sauce.
22. The three chefs recipes were prepared by the chefs themselves on television.
23. Jiro's last name has two *l*s.
24. Have you tried those new fat free potato chips?
25. In the quiet early evening, we could hear the flapping of the geeses wings.

Underlining (Italics)

COMPUTER TIP

If you use a computer, you can set words in italics yourself. Most fonts can be set in italic type.

Italics are printed letters that lean to the right—*like this.* When you handwrite or type, you show that a word should be italicized by underlining it. If your writing were printed, the typesetter would set the underlined words in italics. For example, if you wrote

Zora Neale Hurston wrote Mules and Men.

the sentence would be printed like this:

    Zora Neale Hurston wrote *Mules and Men.*

13a. Use underlining (italics) for titles and subtitles of books, plays, periodicals, films, television series, works of art, and long musical works.

TIPS & TRICKS

Generally, use italics for titles of works that stand alone, such as books, CDs, and television series. Use quotation marks for titles of works that are usually part of a larger work, such as short stories, songs, and episodes of a television series.

Reference Note

For examples of **titles that require quotation marks** instead of italics, see page 343.

SKILLS FOCUS

Use italics correctly. Punctuate titles correctly.

Type of Name	Examples
Books	*Number the Stars* *To Kill a Mockingbird* *Tibet: Through the Red Box*
Plays	*Song of Sheba* *Romeo and Juliet* *Life with Father*
Periodicals	*Sioux City Journal* *The Dallas Morning News* *Highlights for Children*
Films	*Babe: Pig in the City* *The Wizard of Oz* *Oliver & Company*
Television Series	*Under the Umbrella Tree* *Fun with Watercolors* *Reading Rainbow*

MECHANICS

Type of Name	Examples
Works of Art	*The Old Guitarist* *Mona Lisa* *Confucius and Disciples*
Long Musical Works	*The Pirates of Penzance* *The Nutcracker Suite* *A Little Night Music*

NOTE An article (*a, an,* or *the*) before the title of a magazine or a newspaper is not italicized or capitalized when it is part of a sentence rather than part of the title.

EXAMPLES   I deliver **the** *Evening Independent.* [*The* is part of the sentence, not part of the title.]

Is that the latest issue of ***The*** *New Yorker*? [*The* is part of the magazine's title.]

13b. Use underlining (italics) for names of trains, ships, aircraft, and spacecraft.

Type of Name	Examples
Trains	*Stourbridge Lion* *Best Friend of Charleston* *The City of New Orleans*
Ships	*Lusitania* *Flying Cloud* USS *Lexington*
Aircraft	*Solar Challenger* *Hindenburg* *Spirit of St. Louis*
Spacecraft	*Landsat-7* *Discovery* *Enterprise*

┌HELP────
If you are not sure whether an article is part of a title, check the periodical's masthead (the section that lists the publisher, owners, editors, etc.) or the table of contents to find out the official title.

MECHANICS

SKILLS FOCUS
Use italics correctly.

Now and then, writers will use italics (underlining) for emphasis, especially in written dialogue. Read the following sentences aloud. Notice that by italicizing different words, the writer can change the meaning of the sentence.

EXAMPLES
"Are you going to wear the *red* shoes?" asked Ellen. [Will you wear the red shoes, not the blue ones?]

"Are *you* going to wear the red shoes?" asked Ellen. [Will you, not your sister, wear them?]

"Are you going to *wear* the red shoes?" asked Ellen. [Will you wear them, or are you just trying them on?]

Italicizing (underlining) words for emphasis is a handy technique that should not be overused. It can quickly lose its impact.

MECHANICS

For each of the following sentences, write each word or item that should be printed in italics and underline it.

EXAMPLE   1. We saw Rodin's famous statue The Thinker.

1. *The Thinker*

1. The magazine Popular Science reports news about science.
2. Have you ever seen the movie The Shaggy Dog?
3. My favorite painting is Morning of Red Bird by Romare Bearden.
4. The Wright brothers built their first airplane, the Flyer, in 1903.
5. We read the play You're a Good Man, Charlie Brown.
6. On his famous voyage in 1492, Christopher Columbus acted as captain of the ship named the Santa Maria.
7. Which newspaper do you read, the Chicago Sun-Times or the Chicago Tribune?
8. My sister watches Sesame Street every day.
9. Aboard Vostok 1, Yuri A. Gagarin orbited Earth.
10. The book Stuart Little is by E. B. White.

Quotation Marks

13c. Use quotation marks to enclose a ***direct quotation***—a person's exact words.

Be sure to place quotation marks both before and after a person's exact words.

EXAMPLES   Our team leader says, **"**I try to practice every day.**"**

"Let's go home,**"** Jeanne suggested.

Do not use quotation marks for an ***indirect quotation***—a rewording of a direct quotation.

DIRECT QUOTATION   Juan said, **"**The bus is late.**"** [Juan's exact words]

INDIRECT QUOTATION   Juan said that the bus was late. [not Juan's exact words]

SKILLS FOCUS

Use quotation marks correctly.

| DIRECT QUOTATION | Juan asked, "Is the bus late?" [Juan's exact words] |
| INDIRECT QUOTATION | Juan asked whether the bus was late. [not Juan's exact words] |

13d. A directly quoted sentence begins with a capital letter.

EXAMPLES Mrs. Talbott said, "**P**lease get a pencil."

Kristina asked, "**I**s it my turn?"

13e. When an expression identifying the speaker interrupts a quoted sentence, the second part of the quotation begins with a lowercase letter.

EXAMPLE "Will you take care of my lawn and my pets," asked Mr. Franklin, "**w**hile I'm on vacation next month?"

When the second part of a divided quotation is a new sentence, it begins with a capital letter.

EXAMPLE "Yes, we will," I said. "**W**e can use the extra money."

13f. A direct quotation can be set off from the rest of the sentence by a comma, a question mark, or an exclamation point, but not by a period.

(1) If a quotation comes at the beginning of a sentence, a comma, question mark, or exclamation point usually follows it.

EXAMPLES "Dogs make better pets than cats do**,**" said Frank.

"Have you ever had a cat**?**" Donna asked.

"No, and I never will**!**" he replied.

(2) If a quotation comes at the end of a sentence, a comma usually comes before it.

EXAMPLE Maria asked**,** "What makes you say that?"

(3) If a quoted sentence is divided, a comma usually follows the first part and comes before the second part.

EXAMPLE "Oh**,**" Donna commented**,** "he's probably just saying that because he's never had a cat."

HELP

If you need to add explanatory material to a direct quote, use brackets to show that the added material is not part of the original quote.

EXAMPLE

"When she [Christy Delano] made that shot, we shouted for joy!" her teammate said. [The name *Christy Delano* was added so that the reader would know to whom the pronoun *she* refers. The brackets show that the teammate did not say the name.]

HELP

To set off means "to separate."

MECHANICS

SKILLS FOCUS

Punctuate quotations correctly.

13g. A period or a comma should be placed inside the closing quotation marks.

EXAMPLE   "I can't wait to see Matthew Gierhart's new video," James said. "It's supposed to come out next week."

13h. A question mark or an exclamation point should be placed inside closing quotation marks when the quotation itself is a question or an exclamation. Otherwise, it should be placed outside.

EXAMPLES   "What time will you be home from work, Mom?" asked Michael. [The quotation is a question.]

Who said, "All the world's a stage"? [The sentence, not the quotation, is a question.]

"Stop!" yelled the crossing guard. [The quotation is an exclamation.]

What a surprise to hear Susana say, "We're moving back to Puerto Rico in June"! [The sentence, not the quotation, is an exclamation.]

Exercise 2 **Punctuating and Capitalizing Quotations**

Rewrite the following sentences, using commas, end marks, quotation marks, and capital letters where they are needed. If a sentence is already correct, write *C*.

EXAMPLE   1. We're going tubing next Saturday said Carlos.
1. *"We're going tubing next Saturday," said Carlos.*

1. May I go with you I asked.
2. We'd like to go, too added Barbara and Tranh.
3. Barbara asked who will bring tubes for everyone
4. Jim said I'll bring them
5. I offered to bring sandwiches and lemonade.
6. My dad will drive said Carlos he has a van.
7. Tranh told us that the river is fed by a glacier.
8. That means said Barbara that the water will be cold.
9. It should feel good I pointed out if Saturday is as hot as today is.
10. Carlos told all of us to meet him at his house at 8:30 A.M.

MECHANICS

Exercise 3 **Punctuating and Capitalizing Quotations**

Rewrite each of the following sentences correctly, using punctuation and capitalization as needed.

EXAMPLE
1. Clementine Hunter was born in 1887 said María and she died in 1988.

1. *"Clementine Hunter was born in 1887," said María, "and she died in 1988."*

1. Staci said here is a photograph of this self-taught American artist.
2. Clementine Hunter was born in Natchitoches, Louisiana Staci remarked.
3. She started working on a plantation when she was only fourteen María added.
4. When she was fifty-three years old said Staci Hunter decided to do what she loved most—paint.
5. Staci continued she began painting on almost any surface that would hold the paint!
6. Her early pieces were painted on brown paper bags and cardboard boxes María remarked and then on canvas, wood, and paper.
7. Hunter used bright colors Mike explained to paint everyday scenes like this one, called *Wash Day.*
8. It may surprise you to learn added Mike that her paintings sold for as little as twenty-five cents fifty years ago!
9. María asked Mike didn't you say that her paintings are now worth thousands of dollars?
10. Moreover Staci concluded Clementine Hunter's paintings have been exhibited throughout the United States.

Clementine Hunter (c.1945). Photo from the Mildred Bailey Collection, Natchitoches, Louisiana.

Clementine Hunter, *Wash Day.* The collection of Thomas N. Whitehead, courtesy of the Association for the Preservation of Historical Natchitoches, Louisiana, Melrose Plantation.

Revising Indirect Quotations to Create Direct Quotations

Revise each of the following sentences to change the indirect quotation to a direct quotation. Be sure to use capital letters and punctuation marks where they are needed.

EXAMPLE   1. I asked the cashier for change for a dollar.
           1. *"May I please have change for a dollar?" I asked the cashier.*

┌─H E L P─────
You will need
to change some pronouns
and verb forms in Exercise 4.

1. The cashier replied that she was not allowed to make change unless a purchase was made.
2. I said that I needed a new pen.
3. The cashier told me that it cost seventy-nine cents.
4. I said that I would give her $1.79.
5. She told me she could give me change for a dollar.
6. The cashier asked how I wanted the change.
7. I said that three quarters, two dimes, and a nickel would be good.
8. She replied that she did not have any more dimes in her cash register.
9. Then I said that I would gladly take four quarters.
10. She said that was okay but asked why I wanted change.

13i. **When you write dialogue (conversation), begin a new paragraph every time the speaker changes.**

EXAMPLE   In Khanabad, Mulla Nasrudin was sitting in a tea house when a stranger walked in and sat down beside him.
            The newcomer said:
            "Why is that man over there sobbing his heart out?"
            "Because I have just arrived from his hometown and told him that all his winter camel fodder was lost in a fire."
            "It is terrible to be a bearer of such tidings," said the stranger.
            "It is also interesting to be the man who will shortly tell him the good news," said Nasrudin. "You see, his camels have died of a plague, so he will not need the fodder after all."

            Idries Shah, "Camel Fodder"

SKILLS FOCUS

Use quotation marks correctly. Punctuate dialogue correctly.

13j. When a quotation consists of several sentences, put quotation marks only at the beginning and the end of the whole quotation.

EXAMPLE "Will Bao help with the play? Zachary has offered to make costumes," Aaron said.

13k. Use single quotation marks to enclose a quotation within a quotation.

EXAMPLE "Mrs. Engle distinctly said, 'Your book reports are due Thursday,'" Krista told me.

13l. Use quotation marks to enclose the titles of short works such as short stories, poems, newspaper or magazine articles, songs, episodes of television series, and chapters and other parts of books.

Type Of Name	Examples
Short Stories	"The Stone" "All Summer in a Day"
Poems	"Jetliner" "Song of the Sky Loom"
Articles	"Celebrating Our Heritage" "The Giants of Easter Island"
Songs	"Georgia on My Mind" "America the Beautiful"
Episodes of Television Series	"Kali the Lion" "The Trouble with Tribbles"
Chapters and Other Parts of Books	"Energy from the Stars" "I Go to Sea"

NOTE Titles that appear in quotation marks are set in single quotation marks when they appear within a quotation.

EXAMPLE Kris said, "Our class learned 'America the Beautiful' today."

TIPS & TRICKS

In general, the title of a work that can stand alone (for instance, a novel, a TV series, a collection of poems) is in italics. The title of a work that is usually part of a collection or series (for instance, a chapter of a book, an episode of a television series, a poem) is in quotation marks.

Reference Note

For examples of **titles that require italics** instead of quotation marks, see page 336.

SKILLS FOCUS

Use quotation marks correctly. Punctuate quotations correctly. Punctuate titles correctly.

MECHANICS

Exercise 5 Punctuating Quotations and Titles

Rewrite the following sentences, adding single and double quotation marks where they are needed.

EXAMPLE 1. I just finished the chapter The Circulatory System in our health book, Dell told me.

1. "I just finished the chapter 'The Circulatory System' in our health book," Dell told me.

1. Diane is learning the song This Little Rose for her recital.
2. Angelo, can we meet after school tomorrow? We need to practice our presentation, Sam said.
3. I'm sure I heard the announcer say, Schools are closed because of the storm, I said.
4. I can pronounce all the words in Lewis Carroll's poem Jabberwocky, Nina told Lou.
5. Ted said, My dad will pick us up on Saturday at 7:30 A.M. After the race, he is taking us to Lucy Chang's for lunch. Do you like Chinese food?
6. The weather should be nice tomorrow. Let's plan on hiking in the woods, Eric said.
7. Mrs. Banister said, The Fun They Had is a good short story, don't you think?
8. Have you read The Toaster? Sue May asked. It's the funniest poem I know.
9. One article in the newspaper this morning is titled Black Scientists Make History.
10. Strong's new song is Be True, Not Blue, and it's great! Marcie said.

Review A Punctuating Paragraphs in a Dialogue

Rewrite the following paragraphs, using capital letters as well as quotation marks and other marks of punctuation where they are needed.

EXAMPLE [1] What are you writing my grandfather asked.

1. "What are you writing?" my grandfather asked.

[1] Grandpa I said I'm writing a report about your hero, Octaviano Larrazolo. Can you tell me how he helped Mexican Americans?

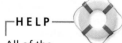
┌HELP
All of the punctuation marks already in Review A are correct.

[2] Grandpa got out his scrapbook. Octaviano did many things for our people he began. In 1912, New Mexico became a state. Octaviano and other Hispanic leaders wanted to be sure that Mexican Americans could hold political office. They wanted to make certain that they would always be allowed to vote. When New Mexico's new constitution was written, Octaviano and the other leaders fought for these rights.

[3] How did Mr. Larrazolo know how to protect the rights of people? I said.

[4] Grandpa replied he had studied law. His knowledge of the law helped him understand the constitution. It also helped him later when he became interested in politics.

[5] When did Mr. Larrazolo become involved in politics I asked.

[6] In 1916, he campaigned for Ezequiel Cabeza de Baca for governor said Grandpa. De Baca was elected, but he died a month later. Another election was held, and Larrazolo became New Mexico's governor.

[7] I asked what are some things that Mr. Larrazolo felt strongly about?

[8] He answered Octaviano believed that public schools should teach children about Mexican American culture. He also was in favor of both English and Spanish being spoken in schools. Here is a picture of him with his daughters.

Photo: Wesley Bradfield. Courtesy Museum of New Mexico, #47660.

[9] What else should I know about Octaviano Larrazolo I asked Grandpa.

[10] Octaviano was elected to the United States Senate in 1928 Grandpa said. He continued to work hard for the rights of Hispanic Americans until he died. If you want to read more about him, I have a copy of an article, Octaviano Larrazolo: New Mexico's Greatest Governor, here in my scrapbook.

Apostrophes

Possessive Case

The *possessive case* of a noun or a pronoun shows ownership or possession.

EXAMPLES   **Heidi's** comb   no **one's** fault

                his jacket   **two weeks'** vacation

                our dog   **my** stepbrother

13m. To form the possessive case of a singular noun, add an apostrophe and an *s.*

EXAMPLES   a student**'s** grant   Tanaka**'s** store

                the child**'s** toy   Tess**'s** painting

> NOTE   A proper noun ending in *–s* may take only an apostrophe to form the possessive case if adding *–'s* would make the name awkward to say.
>
> EXAMPLES   the Netherlands**'** climate
>
>   Ms. Andrews**'** class

Exercise 6   Using Apostrophes for Singular Possessives

For each of the following sentences, identify the word that needs an apostrophe. Then, correctly write the word.

EXAMPLE   1. Kenyans celebrate 1963 as the year of their countrys independence.

           1. *country's*

1. Soon that young nations athletes were setting records in international sports.
2. Leading Kenyas world-class distance runners was Kipchoge Keino, shown on the next page.
3. Keino increased his endurance by running many miles in his homelands mountains.
4. In 1965, he burst into his sports top ranks by setting world records for both the 3,000-meter and the 5,000-meter races.

MECHANICS

5. Training in the mountains helped Keino win a gold medal at Mexico Citys 1968 Olympics.

6. His record in that years 1,500-meter race stood until 1984.

7. In fact, the Kenyan teams runners took home a total of eight medals in 1968.

8. In the 1972 Olympics, Keinos performance won him a second gold medal, this time for the 3,000-meter steeplechase.

9. A silver medal in the 1,500-meter race marked his careers remarkable completion.

10. His victories won Keino the worlds praise and set new standards for all runners.

13n. To form the possessive case of a plural noun that does not end in *s*, add an apostrophe and an *s*.

EXAMPLES   geese**'s** feathers   men**'s** clothing

children**'s** books   feet**'s** bones

13o. To form the possessive case of a plural noun ending in *s*, add only the apostrophe.

EXAMPLES   boxes**'** lids   ten minutes**'** time

beetles**'** shells   the Ozawas**'** address

NOTE   In general, you should not use an apostrophe to form the plural of a noun.

INCORRECT   Two boy's left their books here.

CORRECT   Two **boys** left their books here.

 (side bar label)

MECHANICS

Reference Note

For information about **using apostrophes to form the plurals of letters, numerals, symbols, and words used as words,** see page 353.

> **Exercise 7**   **Writing Plural Possessives**

For each of the following sentences, identify the word that needs an apostrophe. Then, correctly write the word.

EXAMPLE   **1.** Wild creatures survival depends on their ability to adapt.

1. creatures'

1. Animals ways of dealing with cold are fascinating.

SKILLS FOCUS

Use apostrophes correctly in possessives.

2. At night, chickadees feathers are fluffed over the soft down next to their skin.
3. In addition, the birds breathing rates and heartbeats slow, and their body temperatures fall, saving energy.
4. Deers winter coats, made of hollow hairs filled with air, keep body heat from escaping.
5. Soft undercoats of fine hair are many animals thermal underwear.
6. In the picture on the left, you can see how squirrels tails, flattened against their backs and necks, keep them warm when they leave their nests.

7. The picture on the right shows how red foxes tails are used as muffs curled around their heads while they sleep.
8. On grouses toes are comblike structures that make walking in snow easier.
9. In cold weather, fur grows on the bottom of snowshoe hares feet for protection.
10. Some wild creatures survival during freezing temperatures and snow depends on traits like these.

Review B Writing Possessives

Rewrite each of the following expressions by using the possessive case. Be sure to add apostrophes where they are needed.

EXAMPLE   1. the speeches of the politicians
          1. *the politicians' speeches*

1. the books of the children

2. the prize of the winner
3. the bed of the kittens
4. the home of my friend
5. the streets of the city
6. the fish of the teacher
7. the cars of the women
8. the dens of the foxes
9. the fables of Aesop
10. the medal of Rowan
11. the hiding place of the mice
12. the idea of the boss
13. the plans of the builders
14. the diet of moose
15. the climate of the Cook Islands
16. the lawnmower of the Barkers
17. the shoes of the girls
18. the elephants of the zoo
19. the roads of the cities
20. the computer of the company
21. the desks of the students
22. the driveway of the neighbor
23. the tail of the dog
24. the stories of Mark Twain
25. the history of Texas

13p. Do not use an apostrophe with possessive personal pronouns.

EXAMPLES   Is this pencil **yours** or **mine**?

Our apartment is smaller than **theirs.**

Her enchiladas are spicier than **his.**

13q. To form the possessive case of many indefinite pronouns, add an apostrophe and an *s.*

EXAMPLES   either's topic

everyone's favorite

somebody's notebook

Reference Note

For more information about **possessive personal pronouns,** see page 223. For more information about **indefinite pronouns,** see page 80.

SKILLS FOCUS

Use apostrophes correctly in possessives.

MECHANICS

Rewrite each of the following expressions by using the possessive case. Be sure to add apostrophes where they are needed.

EXAMPLE   **1.** the speeches of everybody

       1. everybody's speeches

1. the wishes of everyone
2. the fault of him
3. the answer of no one
4. the album of someone
5. the guess of me
6. the job of neither
7. the color of something
8. the deal of anyone
9. the sweaters of them
10. the notebook of you

Think as a
Reader/Writer

Some people consider contractions informal. Therefore, it is generally best not to use them in formal writing and speech.

Contractions

13r. Use an apostrophe to show where letters, numerals, or words have been left out in a contraction.

A *contraction* is a shortened form of a word, a numeral, or a group of words. The apostrophe in a contraction shows where letters, numerals, or words have been left out.

Common Contractions			
I am	I'm	they have	they've
2009	'09	here is	here's
let us	let's	you are	you're
of the clock	o'clock	she is	she's
movie is	movie's	Bill has	Bill's
he would	he'd	you will	you'll

The word *not* can be shortened to *n't* and added to a verb. The spelling of the verb usually does not change.

SKILLS FOCUS

Use apostrophes correctly in contractions.

EXAMPLES	is not . . . . isn*t	has not . . . . hasn*t
	are not . . . . aren*t	have not . . . . haven*t
	does not. . . . . doesn*t	had not. . . . . hadn*t
	do not . . . . don*t	should not . . . . shouldn*t
	was not . . . . . . wasn*t	would not . . . . wouldn*t
	were not . . . . weren*t	could not . . . . . . couldn*t
EXCEPTIONS	will not . . . . . . **won*t**	cannot. . . . . **can*t**

Do not confuse contractions with possessive pronouns.

Contractions	Possessive Pronouns
It*s [*It is*] raining. **It*s** [*It has*] been a long day.	**Its** tires are flat.
Who*s [*Who is*] your coach? **Who*s** [*Who has*] been in my room?	**Whose** watch is this?
You*re [*You are*] welcome.	**Your** sister won.
They*re [*They are*] late.	**Their** house is next door.
There*s [*There is*] the bell.	That car is **theirs.**

Exercise 9 **Using Apostrophes in Contractions**

For the following sentences, write the word or numeral that requires an apostrophe and insert the apostrophe. If a sentence is already correct, write *C*.

EXAMPLE   **1.** Well be leaving soon.
            1. We'll

1. Youve been a big help.
2. Youd better hurry up.
3. Whose umbrella is this?
4. Were having a fund-raiser for the homeless.
5. I cant find my skateboard.
6. He promised hed wear his seat belt.
7. Lets get tickets to see the concert.

MECHANICS

8. Its time to leave for the party.
9. Its wings are painted blue.
10. Ill wash the car tomorrow morning.
11. Daniel asked the decoration committee whos going to be in charge.
12. Isnt this the book we need?
13. Remember to give your dog fresh water.
14. Stephanie said shell bring a cardboard box from home.
15. This is a picture of my parents in 99, the year before my half-brother was born.
16. If that hummingbird returns to the feeder, Im going to take a picture.
17. Theirs will be the last band to perform.
18. The cold weather doesnt bother Jeremy much.
19. We should be back to school by three o clock.
20. Have you found out yet if youre on the team?

Exercise 10 Writing Contractions

For each of the following sentences, write the contraction of the italicized word or words.

EXAMPLE   1. *We will* see a performance of the puppet theater when we visit the Japan America Theatre in Los Angeles.

1. *We'll*

1. *Have not* you always wondered what goes on backstage at a puppet show?

2. *Here is* an illustration that takes you behind the scenes at a seventeenth-century puppet theater in Japan.

3. The audience *cannot* see all the backstage action because of the curtain.

4. The men *who are* handling the puppets in the picture are very highly trained.

5. They *do not* speak the characters' lines, though.

6. *It is* the man sitting on the right on the platform who narrates the play.

7. As you can see, *he is* accompanied by a musician.

8. On the right are more puppets; *they have* been hung there for future use.

9. In the box at the top, *that is* the Japanese word that means "puppet."

10. As *you will* notice, the Japanese system of writing is very different from ours.

Plurals

13s. Use an apostrophe and an *s* to form the plurals of letters, numerals, and symbols, and of words referred to as words.

EXAMPLES   I think the word *Mississippi* has four *i*'s, four *s* 's, and two *p*'s.

Your *1*'s and *7* 's look alike.

You wrote +'s instead of *x*'s in these math problems.

Try not to use so many *you know* 's when you talk.

Exercise 11 **Forming Plurals by Using Apostrophes**

Correctly form the plural of each of the following items.

EXAMPLE   **1.** *9*
         1. 9's

1. *I*	**6.** #	**11.** *14*	**16.** *B*	**21.** $
2. *t*	**7.** *A*	**12.** %	**17.** *3*	**22.** *
3. @	**8.** *.com*	**13.** *at*	**18.** +	**23.** *uh oh*
4. *it*	**9.** *too*	**14.** ?	**19.** !	**24.** =
5. *6*	**10.** *thou*	**15.** *and*	**20.** *of*	**25.** /

MECHANICS

SKILLS FOCUS

Use apostrophes correctly.

Apostrophes   **353**

Hyphens

13t. Use a hyphen to divide a word at the end of a line.

When you divide a word at the end of a line, remember the following rules:

(1) Divide a word only between syllables.

INCORRECT	Uncle Payat, Aunt Nina, and Ayita will jou-rney eighty miles to join us.
CORRECT	Uncle Payat, Aunt Nina, and Ayita will jour-ney eighty miles to join us.

(2) Do not divide a one-syllable word.

INCORRECT	They are bringing a salad, ham, and rye bre-ad.
CORRECT	They are bringing a salad, ham, and rye bread.

(3) Do not divide a word so that one letter stands alone.

INCORRECT	Is that your family's brand-new car parked a-cross the street?
CORRECT	Is that your family's brand-new car parked across the street?

13u. Use a hyphen with compound numbers from *twenty-one* to *ninety-nine*.

EXAMPLE	Until 1959, the United States had only forty-eight stars in its flag.

13v. Hyphenate a compound adjective when it comes before the noun it modifies.

EXAMPLES	an activity that is well planned
	a **well-planned** activity
	a flavor that is long lasting
	a **long-lasting** flavor

Some compound adjectives are always hyphenated, whether they come before or after the nouns they modify.

Think as a *Reader/Writer*

Hyphens are often used in compound names. In such cases, the hyphen is thought of as part of the spelling of the name.

EXAMPLES

Margaret Bourke-White

Kung-sun Lung

Terry-Jo

Edward Levy-Lawson

If you are not sure whether a compound name is hyphenated, ask the person with that name, or look up the name in a reference source.

SKILLS FOCUS

Use hyphens correctly.

MECHANICS

EXAMPLES   a **brand-new** bicycle

              a bicycle that is **brand-new**

              an **up-to-date** encyclopedia

              an encyclopedia that is **up-to-date**

HELP

If you are not sure whether a compound adjective is always hyphenated, look up the word in a dictionary.

13w. Use a hyphen with the prefixes *all–, ex–, great–, self–,* and with the suffixes *–elect* and *–free.*

EXAMPLES   all-purpose   self-confidence

            ex-students   governor-elect

            great-grandfather   sugar-free

HELP

The prefix *half–* often requires a hyphen, as in *half-life, half-moon,* and *half-truth.* However, sometimes *half* is used without a hyphen, either as a part of a single word (*halftone, halfway, halfback*) or as a separate word (*half shell, half pint, half note*). If you are not sure how to spell a word containing *half,* look up the word in a current dictionary.

Exercise 12   **Using Hyphens Correctly**

Write each of the following words. Add hyphens to show where the word may be divided at the end of a line or where they are needed in a compound number or word. If a word should not be hyphenated, write *do not hyphenate.*

EXAMPLES   **1.** tomorrow

            1. to-mor-row

           2. thirty nine

            2. thirty-nine

           3. theme

            3. do not hyphenate

1. loose
2. twenty nine
3. temporary
4. self esteem
5. children
6. elect
7. principal
8. decorate
9. president elect
10. through
11. immediately
12. eighty three
13. seize
14. broomstick
15. great aunt
16. piano
17. preferred
18. grammar
19. lint free
20. among

MECHANICS

COMPUTER TIP

Some word-processing programs will automatically divide a word at the end of a line and insert a hyphen. Sometimes the program will divide a word at the wrong place. Always check a printout of your writing to see how the computer has hyphenated words at the ends of lines. If a hyphen is used incorrectly, move the word to the next line or divide the word yourself by correctly inserting a "hard" hyphen (one that the computer will not move).

Review C **Using Apostrophes and Hyphens Correctly**

Correctly write the word or letter that needs an apostrophe or a hyphen in each of the following sentences.

EXAMPLE   **1.** Wheres my history book?

　　　　　　1. Where's

1. Do you know where the atlases and the two diction aries are?
2. There are two *rs* in *tomorrow.*
3. The last speaker was the ex president of the Town Council.
4. The tiger cubs arent on view yet.
5. Is that one of Bessie Smiths songs?
6. Someone's gold bracelet is on the counter in the bath room.
7. Forty nine students signed the get-well card.
8. Is that salad dressing fat free?
9. Whos going to the fair this weekend?
10. Its almost time to leave.

Chapter Review

A. Using Underlining (Italics), Quotation Marks, Apostrophes, and Hyphens

Each of the following sentences contains at least one error in the use of underlining (italics), quotation marks, apostrophes, or hyphens. Write each sentence correctly.

1. While taking a bath, I like to sing This Land Is Your Land.
2. Washingtons largest city is named for Chief Seattle.
3. Chapter two is called *The Siamese Cat.*
4. I read Robert Louis Stevensons novel Treasure Island.
5. "I remember making a barometer in the fourth grade. "I had to start over twice before it would work," I said.
6. "Deva, will you please show me how to make a weather vane"? asked Todd.
7. "It took me only forty five minutes to make a sundial," Carlos remarked.
8. We built a model airplane, but it crashed on it's test flight.
9. All student's projects are due next Friday.
10. Raymond read a fascinating article called *The Standing Stones of Wales and Brittany.*
11. When in Corpus Christi, try to visit the USS "Lexington."
12. Which newspaper do you prefer, The New York Times or Newsday?
13. Next time, please be prompt, Joe, said Ms. Lomazzi as I walked through the door ten minutes late.
14. The childrens bikes were in the driveway.
15. "Everyones project must be in on time," Mrs. Tolliver said.
16. "Bill's exact words," said Sean, "were I'll be back at noon."
17. In his English class, my brother Julio is reading the Dylan Thomas poem Fern Hill.
18. Do you know the magazine "Highlights for Children"?
19. Please don't use so many *like*s when you speak.
20. Isn't twenty questions the average length for an exercise of this kind?

B. Revising Indirect Quotations to Create Direct Quotations

Revise each of the following sentences by changing the indirect quotation to a direct quotation. Be sure to use capital letters and punctuation marks where they are needed.

┌H E L P┐

You will need
to change some pronouns
and verb forms in Part B.

21. Our teacher warned us that we could not take any breaks during the exam.

22. Lisa said that she would call me at eight o'clock.

23. Mom told us not to be late.

24. The police officer asked us to wait behind the fence.

25. I asked the museum guard where the *Mona Lisa* was.

26. Taylor said that two hours should be long enough.

27. Stephanie replied that she would be in the city for five days.

28. Dr. Grizzard reminded us to take our vitamins every day.

29. Wendy asked her father if he would drive her to the library.

30. Giulio exclaimed happily that he had never been so surprised in his life.

C. Punctuating a Dialogue

Rewrite the following dialogue, using quotation marks and other marks of punctuation where they are needed. Remember to begin a new paragraph every time the speaker changes.

[**31**] Oh, Travis, said Lucy, when are you leaving? [**32**] I told you, Lucy, replied Travis. I'm planning to leave soon. At around ten o'clock. [**33**] Oh, said Lucy. Listen, Trav, I'm afraid I won't be able to come with you after all. Something has come up. [**34**] Well, Grandma will certainly be disappointed, remarked Travis. She's been looking forward to seeing her two grandkids on her birthday. [**35**] Yes, but that's just it, said Lucy. I haven't bought anything for her birthday yet. I just haven't had the time. [**36**] Well, guess what, Sis. I took care of that yesterday. Travis went over to the desk and took something out of the drawer. [**37**] Your present to Grandma is this framed photograph of me. [**38**] You're kidding, said Lucy. [**39**] And continued Travis, my present to her is this framed photograph of you. What do you think? [**40**] I think you're crazy, but we can discuss that on the way there. Let's go!

Writing Application
Using Apostrophes in a Letter

Contractions and Possessives   You have been so busy at summer camp that you have not had time to write to your best friend. Write your friend a letter telling about your first week at camp. Be sure to use apostrophes correctly to make your meaning clear.

Prewriting   If you have never been to a summer camp, ask a friend or relative who has been to one to tell you about it. Write down some notes on your activities at summer camp. Use your experience or your imagination to describe activities such as sports, crafts, and hiking trips. Also, make some notes about the camp itself.

Writing   Include specific details about the natural setting and special or daily activities at the camp. Tell your friend what you have enjoyed most. Try to give your friend a clear, vivid picture of your first week.

Revising   Ask a friend or a family member to read your letter. Can he or she imagine the activities you have described? If not, revise your letter to make it clearer and more descriptive.

Publishing   Be sure you have used the correct form for personal letters. As you proofread your letter, take extra care with apostrophes. Check your use of contractions and pronouns like *its, it's, your, you're, their,* and *they're*. Also, look for any other errors in grammar, spelling, and punctuation. Exchange letters with a classmate, and see how your camp experiences, real or imagined, are similar and how they are different.

Reference Note

For information about **writing a personal letter,** see "Writing" in the Quick Reference Handbook.

SKILLS FOCUS

Write a letter. Use apostrophes correctly in contractions. Use apostrophes correctly in possessives.

MECHANICS

14 Spelling

Improving Your Spelling

Diagnostic Preview

A. Proofreading Sentences for Correct Spelling

Correctly write the word that is misspelled in each of the following sentences.

EXAMPLE   1. The dog is diging in the flower garden again.
          1. *digging*

1. The children are happyest when swimming in the pool on a hot afternoon.
2. The porch chaires look newer than the tables.
3. Our nieghbor was born in Texas, I believe.
4. The Tolbys bought blueberrys for the party.
5. Uncle Steven is driveing through seven foreign countries on his trip.
6. Is the weather in Arizona ever changable?
7. Five womans auditioned for the leading role in the Broadway production.
8. Have you heard the tunful Peter, Paul, and Mary songs of the sixties?
9. Matthew and Kim bravly rescued the baby raccoon from the muddy ditch.
10. Would you kindly dig up the potatos and let them dry in the cellar?

B. Proofreading Sentences to Correct Spelling Errors

Choose the correct word or words from the choices in parentheses in each of the following sentences.

EXAMPLE   1. Please give (*you're, your*) book orders to me today.
          1. *your*

11. Angela is taking five (*courses, coarses*) this semester.
12. Nora said she was (*already, all ready*) for the banquet.
13. "Please pass me a (*peace, piece*) of bread," Gary said.
14. The (*altar, alter*) at the Spanish mission is marble.
15. The (*plain, plane*) to Ontario is ahead of schedule.
16. People often (*loose, lose*) pennies in stores and on streets.
17. We saw the (*principal, principle*) pass by twice.
18. Whose (*stationery, stationary*) has initials at the top?
19. (*There, Their*) shop sells shirts, dresses, and scarves.
20. "You'd better get these (*breaks, brakes*) fixed right away," the mechanic said.

Good Spelling Habits

The following techniques can help you spell words correctly.

1. **To learn the spelling of a word, pronounce it, study it, and write it.** Pronounce words carefully. Mistakes in speaking can cause mistakes in spelling. For instance, if you say *ad•je•tive* instead of *ad•jec•tive*, you will be more likely to spell the word incorrectly.

   - First, make sure that you know how to pronounce the word correctly, and then practice saying it.
   - Second, study the word. Notice any parts that might be hard to remember.
   - Third, write the word from memory. Check your spelling.
   - If you misspelled the word, repeat the three steps of this process until you can spell the word correctly.

2. **Use a dictionary.** If you are not absolutely sure about the spelling of a word, look it up in a dictionary. Do not guess about the correct spelling.

┌ **HELP** ┐
If you are not sure how to pronounce a word, look it up in a dictionary. In a dictionary, you will usually find the pronunciation given in parentheses after the word. The information in parentheses will show you the sounds used, the syllable breaks, and any accented syllables. A guide to the pronunciation symbols is usually found at the front of a dictionary.

SKILLS FOCUS

Use correct spelling. Use resources to find correct spellings.

MECHANICS

3. Spell by syllables. A *syllable* is a word part that can be pronounced as one uninterrupted sound.

EXAMPLES   ear•ly [two syllables]

av•er•age [three syllables]

Instead of trying to learn how to pronounce and spell a whole word, break it into its syllables whenever possible. It is easier to learn a few letters at a time than to learn all of them at once.

4. Keep a spelling notebook. Divide each page into four columns:

COLUMN 1   Correctly spell any word you have misspelled. (Never enter a misspelled word.)

COLUMN 2   Write the word again, dividing it into syllables and indicating which syllables are accented or stressed. (You will probably need to use a dictionary.)

COLUMN 3   Write the word once more, circling the spot that gives you trouble.

COLUMN 4   Write down any comments that might help you remember the correct spelling.

Here is an example of how you might make entries for two words that are often misspelled.

Correct Spelling	Syllables and Accents	Trouble Spot	Comments
answer	an´•swer	ans(w)er	Silent "w"
advertisement	ad´•ver•tise´•ment	advertis(e)ment	(Study rule 14e.)

5. Proofread for careless spelling errors. Re-read your writing carefully, and correct any mistakes and unclear letters. For example, make sure that your *i*'s are dotted, your *t*'s are crossed, and your *g*'s do not look like *q*'s.

Spelling Rules

ie and *ei*

14a. Write *ie* when the sound is long *e*, except after *c*.

EXAMPLES   ch**ie**f, bel**ie**ve, br**ie**f, rec**ei**ve, c**ei**ling

EXCEPTIONS   **ei**ther, n**ei**ther, prot**ei**n, s**ei**ze

    Write *ei* when the sound is not long *e*, especially when the sound is long *a*.

EXAMPLES   n**ei**ghbor, w**ei**gh, r**ei**ndeer, h**ei**ght, for**ei**gn

EXCEPTIONS   fr**ie**nd, f**ie**rce, anc**ie**nt, misch**ie**f

14
a

TIPS & TRICKS

This verse may help you remember the *ie* rule:
  I before *e*
  Except after *c*,
  Or when sounded like *a*,
  As in *neighbor* and *weigh*.
If you use this rhyme, remember that "*i* before *e*" refers only to words in which these two letters are in the same syllable and stand for the sound of long *e*, as in the examples under Rule 14a.

Exercise 1   Writing Words with *ie* and *ei*

Complete the following letter by adding *ie* or *ei* to each numbered word.

EXAMPLE   I wrote Aunt Hannah a **[1]** br____f thank-you note.
       1. brief

December 12, 2008

Dear Aunt Hannah,

    Thank you very much for the **[1]** sl___gh you recently sent me. I **[2]** rec___ved it on the **[3]** ___ghth of this month, just in time for our first big snowstorm. My new **[4]** fr___nds and I have great fun pulling each other across the **[5]** f___lds in it. The **[6]** n___ghbor's dog races alongside us, barking **[7]** f___rcely all the way.

    So far, I like living here in Vermont, but I can't quite **[8]** bel___ve how different everything is from life in California. Thank you again for your gift.
        Your loving **[9]** n___ce,

       Mai

P.S. If only we had some **[10]** r___ndeer to pull us!

MECHANICS

Prefixes and Suffixes

Prefixes

A **prefix** is a letter or a group of letters added to the beginning of a word to create a new word that has a different meaning.

14b. When adding a prefix to a word, do not change the spelling of the word itself.

EXAMPLES   dis + satisfy = dis**satisfy**

mis + lead = mis**lead**

un + done = un**done**

pre + view = pre**view**

a + typical = a**typical**

Exercise 2   Spelling Words with Prefixes

Combine each of the following prefixes and words to create a new word.

EXAMPLE   **1.** mis + place

1. *misplace*

1. fore + word
2. un + natural
3. in + dependent
4. mis + use
5. un + common

6. im + patient
7. pre + historic
8. mis + spell
9. dis + satisfied
10. re + assert

Exercise 3   Spelling Words with Prefixes

Create ten different words by combining the prefixes given below with the words listed beside them. (You may use a prefix or word more than once.) Check each of your new words in a dictionary. Then, use each word in a sentence.

Prefixes			Words			
un–	mis–	dis–	able	do	judge	place
pre–	over–	re–	cover	trust	pay	informed

EXAMPLE   *1. repay—I'll repay you when I get my allowance.*

MECHANICS

Suffixes

A *suffix* is a letter or a group of letters added at the end of a word to create a new word that has a different meaning.

14c. When adding the suffix *–ness* or *–ly* to a word, do not change the spelling of the word itself.

EXAMPLES   kind + ness = **kind**ness

                  tough + ness = **tough**ness

                  sincere + ly = **sincere**ly

                  slow + ly = **slow**ly

EXCEPTIONS   For most words that end in *y,* change the *y* to *i* before adding *–ly* or *–ness.*

                  happy + ly = happ**ily**

                  friendly + ness = friendl**iness**

14d. Drop the final silent *e* before adding a suffix that begins with a vowel.

Vowels are the letters *a, e, i, o, u,* and sometimes *y.* All other letters of the alphabet are *consonants.*

EXAMPLES   cause + ing = **caus**ing

                  reverse + ible = **revers**ible

                  strange + er = **strang**er

                  adore + able = **ador**able

MECHANICS

SKILLS FOCUS

Spell words with suffixes correctly.

PEANUTS reprinted by permission of United Feature Syndicate, Inc.

EXCEPTIONS Keep the silent e in words ending in *ce* and *ge* before adding a suffix beginning with *a* or *o*.

manage + able = manag**eable**

courage + ous = courag**eous**

notice + able = notic**eable**

14e. Keep the final silent e before adding a suffix that begins with a consonant.

EXAMPLES hope + less = hop**eless**

place + ment = plac**ement**

EXCEPTIONS argue + ment = argu**ment**

true + ly = tru**ly**

┌HELP────
Some words that end with a silent *e* can either keep the *e* or drop it when a suffix is added.

EXAMPLES
judge + ment = judg**ment** *or* judg**ement**

acknowledge + ment = acknowledg**ment** *or* acknowledg**ement**

love + able = lov**able** *or* lov**eable**

Exercise 4 Spelling Words with Suffixes

Combine each of the following words and suffixes to create a new word.

EXAMPLE **1.** sudden + ness

1. *suddenness*

1. active + ity
2. sure + ly
3. state + ment
4. locate + ion
5. courage + ous

6. silly + ness
7. suspense + ful
8. little + est
9. decorate + ed
10. trace + able

┌TIPS & TRICKS┐

When you proofread your own writing, you will find more spelling errors by looking at each word separately. To focus on each word, try using a piece of paper to hide some of the nearby words or lines. You can even cut a slit in a sheet of paper and move it over your writing to show just a few words at a time.

14f. For words that end in a consonant plus *y*, change the *y* to *i* before adding a suffix.

EXAMPLES cry + ed = cr**ied**   lonely + est = lonel**iest**

pretty + er = prett**ier**   lazy + ness = laz**iness**

EXCEPTION Keep the *y* if the suffix begins with an *i*.

carry + ing = carr**ying**

NOTE Keep the *y* if the word ends in a vowel plus *y*.

EXAMPLES stay + ed = sta**yed**   key + ed = ke**yed**

EXCEPTIONS day + ly = daily   pay + **ed** = paid

14g. Double the final consonant before adding *–ing*, *–ed*, *–er*, or *–est* to a one-syllable word that ends in a single vowel followed by a single consonant.

EXAMPLES   beg + ing = be**gging**   sad + er = sa**dder**

chat + ed = cha**tted**   big + est = bi**ggest**

When a one-syllable word ends in two vowels followed by a single consonant, do not double the consonant before adding *–ing*, *–ed*, *–er*, or *–est*.

EXAMPLES   sleep + ing = slee**ping**   cool + er = coo**ler**

treat + ed = trea**ted**   fair + est = fai**rest**

Exercise 5   **Spelling Words with Suffixes**

Combine each of the following words and suffixes to create a new word.

EXAMPLE   **1.** creep + er

     1. creeper

1. say + ing   **6.** beat + ing
2. slim + er   **7.** rely + ing
3. squeak + ing   **8.** easy + ly
4. rainy + est   **9.** chop + ed
5. steady + ness   **10.** play + ed

Review A   **Proofreading Sentences for Correct Spelling**

Most of the following sentences contain a misspelled word. Write each misspelled word correctly. If a sentence is already correct, write *C*.

EXAMPLE   **1.** My grandma often says, "Let sleepping dogs lie."

     1. sleeping

1. It's unnusual weather for this time of year.
2. In 1991, Lithuania regained its independence from the Soviet Union.
3. With Sacagawea's help, the explorers Lewis and Clark maped out the Northwest.
4. Now that Bao Duc is on the team, our hiting has improved.

┌─**HELP**─

In Review A, none of the proper nouns are misspelled.

SKILLS FOCUS

Spell words with suffixes correctly.

5. Serita and I can easyly make enough rice for the class.
6. We visited my grandmother in the Dominican Republic during the rainyest month of the year.
7. Please resstate the question.
8. My sister has the loveliest voice I've ever heard.
9. Former astronaut Sally Ride earned recognition for her courage and steadyness.
10. The temperature has droped at least ten degrees.

Review B Proofreading a Paragraph for Correct Spelling

For each sentence in the following paragraph, correctly write the word or words that are misspelled. If a sentence is already correct, write *C*.

┌─H E L P─┐

Some sentences in Review B contain more than one misspelled word.

EXAMPLE [1] My cousin Chris was very couragous after she was baddly hurt in a car accident.
1. *courageous; badly*

[1] After the accident, Chris found that she truely needed other people. [2] Her friends, family, and nieghbors gladly helped her. [3] However, Chris liked the idea of geting along on her own as much as she could, so she was disatisfied. [4] Fortunatly, she was able to join an exciting program called Helping Hands. [5] This program provides monkeys like this one as friends and helpers for people with disabilities. [6] Chris said that the baby monkeys are raised in loveing foster homes

for four years and then they go to Boston to recieve special training. [7] There, they learn how to do tasks on command, such as opening and closeing doors, turning lights on and off, and puting movies and music into a DVD or CD player. [8] Chris has been happyly working with her own monkey, Aldo, for six months now. [9] Aldo retreives anything that Chris has droped, works the TV remote control, and even scratches Chris's back when it itches! [10] Chris is always jokeing, "Pretty soon Aldo will be writting my book reports for me!"

MECHANICS

Forming the Plurals of Nouns

14h. Follow these rules for spelling the plurals of nouns:

(1) To form the plurals of most nouns, add *s*.

SINGULAR   snack   oven   Juliet   breeze   umbrella

  PLURAL   snack**s**   oven**s**   Juliet**s**   breeze**s**   umbrella**s**

> NOTE   Make sure that you do not confuse the plural form of a noun with its possessive form. In general, you should not use an apostrophe to form the plural of a word.
>
> INCORRECT   The boy's stayed after school for choir practice.
>
>   CORRECT   The **boys** stayed after school for choir practice.
>   [plural]
>
>   CORRECT   The **boys' choir** has practice today. [possessive]

(2) Form the plurals of nouns ending in *s, x, z, ch,* or *sh* by adding *es*.

SINGULAR   glass   fox   buzz   itch   bush   Jones

  PLURAL   glass**es**   fox**es**   buzz**es**   itch**es**   bush**es**   Jones**es**

Reference Note

For a discussion of **possessive forms of nouns**, see page 346. For information on using an apostrophe and an *s* to form **plurals of letters, numerals, symbols, and words used as words**, see page 353.

HELP

Some one-syllable words ending in *z* double the final consonant when forming plurals.

EXAMPLES
  quiz   fez
  qui**zz**es   fe**zz**es

Exercise 6   Spelling the Plurals of Nouns

Spell the plural form of each of the following nouns.

EXAMPLES   **1.** scratch
            1. scratches

            2. ax
            2. axes

1. night
2. dish
3. address
4. lens
5. box
6. branch
7. loss
8. peach
9. waltz
10. Smith

11. complex
12. faucet
13. cobra
14. doctor
15. ditch
16. Sanchez
17. tax
18. glue
19. occurrence
20. radish

MECHANICS

Spell regular and irregular plurals correctly.

(3) Form the plurals of nouns that end in a consonant plus *y* by changing the *y* to *i* and adding *es*.

SINGULAR	country	mummy	berry
PLURAL	countr**ies**	mumm**ies**	berr**ies**

EXCEPTION   With proper nouns, just add *s*.

the Shelby**s**   the Mabry**s**   the O'Grady**s**

(4) Form the plurals of nouns that end in a vowel plus *y* by adding *s*.

SINGULAR	boy	turkey	holiday	Riley
PLURAL	boy**s**	turkey**s**	holiday**s**	Riley**s**

(5) Form the plurals of nouns that end in a vowel plus *o* by adding *s*.

SINGULAR	rodeo	patio	kangaroo	Romeo
PLURAL	rodeo**s**	patio**s**	kangaroo**s**	Romeo**s**

(6) Form the plurals of nouns that end in a consonant plus *o* by adding *es*.

SINGULAR	tomato	echo	veto	torpedo
PLURAL	tomato**es**	echo**es**	veto**es**	torpedo**es**

EXCEPTIONS   auto—auto**s**   Latino—Latino**s**   Soto—Soto**s**

┌─HELP─┐

Form the plurals of most musical terms ending in *o* by adding *s*.

SINGULAR
piano   trio
soprano   cello

PLURAL
piano**s**   trio**s**
soprano**s**   cello**s**

Exercise 7   **Spelling the Plurals of Nouns**

Spell the plural form of each of the following nouns.

EXAMPLE   **1.** story
          1. stories

1. toy
2. apology
3. valley
4. try
5. piano
6. potato
7. emergency
8. chimney
9. radio
10. video

11. journey
12. stereo
13. county
14. hero
15. delay
16. scenario
17. agony
18. solo
19. O'Malley
20. zoo

SKILLS FOCUS

Spell regular and irregular plurals correctly.

(7) The plurals of a few nouns are formed in irregular ways.

SINGULAR	woman	mouse	foot	man	child
PLURAL	wom**en**	m**ice**	f**ee**t	m**en**	child**ren**

(8) Some nouns are the same in the singular and the plural.

SINGULAR AND PLURAL   fowl   sheep   spacecraft   Sioux

(9) Form the plurals of numerals, letters, symbols, and words referred to as words by adding an apostrophe and *s*.

SINGULAR	1990	*A*	+	*and*
PLURAL	1990**'s**	*A***'s**	+**'s**	*and***'s**

Exercise 8 **Spelling the Singular and Plural Forms of Nouns**

Spell the singular form and the plural form of each italicized word in the following sentences.

EXAMPLES 1. We use strong line to fish for *salmon*.
  1. *salmon—singular; salmon—plural*

  2. Field *mice* invaded the food supplies in the tent.
  2. *mouse—singular; mice—plural*

1. Our guide, Robert Tallchief, a *Sioux*, knows all about the animals called llamas.
2. Robert and his father use llamas like the ones shown below to carry equipment people need for hiking and for catching *fish*.
3. The trips are very popular with both men and *women*.

MECHANICS

4. *Children* especially are fascinated and amused by the sure-footed llamas.

5. However, the llama has one very disagreeable habit—if upset, it bares its *teeth* and spits.

6. The Tallchiefs' llama trips have attracted tourists from all over the world, including many *Japanese.*

7. One highlight of these trips is viewing *moose* in their natural habitat.

8. *Deer* thrive in this area of the Northwest.

9. In addition, families of mountain *sheep* clamber up the steep cliffs.

10. Most people who go on the llama trips take many pictures of the wild *geese.*

Review C **Proofreading Sentences for Correct Spelling**

For each of the following sentences, correctly write the word or words that are misspelled. If a sentence is already correct, write *C*.

EXAMPLE
    1. Aunt Dorothy's old-time sayings are echos of her childhood.

    1. *echoes*

1. Aunt Dorothy Kelly talks mostly in expressions from the 1930's and earlyer.

2. If we get into mischeif, she exclaims, "You little monkies!"

3. When my brother's run through the house, she shakes her head and mutters, "Boys will be boys."

4. Every time she can't find her eyeglasses, Aunt Dorothy says, "I've beaten the bushes, looking for them."

5. Aunt Dorothy believes that there are only two things in life that are certain: death and taxs.

6. We've heard her say "There's no use crying over spilled milk" and "Wishs won't wash dishs" about a thousand times apiece.

7. When we want something because our friends have it, Aunt Dorothy says we're trying to keep up with the Jones'.

8. Sometimes we get tired of hearing these little bits of folk wisdom, especially when Aunt Dorothy and all the little Kellies come over to visit for the holidays.

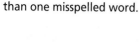

HELP

Some sentences in Review C have more than one misspelled word.

9. However, Aunt Dorothy is so sweet that we just smile and listen to her proverbs and storys.

10. Sometimes she says something really worthwhile, like "There are only two things that money can't buy—true love and home-grown tomatos."

Words Often Confused

People often confuse the words in each of the following groups. Some of these words are **homonyms.** They are pronounced the same, but they have different meanings and spellings. Other words in this section have the same or similar spellings, but have different meanings.

already	[adverb] *at an earlier time* The show has *already* begun.
all ready	[adjective] *all prepared; completely prepared* The floats are *all ready* for the fiesta.
altar	[noun] *a table or stand used for religious ceremonies* My uncle Chee wove the cloth for the *altar.*
alter	[verb] *to change* A flood can *alter* a riverbed.
altogether	[adverb] *entirely* I'm *altogether* lost.
all together	[adjective] *in the same place;* [adverb] *at the same time or place* Is everyone *all together*? Let's sit *all together* at the movie.
brake	[noun] *a device to stop a machine* The front *brake* on my bike squeaks.
break	[verb] *to fracture; to shatter;* [noun] *a fracture; an interruption; a rest* Try not to *break* your promises. Let's take a five-minute *break*.

Reference Note

In the Glossary of Usage in Chapter 10, you can find many other words that are often confused or misused. You can also look them up in a dictionary.

MECHANICS

SKILLS FOCUS

Distinguish between words often confused. Spell frequently misspelled words correctly.

Words Often Confused   **373**

For each of the following sentences, choose the correct word or words from the pair in parentheses.

EXAMPLE   **1.** Can the artist (*altar, alter*) the design?

         1. alter

1. Did you help (*brake, break*) the piñata, Felipe?

2. Who arranged the flowers on the (*altar, alter*)?

3. I've (*all ready, already*) seen that movie.

4. My mom was (*all together, altogether*) pleased with my report card.

5. Don't forget to set the emergency (*brake, break*) when you park on a hill.

6. Our family will be (*all together, altogether*) at Thanksgiving this year.

7. "Will you (*altar, alter*) this sundress for me, Mom?" Angie asked.

8. You were (*all together, altogether*) right about the show times for the movie.

9. The Great Circus Parade is (*already, all ready*) to begin.

10. Unfortunately, handblown glass figurines (*break, brake*) very easily.

TIPS & **TRICKS**

Here's a way to remember the difference between *capital* and *capitol.* There's a d**o**me on the capit**o**l.

capital	[noun] *a city; the location of a government* Havana is the *capital* of Cuba.
capitol	[noun] *a building; statehouse* Our state *capitol* is made of granite.
choose	[verb, rhymes with *shoes*] *to select* Did you *choose* the movie for today?
chose	[verb, past tense of *choose*, rhymes with *shows*] Who *chose* the movie yesterday?
cloths	[noun] *pieces of cloth* My aunt brought these kente *cloths* home from Ghana.
clothes	[noun] *wearing apparel* Bob irons his own *clothes*.

coarse	[adjective] *rough; crude; not fine* Some cities still use *coarse* salt to melt snow on streets and roads.
course	[noun] *a path of action; a series of studies;* [also used in the expression *of course*] What *course* should we follow to accomplish our goal? The counselor suggested several *courses* for us to take. I can't, *of course*, tell you what to do.
desert	[noun, pronounced des'•ert] *a dry, sandy region; a wilderness* Plants and animals of the *desert* can survive on little water.
desert	[verb, pronounced de•sert'] *to abandon; to leave* Don't *desert* your friends when they need you.
dessert	[noun, pronounced des•sert'] *the final, sweet course of a meal* What's for *dessert* tonight?

Exercise 10 Choosing Between Words Often Confused

For each of the following sentences, choose the correct word from the pair of words in parentheses.

EXAMPLE   1. The sand on the beach is (*coarse, course*).

    1. *coarse*

1. The Mojave (*Desert, Dessert*) is located in California.
2. Juan packed lightweight (*clothes, cloths*) to wear on his trip.
3. The sailor set a (*coarse, course*) for the port of Pago Pago.
4. When was the (*capital, capitol*) built, and how long has the state legislature been meeting there?
5. For (*desert, dessert*) we had pears and cheese.
6. Each team must (*choose, chose*) a captain.
7. The polishing (*cloths, clothes*) are by the wax on the shelf.
8. "Of (*coarse, course*) you may go!" Mr. Vance said.
9. The (*capital, capitol*) is the second-largest city in the state.
10. The cooking (*coarse, course*) lasted six weeks last summer.

SKILLS FOCUS

Distinguish between words often confused. Spell frequently misspelled words correctly.

Review D **Proofreading Sentences for Words Often Confused**

For each of the following sentences, correctly write the word that is misused.

EXAMPLE   1. The students are already for the Fall Festival.
             1. *all ready*

1. Throughout history, most societies and cultures, from the hot dessert regions to the cold northern regions, have celebrated the harvest.
2. The Jewish celebration of Sukkot marks the time when the harvest was gathered and the people were already for winter.
3. The most important tradition of Sukkot called for the family to live altogether in a temporary shelter called a sukkah.
4. Today, of coarse, many Jews still celebrate Sukkot but simply eat a meal outdoors under a shelter like the one pictured below.
5. Native Americans believed that without the help of the gods, there would be a brake in their good fortune.
6. During their planting ceremonies, most Native Americans, like the ones at left, dressed in special cloths.
7. To thank their harvest gods, the Chinese and Japanese placed wheat on alters.
8. Today, the Japanese do not altar this tradition much.
9. In most Japanese cities, including the capitol, the people hold parades to thank the ocean for the food it provides.
10. Many families in the United States celebrate Thanksgiving by sharing a meal, often with pumpkin pie for desert.

hear	[verb] *to receive sounds through the ears* When did you *hear* the news?
here	[adverb] *in this place* The mail is *here.*
its	[possessive form of *it*] *belonging to it* You should not judge a book by *its* cover.
it's	[contraction of *it is* or *it has*] *It's* your turn, Theresa. *It's* been a long day.
lead	[verb, rhymes with *need*] *to go first; to be a leader* Will you *lead* the singing, Rachel?
led	[verb, past tense of *lead*, rhymes with *red*] *went first; guided* The dog *led* its master to safety.
lead	[noun, rhymes with *red*] *a heavy metal; graphite used in pencils* *Lead* is no longer used in household paints. Use a pencil with a softer *lead* if you want to draw dark, heavy lines.
loose	[adjective, rhymes with *goose*] *not tight* A *loose* wheel on a bike is dangerous.
lose	[verb, rhymes with *shoes*] *to suffer loss* That sudden, loud noise made me *lose* my place.

Exercise 11 **Choosing Between Words Often Confused**

For each of the following sentences, choose the correct word from the pair of words in parentheses.

EXAMPLE   **1.** Rabbi Epstein (*lead, led*) our group during our tour of Israel.

     1. led

1. We could (*hear, here*) the patter of the rain on the (*lead, led*) roof from a block away.
2. A kimono is a (*loose, lose*) Japanese garment with short, wide sleeves and a sash.
3. Mom said that (*its, it's*) your turn to wash the dishes.

SKILLS FOCUS

Distinguish between words often confused. Spell frequently misspelled words correctly.

4. (*Hear, Here*) is a good article about Black History Month.
5. I hope the team doesn't (*loose, lose*) its opening game.
6. Who will (*lead, led*) the team to victory tomorrow?
7. "Wait (*hear, here*) while I open the door," Peter ordered.
8. The weights were as heavy as (*led, lead*).
9. (*Its, It's*) taken too long to respond to your letter.
10. The (*lead, led*) in this mechanical pencil is almost gone.

passed	[verb, past tense of *pass*] *went* by We *passed* you on the way to school.
past	[noun] *time that has gone by;* [preposition] *beyond;* [adjective] *ended* You can learn much from the *past.* The band marched *past* the school. The *past* week was a busy one.
peace	[noun] *quiet, order, and security* People all over the world long for *peace.*
piece	[noun] *a part of something* I had a delicious *piece* of spinach pie at the Greek festival.
plain	[adjective] *simple; common;* [noun] *a flat area of land* Raul's directions were *plain* and clear. The coastal *plain* was flat and barren.
plane	[noun] *a flat surface; a tool; an airplane* A rectangle is a four-sided *plane* with four right angles. Wood shavings curled from the *plane* to the workshop floor. The *plane* flew nonstop to Atlanta.
principal	[noun] *the head of a school;* [adjective] *chief, main* The vice *principal* is at the high school. The committee's *principal* task is preserving the park.
principle	[noun] *a rule of conduct; a basic truth* Freedom of speech is one of the *principles* of democracy.

TIPS & TRICKS

Here's a way to remember the difference between *peace* and *piece*. You eat a p**ie**ce of p**ie.**

TIPS & TRICKS

To remember the spelling of *principal*, use this sentence: The princi**pal** is your **pal.**

Choosing Between Words Often Confused

For each of the following sentences, choose the correct word from the pair of words in parentheses.

EXAMPLE   **1.** The (*passed, past*) president served two terms, not three.

     1. past

1. The Old Order Amish wear (*plain, plane*) clothes.
2. Many Americans believe that the golden rule is a good (*principal, principle*) by which to live.
3. Mark likes the (*piece, peace*) and quiet of the country.
4. One (*piece, peace*) of the puzzle was missing.
5. Komako used a (*plain, plane*) to smooth the rough edge of the door.
6. We flew in an enormous Singapore Airlines (*plain, plane*) to Frankfurt, Germany.
7. By studying the (*passed, past*), we understand the present.
8. She was (*principal, principle*) of the school for years.
9. Gail Devers quickly (*passed, past*) the other runners.
10. The trees are just (*passed, past*) their lovely fall colors.

Review E   **Proofreading a Paragraph to Correct Errors in Words Often Confused**

For the sentences in the following paragraph, correctly write each incorrect word.

EXAMPLE   **[1]** Often, people don't know how precious something is until they loose it.

     1. lose

[1] Several months ago, my aunt had what we all thought was a plane old cold. [2] In the passed, her doctor had told her there was no cure for a cold, so my aunt didn't even seek treatment. [3] No one knew that she had an ear infection that would led to a hearing loss in one ear. [4] Very soon, my aunt realized that she was hearing only peaces of conversations and could no longer hear out of her left ear. [5] When she went to the doctor, he explained that an infection had caused her to loose hearing in that ear. [6] The doctor gave her a chart showing the principle types of hearing aids. [7] He suggested

the in-the-canal hearing aid because its barely noticeable when in place. [8] It's small size really surprised me. [9] The doctor told my aunt that, of coarse, new advances in hearing technology are being made every day now. [10] Some people who could not here at all before can now be helped.

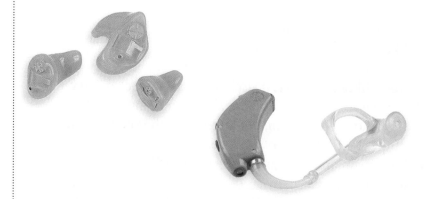

┌ T I P S & T R I C K S ┐

Here is an easy way to remember the difference between *stationary* and *stationery*. You write a lett**er** on station**ery**.

SKILLS FOCUS

Distinguish between words often confused. Spell frequently misspelled words correctly.

stationary	[adjective] *in a fixed position* The desks are *stationary,* but the chairs can be moved.
stationery	[noun] *writing paper* Sarah designs her own *stationery.*
their	[possessive form of *they*] *belonging to them* *Their* pitcher struck out six players.
there	[adverb] *at or to that place;* [also used to begin a sentence] I'll see you *there.* *There* are more than two million books in the Harold Washington Library in Chicago.
they're	[contraction of *they are*] *They're* right behind you.
threw	[verb, past tense of *throw*] *tossed* Zack *threw* the ball to me.
through	[preposition] *in one side and out the other* Let's walk *through* the park.

For each of the following sentences, choose the correct word from the choices in parentheses.

EXAMPLE   **1.** (*Their, They're, There*) goes the space shuttle!

      1. There

1. The 100-yard dash will begin over (*their, there, they're*) by the fence.

2. In a flash, the girls (*threw, through*) everything into (*their, there, they're*) lockers and ran onto the field.

3. The planet earth was once thought to be (*stationary, stationery*) in space.

4. (*Threw, Through*) the door bounded a large dog.

5. Are you sure (*their, there, they're*) not coming?

6. "Who (*through, threw*) the pass that led to the touchdown?" Jill asked.

7. I think that the red envelopes do not go with the pink (*stationery, stationary*) at all.

8. (*They're, Their*) planning to see a Will Smith movie sometime this weekend.

9. We drove (*threw, through*) Kansas and Oklahoma on the way to Texas.

10. (*Their, There*) is a Cajun band playing in the park this afternoon until 4:00.

to	[preposition] *in the direction of; toward* We drove *to* Carson City.
too	[adverb] *also; more than enough* Am I invited, *too*? Your poem has *too* many syllables to be a haiku.
two	[adjective or noun] *one plus one* Ms. Red Cloud's last name is *two* separate words. *Two* of the pandas woke up then.
weak	[adjective] *feeble; not strong* People with *weak* ankles have difficulty ice-skating.
week	[noun] *seven days* The club meets once a *week*.

(continued)

COMPUTER TIP

A computer can help you catch spelling mistakes. Remember, though, that a computer's spellchecker cannot point out homonyms that are used incorrectly. Learn how to proofread your own writing. Never rely entirely on a spellchecker.

MECHANICS

(continued)

who's	[contraction of *who is* or *who has*] *Who's* wearing a watch? *Who's* seen Frida Kahlo's paintings?
whose	[possessive form of *who*] *belonging to whom* I wonder *whose* backpack this is.
your	[possessive form of *you*] *belonging to you* Rest *your* eyes now and then when you read.
you're	[contraction of *you are*] *You're* next in line.

Exercise 14 **Choosing Between Words Often Confused**

For each of the following sentences, choose the correct word from the choices in parentheses.

EXAMPLE   **1.** I wonder (*who's, whose*) won the election.

   1. who's

1. (*Who's, Whose*) story did you like best?
2. Walking (*to, too*) the grocery store, he began to feel (*weak, week*).
3. Does (*your, you're*) dad work for the newspaper, (*to, too, two*)?
4. It took me a (*weak, week*) to complete my project for history class.
5. If (*your, you're*) not making that noise, (*who's, whose*) making it?
6. "Is there (*too, two*) much flour in the tortilla dough?" Alinda asked.
7. Always fasten (*you're, your*) seat belt when (*you're, your*) riding in a vehicle.
8. They asked (*who's, whose*) painting was chosen (*to, too*) be entered in the contest.
9. (*Too, Two*) of the foreign exchange students are from southern India.
10. "See you next (*weak, week*)!" the ballet teacher said to the students cheerfully.

MECHANICS

For each of the following sentences, choose the correct word or words from the choices in parentheses.

EXAMPLE   **1.** Don't (*loose, lose*) your house key.

     1. *lose*

1. Oh, Rebecca, which of these (*to, too, two*) boxes of (*stationary, stationery*) do you like better?
2. The Israelis and the Palestinians met in Madrid, the (*capital, capitol*) of Spain, for the (*peace, piece*) talks.
3. (*Principal, Principle*) Wong raised his hand for silence, and the students waited to (*hear, here*) what he would say.
4. These curtains will likely be hard to (*altar, alter*) because the fabric is so (*coarse, course*).
5. (*Its, It's*) (*all together, altogether*) too easy to confuse similar words.
6. Ruth vowed to (*lead, led*) the life of an exile rather than to (*desert, dessert*) Naomi.
7. Can that (*plain, plane*) (*brake, break*) the sound barrier?
8. We're (*all ready, already*) for the big game against our rivals this (*weak, week*).
9. (*Your, You're*) next chore is to dust; the dust (*clothes, cloths*) are on the counter.
10. The two friends (*passed, past*) the time pleasantly reading (*there, their, they're*) books.

Review **G** **Proofreading a Paragraph to Correct Spelling Errors and Errors in Words Often Confused**

For each sentence in the following paragraph, correctly write each misspelled or misused word. If a sentence is already correct, write *C*.

EXAMPLE   **[1]** Its time to test you're knowledge of South American history.

     1. *It's; your*

    [1] Starting about A.D. 1200, people known as the Incas began too take over the western portion of South America. [2] Look at the map on the next page, and you'll see that thier

MECHANICS

territory included mountains, seacoasts, river valleys, and desserts. [3] The capitol of the Incan empire was Cuzco. [4] The Incas created an impressive road system that connected Cuzco with the rest of there empire. [5] These hard-working people also built storehouses and developped large irrigation projects. [6] To help them manage their huge empire, they used a device called a quipu as their principle method of keeping records. [7] The quipu (shown below) is a series of knotted, colored cords. [8] With it, the Incas recorded such information as the number of people liveing in an area, the movements of the planets, and the amount of goods in storage. [9] The Incan civilization lasted until the Spanish arrived in the mid-1500s'. [10] In only a short time, Spanish conquistadors were able to defeat the Incas and brake up their empire.

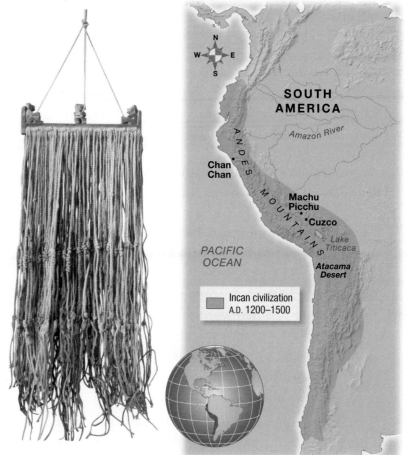

MECHANICS

Chapter Review

A. Proofreading Sentences for Correct Spelling

For each of the following sentences, correctly write the word that is misspelled.

┌─HELP─┐
No proper nouns in the Chapter Review are misspelled.

1. The company's cheif accountant wrote the schedule.
2. Mr. Santander gave a breif speech before the ceremony.
3. Breatheing hard, we finally reached the summit.
4. Chickens and gooses are common fowl.
5. We changed the subject to avoid having an arguement.
6. How many *I*s did you use in your letter to Irene?
7. Mom and Dad have no tolerance for lazyness.
8. Spain and Portugal are two countrys I have always wanted to visit.
9. The new store on the corner will sell computer software, computers, and stereoes.
10. My grandmother's recipe calls for half a clove of garlic and two garden tomatos.
11. Three small active childs came running out of the house.
12. We cut several large branchs off the pine tree.
13. After she ran through the patch of stinging nettles, Alice had itchs up and down her legs.
14. We were surprised to see two pianoes on the stage instead of only one.
15. I am very interested in the history of anceint Egypt.
16. "The last thing we want," said the new sales manager, "is a disatisfied customer."
17. The first thing you notice in San Miguel is the friendlyness of the people.
18. That dinosaur skeleton must have been the bigest thing in the whole museum.
19. Aunt Rina has lost weight; she looks much slimer than she has in a long time.
20. Strawberrys are my favorite fruit.

MECHANICS

B. Choosing Between Words Often Confused

For each of the following sentences, choose from each pair in parentheses the word that will make the sentence correct.

21. Nothing would persuade him to (*altar, alter*) his plans.

22. Berlin is the (*capitol, capital*) of Germany.

23. Sometimes the wisest (*course, coarse*) of action is to do nothing.

24. Samantha tried on the new (*cloths, clothes*) she received on her birthday.

25. For (*desert, dessert*) we had red grapes, strawberries, frozen yogurt, and melon.

26. The vast (*planes, plains*) of Patagonia stretch from the mountains to the ocean.

27. "Your cousins are over (*their, there*)," said Mr. Octavius. "I think this is (*there, their*) luggage."

28. In all the confusion, it was difficult to tell (*whose, who's*) things belonged to whom.

29. We were somewhat surprised when an overloaded pickup truck (*past, passed*) us going uphill.

30. On their way (*too, to*) the train station, they were held up in the (*stationary, stationery*) traffic.

C. Proofreading a Paragraph to Correct Spelling Errors

For each sentence in the following paragraph, correctly write the word or words that are misspelled. If a sentence is already correct, write *C*.

[31] Dublin, the capitol of Ireland, has a beautiful locateion between the sea and the mountains. [32] The city has a rich and interesting passed. [33] The Viking's established Dublin in the mid-800's, though a small settlement had existed previously on the site. [34] Norman soldiers from England captured Dublin in 1170 and built St. Patrick's Cathedral and Dublin Castle their. [35] The castle remained the center of British rule in Ireland throughout the next 700 years. [36] War and piece came and went. [37] By the 1700's, Dublin was growing fast. [38] It's cultural life flourished, and manufacturing and trade increased.

[39] Unfortunatly, between 1916 and 1922, much property was destroyed during the war of independence and a civil war.
[40] Today, Dublin is growing and prosperous and is faceing the challenges common to most modern big citys.

Writing Application

Using Correct Spelling in a Personal Letter

Following Spelling Rules You are writing a letter to congratulate your cousin Mary, who has been awarded first prize in a spelling bee. Write a paragraph expressing your congratulations and saying how important you think it is to use correct spelling. In your paragraph, use at least five words often confused.

Prewriting Jot down a list of reasons correct spelling is important. You might mention making a good impression and making communication easier. Also, compose sentences about how difficult it must be to remember correct spelling in front of an audience and how impressed you are that Mary managed to do so.

Writing Begin your rough draft by stating how hard it is to spell correctly in English and how important it is to continue developing that skill. Then, congratulate Mary on her award and say that her success will inspire you to continue working hard at learning correct spelling.

Revising Have a friend or classmate read your draft. Have you clearly stated the importance of correct spelling? Is your pleasure at your cousin's success clearly described?

Publishing Make sure you have not used any homonyms incorrectly. Then, proofread your letter for any errors in grammar, punctuation, and spelling. You and your classmates may wish to post your letters on a class bulletin board or Web page.

Reference Note

For more about **writing a personal letter,** see "Writing" in the Quick Reference Handbook.

SKILLS FOCUS

Write a letter. Use correct spelling.

MECHANICS

Spelling Words

- contact
  contract
  advance
  depth
  comment
  summit
  sketch
  nonsense
  splendid
  ethnic
  liquid
  impulse

- globe
  grove
  slope
  slice
  roast
  spike
  choke
  praise
  squeeze
  breathe
  gross
  thigh

- shout
  youth
  amount
  pounds
  mountain
  thousands
  proof
  crawled
  account
  launched
  rumors
  saucer

- turtle
  nightmare
  burnt
  curb
  purse
  declare

scarce
inserts
sparkling
source
nervous
warrant

- enough
  though
  straight
  rough
  courage
  eighth
  system
  although
  sleigh
  boulder
  biscuit
  dough

- freight
  foreign
  receive
  receiver
  belief
  relief
  weighed
  reins
  fierce
  heights
  thieves
  achieve

- grandfather
  fairy tales
  bedtime
  cupboard
  upright
  teenager
  thunderstorm
  barefoot
  middle-class
  middle-aged
  bodyguard
  so-called

- grown
  groan
  guest
  guessed
  creek
  creak
  weather
  whether
  sore
  soar
  stake
  steak

- angle
  angel
  costume
  custom
  affect
  effect
  adopt
  adapt
  device
  devise
  decent
  descent

- varied
  centuries
  colonies
  applies
  occupied
  identified
  enemies
  activities
  denied
  allied
  industries
  qualified

- beaten
  musical
  rotten
  German
  Indian
  Roman

explorer
stretcher
critical
criminal
political
original

- escape
  gotten
  velvet
  engine
  insist
  admire
  index
  intense
  further
  frantic
  convince
  instinct

- agent
  evil
  local
  eager
  famous
  fiber
  razor
  vital
  rival
  basis
  cheetah
  scenic

- speaking
  spelling
  wondered
  bragged
  healed
  scrubbed
  answered
  threatened
  admitted
  committed
  referring
  preferred

- insurance
  conference
  ambulance
  absence
  instance
  audience
  allowance
  intelligence
  assurance
  appearance
  obedience
  presence

- activity
  ability
  argument
  personality
  electricity
  championship
  community
  majority
  responsibility
  curiosity
  necessity
  authority

- approach
  accuse
  applause
  affection
  accompany
  assign
  appreciate
  accurate
  association
  apparent
  accustomed
  assistance

- continued
  commander
  commit
  constitution
  confusing
  commence

commotion
commercial
communicate
communities
communication
committee

- elephant
  confident
  instant
  element
  servant
  excellent
  opponent
  permanent
  assistant
  innocent
  significant
  sufficient

- talent
  novel
  treason
  comic
  profit
  token
  weapon
  gopher
  pleasant
  siren
  frigid
  spiral

- habit
  display
  clever
  gather
  empty
  chaos
  suspense
  Saturn
  oval
  orphan
  fatal
  crystal

- media
  fungi
  bacteria
  stimulus
  stimuli
  larvae
  radius
  nucleus
  nuclei
  species
  salmon
  hippopotamus

- curious
  tremendous
  enormous
  obvious
  delicious
  mysterious
  executive
  creative
  fabulous
  legislative
  negative
  sensitive

- unpredictable
  disagreement
  renewal
  unemployment
  unexpectedly
  unfortunately
  unusually
  reproduction
  reconstruction
  disagreeable
  unsuccessful
  uncomfortable

- wonderfully
  thoughtfully
  relationship
  respectively
  naturally
  nervously

gracefully
actively
joyfully
beautifully
successfully
accidentally

- illegal
  impolite
  impossible
  invisible
  irregular
  inexpensive
  impure
  inability
  impatient
  indigestion
  indefinite
  incredible

- descriptive
  description
  prescribed
  inspector
  spectacle
  spectacular
  scribbled
  inscription
  subscription
  spectrum
  spectators
  transcripts

- erupt
  abrupt
  bankrupt
  inject
  disrupting
  disruption
  eject
  reject
  rejected
  rupture
  corrupt
  interrupt

CHAPTER

15 | Correcting Common Errors

┌─ **HELP** ─

The exercises in
Chapter 15 test your
knowledge of the rules
of **standard, formal
English.** These are the
rules you should follow
in your schoolwork.

Reference Note

For more information
about **standard** and **nonstandard English** and
formal and **informal
English,** see page 267.

Key Language Skills Review

This chapter reviews key skills and concepts that pose special
problems for writers.

- **Sentence Fragments and Run-on Sentences**
- **Subject-Verb Agreement**
- **Pronoun-Antecedent Agreement**
- **Verb Forms**
- **Pronoun Forms**
- **Comparison and Placement of Modifiers**
- **Double Negatives**
- **Standard Usage**
- **Capitalization**
- **Punctuation—Commas, End Marks, Semicolons,
  Colons, Quotation Marks, and Apostrophes**
- **Spelling**

Most of the exercises in this chapter follow the same
format as the exercises found throughout the grammar,
usage, and mechanics sections of this book. You will notice,

however, that two sets of review exercises are presented in standardized test formats. These exercises are designed to provide you with practice not only in solving usage and mechanics problems but also in dealing with these kinds of problems on standardized tests.

Exercise 1 Identifying Sentences and Sentence Fragments

Identify each of the following word groups as a *sentence* or a *sentence fragment*. If a word group is a sentence, rewrite it correctly, using a capital letter at the beginning and adding an end mark.

Reference Note

For information on **sentences** and **sentence fragments,** see page 50.

EXAMPLES **1.** the squirrel hopped across the branch

      1. sentence—The squirrel hopped across the branch.

      2. Jeremy's collection of comic books

      2. sentence fragment

1. near the door of the classroom
2. all members of the safety patrol
3. sumo wrestling is popular in Japan
4. please pass me the fruit salad
5. will become a member of Junior Achievement
6. after school Sonya repaired her backpack
7. what an active puppy that is
8. lived in British Columbia for many years
9. do you like the sound of ocean waves
10. on the top shelf of the refrigerator
11. ate goat cheese every day in Norway
12. that's a fantastic idea
13. because rap music is still popular
14. not everyone wants to play the game
15. a tree was placed on top of the completed building
16. when the armadillos enter another state
17. stopped traffic for half an hour
18. John the plumber around noon
19. please return the books by tomorrow afternoon
20. plugged in the computer and nothing happened

COMMON ERRORS

Reference Note

For information on **sentence fragments,** see page 50.

Link to Literature

Exercise 2 Revising Sentence Fragments

Some of the following word groups are sentence fragments. First, identify the fragments. Then, make each fragment a complete sentence by adding (1) a subject, (2) a verb, or (3) both. You may need to change the punctuation and capitalization, too. If the word group is already a complete sentence, write *S*.

EXAMPLE   1. Finished reading an exciting book by Jean Craighead George.

1. *I finished reading an exciting book by Jean Craighead George.*

1. Titled *The Case of the Missing Cutthroats.*
2. A book for young detectives who love nature.
3. In the book, a girl named Spinner goes fishing.
4. During the trip, she catches a giant cutthroat trout.
5. Thought cutthroat trout had died out where she was fishing in the Snake River.
6. Both she and her family are surprised by her catch.
7. Puzzled by the presence of a cutthroat trout.
8. What has happened to the cutthroat trout?
9. Spinner and her cousin Al on an adventure.
10. Hope to find clues that will help them solve the mystery.

Exercise 3 Identifying and Revising Run-on Sentences

Decide which of the following word groups are run-on sentences. Then, revise each run-on sentence by (1) making two separate sentences or (2) using a comma and a coordinating conjunction. You may have to change the punctuation and capitalization, too. If the word group is already a complete sentence, write *S*.

EXAMPLE   1. Both girls enjoy playing soccer one is usually the goalie.

1. *Both girls enjoy playing soccer, and one is usually the goalie.*

or

Both girls enjoy playing soccer. One is usually the goalie.

—HELP—

Most of the sentences in Exercise 3 can be correctly revised in more than one way. You need to give only one revision for each sentence.

Reference Note

For information on **run-on sentences,** see page 431.

COMMON ERRORS

1. Puffins are shorebirds, they have brightly colored beaks and ducklike bodies.
2. Cement is a fine powder it is mixed with sand, water, and small rocks to make concrete.
3. Alicia collects birth dates, she has recorded the birthdays of all her friends and of her favorite movie stars.
4. We may go to the Zuni arts and crafts fair on Saturday we may wait until next weekend.
5. The band placed first in regional competitions, it did not win at the state contests.
6. I plan to go to the Florida Keys someday, I want to skin-dive for seashells.
7. Kerry is having a party tomorrow night, we are planning to go.
8. The school board could vote to remodel the old cafeteria, or they may decide to build a new one.
9. My brother would like to live on a space station someday I would, too.
10. These rocks are too heavy for me to lift, I asked Christy to help me move them.

(Exercise 4) **Identifying and Revising Run-on Sentences**

Identify which of the following word groups are run-on sentences. Then, revise each run-on sentence by (1) making two separate sentences or (2) using a comma and a coordinating conjunction. You may have to change the punctuation and capitalization, too. If the word group is already a complete sentence, write *S*.

EXAMPLE   1. The Navajo woman allowed the children to try on jewelry, it was made out of silver and beautiful turquoise.

1. *The Navajo woman allowed the children to try on jewelry. It was made out of silver and beautiful turquoise.*

1. Sheila liked a ring with one stone in the middle it didn't fit her fingers.
2. She found another ring with three small stones, it was a perfect fit for her.

┌HELP┐

Most of the sentences in Exercise 4 can be correctly revised in more than one way. You need to give only one revision for each sentence.

Reference Note

For information on **run-on sentences,** see page 431.

COMMON ERRORS

3. Aaron picked out a turquoise watchband, and he also found a ring with blue stones and fire agates.
4. The watchband had little pieces of turquoise in the shape of a star he really wanted to buy it.
5. Both Maria and Francine spied a necklace a rough chunk of turquoise was hung from a silver chain.
6. Thad may spend his allowance on a turquoise ring he may save up his money for a watchband.
7. Several children had never seen turquoise before, they wanted to know if the stones were real.
8. The saleswoman's arms were covered with bracelets everyone noticed her.
9. Ruben put six bracelets on his arms, and then he couldn't get all of them off.
10. The group wanted to see more turquoise jewelry the woman had sold many pieces earlier in the day.

HELP

Most of the sentences in Exercise 5 can be correctly revised in more than one way. You need to give only one revision for each sentence.

Reference Note

For information on **sentence fragments,** see page 50. For information on **run-on sentences,** see page 431.

Exercise 5 **Correcting Run-on Sentences and Sentence Fragments**

Decide which of the following word groups are run-on sentences and which are sentence fragments. Then, revise each word group to make one or more complete sentences. Remember to use correct capitalization and punctuation. If a word group is already a complete sentence, write *S*.

EXAMPLES 1. Do you like brightly colored art you should see Faith Ringgold's paintings.

1. *Do you like brightly colored art? You should see Faith Ringgold's paintings.*

2. Uses color boldly and imaginatively.

2. *Ringgold uses color boldly and imaginatively.*

1. Ringgold was born in Harlem in 1930 at a young age, she knew she wanted to be an artist.
2. Today her artwork in museums around the world.
3. Paints on fabric and sometimes uses fabric to frame her paintings.
4. Her creativity led her to invent a whole new art form she decided to call it the "story quilt."
5. Story quilts blend storytelling with painting.

6. One of Ringgold's series of story quilts about an African American woman in Paris.
7. Much of her work represents her African American roots.
8. Ringgold's painting *Tar Beach* is based on her childhood experiences she completed the work in 1988.
9. Shows a playground on the roof of an apartment building.
10. Behind the rooftop lies the George Washington Bridge, a bridge whose string of lights reminded Ringgold of a diamond necklace.

Exercise 6 **Choosing Verbs That Agree in Number with Their Subjects**

For each of the following sentences, choose the form of the verb in parentheses that agrees with the subject.

EXAMPLE   1. Everyone except my twin sisters (*want, wants*) to go to the powwow.

     1. wants

1. Here (*come, comes*) the marching bands in the parade!
2. Several of my friends (*has, have*) trail bikes.
3. I (*don't, doesn't*) like to swim when the water is cold.
4. Neither the guinea pigs nor the hamster (*is, are*) awake yet.
5. (*Has, Have*) Mr. Baldwin and Sherry been talking long?
6. One of the scientists (*was, were*) Isaac Newton.
7. Thunderstorms usually (*don't, doesn't*) bother me.
8. (*Is, Are*) the Chinese cookbooks still on sale?
9. All of the movie (*was, were*) filmed in Vietnam.
10. The boy in the red shoes (*run, runs*) fast.

Exercise 7 **Proofreading Sentences for Correct Subject-Verb Agreement**

Most of the following sentences contain a verb that does not agree in number with its subject. If a verb form is incorrect, write the correct form. If a sentence is already correct, write *C*.

EXAMPLE   1. A carved slice of potato make a good stamp.

     1. makes

1. Images from this type of stamp are called potato prints.

Reference Note

For information on **verb forms,** see page 193. For information on **subject-verb agreement,** see page 170.

Reference Note

For information on **subject-verb agreement,** see page 170.

COMMON ERRORS

2. Both my cousins and my younger brother Michael creates potato prints.
3. It don't cost much to make these prints.
4. A firm potato, a knife, paint, a paintbrush, and paper is the necessary supplies.
5. My friend James find unique shapes and patterns in his mother's old magazines.
6. He then carves these designs on the flat surfaces of cut potatoes.
7. Next, each carved design on the potato slices are coated with paint.
8. Pieces of fabric or a sheet of paper offer a good surface for stamping.
9. Each of my cousins like to make greeting cards with stamped designs.
10. Other uses for a potato stamp includes making writing paper and wrapping paper.

Reference Note

For information on **pronoun-antecedent agreement,** see page 183.

Exercise 8 **Choosing Pronouns That Agree with Their Antecedents**

For each of the following sentences, choose the pronoun in parentheses that agrees with its antecedent.

EXAMPLE   1. The engineers showed (*his, their*) plans for the new bridge.

    1. *their*

1. J. W. and I hope to have (*our, their*) skits ready in time for the talent show.
2. Two boys and one girl have received honors, and all of (*her, their*) parents are very proud.
3. During the last serve, with the crowd watching, Danny's tennis racket flew out of (*his, our*) hand.
4. We treated (*ourselves, themselves*) to Chinese noodles and stir-fried vegetables for supper.
5. The table is made of oak and is quite solid, but one of (*his, its*) legs is broken.
6. The members of the Asian Students Club asked to have (*its, their*) picture taken with the school mascot.

7. Neither Jack nor Charles wants to have (*his, their*) hair cut by Lisa.
8. Arlene asked Samuel to go on the picnic, but (*he, she*) hasn't given an answer yet.
9. The squirrels and the rabbits play in the yard; (*they, it*) seem to have a lot of fun.
10. Each of the girls will receive (*their, her*) own directions.

Exercise 9 **Proofreading for Pronoun-Antecedent Agreement**

Most of the following sentences contain a pronoun that does not agree with its antecedent. If a sentence is incorrect, write the correct pronoun. If a sentence is already correct, write *C*.

EXAMPLES **1.** The asteroids will not hit Earth, but it will come close.
    1. they

    2. Each of the boys thought that their independent project was the best one.
    2. his

1. Dad wrote out the check to the painters although he had not finished the painting job for him.
2. Tom Sawyer tricked his friends into doing his work, but they enjoyed it.
3. Jesse Owens, Willie Mays, and Joe Louis were sports stars in their day, and many people still remember him.
4. Have you ever noticed how the bears at the zoo really enjoy sunning itself?
5. Several of the men in our town plan to donate his time to Habitat for Humanity.
6. Each of the girls wanted to read their report first.
7. Did Randy or Tomás finish cleaning their desk first?
8. Our grandparents gave us a surprise party when we came home from camp.
9. Either José or Andrew will arrive early so that they can help us finish the posters.
10. Each of the cats was chasing their toys.

Reference Note

For information on **pronoun-antecedent agreement,** see page 183.

COMMON ERRORS

HELP

Some sentences in Exercise 10 may have more than one correct answer. You need to give only one answer for each sentence.

Reference Note

For information on **regular verb forms,** see page 194.

Exercise 10 **Using the Principal Parts of Regular Verbs**

Give the form of the italicized verb that will correctly complete each of the following sentences.

EXAMPLE   **1.** *roll*   The dog ____ on its back for us to pet it.

1. *rolled*
or
rolls

1. *climb*   Yesterday the cat ____ the tree.
2. *joke*   I can never tell when Bob is ____.
3. *shop*   My friend and I once ____ all day at a mall in Bloomington, Minnesota.
4. *fill*   Have the fans ____ the auditorium yet?
5. *enter*   Too many cars are ____ the parking lot.
6. *watch*   The class is ____ a film about the ancient Incan culture in Peru.
7. *call*   Who ____ my name a few seconds ago?
8. *measure*   My mother has ____ the space for the new bookcase.
9. *load*   Two men ____ our furniture into the truck.
10. *jump*   A deer has ____ over the fence.
11. *laugh*   We ____ for a long time over Ira's joke.
12. *fix*   Steven is ____ the computer.
13. *wash*   Cora's brother has ____ his new car at least a dozen times.
14. *play*   Have you ____ the soundtrack from that movie for Isaac yet?
15. *walk*   Mother and I ____ three miles on the county road yesterday morning.
16. *talk*   The young boys are ____ about starting their own soccer team.
17. *hammer*   The carpenter ____ the nails into the crossbeam in almost no time at all.
18. *observe*   Benjamin's family is ____ Yom Kippur in the traditional way.
19. *help*   Regular exercise has ____ many people to stay physically fit.
20. *dress*   Are you ____ up for the banquet tonight?

Exercise 11 Using Irregular Verbs

For each italicized verb, give the past or the past participle form that will correctly complete the sentence.

Reference Note

For information on **irregular verb forms,** see page 196.

EXAMPLE 1. *drink* The guests ____ all of the raspberry tea.
1. *drank*

1. *blow* The wind has ____ the kite out of the tree!
2. *shrink* The boy in the movie had ____ to the size of a squirrel.
3. *steal* "I've never ____ anything in my life," Abe declared in his defense.
4. *drive* Pat and Justin ____ go-carts at the park.
5. *freeze* The water in the birdbath has ____.
6. *sink* The toy boat has ____ in the sudsy bath water.
7. *throw* Each athlete has ____ the javelin twice.
8. *sing* The choir ____ at the celebration last night.
9. *swim* Have you ever ____ in warm mineral water?
10. *burst* The balloon ____ when the cat clawed it.
11. *teach* Mrs. Randall has ____ at Rosenwald Middle School for years.
12. *give* Last year I ____ part of my allowance to the United Way.
13. *run* Our car is old and unattractive, but it has ____ well for many years.
14. *eat* Sharon baked two small potatoes and ____ both of them.
15. *fly* "That hawk has ____ over the yard twice," Justin said.
16. *write* Many people have ____ about the Mexican myth of Quetzalcoatl.
17. *begin* It has ____ to snow, but the flakes are very small and dry.
18. *come* "Who ____ to Dad's surprise birthday party?" Miriam asked.
19. *speak* Lin and Jeff have ____ about their tickets to everyone in class.
20. *do* It's a good feeling to know that you have ____ your best.

COMMON ERRORS

Reference Note

For information on **irregular verb forms**, see page 196.

Exercise 12 Proofreading for Errors in Irregular Verbs

Most of the following sentences contain incorrect verb forms. Identify each error, and write the correct form of the verb. If the sentence is already correct, write *C*.

EXAMPLE   1. We have went to the African art exhibit two weekends in a row.

1. *went—gone*

1. Sarah done well at yesterday's track meet.
2. My stepfather brung me a stuffed animal when I was in the hospital.
3. Nickelodeon movie theaters begun to be quite popular in the United States around 1905.
4. Manuel's grandfather come to the United States forty years ago.
5. We seen the Rio Grande when we drove through the state of New Mexico.
6. Chris knew that a basement was a good place to take shelter during a tornado.
7. Judy taked a few minutes to decide what to say.
8. Maria's team choosed the oak tree in her front yard as home base.
9. The poison ivy in the woods gived me a rash.
10. Dr. Seuss wrote the poem "The Sneetches."
11. The blue pitcher that my godparents buyed for me in Denmark is on the table in the living room.
12. Do you remember what running records Carl Lewis breaked?
13. The girls on the front porch have drank their lemonade too quickly.
14. My shirt and pants tore on the barbed wire as I climbed through the fence.
15. Jina's mother and stepfather have went to the same church for thirty-five years.
16. A raccoon felled from the roof of our house, but it was not injured.
17. In a very generous mood, Marsha lended her favorite scarf to Natalie.

18. The family made the giant scarecrow to scare away the grackles from their backyard garden.
19. The young artist drawed a lovely picture of the waves and rocks on the Oregon coast.
20. Gwen catched the ball even though Craig threw it fast and high.

Exercise 13 — Using the Past and Past Participle Forms of Verbs

For the italicized verb in each of the following sentences, give the past or past participle form that will correctly complete the sentence.

EXAMPLE   1. *establish*   Robert D. Ballard, a marine geologist, _____ the JASON Foundation for Education.

    1. established

1. *create*   JASON, an underwater robot, was _____ for scientific research.
2. *build*   JASON was _____ to dive much deeper than humans can dive.
3. *sink*   More than 1,600 years ago, the Roman ship *Isis* _____ in the Mediterranean Sea.
4. *know*   Ballard _____ that students would want to share in the exploration of the wrecked ship.
5. *make*   A network of satellites _____ it possible for many students to see JASON explore the wreck.
6. *see*   Some 250,000 schoolchildren _____ JASON on giant video screens.
7. *ask*   While JASON searched the ship, students _____ questions of Ballard and his team.
8. *take*   Ballard has _____ students on some amazing electronic field trips by televising himself working with JASON.
9. *give*   He has _____ much of his time and energy to involving students in scientific discoveries.
10. *write*   Ballard has _____ about finding the *Isis* and about the 1985 discovery of the *Titanic*, which sank in 1912.

Reference Note

For information on **verb forms,** see page 193.

COMMON ERRORS

Reference Note

For information on **pronoun forms,** see page 223.

Exercise 14 **Choosing Correct Pronoun Forms**

Choose the correct form of the pronoun in parentheses in each of the following sentences.

EXAMPLE   1. The catcher gave (*she, her*) the signal.
1. *her*

1. The winners may be you and (*her, she*).
2. Gregory asked (*her, she*) to the dance.
3. The ending of the movie really amazed Andrew and (*us, we*)!
4. Should Emily and (*they, them*) make the spaghetti?
5. The bus driver gave (*he, him*) a warning.
6. The competition is really between Mario and (*I, me*).
7. Who bought (*her, she*) that opal necklace?
8. The best player on our team is (*him, he*).
9. The next step for Michael and (*them, they*) is to check with the principal.
10. My cousin and (*me, I*) are learning to do origami in our class at the community center.
11. You and (*I, me*) can work together on a report about American Indians of the Southwest.
12. The physical education teacher designed a special exercise program for (*her, she*).
13. The ones who asked to see our pictures from the Miami zoo are (*they, them*).
14. (*Us, We*) always enjoy the plays at the children's theater, especially when they are performed outdoors.
15. (*He, Him*) plays the guitar quite well and has performed in a band.
16. Ms. Ruel asked Kei and (*I, me*) to recite the French nursery rhyme.
17. "I'd like to go to the movies with (*they, them*)," Thi said after meeting Carmela and Tony.
18. Aunt Edna is buying new backpacks for Carl and (*I, me*).
19. Last week (*them, they*) began taking tennis lessons after school.
20. Will you or (*I, me*) be the first one with the correct answer?

Exercise 15 Proofreading for Correct Pronoun Forms

Most of the following sentences contain a pronoun that has been used incorrectly. Identify each incorrect pronoun. Then, write the correct form. If a sentence is already correct, write *C*.

Reference Note

For information on **pronoun forms,** see page 223.

EXAMPLE   1. Cassie sat between Melissa and I at the concert.
            1. *I—me*

1. Who did you meet at the skating rink last night?
2. You and them are the only ones who are going on the hike.
3. My pen pal in Vietnam will soon receive another letter from me.
4. Just between you and I, the other book was much easier to understand.
5. One of the actors in that play was her.
6. The pencils, paints, and colored paper belong to Kimiko and he.
7. Matthew has invited you and I to his party next weekend.
8. Either her or I will make a poster for Black History Month.
9. Who is the fastest runner on the baseball team?
10. They and us went swimming in Lake Travis.

Exercise 16 Choosing Correct Regular and Irregular Modifiers

Choose the correct form of the adjective or adverb in parentheses in each of the following sentences.

Reference Note

For information on **using modifiers correctly,** see Chapter 9.

EXAMPLE   1. The stars tonight look (*more bright, brighter*) than usual.
            1. *brighter*

1. This puzzle book is (*difficulter, more difficult*) than the other one.
2. Kevin is the (*taller, tallest*) of the four Sutherland brothers.
3. The (*most exciting, excitingest*) day of our trip to Indonesia was still to come.
4. I like drawing, but I like painting (*best, better*).
5. If you blend strawberries, bananas, and yogurt really (*good, well*), you'll have a great drink.
6. Felicia had the (*worst, worse*) case of chickenpox of anyone in the sixth grade.

COMMON ERRORS

7. My brothers and I were taught how to wash, iron, and mend clothes, and we are (*gladder, glad*) that we were.
8. Rachel can't decide which of the two wallpaper patterns would look (*prettier, prettiest*) in her room.
9. Our schoolyard has been (*cleanest, cleaner*) since the Ecology Club asked people not to litter.
10. I am going to practice American Sign Language until I sign (*good, well*) enough to communicate easily.

Reference Note

For information on **using modifiers correctly,** see Chapter 9.

Exercise **17** Correcting Errors in the Use of Modifiers

Rewrite each of the following sentences, correcting any errors in the use or placement of modifiers.

EXAMPLE 1. Do you like Western boots or hiking boots most?
1. *most—more*

1. Ernest runs very good, but William can run even better.
2. Katherine is the more curious of the four Matsuo children.
3. Which flavor of frozen yogurt do you think would be worser, cheddar or carrot?
4. Tell me, did you do gooder on this week's spelling test than on last week's?
5. Annie brings homegrown tomatoes to her friends that she picks from her garden.
6. The astronaut met with children who had commanded a mission aboard the space shuttle.
7. Gloria became more worriedly as the storm grew worse.
8. Of the Amazon, Nile, and Mississippi rivers, the Nile is the longer.
9. We rented that scary movie at the video store from which the filmmakers spun off a television series.
10. Have you ever read *Fahrenheit 451*, the novel about book burning by Ray Bradbury?
11. After carefully rehearsing several times, Toni felt confidently about giving her speech.
12. Vincente made a cover for his textbook with his initials on it.
13. Janelle found a recipe for broiling catfish in a cookbook.

14. If you look close at the painting, you can see how tiny the brush strokes are.
15. We looked through the old photo album in the kitchen that we had just found in the attic.
16. It was a large crop, and it grew good, too.
17. Icarus foolish flew nearer to the sun than he should have.
18. In different parts of the world, we have read about unusual customs.
19. Aunt Dee and Uncle Mike enjoyed the broadcast of the symphony in their living room.
20. We found the sheet music for songs your mother used to sing in the piano bench.

Reference Note

For information on **double comparisons** and **double negatives,** see pages 252 and 255.

Exercise 18 **Correcting Double Comparisons and Double Negatives**

Revise each of the following sentences to correct the double comparison or double negative.

EXAMPLE
1. Grandma thought learning to swim would be more harder than it was.
   1. *Grandma thought learning to swim would be harder than it was.*

1. My sister gave me her soccer ball because she never plays soccer no more.
2. You can get a more clearer idea of what the trail is like by looking at this map.
3. We couldn't hardly believe our eyes when we saw what was under the rock!
4. You shouldn't stand nowhere around a tall tree during a thunderstorm.
5. Keisha's uncle Anthony just adopted the most strangest pet I've ever seen.
6. My little sister can't scarcely reach the doorknob without standing on tiptoe.
7. I'm not going to put off practicing my bongo drums no more.
8. That was the most worst movie we've ever seen.

9. Didn't neither of the books have the information you needed?

10. I've read that potbellied pigs learn more faster than dogs do.

Exercise 19 Identifying Correct Usage

For each of the following sentences, choose the word or word group in parentheses that is correct according to the rules of formal, standard English.

EXAMPLE **1.** My aunt Claire was working in Athens, Greece, (*then, than*).

  1. *then*

1. Everyone from the volleyball team is here (*accept, except*) Roseanne.

2. Steve said he thought the new batting lineup looked (*alright, all right*).

3. The two friends felt (*bad, badly*) after arguing.

4. The children helped (*theirselves, themselves*) to the curry.

5. Do you know (*whose, who's*) sunglasses these are?

6. The boys will (*try to, try and*) finish painting today.

7. Be sure to (*bring, take*) your lunch when you go to the park.

8. The ten students in the art class divided all of the construction paper and markers (*between, among*) themselves.

9. (*Who's, Whose*) going to show them how to dance?

10. Heat lightning occurs too far from people for them to hear (*its, it's*) accompanying thunder.

Exercise 20 Correcting Errors in Usage

Each of the following sentences contains an error in the use of formal, standard English. Identify each error, and then write the correct usage.

EXAMPLE **1.** Them fish are called sea horses.

  1. *Them—Those*

1. Where are sea horses found at?

2. Sea horses are found in tropical and temperate waters—not anywheres that is very cold.

3. Baby sea horses often use they're curved tails to hold on to each other.
4. That there sea horse used its tail to grasp some seaweed.
5. Don't you think that it's head looks amazingly like a tiny horse's head?
6. The little fin on a sea horse's back moves so fast that you can't hardly see it.
7. Several students asked the teacher how come the eyes of a sea horse work independently of each other.
8. My stepsisters and I use to look for sea horses when we lived near the coast in California.
9. The teacher reminded us to bring home a parental approval form for the field trip to the city aquarium.
10. When your at the aquarium, remember to stop by the sea horse exhibit.

Reference Note

For information on **common usage errors,** see Chapter 10.

Exercise 21 Proofreading Sentences for Correct Usage

Each of the following sentences contains an error in English usage. Identify each error. Then, write the correct usage.

EXAMPLE 1. Do you all ready know about the Pantanal?

   1. all ready—already

1. The Pantanal is the largest wetland anywheres on earth.
2. To get an idea of it's size, imagine an area about the size of Arkansas.
3. Most of the Pantanal is located inside of Brazil.
4. The area contains a enormous wealth of wildlife.
5. Our science teacher is learning us about the jaguar, the giant anteater, and other animals that live there.
6. The Pantanal may be more important for wading birds such as storks then any other place in South America.
7. In addition, alot of other birds, such as toucans and macaws, live there.
8. The Pantanal has swamps that sometimes have absorbed heavy rains that otherwise might of flooded nearby areas.
9. However, the Pantanal ain't all swamps; it also contains forests.
10. Although the Pantanal is a long ways from where I live, I hope to have a chance to explore it someday.

Grammar and Usage Test: Section 1

DIRECTIONS   In each of the following sentences, a word group is under-lined. Using the rules of formal, standard English, choose the answer that most clearly expresses the meaning of the sentence. If there is no error, choose A. Indicate your response by shading in the appropriate oval on your answer sheet.

EXAMPLE   1. The fish <u>smelled badly</u>, so we didn't buy any.

    (A) smelled badly
    (B) smells badly
    (C) smelled bad
    (D) smelling bad

ANSWER   1.   Ⓐ   Ⓑ   Ⓒ   Ⓓ

1. Roz and <u>I catched</u> fireflies in a jar.
    (A) I catched
    (B) me catched
    (C) I caught
    (D) me caught

2. <u>Fun hiking in the wilderness preserve.</u>
    (A) Fun hiking in the wilderness preserve.
    (B) While having fun hiking in the wilderness preserve.
    (C) Hiking in the wilderness preserve was fun.
    (D) Have had fun hiking in the wilderness preserve.

3. The election resulted in a runoff between <u>he and I.</u>
    (A) he and I
    (B) him and me
    (C) him and I
    (D) he and me

4. In bowling, a strike <u>is when</u> a bowler knocks down all ten pins on the first throw in a frame.
    (A) is when
    (B) occurs when
    (C) is where
    (D) is because

5. Have you heard of Lawrence and Lorne <u>Blair, two brothers who traveled in Indonesia for ten years?</u>

(A) Blair, two brothers who traveled in Indonesia for ten years?

(B) Blair? Two brothers who traveled in Indonesia for ten years.

(C) Blair, two brothers whom traveled in Indonesia for ten years?

(D) Blair and two brothers who traveled in Indonesia for ten years?

6. <u>Is this here</u> drill bit the right size?

(A) Is this here

(B) Is that there

(C) Is this here kind of

(D) Is this

7. <u>Here your car keys.</u>

(A) Here your car keys.

(B) Here are your car keys.

(C) Here's you're car keys.

(D) Here is your car keys.

8. <u>The dog barked the baby awoke.</u>

(A) The dog barked the baby awoke.

(B) The dog barked, the baby awoke.

(C) The dog barked, and the baby awoke.

(D) The dog barking and the baby awoke.

9. I <u>shouldn't of</u> waited to start my essay.

(A) shouldn't of

(B) shouldn't have

(C) ought not to of

(D) oughtn't not to have

10. Mrs. Levine asked <u>how come Darnell and he aren't</u> ready to leave yet.

(A) how come Darnell and he aren't

(B) how come Darnell and him aren't

(C) why Darnell and he isn't

(D) why Darnell and he aren't

COMMON ERRORS

Grammar and Usage Test: Section 2

DIRECTIONS   Read the paragraph below. For each of the numbered blanks, select the word or word group that best completes the sentence. Indicate your response by shading in the appropriate oval on your answer sheet.

EXAMPLE   Two species of elephant __(1)__ today: the African elephant and the Asian elephant.

    1. (**A**) does exist

        (**B**) exists

        (**C**) have been existing

        (**D**) exist

ANSWER   1.   Ⓐ   Ⓑ   Ⓒ   **Ⓓ**

Each of these species has __(1)__ own unique features; for example, the African elephant has __(2)__ ears and tusks than the Asian elephant does. Although different in some ways, both species of elephant __(3)__ strong, intelligent, and social. Both have poor sight and are colorblind but can smell and hear quite __(4)__. Elephants can detect the scent of __(5)__ human who is over a mile away. __(6)__ hearing is so good that they can communicate over distances of more than two miles, using sounds __(7)__ any that humans can hear. Unfortunately, human population growth, farming, industry, and illegal hunting __(8)__ a decline in the elephant population. For instance, poachers have killed thousands of African elephants for their ivory tusks; in fact, from 1979 to the early 1990s, the number of elephants in Africa __(9)__ from 1,300,000 to fewer than 600,000. __(10)__ protect elephants, the trade of ivory was outlawed worldwide in 1989.

---

1. (A) it

   (**B**) its'

   (**C**) it's

   (**D**) its

2. (A) larger

   (**B**) more larger

   (**C**) the more larger

   (**D**) the most largest

3. (A) they are

   (**B**) are

   (**C**) are being

   (**D**) is

4. (A) well

   (**B**) good

   (**C**) better

   (**D**) best

5. (**A**) a
   (**B**) an
   (**C**) the
   (**D**) this

6. (**A**) They're
   (**B**) There
   (**C**) Their
   (**D**) They

7. (**A**) more lower than
   (**B**) lower than
   (**C**) more low then
   (**D**) lower then

8. (**A**) will have caused
   (**B**) causes
   (**C**) are causing
   (**D**) is cause

9. (**A**) shrinks
   (**B**) shrank
   (**C**) shrinked
   (**D**) is shrinking

10. (**A**) 2
    (**B**) Too
    (**C**) Two
    (**D**) To

COMMON ERRORS

Exercise 22 Correcting Errors in Capitalization

Each of the following word groups contains at least one error in capitalization. Correct the errors either by changing capital letters to lowercase letters or by changing lowercase letters to capital letters.

EXAMPLE   **1.** abilene, texas

     1. *Abilene, Texas*

1. the smoky mountains
2. rutherford B. hayes
3. *Alice In Wonderland*
4. university of kansas
5. labor day
6. near lake Placid
7. it's already tuesday!
8. english or Art II
9. washington monument
10. marta Hinojosa, m.d.
11. neptune and other planets
12. second day of hanukkah
13. my Uncle Jack
14. an airplane called *spirit of st. louis*
15. a river running South
16. Bryce canyon national park
17. 912 valentine st.
18. president Cleveland
19. "i'm home!"
20. newbery medal

Exercise 23 Correcting Errors in Capitalization

Correct the capitalization errors in the following sentences either by changing capital letters to lowercase letters or by changing lowercase letters to capital letters.

EXAMPLE   **1.** i went to see a play last saturday.

     1. *I went to see a play last Saturday.*

1. Our drama teacher, ms. soto, took us to see it.
2. the new play was first performed by the south Texas performance company.

3. this theater group's founder and director is the translator, playwright, and theater scholar joe rosenberg.
4. He has established an exchange program for theater students from the united states, mexico, and south america.
5. In addition, mr. rosenberg has written a full-length play titled *saturday stranger,* which was published in germany.
6. Mr. Rosenberg has also edited a Book called *¡aplauso! hispanic Children's theater.*
7. the book includes plays by héctor santiago, roy conboy, and lisa loomer, among others.
8. the plays are printed in both english and spanish.
9. these plays draw on hispanic literary traditions native to such places as mexico, puerto rico, and cuba.
10. Next month the southwest middle school drama club plans to perform one of the plays from this book.

Exercise 24 **Using Periods, Question Marks, and Exclamation Points Correctly**

Reference Note

For information on **using end marks,** see page 309.

For each of the following sentences, write each letter or word that should be followed by a period, question mark, or exclamation point, and add the proper punctuation.

EXAMPLE   1. Senator Jackson, can you meet with our class at 8:15 A M

   1. *A.M.?*

HELP

Some sentences in Exercise 24 need more than one punctuation mark.

1. Please follow me
2. Will you please help me carry my books
3. Where in the downtown library is the new display of Peruvian pottery
4. Watch out for that car
5. Dr Williamson taught me to fly a model helicopter
6. Anthony asked Rose whether her favorite cartoonist is Charles M Schulz
7. One fossil recently discovered in these mountains dates back to 3 million B C
8. What a surprise that was
9. Have you ever brought your skateboard to school
10. The letter addressed to 4613 Sleepy Hollow Blvd, Kingston, NY 12401, must be for Mrs C R Smith

Reference Note

For information on **using commas,** see page 314.

Exercise 25 Proofreading Sentences for the Correct Use of Commas

Each of the following sentences is missing at least one comma. Write the word or numeral that should be followed by a comma, and add the comma.

EXAMPLE 1. Oh I hope we win the track meet when we go to Salina Kansas next week.

1. *Oh, Salina, Kansas,*

1. Sheila ran laps on Monday Tuesday and Wednesday.
2. On February 20 2007 my family had a reunion in San Juan Puerto Rico.
3. Yes that is the dog they adopted from the animal shelter.
4. Because my father is going to teach me to play the guitar soon he is showing me how to tune one now.
5. No I have never read *The Hobbit.*
6. Scissors pins tacks and other sharp items should be kept out of the reach of young children.
7. Athena the Greek goddess of crafts wisdom and war is often shown with an owl on her shoulder.
8. Douglas never leaves shopping carts in parking spaces set aside for people who have disabilities and neither should anyone else.
9. My aunt and I bought nails lumber and paint for the bird-houses we plan to build.
10. Professor Chang will you explain the differences between these two kinds of cells?

Reference Note

For information on **using colons and semicolons,** see page 325.

Exercise 26 Using Semicolons and Colons Correctly

The following sentences lack necessary colons and semicolons. Write the words or numerals that come before and after the needed punctuation, and insert the proper punctuation.

EXAMPLE 1. My grandmother is coming to visit we will meet her at the airport.

1. *visit; we*

1. We picked subjects for our reports I chose sea turtles.
2. Our school day used to start at 8 15 now it starts at 8 00.

3. The following items will be needed for the new playground swings, slides, and picnic tables.
4. The rain just ended maybe we will get a chance to see a double rainbow.
5. We can save water in these ways turning off the faucet while brushing our teeth, pouring only as much as we plan to drink, and taking showers instead of baths.
6. At the farmers' market, shoppers were discussing the recent election they were discussing the weather, too.
7. "Dear Sir or Madam" is one proper way to begin a business letter, but not the only way.
8. Plains Indians include the following peoples Comanche, Osage, Pawnee, Crow, and Blackfeet.
9. At 6 30 A.M. my alarm went off I couldn't believe it was time to get up.
10. My wish list is as follows a mountain bike, good grades, and a happy home.

Exercise 27 **Punctuating and Capitalizing Quotations**

Revise the following numbered items, using quotation marks, other marks of punctuation, and capital letters where needed. If a sentence is already correct, write *C*.

EXAMPLE
1. I admire Marian Wright Edelman said Paul she has worked hard for children's rights.

1. *"I admire Marian Wright Edelman," said Paul. "She has worked hard for children's rights."*

1. In 1973, Edelman founded the Children's Defense Fund, a nonprofit organization that has helped many people said Mr. Knepp.
2. Paul commented that just the other day he had read an article titled Edelman: The Children's Defender.
3. Justin said I'd like to work to protect children's rights, too, one day.
4. Edelman was born in 1939 Paul told us she grew up in Bennettsville, South Carolina.
5. Mr. Knepp said that Marian Wright Edelman is one of our country's greatest civic leaders.

─HELP─

Some sentences in Exercise 27 may be correctly revised in more than one way. You only need to give one revision for each sentence.

Reference Note

For information on **using quotation marks,** see page 338. For information on **using capital letters,** see Chapter 11.

COMMON ERRORS

6. Please tell me more about Edelman's career as a lawyer, Ashley said.

7. She graduated from Yale Law School in 1963 he said And soon became the first African American woman licensed to practice law in Mississippi.

8. Mr. Knepp added Edelman has handled many civil rights cases and has always made community service a priority.

9. did Edelman say that she had been taught as a child to make service a central part of her life? Justin asked.

10. Yes Ashley answered I remember reading that in her autobiography, *The Measure of Our Success: A Letter to My Children and Yours.*

Reference Note

For information on **punctuating dialogue,** see page 342.

Exercise 28 **Punctuating Dialogue**

Revise the following dialogue, adding quotation marks and other marks of punctuation and replacing lowercase letters with capital letters where necessary. Remember to begin a new paragraph each time the speaker changes.

EXAMPLE [1] The legend of Greyfriars Bobby is so moving, Jennifer exclaimed, that I'll never forget it.

1. "The legend of Greyfriars Bobby is so moving," Jennifer exclaimed, "that I'll never forget it."

[1] Bobby was a special dog, Jennifer said, and extremely loyal to his master. [2] Tony asked, "can you believe that Bobby actually lived by his master's grave for fourteen years?" [3] Jennifer said, My cousin went to Edinburgh, Scotland, and saw Bobby's grave. [4] It is in Greyfriars churchyard, near his master's grave. [5] When did Bobby die? Tony asked. [6] He died in 1872, Jennifer replied. [7] "the people in the town fed Bobby and cared for him until his death."

[8] "Bobby slept during the day, Tony recalled because, before his master died, they had worked together at night."

[9] Jennifer said, "yes, his master, old Jock, guarded cattle that were sold at the market." [10] Tony said, In Edinburgh there is a statue of Greyfriars Bobby on top of a drinking fountain for dogs.

COMMON ERRORS

Exercise 29 Using Apostrophes Correctly

Rewrite the following word groups, inserting an apostrophe wherever one is needed.

Reference Note

For information on **using apostrophes,** see page 346.

EXAMPLE   **1.** the womens class

    1. the women's class

1. if theyve gone
2. no ones fault
3. that statues condition
4. so lets try
5. since youre going home
6. that giants castle
7. theirs werent faded
8. the Rockies highest peak
9. when there isnt time
10. these books authors
11. Arkansas governor
12. if everybodys there
13. made all As in school
14. one pueblos history
15. the five camels saddles
16. born in 84
17. and theres the dog
18. the sheeps wool
19. when youll find out
20. two *os* in the word *igloo*
21. arent able to
22. the one whos late
23. when Im tired
24. around 10 oclock
25. those two books pages

Exercise 30 Correcting Spelling Errors

Most of the following words are misspelled. If a word is not spelled correctly, write the correct spelling. If a word is already spelled correctly, write *C*.

Reference Note

For information on **spelling rules,** see page 363.

EXAMPLE   **1.** mispeak

    1. misspeak

1. percieve
2. disolve
3. gladest
4. charging
5. comedies
6. sillyness
7. taxs
8. tryed
9. potatos
10. traceing
11. classes
12. sleigh
13. matchs
14. videoes
15. funnyer
16. toyes
17. schoolling
18. wieght
19. loosness
20. Gomezs
21. managable
22. unatural
23. ladys
24. runing
25. finaly

COMMON ERRORS

Exercise 31 **Choosing Between Words Often Confused**

For each of the following sentences, choose the word or word group in parentheses that will make the sentence correct.

EXAMPLE   1. Matthew suggested that I (*altar, alter*) the first paragraph of my story.
   1. alter

1. Have you (*all ready, already*) finished your latest painting?
2. (*Your, You're*) pets need good food, clean water, warm shelter, and loving attention.
3. Be careful not to (*lose, loose*) any of those puzzle pieces, or we'll have to buy a new puzzle.
4. Chuckwallas are harmless lizards that may grow to be two feet long and live in rocky (*desserts, deserts*) in the United States and Mexico.
5. Manuel dreamed of finding a sunken ship and (*it's, its*) treasure chest.
6. The school (*threw, through*) away tons of paper and cardboard before the recycling program was started.
7. (*Whose, Who's*) planning to bring food and drinks to the fiesta tomorrow?
8. We drove (*passed, past*) the park, across the bridge, and around the lake to the dock.
9. Marcie's enthusiasm for playing in the marching band was (*plain, plane*) to see.
10. The guide (*lead, led*) the scouts through the museum.
11. Former President Jimmy Carter has been greatly involved in efforts to bring (*piece, peace*) to various countries all over the world.
12. In less than one (*weak, week*), Sandra's mother will begin her new job as editor-in-chief of the newspaper's new Washington bureau.
13. (*There, Their*) are many kinds of trees in our neighborhood, and they provide plenty of shade.
14. The gravel in the driveway is (*coarse, course*), but it still feels good on my bare feet.
15. The flagpole itself was (*stationary, stationery*), but the flag flapped in the breeze.

16. "The lamp may (*brake, break*) if you try to carry it on its side and with one hand," Dad cautioned.
17. What is the (*capital, capitol*) of Puerto Rico?
18. Mr. Edgars is a good man whose (*principles, principals*) include honesty and fairness.
19. When we sit outside on the porch, we can't (*hear, here*) the phone ring.
20. We read (*threw, through*) Gary Soto's book of poetry and picked out some poems to memorize.

(Exercise 32) **Proofreading Sentences for Errors in Spelling and Words Often Confused**

For each of the following sentences, identify and correct any error in spelling or usage.

EXAMPLE   **1.** The Iroquois people's name for themselfs means "we longhouse builders."

       1. *themselfs—themselves*

1. In our American history coarse, we learned that the Iroquois constructed large dwellings called longhouses.
2. Years ago, nearly all Iroquois lived in forests and built they're longhouses out of logs and strips of bark.
3. Several individual familys lived in each of these longhouses.
4. When a couple married, the husband would move into the longhouse of his wife's extended family, called a clan.
5. Each family had it's own separate area with a sleeping platform that was raised about a foot above the ground.
6. They kept the longhouse neat by storing many of their belongings on shelfs above their sleeping platforms.
7. Fires were made in hearths in a central corridor, and smoke rose threw holes cut in the longhouse roof.
8. When it rained or snowed, slideing panels were used to close the holes.
9. The biggest longhouses measured more than two hundred feet in length.
10. Such large longhouses could shelter 10 or more individual families at a time.

Reference Note

For information on **spelling rules,** see page 363. For information on **words often confused,** see page 373.

COMMON ERRORS

HELP

Many of the sentences in Exercise 33 contain more than one error.

Exercise 33 Proofreading a Paragraph for Errors in Mechanics

For the sentences in the following paragraph, correct each error in mechanics. If a sentence is already correct, write *C*.

EXAMPLES 1. Have you ever seen the movie *the Wizard of Oz*?
1. *The Wizard of Oz*

2. You may not know that its based on a book.
2. *it's*

[1] The book was written by l. frank Baum. [2] He was born on May 15 1856 in the state of New York. [3] When he was a teenager he was interested in the theater and his father a wealthy oilman gave him several theaters to manage. [4] In 1881 he wrote *The maid of Arran*, a successful play. [5] For many years he worked at several jobs, including storekeeper newspaper reporter and traveling salesman. [6] In 1900 he published a childrens book called *The Wonderful Wizard of Oz*, which was a bestseller for two years in a row. [7] Baum adapted the book into a successful play, and he even made several silent movies about Oz. [8] Baum died in Hollywood California in 1919 and twenty years later the famous film starring Judy Garland as Dorothy was made in the same city. [9] During the making of the film, the actor who played the wizard discovered that L. Frank Baum's name was sewn into the lineing of the wizard's coat. [10] According to Baum's wife, it really was Baum's old coat the movie studio's wardrobe department had bought it at a secondhand clothing shop.

Exercise 34 Proofreading a Business Letter for Correct Grammar, Usage, and Mechanics

HELP

Most items in Exercise 34 contain more than one error.

Correct the errors in grammar, usage, and mechanics in the numbered items in the following letter.

EXAMPLE [1] 254 Thirty second street
1. *254 Thirty-second Street*

254 Thirty-second Street
Syracuse, NY 13210
[1] November 5 2009

Ms. Susan Loroupe
[2] *Syracuse daily times*
598 Seventh Avenue
Syracuse, NY 13208

[3] Dear Ms Loroupe

[4] Thank you for taking time during you're busy workday to show the Van Buren Middle School Journalism Club around the Newspaper's offices.

[5] Us club members are glad to have had the chance to see how newspaper articles are wrote and printed. **[6]** Especially enjoyed seeing the presses—even more then talking with the design artists and editors! **[7]** We were surprised that the presses were so loud and we were impressed by how quick and efficient everyone worked. **[8]** Please thank the artists, to, for showing us how they use computer's to arrange the art and photos on the pages.

Sincerely,

Carlos Lopez

Carlos Lopez
[9] journalism club Secretary
[10] Van Buren middle school

Reference Note
For information on **writing business letters,** see "Writing" in the Quick Reference Handbook.

COMMON ERRORS

Mechanics Test: Section 1

DIRECTIONS Each numbered item below contains an underlined word or word group. Choose the answer that shows the correct capitalization, punctuation, and spelling of the underlined part. If there is no error, choose answer D (Correct as is). Indicate your response by shading in the appropriate oval on your answer sheet.

EXAMPLE [1] Quincy, MA 02158

(A) Quincy, Mass. 02158
(B) Quincy MA, 02158
(C) Quincy, M.A. 02158
(D) Correct as is

ANSWER 1. (A) (B) (C) (**D**)

---

147 Hickory Lane
Quincy, MA 02158
[1] May 11 2009

The Hobby Shop
[2] 2013 forty-First Street
Los Angeles, CA 90924

[3] Dear Mr. Shaw

While I was visiting **[4]** my aunt Laura, who's house is near your store, she bought a model airplane from you. **[5]** Two of my freinds have **[6]** already tryed to help me get the plane to fly, but we haven't been able to. **[7]** Putting the plane together was not difficult; the problem is that the engine will not start. Also, I found no stickers in the box when I opened **[8]** it and the box says that there should be stickers for the plane's wings. I have enclosed the engine and my **[9]** aunt's reciept. I hope that **[10]** youre able to send me stickers and a new engine soon.

Sincerely,

Timothy Martin

Timothy Martin

---

1. (A) May, 11 2009
   (B) May 11, 2009
   (C) May, 11, 2009
   (D) Correct as is

2. (A) 2013 Forty First Street
   (B) 2013 Forty-first street
   (C) 2013 Forty-first Street
   (D) Correct as is

3. (A) Dear Mr. Shaw,
   (B) Dear Mr. Shaw:
   (C) Dear mr. shaw:
   (D) Correct as is

4. (A) my aunt Laura, whose
   (B) my Aunt Laura, whose
   (C) my Aunt Laura, who's
   (D) Correct as is

5. (A) Two of my friends
   (B) To of my freinds
   (C) Too of my friends
   (D) Correct as is

6. (A) all ready tryed
   (B) already tried
   (C) all ready tried
   (D) Correct as is

7. (A) Puting the plane
   (B) Puting the plain
   (C) Putting the plain
   (D) Correct as is

8. (A) it and the box says that their
   (B) it, and the box says that their
   (C) it, and the box says that there
   (D) Correct as is

9. (A) aunt's receipt
   (B) Aunt's receipt
   (C) aunts' reciept
   (D) Correct as is

10. (A) your
    (B) you're
    (C) your'
    (D) Correct as is

Mechanics Test: Section 2

DIRECTIONS   Each of the following sentences contains an underlined word or word group. Choose the answer that shows the correct capitalization, punctuation, and spelling of the underlined part. If there is no error, choose answer D (Correct as is). Indicate your response by shading in the appropriate oval on your answer sheet.

EXAMPLE   1.   Today the school <u>librarian Mr. Woods</u> will show us a film.

        (A) librarian, Mr. Woods
        (B) librarian, Mr. Woods,
        (C) librarian Mr. Woods,
        (D) Correct as is

ANSWER   1.

1. I wonder what the <u>capital of Spain is?</u>
 (A) capital of Spain is.
 (B) capitol of Spain is.
 (C) capitol of Spain is?
 (D) Correct as is

2. The <u>mouses'</u> nest may be in the garage.
 (A) mouses
 (B) mices
 (C) mice's
 (D) Correct as is

3. "What did you <u>see at the park?" asked my grandfather.</u>
 (A) see at the park"? asked my grandfather.
 (B) see at the park," asked my grandfather?
 (C) see at the park? asked my grandfather."
 (D) Correct as is

4. Felix, you've been a naughty kitten this <u>passed week!</u>
 (A) passed weak
 (B) past weak
 (C) past week
 (D) Correct as is

5. Aisha <u>exclaimed, "see</u> how much these crystals have grown!"
 (A) exclaimed, "See
 (B) exclaimed! "See
 (C) exclaimed "see
 (D) Correct as is

6. The Olympic team waved at the <u>crowd, the audience</u> cheered.
 (A) crowd; the audeince
 (B) crowd: the audience
 (C) crowd, and the audience
 (D) Correct as is

7. The <u>Kalahari Desert</u> is in southern Africa.
   (A) Kalahari Dessert
   (B) kalahari desert
   (C) Kalahari desert
   (D) Correct as is

8. <u>"Its snowing,"</u> observed Mrs. Daniels.
   (A) "It's snowwing,"
   (B) "It's snowing,"
   (C) Its snowing,
   (D) Correct as is

9. The Red Cross is asking <u>for: blankets,</u> sheets, and pillows.
   (A) for; blankets,
   (B) for, blankets,
   (C) for blankets,
   (D) Correct as is

10. Robert Frost's <u>poem The Road Not Taken</u> is famous.
    (A) poem *The Road Not Taken*
    (B) poem "The Road Not Taken"
    (C) poem "the Road not Taken"
    (D) Correct as is

PART 2

Sentences and Paragraphs

Writing Effective Sentences

Writing Clear Sentences

Your goal in writing should always be to communicate clearly with your reader. A clear sentence gives your reader just enough information. It does not leave out any important pieces, and it does not run together or string together too many ideas at once. Clear sentences make it easier for your reader to understand what you are saying. You can learn how to spot three enemies of clear writing: *sentence fragments, run-on sentences,* and *stringy sentences.*

Sentence Fragments

What kind of sentence could you write about this picture? You might write something like this:

> The high jumper flips backwards over the bar.

or

> Look at how high the bar is!

or

> How does she know where to jump?

These groups of words say different things, but they have something in common. Each is a *complete sentence.* A **complete sentence** is a group of words that expresses a complete thought.

A part of each thought is expressed by the verb: *flips, look, is, does know, jump.* Another part is expressed by the subject: *high jumper, you, she.* [The *you* is understood in the second sentence even though it is not expressed: (You) Look at how high the bar is!]

A *sentence fragment* is a part of a sentence that is punctuated as if it were a complete sentence. A fragment is confusing because it does not express a complete thought. The following word groups are the example sentences—with some important words left out. Notice how unclear the word groups are when written as fragments.

> **Flips backwards over the bar.** [The subject is missing. *Who* or *what* flips?]

> **At how high the bar is.** [The verb and the understood subject are missing. *What about* how high the bar is?]

> **Where to jump.** [This word group has a subject and a verb, but it does not express a complete thought. *What about* where to jump?]

Use this simple three-part test to help you decide whether a word group is a sentence fragment or a complete sentence.

1. Does the group of words have a *subject*?
2. Does the word group have a *verb*?
3. Does the word group express a *complete thought*?

You know the word group is a complete sentence if you answer "yes" to all three questions above. If you answer "no" to a question, the word group is a sentence fragment.

TIPS & TRICKS

Sometimes a fragment is really a part of a nearby sentence. You can correct the fragment by attaching it to the sentence that comes before or after it.

FRAGMENT
Mark is practicing his hook shot. **Because he wants to try out for the basketball team.**

SENTENCE
Mark is practicing his hook shot because he wants to try out for the basketball team.

When you attach a fragment to a sentence, be sure to check your new sentence for correct punctuation.

Exercise 1 **Recognizing Fragments**

Decide which of the following word groups are sentence fragments and which are complete sentences. Write *S* for a complete sentence; write *F* for a fragment.

1. We visited the pet shop in the mall.
2. A bright-eyed hamster chewing on pieces of carrot.
3. Named him Mustard.
4. Has pouches inside each fat cheek.
5. The pouches are for carrying food.

SKILLS FOCUS

Write clearly and effectively. Identify and correct sentence fragments.

6. Newspaper in lots of little shreds.
7. Making his cage quite comfortable.
8. He is plump and has white and tan fur.
9. A diet of mostly fruit, vegetables, and grain.
10. If you decide to raise hamsters.

Exercise 2 Revising Fragments

Some of the following word groups are sentence fragments. First, identify the fragments. Then, revise each fragment by (1) adding a subject, (2) adding a verb, or (3) attaching the fragment to a complete sentence. You may also need to change the punctuation and capitalization in your revised sentence. If a word group below is already a complete sentence, write *S* on your paper.

EXAMPLE   1. It a stormy Wednesday night.

1. *It was a stormy Wednesday night.*

1. Was watching TV alone.
2. A movie about aliens invading from space.
3. Suddenly, the lights went out on the whole block.
4. Because the batteries in the flashlight were dead.
5. A strange noise in the backyard.
6. After our dog started to bark.
7. Crept slowly to the door and looked out.
8. Two small, glowing eyes in the dark.
9. When I saw it was just the cat from next door.
10. Maybe I should stop watching scary movies.

COMPUTER TIP

You can use your computer to help eliminate sentence fragments. Using the cut and paste commands, you can easily try attaching a fragment to both the sentence before it and the sentence after it. Doing so will allow you to see which sentence makes more sense. Check your writing for correctness and completeness after making changes.

Run-on Sentences

A *run-on sentence* is actually two or more sentences run together without proper punctuation as if they were one sentence. It is often hard to tell where one idea in a run-on ends and the next one begins.

Like sentence fragments, run-on sentences usually appear in your writing because you are in a hurry to get your thoughts down on paper. This mistake happens when you leave out the correct end punctuation (period, question mark, or exclamation point) or when you use a comma to separate the sentences.

There is more than one way to revise a run-on sentence. You can break the run-on into two complete sentences, or you can link the two ideas with a comma and a coordinating conjunction such as *and, but,* or *or.*

RUN-ON	In 1962 John Glenn became the first American to orbit Earth, he made his second space flight on the space shuttle *Discovery* in 1998, when he was 77 years old.
CORRECT	In 1962 John Glenn became the first American to orbit Earth**.** **H**e made his second space flight on the space shuttle *Discovery* in 1998, when he was 77 years old. [The sentence has been broken into two complete sentences.]

or

In 1962 John Glenn became the first American to orbit Earth**,** **and** he made his second space flight on the space shuttle *Discovery* in 1998, when he was 77 years old. [Two complete ideas have been linked by a comma plus *and.*]

NOTE A comma alone is not enough to link two complete ideas in a sentence. If you use just a comma between two complete ideas, you create a run-on sentence.

RUN-ON	Sally Ride was the first American woman in space, she was a member of a shuttle crew.
CORRECT	Sally Ride was the first American woman in space**.** **S**he was a member of a shuttle crew.

Reference Note

For more information about and practice using **commas with coordinating conjunctions,** see page 316.

SKILLS FOCUS

Identify and correct run-on sentences.

Identifying and Revising Run-on Sentences

Decide which of the following groups of words are run-ons. Revise each run-on by (1) making it into two separate sentences, or (2) using a comma and a coordinating conjunction. You may have to change the punctuation and capitalization, too. If the group of words is already correct, write *C*.

1. People constantly search for faster ways to communicate, the Internet is one tool that helps people share information quickly.
2. The earliest form of the Internet was designed over thirty years ago, and it was created to be used by the military.
3. The Internet has changed a great deal since then now it can be used by almost anyone who uses a computer.
4. The first e-mail program was invented in 1972, e-mail is a way to send messages from one computer to another.
5. Twenty years later, scientists in Switzerland created the World Wide Web, and *Internet* quickly became a household word.
6. The scientists planned to use the Web to share research with scientists in other parts of the world the new invention soon interested businesses and government organizations.
7. The programs that make the Internet and the World Wide Web work are very complicated they are not hard to use.
8. Many schools and libraries have computers that are connected to the Internet and the World Wide Web.
9. The World Wide Web began with four newsgroups in 1991, but it soon included millions of sites.
10. Many sites on the World Wide Web focus on school subjects, news, and hobbies, these sites can be useful sources of information.

Stringy Sentences

For variety, you will sometimes want to join sentences and sentence parts with *and*. If you string many ideas together with *and*, though, you create a ***stringy sentence.*** Stringy sentences ramble on and on. They do not give the reader a chance to pause between ideas.

Revise to improve organization. Edit for clarity and detail.

STRINGY   The ostrich is the largest living bird, and it stands nearly eight feet tall, and it weighs over three hundred pounds when it is fully grown, and this speedy bird can run up to forty miles an hour!

BETTER   The ostrich is the largest living bird. It stands nearly eight feet tall, and it weighs over three hundred pounds when it is fully grown. This speedy bird can run up to forty miles an hour!

In the revised version, only two ideas are linked by *and*. These ideas can be combined into one sentence because they are closely related. Notice that a comma is used before the word *and*. The comma is also necessary to show a slight pause between the two complete ideas.

Exercise 4 **Identifying and Revising Stringy Sentences**

Some of the following sentences are stringy. Revise each stringy sentence by breaking it into two or more sentences. If an item is already correct, write *C*.

1. Thomas and José were playing softball at school, and Thomas hit the ball very hard, and then he saw it roll under the steps of the library.
2. Thomas peered under the dark steps to recover his ball, and when he reached for it, he saw a giant raccoon, and Thomas wasn't sure what to do next!
3. José told Thomas that raccoons are fierce fighters, and then José warned him not to anger the raccoon, and by this time, other softball players had gathered to offer advice.
4. Thomas finally rolled the ball out from under the steps with a baseball bat. The raccoon stayed completely still, and it hissed and looked fiercely at the group. Then Thomas saw why the raccoon was behaving so strangely.
5. Five baby raccoons were hiding behind the mother, and they were too small to protect themselves, and the mother raccoon was trying to frighten the softball players away!

Revising Sentence Fragments, Run-on Sentences, and Stringy Sentences

Decide which of the following word groups are fragments, run-ons, or stringy sentences. Then, revise each of these word groups to make it clear and complete. Remember to add correct capitalization and punctuation. If a word group is already clear and complete, write *C* for *correct*.

1. Not all animals see the world in the same way humans see the world.
2. See only light and dark shapes.
3. Squids and octopuses have very advanced eyes they see almost as well as humans.
4. The jeweled squid lives deep underwater in the Indian Ocean, it has white, blue, and red lights around its eyes to help it see in the dark water.
5. Several other sea creatures have their own "headlights," and these lights are sometimes produced by helpful bacteria, and the fish store the bacteria in special skin pouches.
6. Some owls can catch mice in total darkness by hearing alone others can find a mouse by the light of one candle placed nearly a quarter of a mile away from the mouse.
7. Grazing animals must have a wide field of vision so that they will know when an enemy is coming.
8. Rabbits and deer eyes on the sides of their heads.
9. Mammals that hunt other animals for food must be able to judge distance well, therefore their eyes are usually located toward the front of their faces.
10. Most apes do not hunt other animals for food, but their eyes are in much the same position as human eyes, and apes also see the same range of colors humans see.

Combining Sentences

Good writers usually use some short sentences, but they don't use them all the time. An entire paragraph of short sentences makes writing sound choppy. For example, notice how dull and choppy the following paragraph sounds.

```
    Quicksand is really just sand. The
sand is wet. The sand is loose. You can
sink in quicksand. It will not actually
suck you down. You might get caught in
quicksand. You can lie on your back. You
can float. Then you can roll or wriggle.
Your movements must be slow. You can get
to solid ground this way.
```

Now, see how the writer has revised the paragraph by combining some of the short sentences. Notice how sentence combining has helped to eliminate some repeated words and ideas. The result is a smoother paragraph that has much more variety.

```
    Quicksand is really just wet, loose
sand. You can sink in quicksand, but it
will not actually suck you down. If you
are caught in quicksand, you can lie on
your back and float. Then you can slowly
roll or wriggle to solid ground.
```

You can combine sentences in several different ways. Sometimes you can insert a word or a group of words from one sentence into another sentence. Other times you can combine two related sentences by using a connecting word.

Inserting Words

One way to combine two sentences is to pull a key word from one sentence and insert it into the other sentence. Sometimes you can just add the key word to the first sentence and drop the rest of the second sentence. Other times you will need to change the form of the key word before you can insert it.

TIPS & TRICKS

To get ideas for a variety of ways to organize your ideas into sentences, look at sentences written by professional authors. Try imitating the style of a favorite author by using similar sentence structures in your own sentences or paragraphs.

SKILLS FOCUS

Combine sentences for effective writing.
Combine sentences by inserting words.

When you change the forms of key words, you often add endings such as –ed, –ing, –ful, and –ly to make adjectives and adverbs.

EXAMPLES
skill → skilled
crash → crashing
use → useful
quiet → quietly

Using the Same Form	
Original	Dr. Martin Luther King, Jr., was a civil rights leader. He was an American.
Combined	Dr. Martin Luther King, Jr., was an **American** civil rights leader.

Changing the Form	
Original	He was famous for his brilliant speeches. His fame was international.
Combined	He was **internationally** famous for his brilliant speeches.

Exercise 5 **Combining Sentences by Inserting Words**

Each of the following items contains two sentences. Combine the two sentences by taking the italicized key word from the second sentence and inserting it into the first sentence. The directions in parentheses will tell you how to change the form of the key word if you need to do so.

EXAMPLE **1.** Chief Joseph was a Nez Perce Indian chief who fought for his people. He was a *brave* fighter. (Add –ly.)

1. Chief Joseph was a Nez Perce Indian chief who fought bravely for his people.

1. The name Joseph was given to his father by missionaries. The missionaries were *Christian.*

2. His name, Hin-mah-too-yah-lat-ket, means "thunder rolling down the mountains." That is his *Nez Perce* name.

3. Chief Joseph fought the United States Army to defend his people's homeland. The fighting was *fierce.* (Add –ly.)

4. When he realized he could not win, he led the Nez Perce band more than one thousand miles. The band was in *retreat.* (Add –ing.)

5. Chief Joseph's surrender speech is famous. The speech is *moving.*

Inserting Groups of Words

Often, you can combine two related sentences by taking an entire group of words from one sentence and adding it to the other sentence. When the group of words is inserted, it adds detail to the information in the first sentence.

ORIGINAL	The first known baseball game was played in 1846. It was played in Hoboken, New Jersey.
COMBINED	The first known baseball game was played in 1846 **in Hoboken, New Jersey.**

ORIGINAL	The game ended with a score of 23–1. It was played by the New York Baseball Club and the Knickerbockers.
COMBINED	**Played by the New York Baseball Club and the Knickerbockers,** the game ended with a score of 23–1.

ORIGINAL	The players were all amateurs. They were in the first organized baseball league.
COMBINED	The players **in the first organized baseball league** were all amateurs.

Sometimes you will need to put commas around the group of words you are inserting. Ask yourself whether the group of words renames or identifies a noun or pronoun in the sentence. If it does, it is an *appositive phrase* and generally needs a comma or commas to set off the word group from the rest of the sentence.

ORIGINAL	The All-American Girls Professional Baseball League had ten teams at its 1948 peak. The league was the subject of a 1992 movie.
COMBINED	The All-American Girls Professional Baseball League, **the subject of a 1992 movie,** had ten teams at its 1948 peak.

ORIGINAL	Baseball is a sport that is popular with people of all ages. It is played in countries around the world.
COMBINED	Baseball, **a sport that is popular with people of all ages,** is played in countries around the world.

TIPS & TRICKS

If you move a phrase from one sentence to the *beginning* of the other sentence, you may need to add a comma after the introductory phrase.

Reference Note

For more information about and practice using **commas with appositive phrases,** see page 318.

SKILLS FOCUS

Combine sentences by inserting phrases. Use phrases correctly. Identify and use appositives and appositive phrases correctly.

After you combine two sentences, be sure to read your new sentence carefully. Then, ask yourself the following questions:

- Is my new sentence clear?
- Does it make sense?
- Does it sound better than the two shorter sentences?

If you answer "no" to any of the above questions, try to combine the sentences in a different way. Then, ask yourself the questions again.

Exercise 6 Combining Sentences by Inserting Word Groups

Combine each pair of sentences by taking the underlined word group from the second sentence and inserting it into the first sentence. Be sure to add commas if they are needed.

EXAMPLE
1. Jorge read *Storm Chaser: Into the Eye of a Hurricane* for his science report. Jorge is <u>a boy in my class</u>.

1. *Jorge, a boy in my class, read* Storm Chaser: Into the Eye of a Hurricane *for his science report.*

1. *Storm Chaser* is an exciting book. It is by <u>Keith Elliot Greenberg</u>.
2. The book is a true story about a pilot named Brian Taggart, who flies a P-3 airplane. He flies the airplane <u>directly into dangerous storms</u>.
3. Taggart works for the National Oceanic and Atmospheric Administration. He is <u>trained in the study of</u> <u>weather</u>.
4. Scientists aboard his P-3 collect information about hurricanes. The scientists collect this information <u>using computers and other machines</u>.
5. Pilots like Brian help weather forecasters predict where and when a storm will hit land. These pilots are <u>called "hurricane hunters."</u>

Using Connecting Words

Reference Note

For more information about and practice using **conjunctions,** see page 112.

Another way you can combine sentences is by using connecting words called **conjunctions.** Conjunctions allow you to join closely related sentences and sentence parts.

Joining Subjects and Verbs

Sometimes two sentences are so closely related that they have the same subjects or verbs. If two sentences have the same subject, you can combine them by making a *compound verb.* If the sentences have the same verb, you can combine them by making a *compound subject.*

The conjunction you use is important. It tells your reader how the two subjects or verbs are related to one another.

- Use *and* to join similar ideas.

ORIGINAL   The Sun Dance is an American Indian tradition. The Spirit Dance is an American Indian tradition.

COMBINED   **The Sun Dance and the Spirit Dance** are American Indian traditions. [compound subject]

- Use *but* to join contrasting ideas.

ORIGINAL   Mike will cook the main course. Mike will buy the dessert.

COMBINED   Mike will **cook** the main course **but buy** the dessert. [compound verb]

- Use *or* to show a choice between ideas.

ORIGINAL   Sara Tallchief may be elected president of the student council. Frances O'Connor may be elected president of the student council.

COMBINED   **Sara Tallchief or Frances O'Connor** may be elected president of the student council. [compound subject]

When you use the conjunction *and* to link two subjects, your new compound subject will be plural. Remember to make the verb plural, too. A verb must agree with the subject in number.

EXAMPLE
Carlos and Hannah play on the same team. [The plural subject *Carlos and Hannah* takes the plural verb *play.*]

Exercise 7 **Combining Sentences by Joining Subjects and Verbs**

Use *and, but,* or *or* to combine each of the following pairs of sentences. If the sentences have the same verb, make one sentence with a compound subject. If the sentences have the same subject, make one sentence with a compound verb. The hints in parentheses will help you.

EXAMPLE   1. The climbing perch is a fish that can walk. The mudskipper is a fish that can walk. (Join with *and.*)

1. *The climbing perch and the mudskipper are fish that can walk.*

Combine sentences by using coordinating conjunctions. Identify and use compound verbs. Identify the compound subject of a sentence.

1. Climbing fish have side fins that work much like feet. Mudskippers have side fins that work much like feet. (Join with *and*.)
2. Mudskippers walk on mud flats. Mudskippers even climb trees. (Join with *and*.)
3. Walking catfish are native to the East Indies. They have been seen in Florida. (Join with *but*.)
4. You might find walking catfish in warm, muddy water. You might find climbing perch in warm, muddy water. (Join with *or*.)
5. Mudskippers can hop more than a yard at a time. Mudskippers can catch insects as the insects fly. (Join with *and*.)

Joining Sentences

Sometimes you may want to combine two related sentences that express equally important ideas. You can connect the two sentences by using a comma and *and, but,* or *or.* The result is a ***compound sentence.***

| ORIGINAL | A group of frogs is called an *army*. A group of turtles is called a *bale*. |
| COMBINED | A group of frogs is called an *army*, **and** a group of turtles is called a *bale*. |

Other times you may want to combine two sentences that are related in a special way. One sentence helps explain the other sentence by telling *who, what, where, when, why,* or *how.*

A good way to combine these sentences is to add a connecting word that shows the special relationship. In this kind of sentence combining, you create a *complex sentence.*

ORIGINAL   The drawbridge was pulled up. The enemy knights could not get into the castle.

COMBINED   **When** the drawbridge was pulled up, the enemy knights could not get into the castle.

ORIGINAL   Their leader had not counted on the princess. The princess knew how to operate the drawbridge.

COMBINED   Their leader had not counted on the princess, **who** knew how to operate the drawbridge.

Reference Note

For more about **complex sentences,** see page 145.

Some connecting words that you can use to create complex sentences are given below. The word that you choose will depend on what you want your sentence to say.

after	before	so that	when	who
although	how	that	whether	whom
as	if	until	which	whose
because	since	what	while	why

Exercise 8   Combining Complete Sentences

Following are five pairs of short, choppy sentences that need improving. Make each pair into one sentence by using the connecting word given in parentheses. Be sure to change the capitalization and the punctuation where necessary.

EXAMPLE   1. Planets move quickly. Stars move slowly. (but)
           1. *Planets move quickly, but stars move slowly.*

1. I would like to learn more about stars. They are interesting and beautiful. (because)
2. Planets do not give off light of their own. Stars do. (but)
3. Some stars are fainter than our sun. Some are many times brighter. (and)
4. Our sun will change. The change will be slow. (but)
5. We must continue to study the stars and planets. We will understand how we fit into our vast universe. (so that)

SKILLS FOCUS

Identify and use complex sentences.

The following paragraph sounds choppy because it has too many short sentences. Use the methods you have learned in this section to combine some of the sentences. After you have revised the paragraph, read the choppy version and the new version aloud. You will notice how much better the paragraph sounds after you have revised it.

EXAMPLE   Ancient cities provide information. The information is about how people lived.

Ancient cities provide information about how people lived.

    Some of the world's oldest cities have been found in Sumer. Sumer is the land between the Tigris and the Euphrates rivers. These early cities began as villages. The villages were made of farms. Eventually, Sumerian merchants began to trade with their neighbors in the mountains. The Sumerians sold the mountain people grains. The mountain people sold the Sumerians lumber, stone, and copper. Over five thousand years ago, Sumerians invented a system of writing. They invented their writing system to keep track of their trading. We know much about how ancient Sumerians lived. They left us many written records.

Review **C** Writing Clear Sentences

The following paragraph is hard to read because it contains some sentence fragments and run-on sentences as well as choppy and stringy sentences. Identify **two** fragments, **one** run-on, and **two** stringy sentences. Then, revise those sentences using the methods you have learned. Also, combine sentences in at least **two** other places.

Sumo wrestling is an unusual sport, not only because of the unique and impressive appearance of the athletes. On average weigh 330 pounds and dress in traditional loincloths. Sumo is based in myth. It is also based in ritual. There is a myth that the Japanese people gained control of Japan when a god won a sumo match with another leader. From a rival group. The earliest sumo matches, dating back over 1500 years, were rituals performed to ensure a good harvest, and sumo later became a way to entertain royalty, and Japan then entered a time of military rule, and sumo wrestlers were used in fighting. When peace returned, sumo became entertainment again, it came to be known as the national sport of Japan. The ritual elements of early sumo remain today. At tournaments, each day opens with a colorful and exciting ritual performed by the wrestlers. The ritual is called *dohyo-iri*. *Dohyo-iri* means "entering the ring." In this ceremony the wrestlers enter the ring, and then the highest ranked wrestler comes into the ring, and he claps and stomps on the ground in a very formal way, and when he is finished other highly ranked wrestlers repeat the clapping and stomping. The ceremony symbolically drives evil spirits away. The world got to see this ceremony when it was part of the 1998 Winter Olympics opening ceremony in Nagano, Japan.

┌─HELP───

To make sure you catch all of the errors listed in the instructions, try one of the following methods. (After you correct the errors, remember to choose two other places to combine sentences.)

- Use a sticky note to label each type of sentence error you find; then, see which sentence errors listed in the instructions you have not yet found.

- Make a copy of this paragraph and highlight each type of error in a different color.

17 Learning About Paragraphs

internet **connect**

GO TO: go.hrw.com
KEYWORD: EOLang

What Is a Paragraph?

A *paragraph* is a group of related sentences. Often a paragraph is part of a longer piece of writing. For example, in a paper about a visit to a wildlife park, one paragraph might focus on the apes and monkeys. Other paragraphs in the paper could each focus on another type of animal. In this way, the paragraphs would give readers a clear idea of what they might experience at the wildlife park.

Why Use Paragraphs?

Has a friend ever sent you a letter made up of one enormous paragraph? Did you find it hard to follow his or her ideas? Breaking a long piece of writing into paragraphs is more than just a way to give your reader's eyes a rest. Breaking writing into paragraphs is like providing a map for your reader. Paragraphs guide your reader through a piece of writing by showing where one idea (or setting, or speaker) ends and the next begins. Paragraphs also make it easier for your reader to understand the main point of a piece of writing.

What Are the Parts of a Paragraph?

Paragraphs are not all alike, but many of them have the same parts. Most paragraphs have a *main idea, a topic sentence,* and *supporting sentences.* In some paragraphs a *clincher sentence* ends the paragraph and ties the details together.

The Main Idea and Topic Sentence

All of the sentences in a paragraph usually point to a single main idea. This **main idea** is the main point, or central message, of the paragraph. Sometimes an author states the main idea in a **topic sentence.** When a paragraph has a topic sentence, it is often the first or second sentence of the paragraph. Sometimes, though, the topic sentence comes in the middle or at the end of the paragraph. In the following paragraph, the topic sentence comes at the end. Notice that all of the other sentences in this paragraph support, or point to, the main idea stated in the topic sentence.

> He thought he had failed in his life's work. Others agreed with him. He died poor and bitterly disliked. To us today, this rejection seems strange. He had helped to free five South American countries from Spanish rule. He had won major victories on the battlefield. He was anything but a failure. Over time, people began to accept the truth. Monuments were built to honor him. People started to celebrate his birthday. Today, Simón Bolívar is regarded as one of Latin America's greatest heroes.

Exercise 1 **Identifying Main Ideas and Topic Sentences**

How good are you at identifying main ideas and topic sentences? Each of the following paragraphs has one main idea. Read each paragraph, and try to identify its main idea. If the

Some paragraphs, such as those in narrative writing, will have a main idea without including a topic sentence. When reading a paragraph without a topic sentence, the reader must find the main idea by paying attention to the supporting details. A main idea that is not directly stated in a topic sentence is called **an implied main idea.** In your own writing, especially writing you do for school or on tests, you should generally tell readers the main idea of every paragraph with a topic sentence.

Identify the main idea.
Identify the topic sentence.

paragraph has a topic sentence, tell what it is. If there is no topic sentence, state the main idea in your own words.

1.   Unlike domestic cattle today, the wild buffalo on the plains were very hardy animals. They lived and thrived when other animals, especially cattle, might have died. When winter blizzards hit the plains and prairies, the buffalo did not drift with the storm like cattle. Instead, they faced into the storm, either standing still waiting for the storm to pass or slowly heading into it. In this way the storm passed faster for the buffalo than it did for cattle, who would drift with the storm and frequently die from the elements.

David A. Dary, *The Buffalo Book*

2.   It was a warm tropical evening in Puerto Rico. Roberto Clemente was playing with a group of boys on a muddy field in Barrio San Antón. It was nothing at all like the great stadium in San Juan. There were bumps and puddles, and the outfield was full of trees. The bat in Roberto's hand was a thick stick cut from the branch of a guava tree. The bases were old coffee sacks. The ball was a tightly-knotted bunch of rags.

Paul Robert Walker, *Pride of Puerto Rico*

3.   Comets, asteroids, and meteors are the speed demons of the solar system. The average comet moves at 129,603 miles per hour; an asteroid's average speed is 39,603 miles per hour. Using radar, astronomers have clocked one meteor whizzing along at 164,250 miles per hour.

Time-Life Books, *Forces of Nature*

Supporting Sentences

Supporting sentences have details that support, explain, or prove the main idea. Supporting sentences may be *facts*, *examples*, or other kinds of details such as *sensory details*.

- **Facts** are statements that can be tested and proved true. They can be checked in reference books or through firsthand observations. They often include **statistics,** or information based on numbers.

- **Examples** are specific instances of an idea. T-shirts and sunglasses are examples of things you wear.

- **Sensory details** are details that you see, hear, taste, touch, or smell. They make descriptions come alive for the reader.

In the following paragraph, notice that the writer uses a sensory detail and three facts. The supporting sentences explain the main idea that is stated in the first sentence.

Your bones resist breaks in two ways.	Topic sentence
Not only are they as strong as steel, but they	Example
also have the ability to stretch like a rubber	Sensory detail
band. Bone is made of hard mineral crystals.	Fact
These crystals give bone enough strength to	Fact
withstand thousands of pounds of weight	
without breaking. Also in bone is a stretchy	Fact
material, called fiber, which prevents bone	
from easily snapping when bent.	

Exercise 2 **Collecting Supporting Details**

Perhaps you collect details about the life of your favorite movie actor or TV star. In the same way, you can gather details about your main idea for a paragraph. Choose one of the main ideas on the following page. Then, make a list of three or four details that support it. Try to use at least one fact, one example, and one sensory detail.

SKILLS FOCUS

Identify supporting sentences. Support, develop, and elaborate ideas in writing.

EXAMPLE 1. Main Idea: Stamp collecting is a useful hobby.
1. *Details:* *(1) Stamps can be educational.*
(2) One stamp series shows drawings of twenty different insects.
(3) The drawings are brightly colored.

1. Skateboarding (or another sport) requires skill.
2. My room is always messy (or neat).
3. I cannot stand snakes (or spiders, worms, or storms).

The Clincher Sentence

Once you have written a topic sentence and supporting sentences that reinforce your main idea, you may want to give your paragraph a strong finish. One way to do this is to make the concluding (last) sentence of your paragraph a *clincher sentence*. A **clincher sentence** ties together the information in your supporting sentences and reminds your reader of the importance of your main idea. Notice how the last sentence of the following paragraph ties the whole paragraph together.

> The shark's survival, which goes back 400 million years, is threatened by only one serious predator—humans. Commercial and sport fishers take more than one million sharks a year from the Gulf of Mexico alone. Each year fewer than seventy-five shark attacks on people are reported, most of which are not deadly. Clearly, we are much more dangerous to sharks than they are to us.
>
> "Introduction to Sharks," *Ocean of Know* Web site

Not every paragraph needs a clincher sentence. However, clincher sentences are often a good way to make your main idea stick in the reader's mind.

SKILLS FOCUS

Summarize main ideas.
End with a clear
conclusion.

Exercise 3 Developing a Clincher Sentence

Write a clincher sentence for each of the following short paragraphs. Remember that a clincher sentence wraps up the information in a paragraph without just repeating it.

1. Guide dogs for the blind are more than just pets. They go almost everywhere with their owners. Unlike most pets, guide dogs wear special harnesses that help them direct their owners safely through unfamiliar places. Because they are trained to ignore strangers unless the strangers are in their owners' way, guide dogs should not be petted while they are working.

2. Every year, lightning kills many people. This happens because many people do not know what to do when a thunderstorm strikes. Some try to take shelter under tall trees that attract lightning strikes. Others think that if they only hear thunder and see no lightning there is no danger of being struck.

What Makes a Good Paragraph?
Coherence

A good paragraph needs more than a clear main idea and supporting details, facts, or examples. It also needs to have *coherence*. *Coherence* occurs when the details in a paragraph are arranged and connected in a way that makes sense to the reader. You can create coherence by following two steps. First, arrange your ideas in an order that helps your reader understand them. Then, connect your ideas with transitional words and phrases (like *first* and *then* in this paragraph), which will be discussed starting on page 453.

Organizing Ideas

To help get your ideas across clearly, arrange the information in your paragraphs in a sensible way. Here are two useful ways to order information.

- *Spatial order* presents details according to their location.

- *Chronological order* presents details in the order in which they happen.

SKILLS FOCUS

Evaluate the coherence of a text. Write cohesively and coherently. Organize drafts.

Spatial Order   If you were describing the inside of a house, you probably would not include a description of the couch in a paragraph about the bathroom. You would not describe the kitchen sink in a paragraph about the bedroom, either. If you did, your reader would be confused about what can be found where.

Spatial order organizes details according to their location. When you describe something—a room or a sports arena, for example—you often use spatial order to give details as your eyes move from left to right or right to left. You might also arrange details from far away to close up or from close up to far away. Notice how the writer of the following paragraph uses spatial order to describe the view of Niagara Falls from above.

> . . . At altitude you see it all at once. You see Lake Ontario on one side, Lake Erie on the other, and linking them the thirty-four-mile Niagara River. Then, coming down lower, you see the falls them-selves—where the river, along a front almost a mile wide, plunges over a 167-foot cliff and flows off through a deep, narrow gorge seven miles long. . . .
>
> Wolfgang Langewiesche, "The Spectacle of Niagara"

SKILLS FOCUS

Organize writing by spatial order.

How would you describe a pond or creek, a city street, or the contents of a fish tank? Work in a group with one or two other students. Choose one of the subjects below, and list the details that describe it. Then, arrange the details in spatial order.

1. a grocery store
2. a bicycle
3. a park or building near your school
4. a painting or photograph you have seen
5. a local park or playing field

─HELP─

When writing a descriptive paragraph, brainstorm and arrange ideas at the same time by creating a map or sketch. For example, if you are describing a bicycle, sketch it. Then label the sketch with details that describe each of the bicycle's parts. Use the labels as notes for your descriptive paragraph.

Chronological Order What happens after Dorothy is blown by a tornado to the land of Oz? How do you build a model ship in a bottle? What causes a solar eclipse? When you answer these questions, you explain how the event or action happens over time. To explain how something happens, you use chronological, or time, order.

Chronological order helps you tell a story (what happens to Dorothy in the land of Oz) or explain a process (how to build a model ship in a bottle).

- **Using chronological order to tell a story** Some stories are true, and some are made-up. The following paragraph is from a book of fiction.

> Strangely, when Ramona's heart was heavy, so were her feet. She trudged to the school bus, plodded through the halls at school, and clumped home from the bus after school. The house felt lonely when she let herself in, so she turned on the television set for company. She sat on the couch and stared at one of the senseless soap operas Mrs. Kemp watched. They were all about rich people—none of them looking like Howie's Uncle Hobart—who accused other people of doing something terrible; Ramona didn't understand exactly what, but it all was boring, boring, boring.
>
> Beverly Cleary, *Ramona Forever*

SKILLS FOCUS

Organize writing by chronological order.

Paragraphs that tell a story do not always have a main idea. However, as you see in the paragraph on the previous page, the events in the paragraph do follow one another. This makes the paragraph easy to understand.

- **Using chronological order to explain a process** When your friend explains how to make a certain meal, he or she is explaining a process. The instructions for that process will be in step-by-step (chronological) order.

Notice how the writer of the following paragraph uses chronological order. He explains, step by step, how to get ready to make a simple movie using clear film and markers.

> After you have assembled your materials you will need a place to work. A desk or drawing table that is well lighted is best. Tape down a sheet of white construction paper on top of the desk. Next, unwind some of the film from the reel and tape it down to the construction paper with clear tape.
>
> Stephen Mooser, *Lights! Camera! Scream!*

NOTE There are two other ways to organize ideas in paragraphs. One way is in *order of importance*. When you use **order of importance,** you arrange details from most important to least important or from least important to most important. For instance, if you were writing a paragraph about your summer vacation, you could begin with the least exciting detail and save the most exciting detail for the end of the paragraph. The other way to organize ideas is in *logical order*. When you use **logical order,** you arrange ideas into groups. For example, if you were writing about frogs, you could discuss their diet at the beginning of the paragraph and their life cycle at the end.

SKILLS FOCUS

Write to explain.
Organize writing by order of importance.
Organize writing by logical order.

Exercise 5 **Using Chronological Order to Develop Paragraphs**

Telling a story can be fun. Explaining a process can be easy. In this exercise you will develop these skills.

1. Write a group story. Work as a whole class or in smaller groups. Begin with one of the following "starters" or with one of your own. Then, take turns adding a sentence to the story. Be sure the events of the story are in chronological order.
   a. Late one night, a Texas rancher named Ellison looked out across his pastures. He was amazed to see big, strange lights bouncing playfully across the land.
   b. Monika was exploring a cave last weekend when she discovered a small pile of very old bones. At first the bones were a mystery.
2. Choose one of the following processes. Then, list three or more steps needed to complete the process. List the steps in chronological order.
   a. how to introduce yourself to someone
   b. how to make a paper airplane
   c. how to prepare a healthful lunch

Words That Connect Ideas

Carefully arranged ideas help make a paragraph coherent. Sometimes it is easy to tell how ideas are related. In a story, for example, one event usually follows another. This order helps you understand what happens in the story.

Sometimes, though, the reader needs help to see how ideas are arranged. Special words help show how ideas are related. These words are called **transitional words and phrases.** They are connectors that tie one idea to another, one sentence to another, or one paragraph to another. The following chart lists some common transitional words and phrases.

Transitional Words and Phrases		
Showing Similarities	also	another
	in addition	too
	and	like
Showing Differences	although	however
	but	instead
Showing Causes and Effects	as a result	since
	because	so

(continued)

COMPUTER TIP

If the computers at your school are arranged in a network, you may be able to use them to do collaborative writing. Some types of computer networks allow writers sitting at different computers to work together on the same piece, to read each other's work, and to make suggestions and comments that all group members can see.

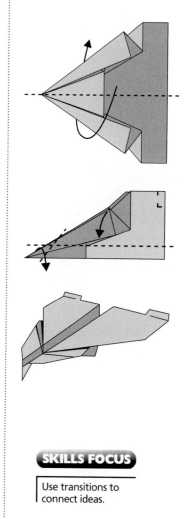

SKILLS FOCUS

Use transitions to connect ideas.

(continued)

Transitional Words and Phrases		
Showing Time	after before finally first	next second then when
Showing Place	above around across behind	here nearby there under
Showing Importance	first last	mainly most important

The following paragraph is about Babe Didrikson Zaharias, a great athlete. In 1932, she was the entire winning track "team" for an insurance company in Dallas, Texas. Notice how the underlined transitional words connect the ideas.

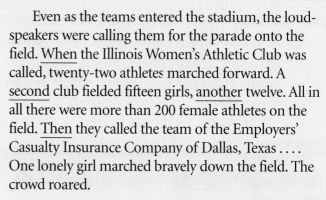

Even as the teams entered the stadium, the loud-speakers were calling them for the parade onto the field. When the Illinois Women's Athletic Club was called, twenty-two athletes marched forward. A second club fielded fifteen girls, another twelve. All in all there were more than 200 female athletes on the field. Then they called the team of the Employers' Casualty Insurance Company of Dallas, Texas . . . . One lonely girl marched bravely down the field. The crowd roared.

Harry Gersh, *Women Who Made America Great*

NOTE If you have trouble connecting ideas with transitional words, your paragraph may lack *unity*. A paragraph has **unity** when all of its sentences work together to support the main idea. For example, a paragraph about your pet turtle might describe the markings on its shell, but not what your pet cat looks like. The information about your cat is not related to your main idea.

Evaluate the unity of a text.

Identifying Transitions

The transition words in the following paragraphs show how one idea is related to another. Identify the transitions in each of the paragraphs. Use the chart on pages 453–454 to help you.

1. Building an igloo calls for skill and experience. First, the builder locates a site in firmly packed snow. Next, while standing in the outlined igloo, the builder cuts the snow into blocks of different sizes. Large blocks are used for the bottom layer, and thinner blocks are used for the walls. After the blocks are cut, the builder trims the top edge of each block to help the walls slope inward. Finally, the blocks are stacked to create a dome.

2. A polar bear's fur looks white at a glance, but a closer look reveals a different color. Each hair is a transparent tube. When the hairs are clear, the bear appears to be white. However, tiny green plants called algae can grow inside the hairs. As a result, the bear looks green.

Elaboration

A good paragraph *elaborates* (explains or illustrates) the supporting facts and details so that the reader has a clear picture of the main idea. To elaborate, illustrate your main idea by using more than one detail, fact, or example.

The following paragraph has a main idea and supporting details, but the writer has not elaborated on the idea.

    The Great Pyramid at Giza, Egypt, is
one of the Seven Wonders of the Ancient
World. The pyramid is one of the most
famous structures in the world. Built
about 4,500 years ago as the tomb of
King Khufu, the Great Pyramid is also
one of the largest monuments to a
single person.

Reference Note

For more on **supporting details,** see page 447.

SKILLS FOCUS

Support, develop, and elaborate ideas in writing.

Now, read the revised paragraph. Notice how the writer has elaborated on the main idea and details by including more information.

The Great Pyramid at Giza, Egypt, is one of the Seven Wonders of the Ancient World. The pyramid is one of the most famous struc-

New fact tures in the world. In fact, it is visited by more than a million

New detail tourists each year. Many millions more recognize its familiar shape from postcards and photographs. Built about 4,500 years ago as the tomb of King Khufu, the Great Pyramid is also one of the largest monuments to a single person. At

New fact 450 feet, it is almost one and one-half times as tall as the Statue of Liberty and nearly three times taller than the Arc de Triomphe in Paris.

Exercise 7 **Elaborating Details**

The paragraph on the next page does not have enough elaboration. Add details, facts, or examples to improve the paragraph.

Most of us do not think about the importance of electricity until the power goes out. Many everyday activities require electricity. After sundown, our reliance on electric power increases. Can you imagine how different life must have been before we had electricity and appliances?

┌ TIPS & TRICKS ┐

When elaborating, look closely at each supporting sentence. Ask yourself whether you can add any information to explain or illustrate what you say in each sentence.

What Are the Types of Paragraphs?

There are four different types of paragraphs.

Types of Paragraphs	
Narrative	used to tell a story or recount an event
Descriptive	used to describe a person, animal, scene, or object
Expository	used to provide information, including facts, instructions, and definitions
Persuasive	used to share opinions and convince others to agree with those opinions and sometimes take action

Which type of paragraph you write depends on your *purpose for writing.* If you want to **entertain** your readers or **express** yourself, you may write narrative or descriptive paragraphs. If you want to **inform** your readers about something or **explain** something, you may write expository or narrative paragraphs. If your purpose is to **influence** or **persuade** your readers to agree with your opinion about an issue, you will probably write persuasive paragraphs.

Different types of paragraphs can be written about the same subject. Notice that each of the following paragraphs is about volunteer activities, but each represents a different type of paragraph.

SKILLS FOCUS

Create various kinds of texts in the different writing modes. Determine the writer's purpose.

Narrative Paragraphs

Reference Note

For more on **chronological order,** see page 451.

Narrative paragraphs tell a story or describe an event or sequence of events. In narrative paragraphs, details are usually arranged in chronological order. Short stories are examples of narrative writing. However, narrative writing is also found in newspaper articles and in history books—anywhere that a writer wants to recount events from beginning to end.

> Joseph J. Gebhardt started reading for the blind around 1967. For years he had been playing guitar with a local band . . . and had bought a reel-to-reel recorder with the idea of immortalizing them. One night he heard an ad seeking readers for the blind and decided he'd had enough of being drowned out by . . . trombones. For a while he read *Science* magazine, but later he concentrated on *Smithsonian,* which he's been reading ever since.
>
> "Reading for the Blind," *Smithsonian*

Descriptive Paragraphs

Reference Note

For more on **spatial order,** see page 450.

Descriptive paragraphs create a mental picture of a person, animal, scene, or object by describing the details. The following paragraph uses spatial order to describe the plan for a monument to be built in honor of volunteers.

> Atop the monument will be a bald eagle with its thirty-foot wings outstretched, as if ready to take flight. At the base of the monument will be a nine-foot-tall, black granite monolith dedicated to all volunteers who have died during a volunteer activity. . . . Extending outward from the monument will be The Walls of Tribute. These walls, along with other Walls of Tribute located throughout the complex, will contain the names of volunteers who have given one thousand hours or five years of volunteer service.
>
> "Side View of Complex," *Friends of Volunteers* Web site

Expository Paragraphs

Expository paragraphs are used to explain subjects or ideas. Expository paragraphs can list facts or explain a process. Some expository paragraphs, like the one below, follow a *cause-and-effect* pattern. This paragraph explains the effects (or results) of a massive volunteer cleanup.

Cause	In 2004, approximately 158,000 volunteers picked up nearly four million pounds of garbage along the coasts of the United States.
Effect	As a result, both people and sea animals can enjoy cleaner and safer environments. Glass
Effect	bottles, lumber, and syringes are less of a threat to barefooted beachgoers. Fewer
Effect	seabirds, fish, and crabs will die entangled in plastic can holders, fishing nets, and fishing line. People put trash in the oceans, but by volunteering their time to help clean up after themselves, people are also the solution to the problem.

Persuasive Paragraphs

Persuasive paragraphs express an opinion about an issue. An *issue* is a topic about which people might disagree. A writer uses supporting details, or reasons, in a persuasive paragraph to convince readers to agree with his or her opinion. Sometimes, the writer of a persuasive paragraph encourages readers to take action on a particular issue.

> . . . Your community is really one of your best friends. It's only natural that you give something back as a way to say thanks. That could include raising money for a local charity, volunteering to clean
>
> *(continued)*

(continued)

up your neighborhood, visiting nursing home residents on a regular basis, or collecting food for a local shelter. The possibilities are endless and whatever you do, your community will be grateful.

"Volunteering—It's So Easy, a Kid Can Do It,"
GirlZone Web site

Exercise 8 Identifying Types of Paragraphs

In a group with two or three students, look for examples of each of the four types of paragraphs: narrative, descriptive, expository, and persuasive. To find your paragraphs, look in magazines, newspapers, or books, or on Web sites. As a group, answer the following questions for each paragraph.

1. Which type of paragraph would you say this is? Why?
2. What was the writer's purpose for writing each paragraph—to entertain, express, inform, or influence? Was the writer successful in achieving his or her purpose? Why or why not?

Reference Note

For more on identifying **author's purpose,** see page 646.

How Are Paragraphs Used in Longer Pieces of Writing?

Paragraphs can exist by themselves, or they can be grouped together as a longer piece of writing. To make a longer piece of writing complete from beginning to end, there are two types of paragraphs you should add to the **body,** or main part, of a piece. These are *introductory paragraphs* and *concluding paragraphs.*

An **introductory paragraph** is like an introduction between two people. It gives your ideas a chance to say "hello" to the reader. An introductory paragraph is a way to get the reader interested in—and ready for—your ideas.

At the opposite end of a longer piece of writing is the **concluding paragraph.** It says "goodbye" to the reader, leaving him or her with a clear idea of what your piece was about.

Reference Note

For more on writing **introductory** and **concluding paragraphs,** see pages 789 and 790 in the Quick Reference Handbook.

Dividing a Longer Piece of Writing into Paragraphs

When you write a paper or article, you should divide it into paragraphs. There are two main reasons you should do this:

- to give your reader's eyes a rest,
- to give your reader a chance to pause, and
- to show a change.

Writing nonstop without paragraph breaks is much like talking nonstop without taking a breath. If you talk without changing your tone of voice or without pausing now and then, people listening to you will have a hard time following what you are saying. Changes and breaks are as important to good writing as they are to clear speech.

To help make your reader aware of each idea in your composition, start a new paragraph when one of the following occurs:

- you need to express a new or different main idea
- you explain a different part of your subject or another step in the process
- you provide a different reason to support your opinion
- the time or location changes
- a different person or character speaks

Exercise 9 **Dividing a Piece into Paragraphs**

The following selection needs to be divided into separate paragraphs. Decide where to begin new paragraphs by watching for any of the changes noted above.

```
    Some jobs are dangerous, and some
jobs are a little scary. For a biospe-
leologist (bī'ō•spe'le•äl'ə•jist)—a
scientist who studies life underground—
a day on the job can be both. The bugs and
salamanders a biospeleologist collects may
not be dangerous, but getting to them is.
```
                                          (continued)

(continued)

```
Sometimes, these scientists lower them-
selves thousands of feet into rocky
caverns that have never seen the light of
day. Other times, they crawl through cold
underground streams that are only inches
from the rock top above them. Either way,
these scientists are searching for blind
scorpions; small, jumping bugs called
springtails; and other creatures that live
in total darkness. This job is not for
people afraid of the dark or of bugs. It
is a job, though, for people with a sense
of adventure and an interest in finding
out just how the world under our feet
really works.
```

Review A **Writing a Narrative Paragraph**

Narration can be used to tell true stories or made-up stories. Write a narrative paragraph in which you use chronological (time) order to organize the details. Before writing your paragraph, review the order of your details to make sure the order makes sense. Here are some ideas to get you started.

- Tell how you learned to do a new activity such as riding a bike, swimming, or using a computer.
- Retell a children's story you remember.

Review B **Writing a Descriptive Paragraph**

Write a descriptive paragraph. Remember to use details to give the reader a sense of how your subject looks, smells, feels, sounds, and tastes. Use spatial order to arrange your details. Here are some ideas for a topic.

- Describe a person or place that is important to you.
- Describe your favorite food.

Review C Writing an Expository Paragraph

You will probably use expository writing more often than narrative, descriptive, or persuasive writing. You will use it to answer test questions or to give instructions. Write an expository paragraph to explain what you know about a subject. Remember to support your main idea by using details, facts, and examples. Here are a few ideas for subjects.

- Explain how to do something simple, such as making a sandwich.
- Explain why you enjoy your favorite hobby or activity.

Review D Writing a Persuasive Paragraph

Simply asking for something does not always get you what you want. To be persuasive, sometimes you have to *write* about what you want. Write a persuasive paragraph. Remember to give your reader reasons to believe your ideas. Here are some ideas for topics.

- Share your opinion about a school or community issue. For example, you might propose a recycling center for paper and cans at your school, or you might suggest that your community build a new public pool.
- Ask a local business to contribute to a fund-raiser for your school club.

PEANUTS reprinted by permission of United Feature Syndicate, Inc.

Communications

The Reading and Writing Processes

Do these situations sound familiar? While reading, you suddenly realize you have read the same sentences several times without gaining any meaning from them. While writing, you stare at the single sentence you have written, unable to think of anything else to write. When you find yourself stuck, step back and look at the processes of reading and writing.

Think as a Reader

The reading you do in school requires you to think critically about information and ideas. In order to get the most from a text, prepare your mind for the task before you read, use effective strategies while you read, and take time to process the information after you read.

- **Before Reading** Get your mind in gear by considering your purpose for reading a particular piece of writing and by thinking about what you already know about the topic. Preview the text by skimming a bit and considering headings, graphics, and other features. Use this information to predict what the text will discuss and how challenging it will be to read.

- **While Reading** As you read, figure out the writer's main idea about the topic. Notice how the text is organized (by cause and effect or in order of importance, for example) to help you find support for that point. Connect the ideas to your own experiences when you can. If you get confused, slow down, re-read, or jot ideas in a graphic organizer.

- **After Reading** Confirm and extend your understanding of the text. Draw conclusions about the writer's point of view, and evaluate how well the writer communicated the message. Use ideas in the text to create a piece of art, to read more on a related topic, or to solve a problem.

Think as a Writer

A perfect text seldom springs fully formed from your mind; instead, you must plan your text before you write and work to improve it after drafting.

- **Before Writing** First, choose a topic and a form of writing, such as a poem or an editorial. Decide who your readers will be and what you want the text to accomplish. Develop ideas based on your knowledge and on research. Organize the ideas, and jot down your main point.

- **While Writing** Grab attention and provide background information in an introduction. Elaborate your ideas to support your point, and organize them clearly. Then, wrap things up with a conclusion.

- **After Writing** To improve a draft, evaluate how clearly you expressed your ideas. Ask a peer to suggest areas that need work. Then, revise. Proofread to correct mistakes. Share your finished work with others, and reflect on what you learned.

You may have noticed that the reading and writing processes involve similar strategies. The chart below summarizes these similarities.

The Reading and Writing Processes

Reading   Writing

Before

Reading	Writing
■ Determine your purpose for reading. ■ Consider what you already know about the topic. ■ Preview the text to make predictions about what it will include.	■ Identify your writing purpose and your audience. ■ Draw upon what you know about the topic, and do research to find out more. ■ Make notes or an outline to plan what the text will include.

While

Reading	Writing
■ Figure out the writer's main ideas. ■ Look for support for the main ideas. ■ Notice how the ideas in the text are organized.	■ Express your main ideas clearly. ■ Support them with details, facts, examples, or anecdotes. ■ Follow prewriting notes or an outline to organize your text so readers can easily follow your ideas.

After

Reading	Writing
■ Evaluate the text to decide how accurate it is and its overall quality. ■ Relate what you have read to the world around you by creating something, reading further, or applying ideas. ■ Reflect on what you have read.	■ Evaluate and revise your text. Use peer editors' comments to help improve your work. ■ Relate your writing to the world around you by publishing it. ■ Reflect on what you have written.

The Reading and Writing Workshops in this book provide valuable practice for strategies that will help you effectively use these related processes.

18 Sharing Our Stories

Reading Workshop

Reading an Autobiographical Incident

Writing Workshop

Writing About a Life Experience

Speaking and Listening

Telling a Story

D o you wonder what it is like to fly over the ocean alone in a small plane? Would you like to know what it is like to live in a different country? You can learn about these experiences by reading *autobiographical incidents*. An **autobiographical incident** is a true story about a specific event in a writer's life. Not only do you learn about the event, but you also learn why the experience is important to the writer. Because writers share, or express, their thoughts and feelings, an autobiographical incident is an example of **expressive writing.**

You also share autobiographical incidents. When you talk with your grandmother about your track meet, for example, you are telling a story about yourself. Writing an autobiographical incident is a great way to express what you think and feel.

> **Narration/ Description**

YOUR TURN 1   Sharing Experiences

List the topics of three memorable experiences that you would not mind sharing. Then, discuss the following questions with a partner.

- Why are these experiences memorable?
- What did you learn about yourself from these experiences?

GO TO: go.hrw.com
KEYWORD: EOLang 6-18

WHAT'S AHEAD?

In this section you will read an autobiographical incident. You will also learn how to

■ form generalizations

■ construct a flowchart to understand chronological order

Reading an Autobiographical Incident

If you want to bring about a change, you have to take action. Many people throughout the history of the United States have dared to do just that. These people stood up for what they believed, and their actions led to positive changes in U.S. society. Rosa Parks was one of those people. On December 1, 1955, in Montgomery, Alabama, Rosa Parks challenged a law that said African Americans must sit in a separate section from whites on public buses. Read about the incident in the excerpt from her autobiography on the next page.

Preparing to Read

READING SKILL

Making Inferences: Forming Generalizations A **generalization** is a statement that applies to many individuals or experiences, not just a specific person or experience. As you read the following excerpt, think about what you could say about Rosa Parks's experience that would also be true for others who have experienced discrimination.

READING FOCUS

Chronological Order Rosa Parks tells her story in **chronological order.** She starts with the first event and ends with the last. As you read, pay attention to the order, or **sequence,** of events. How does chronological order help you understand the story?

Jot down answers to the numbered active-reading questions in the shaded boxes. The underlined words will be discussed in the Vocabulary Mini-Lesson on page 477.

from Rosa Parks: My Story

BY ROSA PARKS
with Jim Haskins

When I got off from work that evening of December 1, I went to Court Square as usual to catch the Cleveland Avenue bus home. I didn't look to see who was driving when I got on, and by the time I recognized him, I had already paid my fare. It was the same driver who had put me off the bus back in 1943, twelve years earlier. He was still tall and heavy, with red, rough-looking skin. And he was still mean-looking. I didn't know if he had been on that route before—they switched the drivers around sometimes. I do know that most of the time if I saw him on a bus, I wouldn't get on it.

> **1. What is the first event in Rosa Parks's story?**

I saw a vacant seat in the middle section of the bus and took it. I didn't even question why there was a vacant seat even though there were quite a few people standing in the back. If I had thought about it at all, I would probably have figured maybe someone saw me get on and did not take the seat but left it vacant for me. There was a man sitting next to the window and two women across the aisle.

> **2. Do you think the order of the first two paragraphs could be switched? Why?**

The next stop was the Empire Theater, and some whites got on. They filled up the white seats,[1] and one man was left standing. The driver looked back and noticed the man standing. Then he looked back at us. He said,

---

1. **white seats:** seats on a public bus that only white people could occupy.

"Let me have those front seats," because they were the front seats of the black section.[2] Didn't anybody move. We just sat right where we were, the four of us. Then he spoke a second time: "Y'all better make it light on yourselves and let me have those seats."

3. Why did the bus driver tell the black passengers to give up their seats?

The man in the window seat next to me stood up, and I moved to let him pass by me, and then I looked across the aisle and saw that the two women were also standing. I moved over to the window seat. I could not see how standing up was going to "make it light" for me. The more we gave in and complied, the worse they treated us.

4. How many seats did the bus driver need so all the white passengers could sit down?

I thought back to the time when I used to sit up all night and didn't sleep, and my grandfather would have his gun right by the fireplace, or if he had his one-horse wagon going anywhere, he always had his gun in the back of the wagon. People always say that I didn't give up my seat because I was tired, but that isn't true. I was not tired physically, or no more tired than I usually was at the end of a working day. I was not old, although some people have an image of me as being old then. I was forty-two. No, the only tired I was, was tired of giving in.

The driver of the bus saw me still sitting there, and he asked was I going to stand up. I said, "No." He said, "Well, I'm going to have you arrested." Then I said, "You may do that." These were the only words we said to each other. I didn't even know his name, which was James Blake, until we were in court together. He got out of the bus and stayed outside for a few minutes, waiting for the police.

5. Why do you think the bus driver insisted that Rosa Parks move?

As I sat there, I tried not to think about what might happen. I knew that anything was possible. I could be manhandled or beaten. I could be arrested. People have asked me if it occurred to me then that I could be the test case the NAACP[3] had been looking for. I did not think about that at all. In fact if I had let myself think too deeply about what might happen to me, I might have gotten off the bus. But I chose to remain.

6. Why do you think Rosa Parks decided not to give up her seat?

---

2. black section: the back of a public bus, where African Americans were allowed to sit.

3. NAACP: National Association for the Advancement of Colored People, an organization that fights for the equal treatment of African Americans and other minority groups.

Making Inferences: Forming Generalizations

Read Between the Lines   An author will not always give you every detail of a story. Sometimes you will need to make educated guesses about what is happening. Educated guesses are called **inferences.** To make inferences, combine clues that the author provides with what you already know about the subject.

Example: **What you read:** The little boy fell on the floor kicking and screaming while his mother held the football.

+ **What you know:** My mother took my toys away when I was in trouble, and I would get very mad.

Inference: The little boy misbehaved, so his mother took the football away from him.

Reference Note

For more on **inferences,** see page 740 in the Quick Reference Handbook.

One type of inference is a *generalization.* A **generalization** is a statement that applies to many different situations or people even though it is based on specific situations or people.

Example: **What you read:** Emma and Miguel do their math homework. Emma and Miguel make *A's* in math.

+ **What you know:** I do my homework in science, and I make good grades.

Generalization: Doing your homework usually leads to good grades.

TIP Generalizations use words like *many, usually, some, overall, most,* and *generally.* What clue word does the generalization in the example use?

Notice that the generalization above doesn't apply just to Emma and Miguel or to math homework. It is a general statement that is true for many different people and school subjects.

Read the paragraph on the next page. Then, form a generalization by using personal knowledge as well as information in the paragraph. Use the steps that follow the paragraph if you need help.

SKILLS FOCUS

Make inferences from a text. Make generalizations from a text.

TIP Be careful not to make *faulty generalizations*. If you can find an exception to your generalization, then it is faulty. Faulty generalizations tend to include words like *all, none, never, always,* and *every*.

Faulty Generalization: Doing your homework *always* leads to good grades.

> In 1848, Elizabeth Cady Stanton and Lucretia Mott organized the first women's rights convention. Through their efforts and the persistence of women after them, women eventually gained the right to own property and to vote. In the 1960s, Cesar Chavez helped migrant workers by forming a union, the United Farm Workers. He began strikes and boycotts that won union members better wages and working conditions. Ed Roberts began the movement for the rights of the disabled when he started a program to help disabled students in the 1960s. Other people joined the cause, and eventually Congress passed the Americans with Disabilities Act in 1990. This act made it illegal to discriminate against people with mental or physical disabilities.

Reference Note

For more on **generalizations,** see page 739 in the Quick Reference Handbook.

THINKING IT THROUGH **Forming Generalizations**

▶ **STEP 1** Read the entire passage. Look for similarities and connections between the details in the passage.

Stanton and Mott helped women. Chavez helped migrant workers. Roberts helped disabled people. They all made a difference.

▶ **STEP 2** Connect the details in the passage to something you already know.

My parents organized a petition to keep a park from becoming a parking lot. The mayor agreed.

▶ **STEP 3** Form a generalization that combines what you read with what you know.

People can often make a difference when they stand up for what they believe.

▶ **STEP 4** Check your answer. Make sure your generalization
- is not faulty (look for a faulty generalization clue word)
- is reasonable, based on the information in the passage.

I say often, not always. My generalization is reasonable because all the details I read were about people who did something and made a difference.

SKILLS FOCUS

Identify faulty reasoning and unsupported inferences.

YOUR TURN 2 **Forming Generalizations**

Re-read the reading selection on pages 471–472. Using the steps in the Thinking It Through on page 474, form a generalization about what sometimes happens when people take a stand against something they believe is unfair. Be prepared to support your generalization with information from the reading selection and from your own knowledge.

Chronological Order

READING FOCUS

It Goes Like This   Like a fictional story, an autobiographical incident has a beginning, middle, and end. The writer uses **chronological** (or time) **order** to tell which event happened first, second, third, and so on. If the events were not written in chronological order, you might have a hard time picturing the story in your mind. Read the following autobiographical incident. Which event happened first? second? third?

> While visiting our grandmother, my sister and I decided we would have a picnic lunch. We packed a bag and walked to the field behind my grandmother's house.
>
> We chose a nice, shady spot under a big tree. Tamara had started to spread out the blanket when all of a sudden she began to scream and fling her arms wildly. Before I could ask her what was wrong, I was screaming, too. We both ran to the house.
>
> My grandmother heard the noise and came out to see what was wrong. She found that Tamara and I had been stung several times. We definitely upset a family of yellow jackets when we laid our blanket on top of their nest.

Flowcharts are graphic organizers that can help you see the events of an autobiographical incident in the order in which they occurred. In the flowchart on the next page, notice that only major events of the incident above are listed. Details are left out.

SKILLS FOCUS

Identify and understand chronological organization.

First Event: My sister and I went out to have a picnic lunch.	→	Second Event: We screamed and ran to the house.	→	Third Event: We found out we had been stung by yellow jackets.

To tell the difference between a major event and a supporting detail, look for action. For instance, what is more important: that the picnic spot was nice and shady, or that the narrator and her sister screamed and ran to the house? The main event in that paragraph is the action of the narrator and her sister.

YOUR TURN 3 Charting Chronological Order

Copy the following flowchart onto your paper. Then, read the list of events and details taken from *Rosa Parks: My Story* below. Decide which sentences are supporting details and which are major events. Place the major events in the flowchart. When you are done, re-read the reading selection on pages 471–472 to see if you listed the major events in the correct order.

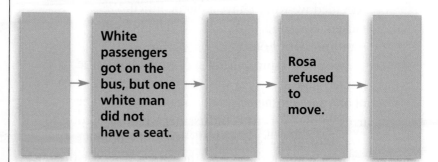

The bus driver told the African American passengers to move.

The bus driver's name was James Blake.

Rosa waited for the police.

Rosa got on the bus after work to go home.

The bus driver was tall, heavy, and had a red face.

SKILLS FOCUS

Create a graphic organizer to enhance comprehension of text. *(page 477):* Use context clues in words, sentences, and paragraphs to decode new vocabulary. *(page 478):* Make inferences from a text.

Context Clues

As you read an autobiographical incident, you may discover that the author uses unfamiliar words to tell about his or her experience. One way to determine the meaning of an unfamiliar word is to use *context clues*. A word's **context** is made up of the words and sentences that surround it. Try using context clues to understand the underlined word in this passage taken from Rosa Parks's autobiography.

I wasn't frightened at the jail. I was more <u>resigned</u> than anything else. I don't recall being real angry, not enough to have an argument. I was just prepared to accept whatever I had to face. I asked again if I could make a telephone call. I was ignored.

Rosa Parks, *Rosa Parks: My Story*

THINKING IT THROUGH   **Using Context Clues**

STEP 1 Look at the context of the unfamiliar word. See if the words and sentences around it provide clues to the word's meaning.	The passage says that Rosa was not frightened or angry. It also says she was "prepared to accept" anything.
STEP 2 Use the context clues to make a guess at the unfamiliar word's meaning.	Since Rosa was not frightened or angry, and she could accept anything, I think resigned means "prepared to accept whatever happens."
STEP 3 Check your definition by inserting it in the passage in place of the unfamiliar word.	"I wasn't frightened at the jail. I was more <u>prepared to accept whatever happened</u> than anything else." That makes sense.

PRACTICE

Using context clues, figure out the meanings of these words. The words are underlined in *Rosa Parks: My Story.*

1. recognized (page 471)
2. vacant (page 471)
3. complied (page 472)
4. manhandled (page 472)
5. occurred (page 472)

Making Inferences

When you take a reading test, you may be asked to make an inference. Read the passage below and the question following it. How would you answer the question?

Citizens in Montgomery organized a bus boycott to protest the arrest of Rosa Parks. Leaflets were distributed encouraging African Americans not to ride the bus. Not using public transportation was very difficult for families without cars, so other means of transportation were made available. Black-owned cab companies helped those without cars by charging cheap fares. In addition, car owners and local churches formed car pools.

You can tell from the passage that during the Montgomery bus boycott

A. most African Americans stayed home

B. all African Americans refused to ride the bus

C. many African Americans supported one another

D. all African Americans used taxis to get around

THINKING IT THROUGH   **Making Inferences**

▶ **STEP 1** Read the passage and the question to see what it is asking you.

▶ **STEP 2** To identify the best response, look at each of the answer choices and ask yourself these questions:

■ Is there information in the passage that supports this answer choice?

■ Does this statement cover all the information in the passage?

■ Is the answer free of faulty generalization words such as *all, none, never, always, every?*

▶ **STEP 3** After evaluating each answer choice, choose the best one.

"You can tell" tells me I will make an educated guess, or an inference.

Answer A—The passage does not mention African Americans staying home.

Answer B—Right away I see a faulty generalization clue word—all. I don't know if all African Americans refused to ride the bus.

Answer C—I can find specific information to support this choice.

Answer D—Yes, they did use taxis, but they also carpooled. D also has a faulty generalization word—all.

I think answer C is the best answer. I can support it with information from the passage.

Writing About a Life Experience

On the first day of school, you are given your first assignment—*Tell the class one thing you did this summer.* "This is easy," you think. "I'll talk about my rafting trip." You begin by telling when and where you went, and who was with you. Then, you describe the trip, particularly the dangerous parts. As you share your experience, your teacher and classmates learn something about you. You discover something about yourself, too. It is obvious that you like rafting, but your story also reveals that you like action.

You can discover more about yourself through **expressive writing.** In this workshop you will have an opportunity to share your thoughts and feelings about a single experience from your life by writing an **autobiographical incident.** You will use details that tell the reader what happened and how you felt about the incident.

Prewriting

Choose an Experience

Who? Me?   What is the one subject you know the best? Why, *you* are, of course. You have probably had many experiences that you can write about. The first step in writing an autobiographical

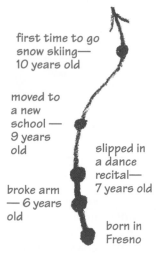

first time to go
snow skiing—
10 years old

moved to
a new
school —
9 years
old

slipped in
a dance
recital—
7 years old

broke arm
— 6 years
old

born in
Fresno

| KEY CONCEPT

incident is choosing one particular experience. If you need help coming up with one, consider these suggestions.

- Think about an experience that defines an emotion. When were you most happy, scared, surprised, sad, or angry?
- Brainstorm with your friends and family members. Ask them to recall a memorable experience that involves you.
- Look at your journals and at letters or pictures you have saved.
- Draw a road map of your life like the one to the left. Start with your birth and list all the important events that have happened to you up to now, such as your first day of kindergarten, the day your little sister was born, and the time your baseball team won the city championship.

You Be the Judge   Once you have a list of experiences, you want to choose the one that will make the best autobiographical incident to share with an audience. **The best experience is one that is meaningful, or important, to you.** Ask yourself the questions below to decide which experience is most meaningful.

Question	Example
Do I remember the experience well?	If you cannot remember all the details, you will not be able to provide a complete picture of the experience. For instance, family members may have told you about your first step, but do *you* remember all the details?
Why is this experience important?	The reader should know how you felt about this experience or what you learned from it. For example, you might say that forgetting your lines in the school play was your most embarrassing moment.
Am I willing to share this experience?	You should feel comfortable letting other people read about your experience. For example, you might not want to share your first crush with the whole class.

SKILLS FOCUS

Choose a topic to write about. Brainstorm to generate ideas. Use graphic organizers to generate ideas. Include the meaning of the experience. *(page 479):* Write autobiographical narratives.

 **Choosing an Experience**

Make a list of your experiences. Then, choose one experience to share by answering the questions in the chart above.

Think About Purpose and Audience

FYI... You are telling a story to a group of people when someone interrupts to ask, "How old were you?" Before you can speak, your best friend answers, "Third grade, right?" You agree and continue, only to be stopped again with another question. Again, your best friend answers. Why does your best friend understand the story when everyone else does not?

Before you begin writing your autobiographical incident, think about your purpose and audience. **Your purpose is to express your thoughts and feelings by sharing an experience with an audience.** Because you may not know exactly who your audience is, you should write as if your audience knows nothing about you. In order for your audience to understand your incident fully, you will need to provide **background information,** facts that set up the story. The four *W*'s—*What? When? Who? Where?*—will help you think about the information your audience needs.

KEY CONCEPT

- **What:** What is the incident? What happened?
- **When:** When did this event happen? How old were you?
- **Who:** Besides you, who was involved?
- **Where:** Where did this event take place? What was this place like?

> What? slipped during a dance recital
>
> When? an October night when I was seven years old
>
> Who? me, my parents, my dance teacher, my classmates, and their friends and families
>
> Where? on an auditorium stage that had very bright lights

YOUR TURN 5 — Thinking About Your Audience

Ask yourself *What? When? Who? Where?* to help you think of background information you should give your audience. Write your answers on a sheet of paper or in a learning log.

TIP Part of your **style**—how you say things—is your **voice**—the *sound* of your writing. Most good writing sounds like speech. You can develop your voice by choosing words that sound like you yet fit your audience and purpose.

Describe the voice in each sentence below:

1. I was so embarrassed! I wanted to crawl under the stage.

2. I doubt that I had ever been as embarrassed as I was at that moment.

SKILLS FOCUS

Write to express. Include thoughts and feelings. Plan writing by targeting an audience. Include background information. Plan writing by developing voice.

Recall Descriptive Details

You Had to Be There   You ask a friend about the movie he saw the other night. "Oh, it was great! First, the bad guy terrorizes the city. In the end, though, the good guy wins." It doesn't sound so great to you. Why not? Your friend left out the details.

Details will allow your readers to experience an incident just as if they were there. Two types of details that you should include in your essay are *action details* and *sensory details.*

- **Action details** tell what events occurred and what people said.

> After waiting thirty minutes, I finally made it through the ticket line. I raced to the roller coaster only to find another long line.
>
> "Will I ever get to have fun?" I moaned to my friend.

- **Sensory details** describe what you see, hear, taste, feel, and smell.

> The coaster went click, click, click as it slowly went uphill. Sweat trickled down my neck as we reached the top.

To re-create your memory, picture the incident in your mind. In a chart like the one below, record the details that you "see."

Action Details	Sensory Details
Beginning: lined up backstage, then walked onto stage. My dance teacher said, "Break a leg!"	black leotard, sequined belt flowery smell of hair spray announcer's booming voice
Middle: doing a routine with wooden boxes, was supposed to put one foot on the box next to me, missed and slipped—everyone else was on their box except me	heard audience laughing felt hot, face turned red dance teacher had said if we made a mistake to keep smiling
End: curtain dropped, I cried	sobbing, salty tears

KEY CONCEPT ➤

TIP You can decide if a detail is necessary by asking yourself, "What was most important about my experience?" For instance, if the most important part of your vacation was going whale watching, then your details should be about whales. Leave out the details that do not describe the whales.

Reference Note

For more information and practice on **punctuating dialogue,** see page 342.

SKILLS FOCUS

Support ideas/theses with relevant evidence and details. Develop descriptions with action details. Develop descriptions with sensory details. Use graphic organizers to generate ideas. *(page 483):* Organize writing by chronological order.

 **Recalling Details**

Create a detail chart like the one above. List action and sensory details from the beginning, middle, and end of your incident.

CRITICAL THINKING

Arranging Ideas

My mom was not happy. Tony and Najla stared at me with open mouths. I hit the ball. It went crashing into the living room window. Tony, Najla, and I were playing baseball in the street. Najla pitched the ball. "I'm in trouble now," I said.

Wait a minute. What just happened? The mother was angry before the ball broke the window? The narrator is in trouble for playing in the street or because the ball crashed into the living room? This story is confusing.

In order to help their readers understand an incident, writers usually tell events in *chronological order*. Using

chronological order means telling the events of a story in the order that they happened, starting with the first event, going to the second, then the third, and so on. Chronological order helps the reader follow the action of the incident. You can see that a story written chronologically is much easier to understand than one that is not.

Tony, Najla, and I were playing baseball in the street. Najla pitched the ball to me. I hit the ball, and it went crashing into the living room window. Tony and Najla stared at me with open mouths. "I'm in trouble now," I said. My mom was not happy.

PRACTICE

Read the following list of events. Then, rewrite the events in chronological order on your own paper.

look at the clock, it is 6:50 A.M.

get dressed, it is 6:55 A.M.

alarm goes off at 6 A.M.

grab my books, it is 6:59 A.M.

get on the bus at 7 A.M.

take a shower

jump out of bed

hit the snooze button

breathe a sigh of relief, "I barely made it!"

 TIP To arrange events in chronological order, you can create a numbered list, draw a **flow-chart,** or make a **time line.** Choose one of these methods when you write your answer.

Reference Note

For more on **flowcharts,** see page 475. For more on **time lines,** see page 548.

Writing

Autobiographical Incident

Framework   **Think as a Reader/Writer**

Introduction
- Attention-grabbing opening
- Background information

Start your paper with an **interesting opening.** You might ask a question or give a hint about why this incident is important to you. Or, like the writer of the model to the right, you might set the scene. Provide **background information** by telling your reader what the incident is, who was involved, where the incident took place, and when it happened.

Body
- Beginning of incident (action details and sensory details)
- Middle of incident (action details and sensory details)
- End of incident (action details and sensory details)

- Write the events in **chronological order.**
- Write about the beginning of your incident in the first paragraph of the body, the middle of the incident in the second paragraph, and the end of the incident in the third paragraph.
- Describe each part of the incident using **action details** and **sensory details.**

Conclusion
- Reason this incident is important to you

Explain how this incident affected you. **Why is it important? What does it mean to you?** Leave your reader with a complete picture of what occurred and how you felt.

YOUR TURN 7
Drafting Your Autobiographical Incident

Now it is your turn to write an autobiographical incident. As you write, refer to the framework above and the Writer's Model on the next page.

A Writer's Model

A Night to Remember

It was a cool October evening. Excitement and family members filled the auditorium. I was only seven years old, but I was the center of attention. Finally, after weeks of preparation, I would show off all my hard work in a dance recital. Everything would be perfect—so I thought.

I waited backstage all dressed up in my black leotard and tights with a gold sequined belt. My hair was pulled back in a French braid, and a strong flowery smell of hair spray hung around me. In a booming voice, the master of ceremonies announced that my class was next. As I pranced proudly onto the stage and into the hot, bright stage lights, my dance teacher whispered, "Break a leg!"

My dance class was doing a routine with boxes two feet by two feet, made of wood. During part of the routine, the entire class was standing in a line on top of our boxes facing the audience. All I had to do in the next move was put one foot on the box next to mine and keep my other foot on my box. It really was an easy move. I was concentrating so much on maintaining the huge smile I had plastered on my face and keeping my head up that I did not look where I was going. I missed my partner's box altogether and slipped. There I was standing on the stage floor when my classmates were on top of their boxes. I could hear giggles coming from the audience, and I felt the heat rush to my face. I remembered my dance teacher had told my class during rehearsal, "If you make a mistake, keep smiling so the audience will not notice." I did my best to follow her advice as I continued with the routine.

Attention-grabbing opening

Background information

Beginning of incident

Sensory details

Action details
Middle of incident

Action details

Sensory details

(continued)

(continued)

End of incident

Sensory details

Action details

Reason this incident is
important

When the curtain dropped, so did my hopes for the evening. I sobbed loudly, tasting the salt from the tears that streamed down my face. I ran backstage, but no one could console me. I just wanted to be left alone.

Recently I realized I *had* been a star that night. I was embarrassed, but I fought the urge to run off the stage. Instead, I finished the routine with a smile on my face. Now when friends and family laugh about the time I slipped during a dance recital, I can laugh too.

Designing Your Writing

Illustrating Your Autobiographical Incident Illustrations, such as drawings or photographs, can enhance your written description and show why an incident is important and meaningful to you. For instance, say you are writing about the time you received your best present—a puppy. You could include a picture of yourself hugging the puppy with a red ribbon around its neck. The picture shows how excited you were when you got your dog. The writer of the Writer's Model included a photo that was taken the exact moment she slipped during the dance recital. The picture definitely illustrates her embarrassment. There are several ways you can include pictures in your paper. You can paste snapshots on a piece of paper, scan pictures on the computer, or even draw your own illustrations.

SKILLS FOCUS

Support ideas/theses with illustrations. Use technology for effective writing.

A Student's Model

In the following paper, Anthony C. Rodrigues, a middle school student from Cumberland, Rhode Island, writes about what he learned from a soccer game. Anthony suggests that writers should make "an organizational chart" of action and sensory details to re-create the experience.

In the Net

It was two o'clock on a Sunday afternoon, and I was on my way to my championship soccer game. As I rode up to the field and entered the parking lot, I wondered if this game was going to be like the other years when our team made it to the semifinals but then lost in the championship game. I looked at the field and I remembered seeing the pine trees in the background, but it was difficult to concentrate on their beauty because I was so nervous.

Background information

One by one the players arrived and the coach told us to begin our warm-up drills and to take shots on our goaltender. I wondered if during the game I was going to shoot as well as I had in warm-ups.

Beginning of incident

Finally, it was time. I was in the starting lineup, playing halfback. The whistle blew and the game had officially started. In the first half our team played exceptionally well, but at half time the score was 0–0, and we were all exhausted and cold. In the beginning of the second half we scored a goal. The crowd went up with a roar, and the players were running down the field yelling and screaming. I started to believe that maybe we would win. The second half went on and on. We maintained our 1–0 lead.

Middle of incident

We went on to win the game 1–0. I was so excited that I had won my first championship game in all of my six years playing soccer. I learned that anything is possible if I put my mind and soul into it.

End of incident

Reason this incident is important

Revising

Evaluate and Revise Content, Organization, and Style

Take Two When you are ready to evaluate your essay or a classmate's, you should read the essay twice. In the first reading, look at the essay's content and organization, using the guidelines below. In the second reading, focus on the sentences, using the Focus on Word Choice on page 490. For both readings, be sure to **collaborate** or have a **writing conference** with a classmate to discuss your evaluation.

➤ **First Reading: Content and Organization** Use the chart below to evaluate and revise your autobiographical incident.

Guidelines for Self-Evaluation and Peer Evaluation

Evaluation Questions	Tips	Revision Techniques
❶ Does the introduction grab the reader's attention?	**Underline** the question or hint that makes the beginning interesting.	If needed, **add** a question or a hint about the incident's importance.
❷ Does the introduction include enough background information to help the reader understand this incident?	**Circle** information about what the incident is, who was involved, where it took place, and when it happened.	If necessary, **add** sentences that provide background information for the reader.
❸ Are the action details in chronological order?	**Put a number** by each action detail and check that the numbers match the order in which the action happened.	If necessary, **rearrange** action details so that they are in chronological order.
❹ Do sensory details help the reader experience the incident?	Use a colored marker to **highlight** the sensory details.	**Elaborate** on each action detail as needed by adding sensory details that describe what was seen, heard, tasted, felt, or smelled.
❺ Does the conclusion tell why the incident is important to the writer?	**Put a check mark** next to the passage that explains why the event is important.	If needed, **add** thoughts or feelings that will relate the importance of the incident.

ONE WRITER'S REVISIONS This revision is an early draft of the autobiographical incident on page 485.

> There I was standing on the stage floor when my class-mates were on top of their boxes. I missed my partner's box altogether and slipped. I could hear giggles coming , *and I felt the heat rush to my face.* from the audience. I remembered my dance teacher had told my class during rehearsal, "If you make a mistake, keep smiling so the audience will not notice."

move

elaborate

Think as a Reader/Writer

1. Why do you think the writer moved a sentence?
2. Why do you think the writer added information to the paragraph above?

> **Second Reading: Style** You have revised your essay so that it is well organized and complete. Now, you will check that you have written your autobiographical incident using the best possible sentences. One way to improve your sentences is to use *exact verbs*. **Exact verbs** make your writing better because they accurately express a specific action.

When you evaluate your autobiographical incident for style, ask yourself whether your writing includes verbs that accurately describe certain actions. As you re-read your incident, mark an *X* through ordinary verbs that are not very descriptive. Then, replace the dull verbs with more descriptive ones. The Focus on Word Choice on the next page can help you learn to use exact verbs.

Exact Verbs

One of your purposes when you are writing an autobiographical incident is to help your readers see the action. Exact verbs can help you accomplish your goal. Exact verbs make your writing style more vivid and precise. Look at the following examples. Notice how exact verbs paint a more specific picture of an event in your mind—they make the action come alive.

Dull Verbs	Exact Verbs
Jesse *ate* his dinner.	Jesse *gobbled down* his dinner.
Natalie *said,* "I'm leaving!"	Natalie *screamed,* "I'm leaving!"
Brian *went* to the store.	Brian *raced* to the store.

COMPUTER TIP

You can use the thesaurus function to replace dull verbs with exact verbs. Highlight the verb you want to replace, and the thesaurus will list other verbs with the same or similar meanings. From the list, you can choose the exact verb that accurately describes the action.

ONE WRITER'S REVISIONS

> *pranced*
> As I ~~walked~~ proudly onto the stage and into the hot,
> *whispered*
> bright stage lights, my dance teacher ~~said,~~ "Break a leg!"

Think as a Reader/Writer

How did replacing dull verbs with exact verbs improve the sentence above?

SKILLS FOCUS

Use appropriate word choice and precise wording. Revise to refine word choice. Use technology to revise texts. *(page 491):* Proofread one's own writing in preparation for publishing. Capitalize proper nouns and adjectives correctly.

YOUR TURN 8 — Evaluating and Revising Your Autobiographical Incident

- First, evaluate and revise the content and organization of your paper, using the guidelines on page 488.
- Next, use the Focus on Word Choice above to see if you need to replace dull verbs in your paper with exact verbs.
- If a peer evaluated your paper, think carefully about your peer's comments as you revise.

Proofread Your Narrative

Correctness Counts Errors in your final draft will be distracting to your readers. If you have another person proofread your narrative, you will be less likely to overlook mistakes.

Capitalizing Proper Nouns

As you write your autobiographical incident, you will use **nouns,** words that name people, places, things, and ideas. There are two kinds of nouns: *common* and *proper.* A **common noun** names any one of a group of persons, places, things, or ideas. A **proper noun** names a particular person, place, thing, or idea, and begins with a capital letter. Here are some examples of common and proper nouns.

Common Nouns	Proper Nouns
city	Boston
religion	Judaism
basketball player	Michael Jordan
teacher	Mr. Williams

Notice that the title *Mr.* is capitalized in the example above. Capitalize a title that comes *immediately* before the person's name.

Example:
Washington, D.C., was named after President George Washington.

Most titles are not capitalized when they are not immediately followed by a name.

Example:
The first president was George Washington.

PRACTICE

Capitalize the proper nouns in the following sentences.

Example:
1. My vacation to visit aunt sue in england was the best.

*1. aunt sue ➤ Aunt Sue
england ➤ England*

1. I spent the entire month of july living in london.
2. In one day, we visited the tower of london and buckingham palace.
3. Riding on a boat down the thames river was exciting for my aunt and me.
4. I was hoping to see prince william, but he was in scotland with his father.
5. It took over ten hours for me to travel from london's gatwick airport to george bush intercontinental airport.

For more information and practice on **capitalizing proper nouns,** see page 287.

Publish Your Essay

Extra, Extra Read All About It You are finally ready to share your experience with others. After all, that is the purpose of writing an autobiographical incident. How do you go about getting an audience to read your essay?

- One audience could be an older you. Create a scrapbook of your life with the first entry being your autobiographical incident. It will be fun to look back on these memories later in life.

- Make an illustrated book of all the autobiographical incidents from your class. Place the book in your school library for other students to read.

- Create a "Me" poster you could share with your class. Include your autobiographical incident along with pictures and mementos that tell your hobbies, likes and dislikes, and plans for the future.

PORTFOLIO

Reflect on Your Essay

Building Your Portfolio Your essay is finally written and published. Now, take the time to think about *what* you wrote and *how* you wrote. Reflecting on work that you have completed will make you a better writer in the future.

- What did you find difficult when writing about yourself? What did you find easy?

- Think back on all the steps you took before you actually began writing your autobiographical incident. Which of these steps would you use again when writing another paper?

TIP As you proofread your essay, use a dictionary to make sure you have spelled words correctly. Don't guess about the correct spelling.

SKILLS FOCUS

Publish in a variety of formats. *(page 493):* Write descriptive essays. Use descriptive strategies. Write legibly. *(page 494):* Write short stories or poems. Incorporate specific narrative action. Use figurative language. Use correct spelling.

YOUR TURN 9 Proofreading, Publishing, and Reflecting on Your Essay

- Correct grammar, usage, and mechanics errors. Pay particular attention to the capitalization of proper nouns.

- Publish your essay using one of the suggestions above.

- Answer the Reflect on Your Essay questions above. Write your responses in a learning log, or include them in your portfolio.

Writing Description for Tests

In an essay test, you may be given a question that asks you to describe a person, place, or thing. Your description should include action details and sensory details. Read the following descriptive writing prompt. How would you answer this type of essay question?

Think about your friends. Choose one and write a letter to your teacher in which you describe your friend. In your letter, describe in detail what your friend looks like and how your friend acts.

> **TIP** Handwriting is important when answering an essay question. Your teacher or another test grader will not be able to read your answer if your handwriting is not **legible,** or easy to read. To make sure your answer is legible, use your best handwriting. You can print or write in cursive. Choose the style that will be easier for others to read.

THINKING IT THROUGH | Writing a Description

▶ **STEP 1** Read the prompt to see what it is asking you to do. What is your topic? Who is your audience?

The prompt is asking me to write a letter describing a friend. I will describe how my friend Reggie looks and acts. The audience is my teacher.

▶ **STEP 2** List action and sensory details that describe your subject. To picture the details, close your eyes and imagine the subject right in front of you.

Action details: makes good grades, does nice things (shared his sandwich), plays baseball

Sensory details: has curly, short, black hair and brown eyes, is tall (5 feet 3 inches) and thin (about 95 pounds), has a squeaky voice, smells like apples because he always uses apple shampoo

▶ **STEP 3** Decide how you will organize your details. Then, write your description.

First paragraph: I will tell what Reggie looks like.
Second paragraph: I will tell how he acts.

▶ **STEP 4** Read your description, checking for details that allow your reader to see your subject clearly.

I will check to see that I have a really good description of what Reggie looks like and how he acts.

Literature

Writing a Narrative Poem

Just as there are different types of stories—funny, sad, scary—there are different ways to present them to an audience. One way to present a story is by writing a narrative poem. A **narrative poem** has characters and a beginning, middle, and end. When you wrote your autobiographical incident, you wrote a *prose* narrative. Now you have a chance to be a poet by writing a narrative *poem*.

Start with the Basics It is not difficult to create a poem once you understand how poems are written. Poets say things in unusual ways. They often use very few words, so they have to select their words very carefully. Poets use sounds and figurative language to express their thoughts and feelings and to paint a picture of people, places, things, and actions.

The following list will provide you with the definitions and examples of the most common poetic elements.

Alliteration is the repetition of consonant sounds, especially sounds at the beginning of words.

Sara certainly saw Sam sail to Sardinia.

Bobby built rubber baby buggy bumpers.

Figurative Language is descriptive language that is not meant to be taken literally. Figurative language is used to express an idea by making a comparison that will give readers a clearer picture of the idea. For example, saying a noise is loud is not as clear as comparing the noise to eighty bowlers all making strikes at the same time. Three types of figurative language are *personification, simile,* and *metaphor*.

■ **Personification** is describing something that is not human, such as an animal or object, as if it were human by giving it human qualities.

The *joyful* sparrow chirped *hello.*

Each morning the alarm clock *screams* at me to get out of bed.

■ **Simile** compares two different things using the word *like* or *as.*

Like a statue, I sat motionless.

The leaves fell as quietly *as* a whisper.

■ **Metaphor** compares two different things by saying one is the other.

He *is* a bottomless pit, eating everything in sight.

When she first wakes up in the morning, her hair *is* a tangled bird's nest.

Seeing Is Believing Read the narrative poem on the next page. What event is the poet relating? What are his thoughts and feelings? What other examples of alliteration or figurative language can you find?

Foul Shot
by Edwin A. Hoey

With two 60's stuck on the scoreboard
And two seconds hanging on the clock,
The solemn boy in the center of eyes,
Squeezed by silence,
Seeks out the line with his feet,
Soothes his hands along his uniform,
Gently drums the ball against the floor,
Then measures the waiting net,
Raises the ball on his right hand,
Balances it with his left,
Calms it with fingertips,
Breathes,
Crouches,
Waits,
And then through a stretching of stillness,
Nudges it upward.
The ball
Slides up and out,
Lands,
Leans,
Wobbles,
Wavers,
Hesitates,
Exasperates,
Plays it coy
Until every face begs with unsounding
screams—
And then

        And then

                And then,
Right before ROAR-UP,
Dives down and through.

Figurative language: personification—silence is squeezing the boy

Alliteration—lands and leans

Alliteration—wobbles and wavers

Figurative language: personification—the ball is playing it coy

---

TIP As you read the narrative poem, notice that

- the incident can be the title of the poem
- a narrative poem does not have to be auto-biographical
- events are written in chronological order so the reader can understand the incident
- placing one word on a line can emphasize that word or thought
- exact verbs provide an accurate description of the action

Got the Idea? How did the author of "Foul Shot" fit a story into a poem? As you can see, the author based his poem on a specific incident. The poem describes, in order, the events that happened during a free-throw shot. The poet did not take five pages to describe the incident, nor did he just list the events by saying, "The boy bounced the ball a few times, threw it, and it went into the basket." Instead, he selected his words carefully and used alliteration and figurative language. The poet's words put you there in the gym. You can see the action clearly and feel the crowd's hopes and the boy's nervousness.

The Ball Is in Your Court Now that you have read an example, try writing your own narrative poem by following the steps below.

1. Brainstorm an incident to write about that you don't mind sharing with others. The incident could be the title of your poem.

2. In the first stanza (group of lines), describe where the character is and how he or she feels. You can write about yourself or a **fictional,** or made-up, character.

3. In the second stanza, describe what the character is doing and what he or she is thinking. Remember, each line does not have to be a complete sentence. You can write a phrase or one word on a line.

4. In the last stanza of your poem, tell how the incident ends.

Making It Better Once you have written the basic events that make up your narrative poem, you can revise your poem. You want to make sure you have used the best words to relate your ideas and feelings. Use the following suggestions to add poetic sounds and descriptions to your poem. Remember, a poem does not have to rhyme unless you want it to. There are other poetic elements you can use. Look for places where you can

- make several words that are near each other all begin with the same sound
- give human qualities to a feeling, animal, or object
- compare two unlike things using *like* or *as*
- compare two unlike things by saying one *is* the other

YOUR TURN 10 **Writing and Revising a Narrative Poem**

Write a narrative poem using the steps above. Then, revise your poem by adding as many of the poetic elements on page 494 as you can. Make a clean copy of your narrative poem and share it with a friend or give a **dramatic presentation** of your poem to your class.

Telling a Story

The art of storytelling has been around for a very long time. Before people could write, they told stories. Early storytellers would explain things in nature, teach lessons, and retell historical events. The **oral tradition** continued as these stories were passed from one generation to the next.

People still enjoy listening to a good story. In order to make a story entertaining, storytellers plan and practice before sharing a story with an audience. You can use the following guidelines as you prepare to tell a story.

Plan Your Story

To keep your audience's attention, plan to give them what they want—action. Choose an incident that has more "doing" than "describing." Your story will be more interesting if it keeps moving with action details.

You should also plan to tell your story in **chronological order.** You want your audience to be eager to find out what will happen next. Build **suspense** by saving the outcome until the very last moment. Jotting down the events on note cards will help you. Use three note cards, one each for the beginning, middle, and end of your story.

Your audience will also want **background information.** What will the audience need to know to understand your story? Answer this question before you begin practicing.

Practice Your Story

Before you tell your story in front of an audience, you will need to practice what you have planned. You will also need to practice making your story entertaining. How do you do that? It's simple.

WHAT'S AHEAD?

In this section you will tell a story. You will also learn how to

- **keep your audience's attention**
- **make your story entertaining**
- **understand your audience's needs**

 TIP Use formal language when telling your story. Use informal language, such as slang, only when a character is speaking and you are sure your audience will understand it.

SKILLS FOCUS

Deliver short stories. Incorporate suspense when presenting short stories. Establish a context when presenting short stories. Use informal, standard, and technical language appropriately.

Speak Out Your voice is the most important tool when telling a story, so use it. Practice speaking loudly enough for the people in the back row to hear; talk slowly and clearly enough for your audience to understand you. Also, practice changing the levels of your voice to change the mood. For instance, whispering adds suspense, and yelling suddenly can show surprise. You can even change your voice entirely. Try using different voices so the audience will know when different characters are speaking.

Show and Tell Words alone cannot express a story fully. Facial expressions and gestures are important as well. Don't tell everything; practice showing your actions. If you were telling a story about falling off your mountain bike, you might fall to the floor, grab your knee, and grimace as if in pain. You can include **sensory details** in your story by using gestures, too. For example, covering your ears shows that you heard a loud noise.

Practice Makes Perfect Practice telling your story in front of a friend and let your friend make suggestions on how you can improve your presentation. Make sure that you tell your story to your friend the same way you would tell it to a real audience. Keep the events in order, include background information, and use your voice and gestures.

Share Your Story

As you share your story, maintain eye contact with your audience. By looking at your audience, you can tell what they need. If the faces in your audience look puzzled, give background information or a more detailed explanation. If your audience is distracted or, worse, falling asleep, wake them up by performing an action or speaking in a different voice. The more lively you are, the more your audience will enjoy your story. Have fun. Telling a story should be an enjoyable experience for the audience and for you.

Reference Note

For more on adjusting **volume, rate, pitch** (your voice's highs and lows), and **tone** (or mood), see page 756. For more on **oral interpretation,** see page 759.

SKILLS FOCUS

Demonstrate effective verbal techniques when speaking. Demonstrate effective nonverbal techniques when speaking. Practice/rehearse before presenting oral messages. Adapt presentation according to audience feedback when speaking.

YOUR TURN 11 **Telling a Story**

Follow the guidelines above to share a story and make connections with your classmates. As you tell your story and listen to your classmates' stories, do you notice similar experiences?

18 Choices

Choose one of the following activities to complete.

▶ **CAREERS**

1. When I Grow Up Read an autobiography or biography about a person who has a career that interests you. When you are finished, write a **journal entry** telling one thing that surprised you about the person and the career.

▶ **SPEECH**

2. Telling Tales All cultures have stories that are passed on from one generation to the next. These stories, called folk tales, come from the **oral tradition.** Even though folk tales reflect the particular culture that created them, tales from different cultures have common features, such as talking animals. Compare two folk tales from different cultures, and present your findings to your class in an **oral report.**

▶ **DRAMA**

3. Another Life With a few other classmates, present a **dramatic interpretation** of a play based on the life of a real person. For example, *The*

Miracle Worker is about Helen Keller. You can find plays in the drama section of your school or local library.

▶ **WRITING**

4. Larger Than Life Write a **tall tale,** a story full of exaggerations, by taking a real incident and describing it with larger-than-life details. For instance, say you went fishing and caught a two-pounder that did not put up much of a fight. In your tall tale, however, the fish weighed twenty pounds, and it took you *and* a friend to drag it into the boat! If you wish, produce your tale as a **puppet show** or **skit.**

▶ **TECHNOLOGY**

5. You've Got Mail If you have access to e-mail, send an **e-mail message** to a friend describing an event that has just occurred in your life. Give background information so your friend will understand what happened.

◀ PORTFOLIO

SKILLS FOCUS

Analyze and understand elements and features of nonfiction and informational texts. Write a journal. Research topics when preparing oral messages. Present oral messages. Organize and present oral interpretations: plays. Write short stories or poems. Elaborate with explanations. Use effective representing strategies. Correspond with writers by e-mail.

19

Reporting the News

Reading Workshop

Reading a Newspaper Article

Writing Workshop

Writing a Newspaper Article

Viewing and Representing

Producing a Newspaper

Viewing and Representing

Producing a TV News Segment

Y ou and your classmates are riding the bus to school when suddenly the bus stalls. The bus driver tries to start the bus, but is unsuccessful. A trip that normally takes thirty minutes has turned into a two-hour ordeal. This event has made a big impression on you, but you probably will not see it reported on tonight's newscast or in tomorrow's newspaper. What makes some events worth reporting in the news and others not? Newsworthy events are not just recent events. They must also affect many people or simply grab people's attention.

> **Informational Text**
>
> Exposition

YOUR TURN 1 Looking at the News

Find an example of a news story. You can watch the news on television, listen to the news on the radio, or find a news article in a newspaper or magazine. Then, answer the following questions about the story you found.

- What event is the news story about?
- Who would want to know about this event?
- Why do you think this event made the news?

> **internet connect**
>
> **go.hrw.com**
>
> **GO TO:** go.hrw.com
> **KEYWORD:** EOLang 6-19

Reading a Newspaper Article

WHAT'S AHEAD?

In this section you will read a news article. You will also learn how to

- **identify the main idea of a news article**
- **recognize the pattern of a news article called inverted pyramid structure**

Can an orphaned baby whale survive without its parents? Students in California are asking the same question. They have been logging onto the Internet to check the status of the baby whale ever since she was returned to the ocean. What started as a history project focusing on current events has turned into something more. Find out what students have learned from this project by reading the news article on the next page.

Preparing to Read

READING SKILL

Main Idea The **main idea** is the most important point a writer wants to make. Sometimes the main idea is *stated*. This means it will be written in a sentence or two. Other times the main idea is *implied*, or suggested. In that case, you will have to look for clues to figure out the writer's most important point. As you read the following article, see if you can figure out the main idea.

READING FOCUS

Inverted Pyramid Structure A news event is made up of many details that answer the *5W-How?* questions.

- *Who* was involved?
- *What* happened?
- *When* did the event take place?
- *Where* did the event occur?
- *Why* did the event happen?
- *How* did the event happen?

News writers organize these details in an **inverted pyramid** (upside-down triangle) **structure** that begins with the most important details and ends with the least important details. Why do you think news articles are organized this way?

Read the following news article. In a notebook, write the answers to the numbered active-reading questions in the shaded boxes. The underlined words will be discussed in the Vocabulary Mini-Lesson on page 508.

FROM LOS ANGELES TIMES; ORANGE COUNTY EDITION

Whale Watch: Kids Use Internet to Track Progress of Newly Freed J. J.

BY LISA RICHARDSON

MISSION VIEJO—Marine experts from Sea World are using the latest radio transmission technology to monitor J. J., the newly freed gray whale.

Ten sixth-graders at Barcelona Hills Elementary School in Mission Viejo are doing the same thing, using the Internet.

Since the fifteen-month-old whale was orphaned last year, the group has followed her arrival at Sea World, how she has adapted to her handlers and, most recently, her return to the ocean and ride to freedom Tuesday.

The group has amassed an encyclopedic amount of whale knowledge over the months, and students can spout whale family classifications, whale dietary habits, and whale growth patterns with ease.

The group, students of history teacher Kaye Denison, spent most of Thursday morning on the Internet, checking reports on the whale's progress.

Having followed J. J. for so long, the eleven- and twelve-year-olds have put some thought into why—beyond scientific reasons—saving her life and studying her is important.

They have concluded that even if animals and mammals don't love human beings, it's natural for humans to love them.

At their school, the kids care for frogs, snakes, a chameleon, a skunk, an iguana, fish, and water turtles. They are sure the animals are indifferent toward them, but it doesn't stop them from liking the creatures.

"I heard on the news that you're not lonely and your life is not so stressful with animals in it, and I think it's true," said Sean Kingsmill, twelve.

"I mean, people are lonely," A. J. Young said.

1. What have the sixth-graders been doing for several months?

2. How are the students keeping track of J. J.'s progress?

"For example, wouldn't you be lonely if you didn't live at all with anybody, and wouldn't you want a dog or something?"

Learning about the whale has been fun. They know that J. J. weighs more than 17,000 pounds, is 29 feet long, and gains 2 pounds every hour. Killer whales are natural enemies of gray whales, and while adults eat plankton,[1] J. J. existed mostly on a mixture of milk, powdered fish, and warm cream passed through a tube into her stomach.

"It's important to save her because they come from an extinct [endangered] species, and it's good since they're coming back up," said Danielle Howannesian, eleven. "Besides, babies are always cute."

---

1. **plankton:** microscopic animals and plants.

3. Do you think the information in the second paragraph above should appear earlier in the article? Why or why not?

It is largely affection for the baby whale that keeps them interested in her plight.

They sympathized with J. J.'s orphanhood and her efforts to learn survival skills. When she was released, the group felt bad for the whale's disappointed handlers, who said J. J. did not make her typical sound of gratitude before swimming away. But they believe J. J. will miss her handlers after awhile. . . .

For now the group relies on updates posted to the Sea World Web site . . . , but by next Friday, the satellite tracking system should begin receiving transmissions directly from J. J., and the students will have access to more current information.

But the class doesn't spend all its time on J. J. For another project in Denison's class, the children had to pre-

4. According to the first paragraph above, why does this project interest students?

tend they were Hollywood location scouts and, using computers, map important sites in ancient Egypt. The project was coupled with lessons on chemical warfare in neighboring Iraq and political tension in the region.

"My class is actually an ancient history class, but because we're really involved in current events, we tie in whatever is happening in the world," Denison said.

Members of the "Barcelona Hills J. J. Fan Club"—what one student dubbed the group—say they will follow the whale's progress until they are sure she is safe or has joined a pod of whales.

"We've been with it this long," said Lindsay Murray, twelve. "We have to make sure that she's going to be OK."

5. Is the information in the two paragraphs at the top of this column necessary to understand the class's "J. J." project? Why or why not?

Main Idea

READING SKILL

Behind the Wheel   What do a bicycle wheel and a news article have in common? You may have noticed that the spokes on a bicycle wheel lead directly to the hub, which is the central point of the wheel. News articles also have a central point, or **main idea.** All the details lead the reader to the main idea, which can be stated or implied. A **stated main idea** is one that is written out in a sentence or two.

TIP   Whether you are reading a newspaper article, a short story, or a research report, you should look for a main idea. Finding the main idea will help you understand the supporting details.

Example:
Brian Caspar's quick thinking saved his friend's life.

An **implied main idea,** or suggested main idea, is not found in a specific sentence. The reader must look at how the supporting details are related to figure out the implied main idea.

Example:
Brian Caspar found his friend lying unconscious on the floor. After calling 911, Brian began CPR before paramedics arrived. His friend is now in stable condition.

All the details in the example above support the main idea: Brian thought quickly and saved his friend's life.

Read the news article below. Can you identify the main idea? Use the Thinking It Through steps on the next page if you need help.

> To make room for a new playground, Urban Demolition, Inc., used dynamite to demolish the old Paramount Theater on Elm Avenue last Wednesday.
> The demolition took approximately nine seconds from start to finish. Dust hovered over Elm Avenue and the surrounding areas for several hours.
> Urban Demolition crews estimate that it will take a week for them to clear the rubble.

SKILLS FOCUS

Identify the main idea.
Identify supporting sentences.

Identifying the Main Idea in a News Article

▶ **STEP 1** Identify the main idea by asking, "*Who* (or *what*) did *what* and *why*?"

▶ **STEP 2** Check to see that you identified the main idea by asking, "Do all the details support my answer?"

Urban Demolition, Inc., demolished the Paramount Theater to make room for a playground.

The details tell me how long it took, what happened afterward, and what will happen in the future. They all relate to the demolition.

YOUR TURN 2 Identifying the Main Idea

Re-read the news article on pages 503–504. Then, use the Thinking It Through steps above to identify the main idea.

READING FOCUS

Inverted Pyramid Structure

Why Save the Best for Last?   After dinner, you can have dessert. After you clean your room, you can see your friends. Have you ever asked yourself, "Why do I have to *wait* for all the good stuff?" You don't have to wait when you read a news article.

Lead
(5W-How?
questions)
Details
Details
Details

News articles are arranged in an **inverted pyramid structure.** An inverted pyramid is an upside-down triangle. The wide part of the triangle holds the *lead*. The **lead,** which can be more than one paragraph long, is the beginning of a news article. It summarizes the most important information about an event by answering the *5W-How?* questions: *Who? What? When? Where? Why?* and *How?* Readers who are in a hurry can understand the event by reading just the lead.

The rest of the news article provides readers with more information about the event. The details are presented in order from most important to least important. Why? If an article is longer than the amount of space the news editor has set aside for it, some of the information will need to be cut. Cutting is easy when the least important details are at the end of the article. The news editor can start at the end and cut details until the article fits its assigned space. An inverted pyramid structure saves time for both the reader and the news editor.

Cut to Fit   Edie, a newspaper editor, has room for a four-paragraph article, but the following article has five paragraphs. Notice how Edie rearranged the details so that the important ones are at the beginning, then cut the unimportant details so the article now has only four paragraphs.

TIP The paragraphs in a newspaper article are usually very short, sometimes only one or two sentences. Shorter paragraphs with fewer details make reading a news article easier and more efficient.

> Malcolm Scott, CEO of Happy Faces Corporation, announced plans today to build a new amusement park west of downtown.
>
> ~~"I can't wait for the park to open," said eleven year old Hector Garza. "I will be the first one in line."~~
>
> "We want to give people, especially kids, a fun and exciting place to visit," said Scott.
>
> The park will be a good source of entertainment, say city officials. It will also create jobs and bring additional money to the community from tourists.
>
> Construction for the new amusement park will begin in September and should be completed by the end of April. The grand opening is scheduled for the beginning of May.

Answers to *who, what,* and *where*

Answers to *why*

Answers to *how* and *when*

TIP How does an editor decide which details are less important than others? You already know that the *most* important details answer the *5W-How?* questions about the topic. Among the details that follow the lead, those judged more important than others might be ones that

- are more recent
- concern more readers
- are more attention-grabbing

YOUR TURN 3 Editing a News Article

Make a copy of the news article on pages 503–504. In a group, re-read it with news editors' eyes.

- After reading, discuss whether the answers to the *5W-How?* questions are in the lead. If they are not, rearrange the paragraphs so that the answers are at the beginning.

- Then, cut the least important details in the article so it will fit in a space for a fifteen-paragraph article. You will need to cut four paragraphs. Use the second Tip in the margin above to decide which details are less important.

SKILLS FOCUS

Read for details. *(page 506):* Identify and understand order-of-importance organization. Identify the lead and understand its purpose. *(page 508):* Identify and use correctly multiple-meaning words. *(page 509):* Identify the main idea.

Multiple-Meaning Words

When you read the newspaper, do you ever get confused by a word you have known for years? When that happens, you have probably stumbled upon a **multiple-meaning word**, a word with more than one meaning.

■ A multiple-meaning word can have two or more very different definitions.

Examples:

Marcus *filed* the papers. (to put in place)

The band members *filed* onto the field. (to move in a line)

■ A multiple-meaning word can be used as more than one part of speech.

Examples:

If you know the answer, raise your *hand*. (part of the body—noun)

Can you *hand* me the hammer, please? (to give by hand—verb)

THINKING IT THROUGH **Understanding Multiple-Meaning Words**

The following steps can help you find the correct meaning of a multiple-meaning word. The example below is from the reading selection.

Example:

"Members of the 'Barcelona Hills J. J. Fan Club'—what one student dubbed the group . . ."

I think dubbed means "you record over the original," but that definition doesn't make sense here.

▶ **STEP 1** Look at how the word is used in the passage. What do the words and sentences around it tell you?

The sentence says that one student dubbed the class the "Barcelona Hills J. J. Fan Club." It sounds like dubbed means "to name."

▶ **STEP 2** Check your definition in the original sentence. Ask yourself, "Does this definition make sense?"

"Members of the Barcelona Hills J. J. Fan Club—what one student named the group . . ." That makes sense to me.

PRACTICE

Use the steps above to define the following multiple-meaning words. The words are underlined for you in the reading selection.

1. marine (page 503)
2. spout (page 503)
3. concluded (page 503)
4. scouts (page 504)
5. pod (page 504)

Answering Main Idea Questions

Just as a lead will tell you the most important points of a news article, a main idea will tell you the central point of a reading passage. When you take a reading test, you may be asked to identify the main idea of a reading selection. Read the following passage and question. How would you answer the question?

Gray whales exhibit a number of interesting behaviors. They often show their flukes, or tails, when they dive. A diving whale is said to be *sounding.* Gray whales can also leap out of the water and fall back, creating a big splash. This type of behavior is called *breaching. Spyhopping* occurs when a whale peeks its head vertically out of the water, possibly to see above the surface. You can see the behaviors of gray whales off the west coast of the United States from late fall until early spring.

What is the main idea of this passage?

A. Whale watching is a fun activity.

B. Whales can leap out of the water.

C. Spyhopping allows whales to see above the surface.

D. Gray whales display many interesting behaviors.

THINKING IT THROUGH   **Identifying the Main Idea**

▶ **STEP 1** Decide what the question asks.

I need to find the main idea.

▶ **STEP 2** Look at what all the details have in common. The details should point to the main idea. **Hint:** Pay attention to the first and last sentences. Sometimes you may find a sentence that states the main idea.

All of the details describe the behaviors of gray whales. The first sentence tells me that gray whales have different behaviors, and the last sentence tells me where and when I can see them.

▶ **STEP 3** State the main idea in your own words. Then, look for an answer that closely matches your own. Rule out answers that are obviously wrong.

Gray whales exhibit three different behaviors. Answer choice D says something like that.

▶ **STEP 4** Check to make sure that the details in the paragraph or passage support your answer.

The different behaviors of gray whales are sounding, breaching, and spyhopping. Those details support my answer.

Writing a Newspaper Article

In this workshop you will write a newspaper article. You will also learn how to

- **choose a newsworthy event**
- **organize and evaluate details**
- **analyze cause and effect**
- **vary sentence structure**
- **correct run-on sentences**

The headlines read "Mayor Honors Sixth-Grade Student," "Wind Rips Roof off Middle School," and "Girl Saves Brother from Shark Attack." Interesting events occur every day everywhere—even where you live. Would you like to be the one to tell the story? You can, by writing a news article.

News articles are a form of **expository,** or **informative,** writing. They provide readers with information about events that have happened recently. In this Writing Workshop you will write a newspaper article. Your article will explain an interesting event of your choice.

Prewriting

Choose and Evaluate an Event

Look and Listen Interesting events will not just fall into your lap. To find one, you may need to do a little digging. You won't be digging with a shovel, though. Instead, you will use your eyes and ears. Here are some suggestions you can use to find an event that has already happened.

- Talk to presidents and sponsors of clubs at your school about events that have happened recently.
- Ask members of local organizations, such as the PTA or city council, about recent decisions they have made.
- Make a list of recent events you have observed firsthand.

SKILLS FOCUS

Write to report. Use writing as a tool for learning and research.

Is It Worth It?   Would you spend all your time gathering, organizing, writing, revising, and publishing information about an event if no one is going to find your article interesting? Of course not. **Make your time and the readers' time worthwhile by writing about an event that is newsworthy.** An event is newsworthy if it has at least one of the following characteristics.

◀ **KEY CONCEPT**

Newsworthy Characteristic	Example
The event . . .	
makes a difference in people's lives	World leaders announce plans to help nations' starving people.
is current	A hurricane slams into the East Coast.
involves people who are famous or in power	A famous singer gives a free concert.
touches people's emotions	Students organize a fund-raiser to help an animal shelter buy supplies.

TIP Events can have more than one newsworthy characteristic. For instance, a school newspaper's story about the volleyball team's win in the state tournament is current *and* touches people's emotions. Reporters look for events with more than one newsworthy characteristic so more people will read their articles.

An article's newsworthiness also depends on the purpose of the newspaper. For example, school or community newspapers generally focus on local events. However, city and national newspapers focus on a range of events, from local to worldwide.

YOUR TURN 4 Choosing and Evaluating an Event

- Make a list of events that have happened recently in your school or community.

- Then, evaluate each event on your list by looking for newsworthy characteristics. (Assume you are writing for a community or school newspaper.)

- Choose the event with the greatest number of newsworthy characteristics as the subject of your news article.

SKILLS FOCUS

Engage the interest of the reader. Choose a topic to write about. Narrow the focus of the topic.

Identify Your Audience

Who Wants to Know? The school board meeting is over. Your teacher wants to know if the school board approved a pay raise for teachers, but you want to know what the board decided about school uniforms.

Different events interest different people. The people who will be interested in the event you have chosen are your **audience.** To figure out the audience for your news article, ask yourself, "Who will be interested in this event, and why?"

Here is how a student identified his news article's audience.

> Event: I am writing about the principal approving a longer passing period between classes at my school.
>
> Audience: I think teachers and students will be interested because this event happened at school, and the longer passing period will affect them.

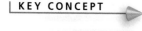 **Identifying Your Audience**

In your notebook, complete the sentences below to identify the audience for your news article.

Event: I am writing about _____.

Audience: I think _____ will be interested because _____.

Gather Details

Just the Facts Your friend tells you he saw a famous sports star. You want to know all about it. "Who? When? Where? Tell me!" you beg.

Just as you want all the facts of your friend's encounter with a sports star, **your audience will want all the facts of the newsworthy event.** Answers to the *5W-How?* questions will provide your readers with the facts, or details, of the event. The following chart shows specific questions you should try to answer as you gather the details for your news article.

Who?	Who was involved in the event? (Names are important, but also try to get other details about the people involved, such as titles, ages, or professions.)
What?	What was the event?
When?	When did the event occur? (Get the time and date of the event.)
Where?	Where did the event take place? (Find out the address or location.)
Why?	Why did the event happen?
How?	How did the event happen? (List the smaller events that made up the event.)

The *5W-How?* questions will give your audience the basic information about the event, but some readers will want to know even more. To help your audience fully understand the event, find the answers to these questions as well.

- What are the effects of the event?
- How do people feel about the event?

TIP A news article's **voice** is *objective,* or factual. When you write a news article, use words that simply state the facts. For instance, instead of writing about a "cute cocker spaniel," stick to the facts and write about a "one-year-old cocker spaniel." The dog's age is a fact because it can be proven. "Cute," on the other hand, is a matter of opinion.

Get to the Source You know what information you need, but how do you go about getting the answers to your questions? **Gather details for your news article by interviewing people who witnessed the event or played a part in it.** Even if *you* observed the event firsthand, you should still talk to other people.

As you interview, take notes about what people say, but also record a few direct quotations. In other words, write down what people say word-for-word instead of summarizing. Readers find direct quotations interesting because they have more force than a summary. You can see the power of a direct quotation in the example on the next page.

KEY CONCEPT

SKILLS FOCUS

Answer the *5W-How?* questions as a way to plan writing. Take notes from relevant and authoritative sources. Quote sources.

Summary: Neil Armstrong was the first man to walk on the moon. Armstrong felt his first step was an exciting moment not only for him but for the rest of the world as well.

Direct Quotation: Neil Armstrong was the first man to walk on the moon. As he made his first step he said, "That's one small step for [a] man, one giant leap for mankind."

The following example shows the notes one student took as he interviewed people. Notice that he includes details that answer the *5W-How?* questions, information about the effects of the event, and people's reactions to it. The student also recorded direct quotations that support some of the details.

Who? Principal Reyes

What? He approved a longer passing period between classes.

When? He announced it at today's pep rally.

Where? Main Street Middle School

Why? Principal Reyes agreed that students needed more time to go to their lockers and the restroom between classes.

How? Morgan Sykes passed a petition around last Wed. and Thurs. It was given to Principal Reyes on Fri.—134 people signed it.

What are the effects of the event? Starts Oct. 7. Classes—5 minutes shorter except 7th period. Passing period—5 minutes longer. School is still over at 3:00 P.M.

How do people feel about the event?
Negative reaction: Toby Washington, 7th grade: "I like my classes. I don't want them to be five minutes shorter. Those five minutes give me a chance to start my homework."

Positive reaction: Paul Brook, 6th-grade history teacher: "I'm so happy that instruction will not be interrupted by students leaving class to go to the restroom or their lockers."

Positive reaction: Joanna Tran, 6th grade: "The extra time will help me clear my head after one class and gear up for the next."

SKILLS FOCUS

Provide balanced, unbiased support.

Organize and Evaluate Details

Go Ahead, Spoil Them! Your readers not only want information about an event, they want to read the most important information first. Give your readers what they want by organizing the details you have gathered in a logical progression—an inverted pyramid structure. **In an inverted pyramid structure, the most important details appear at the beginning of a news article, and the least important details appear at the end.** The inverted pyramid structure of a news article looks like this:

Reference Note

For more on **inverted pyramid structure,** see page 506.

◀ KEY CONCEPT

Lead (answers the *5W-How?* questions)
Most important details
Less important details
Least important details

To arrange your details in an inverted pyramid structure, start by identifying the details that will go in the *lead*. The **lead** is the beginning of an article, and it provides the answers to the *5W-How?* questions. If your audience reads only the lead, they will still have an idea of what happened.

Once you know which details go in the lead, evaluate the remaining details, and arrange them in descending, or decreasing, order of importance. How do you organize details from most important to least important? Look at your details about the effects of the event and people's reactions to it. Think about your audience and ask yourself the questions on the following page.

SKILLS FOCUS

Organize writing by order of importance. Evaluate appropriateness of sources.

- **Which details would give my audience a better understanding of the event?** The answer to this question will point to the most important details, the ones that will follow the lead.

- **What additional information is likely to interest my *whole* audience?** You have identified information for the lead and other important details of the event. Look over your remaining notes. What *other* information is likely to interest *all* your readers? This information, though less important than the lead, is important enough for the middle of the article.

Reference Note

For more on **evaluating details,** see the second Tip on page 507.

- **What information might interest *just a few members* of my audience?** Your audience may contain a group with a special interest in certain details. The "least important" details may still be of interest to this group. These types of details go at the end of the article.

This is how the student writing about the passing period change arranged the details for his news article.

Lead: answers to the 5W-How? questions

Most important details:
—information about when the passing period starts and the effect on class time, passing period time, and school hours

Less important details:
—information about how students feel about the longer passing period
—positive quotation from Joanna Tran and negative quotation from Toby Washington

Least important details:
—information about teachers appreciating the extra time as much as the students do and positive quotation from Paul Brook

YOUR TURN 7 **Organizing and Evaluating Details**

Organize your details in an inverted pyramid structure. First, place the answers to the *5W-How?* questions in the lead. Then, arrange the remaining details from most important to least important by asking yourself the questions that appear at the top of this page.

SKILLS FOCUS

(page 517): Analyze causes and effects.

CRITICAL THINKING

Analyzing Cause and Effect

Have you ever set a series of dominoes upright in a row? When the first domino in line tips over, it causes the next one to fall, which causes the next one to fall, and so on. Analyzing a cause-and-effect chain is like watching a chain of dominoes, because it involves looking at how one thing leads to another.

Below is an example of a cause-and-effect chain. Can you see how each cause leads to an effect, which then causes another effect, and so on?

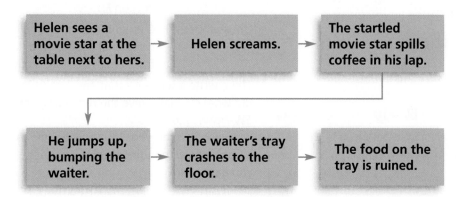

Your news article will explain the causes and the effects of an event. As you write, make sure that the relationships between the causes and effects are clear. If you leave out a portion of the cause-and-effect chain, your audience may not fully understand the event. For example, suppose your little brothers are happily playing together in the living room. You leave to get a snack. When you come back, one brother is crying, and the other brother is yelling. What happened? You missed what caused your brothers to fight. Causes and effects need to be connected clearly in order for them to make sense.

PRACTICE

Create five cause-and-effect chains. The following causes will be the first step in each chain. Use your imagination and experience to complete the chains. Each chain should have at least three steps.

1. A river overflows due to heavy rain.

2. A tornado is seen near town.

3. Sixth-grade students take snacks to a local nursing home.

4. Ms. Martinez, a science teacher, wins the Teacher of the Year award.

5. Greg Goldstein sings off-key during the choir's concert.

News Article

Framework	Think as a Reader/Writer

Lead
- Attention-grabbing opening
- Answers to the *5W-How?* questions

Capture your audience's attention by beginning your article with an unusual or interesting detail.

Detail   Several animals escaped from Pete's Pets on Friday.

Unusual Detail   Charlie the chimpanzee led several of his animal friends on a daring escape from Pete's Pets on Friday.

Then, write a sentence that answers, at least, "*Who* did *what?*" Finally, give the remaining answers to the *5W-How?* questions.

    Keep in mind your lead may be one to three short paragraphs, depending on the amount of information you gathered.

Body
- Most important details
- Less important details
- Least important details

- Organize the remaining **details** in an inverted pyramid structure. Refer to your responses to Your Turn 7 for the order of these details. Be sure the remaining details include information about the effects of the event and people's reactions to it.
- Group the details in short paragraphs.
- Place **direct quotations** after the details they support.

YOUR TURN 8 **Writing Your News Article**

Now it is your turn to write a news article. As you write,
- keep your audience in mind
- order your details so that the most important ones come first and the least important ones come last
- refer to the framework above and to the Writer's Model on the next page

A Writer's Model

The final draft below closely follows the framework for a news article on the previous page.

Principal Approves Longer Passing Period

A major change has taken place at Main Street Middle School: The period between each class is now five minutes longer. Principal Alan Reyes approved the longer passing period. His decision was announced at today's pep rally in Loftus Gymnasium.

Eighth-grader Morgan Sykes started the petition that led to the longer passing period. She passed the petition to other students last Wednesday and Thursday. When Principal Reyes received it last Friday, 134 students had signed it.

Principal Reyes agreed that students need extra time between classes. With a longer passing period, students will not have to leave class to go to their lockers or the restroom.

The longer passing period will go into effect on Monday, October 7. From now on, each class except seventh period will be five minutes shorter, and the passing periods will be five minutes longer. School will still be over at 3:00 P.M.

Most students are happy about the change, and they are already making plans for the extended passing time. Sixth-grader Joanna Tran said, "The extra time will help me clear my head after one class and gear up for the next."

At least one student disapproved of the new passing period. "I like my classes. I don't want them to be five minutes shorter," said seventh-grader Toby Washington. "Those five minutes give me a chance to start my homework."

Most teachers will enjoy the extra time as much as the students will. "I'm so happy that instruction will not be interrupted by students leaving class to go to the restroom or their lockers," said sixth-grade history teacher Paul Brook.

Annotations (margin):

- Attention-grabbing opening
- Answer to *where*
- Answers to *what* and *who*
- Answer to *when*
- Answer to *how*
- Answer to *why*
- Most important details
- Less important details
- Quotation
- Quotation
- Least important details
- Quotation

A Student's Model

When you write a news article, you want to choose a newsworthy topic. Natalie Banta and Amy Tidwell, reporters for Olympus Junior High's online newspaper the *Olympian,* write about an important school event—the principal leaving.

Attention-grabbing opening

Answers to *who, what, why,* and *how*

Answer to *when*

Most important details

Less important details

Least important details

Mr. Sagers Moves to Cyprus High

Maybe you have heard the rumor about Principal Sagers leaving Olympus Junior High School. Well, it is true. Mr. Sagers was promoted to be the principal of Cyprus High.

The new principal of Olympus Junior High (OJH) will be Linda Mariotti. She has been the assistant principal at Bonneville and at Granite High, a coordinator at the Jones Center, and a language specialist. We will meet her next September.

When we asked Principal Sagers what he would miss the most about OJH, he answered that he would miss the attitude of the community. "Everyone seems to have high expectations of learning," he said.

Some of Principal Sagers's greatest accomplishments have been in the area of technology. He said, "We've achieved a lot [in the area of technology] in the last two years. We've also tried to create a positive climate and beautify the school." If Principal Sagers were not leaving, he would continue increasing literacy. "The goal was to identify all students not reading on their grade level. We're using technology as a vehicle to enhance instruction," he said.

It is hard to go to a new school for everyone, but Principal Sagers said, "The first year at a new high school [for a principal] is extremely difficult. It's always hard to start over as a new leader."

Evaluate and Revise Content, Organization, and Style

Check and Check Again As you look over a peer's article or your own, you should do at least two readings. First, focus on the article's content and organization. The guidelines below will help you edit your article. Then, in your second reading, go back and look for ways to make sentences stronger by using the Focus on Sentences on page 523.

➤ **First Reading: Content and Organization** Use the chart below to look for ways to improve the content and organization of your news article. Respond to questions in the left-hand column. If you need help answering the questions, use the tips in the middle column. If necessary, make the changes suggested in the right-hand column.

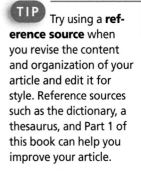

TIP Try using a **reference source** when you revise the content and organization of your article and edit it for style. Reference sources such as the dictionary, a thesaurus, and Part 1 of this book can help you improve your article.

Guidelines for Self-Evaluation and Peer Evaluation		
Evaluation Questions	**Tips**	**Revision Techniques**
❶ Does the lead answer the *5W-How?* questions?	**Circle** the answers to the questions *who, what, when, where, why,* and *how.*	If needed, **add** answers to the *5W-How?* questions at the beginning of the news article.
❷ Are details in the body given in order from most important to least important?	**Put a star** next to the details that help the reader better understand the event. **Put a check** next to the details that are not as important and could be cut.	If necessary, **rearrange** the details so those with a star next to them directly follow the lead and those with a check are at the end of the article.
❸ Does the body include details that explain the effects of the event and people's reactions to it?	**Underline** the details that explain the effects. **Put a box** around the details that show people's reactions.	**Add** details that explain the effects and people's reactions if these details are missing.
❹ Does the article include quotations that support the details of the article?	**Highlight** each quotation. **Draw an arrow** to the detail each quotation supports.	If needed, **elaborate** the details by adding quotations.

ONE WRITER'S REVISIONS This revision is an early draft of the news article on page 519.

The longer passing period will go into effect on Monday, October 7. From now on, each class except seventh period will be five minutes shorter, and the passing periods will be five minutes longer. School will still be over at 3:00 P.M.

rearrange

Principal Reyes agreed that students need extra time between classes. *With a longer passing period, students will not have to leave class to go to their lockers or the restroom.*

add

PEER REVIEW

As you look at a peer's news article, ask yourself these questions:

- What makes this article newsworthy?
- How do people feel about this event? Is more than one viewpoint presented?

Think as a Reader/Writer

1. Why do you think the writer changed the order of the two paragraphs?
2. How did adding a sentence improve the writing?

▷ **Second Reading: Style** Now that you have revised the content and organization of your news article, you can **edit** the individual sentences. You can improve your sentence style by using a variety of sentences—short sentences and long sentences. An article with too many short, choppy sentences or too many long, complex sentences will be difficult to read.

SKILLS FOCUS

Develop writer's style. *(page 521):* Revise by adding or replacing text. Revise by rearranging text. Revise by elaborating. Evaluate others' writing. Use reference materials for revising drafts.

When you evaluate your news article for style, ask yourself whether your writing has a variety of sentences—both short and long. As you re-read your article, draw a wavy line under short sentences, especially ones that contain eight words or fewer. Look over your work. Does your news article seem to have mainly short sentences? If so, combine some of the short sentences by using *and, but,* or *or.* (Keep some short, effective sentences for variety, though.)

Varying Sentences

A news article presents the facts simply and quickly. That does not mean, however, that all its sentences will be short. A series of short sentences can bore the audience. To vary your sentences, use *and, but,* or *or* to combine two short sentences.

All Short Sentences: An ice storm surprised downtown workers last night. Road crews responded. They were not prepared for the severity of the storm. The storm continued until 10:00 P.M. Roads remained icy. Workers found they had two options. They could risk driving. They could stay in their offices.

A Variety of Sentences: An ice storm surprised downtown workers last night. Road crews responded**, but** they were not prepared for the severity of the storm. The storm continued until 10:00 P.M.**, and** roads remained icy. Workers found they had two options. They could risk driving**, or** they could stay in their offices.

> **TIP** A comma generally comes before the *and, but,* or *or* that connects two short sentences.

ONE WRITER'S REVISIONS

School will still be over at 3:00 P.M.

Most students are happy about the change$_\wedge$, *and* They are already making plans for the extended passing time.

Think as a Reader/Writer

How did combining the sentences improve the writing?

YOUR TURN 9 · Evaluating and Revising Your News Article

Evaluate and revise the content and organization of your news article, using the guidelines on page 521. Then, use the Focus on Sentences above. If your class did peer evaluations, consider your peer's comments as you revise.

SKILLS FOCUS

Vary types of sentences for effective writing. Combine sentences for effective writing.

Publishing

Proofread Your News Article

Upon Close Inspection . . .   Mistakes in a news article will distract readers from the facts. Have another person proofread your article to find mistakes you might have missed.

Grammar Link

Correcting Run-on Sentences

Sometimes when you write, your pencil cannot keep up with your thoughts. When this happens, you may write *run-on sentences*. A **run-on sentence** is really two or more sentences that are written as one.

Mick loves old movies he also loves to read.

One way to correct a run-on sentence is to divide the sentence into separate sentences.

Mick loves old movies. He also loves to read.

You can also turn a run-on sentence into a compound sentence by adding a comma and *and, but,* or *or.*

Mick loves old movies**, but** he also loves to read.

Example:

1. I like the longer passing period my friend does not.

1. *I like the longer passing period. My friend does not.*

   I like the longer passing period, but my friend does not.

1. The passing period will be five minutes longer school will still be over at 3:00.

2. Morgan Sykes talked at the pep rally she received a standing ovation.

3. The students signed the petition asking for a longer passing period the principal agreed with them.

4. Students can use the extra time to go to their lockers they might use the time to go to the restroom.

5. Students will not miss important information by leaving class to go to their lockers or the restroom.

For more information and practice on correcting **run-on sentences,** see page 431.

PRACTICE

Correct the run-on sentences to the right. First, divide the run-on sentence into separate sentences. Then, rewrite the run-on sentence as a compound sentence by adding a comma and *and, but,* or *or.* If a sentence is correctly punctuated and is not a run-on, write C on your paper.

Publish Your News Article

Spread the News   Before you publish your article, you will need to write a *headline*. A **headline** is an attention-grabbing title for a news article. A good headline will summarize the event in a short sentence that contains an action verb. Action verbs are important because they tell the reader specifically what happened. Look at the examples below.

Examples:
Sixth-Graders **Adopt** Terence the Tarantula
Teachers **Ban** Homework Next Week

   After writing a headline for your article, publish it using one of the following ideas.

- With your classmates, publish your articles together in a newspaper and distribute it to your class.
- Record your article and show it to your class as part of a news segment. See pages 531–534 for more information.
- Submit your article to your school or community newspaper.

Reflect on Your News Article

Building Your Portfolio   Now, take time to reflect on what you have done. Answer these questions.

- How is a lead for a news article like other introductions for other types of writing? How is it different?
- Would you use interviewing to gather information for other types of writing? Why or why not?

Make your news article look like a real one by typing it in **columns,** or vertical rows. Measure the width of a real newspaper column and set the margins of your document to the same width. Then, select the justify option to make straight edges at both the left and right margins.

   Before you print your article, use the print preview feature to see what it will look like.

PORTFOLIO

YOUR TURN 10   **Proofreading, Publishing, and Reflecting on Your News Article**

- Correct spelling and punctuation mistakes. Make sure your article does not contain run-on sentences.
- Write a headline for your article and publish your article using one of the suggestions above.
- Answer the questions from Reflect on Your News Article above. Record your responses in a learning log, or include them in your portfolio.

SKILLS FOCUS

Refine text for a general audience. Use technology to publish texts. Design documents in preparation for publishing. *(page 524):* Proofread one's own writing in preparation for publishing. Identify and correct run-on sentences. *(page 526):* Write problem-solution essays. Present reasonable solutions.

Writing a Newspaper's Advice Column

You have a problem, and you are unsure how to solve it. Of course, you could turn to a friend or relative for help. Would you consider writing to the newspaper? Newspapers feature a special kind of **problem-solution writing** called an advice column. Newspaper advice columns provide information on how to solve all sorts of problems, from personal and financial to car and home repair. They are designed to be entertaining as well as informative.

What Is Your Problem?

Advice columns consist of two parts—the readers' problems and the columnist's answers. Newspapers publish these letters and responses to offer help not only to the person writing the letter but also to other readers who may have a similar problem. Maybe you can identify with this reader's problem below:

> Dear Pat the Problem Solver,
>
> My little brother always gets me in trouble by starting arguments. Then, when my mom comes to see what we are arguing about, he blames me for starting it. I try to explain my side of the story, but it's my word against his. What can I do to keep from being accused of a crime I have not committed?
>
> *Falsely Accused*

Help Is on the Way

What is the solution? An advice columnist does more than just provide the reader with an answer. In a response, you can usually find these items.

- **a restatement of the problem** The first thing an advice columnist does is restate the reader's problem. By restating the problem, the columnist lets the reader know that he or she understands what is wrong.

- **a solution** The next part of the response is the advice. Columnists give readers advice that they can actually use. The advice columnist will offer a solution that the reader can carry out to make the situation better.

- **an example** The final part of the response is an example that shows that the recommended solution really works. The advice columnist may give a personal example or one from someone else who tried the same solution. Readers are more likely to try the advice if they read that the solution has already worked in another situation.

Read the response Pat the Problem Solver wrote to Falsely Accused on the next page. The elements listed above are labeled for you.

Dear Falsely Accused,

Brothers and sisters often start arguments and then try to pass the blame to someone else. There are two ways you can handle this type of situation. One way is to avoid arguing. When your brother wants to start a fight, walk away and ignore him. However, if you simply cannot hold your tongue, the second way is to discuss (not argue about) the issue in front of your parents. This will keep your little brother (and you) in line. When my little sister wanted to argue, I would ignore her or tell her we should ask our parents what they thought. Suddenly, she would drop the issue. My sister no longer had the fun of seeing me mad or in trouble. Good luck!

Pat

Restatement of the problem

Solution

Example

YOUR TURN 11 Writing a Newspaper's Advice Column

Pretend you are an advice columnist. Choose one of the following letters. Then, use the guidelines on page 526 to write a response. To publish your response, consider producing a newspaper in which you include an advice column or presenting your response in an oral presentation.

My father is coach of the soccer team. He made someone else goalie even though he knew that I wanted the position and that I am a good goalie. He said he didn't choose me because he didn't want to show favoritism. Can you help?

A Fan of Fairness

I just moved to a small school where everyone else has known each other since kindergarten. It has been really hard to make friends, and my shyness doesn't help. Do you have any suggestions?

New Kid in Town

Producing a Newspaper

WHAT'S AHEAD?

In this section you will produce a newspaper. You will also learn how to

- organize news articles into sections
- write editorials
- design the layout of a newspaper

You and your classmates have written a variety of news articles that would interest others, so why not publish them in your own newspaper? Working with a small group, you can follow the guidelines below to produce a newspaper.

Make a Plan

Use What You Have To fill the pages of your newspaper, you can use the articles you and your group members wrote in the Writing Workshop. First, gather the articles together. Then, put the ones about school events in one stack and ones about community events in another stack.

Hand Out Assignments Your newspaper should include school articles and community articles. If you need more of one type of article, brainstorm a list of story ideas and choose a "reporter" to investigate and write an article.

In addition to school and community news, you will also need two *editorials* and an *editorial cartoon*. **Editorials** are articles that try to persuade readers to think or act a certain way. For instance, you may want to persuade others that your community needs to create bike lanes on busy streets. In the editorial, you would clearly state your opinion and support it with evidence—facts and examples. At the end of the editorial, you would ask your readers to take some action, such as signing a petition or changing a habit. You can also express your opinion in an **editorial cartoon.** Drawing a cyclist riding on top of cars because no room is available on the street would show that bike lanes are needed.

TIP The outline of an editorial looks like this:

Opinion statement
    First reason
        Fact or example
    Second reason
        Fact or example
    Third reason
        Fact or example
Call to action

Reference Note

For more on **persuasive writing,** see page 689. For more on **editorial cartoons,** see page 786 in the Quick Reference Handbook.

The Name Game   Before you put your paper together, you should decide on an original name for your newspaper. The name should be related to your school or community and appeal to readers. For example, if your school's mascot is an alligator, you could call your newspaper the *Gator Gazette*.

Put It Together

To put your newspaper together, use the instructions in Designing Your Writing below.

Designing Your Writing

Newspaper Layout   If your newspaper is clearly organized and appeals to the eye, people will be eager to read it. Your newspaper will consist of four pages. Each page will represent a section.

Page 1—The front page will have a **flag,** the title of the newspaper and the date of publication, across the top. It will also include the most newsworthy school article and the most newsworthy community article.

Page 2—School news section

Page 3—Community news section

Page 4—Editorial section

Follow these steps to design the layout of your newspaper.

- First, draw what each newspaper page will look like on an $8\frac{1}{2}'' \times 11''$ piece of paper. Use ××× to represent headlines, ≡ to indicate articles written in columns, and ⊠ to stand for pictures or graphics. As you design the layout, keep in mind the following guidelines.

  1. Articles in a newspaper should fill a square or rectangular block. Blocks help readers know where an article begins and ends. Look at the examples to the right.
  2. Generally, headlines should not be placed side by side. Headlines attract readers to the article because they are written or typed in a larger size than the articles. If two headlines are next to one another, readers will have difficulty separating them. Look at the difference in the examples to the right.
  3. Each page should have one image. Your group can paste or scan actual photographs onto the pages. If you do not have photographs, you can draw pictures. Make sure that the picture or photograph is related to the topic of the article.

TIP   You can add more pages to your newspaper by including other sections, such as sports, movie reviews, and classified ads.

Poorly Designed

Well Designed

Here is an example of one group's drawing of their newspaper's layout.

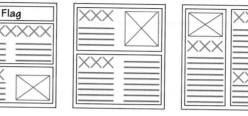

Front page **School news** **Community news** **Editorials**

- After you have decided on the placement of the articles, you can begin to make the pages of the newspaper. Tape two $8\frac{1}{2}'' \times 11''$ pieces of paper together like a book. Fold the taped paper in half to make four pages. Set your newspaper pages aside.

Reference Note

For more on laying out articles in **columns,** see the Computer Tip on page 525.

- On separate pieces of paper, write or type the articles in columns that are two or three inches wide. On an $8\frac{1}{2}'' \times 11''$ piece of paper, you can fit three 2-inch columns or two 3-inch columns. You also need to write or type the flag and headlines, and draw or print the images.

- Finally, glue the flag, the articles, the headlines, and the pictures onto the pages of the newspaper.

TIP If a news article is too long to fit within the block you have assigned to it, you can cut the article from the bottom. The least important details are at the end because you arranged them in an inverted pyramid structure.

YOUR TURN 12 Producing a Newspaper

In a group, use the following steps to produce a newspaper.

- First, decide whether the articles you wrote in the Writing Workshop are school news or community news.

- Next, assign some reporters to write editorials and others to draw editorial cartoons. If you need more school or community articles, assign reporters to write them, too.

- Then, use the guidelines in Designing Your Writing on pages 529–530 to design the layout of your newspaper.

- Finally, when your newspaper is complete, place it in your school's library so other students can read it.

SKILLS FOCUS

(page 528): Create class newspapers. Write an editorial.
(page 529): Design documents in preparation for publishing. Understand how graphics and drawings enhance communication.

Producing a TV News Segment

Watching a news segment on TV can affect you differently than simply reading a newspaper article or listening to a news story on the radio. The visual images that you see on TV can make you feel as if you are witnessing an event firsthand. In this section you and a few classmates will work together to produce a short news segment (around three minutes) that will help others experience the excitement of a news event.

Select Your Story

Look over the articles you and your group members wrote for the Writing Workshop. Which one is most newsworthy? Which news article has the greatest potential for interesting visuals? Identify the news article that is both newsworthy and has visual interest, and use it as the story for your news segment.

Choose Your Part

In your group, decide who will play each of the following roles.

- **Producer** The producer coordinates the production and is a link between the camera person and the anchor and reporter. The producer signals the camera person to start and stop recording and points to the anchor or reporter to begin talking. He or she also keeps the cue cards ready for the anchor and reporter to use if they need help with their lines.
- **Camera Person** The camera person is responsible for operating the video camera and recording the news segment.

WHAT'S AHEAD?

In this section you will produce a television news segment. You will also learn how to

- recognize the different roles of a television production team
- convert a news article into a script
- perform, record, and evaluate your news segment

Reference Note

For more on **newsworthy characteristics,** see page 511.

SKILLS FOCUS

Create TV news programs.

- **Anchor** The anchor introduces the news story and the reporter. The anchor almost always sits behind a desk in the studio. Your group can create a studio by setting up a table or desk and chair in front of a solid-color background.
- **Reporter** The reporter presents the details of the event, usually from the scene where the event occurred. If your group cannot get to the scene, the reporter can sit in the studio. Sometimes the reporter sits beside the anchor. Other times the reporter is located in a different part of the studio. The reporter may also interview people who witnessed or were involved in the event.

Prepare the Script

A script tells what will be *said* and *shown* in the news segment. It consists of two parts, audio and video. The audio part includes the music and words that people will hear in your news segment. The video part shows what people will see as they watch your news segment. Look at the example below.

Video: What Is Seen	Audio: What Is Heard
Shot of the studio with anchor behind desk (Begin recording when music starts.)	Begin music
Move in to a close-up shot of anchor	Fade music
Close-up shot of anchor (Put camera on pause.)	Anchor: Good evening. I'm Fatima Rahman. Tonight we bring you a story about the decision of Main Street Middle School's Principal Reyes to extend the passing period. We go now to our reporter on the scene, Kyle Lucas. Kyle . . .
Close-up shot of reporter outside principal's office (Begin recording when reporter speaks.)	Reporter: Thank you, Fatima. I'm here at Main Street Middle School where today Principal Reyes announced . . .

SKILLS FOCUS

Develop an organizational plan when creating media messages. Prepare scripts. Use video when creating media messages. Use sound when creating media messages.

Your group is now ready to write its own script. To turn the news article you have chosen into a script for the news segment, fold a piece of paper in half to create two columns. Label one column *Video* and the other *Audio.* Then, follow the steps below.

Writing a Script	
Step 1	**Write the anchor's dialogue.** In your article's lead, find the answer to the question "Who did what?" The answer will be what the anchor says to introduce the news story. The anchor will also introduce the reporter.
Step 2	**Write the reporter's dialogue.** The reporter will tell the remaining information in the lead and the body of the news article. The reporter will also interview the real people involved in the event or classmates playing the parts. This way, the quotes that are in the article will also be in the news segment.
Step 3	**Write the camera shots.** Next to the dialogue, write the directions for the camera person. The camera person will need to know what images to shoot and when to start and stop recording.
Step 4	**Make cue cards.** Transfer the dialogue to large pieces of poster board. Write in big letters so the anchor and reporter can use the cards for reference.
Step 5	**Decide on hand signals.** The producer will give hand signals to tell the rest of the group when to start and stop. That way, the producer's voice will not be heard on the video.

TIP Your group may choose to complete the steps in this chart together, or you may assign specific tasks to different group members.

Practice Your Performance

Practice does make perfect, so you should have several practice sessions before filming your news segment. Time your practices so your group can be sure the segment will not run more than the time your teacher allows.

TIP Check with your teacher to see if your school has video equipment. If not, you can perform your news segment live.

All for One and One for All   Each group member should practice his or her role.

■ The **producer** should be familiar with the script so that he or she knows when to use hand signals. He or she should also keep the cue cards ready and in order while recording so the anchor and reporter can use them.

- The **camera person** should practice using the video recorder. He or she should know how to start, stop, pause, and focus the camera. The camera person should also practice moving in for close-ups and pulling back for long shots.

- The **anchor** and **reporter** should be familiar with their lines so that they depend on cue cards as little as possible. Unless they are interviewing someone, they should practice looking directly into the camera when speaking. The anchor and reporter should speak slowly, clearly, and loudly enough for the microphone to pick up their voices.

All Together, Now   Once your group has practiced a few times and feels confident, do one practice run with the camera. As you watch the video, look for errors your group can avoid the next time you record. For instance, if the camera person notes problems with shaking or blurring, he or she can try to avoid those same mistakes by holding the camera more steady and focusing more carefully. The anchor and reporter can listen for misreadings or quiet voices. The producer can make sure the transitions between shots are smooth.

Record and Evaluate Your News Segment

Now that you have practiced, record a final time. Follow the instructions in your script to create your news segment.

When you are finished, evaluate your news segment. How does it look? With your group, watch the video and ask yourselves the following questions about language, medium, and presentation.

- **Language:** Are the details of the event told clearly and completely?

- **Medium:** Do the sounds and images used enhance the written story?

- **Presentation:** Do the anchor and reporter speak clearly and look directly into the camera? Are camera shots steady and focused?

SKILLS FOCUS

Reflect critically on media message produced.

YOUR TURN 13   Producing a TV News Segment

Follow the guidelines beginning on page 531 to produce a TV news segment. When you finish, share it with your classmates.

19 *Choices*

Choose one of the following activities to complete.

▶ CAREERS

1. Behind the News There are many careers in the field of journalism, such as newspaper reporter, TV reporter, newspaper editor, TV anchor, and TV producer. Research one of these careers to find out the education and training required and the average salary a person in that position would make. You may call your local TV station or newspaper, contact a university, or use the Internet to find information. Use what you learn to write a **report**.

▶ CROSSING THE CURRICULUM: ART

2. Express Yourself
Editorial cartoons use pictures and symbols to express opinions about different events. You can create an **editorial cartoon** about a current situation in your school or community. The cartoon should show the event and your opinion about it. Limit the words in your cartoon to the title and, if necessary, brief dialogue between characters.

▶ WRITING

3. What's the Story? Turn your newspaper article into a **short story.** Your story should include everything that your article does—the details of the newsworthy event and the people involved. However, your purpose will be to entertain rather than to inform. Use plenty of descriptive language and action verbs to make the reader feel as if he or she actually witnessed the event.

▶ CROSSING THE CURRICULUM: SCIENCE

4. Tell Me Why Write a brief **article** that answers a frequently asked *why* question about science. Begin the article with a question, such as "Why do people get the hiccups?" or "Why do leaves change colors and fall in autumn?" Then, do enough research to answer the question. Ask your science teacher to help you find the most up-to-date material. Submit your article to a class or school newspaper.

PORTFOLIO

Explaining How

Reading Workshop

Reading a "How-to" Article

Writing Workshop

Writing a "How-to" Paper

Viewing and Listening

Viewing and Listening to Learn

Here is a riddle for you: How are you and a computer alike? Computers follow a set of instructions to perform a function, and so do you. Think about it. In math class, for instance, your teacher tells you how to turn an improper fraction into a mixed number. This evening, you may heat up a frozen dinner by following the instructions on the box. The instructions you listen to, view, and read are all designed to teach you to complete a process.

Once you know how a process is done, you can share that information by giving instructions. Whether you share instructions orally, in writing, or through a demonstration, your goal is still the same: to teach others what you know.

Informational Text

Exposition

YOUR TURN 1 Examining a Process

Find an example of instructions for how to do or how to make something. Share your example with a partner and discuss the following questions.

- Do the instructions tell you how to do something or how to make something? What process do they explain?
- Do you think you could follow the instructions? Why or why not?

internet connect

go. hrw .com

GO TO: go.hrw.com
KEYWORD: EOLang 6-20

Reading a "How-to" Article

WHAT'S AHEAD?

In this section, you will read a "how-to" article. You will also learn how to

■ make predictions

■ form mental images from specific language

Holidays are a special time for families and friends to gather together and celebrate. Holidays are also a great time to do fun activities. Maybe you have made a card for Valentine's Day, planned a picnic for the Fourth of July, or planted a tree for Earth Day. You will read about one of these activities on the following pages. You will also read about a holiday activity that children take part in halfway around the world. Every May fifth, Japanese children make windsocks called *koinobori* (koi•nō´bô•ri) to hang outside their homes to celebrate Children's Day. The instructions for making *koinobori* appear in "Making a Flying Fish" on page 541.

Preparing to Read

READING SKILL

Making Predictions   A **prediction** is a guess you make about what will happen next. As you read instructions, you may predict what you will do with the supplies that are listed, what the outcome of a step will be, or what the final product will look like. Predictions give you a purpose for reading. You can find out whether your prediction is right by reading further and finding out what happens.

READING FOCUS

Forming Mental Images   Writers of "how-to" articles use **specific language** to name and describe the parts and the activities involved in a process. As you read the "how-to" article on page 541, look for words and phrases that create a picture in your mind of the steps for making a windsock.

Making Predictions

I Wonder What Will Happen   As you enter your math class, you see that you have a substitute teacher. You go to your seat, get out your review, and begin studying for the test you are about to take. After the bell rings, the substitute announces that the test has been canceled for today. Your friend will have the same substitute teacher later that day, so you go to tell her that her test will be canceled, too. How do you think she will react to the news that the test has been canceled? What if you find out your friend spent four hours studying last night? Now, what do you think her reaction will be? Has your prediction changed?

In life, you are constantly making predictions and adjusting them. For instance, your mind may follow this pattern:

1. **what you know**	There is no math test today.
2. **your prediction**	My friend will be happy.
3. **new information**	My friend studied for four hours.
4. **adjusted prediction**	My friend will not be happy.

Your mind also makes predictions when you read. The flowchart below shows what your mind is doing as you make a prediction.

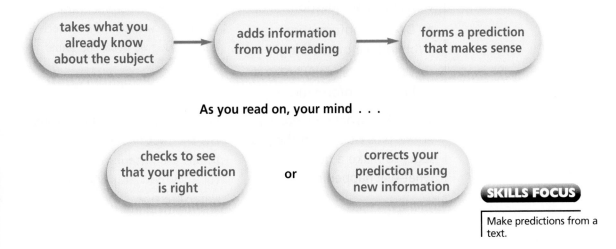

Your mind . . .

takes what you already know about the subject → adds information from your reading → forms a prediction that makes sense

As you read on, your mind . . .

checks to see that your prediction is right   **or**   corrects your prediction using new information

SKILLS FOCUS

Make predictions from a text.

Try making a prediction now. The following paragraph is from a set of "how-to" instructions for an Earth Day activity. Read the list of materials and steps. Think about what you already know about the subject. Then, make a prediction about what you think the next step will be. If you need help, use the steps in the Thinking It Through below the instructions.

> To plant a tree, you should gather the following materials: tree, shovel, mulch, and a watering can. First, dig a hole twice as deep as the tree's container. The hole should also be twice as wide as the container. Second, remove the container and place the tree in the hole. Then, using the same soil you removed, fill the hole. When the hole is completely filled, apply a two-inch layer of mulch around the base of the tree.

THINKING IT THROUGH — Making Predictions

STEP 1 Read a part of the passage. Ask yourself, "What is the passage explaining or telling?"

The passage is telling me how to plant a tree.

STEP 2 Consider the information you have just read. Ask yourself these questions:
- "Does the information remind me of anything?"
- "What do I already know about this information?"

The information reminds me of the time when I helped my mom plant a tree in our backyard. I already know about the materials because we used the same materials.

STEP 3 Use what you already know, plus clues from the passage, to make a guess about what will happen next.

I have already been told to plant the tree, but I haven't been told to use the watering can yet. I think the next step will tell me to water the tree.

Read the following article. In a notebook, write down the answers to the numbered active-reading questions in the shaded boxes. If necessary, use the Thinking It Through steps on page 540 for the questions that ask you to make a prediction. The underlined words will be used in the Vocabulary Mini-Lesson on page 544.

Making a Flying Fish

by Paula Morrow
from FACES

Japanese boys and girls have their own special day each year on May 5. It is called Children's Day and is a national holiday. This is a time for families to celebrate having children by telling stories, feasting, going on picnics, or visiting grandparents. . . .

A special feature of Children's Day is the *koinobori* (koi•nō′bô•ri) that families display in their yards—one for each child in the family. A tall pole is placed in the garden. . . . Fish made of cloth or strong paper are attached to the pole. Each fish has a hoop in its mouth to catch the wind. The largest fish is for the oldest child, and the smallest is for the youngest.

These fish represent a kind of carp known as a strong fighter.

> **1. Based on this paragraph, predict what materials might be discussed later in the selection.**

These carp battle their way upstream against strong currents. When the *koinobori* dance in the wind, they remind the children of carp leaping up a waterfall. This is

supposed to inspire children to be equally brave and strong.

You can make your own *koino-bori* and fly it from a pole or hang it from your window on May 5. In that way, you can share Children's Day with the boys and girls of Japan.

You need an 18- by 30-inch piece of lightweight cloth (cotton, rayon, or nylon), felt-tip markers, a needle and thread, scissors, a narrow plastic headband, and string.

2. Make a prediction about what you might do with the needle and thread based on this paragraph.

First, choose a piece of cloth with a bright, colorful pattern or decorate it yourself with felt-tip markers. Fold the fabric in half lengthwise, with the bright side on the inside. Sew a seam ½ inch from the long (30-inch) edge, making a sleeve.

3. What do you predict the "sleeve" will be used for?

On one end of the sleeve, make a 1-inch-wide hem by turning the right side of the fabric over the wrong side. Then, sew the hem,

leaving three 1-inch-wide openings about 5 inches apart.

Make cuts 5 inches deep and 1 inch apart all around the unhemmed end of the sleeve to form a fringe. This is the fish's tail.

4. How do you know how long the fringe will be?

Next, turn the sleeve right side out. With . . . a felt-tip marker, add eyes near the hemmed (head) end (away from the fringed tail).

Thread the narrow plastic headband into the hem through one of the openings. Continue threading it until the open part of the headband is hidden.

Then, tie a 12-inch-long piece of string to the headband at each of the three openings. Tie the loose ends of the strings together.

Finally, hang your windsock from the strings on a tree limb, a clothes pole, or the eaves of your house. On windy days, it will dance like a carp swimming upstream against a waterfall!

5. What word lets you know this is the last step?

one-inch opening

one-inch hem

Sleeve

right side of fabric

wrong side of fabric

Forming Mental Images

It's All in Your Head   Pictures in your first books probably helped you understand the words. Even though the books you read today may lack pictures, you can create your own **mental images**—pictures in your mind—using the words on a page.

Most writers of "how-to" instructions know that they should use specific language to describe a process. As a reader, you can use these specific words and phrases to come up with a mental image.

The chart below gives examples of different kinds of specific language. As you read, think about how these examples help a reader *visualize*, or create a mental picture of, a process.

TIP Drawing the instructions you read will help you understand a process better. Drawing can make it easier to picture a process. What do you picture when you read, "Turn the poster over and shake gently to remove any excess glitter"? Is it something like this?

Specific Language	Examples
Numbers	12 x 15 inches, 3 pieces, 450 degrees
Descriptive Words	small circle, large piece of fabric, hollow pipe
Exact Verbs	fold, turn, hang, sprinkle, twist
Comparisons	sew cloth like a sleeve, fold like a hot dog bun
Transitions	after, first, next, finally; above, below, behind, into

SKILLS FOCUS

Describe mental images that text descriptions evoke.
(page 544): Demonstrate knowledge of literal meanings of words and their usage.
(page 545): Make predictions from a text.

YOUR TURN 2   Forming a Mental Image

Find examples of specific language in the selection on pages 541–542. Choose one example and draw a picture of what you see in your mind. Share your drawing with a classmate who drew the same example and discuss the similarities and differences.

Compound Words

As you read a "how-to" article, you may find words that are unfamiliar to you. Some of these unfamiliar words may be *compound words*. **Compound words** are formed by putting together two or more words to make a new word. A compound word might be written as one word, as separate words, or as a hyphenated word.

Examples: roadrunner
free fall
ice-skating
hand-me-down

Discovering the Meanings of Compound Words

Here is one example of a compound word from "Making a Flying Fish":

You need an 18- by 30-inch piece of lightweight cloth.

STEP 1 Break the compound word down into its parts.

Lightweight breaks down to light and weight.

STEP 2 Define each of the parts.

The word light means "not very heavy." Weight means "how much something weighs."

STEP 3 Use the definitions of the parts to come up with a full definition.

Lightweight must mean "not weighing very much."

STEP 4 Check that your definition makes sense by inserting the definition for the compound word into the sentence.

"You need an 18- by 30-inch piece of not weighing very much cloth." The definition makes sense to me.

PRACTICE

Define the meanings of the following compound words by using the steps in the Thinking It Through above. The words are underlined in "Making a Flying Fish."

1. felt-tip
(page 542)

2. headband
(page 542)

3. windsock
(page 542)

4. upstream
(page 542)

5. waterfall
(page 542)

Making Predictions

Some reading tests may ask you to make predictions. Read the following passage and question. How would you answer the question?

> Several Mexican holidays are celebrated in the United States. One is Cinco de Mayo. Cinco de Mayo is a national holiday in Mexico. On May 5, 1862, a small group of Mexican patriots defeated an invasion by the French army in Puebla, Mexico. Today, Cinco de Mayo is recognized as a celebration of not only that victory but also of Mexican culture.

Based on the information in this paragraph, what might the next paragraph be about?

A. how the French invaded Mexico

B. other Mexican victories

C. how Cinco de Mayo is celebrated

D. French holidays

THINKING IT THROUGH   **Making Predictions**

▶ **STEP 1** Read the passage and the question. Try to answer the question in your own words.

I think the next paragraph will talk more about other Mexican holidays.

▶ **STEP 2** Look for an answer choice that closely matches your own.

The answer choices don't really say the same thing as my prediction, so I will go to the next step.

▶ **STEP 3** If no answer choice matches your prediction exactly, look at each answer choice and ask,

■ "Does the choice make sense?"

■ "Is this choice supported by information in the passage?" If you cannot support the choice, then it is not the correct one.

If you answer "yes" to both questions, you may have found the right answer.

A—The author has already told me how the French invaded Mexico.

B—The author does not mention other Mexican victories.

C—The passage says that Cinco de Mayo is celebrated to honor Mexican culture. The author could discuss how it is celebrated.

D—The passage is talking about a Mexican holiday, not French holidays.

I think the correct answer is C.

Writing a "How-to" Paper

WHAT'S AHEAD?

In this workshop you will write a "how-to" paper. You will also learn how to

- **create a time line**
- **elaborate ideas with specific language**
- **use transitional words**
- **use commas in a series**

"**M**mm, mmm. No one makes a smoothie as well as you do!" Everyone knows how to make something, whether it is a simple product such as a delicious fruit smoothie or a more complicated one such as a two-level treehouse. Whether the process is easy or difficult, making things takes knowledge and talent. What special skills do you have?

In this workshop you will have an opportunity to share your knowledge with others by writing a "how-to" paper. You will use specific details and **transitional words,** words that connect one idea to another, to give exact instructions for making a product.

Prewriting

Choose a Topic

I Know, I Know   Follow the rule successful writers live by: *Write about what you know.* Brainstorm a list of products that you have successfully made before. Consider the following questions.

- Look around your house. What have you built or made?
- What school projects have you made in the past?
- What is your favorite recipe to make?

SKILLS FOCUS

Write an explanation. Brainstorm to generate ideas. Choose a topic to write about.

How Do I Decide?   Once you have listed several products, you will need to evaluate them to choose the best one to write about. The chart on the next page shows how one student decided on one of three topics by asking questions about each topic.

Topic	Have I made this product before, and do I know the process well?	Does this process have a manageable number of steps (between three and five)?
Paper swan	yes	no—it has over five steps
Snowman decoration ✓	yes	yes—it has about five steps
Soapbox car	not really—I helped my big brother make it	no—this probably takes more than five steps

After evaluating each of his topics, the student whose chart appears above chose the topic that had the most *yes* answers. His "how-to" paper will tell others how to make a snowman decoration.

Think About Purpose and Audience

Show Some Consideration Your friend teaches you a great magic trick. You amaze your little brother with the trick, and he begs you to teach it to him. After you explain it twice, your brother is still confused. Obviously, you need to explain the trick to him in a different way.

Your purpose for writing instructions is to teach someone how to make something. That person could be a teacher, a friend, or even a young child. Before you begin to write, you should consider what information your audience will need. To do that, use the steps in the Thinking It Through below.

KEY CONCEPT

THINKING IT THROUGH **Considering Your Audience**

▶ **STEP 1** Identify your audience.

My audience will be fourth-graders.

▶ **STEP 2** What words should you define so your audience can understand the process?

The snowman decoration has a muffler. Fourth-graders may not know that a muffler is a scarf.

▶ **STEP 3** Ask yourself, "What steps caused me trouble?" How can you make those steps clearer?

I had a problem keeping the sequin eyes in place. I used straight pins to hold them until the glue dried.

SKILLS FOCUS

Decide on a purpose for writing. Plan writing by targeting audience.

YOUR TURN 3 — Choosing a Topic and Thinking About Your Audience

Brainstorm a list of products that you have made. Then, make a chart like the one on page 547 and evaluate each product as a possible topic for your "how-to" paper. Choose the product that has the most "yes" answers in the chart.

Once you have a topic, choose an audience. Then, think about the information your audience will need by completing the steps in the Thinking It Through on page 547.

| KEY CONCEPT

Plan Your Instructions

As Easy as 1, 2, 3   Imagine the frustration of trying to build a model car if the instructions described painting the model before the car was even put together. **Putting steps in the correct order makes the process easier to understand.** Most "how-to" papers are written in **chronological order,** or time order.

One way to think of the steps in chronological order is to imagine yourself making the product. As you perform each step, write it on a time line, recording the **progression,** or order, of the process. Then, look over your steps and add anything you left out.

Steps to make a snowman decoration:

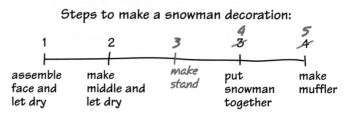

Next, brainstorm the materials you need to make the product. Think carefully about everything you need. If you forget to list a material, your reader will not be able to make the product.

TIP   Look over your time line for steps that may distract the reader. Ask yourself, "Does my audience already know how to do this step?" If the answer is "yes," then you do not need that step.

For example, if you were writing instructions for making a peanut-butter-and-jelly sandwich, it would not be necessary to tell readers to open the jar of jelly. They would already know to do that.

SKILLS FOCUS

Organize writing by chronological order. Use graphic organizers to generate ideas. *(page 549):* Support, develop, and elaborate ideas in writing. Use appropriate word choice and precise wording.

YOUR TURN 4 — Planning Your Instructions

Write the steps for making your product in chronological order on a time line. Then, list the needed materials.

Elaboration: Using Specific Language

Suppose a friend gave you the following recipe for making Zesty Bagels. Could you follow the directions?

Zesty Bagels

Step 1: Gather materials—pan, bagels, sauce, olives, mushrooms, cheese.

Step 2: Place bagels on pan and pour sauce.

Step 3: Put on toppings.

Step 4: Bake.

As you read the steps, you probably asked yourself many questions. *How many bagels do I need? What are the measurements for the toppings? How long do I bake the bagels and at what temperature?* The recipe leaves you guessing because your friend's directions are not specific.

To help a reader understand a process, you should write your instructions using **specific language.** For example you can give *numbers* to tell how much or how many, such as "six plain bagels." You can also describe supplies using *descriptive words*, such as "finely chopped mush-

rooms." *Exact verbs* (V) and *transitions* (T) will help tell a reader exactly what to do and where to put supplies.

V

Sprinkle black olives, mushrooms, and

T

cheese evenly **over** the sauce.

Notice how specific language eliminates all guesswork in the recipe below.

Zesty Bagels

Step 1: Gather these materials: a cookie sheet, 6 plain bagels cut in half, 18-ounce jar of spaghetti sauce, ¼ cup chopped black olives, 6 finely chopped mushrooms, and 1 cup grated Parmesan cheese.

Step 2: Place bagel halves on cookie sheet. Evenly spread 1 tablespoon of spaghetti sauce over the face of each bagel.

Step 3: Sprinkle black olives, mushrooms, and cheese evenly over the sauce.

Step 4: Bake in oven at 350 degrees for 15–20 minutes. When done, remove from oven and cool.

PRACTICE

Read the following steps. Then, rewrite the instructions, adding specific language. For more information on specific language, see the chart on page 543.

Directions for Preparing a Can of Soup

Step 1: Gather supplies.

Step 2: Heat soup.

Step 3: Serve.

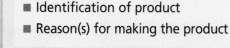

Writing

"How-to" Paper

Framework   **Think as a Reader/Writer**

Introduction
- Attention-grabbing opening
- Identification of product
- Reason(s) for making the product

Grab your reader's attention quickly with an interesting introduction. For example, you could **ask questions** to get your reader involved in your paper. Also, **clearly state reasons** why your reader will want to learn to make the product you will explain.

Body
- List of materials
- Step 1 (with specific language)
- Step 2 (with specific language)
- Step 3 (with specific language) and so on

In the first body paragraph, **list the materials your reader needs** to make the product. One way to list the materials is to put them in the order in which your readers will use them. Another way is to group similar types of materials together. Then, write the steps in the correct **chronological order.** As you write, you should

- place each step in a **separate paragraph**
- elaborate on each step with **specific language.** Specific language includes numbers, exact verbs, comparisons, transitions, and descriptive words. (See mini-lesson on page 549.) Transitions are especially useful because they create **coherence.** That is, they show how all the ideas connect.

Conclusion
- Restatement of reason(s) and/or
- Suggestions for using or displaying the product

Restate the reasons for making the product. You can also suggest **ways to use or display** the product.

 Drafting Your "How-to" Paper

Now it is your turn to draft a "how-to" paper. As you write, refer to the framework above and the Writer's Model on the next page.

A Writer's Model

The final draft below closely follows the framework for a "how-to" paper on the previous page.

A Snowman of Style

Are you at home with nothing to do? Are you eager to do something fun? If so, you can make a snowman. It is easy and fun, and you can make one without snow.

Picture a plump snowman with bright shiny eyes, a muffler, and a black hat. You can make the same winter wonder with these materials, which you can find at many hobby and craft stores:

a 5-inch, a 4-inch, and a 3-inch foam ball
two 12-inch black pipe cleaners
one 1-inch orange pipe cleaner
a 2-inch piece of black yarn
three medium-size buttons
two medium-size sequins
a 1- × 15-inch piece of bright cloth
an 8½- × 11-inch piece of black paper
a 2-inch black pompom
two straight pins
scissors
white glue

The first step is making the snowman's face and hat. The orange pipe cleaner will be the nose. Push the pipe cleaner into the center of the smallest foam ball until it sticks out about ½ inch. Next, make the mouth using the black yarn. Happy snowmen wear smiles. Confused snowmen have mouths like a series of mountain peaks. Choose an emotion for your snowman, and glue the black yarn down to match the feeling you are trying to create. To make the eyes, glue down the two sequins. Use the straight pins to pin the eyes in place while they dry.

Attention-grabber

Identification of product

Reasons for making the product

List of materials

Step one

(continued)

Snowmen often wear hats. You can make one by cutting a 3-inch circle of black paper. Pin the circle to the top of the snowman's head. Glue the black pompom to the center of the paper, and set the head aside to dry.

Step two

Next, you will make the snowman's middle using the 4-inch foam ball. Cut one of the black pipe cleaners in half to make the arms. Shape each pipe cleaner like a tree branch or jagged line. Then, push each arm in place on the sides of the ball. The three black buttons will make the snowman's shirt. Glue them down the front of the ball. Set the middle aside to dry.

Step three

While you are waiting for the face and middle to dry, you can make a stand to keep your snowman from falling over. Cut a 1- × 5-inch piece of black paper. Form it into a ring by gluing the ends together.

Step four

When everything is dry, you are ready to put the snowman's body together. Take your last black pipe cleaner and cut four 2-inch pieces. Push two of the pipe cleaners in the top of the 4-inch foam ball 1 inch apart. Push the other two pipe cleaners in the bottom of the 4-inch ball 1 inch apart. Make sure you use two pipe cleaners because they will keep the snowman from wobbling. Then, push the snowman's head on top of the pipe cleaners to attach it to the 4-inch ball. Push the 5-inch ball on the bottom pipe cleaners to finish making the snowman's body.

Step five

The final step is making a muffler for your snowman. A muffler is a long fringed scarf that wraps around the neck. The strip of cloth will make the muffler. Create fringe by making cuts into each end of the fabric. Once that is done, tie the muffler around the snowman's neck.

Suggestions

You can make a variety of snow people by changing the style of the hat and clothing. Make a snow woman or snow child. Give your snow person a job. Doctors wear stethoscopes around their necks, and movie stars wear sunglasses. No matter what type of snowman you choose to create, making one is easy and fun.

Restatement of reasons

Illustrating Steps in a Process When you are writing a "how-to" paper, consider using pictures to help readers understand what you are writing about. You can show readers how to complete individual steps by drawing pictures of the materials and using arrows or lines to show the action that will take place. You can also provide an illustration of the final product so that readers will know what their product should look like. To illustrate your "how-to" paper, you can print or scan images using a computer, cut out pictures from magazines, or even draw graphics by hand. Below is an illustration drawn by the writer of the Writer's Model to help readers understand one step in his "how-to" paper.

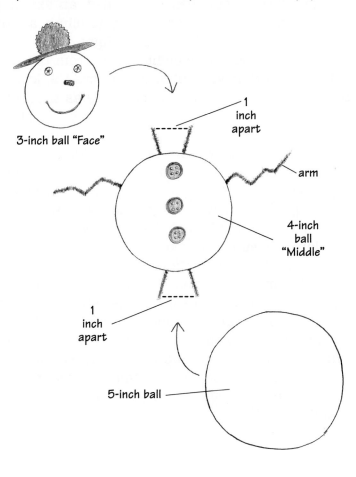

3-inch ball "Face"

1 inch apart

arm

4-inch ball "Middle"

1 inch apart

5-inch ball

SKILLS FOCUS

Design documents in preparation for publishing. Support ideas/theses with illustrations.

A Student's Model

It is important to have detailed knowledge and enthusiasm about the product you are explaining in your "how-to" paper. Stephanie Thompson wrote the following paper as a middle school student in St. Peters, Missouri. In it, she shares her knowledge and enthusiasm as she provides the instructions for growing ivy.

Make It Grow

Attention-grabbing opener

Have you ever tried growing ivy from a clipping? It is not as hard to do as it might seem. To get started, the following supplies are needed: an existing ivy plant, a fence or trellis for the ivy to climb, a pan about two inches deep, water, and sunlight.

List of supplies

Step one

First, cut about seven or eight leaves from the ivy plant. Make sure that you cut above where the leaf joins the stem, and cut at the same angle as the leaf grows. Then, fill the pan with water and place each leaf in the water. Let the leaves soak until they form roots that are about three to four inches long.

Step two

Step three

When the roots reach the desired length, it is time to find the best location for the ivy to grow. Although ivy is a hardy plant, it does need some care when it is grown from a clipping. Look for a place where there is plenty of sunlight, good drainage, and where no animals can damage it. Make sure that there is a fence or trellis in the location for the ivy to climb.

Step four

Next, hook the ivy leaves on to the fence or trellis so that the roots are almost touching the ground. As they receive sunlight and moisture from the dew, the roots will grow into the ground and the leaves will continue to sprout upward. In no time the ivy will be covering the fence or trellis, and you can start all over again!

Evaluate and Revise Content, Organization, and Style

Two Is Better Than One When revising your paper or a peer's, you should read the rough draft twice. First, look at the content and organization, using the guidelines below. The second time you read, concentrate on the sentences, using the Focus on Sentences on page 557.

▶ **First Reading: Content and Organization** Use the chart below on your first reading. It will help you evaluate a "how-to" paper and revise its content and organization.

Guidelines for Self-Evaluation and Peer Evaluation		
Evaluation Questions	**Tips**	**Revision Techniques**
❶ Does the introduction give a reason for making the product?	**Put brackets** around the reason.	If needed, **add** a reason for making the product.
❷ Does the body list all the materials needed to make the product?	**Circle** all the supplies needed to make the product.	**Add** any supplies that have been left out.
❸ Are the steps of the process in the correct chronological order? Is each step in a separate paragraph?	**Write a number** next to each step in the margin of the paper.	If needed, **rearrange** the steps so they are in the correct order and so that each step is in its own paragraph, as needed.
❹ Is each step described with specific language?	**Underline** numbers, descriptions, comparisons, verbs, and transitions.	If necessary, **elaborate** on the steps by adding specific details.
❺ Does the conclusion restate the reason for making the product and/or give suggestions on how to use the product?	**Put a star** beside the sentence that restates the reason. **Draw a wavy line** under the suggestions for using the product.	If needed, **add** a restatement of the reason for making the product. **Add** some suggestions for how to use the product.

ONE WRITER'S REVISIONS Here is an early draft of the "how-to" paper on pages 551–552.

> Next, you will make the snowman's middle using the 4-inch foam ball. Cut one of the black pipe cleaners in half
>
> *elaborate*   *Shape each pipe cleaner like a tree branch or jagged line.*
>
> to make the arms. Then, push each arm in place on the sides of the ball. The three black buttons will make the snowman's shirt. Glue them down the front of the ball. Set
>
> *rearrange*   the middle aside to dry. ¶ While you are waiting for the face and middle to dry, you can make a stand to keep your snowman from falling over. Cut a 1- × 5-inch piece of black paper. Form it into a ring by gluing the ends together.

Think as a Reader/Writer

1. How does adding a sentence improve this part of the instructions?
2. How does breaking the one paragraph into two paragraphs make the instructions clearer?

> **Second Reading: Style**   You have improved the content and organization of your paper. Now you will concentrate on the style of your sentences. One way to improve your style is to use transitional words, such as *first, next,* and *finally.* Transitional words connect one idea to another.

When you evaluate your "how-to" paper for style, ask yourself whether your writing has transitional words connecting one step to another, creating coherence. As you re-read your paper, highlight each transitional word. Are there any paragraphs with few or no transitional words? If so, add transitional words to paragraphs that need them.

Transitional Words

A reader should be able to follow your ideas as easily as a driver follows road signs. Adding **transitional words** between your thoughts will steer the reader in the right direction. Notice how the underlined transitional words make this paragraph easy to read and understand.

Sentences

> To make a tie-dyed shirt, <u>first</u> you will need to wrap rubber bands around several parts of a T-shirt. <u>Next,</u> fill a tub or sink with dye. <u>Then,</u> dunk the shirt into the dye. Rinse the shirt with water and hang to dry. <u>Finally,</u> take off the rubber bands when the shirt is completely dry.

TIP Listed below are common transitional words for chronological order, the order used to explain a process.

after	next
before	often
finally	then
first	when

ONE WRITER'S REVISIONS

The orange pipe cleaner will be the nose. Push the pipe cleaner into the center of the smallest foam ball until it sticks out about ½ inch. *Next,* ~~You will~~ make the mouth using the black yarn.

Think as a Reader/Writer

How did adding a transitional word make this part of the instructions clearer?

Evaluating and Revising Your "How-to" Paper

First, improve content and organization using the guidelines on page 555. Then, use the Focus on Sentences above to add transitional words to your paper. If a peer evaluated your paper, consider his or her suggestions as you revise.

SKILLS FOCUS

Use transitions to connect ideas.

Publishing

Proofread Your Paper

Clear the Path Reading a paper full of errors is like running an obstacle course: Progress is often slow. If you *and* a peer proofread your paper, you are more likely to catch distracting mistakes.

Grammar Link

Using Commas in a Series

When you write a "how-to" paper, you may list materials or give directions in a series. A series consists of three or more items written one after the other.

Use commas to separate three or more items in a series.

Incorrect   Get out a pen, and paper.

Correct   Get out a pen, a ruler, and paper.

To make the meaning of a sentence clear, use a comma before the *and* or *or* in a series.

Unclear   Lori's favorite sandwiches are turkey, ham and cheese. [Does Lori have two or three favorite sandwiches?]

Clear   Lori's favorite sandwiches are turkey, ham, and cheese.

Do not use commas if *all* of the items are joined by *and* or *or*.

Incorrect   You can throw, or roll, or bounce the ball.

Correct   You can throw or roll or bounce the ball.

PRACTICE

Some of the sentences below need commas. Refer to the rules to the left to decide when to use commas. If a sentence needs commas, rewrite the sentence, adding commas where they are needed. If a sentence is correct, write C.

Example:

1. Your snow woman could have long hair a lace collar and earrings.

1. *Your snow woman could have long hair, a lace collar, and earrings.*

1. Glue the eyes hold them with a pin and allow them to dry.

2. My snowman has green eyes a red scarf and blue buttons.

3. Miguel gave his snow teen a headset a T-shirt and a book bag.

4. A snow baby has a bib cap or bow.

5. You can place your snowman on a shelf or a table or a countertop.

For more information and practice on **commas,** see page 314.

Publish Your Paper

Tell Them How It Is Done   Since you are the expert, you can share your instructions with others. How do you get your paper to your audience? Use the following suggestions to get people to read your "how-to" paper.

- If you wrote your "how-to" paper for a younger audience, make copies of your instructions and give them to an elementary teacher. If your audience is your classmates, ask your teacher if you can demonstrate how to make your product in class.

- Gather all the "how-to" papers in your class and organize them into categories such as recipes, crafts, and decorations. Compile a "how-to" book and place it in your school's library.

PORTFOLIO

Reflect on Your Paper

Building Your Portfolio   Now that you are finished writing and publishing, take a moment and reflect on your "how-to" paper. Remember your purpose for writing, and think about how your paper will achieve that purpose. Reflecting on a paper you have already completed will help make your next one better.

- Which step in your paper is the easiest to follow? What makes this step clear and easy to understand?

- You created a time line to list your steps in order. In what other types of writing would a time line be useful?

- Take time to examine all the papers in your portfolio. What is one goal you would like to work toward to improve your writing?

YOUR TURN 7 Proofreading, Publishing, and Reflecting on Your Paper

- Correct any grammar, usage, and mechanics errors. Pay attention to spelling and punctuation, particularly the use of commas in a series.

- Publish your paper so others can use your instructions.

- Answer the questions from Reflect on Your Paper above. Record your responses in a learning log, or include them in your portfolio.

COMPUTER TIP

Use the **spellchecker** feature on your computer when you edit your paper to catch and correct misspelled words. However, a spellchecker cannot check homonyms such as *its* (showing possession) and *it's* (it is).

SKILLS FOCUS

Publish in a variety of formats. Publish for a variety of audiences. *(page 558):* Proofread one's own writing in preparation for publishing. Use commas correctly to separate items in a series. *(page 560):* Write instructions. *(page 561):* Describe an object or animal. Develop descriptions with sensory details. Use prepositional phrases to elaborate written ideas. Use adverbs to write vividly. Use figurative language. Organize writing by spatial order.

MINI-LESSON TEST TAKING

Writing Instructions

Sometimes an essay test may ask you to write instructions, such as how to do or how to make something. Read the prompt to the right. How would you respond to this prompt on a test?

A new student in your school needs to find the cafeteria. Write the directions for walking from your classroom to the cafeteria.

THINKING IT THROUGH — Writing Instructions for Tests

▶ **STEP 1** Read the prompt. Find out
  - what it is asking you to explain
  - who your audience is

The prompt is asking me to explain how to get from my classroom to the cafeteria. A new student will be reading my instructions.

▶ **STEP 2** List the materials, if any, you would need to complete the process. Provide definitions of key terms, if necessary.

The new student will not need any materials to learn the way to the cafeteria. There are no terms to define.

▶ **STEP 3** Create a time line to list the steps of the process in order.

Step 1	Step 2	Step 3	Step 4
Turn right out of the class-room door.	Go to the end of the hall and turn right again.	Take the first left.	Go through the double doors, and the cafeteria will be on your left.

▶ **STEP 4** Write your instructions in paragraphs. Remember to use specific language.

I will give specific locations and use directions, such as right and left.

▶ **STEP 5** Review your instructions, checking to make sure that
  - you listed any materials needed
  - your steps are in order
  - you have not left out any steps
  - you have included specific language

I don't need materials, and my steps are in order. I can add a specific detail to step 3, though. The first left will come after a water fountain. I also need to explain where the student will find the double doors in Step 4.

Writing a Descriptive Paragraph

You are reading instructions for building a basketball backboard. Does having a picture of the backboard in your mind make understanding the instructions easier? It certainly does. You know what the final product looks like, so you already have an idea of what you need to do to make it.

Here's an opportunity for you to help the readers of your "how-to" paper. You will write a **descriptive paragraph** about the product they will make. The written description will help your audience create a mental picture, making the instructions easier to follow.

Do You See What I See? To describe something another person has not seen, you can use descriptive words and phrases to paint a picture in that person's mind. What kinds of descriptive words and phrases help someone picture an object? The following chart provides some examples for you.

Descriptive Words and Phrases	Definitions	Examples
Sensory Details	Details that express what you experience through your five senses—What you hear, see, taste, touch, and smell	sight—blue, tall, leaning hearing—pops, hisses, whispers taste—sweet, salty, sour touch—hot, soft, rough smell—smoky, fresh, spicy
Location Words	Words that describe where something is located	across from next to on the top to the right near to the left
Figurative Language	**Simile**—Language that compares two unlike things using *like* or *as*	The wire is rigid and curled *like* corkscrew pasta. The eyes are *as* shiny *as* emeralds.
	Metaphor—Language that compares two unlike things saying one *is* the other	The string *is* a lifeline keeping the two parts together.

First Things First To write a descriptive paragraph, you first need to decide what *spatial order* you are going to use to organize your description. **Spatial order** organizes the details according to their location. You might describe a product from right to left, from top to bottom, or from far away to close up. Choosing an order first will help you be organized as you observe and list all the important details about your product.

For instance, if you choose to describe your product from the left to the right, you will look at the left side of the product and list the details. Then, you will observe the middle of the product, and then the right side, writing down details as you go. You should describe what the product looks like, but you should also consider other sensory details. Does your product make a sound? How does it taste or smell? What does it feel like? Make sure you use location words to tell where the sensory details are located.

To help organize your details in the spatial order that you chose, list them in a chart as you observe your product. The chart below shows a top-to-bottom order for describing a foam snowman.

Spatial Order	Sensory Details and Location Words
Top	small foam ball, black hat on top, fluffy pompom in the center, green sequin eyes, orange nose, black yarn mouth that smiles
Middle	medium foam ball; soft, blue muffler around his neck; three black buttons down the front; black arms stick out
Bottom	large foam ball, black stand made out of paper

Ready, Set, Write Once you have your information in a chart, you are ready to write a descriptive paragraph. All you have to do is follow the order that you chose and write complete sentences using the details that you listed.

When you are finished with your first draft, **elaborate** on your description by adding figurative language. To add figurative language, look at the details to see what comparisons you can make. In the chart above, for instance, the snowman has a mouth that smiles. To whom can a smiling snowman be compared? The snowman smiles like a child with a new toy. The snowman also has green eyes made of sequins. Can you compare his eyes to anything?

Now Picture This   The following is an example of a descriptive paragraph that could be included with the Writer's Model on pages 551–552. You can see how the writer uses sensory details, figurative language, location words, and spatial order to describe the snowman decoration. Do you see how adding description will help readers make the snowman?

> My snowman is not a typical snowman made of snow. He does not have to be kept outdoors, and he will not melt. Instead, my snowman is a decoration made of three foam balls, 3 inches, 4 inches, and 5 inches in diameter. He can be placed anywhere and enjoyed anytime. The smallest foam ball is my snowman's head. On top of the head sits a black hat with a fluffy, black pompom in the center. The snowman's eyes are green, sparkling sequins, and his nose is bright orange. The black yarn of his mouth is made to smile like a child with a new toy. The middle foam ball makes his body. He is dressed with a soft, blue muffler around his neck and three shiny black buttons down his front. His arms are also black, and they stick out from his body like branches of a tree. The largest foam ball is on the bottom, and it sits in a circular stand made of black paper. The stand is an anchor keeping the snowman in place.

description begins at the top

sensory details and figurative language

description moves to the middle

sensory details and figurative language

description ends at the bottom

figurative language

YOUR TURN 8   **Writing and Revising a Descriptive Paragraph**

Write a descriptive paragraph using the suggestions above. Remember to

- use spatial order to organize your paragraph
- describe the product with sensory details and location words
- revise your paragraph by adding figurative language

When you have finished writing and revising, make a final draft and include it with your "how-to" instructions.

Viewing and Listening to Learn

WHAT'S AHEAD?

In this section you will learn how to listen to and watch instructions in different forms. You will also learn how to

- understand instructional charts and graphics
- summarize "how-to" instruction in computer software
- take notes while watching directions on TV or video

You and your friend are neck and neck as you swim to the side of the pool. You both turn at the same time, but you come out ahead. Why? You know how to do a flip turn. You hold on to the lead and declare a victory as you touch the other side.

"Where did you learn to do that?" your friend asks.

You confess, "I learned how from TV."

Instructions come in many forms. Not only can you read a how-to paper, you can also learn how to do or make something from **charts and graphics, computer software,** and **"how-to" videos** or **TV shows.** To follow instructions in these forms, you will need to work on your viewing and listening skills.

Charts and Graphics

SKILLS FOCUS

Understand how media tools enhance communication. Understand how graphics and drawings enhance communication. Analyze charts used to support text in media. Analyze graphics used to support text in media.

Charts and graphics provide you with the same information as a "how-to" paper. Both tell the materials, the instructions, and the order in which you should do the instructions. However, charts and graphics do not rely only on words. They *show* the steps in a process by using pictures, symbols, and labels.

One type of chart is a flowchart. Look at the flowchart on the next page. The steps are easy to follow because arrows direct you from one step to another. Labels, such as Step 1, Step 2, and Step 3, also help you see the order of the steps, and the instructions are brief and to the point.

How to Make a Friend

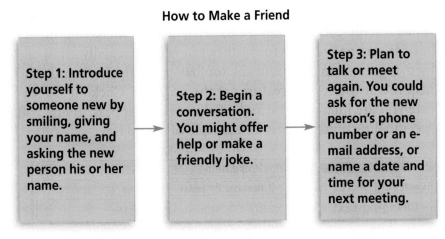

Step 1: Introduce yourself to someone new by smiling, giving your name, and asking the new person his or her name.

Step 2: Begin a conversation. You might offer help or make a friendly joke.

Step 3: Plan to talk or meet again. You could ask for the new person's phone number or an e-mail address, or name a date and time for your next meeting.

Now, look at the graphic below. This type of graphic is called a diagram. The diagram shows how to fold a blanket like a sleeping bag. As on the flowchart, the steps are labeled, but pictures and symbols give the instructions. These features make it easy to understand what the diagram is demonstrating.

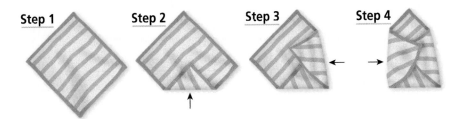

Step 1   Step 2   Step 3   Step 4

YOUR TURN 9 Understanding Charts and Graphics

Answer the following questions about the flowchart and diagram above.

■ What material do you need to make the sleeping bag? How is the material presented?

■ How are the instructions presented in the flowchart and the graphic? Do words, pictures, or symbols tell you what to do?

■ What order is used in the flowchart and the graph (chronological? spatial?)? How is that order shown in each?

Computer Software

Most software, including word-processing programs, computer games, and encyclopedias, comes with built-in "how-to" instructions, usually called a help menu. Help menus are set up differently from one program to another, but you can usually get to one by using the help button in the toolbar or on the keyboard. The help menu will list the features of the program. Click on the feature you are interested in, and a help box will appear, giving you specific directions. Here is an example of a help box.

☐ ═══════════ **Word Help** ═══════════ ⊞⊟

[Contents] [Search] [Back] [History] [Index] [On Top]

Changing text color

You can apply color to text. To display color, you must have a color monitor; to print color, you must have a color plotter or a color printer.

To change text color

1. Select the text you want to change, or position the insertion point where you want to begin typing text with the new color.
2. From the Format menu, choose Font.
3. Select the Font tab.
4. In the Color box, select the color you want.
   Word comes with 16 predefined colors. Auto, which is black, is the default.
5. Choose the OK button.

Tip
You can change the color of text throughout a document. See Replacing text and formatting.

◄ ───────────────────── ► ▒

Screen shot reprinted by permission from Microsoft Corporation.

SKILLS FOCUS

Analyze technical directions. Follow technical directions and steps in a process. Summarize to enhance comprehension of text. Create a graphic organizer to enhance comprehension of text.

You may find that you go to the same item in a help menu again and again. How can you remember the steps in a process so that you don't have to keep returning to the menu? Summarizing the instructions in a flowchart can help you remember them. To do that, read each step and write down only the important words and details. Use arrows to show the sequence of steps. A flowchart for the instructions in the help box above might look like this:

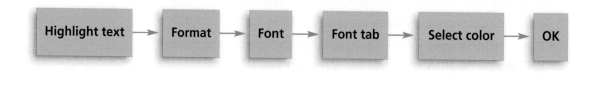

Highlight text → Format → Font → Font tab → Select color → OK

Summarizing Instruction

Create a flowchart that summarizes the steps in the following help box.

Word Help

| Contents | Search | Back | History | Index | On Top |

Inserting symbols

Symbols and special characters in non-ANSI fonts, such as the Symbol font, are "protected" when you insert them by using the Symbol dialog box. A protected character is the same as a regular character except that you cannot change the font.

To insert symbols with the Symbol command

1. Position the insertion point where you want to insert the symbol.
2. From the Insert menu, choose Symbol.
3. In the Font box, type or select the font that contains the symbol you want to insert.
4. Double-click the symbol character you want. Word inserts the character in the point size of the text that precedes the insertion point. If you cannot find the symbol you're looking for, try selecting another font in the Font box.

   To see an enlarged version of the symbol in the dialog box, click the symbol character, or use the arrow keys to move to the symbol.
5. To insert another symbol, position the insertion point in the document, and then repeat step 4.
6. When you finish inserting symbols, choose the Close button.

Screen shot reprinted by permission from Microsoft Corporation.

SKILLS FOCUS

Listen to comprehend/gain information. Listen and respond to directions/explanations. Take notes when listening.

TV and Video

There are "how-to" programs and videos about a variety of topics, but popular ones include cooking, exercise, and home repair. "How-to" programs and videos are very helpful—not only do you *hear* the directions, you also *see* the steps.

When you watch "how-to" instructions on TV or on video, you are doing two things at once. First, you are *listening to* and *viewing* the information. At the same time, you are *trying to understand* how to do the steps in the process. If you are watching a TV program, you cannot ask questions. If you are watching a video, you might hit "pause" or "rewind," but having control over the video player is not always possible. However, you can get a better understanding of the steps of a process if you take notes. The

following chart gives useful suggestions for taking quick and complete notes while viewing "how-to" instructions.

> **TIP** The guidelines below can apply to viewing *any* informative video. Always watch for important facts, on-screen graphics, and ideas emphasized through repetition or dramatic phrasing. In addition, always take a minute after viewing to record important points and to think about the video producer's purpose.

Note-Taking Guidelines	
Guidelines	**Tip**
Prepare to listen.	Think about your purpose for listening, and prepare to focus on the message by eliminating distractions.
Listen to each step.	Clue words such as the transitions *first, second, then,* and *finally* will let you know when a step begins and ends.
Create an outline of the steps.	Organize your notes by numbering steps as they are presented.
Take notes on each step.	Do not try to write every word. Instead, make a note of each major idea and its support. Listen for words and phrases that are repeated. Watch for on-screen graphics.
Listen for a conclusion.	Major points may be repeated.
Check your notes.	Make any necessary additions or corrections. Summarize the information while it is still fresh in your mind. If possible, discuss the message with others who viewed it. Compare your different perceptions of the message, and add to your notes any points you may have missed.

 **Taking Notes to Learn**

- Watch a "how-to" program on TV or find a "how-to" video at a video rental store or at your local library.
- Use the note-taking guidelines above to take notes.
- After viewing the video, take five minutes to complete the following sentence starters:

  The producers created this video to _____.

  The most important facts or ideas were _____.

20 *Choices*

Select one of the following activities to complete.

▶ CROSSING THE CURRICULUM: SCIENCE

1. How Did That Happen? Use your science book to find information on how something occurs, such as how fish breathe underwater or how taste buds work. Create a **flowchart** or **graphic** that shows the steps of the process. You can use drawings, magazine cutouts, or computer art to illustrate the steps.

▶ CROSSING THE CURRICULUM: SPEECH

2. You Be the Teacher Choose a product and learn how to make it by listening to someone or by watching a "how-to" program. Then, demonstrate how to make it for your class. Select something entertaining, unique, or appealing to others your age.

Give clear, precise **directions** as you show classmates how to make the product. Use visuals to help your audience understand the process.

▶ CAREERS

3. Do You Have What It Takes? Choose a career that interests you. Find out what sort of training, education, and skills you would need to pursue that career by looking in books in the library, using informational Web sites, or interviewing people who are in that career field. Write a **letter** to a friend explaining how to enter the profession you choose.

▶ WRITING

4. Games People Play Invent a game. Your game could be a board game, an athletic game, a card game, or any other type of game. Write the **instructions** for playing your game. First, state the goal of the game. Is the goal to advance to the center of the board, put a ball through a basket, or get rid of all of your cards? Next, write all the steps required for playing the game. Finally, provide the instructions and materials needed to play the game for a group of your classmates.

PORTFOLIO

SKILLS FOCUS

Use graphics to convey information. Give directions orally. Read print and Internet sources to research questions or information. Write a letter. Write instructions.

21

Comparing and Contrasting

Reading Workshop

Reading a Comparison-Contrast Essay

Writing Workshop

Writing a Comparison-Contrast Essay

Viewing and Representing

Comparing Ideas in Photographs

B aked potato or salad? Art or band? You make choices every day. Sometimes those choices are easy, such as deciding on a baked potato for lunch. Other choices require more thought, such as choosing an elective in school. How do you make these important decisions? One way is to **compare** and **contrast** the two choices: You can look at how the two things are alike and how they are different. Once you understand the similarities and differences, you are ready to make a decision.

Comparing and contrasting is useful in other ways, too. Comparison-and-contrast structure may be used to define something unfamiliar by comparing it to something well known. For instance, did you know that the English sport rugby is like American football? Comparing and contrasting two subjects is a great way to share useful or interesting information with others.

> **Informational Text**
>
> **Exposition**

YOUR TURN 1 Practicing Comparing and Contrasting

Answer the following questions, and then discuss them with a few classmates. Share your group's findings with the class.

- How are fifth grade and sixth grade different?
- How are fifth grade and sixth grade alike?

internet connect

go. hrw .com

GO TO: go.hrw.com
KEYWORD: EOLang 6-21

WHAT'S AHEAD?

In this section you will read a comparison-contrast essay. You will also learn how to

- **identify points of comparison**
- **examine two comparison-contrast structures**

Reading a Comparison-Contrast Essay

The two men faced each other down, ready for the big fight. One was the clear favorite; the other was a rookie. Who would win? The event had all the drama of a boxing match, but this was a debate. The following comparison-contrast essay shows how television made the presidential debate between John F. Kennedy and Richard M. Nixon different from previous ones. The debate was not just a war of words. Other elements made one candidate more successful than the other. Read on to see if you can identify those winning elements.

Preparing to Read

READING SKILL

Points of Comparison   Not every similarity and difference between two subjects is important, so an author must choose the most important areas to compare and contrast. These areas are called the author's **points of comparison.**

READING FOCUS

Comparison-Contrast Structure   The **structure,** or organization, of a comparison-contrast essay can help a reader see the similarities and differences more clearly. A writer may give all the information about one subject and then all the information about the other subject, or the writer may shift back and forth between the subjects. As you read Edward Wakin's essay on the next page, try to follow the organization he uses.

Read the following essay. In a notebook, jot down answers to the numbered active-reading questions in the shaded boxes. The underlined words will be discussed in the Vocabulary Mini-Lesson on page 578.

from HOW TV CHANGED AMERICA'S MIND

THE NIXON- KENNEDY PRESIDENTIAL DEBATES

BY EDWARD WAKIN

A trim, tanned presidential candidate dressed smartly in dark suit, dark tie, and blue shirt stood at the podium on the left in the Chicago studio of WBBM–TV. He looked <u>vigorous</u>, confident, and businesslike.

His opponent at the other podium wore a light suit, pale tie, and a shirt with a collar that was too big for him. He looked tired, nervous, and in need of a shave.

> **1. In the first two paragraphs, are the two candidates shown as being similar or different? How?**

Both faced the <u>pitiless</u> eye of TV cameras carrying the first televised presidential debate. For one hour of prime time on all three networks, 75 million Americans watched on the evening of September 26, 1960.

> **2. Whose appearance does the writer describe first, Nixon's or Kennedy's? Whose experience does he describe first?**

The candidate on the left side, Democrat John F. Kennedy, looked nothing like the underdog he was supposed to be. An <u>unproved</u> junior senator from Massachusetts, he faced the highly experienced Republican candidate, Richard M. Nixon.

Kennedy needed national exposure. Nixon was seasoned and already nationally known. Twice elected vice president, Nixon had prepared himself for eight years to take over from President Dwight D. Eisenhower.

TV critic Robert Lewis Shayon described the televised debate as if it were a boxing match: "The atmosphere was clearly that of a prizefight: the referee (producer) instructing the champ and the challenger (the candidates), the seconds (advisors) milling around, and the 'come out fighting' handshake."

The rules of the match called for an eight-minute opening statement by Kennedy followed by eight minutes from Nixon. Then a panel of four reporters would ask questions.

Kennedy won.

He won on style and image—two key ingredients for success on TV. Nixon challenged and rebutted[1] what Kennedy said as if he were out to win debating points. He addressed Kennedy rather than the TV viewers.

On the other hand, as the celebrated chronicler[2] of presidential campaigns Theodore H. White noted, Kennedy "was addressing himself to the audience that was the nation."

> **3. Whom does each of the candidates address during the debate?**

Kennedy came across as assured, energetic, <u>dynamic</u>. The camera was his friend.

Nixon came across as <u>uncomfortable</u> and ill at ease.

Nixon lost not on what he said, but on how he appeared. TV viewers saw Nixon as a gray man against the studio's gray backdrop. They saw Nixon forcing nervous smiles and perspiring under the studio lights. He "looked terrible," historian David Culbert stated.

> **4. Are Kennedy and Nixon alike or different in the way they come across to the audience?**

At one point, the camera showed Nixon wiping perspiration from his brow and upper lip as he listened to Kennedy. When the camera was on Kennedy listening, he looked attentive, alert, and self-assured.

> **5. When listening, what does each candidate do?**

Neither candidate said anything that was memorable or headline making. The importance of style and image became obvious when audience <u>reactions</u> to the televised and radio versions were compared. Those who heard the debate on radio thought Nixon had won!

> **6. What similarity do Kennedy and Nixon share?**

But what counted was the televised debate. Half the country had watched it. White had a clear verdict: "In 1960 television had won the nation away from sound to images, and that was that."

---

1. rebutted: provided opposing arguments in a debate.

2. chronicler: person who records historical events.

Think as a Reader/Writer: First Thoughts

1. **Name one thing about Kennedy and Nixon that the author compares.**
2. **Was the article's organization easy to follow? Why or why not?**

Points of Comparison

READING SKIL

The Same, Only Different? Your two closest friends are probably both alike and different. To help someone understand these two friends, however, you wouldn't discuss every similarity and difference. Is it really important to know that one friend has a blue bike helmet while the other has a white bike helmet? You would focus on more important areas, such as personality and hobbies. These main areas would be your **points of comparison.**

A writer does not always announce points of comparison directly. A reader can usually figure out what they are, though, by looking at the details the writer provides.

Look back at the first two paragraphs of "The Nixon-Kennedy Presidential Debates" on page 573. Can you identify the first point of comparison? If you have trouble, look at the chart below.

THINKING IT THROUGH

Identifying Points of Comparison

STEP 1 Does the first paragraph talk about one subject or both? Write down the topic of the paragraph.	*The first paragraph is about what Kennedy wore and how he looked confident.*
STEP 2 Read the next paragraph and write down what it is about.	*This paragraph is about what Nixon wore and how he looked tired and nervous.*
STEP 3 Identify the author's first point of comparison. Repeat the process until you have identified all points of comparison.	*The author talks about the candidates' overall appearance. This is the first point of comparison.*

TIP Sometimes you can identify the point of comparison by reading one paragraph. If an author provides information about both subjects in one paragraph, you can skip Step 2.

SKILLS FOCUS

Read for details.

TIP Paragraphs providing background information may interrupt the author's points of comparison. You should keep reading to find details that describe one subject or both.

 Identifying Points of Comparison

Use the steps in the Thinking It Through on page 575 to identify and list the points of comparison in the reading selection that begins on page 573. You will use your list of points of comparison in the Your Turn on the next page. **Hint:** You should find at least four points of comparison.

READING FOCUS

Comparison-Contrast Structure

A Question of Style   Everything has a style. Sports cars have a specific look. You dress in a certain way. Even a comparison-contrast piece has a particular appearance. Not all comparison-contrast writings look just alike, though, because they can be organized in different ways. Two common patterns of organization for comparison-contrast writing are the *block style* and the *point-by-point style*. You can identify the structure of a comparison-contrast piece by looking at the points of comparison.

Block Style   A comparison-contrast piece organized in the **block style** discusses all the points of comparison for the first subject and then all the points of comparison for the second subject. Suppose you are reading a comparison-contrast article about going to the movies versus renting a video. The points of comparison are *cost* and *choice of movies*. Here is how a writer using the block style would organize the article.

Subject 1: going to the movies	cost
	choice of movies
Subject 2: renting a video	cost
	choice of movies

 **SKILLS FOCUS**

Identify and understand comparison-contrast organization.

In block style, the writer would first discuss going to the movies. The writer would tell about the ticket prices and the choices of movies available. Then, the writer would discuss renting a video. You would read about how much a video costs and what choices you have when renting a video.

Point-by-Point Style A comparison-contrast piece organized in the **point-by-point style** goes back and forth between two subjects. It explains how the two subjects are alike and different for *one* point of comparison. Then, it explains how they are alike and different for the *next* point of comparison, and so on. The example below shows how the movies-versus-video comparison would be organized in point-by-point style.

Point of Comparison 1: cost	going to the movies
	renting a video
Point of Comparison 2: choice of movies	going to the movies
	renting a video

In point-by-point style, the writer would discuss cost first. You would read about how much going to the movies costs in comparison to renting a video. Then, you would read about the choice of movies you have when you go to the movies, followed by a discussion of the choice of movies available at a video store.

TIP Did you notice how the point-by-point style always discussed movies first and videos second? This **predictable order** makes it easy for a reader to understand and follow the points of comparison.

? Look back at the block style organization on the previous page. What is predictable about the order in the block style?

YOUR TURN 3 Identifying Comparison-Contrast Structure

Use your list of points of comparison from Your Turn 2 to identify the organization of the reading selection. Overall, does the article tend to use the block style or the point-by-point style? Support your answer with examples from the essay. **Hint**: Do all the details about Kennedy come before the details about Nixon (block style), or do the details switch back and forth between Kennedy and Nixon (point-by-point style)?

SKILLS FOCUS

(page 578): Use prefixes to interpret and create words. Use suffixes to interpret and create words. *(page 579):* Identify supporting sentences.

Prefixes and Suffixes

A comparison-contrast piece may contain unfamiliar words. Knowing the meanings of common *prefixes* and *suffixes* may help you figure out these words' meanings. A **prefix** is a word part added *before* the root. A **suffix** is a word part added *after* a root. The **root** is the main part of the word. The charts below provide you with the definitions of common prefixes and suffixes.

Prefix	Definition	Example
un–	not	uneven
re–	again	rerun
pre–	before	preview
semi–	half	semifinals

Suffix	Definition	Example
–ous	characterized by	victorious
–ion	act or condition of	inspection
–ic	nature of	angelic
–less	without	careless

THINKING IT THROUGH   Using Prefixes and Suffixes

Here is an example based on the word *uncomfortable* from page 574.

STEP 1 Separate any prefixes or suffixes from the word's root. Define the root.

Un– is a prefix and –able is a suffix. Comfort is the root. It means "free from worry."

STEP 2 Add the prefix or suffix to the root, and define the word. If you have another prefix or suffix, add it and define the word.

I'll add –able. Comfortable means "able to be free from worry." I'll add un–. Uncomfortable means "not able to be free from worry."

STEP 3 Check your definition by placing it in the original sentence.

"Nixon came across as not able to be free from worry and ill at ease." That works.

PRACTICE

Using the steps above, figure out the meanings for the following words underlined in "The Nixon-Kennedy Presidential Debates."

1. vigorous (page 573)
2. pitiless (page 573)
3. unproved (page 573)
4. dynamic (page 574)
5. reactions (page 574)

Recognizing Supporting Details

Maybe you have had this experience: Your friend tells you, "I met this person the other day who reminds me so much of you." Your first question would probably be "How are we alike?" You want **supporting details** that show how this other person is like you. A reading test may ask you to identify supporting details that show how two subjects are alike or different. Suppose the following passage and the question below it were in a reading test. How would you answer the question?

Sonja and Maria sometimes seem like the same person. First, they look alike, since each has shiny black hair and big brown eyes. They also have the same interest in collecting stamps from all over the world. They have similar families, too. Sonja has four brothers and Maria has three brothers. Although they complain about their brothers sometimes, each is proud to be the only sister.

What is similar about Sonja and Maria's appearance?

A. They like to wear the same clothes.

B. They both have dark hair and brown eyes.

C. They both have beautiful curly hair.

D. They both are the only sister.

THINKING IT THROUGH   **Recognizing Supporting Details**

▶ **STEP 1** Identify what detail the question is asking about.

This question asks about the girls' appearance.

▶ **STEP 2** Scan the passage to find the section where this detail is discussed.

The passage doesn't use the word "appearance," but it talks about what the girls look like.

▶ **STEP 3** Find the place in the passage that gives you the answer.

The sentence about their "shiny black hair and big brown eyes" holds the answer.

▶ **STEP 4** Look for the choice that best matches your answer. It may not be stated in the same words, but it should mean the same thing.

Choice D talks about their families. That leaves choices A, B, and C. Clothes are not mentioned, so choice A is not right, and choice C does not match the information in the passage. Choice B is the correct answer.

Writing a Comparison-Contrast Essay

You and your best friend wear the same brand of tennis shoes, save your allowances, and spend too much time on the phone. You seem exactly alike, but are you really? You keep your room neat and organized, while your friend's room is always messy. You love Mexican food, but your friend prefers Thai food. You and your friend share many similarities, but you also have differences. Whenever you recognize that two things are both alike and different, you are comparing and contrasting.

You can understand many things by comparing and contrasting two subjects. In letters, reports, journal entries, and tests, you will find many occasions to write about how two subjects are alike and different. This workshop will prepare you.

Choose and Narrow Two Subjects

Apples and Oranges?   Maybe you have heard this statement: "That's like comparing apples and oranges!" This expression means that you should only compare things that are alike, such as a red apple with a green one. If you think about it, though, comparing apples and oranges makes sense. They are similar enough to be compared, yet different enough to contrast with each other. **When you choose two subjects for your comparison-contrast essay, make sure they have basic similarities as well as differences.**

You should also choose two subjects you know well. For example, you probably know apples and oranges well enough to give specific details about their similarities and differences. What other subjects do you know well? **Brainstorm** about these categories:

- two TV shows
- two people, such as relatives, friends, or movie or sport stars
- two holidays
- two sports
- two musical groups

Set Your Limits The two subjects you choose should be narrow enough for you to write about in an essay. For instance, you could compare apples and oranges in a short essay, but to compare fruits and vegetables, you would need to write a book. Use the steps in the following Thinking It Through to figure out if you need to narrow your subjects.

KEY CONCEPT

TIP One way to choose two subjects for a comparison-contrast essay is to pick a category first. Then, select two subjects within that category. For example, apples and oranges are part of the same category—fruit. Apples and motorcycles are from two different categories—food and transportation—so comparing them would be difficult.

THINKING IT THROUGH **Narrowing Your Subjects**

▶ **STEP 1** Write down a possible subject you know well.

big pets and small pets

▶ **STEP 2** Ask yourself, "Can I break down my subjects into smaller or more specific groups?"

These subjects seem too big. Maybe I should focus on pets I have actually had, like dogs, cats, fish, hamsters, and hermit crabs.

▶ **STEP 3** Choose two specific groups that could be discussed in an essay. These are your narrowed subjects.

Since I have a dog and a hamster as pets, I can talk about those in a short essay. They will be my two subjects.

SKILLS FOCUS

Write comparison-contrast essays. Compare topics. Narrow the focus of the topic.

Make a list of possible subjects to compare and contrast. Consider the following questions to help you choose two subjects you can write about in your essay.

- Are the subjects alike enough to make a comparison?
- Do I know enough about the subjects to provide details?
- Are the subjects narrow enough to discuss in an essay? (Use the Thinking It Through steps on page 581.)

Consider Purpose and Audience

A Reason for Everything   Comparing apples and oranges might make sense, except for just one thing: Who cares about them? Most people already know how apples and oranges are alike and different. In other words, there is no strong **purpose** or **audience** for the essay. To determine a specific purpose and audience, first ask yourself the reason for comparing and contrasting the two subjects. Then, ask yourself who would be able to use the information.

Subjects: *dogs and hamsters*

Purpose: What is the reason for comparing and contrasting dogs and hamsters?	✓ *to help people choose a family pet* *to help students from other countries understand two American pets*
Audience: Who would be able to use this information?	✓ *students and families who want a pet* *students from other countries who do not have dogs or hamsters as pets*

SKILLS FOCUS

Decide on a purpose for writing. Plan writing by targeting audience.

The student whose chart is shown above chose to help other students and families decide on a family pet. Because her essay will help readers choose a pet, the student will need to provide more information about caring for these pets. Once you have identified your purpose and audience, you can decide what background information or definitions to include in your essay.

Determine your specific purpose and audience for the subjects you have chosen. Create a chart like the one on page 582. Then, think about the background information and definitions your audience will need. Use the following questions to guide you.

- What is the reason for comparing and contrasting the two subjects you have chosen?
- Who would be able to use this information?
- What background information will I need to provide?
- What words will I need to define?

TIP The **voice** of your essay should match your purpose. For example, with a serious purpose such as helping families choose a dog, you would choose words that give specific, direct information: You might refer to a "Lab-Poodle mix" instead of "a mutt." If you want to show the humor in caring for dogs, you might use words that express a lighter tone, such as *pooch, pup,* or *canine comrade.*

Think of Points of Comparison

Generally Speaking   How are your two subjects alike? How are they different? As you answer these questions, **begin to notice the larger areas in which you find both similarities and differences.** These areas will be the points of comparison that will help you organize your essay.

KEY CONCEPT

THINKING IT THROUGH   **Choosing Points of Comparison**

Here is how to choose the points of comparison for your comparison-contrast essay.

▶ **STEP 1** Think about the subjects of your comparison-contrast essay. What points do they share?

When I think of dogs and hamsters, I think about how they look and act, what they need to survive, how they relate to people, and how long they live.

▶ **STEP 2** Choose two or three of these points of comparison for your essay. Select the ones that you know well so you can provide specific details.

Because I take care of both pets, I can give lots of details about what they need. I also know how they relate to people.

SKILLS FOCUS

Plan writing by developing voice. Plan writing by organizing ideas and information.

YOUR TURN 6 · Choosing Your Points of Comparison

Decide on the points of comparison you will use by following the steps in the Thinking It Through on page 583.

Gather Support and Organize Information

TIP Since you are writing to inform, you want to be sure your details are accurate. If you are unsure about a detail, use **reference materials** and other **resources.** Look up and verify your information in books, in magazines, or on the Internet. You can also verify information by asking teachers or friends who are experts on the subjects you have chosen.

A Leg to Stand On   Strong bones support your body just as details support a good essay. How do you get details that will provide the support your ideas need? Start by listing as many details as possible for each point of comparison. Just be sure each detail relates directly to your point of comparison. If it does not, it will weaken, not support, your point.

Getting Organized   A Venn diagram can help you organize your details. To make a Venn diagram, draw two overlapping circles like the ones in the student's example below. In the example, the points of comparison are listed to the left of the circles. Each circle represents one of the subjects. The overlapping section includes the details that the subjects have in common. The sections that do not overlap include the details that make each subject different.

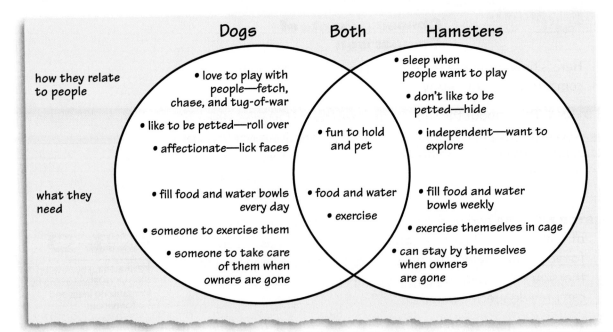

Dogs — **Both** — **Hamsters**

how they relate to people
- love to play with people—fetch, chase, and tug-of-war
- like to be petted—roll over
- affectionate—lick faces

- sleep when people want to play
- don't like to be petted—hide
- independent—want to explore

- fun to hold and pet

what they need
- fill food and water bowls every day
- someone to exercise them
- someone to take care of them when owners are gone

- food and water
- exercise

- fill food and water bowls weekly
- exercise themselves in cage
- can stay by themselves when owners are gone

YOUR TURN 7 — Gathering and Organizing Support

Brainstorm a list of details for your two points of comparison. Organize your details in a graphic organizer like the Venn diagram on page 584.

Reference Note

For more on **evaluating details,** see page 587.

Develop a Main Idea Statement

My Point Is . . . Have you ever had a conversation with someone who gives you an endless list of details? The entire time that person is talking, you are thinking, "What is the point of all this?" In an essay, you can get to the point by writing a **main idea statement,** or **thesis.** This statement is similar to a topic sentence for a paragraph except that it summarizes the main idea of the entire essay. The main idea statement for your comparison-contrast essay will tell readers the subjects you are comparing and contrasting, the purpose of your essay, and your points of comparison. You can write a main idea statement in one or two sentences. See how one student wrote a main idea statement in the example below.

Subjects: dogs and hamsters

Purpose: helping students and families decide on a family pet

Points of comparison: how dogs and hamsters relate to people and what dogs and hamsters need

Main idea statement: Dogs and hamsters both make good family pets, but they are different in the way they relate to people and in their needs.

YOUR TURN 8 — Writing a Main Idea Statement

Think about the subjects, purpose, and points of comparison for your comparison-contrast essay. Then, write a main idea statement to communicate these ideas.

SKILLS FOCUS

Brainstorm to generate ideas. Use graphic organizers to generate ideas. Include a statement of thesis/main idea. Use reference materials when writing. Gather information and sources.

Arranging Details

What Goes Where?   You will organize your essay using the block style, which presents all the information about one subject and then all the information about the other subject. Here is how the student using the block style would arrange the points of comparison for dogs and hamsters.

> **Subject 1: Dogs**
>
> > how they relate to people
> >
> > what they need
>
> **Subject 2: Hamsters**
>
> > how they relate to people
> >
> > what they need

As you can see, the block style presents the points of comparison in the same order for both subjects. For each subject, how the pet relates to people is discussed first, and what the pet needs is discussed second. Follow the same structure in your essay.

TIP   For short comparison-contrast essays, the block style is a good way to group similar ideas together. The arrangement of ideas based on similarities is called **logical order.** However, there are other ways to achieve logical order. The chart on page 577 shows the point-by-point style. Still another type of structure is the **modified block style.** In this style, all the *similarities* for the points of comparison are discussed. Then all the *differences* for the points of comparison are discussed. The modified block style looks like this:

Similarities of rugby and football:	rules
	equipment
Differences between rugby and football:	rules
	equipment

SKILLS FOCUS

Organize writing by block order. Organize writing by logical order. Organize writing by point-by-point order. *(page 587):* Support ideas/theses with relevant evidence and details. Evaluate sources before writing.

YOUR TURN 9   Arranging Details

Arrange the points of comparison for your comparison-contrast essay as in the student example above. Check to see that the points of comparison are in the same order for each subject.

Evaluating Details

When you write a comparison-contrast essay, it is important that your details provide **logical support** for the points of comparison. A feature of logical support is *relevance*. **Relevant details** are related to the point they support. Examine the Venn diagram to the right. Can you identify any details that do not support the point of comparison "appearance"? The details that do not support the point of comparison "appearance" would be either listed with a different point of comparison or removed from the essay.

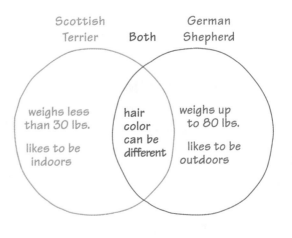

Scottish Terrier

Both

German Shepherd

weighs less than 30 lbs.

likes to be indoors

hair color can be different

weighs up to 80 lbs.

likes to be outdoors

PRACTICE

Look at the example below and evaluate the details for each point of comparison. Decide whether any detail does not belong with the point of comparison where it is listed.

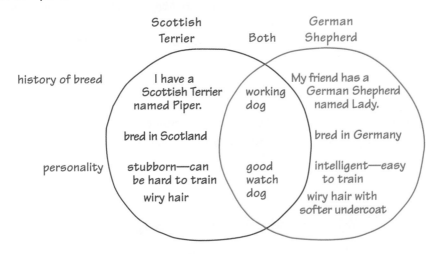

Scottish Terrier

Both

German Shepherd

history of breed

I have a Scottish Terrier named Piper.

working dog

My friend has a German Shepherd named Lady.

bred in Scotland

bred in Germany

personality

stubborn—can be hard to train

wiry hair

good watch dog

intelligent—easy to train

wiry hair with softer undercoat

Writing

Comparison-Contrast Essay

Framework	**Think as a Reader/Writer**

Introduction
- Attention-grabbing opener
- Main idea statement

Pull your reader in right away with an **interesting beginning.** You could begin with a mysterious statement which you go on to explain, as the writer of the model to the right did. You could also begin with a funny story or a question. Then, include your **main idea statement** so that the reader understands exactly what you are comparing and contrasting.

Body
- Subject #1
  Point of comparison #1
  (with logical support)
  Point of comparison #2
  (with logical support)
- Subject #2
  Point of comparison #1
  (with logical support)
  Point of comparison #2
  (with logical support)

Here you will point out how the two subjects are alike and different for at least two points of comparison.

- Present your first subject by discussing both **points of comparison** in the first body paragraph.
- When you present your second subject in the next paragraph, discuss the **points of comparison** in the same order.

To help you discuss the similarities and differences, use **transitional words.** Transitional words that show similarities are *also, like, in addition,* and *another.* Transitional words that point out the differences are *on the other hand, but, however,* and *unlike.*

Conclusion
- Summary of body paragraphs

Briefly **sum up** the result of the comparison. **Relate** your summary to the main idea you included in the first paragraph.

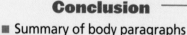  **Drafting Your Essay**

Write a comparison-contrast essay. As you write, refer to the framework above and the Writer's Model on the next page.

A Writer's Model

The final draft below closely follows the framework for a comparison-contrast essay on the previous page.

Puppy Love or Hamster Heaven?

Your friends have one, maybe even two or three. The neighbors have one. Does it seem that everyone has one but you? No, it is not the latest video game, but something much more fun—a family pet. Dogs and hamsters both make good family pets, but they are different in the way they relate to people and in their needs.

Dogs and hamsters are both fun to hold and pet, but they relate to people in different ways. For instance, dogs enjoy human contact. They love to play fetch, chase, and tug-of-war with their owners. Dogs like to be petted, and most dogs will roll over to have their bellies rubbed. Dogs are also affectionate and love licking their owners' faces. However, dogs need lots of care, too. They need fresh food and water every day, and they need regular exercise. They also need someone to take care of them when their owners go out of town.

Hamsters are very different from dogs. Having contact with people is not important to them. They like to sleep when people want to play. Unlike dogs, hamsters do not like being petted. Many will hide when their owners want to pick them up. Hamsters are also very independent. They like to spend their time exploring. Hamsters may be low on affection, but they need less daily care than dogs do. They need food and water just as dogs do, but an owner usually fills up the food and water dishes only once a week. Hamsters need exercise too, but they get their exercise by running on wheels in their cages. If their owners go out of town, hamsters can be left alone.

Dogs and hamsters both make good pets. Dogs provide plenty of affection, but they are also high maintenance. Hamsters are definitely low maintenance, but they are also less cuddly. The choice is yours.

Attention-grabbing opener

Main idea statement

Subject 1: First point of comparison

Supporting details

Second point of comparison

Supporting details

Subject 2: First point of comparison

Supporting details

Second point of comparison

Supporting details

Summary of body paragraphs

A Student's Model

When you write a comparison-contrast essay, make sure you have a purpose for writing. Matthew Hester, a middle school student from Laurel Hill, Florida, wants to help his audience make a decision. He compares two types of collections that may interest beginner collectors.

A Collection Question

Attention-grabbing opener

Collecting is very popular today. Collectors have their own magazines, television shows, and Internet sites. If you are thinking about starting a collection, I suggest considering trading cards or airplane models.

Main idea statement

They are both good investments and fun, but they differ in storage and use.

Subject 1: First point of comparison

Collecting trading cards is an enjoyable hobby. They are easy to store and transport in bags, boxes, or notebooks.

Second point of comparison

Trading cards with friends is a super way to spend an afternoon. Cards also provide adventure and challenge as you seek that one card essential to completing your set.

Subject 2: First point of comparison

Model collecting differs from card collecting in several ways. Model airplanes require more storage space than cards do and are more difficult to transport due to their larger size.

Second point of comparison

However, models do allow for more realistic play. The zooming and swooshing of miniature airplanes give the feeling of being in the center of the action.

Summary of body paragraphs

Trading cards and model airplanes both make good collections due to their current and possible future value. This makes them a wise investment for your allowance dollars. Trading cards are excellent choices if you have limited storage space and enjoy a challenge. Model airplanes are better if your storage space is unlimited and you enjoy live-action play. If you have trouble deciding, join me in collecting both. Either way, start your collection today!

Evaluate and Revise Content, Organization, and Style

Double Vision   Look twice when you evaluate a peer's paper or your own. On the first reading, concentrate on content and organization, using the guidelines below. The second time you read the essay, pay attention to the sentences, using the Focus on Sentences on page 593.

▶ **First Reading: Content and Organization**   Use this chart to evaluate and revise your essay so the ideas are clear.

Guidelines for Self-Evaluation and Peer Evaluation		
Evaluation Questions	**Tips**	**Revision Techniques**
❶ Does the introduction state the main idea?	**Underline** the main idea statement.	**Add** a main idea statement if one is missing.
❷ Does the first body paragraph discuss the first subject with at least two points of comparison?	**Put a star** next to each point of comparison.	If there is no clear point of comparison, **add** one or **revise** an existing one.
❸ Does the second body paragraph discuss the second subject using the same points of comparison in the same order?	**Draw a wavy line** under each point of comparison.	If the same points of comparison are not used, **add** one or **revise** an existing one. **Rearrange** the points of comparison if they are not in the same order.
❹ Do relevant details logically support each point of comparison for both subjects?	**Put a check mark** next to the supporting details for each point of comparison. **Underline** any details that do not support the point of comparison.	If needed, **elaborate** on a point of comparison by adding details. **Delete** details that do not directly support the point of comparison.
❺ Does the conclusion summarize the body paragraphs and refer to the main idea?	With a colored marker, **highlight** the summary.	If needed, **add** a brief summary that is related to the main idea.

ONE WRITER'S REVISIONS This revision is an early draft of the essay on page 589.

delete

elaborate

> Hamsters are very different from dogs. Having contact with people is not important to them. They like to sleep when people want to play. ~~I have to go to bed by 10:30.~~ Unlike dogs, hamsters do not like being petted. *Many will hide when their owners want to pick them up.* Hamsters are also very independent. They like to spend their time exploring.

PEER REVIEW

As you evaluate a peer's paper, ask yourself the following questions:

- What points of comparison does the writer discuss?
- Who will be able to use this information?

Think as a Reader/Writer

1. Why do you think the writer deleted a sentence in the paragraph above?

2. Why do you think the writer added a sentence to the paragraph?

▷ **Second Reading: Style** During your first reading, you looked at what you said in your essay and how you organized your ideas. Now, focus on how your essay *sounds*. Good writing has an easy rhythm that is not choppy. To achieve an easy rhythm, writers use a variety of sentences in their essays. They avoid long series of short sentences by combining two short sentences into one sentence.

When you evaluate the rhythm of your comparison-contrast essay, ask yourself whether you have combined sentences so that they are not choppy. As you re-read your essay, underline any short sentence that repeats several words or a phrase from the sentence before or after it. Then, combine sentences by cutting repeated words and inserting necessary words or phrases.

SKILLS FOCUS

Develop writer's style. *(page 591):* Evaluate one's own writing. Revise by adding or replacing text. Revise by rearranging text. Revise by elaborating. Revise by deleting text.

Combining Sentences

Good writers use some short sentences. Too many short sentences are a problem. Many short sentences in a row bore readers. The ideas in the previous three sentences are important for writers to know, but you might have found it difficult to pay attention to them. Their choppy sound and their repeated words and phrases probably bothered you. Combining short, choppy sentences can be as easy as moving a word or phrase from one sentence to another.

Choppy Sentences	~~The car was~~ black. The car was hot. [move a word]
Combined Sentence	The black car was hot.
Choppy Sentences	Jamal played disc golf. ~~He played~~ in the afternoon. [move a phrase]
Combined Sentence	Jamal played disc golf in the afternoon.

ONE WRITER'S REVISIONS

They love to play fetch and tug-of-war with their owners.

~~Dogs also like to play~~ chase.

Think as a Reader/Writer

How does combining the two sentences improve the writing?

YOUR TURN 11 — Evaluating and Revising Your Comparison-Contrast Essay

First, evaluate and revise the content and organization of your essay, using the guidelines on page 591. Then, use the Focus on Sentences above to see if you need to combine any choppy sentences. Finally, if a peer evaluated your paper, think carefully about his or her comments as you revise.

SKILLS FOCUS

Combine sentences for effective writing.

Publishing

Proofread Your Essay

Look Out Two sets of eyes are better than one when trying to find mistakes. After you proofread your essay, see if you can catch more mistakes by enlisting the help of another proofreader.

Grammar Link

Using Comparatives Correctly

In a comparison-contrast essay, you have to make comparisons. When you make comparisons between two subjects, you use the **comparative** form of adjectives and adverbs. To write comparatives correctly, follow the guidelines.

The comparative form of one-syllable modifiers is usually made by adding *–er.*

Modifier	Comparative Form
fast	faster

Some two-syllable modifiers form the comparative by using *more.*

Modifier	Comparative Form
nervous	more nervous

Modifiers with three or more syllables use *more* to form the comparative.

Modifier	Comparative Form
successful	more successful

Be sure not to use *–er* together with *more.* That combination is never correct.

Incorrect Mandy always arrives more earlier than Liza.

Correct Mandy always arrives *earlier* than Liza.

PRACTICE

Complete each of the following sentences with the correct form of the given modifier.

Example:

1. **quickly**   Sam finished his test _____ than Liam.

1. more quickly

1. **lovable**   I think dogs are _____ than hamsters are.

2. **small**   Hamsters are _____ than dogs.

3. **playful**   Hamsters are _____ at night than during the day.

4. **frequently**   Dogs have to be fed _____ than hamsters.

5. **easy**   Do you think hamsters are _____ to take care of than dogs?

For more information and practice on **comparatives,** see page 245.

Publish Your Essay

Experience to the Rescue   Your experience with the two subjects you wrote about in your comparison-contrast essay can provide information that people need and want. What is the best way to reach the audience who will benefit from your experience?

- Does the topic of your comparison-contrast essay relate to a school subject? Did you compare two sports? two artists? two countries? Make copies of your essay and share them with teachers. They might use your essay in their classes.

- Display your essays and those of your classmates on a wall in your school. Invite teachers, parents, and other students to view the "Authors' Wall."

TIP Grab potential readers by giving your essay an attention-getting title that creatively reflects your topic.

Designing Your Writing

Creating a Bar Graph   A quick and visual way to show your readers the similarities and differences between two subjects is to provide a bar graph. Each point of comparison can be a separate graph. Some word-processing programs allow you to create graphs, or you can draw one by hand. Either way, make sure you use colors and provide a **legend,** or explanation of what each color represents. Colors will help your reader identify each subject in your graph. Below, see how the writer of the Writer's Model used a bar graph that includes a legend to compare the needs of hamsters and dogs.

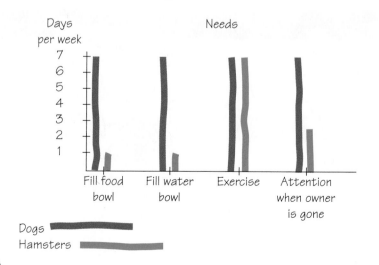

Days per week

Needs

7 6 5 4 3 2 1

Fill food bowl   Fill water bowl   Exercise   Attention when owner is gone

Dogs
Hamsters

TIP   By looking at the bar graph to the left, readers can tell which pet needs more daily care.

? Do you know which pet has more needs?

SKILLS FOCUS

Proofread one's own writing in preparation for publishing. Use the comparative forms of modifiers correctly. Publish in a variety of formats. Publish for a variety of audiences. Design documents in preparation for publishing.

Reflect on Your Essay

Building Your Portfolio   Take time to reflect both on the process of comparing and contrasting two subjects and on the process of writing your essay. Thinking about how you wrote this assignment will help you when you write your next paper.

- Do you think the two subjects you wrote about are more similar or more different? Why?

- Before you wrote your essay, you arranged your ideas in a certain order. Did you find that helpful? Why or why not?

- Think about the reason why you compared the two subjects you chose. How does your essay achieve that purpose?

YOUR TURN 12   Proofreading, Publishing, and Reflecting on Your Essay

- Correct grammar, usage, and mechanics errors.

- Publish your essay by following one of the suggestions on the previous page.

- Answer the questions from Reflect on Your Essay above. Record your responses in a learning log, or include them in your portfolio.

HAGAR THE HORRIBLE reprinted with special permission of King Features Syndicate, Inc.

Writing a Classification Essay

A common question on essay tests is one that asks you to classify the similarities and differences between two subjects or the good and bad points about one subject. You must quickly determine how to generate ideas. A T-chart can help. Suppose the prompt to the right appeared on a writing test. How would you approach it?

Think about your language arts class and your science class. They are alike in some ways and different in other ways. Write a composition in which you explain how your language arts and science classes are alike and how they are different.

THINKING IT THROUGH

Writing a Classification Essay

STEP 1 Identify what the prompt is asking you to do.

It asks me to explain how my language arts and science classes are alike and different.

STEP 2 Think of at least two points of comparison. Then, create a T-chart and fill it in with supporting details.

	Similarities	Differences
What I learn	information about people and events	L. A. – grammar, writing Sci. – plants, animals
What I do	homework write papers read	L. A. – act out plays, write essays Sci. – labs, draw diagrams

STEP 3 Plan how you will develop your essay.

I'll use block style. I'll talk all about language arts in the first body paragraph and science in the second body paragraph.

STEP 4 Write your essay. Make sure to elaborate on the supporting details from your T-chart with facts, examples, and explanations.

Connections to Life

Comparing Documentaries

Is truth stranger than fiction? Many film-makers and writers would answer with a booming "Yes!" Filmmakers who want to show that truth is interesting will make a *documentary*. A **documentary** is a non-fiction film that creatively portrays an actual event, person, place, thing, or issue.

Filmmakers have the same reasons for producing documentaries as writers have for writing essays, articles, stories, or poems. Their purposes are *to inform, to entertain, to persuade,* and *to express themselves.* Like many writers, filmmakers may also have the purpose of *making money.* Every documentary will have at least one of these purposes. In fact, a documentary, like a written work, may have several purposes.

Two of a Kind?   For this assignment, you will compare the purposes of two documentaries on the same topic. To do that, ask yourself the questions to the right.

- Does the filmmaker provide facts and explanations about a topic? If so, the purpose may be **to inform.**

- Does the filmmaker focus on a famous person, a funny event, or an attention-grabbing topic? Does the documentary contain flashy graphics, an appealing soundtrack, and eye-catching camera-work? If so, the purpose may be **to entertain.**

- Does the filmmaker appeal to viewers' emotions and try to get the viewers to think a certain way? If so, the purpose may be **to persuade.**

- Does the filmmaker explore a topic using a first-person narrator who reveals his or her inner thoughts about the topic? If so, the purpose may be **to express.**

- Does the filmmaker focus on a popular topic? If so, the purpose may be **to make money.** The larger the audience a documentary attracts, the more ads the network can sell.

YOUR TURN 13   Comparing Documentaries

View two documentaries on the same topic. As you watch, take notes on how information is presented in each, using the questions above as a guide. Then, write a paragraph or two comparing the two documentaries. Discuss how the documentaries' purposes are similar, and how they are different.

Comparing Ideas in Photographs

W hen you look at a photograph of yourself, what do
you see? You see yourself, right? The picture shows
the color of your eyes and hair, the shape of your nose and
mouth, and the style of clothing you wear. Actually, while the
person in the picture certainly seems to look like you, it is not
the *real* you.

Photographs vs. Reality

Many people believe that photographs truly represent reality, but
they do not. In truth, photographs, like all illustrations, only resemble an actual person, place, thing, or event. What you see in a
photograph is not the same as what you see in real life because
photographs have the following unique characteristics.

- **Photographs are two-dimensional and flat.** If you took a picture
  of the palm of your hand, could you turn the picture over and
  see the top of your hand? No. The photograph shows only one
  side. In real life, you can view all sides.

- **Photographs are easily reproduced and distributed.** It is easy to
  make copies of your birthday party pictures and send them to
  relatives and friends. Although it might be fun, it would be impossible to reproduce the real party over and over again.

- **Photographs contain a single point of view.** When you look at a
  head-on photograph of a baseball player hitting a baseball, you
  are looking at the action from the photographer's point of view.
  You do not see what the hitter sees. Photographers use the element of point of view to show how an image looks from a specific position.

WHAT'S AHEAD?

**In this section you will
compare ideas in pho-
tographs. You will also
learn how to**

- **explain the differ-
  ence between a pho-
  tograph of an object
  and the real object**

- **analyze how photo-
  graphs provide infor-
  mation**

SKILLS FOCUS

Analyze and evaluate
images and illustrations.
Understand how pictures
enhance communication.

Photographs Provide Information

Even though looking at a photograph is not the same as actually seeing the real thing, photographs are helpful because they provide information in an easily accessible way. For example, if you want to know what a Tasmanian devil looks like, you could visit the nearest zoo, fly to Tasmania, or look at a photograph. The easiest choice, of course, would be to look at a photograph.

Photographs are also a powerful partner to the written and spoken word. In a newspaper, for instance, you might read about an erupting volcano. Not until you look at the picture that accompanies the article would you fully understand the massive destruction the volcano caused. Because photographs are so powerful and easy to reproduce, they are a popular form of media. Look in any magazine, newspaper, or textbook and you will find many photographs. You should be aware, however, that the information photographs provide can be changed by adjusting the *camera angle,* by *cropping* the photograph, and by using *captions.*

Up, Down, Sideways   A photographer can change the appearance of a person, place, thing, or event by changing the **camera angle.** Look at the examples below. In the picture on the left, the photographer stood on a ladder and shot the picture looking down. Do you see how the boy looks small and rather fragile? Now, look at the picture on the right taken of the same boy from a low angle. From this point of view, the boy looks big and powerful, even a little intimidating.

TIP Photography is not the only media form that provides information.

? Can you think of any others? **Hint:** The paragraph to the right can give you a few answers.

SKILLS FOCUS

Determine how media use enhances information. Determine how media use manipulates information. Identify false or misleading information in media messages.

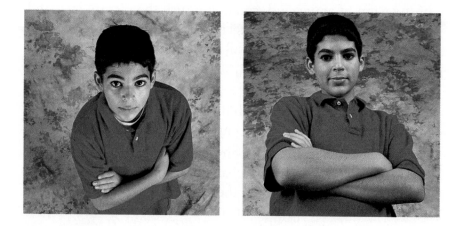

What's Missing? Photographs can be **cropped,** or cut, so background details do not distract the viewer from the main subject. However, cropping can change the meaning of a picture, as you can see below. In the picture on the left you see a spaceship hovering in the sky. In the picture on the right, though, you see what was cut from the first picture. Aliens are not landing; a girl is holding the spaceship by a string.

More Than Words Some photographs have **captions,** which are like titles. A caption provides viewers with a summary of what is shown in a picture. Captions can be neutral, giving only facts, or they can show a positive or negative attitude toward the subject. Look at the pictures and captions below and on the next page. You can see that the images are the same, but the captions show two very different attitudes toward grizzly bears.

Enjoying the spring weather, a mother bear and her young relax by the riverside.

TIP What attitude toward bears does this caption express?

SKILLS FOCUS

Identify captions and understand their purpose. Identify bias in the media.

Here is the same picture with a different caption. Notice how the caption changes what you "see" in the photo.

Rangers warn park visitors not to approach mother grizzly bears. They will fiercely protect their cubs.

YOUR TURN 14 Comparing Ideas in Photographs

- Look at the photograph on the left below, while covering up the photo next to it. How do you feel about the subject? Write a caption for the photograph that summarizes what you see and expresses your feelings.

- Next, look at the photograph on the right. How do you feel about the subject now? Write a caption for the photograph that summarizes what you see and expresses your feelings.

- Finally, write a paragraph in which you compare the two photographs. Explain how the differences in the way each photo is presented may have affected the captions you wrote.

21 *Choices*

Choose one of the following activities to complete.

▶ CAREERS

1. Tool Time Comparing and contrasting two subjects is a favorite tool of journalists, consumer advocates, scientists, sports commentators, and campaign managers for politicians. Find examples of how comparing and contrasting is used in these fields or in other fields. Then, write a **report** that describes examples of how people in their fields make comparisons.

▶ VIEWING AND REPRESENTING

2. News Views Give a short **oral report** comparing how two news sources—for example, a network TV newscast and an Internet news site—present the same story. Choose a recent situation or event that catches your interest, and look in two sources for reports about it. Compare and contrast the treatment of the story, including the story's focus, the amount of detail provided, and the viewpoints that are presented.

▶ CREATIVE WRITING

3. It's Like This Compose a **humorous poem** about a person, place, thing, or idea using similes. A simile is a comparison of two unlike things using *like* or *as.* For example, you could write a simile poem about happiness that begins, "Happiness is like a day without homework." In the rest of the poem, you would explain in a funny way the ways in which these two things are alike.

▶ CROSSING THE CURRICULUM: MUSIC

4. The Beat Goes On Does your favorite musician or band follow the same formula from one album to the next? Find specific examples that show how the musician or band has changed or stayed the same over time. You might focus on lyrics, style, vocals, or other areas. Give a **multimedia presentation,** using audio or audio-visual clips to demonstrate your points.

PORTFOLIO

SKILLS FOCUS

Identify and understand comparison-contrast organization. Write to report. Present oral messages. Compare and contrast media coverage. Identify metaphors and similes. Write short stories or poems. Integrate multimedia and technology into presentations.

22 Responding to a Novel

Reading Workshop

Reading a Book Review

Writing Workshop

Writing a Book Review

Viewing and Representing

Comparing Media: Film, TV, and Literature

Y ou stand staring at the rows of bookshelves in your school library. You need to choose a book to read, but how can you? With so many books to choose from, it sometimes seems impossible to settle on just one.

One way to choose a book is to read a book review. A **book review** tells what a book is about and the reviewer's opinion of the book. You can find book reviews in many newspapers and magazines. Some sites on the Internet are devoted entirely to book reviews.

Book reviewers help readers sort through the many choices they have when deciding what to read. Reviewers base their ideas about books on careful reading and on knowledge of what makes a book good. You can be a book reviewer, too. You can use your skills as a reader to judge a book. Then, by sharing your ideas, you will help others decide if a book might be good to read.

Informational Text

Exposition

 Reviewing a Book

With a partner, think of a book that you liked and give two reasons why you liked it. Then, think of a book you disliked and give two reasons why you disliked it. Discuss your reasons.

internet**connect**

go. hrw .com

GO TO: go.hrw.com
KEYWORD: EOLang 6-22

Reading a Book Review

WHAT'S AHEAD?

In this workshop you will read a book review. You will also learn how to

■ identify the elements of a novel

■ identify a writer's point of view

"**H**ilarious," "humorous," and "sarcastic" are words a reviewer uses in the review of the book *Catherine, Called Birdy*. Does this description make you interested in knowing more about the book? Read the following book review to see more of the reviewer's ideas about the book. Will it be a "thumbs up" or "thumbs down" review?

Preparing to Read

READING FOCUS

Elements of a Novel   A novel does not just happen. A writer must put certain parts, or **elements,** into a book. Plot, character, setting, and a problem—a novel must have these elements, just as a baseball team needs a pitcher, a catcher, infielders, and outfielders. Reviewers focus on the elements of a novel when they read novels and when they write reviews about them. Notice which elements are mentioned in the review of *Catherine, Called Birdy* by Karen Cushman.

READING SKILL

Point of View   We all have an attitude sometimes. Book reviewers specialize in having an attitude, and they will let you know what it is. The attitude of the reviewer (or of any writer) toward his or her topic is sometimes called the **point of view.** A book review will often end with a statement telling you whether the reviewer recommends reading the book. Long before you reach the end of a review, though, you will know how the reviewer feels. The reviewer's point of view will come across in the words he or she uses to talk about the book. What is the point of view of the reviewer of *Catherine, Called Birdy*?

Read the following book review. In a notebook or on a separate sheet of paper, jot down answers to the numbered active-reading questions in the shaded boxes. The underlined words will be discussed in the Vocabulary Mini-Lesson on page 611.

from Great Books for Girls

❦

Catherine, Called Birdy

BY KAREN CUSHMAN. 1994. CLARION. AGES 12–14.

Reviewed by Kathleen Odean

Catherine, daughter of a small-time nobleman in medieval England, is hilarious. In a diary format she records her daily life, the <u>outrages</u> she suffers as a girl, and her often humorous <u>assessment</u> of things. She longs to be outside <u>frolicking</u> instead of inside sewing, and she <u>chafes</u> at her lessons in ladylike behavior. Birdy is the sort of girl who organizes a spitting contest and starts a mud fight. She makes a list of all the things girls cannot do, such as go on a crusade,[1] be a horse trainer, laugh out loud, and "marry whom they will." She battles with her father, who wants to marry her off to the highest bidder, no matter how <u>repulsive</u>. Many of her best sarcastic remarks are reserved for him, and she irritates him whenever possible. She has a lively sense of humor and a <u>palpable</u> love of life. Few fictional characters are so vivid and funny—do not miss this one.

> **1.** Who or what is the focus of the reviewer's comments?

> **2.** What does the reviewer think about the book?

> **3.** Does this review make you want to read the book? Why or why not?

---

1. crusade: In the eleventh, twelfth, and thirteenth centuries, Christian nations repeatedly sent armies to the Holy Land, the region that is now made up of parts of Israel, Jordan, and Egypt. These armies repeatedly tried but failed to win back the Holy Land from the Muslims. These missions were called crusades.

| READING FOCUS |

Elements of a Novel

A Recipe for Greatness   When you cook, you must have certain ingredients for a dish to turn out well. A spaghetti dinner, for example, needs pasta and a good sauce.

Good stories and novels have several ingredients, or **elements**. A book reviewer will tell you about the elements of a particular novel. The reviewer will also let you know if he or she thinks the novelist got the recipe right. The chart below defines some elements of stories and novels and provides examples from a fairy tale you may know.

Elements of Stories and Novels	Examples from "Snow-White"
The **plot** is a series of related events that make up a story. The events revolve around a central problem, or **conflict**, which must be resolved before the story ends.	A jealous queen wants to kill her beautiful step-daughter, Snow-White. Snow-White hides in the forest. She lives in a cottage with seven dwarfs. The queen tricks Snow-White into eating a poisoned apple that makes her appear dead. Snow-White is rescued by a prince.
The **main character** is the central person in the story.	Snow-White is the main character.
The **setting** is the time and place of a story.	The story is set a long time ago in a forest.

 Identifying Elements of a Novel in a Book Review

Re-read the review of *Catherine, Called Birdy* on page 607. Find the elements of the novel by answering the following questions.

- **Plot:** What does the reviewer tell you about what happens?
- **Character:** Who is the main character? What is she like?
- **Setting:** Where and when do the events take place?

 **SKILLS FOCUS**

Identify elements of a text.

Point of View

Grade "A" Quality   A book reviewer's job is to evaluate, or judge the quality of, a novel. A reviewer's **point of view** often comes through in the way he or she discusses the elements of the novel. Positive or negative words reveal the reviewer's attitude toward the book.

Read the following review of the fairy tale "Snow-White." Look for the reviewer's point of view by noting which elements the reviewer mentions and whether he or she uses positive or negative words. If you need help, the Thinking It Through that follows the review will guide you.

> The character of Snow-White is unbelievably good and beautiful, but she is also much too trusting. Her beauty keeps the hunter and wild animals from harming her and provides her a charming home in the forest. However, her beauty does not hide her helplessness. She knows that the queen is trying to kill her, yet she continues to talk to strange women who come to the dwarfs' house. Three times she accepts deadly gifts from the disguised evil queen. Three times she survives. Anyone else would probably not be so lucky. Her character leaves the reader wondering how she manages to live happily ever after.

TIP   Reviewers use **positive words** (such as *powerful, exciting, fascinating*, and *funny*) to praise or compliment a novel. They use **negative words** (such as *weak, boring, unrealistic*, and *silly*) to criticize a novel.

THINKING IT THROUGH

Identifying Point of View

▶ **STEP 1** You can make a chart like the one on the next page to analyze a book review. In the middle column, note positive or negative words and phrases the reviewer uses to discuss each element. You may write *none* if the reviewer does not discuss a certain element.

▶ **STEP 2** Based on the negative or positive words that the reviewer uses, decide what his or her point of view is. Write the point of view in the right-hand column of the chart. If the element is not discussed, you may leave the space blank.

SKILLS FOCUS

Identify and trace the development of an author's point of view in a text.

Element	Positive or Negative Words and Phrases	Reviewer's Point of View
Plot	none describing plot	
Main Character	positive: good, beautiful, lucky negative: unbelievably, much too trusting, helplessness	Snow-White is beautiful, but that does not make her a great character.
Setting	positive: charming negative: none	There is not enough information to tell.

▶ **STEP 3** Put it all together. Look at the positive and negative words and phrases and decide what the reviewer thinks.

The reviewer does not think "Snow-White" is a good story because the main character is too helpless and unbelievably lucky.

  **Identifying a Reviewer's Point of View**

Re-read the review of *Catherine, Called Birdy* on page 607. Then, use the Thinking It Through steps to identify the reviewer's point of view. Be prepared to explain *why* you think the reviewer takes the point of view you have identified.

SKILLS FOCUS

(page 611): Use context clues in words, sentences, and paragraphs to decode new vocabulary. Identify and use Greek, Latin, and Anglo-Saxon roots and affixes to understand vocabulary. Use reference aids to clarify meanings and usage.
(page 612): Use context clues in words, sentences, and paragraphs to decode new vocabulary.

VOCABULARY

Wordbusting Strategy (CSSD)

A reviewer may use very specific words to communicate exactly what he or she thinks of a book. Often, the word *good* is just not good enough.

When you come across an unfamiliar word in a book review, you can use a four-part strategy called **Wordbusting.** The letters *CSSD* can help you remember the steps of the strategy. Use only as many steps as it takes to understand the word.

- **Context** Use clues from the words and sentences around the word.
- **Structure** Look for familiar roots, prefixes, or suffixes.
- **Sound** Say the word aloud. It may sound like a word you know.
- **Dictionary** Look up the word.

THINKING IT THROUGH — Using the Wordbusting Strategy

Here is an example of Wordbusting, using the word *outrages* from the review of *Catherine, Called Birdy.*

▶ **Context:** "In a diary format she records her daily life, the *outrages* she suffers as a girl, and her often humorous assessment of things."

In the sentence, outrages are something she suffers. Suffers tells me that outrages are bad.

▶ **Structure:** out + rage + s

Rage means "anger," so the word must have something to do with getting mad.

▶ **Sound:** ou t´ rāj´ iz

It sounds like out and rage. I think an outrage must be something that makes you mad.

▶ **Dictionary:** *Outrages* are acts that hurt someone or disregard a person's feelings.

My definition is pretty close.

PRACTICE

Use the Wordbusting strategy to figure out the meanings of the words to the right. The words are underlined in the review of *Catherine, Called Birdy* on page 607, so you can see the context of each word. After each definition, list the steps of CSSD that you used for that word.

1. assessment
2. frolicking
3. chafes
4. repulsive
5. palpable

Answering Questions About Unfamiliar Vocabulary

Reading tests may ask you to identify the meanings of new words. The words may be technical or specialized terms that you normally do not use. To figure out their meanings, you must find clues in the reading passage. Look at the reading passage below and the test question that follows it. Then, use the Thinking It Through steps to figure out the answer.

> In the Middle Ages, books and other documents had to be copied by hand. Professional writers, called scribes, copied documents onto a kind of paper made from sheepskin. Often, many scribes sat together in a scriptorium, writing with ink and quill pens made from feathers. Scribes left wide margins on pages so that artists could draw colorful illustrations. When the handmade pages were complete, they were sewn together into a book.

You can tell from the passage that a scriptorium is

A. a person who copies documents

B. a pen made from feathers

C. a room where scribes work

D. a book made from sheepskin

THINKING IT THROUGH **Answering Questions About Unfamiliar Vocabulary**

▶ **STEP 1** Read the whole passage and get a sense of what it is about.

The passage is about how scribes copied documents in the Middle Ages.

▶ **STEP 2** Look at the context of the word. Pay attention to words near the new term that may provide a clue to the word's meaning.

The passage tells me that scribes sat in a scriptorium. I can tell from the words "sat" and "in" that a scriptorium is a building or room.

▶ **STEP 3** Check your answer against the items in the test question.

A is wrong. The people who copied are scribes.

B does not match my answer.

C matches my answer. This is correct.

D is wrong. The scribes would not sit in a book.

Writing a Book Review

You have just taken a journey. Maybe you went back in time or visited a foreign land. Perhaps you fought dragons, danced with royalty, and conquered evil. How did you do these wonderful things? You read a book, of course.

You think that all your friends should visit the world in the book you have just read. You can show your friends this world by writing a **book review.** In this workshop you will write a book review about a young adult novel. You will summarize the book and tell whether you think it is worth reading.

WHAT'S AHEAD?

In this workshop you will write a book review. You will also learn how to

- **preview and summarize a novel**
- **identify the elements of a plot**
- **replace clichés with your own words**
- **use appositives**

Select a Novel

Plucky Heroines in the City   For this review, you will read a young adult novel. Think of the types of characters or settings you like to read about in novels. Then, look for a book with the type of character or setting that interests you most. To find a book, you might

- browse in bookstores—in person or online
- ask friends for recommendations
- go to the HRW Web site
- ask a librarian or media specialist for suggestions
- read some book reviews
- look for a new book by one of your favorite authors

SKILLS FOCUS

Analyze a short story. Choose a topic to write about. Confer with teachers to generate ideas. Analyze published examples as models for writing.

Preview of Coming Attractions   Once you have found several possible choices for your book review, **preview** each one to make your final decision. One student previewed *Tuck Everlasting* by Natalie Babbitt by following the steps in the Thinking it Through below.

THINKING IT THROUGH   Previewing a Novel

▶ **STEP 1 Look at the cover.** Is there something that makes you interested in the book?

The front cover has a mysterious pair of eyes on it. The back cover has a quotation that makes me curious about the book.

▶ **STEP 2 Read the book jacket summary.** What does the summary tell you?

The story is about a young girl who is kidnapped by a family who drank from a spring that lets them live forever.

▶ **STEP 3 Skim some pages.** Do you like the way the characters are shown? Do you see any interesting action taking place?

There are lots of examples of dialogue, and I like to hear the characters talking. Somebody escapes from jail.

▶ **STEP 4 Consider what you have found.** Does the book look interesting? Do you want to know more about the characters?

Yes, I want to know more about these characters. I think that this is a good choice for me.

| KEY CONCEPT

Read Your Novel

SKILLS FOCUS

Preview a text. Identify and analyze literary elements. *(page 615):* Create notes to enhance comprehension of text. Decide on a purpose for writing. Plan writing by targeting an audience.

Please Note . . .   As you read the book you have chosen, remember that you will be writing about it later. Keep nearby a sheet of paper divided into three columns. Label the columns *plot, setting,* and *main character.* Fill in the columns by answering the questions at the top of the next page as you read. Include page numbers next to important notes. The page numbers will help you if you need to go back and re-read some sections of the novel.

Plot	Setting	Main Character
■ What are the key events of each chapter? ■ What problem does the main character face? ■ How is the problem solved?	■ Where does the story take place? ■ When does the story take place? ■ How much time passes in the story?	■ Name: ■ Age: ■ What does the character look like? ■ What does the character like to do or play or eat?

YOUR TURN 4 **Selecting and Reading a Novel**

Brainstorm a list of the types of novels you like to read. Follow the Thinking It Through steps on page 614 to preview a few novels and choose one that you think you will enjoy. Then, read your book and take notes in a three-column chart based on your answers to the questions above. Save your notes for later.

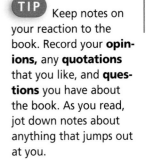

TIP Keep notes on your reaction to the book. Record your **opinions,** any **quotations** that you like, and **questions** you have about the book. As you read, jot down notes about anything that jumps out at you.

Think About Purpose and Audience

The Big Picture You have read your book and are ready to tell people what you think. Before you begin, think about

■ the **purpose** of your book review
■ the people who will be reading it (your **audience**)

Your purpose for writing a book review will be closely linked to your audience and to *their* purpose for reading the review. Here are some questions and possible responses to help you think about your audience and their purpose.

Who is the audience for my book review?	Why might these people read my book review?	What types of information might interest my audience?
classmates	to decide whether to read a book	What is the book about?
community librarian	to decide whether to get a book for the library	What type of book is it? (mystery, fantasy, western, general fiction, and so on)
parents	to decide if a book is right for younger readers	How easy (or difficult) is it to read?
gift shoppers	to decide whether to buy a book as a gift	How much does it cost?

The audience for the review of *Tuck Everlasting* will be the student's classmates. Their purpose for reading will be to decide whether to read the book themselves. This audience will probably want to know what the book is about, but not how it ends. They might also be interested in knowing how easy or difficult the book is to read.

YOUR TURN 5 Thinking About Purpose and Audience

Use the chart at the bottom of page 615 to help you consider your audience and their purpose for reading your review.

Gather and Organize Details

You Get the Idea If you want people to read the book you have chosen, you need to say more about it than "It's good." You need to give them a *summary* of the book. A **summary** of a piece of writing includes only the key ideas of the piece. When you summarize a novel, you will briefly retell the important events. The notes that you took while you read your novel and the instructions on page 618 will help you write your summary.

There Is More to the Story If a story were plot alone, it would not be much fun to read. Readers will be more interested in plot events if they know something about the people and places involved. When you write a summary, include a description of the characters and the setting. The chart below contains examples from *Tuck Everlasting*.

Character	Who is the main character? What is he or she like?	The main character is Winnie. She is a spoiled only child who is bored and tired of being told what to do.
Setting	Where and when does the story take place?	The novel is set in 1880 in the village of Treegap.
Plot	What problem does the main character face? How does he or she deal with the problem?	Winnie has to decide if she should keep the Tucks' secret—the fountain the Tucks drink from that gives them eternal life. She decides to help them. Helping them makes her brave.

Identifying the Elements of a Plot

Once upon a Time Most fairy tales begin with "Once upon a time . . ." and end with ". . . happily ever after." The plot in between is usually easy to follow. Novels, on the other hand, usually have a more complicated plot. However, they, too, follow a plot pattern.

- Most stories begin with a **basic situation** in which you learn about the characters and the setting.

- The main character usually runs into a **conflict,** or problem, early in the story.

- This problem sets in motion a series of events, or **complications,** that make up the action of the story.

- All of these events build to a high point, the **climax.** The climax is the most exciting moment in the plot.

- Following the climax is the **resolution,** or outcome. In this part of the story, we see how everything works out for the main character.

A **plot line** helps you figure out all the important steps of a plot. Below is an example of a plot line for *Tuck Everlasting.*

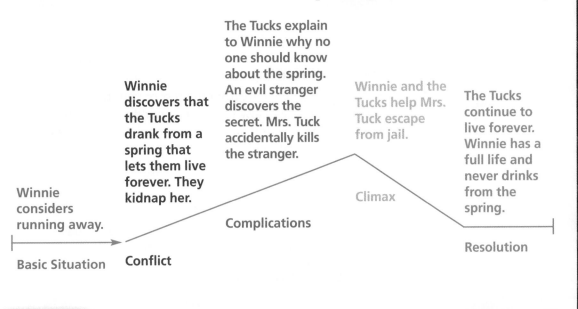

The Tucks explain to Winnie why no one should know about the spring. An evil stranger discovers the secret. Mrs. Tuck accidentally kills the stranger.

Winnie discovers that the Tucks drank from a spring that lets them live forever. They kidnap her.

Winnie and the Tucks help Mrs. Tuck escape from jail.

The Tucks continue to live forever. Winnie has a full life and never drinks from the spring.

Winnie considers running away.

Climax

Complications

Basic Situation   Conflict

Resolution

PRACTICE

Create a plot line for the novel that you read.
(**Hint:** As you decide which events are the most important, think about what sticks out in your mind. What are the events that any reader would need to know for the story to make sense?)

Order! Order! You may want to begin your summary with details about character and setting. Then you can start summarizing the plot. Follow **chronological order,** telling what happens in the beginning and middle of the novel but do not tell how the novel ends, unless your audience is a group (such as librarians) who would prefer to know. **When you write your summary, use transitions like *first, next,* and *last* to link the details of the plot together.**

KEY CONCEPT

YOUR TURN 6 Gathering and Organizing Details

Record details from your reading notes about plot, main character, and setting in a chart like the one on page 616. Put a number next to each detail in your chart to show the order in which you will present the details when you write your summary.

Designing Your Writing

Highlighting a Quotation Book reviews sometimes highlight a quotation from the book. The stand-alone quotation sparks the reader's curiosity. To include a quotation, follow these guidelines.

- Select a quotation by thinking about what the main character says or does at an important moment in the book.
- Set the quotation apart from the rest of your book review by placing it directly below your title and indenting it on both sides. List the title and author of the book beneath the quotation, indented on the left side. Here is an example.

> A Review of Natalie Babbitt's <u>Tuck Everlasting</u>
>
> She would try very hard not to think of it, but sometimes, as now, it would be forced upon her. She raged against it, helpless and insulted, and blurted at last, "I don't want to die."
>
> <u>Tuck Everlasting,</u> by Natalie Babbitt
>
> If you could live forever just by drinking water, would you do it? The Tuck family unknowingly does just that in Natalie Babbitt's fantasy novel <u>Tuck Everlasting</u>. . . .

Preparing Your Evaluation

Four Stars ★★★★   After you have prepared notes for your book's summary, you should think about your *evaluation.* The evaluation is the last part of a book review. In an **evaluation,** you

- tell readers why you like or dislike the book
- include a recommendation to read or not to read the book

It is important to know whether or not you would recommend the book. After all, you want your **point of view,** or attitude, about the book to come across throughout your review. Also, remember who your audience is when you make your recommendation. For example, you might think a book is too easy to read, but if your audience is younger readers, the reading level might be just right for them.

Here are two example evaluations based on *Tuck Everlasting.*

> The question of whether Winnie would drink from the spring remained open through the whole book. I could tell she might go either way, so the suspense was great. I enjoyed watching Winnie discover a world beyond her sheltered life. I would recommend <u>Tuck Everlasting</u> to readers who wonder what it might be like to live forever and who like suspense and fantasy.

> Winnie's conflict over whether she would tell the Tucks' secret ended early in the book. From then on, I knew exactly how the book would end, and I found too many parts of the story unbelievable. I thought Winnie was weak and boring. She liked rules and order too much, and she hated getting dirty. I would not recommend the book except to big fans of fantasy.

TIP Your **voice** shows your **point of view,** or attitude, about the book. Use positive words for characters and events that you like. Use negative words to describe characters you do not like and parts of the plot that do not work. For more on **point of view,** see page 609.

YOUR TURN 7 Preparing Your Evaluation

Write an evaluation of the young adult novel you read for your book review. State clearly why you like or dislike the book and whether you think others should read the book or not.

SKILLS FOCUS

Develop an interpretation. Justify an interpretation using textual evidence. Plan writing by developing voice. Use connotation and denotation in writing.

Book Review

Framework	Think as a Reader/Writer
Introduction ■ Attention grabber ■ Statement of author and title	Get your readers' attention by **introducing the topic of the book** in an interesting way. You may use a quotation, dialogue, a question, a metaphor or simile, or a slice of action to get your readers' attention. Be sure to identify the **author and title.** You might also tell readers what **type of book** it is: mystery, fantasy, historical fiction, and so on.

Body
■ Summary
   Details about setting
   Details about main character
   Details about plot
	A **plot summary** should follow **chronological,** or time, **order.** Start with the beginning events, followed by the middle events, but do not reveal the novel's ending unless you think your audience would prefer to know it.
	
	Use **transition** words to give your paper *coherence.* In a **coherent** composition, one idea flows logically to the next. For more on **transitions,** see page 453.

Conclusion
■ Evaluation
   Reason
   Recommendation
	Write your **evaluation.** Give readers at least one **reason** why you like or dislike the book. Finally, make a **recommendation** to your readers: Should they read the book or not?

YOUR TURN 8   Drafting Your Book Review

Now it is your turn to draft a book review. As you write,

■ keep your audience in mind

■ refer to the framework above and the Writer's Model on the next page

A Writer's Model

The final draft below closely follows the framework for a book review.

TIP The highlighted words show the writer's point of view about the book's main character.

A Review of
Natalie Babbitt's *Tuck Everlasting*

If you could live forever just by drinking water, would you do it? The Tuck family unknowingly does just that in Natalie Babbitt's fantasy novel *Tuck Everlasting*. Living forever is complicated, though, especially when other people discover the secret.

Winnie, a lonely, sheltered, and spoiled only child, lives in a house at the edge of a village called Treegap. One hot August day in 1880, she discovers the Tuck family and the magic spring that lets them live forever. The Tucks are kindhearted, but they do not want anyone to know their secret. To keep Winnie from telling what she has seen, the Tucks kidnap her and take her to their home. There, Mr. Tuck explains why no one else should know about the spring. He feels that living forever is a lonely and empty experience. No one has ever talked to Winnie about such important things before. Winnie begins to see the world a bit differently and becomes friends with the Tucks. The next day, however, an evil stranger threatens to tell the secret. Mrs. Tuck gets upset and accidentally kills the man when he tries to take Winnie away. The Treegap constable takes Mrs. Tuck to jail. Next, Winnie bravely helps rescue Mrs. Tuck from jail. Winnie courageously struggles with some tough decisions. For starters, she must decide whether to keep the Tucks' secret. She also faces the opportunity to drink from the spring and live forever with the Tucks.

Tuck Everlasting is excellent. It is full of suspense as Winnie makes choices, takes risks, and learns about life. Although it is a fantasy book, it contains some truths about life. I recommend it to anyone who has ever dreamed about living forever or has had to make a tough choice.

Attention grabber

Statement of author and title

Summary: Details about main character

Details about setting

Details about plot

Evaluation and reason

Recommendation

A Student's Model

When you write a book review, you want your point of view about the book to be obvious. Diana DeGarmo, a sixth-grade student from Sand Springs, Oklahoma, makes her feelings known by clearly describing the main character and her situation in the following book review.

A Review of
Out of the Storm by Patricia Willis

Attention grabber

When single mother Vera lost her job in Garnet Creek, the family had to move to a new town.

Statement of author and title

Patricia Willis, author of *Out of the Storm*, wrote this story from the viewpoint of Mandy, Vera's twelve-year-old daughter.

Summary

Mom and nine-year-old Ira adjusted to the new setting quickly, but Mandy resented everything about their new location. She held on to a dream that she and her deceased father had, and that dream prevented her from accepting her new life. She resented living with grumpy Aunt Bess and detested having to tend the sheep.

Mandy lived with her unhappiness and pitied herself until several incidents happened that made her realize that she was not the only kid who did not have a perfect life. She also found that others had dreams and perhaps by forgetting herself and helping someone else, she might find real happiness.

Evaluation

I think if a reader is looking for a book that tells of a family's struggle to live, *Out of the Storm* by Patricia Willis would be a good choice. I really liked this book because it showed characters learning to tough out bad situations. I also like the book's motto, "Sometimes it takes something Bad to make you see the Good."

Revising

Evaluate and Revise Content, Organization, and Style

A Second Look Once you have written a first draft, you need to think about how to improve it. Do this by taking a break from your review and then reading the draft twice. In the first reading, focus on your ideas. Do they make sense? Are they in the right order? The guidelines below will help you decide. In the second reading, look at your words and sentences. The Focus on Word Choice on page 625 will help you.

> **COMPUTER TIP**
>
> If you use a computer to write your review, you can use the underlining feature for Tips 1, 3, and 5. For Tip 2, highlight or color the text on your screen.

▶ **First Reading: Content and Organization** Use the following chart to evaluate and revise your book review.

Guidelines for Self-Evaluation and Peer Evaluation		
Evaluation Questions	**Tips**	**Revision Techniques**
❶ Does the introduction grab the reader's attention and give the book's author and title?	**Put a check mark** next to any interesting statements. **Underline** the title and author of the book.	**Add** a quotation, question, or interesting statement to the introduction. **Add** the book's title and author if necessary.
❷ Does the summary include information about the book's setting and main character?	**Highlight** the book's setting. **Draw a wavy line** under information about the main character.	**Elaborate** with details about the book's setting and main character.
❸ Does the summary retell the book's major plot events? Does it give details that would interest readers?	**Put a star** next to each major plot event. **Underline** any information that would appeal to the review's audience.	**Delete** unimportant plot events and information. **Add** any important plot events missing from the summary.
❹ Does the summary show how the major events are connected?	**Draw a box around** each word that shows how the events are related.	**Add** transition words or **rearrange** events to make their order clearer.
❺ Does the conclusion include a clear evaluation with at least one reason? Does it include a recommendation?	**Underline** the evaluation. **Draw two lines** under the reason or reasons given for it. **Circle** the recommendation.	**Add** reasons to the evaluation, if necessary. **Add** a recommendation, if necessary.

Quick guide

ONE WRITER'S REVISIONS This revision is an early draft of the book review on page 621.

elaborate

, a lonely, sheltered, and spoiled only child,
Winnie lives in a house at the edge of a village called Treegap. One hot August day in 1880, she discovers the Tuck family and the magic spring that lets them live for-

delete

ever. ~~She had been following a frog into the forest.~~ The Tucks are kindhearted, but they do not want anyone to

add

know their secret. *To keep Winnie from telling what she has seen, the Tucks kidnap her and take her to their home.*

PEER REVIEW

If you are evaluating a peer's book review, ask yourself these questions:

- Do I understand what the book is about?
- Do I know what the writer thinks of the book?
- Does the book review make me want to read the book? Why or why not?

Think as a Reader/Writer

1. Why do you think the writer elaborated by adding words to the first sentence?
2. Why do you think the writer deleted a sentence from the paragraph above?
3. Why do you think the writer added the last sentence?

▶ **Second Reading: Style** Now that you have looked at the big picture, it is time to focus on your sentences. There are many ways to edit sentences. One way is to eliminate *clichés*. **Clichés** are expressions that have been used so often they have lost their original meaning. When you hear or read a cliché, you probably do not even bother to picture the image in your mind. As a writer, the last thing you want is to have your readers ignore your ideas.

When you evaluate your book review for clarity and originality, ask yourself whether your writing contains any overused words or phrases—ones that you have heard so often that their original meanings seem lost. As you re-read your review, circle every word or phrase that you think is a cliché. Then, replace each cliché with your own words.

SKILLS FOCUS

Evaluate others' writing. Develop writer's style. *(page 623):* Evaluate one's own writing. Revise by adding or replacing text. Revise by rearranging text. Revise by elaborating. Revise by deleting text.

Clichés

When you are writing about a book you have read, you may want to use certain familiar expressions. However, clichés will weaken the punch of your writing. Here are some examples of clichés. See if you can think of others.

It is **raining cats and dogs.**   She is **as busy as a bee.**

Replacing clichés with more original wording will make your meaning clearer and your writing more interesting.

The rain is pummeling the ground.

She zips around from 7:00 A.M. until 7:00 P.M. each day.

ONE WRITER'S REVISIONS

There, Mr. Tuck explains why no one else should

know about the spring. He feels that living forever is

a lonely and empty experience.

~~no bowl of cherries.~~

Think as a Reader/Writer

How did replacing the cliché "bowl of cherries" with another phrase improve the sentence above?

YOUR TURN 9

Evaluating and Revising Your Book Review

- First, evaluate and revise the content and organization of your review by using the guidelines on page 623.

- Next, replace any clichés in your writing. Use the guidelines on page 624 and the Focus on Word Choice above to help you.

- If a peer read your paper, think carefully about his or her comments before you revise.

SKILLS FOCUS

Revise to refine word choice.

Publishing

Proofread Your Book Review

Getting It Right   Now you need to proofread, or **edit,** your book review. If you have too many errors in your book review, your readers may not take your recommendation seriously. To make sure you catch every error, also have a classmate proofread your review.

Grammar Link

Using Appositives

An **appositive** is a noun or pronoun that identifies or describes another noun or pronoun. An **appositive phrase** includes an appositive and its modifiers. Appositives and appositive phrases often answer the question *Who?* or *What?*

Appositive: My Spanish teacher, **Ms. Alvarez,** was born in Cuba. [*Ms. Alvarez* identifies *who* the Spanish teacher is.]

Appositive Phrase: I am interested in geology, **the study of the earth and rocks.** [*The study of the earth and rocks* explains *what* geology is.]

Appositives that are not essential to the sentence are set off with **commas.**

Our new gym teacher**, Mr. Samson,** trained as a gymnast. [The name *Mr. Samson* is extra information. Commas must be used to set it off.]

Commas are not needed if the appositive is essential to the meaning of the sentence.

My brother **Abdul** wants to be a gymnast. [The speaker has more than one brother.]

PRACTICE

Copy the sentences below on your own paper. Underline the appositive in each sentence, and insert commas where needed.

Example:

1. Last week I read *Tuck Everlasting* a novel about living forever.

1. *Last week I read* Tuck Everlasting**,** *a novel about living forever* .

1. The novel a fantasy for young adults is set a long time ago in a small village.

2. The main character Winnie Foster learns many things in the book.

3. Angus Tuck head of the Tuck family talks to Winnie about the loneliness of living forever.

4. Mae Tuck a character in the book accidentally kills a man.

5. The Tucks' son Jesse wants Winnie to drink from the spring. (They have two sons.)

For more information and practice on **punctuating appositives,** see page 318.

Publish Your Book Review

Read All About It   Finally, your book review is finished. Your goal was to write a review that would inform others about a book. How will you get your audience to read your review? Here are some suggestions.

■ Find a Web site or online bookstore that asks for reader reviews of young adult literature, and send in your review.

■ Create a reading suggestion bulletin board in your classroom. Post a copy of your book review there. If you have access to a school Web site, help create a Web page for all the book reviews written by your classmates.

■ Deliver your book review as an **oral response** to the novel. Summarize the book for your listeners, and then explain your evaluation. Be sure to provide clear reasons why you like or dislike the book.

Reflect on Your Book Review

PORTFOLIO

Building Your Portfolio   Take time to think about your book review now that it is finished. What did you learn from it? Good writers are always learning from their writing. You can, too, by answering the following questions.

■ What did you find easy or difficult about writing a summary?

■ When else could you use summary writing?

■ Which evaluation guideline (page 623) was most helpful in evaluating and revising your book review? Why?

YOUR TURN 10 Proofreading, Publishing, and Reflecting on Your Book Review

■ Correct any punctuation, spelling, or grammar errors in your book review. Look closely at any appositives you used.

■ Publish your book review so that others can read it.

■ Answer the questions from Reflect on Your Book Review above. Record your responses in a learning log, or include them in your portfolio.

Connections to Literature

Writing a Short Story

Like a novel, a short story has characters, a setting, and a conflict. Because short stories are usually only a few pages long, they deal with just a few characters, a single setting, and a simple plot. As a result, short stories often seem more focused than novels. The challenge in writing a short story is getting the focus just right. Here is an opportunity to write your own short story.

Read All About It   Read the beginning of the story "Ta-Na-E-Ka." Notice how the writer introduces the main character, setting, and conflict.

As my birthday drew closer, I had awful nightmares about it. I was reaching the age at which all Kaw Indians had to participate in Ta-Na-E-Ka. Well, not all Kaws. Many of the younger families on the reservation were beginning to give up the old customs. But my grandfather, Amos Deer Leg, was devoted to tradition. He still wore handmade beaded moccasins instead of shoes and kept his iron-gray hair in tight braids. He could speak English, but he spoke it only with white men. With his family he used a Sioux dialect. . . .

Eleven was a magic word among the Kaws. It was the time of Ta-Na-E-Ka, the "flowering of adulthood." It was the age, my grandfather informed us hundreds of times, "when a boy could prove himself to be a warrior and a girl took the first steps to womanhood."

"I don't want to be a warrior," my cousin Roger Deer Leg confided to me. "I'm going to become an accountant."

"None of the other tribes make girls go through the endurance ritual," I complained to my mother.

Mary Whitebird, "Ta-Na-E-Ka"

Plot a Course   Every project needs a plan. Here is a plan to help you write your story.

1. **Brainstorm characters, settings, and conflicts.** Make a chart like the one below to generate ideas. For each column, think of all the possibilities you can imagine. One example is given.

Main Character	Setting	Conflict
Hector, an 11-year-old detective	a shopping mall	A storm knocks out all the electricity.

2. **Choose a main character, a setting, and a conflict.** To create a story beginning, select one idea from each column in your chart. You can mix and match, choosing the character, setting, and conflict that give you the most interesting ideas.

3. **Generate details about character and setting.** To come up with details, answer the following questions.

Main Character	■ What does he or she like to do?
	■ How old is the character?
	■ What does he or she look like?
Setting	■ Where does the story take place?
	■ When does the story take place?
	■ What **sensory details** will help the reader imagine the setting?

4. **Map out the plot of your story.** Think of details for your plot, using the questions that follow. You may want to use a plot line like the one shown on page 617.

Questions:
■ What events happen because of the conflict?
■ How can you create **suspense,** keeping the reader wondering what will happen next?
■ What happens first, second, or later?
■ What event will be the climax?
■ How will the conflict be settled?

Getting Started Once you map out your plot, start writing. If you need help getting started, look again at the first paragraphs of "Ta-Na-E-Ka." You may find it easier to begin in the middle of your story, and then write the beginning and the ending. Finally, remember that a good story has suspense, dialogue, description, and sensory details, and that its resolution ties up loose ends.

YOUR TURN 11 Writing a Short Story

Write a draft of a short story by following the steps you have just read. Exchange your draft with a partner. Read your partner's draft and look for the story elements of character, setting, and plot. Are any missing? Share your ideas with your partner. Then, revise your story as necessary.

After you have written the story, consider preparing a **dramatic interpretation** of it or a **play** based on it to present to your class. (For information on **dramatic interpretation,** see page 759 in the Quick Reference Handbook.)

Writing an Essay About a Poem's Sound Effects

Poets play with words to give their readers new ways of looking at the world. In just a few words, a poem can express a wealth of meanings. Many poems rely partly on the sounds of words to convey meaning. You can recognize and appreciate a poem's **sound effects** when you understand some of the special techniques poets use. In this section, you will choose a poem and write an essay analyzing its sound effects.

Sound Effect Check Poets often choose and arrange words to create sound effects. They may try to imitate a specific sound (such as the wind's howling or a bee's buzzing) or to create a mood (such as excitement or joy). Sound effects may provide a clue to a poem's meaning. Three kinds of sound effects are rhyme, rhythm, and repetition.

Rhyme is the repetition of vowel sounds and all sounds following them.

shelf and *elf*   *comb* and *gnome*

Rhyme is used to emphasize ideas, organize the poem, and entertain the reader.

Rhythm is a musical quality created by the repetition of stressed (´) and unstressed (˘) syllables in a line or by the repetition of certain sounds.

You may notice the rhythm of words when you talk. Poets sometimes empha-

size the rhythm and pattern of words to imitate actions described in the poem.

> Hŏw dóth thĕ líttlĕ crócŏdíle
> Ĭmpróve hĭs shíning táil,
> Ănd poúr thĕ wáters ŏf thĕ Níle
> Ŏn évery góldĕn scále!
>
> Lewis Carroll,
> "How Doth the Little Crocodile"

Repetition is the effect of repeating a word, phrase, or line throughout a poem. Repetition creates rhythm, helps organize a poem, and emphasizes feelings or ideas. Notice the repetition in the following poem.

> Last night I dreamed of chickens,
> there were chickens everywhere,
> they were standing on my stomach,
> they were nesting in my hair,
> they were pecking at my pillow,
> they were hopping on my head,
> they were ruffling up their feathers
> as they raced about my bed.
>
> Jack Prelutsky,
> "Last Night I Dreamed of Chickens"

Jump In Read the poem on the next page. What sound effects can you find? (Hint: Read the poem aloud, and listen.)

Whenever the moon and stars are set,
  Whenever the wind is high,
All night long in the dark and wet,
  A man goes riding by.
Late in the night when the fires are out,   5
Why does he gallop and gallop about?

Whenever the trees are crying aloud,
  And ships are tossed at sea,
By, on the highway, low and loud,
  By at the gallop goes he.   10
By at the gallop he goes, and then
By he comes back at the gallop again.

Robert Louis Stevenson, "Windy Nights"

First Impressions In order to analyze a poem's sound effects, you need to hear them. Read the poem aloud, and jot down your impressions or feelings about it. The following questions can help you identify your response to any poem. Sample responses to "Windy Nights" are provided.

- What did you think about when you read the poem? I thought about a windy night and the sounds that the wind makes.

- Do you like the poem? Why or why not? Yes, I like the way it repeats words.

A Closer Look Now, re-read the poem, listening more closely to its sound effects. Think about the following questions as you re-read the poem. Find examples in the poem to answer the questions. (Note the line numbers where you find your examples. You will need to use those examples for support in your essay.)

- Does the poem use rhyme?
- Does the poem have rhythm?
- Does the poem use repetition?
- What do the sound effects add to the poem? Would the poem be as effective without the sound effects?

What's the Plan? By now, you have a lot of information about the poem. You know what you think about it and the sound effects it uses. The next step is to organize your ideas before you draft your essay. Use the notes that you have taken on the poem, and put your ideas in a graphic organizer like the one below.

Introduction
- **Mention the poem's title and author.**
- **Explain what the poem is about—summarize major events, ideas, or images.**

Body
- **Explain your conclusion about how sound effects are used in the poem.**
- **Provide one quotation or example from the poem as evidence for each type of sound effect.**

Conclusion
- **State whether you like the poem.**
- **Explain why you do or do not like it.**

For Example   Below is an analysis of the sound effects in "Windy Nights." Notice that the writer mentions the three kinds of sound effects in the poem and provides examples with their line numbers.

"Windy Nights" by Robert Louis Stevenson is a poem about the noises of a windy night. The poet talks about a man riding a horse, but he is really talking about the wind. The sound effects in the poem help me hear and feel a windy night.

The poem uses rhyme, rhythm, and repetition. The rhyming words are in a regular pattern. For example, the words at the ends of every other line rhyme ("set" and "wet" in lines 1 and 3). Then, there are two rhymes in the last two lines of each stanza ("out" and "about" in lines 5 and 6). This reminds me of the way the wind keeps coming back over and over. The rhythm of the poem also reminds me of the wind. Words like "whenever" (lines 1, 2, and 7) and "gallop" (lines 6, 10, 11, and 12) have the rhythm of a galloping horse. The repetition of these words makes the idea of the wind seem even stronger. The repetition of the word "by" in the last four lines makes me think of a night when the wind will not stop.

I like the poem "Windy Nights." At first, I did not know why the poet talks about a man riding. Then, the repetition of the word "gallop" made me realize that the rider is the wind. I like the way the sound of the poem makes the meaning come alive.

YOUR TURN 12 **Writing About a Poem's Sound Effects**

■ Find a poem that contains sound effects. (Ask your teacher or librarian to help you.) Jot down your response to the poem. How do the sound effects help express the poem's meaning?

■ Use the questions and the graphic organizer on page 631 to prepare a short essay that analyzes the sound effects in the poem.

■ Revise your essay and check your final copy for spelling, punctuation, and grammar errors. (If you wish, present your ideas as an **oral response to literature** instead.)

Comparing Media: Film, TV, and Literature

WHAT'S AHEAD?

In this section you will compare a book and a film or TV show of the same type. You will also learn how to

- identify the elements of a novel and techniques used in a film
- make generalizations about a genre

"I will wait until the movie comes out." So many books are made into films that you might be tempted to stop reading and only see movies. What would you lose if you did that? Books, movies, and television all tell stories, but they tell them in different ways.

Read the Book and Watch the Show

Use Your Critical Eye For this workshop you will work with a partner to compare the main characters in books and movies or TV shows of the same type or *genre*. **Genre** (zh än′rə) is a French word meaning "type" or "class." Works of the same genre share certain characteristics. For example, the main character in detective novels, films, and TV shows is often a private investigator who has one faithful friend but who tends to make other people angry. The investigator also shows great determination, especially if he or she gets injured while trying to solve the mystery.

Other genres include fantasy/science fiction, westerns, animal stories, war/spy stories, sports stories, and historical fiction. Can you think of an example for each of these genres?

Be Choosy With your partner, select a genre. From that genre, each of you should select a book that you have read before. Then, you should each watch a different film or TV show from the same genre. The following chart will give you some ideas.

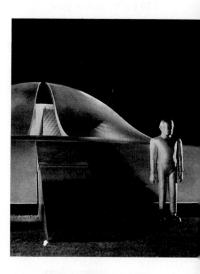

Possible Book and Movie/TV Combinations by Genre		
Genre	**Books**	**Movies/TV Shows**
Science Fiction Stories	*Fantastic Voyage* by Isaac Asimov	*The Day the Earth Stood Still*
	The Time Machine by H. G. Wells	*Star Trek*
Animal Stories	*Call of the Wild* by Jack London	*Wild America*
	The Yearling by Marjorie Kinnan Rawlings	*Fly Away Home*
War Stories	*Number the Stars* by Lois Lowry	*The Diary of Anne Frank*
	Zlata's Diary by Zlata Filipovic	*Empire of the Sun*
Sports Stories	*Hoops* by Walter Dean Myers	*Brian's Song*
	The Contender by Robert Lipsyte	*Wild Hearts Can't Be Broken*
Mysteries	*I Am the Cheese* by Robert Cormier	*Fairy Tale: A True Story*
	The A.I. Gang: Operation Sherlock by Bruce Coville	*From the Mixed-Up Files of Mrs. Basil E. Frankweiler*
Westerns	*Jimmy Spoon and the Pony Express* by Kristiana Gregory	*Shane*
	The Long Chance by Max Brand	*Gunsmoke*

TIP Rent the video or check it out from the library. If you do not see a combination that you like in the chart above, talk to a librarian or your teacher to get suggestions.

Reading at the Movies   Books, TV, and films have their own **media languages**—special ways of making meaning. The boldface terms below give you some of the language *you* will need to talk about the effects of these media.

How to Be a Character   To create a believable character, a writer uses *characterization*. **Characterization** is the process of showing a character's personality. The writer can directly tell you what a character is like by using **description.** Writers can also indirectly show you what a character is like. When a writer uses **narration** (telling the events of a story) to tell us what a character is doing, for example, we get ideas about that character's personality. Another way that writers give us indirect information about character is through **dialogue.**

Like novelists, filmmakers and TV writers use narration and dialogue. Films and TV, though, have some additional techniques for showing character.

- **Facial expression and body movement:** Close-ups of actors' faces help reveal characters' feelings. A character may show confidence or fear by the way she walks. A nervous character might constantly wiggle a foot or play with a pen while he is talking.

- **Sound:** Music can be used to say something about characters. For example, the appearance of a threatening character may be accompanied by scary music. A filmmaker may also use different types of music to reflect a character's changing moods.

Tools of the Trade The Venn diagram below reviews some of the tools available to writers, TV show producers, and filmmakers. As you read the book and watch the TV show or movie you have chosen, think about how these tools are used to create character as well as other elements, such as setting and conflict.

writer   both   TV/filmmaker

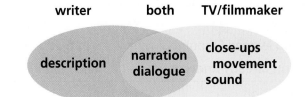

description   narration dialogue   close-ups movement sound

Compare the Book and Movie or TV Show

What's the Difference? After you have read your book and watched your movie or TV show, you will compare the main characters in your two examples. The following charts compare the main characters in two fairy tales: a print version of "Sleeping Beauty" and a TV movie version of *Cinderella*. Make similar charts for the book and film or TV show you chose.

SKILLS FOCUS

Understand how media tools enhance communication. Understand how motion enhances communication. Understand how music enhances communication.

Story: "Sleeping Beauty" by Charles Perrault	
Main Character and Description	**Techniques Used to Create Element**
The princess: She is lovely, sweet tempered, and clever. She sings and dances. She doesn't do much in the story, but everyone loves her.	Description: The princess is described to us. Narration: The narrator explains what happens to the princess, who does not take any action. Dialogue: There are only a few lines of dialogue, and they don't tell us much.

Movie: *Cinderella*	
Main Character and Description	**Techniques Used to Create Element**
Cinderella: She is pretty, sweet, and kind, but her costumes are plain and tattered. She wants to be treated with respect.	Narration: The fairy godmother narrates what is happening. Facial expressions: Close-ups of Cinderella show her sadness when her family treats her badly and her joy when she dances with the prince. Sound: Cinderella sings happy songs when she is happy. She also sings songs that tell us about her dreams. Dialogue: The things she says tell us how she feels.

Reference Note

For more on **generalizations,** see page 739 in the Quick Reference Handbook.

Once you have completed your chart, get together with your partner to make a generalization about the main character in the genre you chose. To make a **generalization**—a statement about the general characteristics of something—use the equation below.

What you learned (about main character in that genre)

\+ What you already know

Generalization

Here is a generalization about the main character in a fairy tale.

> The main character in a fairy tale is often a girl who is sweet and beautiful and loves to sing.

This generalization can be supported by information in the chart, plus what the student's partner discovered, plus what both students know from hearing other fairy tales.

 **Comparing Media and Making Generalizations**

Choose a book and a movie or TV show from the same genre. Follow the steps on pages 633–636 to make a chart comparing the main characters in the book and the movie or TV show. Then, working with a partner, make a generalization about the main characters in that genre. Support your generalization with evidence from your partner's and your own charts.

SKILLS FOCUS

Make generalizations from a text. Assess how language, media, and presentation contribute to message.

22 *Choices*

Choose one of the following activities to complete.

▶ **VIEWING AND REPRESENTING**

1. More than One Way
Respond to a movie that made a strong impression—good or bad—on you. Choose one of these options:

- Present an **oral review,** using the same strategies you used in your book review.
- Express your thoughts about the movie in a **poem** or a one-paragraph **reflection.**

▶ **WRITING**

2. That's What I Think
Share your thoughts about a novel by writing **e-mails** or **letters** to a pen pal. Discuss the main character, setting, and plot, as well as your reactions. Discuss your pen pal's book, too. Write at least two letters or e-mails each.

▶ **CONNECTING CULTURES**

3. It's a Small World The German "Aschenputtel," the Chinese "Yeh-Shen," and the English "Cinderella" are different versions of the same story. Read them, or read several versions of another story. Create **charts** comparing the stories' characters, settings, and plot events.

▶ **TECHNOLOGY**

4. Virtual Critic
Collaborate with a group to create a **database** of reports on educational computer games. As a group, decide which elements to evaluate or rank (sound effects, difficulty level, graphics, and so on). Then, create **forms** for evaluating the games. Each member should then choose a game, play it, and complete the form. Once you have all the information, the group will create a database **record** about each of those games.

▶ **CREATIVE WRITING**

5. All Together Now
Collaborate with a group of classmates in writing an original **short story** in response to a work you have all read. Each person in the group should write a paragraph. Discuss and revise the paragraphs as a group. Read your final version to the class, and discuss your experience of working as a group.

PORTFOLIO

SKILLS FOCUS

Present oral messages. Write short stories or poems. Write to reflect on ideas. Correspond with writers by e-mail. Write a letter. Summarize and organize information from one or more sources by taking notes, outlining ideas, and making charts. Interact with writers to reflect the practical use of writing.

23 | Sharing Your Research

Reading Workshop

Reading an Informative Article

Writing Workshop

Writing a Research Report

Speaking and Listening

Giving and Evaluating a Research Presentation

Informational Text

Exposition

You just heard the greatest album of all time. You want to know everything about the group—Where are they from? How do they get ideas for songs? What other recordings have they made? Finding answers to these questions requires research.

From sixth-graders to research scientists, people need to find and share information with others. One way for people to share this information is by writing a research report. Research reports are based on reliable sources—experts, informative books or articles, videos, or Internet sources. A research report writer pulls together information from different sources and presents it along with his or her own thoughts on a subject.

YOUR TURN 1 Seeking Information

With a few classmates, make a list of some subjects you have researched in the past, such as a hobby or sport, something in nature, or an interesting person. Then, discuss these questions:

- What sources did your group use to find information?
- Which sources were easy to use? Why? Which sources were difficult to use? Why?

internet**connect**

go. hrw .com

GO TO: go.hrw.com
KEYWORD: EOLang 6-23

Reading an Informative Article

In this section you will read an informative article. You will also learn how to

- **draw conclusions**
- **recognize an author's purpose for writing**

What is a gold rush? Who were the original Forty-Niners? Why is California known as "the Golden State"? You will find the answers to these questions and more as you read "The California Gold Rush," the informative article on the next page.

Preparing to Read

READING SKILL

Making Inferences: Drawing Conclusions An **inference** is an idea a reader forms, based in part on what he or she has read, seen, or experienced. One type of inference is a *conclusion*. Readers draw **conclusions** by putting together the pieces of information a writer presents and adding their own knowledge to that information. For example, details such as an eye patch, a wooden leg, and a parrot perched on a person's shoulder are clues that can lead readers to conclude that the person being described is a pirate. As you read the following article, try to draw conclusions about the gold rush in California.

READING FOCUS

Author's Purpose An **author's purpose** is the reason the author writes a piece. In the following article, Kathy Wilmore answers questions like these about the California gold rush: *Who was involved? What did they do? Why? How did it start? How did it turn out?* The fact that the article answers such questions gives you a clue about why the author wrote it.

Read the following selection. In a notebook, jot down answers to the numbered active-reading questions in the shaded boxes. Underlined words will be used in the Vocabulary Mini-Lesson on page 648.

from Junior Scholastic

THE CALIFORNIA

GOLD RUSH

BY KATHY WILMORE

1 For seventeen years—ever since leaving his New Jersey home at age eighteen—James Wilson Marshall kept moving farther and farther west in search of a better life. In 1845, he went to California, which was part of Mexico then, and things finally seemed to turn around for him. A businessman named John A. Sutter gave him a job building a sawmill in a remote wilderness area in northern California. Build it, Sutter told him, and you can run the place for me. Sutter was looking to make a tidy profit; Marshall was just hoping to make a living. But on January 24, 1848, Marshall was <u>momentarily</u> distracted from his work. A glint of light caught his eye—and sleepy California was never the same again.

1. Why do you think the author tells you so much about James Marshall?

"To See the Elephant"

2 In January 1848, California had a <u>population</u> of only 15,000 people. By the time December 1849 came around, the population was up to 100,000 and climbing. Why such a boom? Blame it on that glint that caught James Marshall's eye.

3 One cold and rainy day soon after, Marshall arrived at Sutter's house with "some important and interesting news." Sutter studied the stuff that Marshall had brought and

2. What was the glint that caught Marshall's eye?

realized it was gold. He was not happy.

4   "I told [my employees] that I would consider it as a great favor if they would keep this discovery secret only for six weeks, so I could finish [building] my large flour mill at Brighton. . . . [I]nstead of feeling happy and contented, I was very unhappy, and could not see that it would benefit me much, and I was perfectly right in thinking so."[1]

5   Sutter's employees promised not to tell, but word leaked out. . . .

6   By 1849, the gold rush was on. People poured into California from all points of the compass. They arrived by ship or overland trails, crossing North America by wagon train, riding horses or mules, and even on foot.

7   These hopeful thousands, the first large wave of whom arrived in 1849, were known as Forty-Niners. Many had sold everything they owned to pay their way to California.

3. Why were the first miners called Forty-Niners?

8   Ask a Forty-Niner why, and he or she was likely to reply, "I am going to see the elephant"—that is, to find something wonderful and rare.

---

1. From "The Discovery of Gold in California" by Gen. John A. Sutter, *Hutchings California Magazine* (November 1857).

"A Dog's Life"

Dreaming of gold was easy, but find-   9 ing it was anything but. Miners faced hours of strenuous work. Some were able to reach out and pick up a gold-filled nugget, but that was rare.

Most miners spent hours slam-   10 ming pickaxes into rocky soil, or scooping up panfuls of riverbed mud and rinsing it to find tiny grains of gold. They lived in rough, makeshift camps far from "civilization," with little shelter from cold mountain winds and rain. As William Swain described camp life in a letter sent home in 1850:

"George, I tell you this mining   11 among the mountains is a dog's life. . . . [T]his climate in the mines requires a consti- tution like iron. Often for weeks during the rainy season it is damp, cold, and sunless, and the labor of getting gold is of the most laborious kind. Exposure causes sickness to a great extent for, in most of the mines, tents are all the habitation [home] miners have."[2]

4. Why do you think the author includes quotes such as this one in the article?

Making a Go of It

Thousands of Forty-Niners made   12 the trek to California with the idea

---

2. From a letter from California by William Swain, January 6 & 16, 1850.

of striking it rich, then returning home to spend their wealth. But for every Forty-Niner whose labor paid off handsomely, countless others had to find other ways of making a living.

13   Among those were thousands of Chinese. Word of "Gold Mountain"—the Chinese name for California—lit new hope among poverty-stricken peasants in China. In 1849, only 54 Chinese lived in California; by 1852, the number had risen to 14,000.

14   Chinese miners faced the resentment of many white Forty-Niners who saw them as unfair competition. . . . Looking for less risky ways of earning a living, many Chinese turned to service work: cooking meals, toting heavy loads, and washing clothes. Miners happily plunked down money for such services.

15   The Chinese were not the only Forty-Niners to make a go of things at something other than mining. One of the biggest success stories was that of a Bavarian immigrant named Levi Strauss. Strauss, a tailor, hoped to make his fortune by making and selling tents. But he found that another item he made was more popular: the heavy-duty work pants that became known as those "wonderful pants of Levi's." His blue jeans business prospered, and Strauss became one of the wealthiest men in California.

From Fortune to Misfortune

What of Sutter and Marshall, the men who started it all?   16

17   Sutter's workers all quit and poured their efforts into finding gold. When the first Forty-Niners arrived, they overran Sutter's land, wrecked his mills and farmlands, and even killed his cattle for food. . . .

5. Do you think Sutter was right to be unhappy when Marshall first discovered gold? Why or why not?

18   Marshall's hope of earning a living by running the mill was destroyed when the workers quit and it was wrecked by treasure seekers. He became a drifter, then a poor farmer.

The Golden State

For California, however, the gold rush brought long-lasting benefits. California had become U.S. territory as a result of the treaty ending the Mexican War. That was signed on February 2, 1848—just eight days after Marshall spied that first glint of gold. California became the thirty-first state on September 9, 1850. In that short time, it grew from a place of scattered settlements to one of bustling seaports and boomtowns. Whether or not they ever had the thrill of "seeing the elephant," thousands of restless Forty-Niners found a place to call home. ■   19

Think as a Reader/Writer: First Thoughts
1. Why do you think the author wrote this article?
2. What qualities helped people succeed during the gold rush?

| READING SKILL |

Making Inferences: Drawing Conclusions

Add It Up   Suppose you are watching a mystery on TV in which a character sneaks into a room, then races from the room carrying a small box. Another character enters the room and screams, "My jewelry has been stolen!" What happened? In order to understand the story, you will need to draw a *conclusion*.

A **conclusion** is a judgment a reader makes about a text based on details the author provides and on what the reader already knows about the subject. Here is an example.

What you read: The Maximizer, the most powerful superhero, has captured the evil Dr. Z. Suddenly, Dr. Z throws a glowing liquid at the Maximizer, who collapses.

+ **What you know:** In other comic books, the superhero usually has one big weakness, which his or her enemy discovers at some point.

Conclusion: Dr. Z has discovered the Maximizer's weakness. The glowing liquid makes the Maximizer helpless.

Read the following paragraph and try to draw a conclusion based on the details in it. If you have trouble reaching a conclusion, use the Thinking It Through steps on the next page.

> In 1901, the first cars were being mass-produced in the United States. They were popular and sold well. In that same year, a huge oil field was discovered at Spindletop, near Beaumont, Texas. Within three months, the population of Beaumont had grown from nine thousand to fifty thousand.

SKILLS FOCUS

Make inferences from a text. Draw conclusions.

THINKING IT THROUGH

Drawing Conclusions

STEP 1 Identify the topic of the passage and look for the details about it.

Topic: cars and oil

Details: Cars were mass-produced, and a huge oil field was discovered in the same year. The town where oil was discovered grew.

STEP 2 Think about what you already know about the topic. How can you connect the details to your own knowledge or experiences?

I know cars use oil and gasoline. I also know people rush to places where big discoveries are made—the way the Forty-Niners rushed to California—because they hope to get rich.

STEP 3 Connect your knowledge or experiences you recalled from Step 2 with the details you identified in Step 1 to draw a conclusion about the subject.

Conclusion: People knew cars would need oil, so many people rushed to the place where it was discovered, hoping to get rich.

YOUR TURN 2 Drawing Conclusions

Use the Thinking It Through steps above to draw conclusions about the following parts of "The California Gold Rush." Read each passage listed and draw a conclusion by answering the question that follows each item on the list. Be prepared to support your conclusions with details from the reading selection.

- Paragraphs 3 and 4: Why did Sutter react as he did to the discovery of gold?

- Paragraph 15: What did the gold rush have to do with one businessman's making a fortune from the sale of work pants?

- The section titled "From Fortune to Misfortune": Was the gold rush lucky for Sutter? Why?

Author's Purpose

What's the Point? When you read a comic book, you usually are reading to be entertained. The creator of that comic book most likely wrote it for exactly that purpose. Sometimes, though, writers use the comic-book form in order to express themselves—to tell about something meaningful that happened to them or to share their own feelings about something they think is important. Whether they write comic books or research reports, writers write for a **purpose,** or reason. Being aware of an author's purpose can help you set your own purpose for reading.

The following chart explains the four main purposes for writing. In the right-hand column, it gives clues that you can look for in a piece of writing to figure out an author's purpose.

Purpose	Explanation	Clues
to inform	Informative writing teaches something. It answers *Who? What? Where? When? Why?* and *How?* questions. It can explain the way bats navigate, how a firefighter made a daring rescue, or how to play a game.	• dates • names of real people and places • facts, maps, and charts • helpful headings • quotations from real people
to express a belief or feeling	Expressive writing shares a writer's beliefs or feelings about something. Poems and personal essays are examples of expressive writing.	• words about feelings • use of *I* • value words like *best, worst, great*
to be creative or entertain	Creative writing tells a story, uses drama or humor, or plays with language. Examples include novels, short stories, poems, and plays.	• a story with a beginning, middle, and end • dialogue • rhyme • humor • suspense
to influence or persuade	Persuasive writing tries to convince the reader to share the writer's opinion or to take some action. Examples include editorials, persuasive essays, reviews, and advertisements.	• opinions supported by reasons, facts, or examples • words like *should, must, have to* • value words like *best, worst, great*

Can you figure out the author's purpose in the following passage? You can if you look for clues from the chart on page 646.

> Although history tells about the taming of the American West, an important part of that story is often left out. History books should emphasize the contributions of Chinese immigrants. Chinese workers provided much of the labor for early railroads and took jobs that others considered too dangerous. They suffered from low pay, unfair laws, and frequent attacks by other groups. These people who helped to build the modern West should be honored.

Here is how one student identified clues in this paragraph to figure out the author's purpose.

Clues	What They Tell Me About Purpose
The paragraph includes facts about Chinese workers in the West.	The purpose could be to inform. These facts also seem to back up an opinion, though, so I think the purpose is probably to persuade.
The word <u>should</u> is used twice.	The purpose is definitely to persuade.

YOUR TURN 3 Identifying the Author's Purpose

- Re-read "The California Gold Rush" on pages 641–643. Alone or with a partner, look for clues from the chart on page 646.

- List the clues you find and identify the purposes they point to, as in the above example.

- Finally, look over your list of the clues and purposes you have found in the article, and choose the purpose that you have listed most often.

SKILLS FOCUS

Determine the writer's purpose.
(page 648): Identify and understand etymology/ word origins/roots. Use prefixes to interpret and create words. Use suffixes to interpret and create words. Use context clues in words, sentences, and paragraphs to decode new vocabulary.

Word Roots

An informative article on a subject you know little about may contain unfamiliar words. You can often figure out the meaning of a word if you recognize its *root*. A **root** is the main part of a word. For example, the words *personality* and *impersonal* have the same root—*person*. Word roots like *person* can stand alone, but some roots cannot. The chart to the right gives examples of such roots. These roots need word parts called *prefixes* and *suffixes* to become words. A **prefix** is a word part that may be added to the beginning of a root to change the root's meaning. A **suffix** may be added to the end of a root. (For more on **prefixes** and **suffixes,** see page 578.)

Word Root	Meaning	Examples
–civi–	relating to townspeople	uncivilized
–migr–	to move	migrate
–popul–	people	unpopular

THINKING IT THROUGH **Using Word Roots**

Here is an example based on a word from the reading selection.

▶ **STEP 1** Peel off the prefixes and suffixes to identify the unfamiliar word's root.

The word is <u>population</u>. I can peel off the suffix -ation. That leaves <u>popul</u>-.

▶ **STEP 2** Use what you know about the root and the word's context to come up with a definition for the unfamiliar word.

I know <u>popul</u>- means "people." The words around <u>population</u> tell me how many people lived in California. <u>Population</u> must mean "the number of people."

▶ **STEP 3** Replace your definition in the original sentence to see if it makes sense.

"In January 1848, California had <u>a number of</u> only 15,000 people." That makes sense to me.

PRACTICE

Use the steps above to define the following words. They are underlined for you in the reading selection. For help with meanings of prefixes and suffixes, see pages 749–750.

1. momentarily (page 641)
2. civilization (page 642)
3. laborious (page 642)
4. immigrant (page 643)
5. settlements (page 643)

Answering Questions About Tables

Informative texts, including passages found on reading tests, often list factual information in table form. A table, which may have one or many columns, organizes facts into categories to help a reader quickly find information. The categories are usually listed as column headings. To read a table, read the column headings, and then look at the information in each column. When looking at information in the form of dates, notice the amount of time between dates.

The table to the right contains information about important discoveries in history. Study the information, and answer the question below the table.

Century	Discovery
16th	the fact that Earth circles the sun the existence of bacteria
17th	the power of gravity
19th	how to generate electrical current the existence of electrons
20th	bacteria-killing antibiotics the structure of DNA

According to the information in the chart, for how many centuries did people know about bacteria without knowing how to kill bacteria?

A. 20   **B.** 4   **C.** 2   **D.** 16

THINKING IT THROUGH   **Answering Questions About Tables**

STEP 1 Read the question, and identify the information you need to find in the chart.

I need to find when bacteria were discovered and when something that kills bacteria was discovered.

STEP 2 Identify the information in the chart that you can use to answer the question.

The chart says bacteria were discovered in the 16th century and antibiotics were discovered in the 20th century.

STEP 3 Decide what you need to do with the information to come up with an answer.

I need to figure out how long it was between these discoveries. If I count—16, 17, 18, 19, 20—I get five centuries.

STEP 4 If none of the choices matches your answer, cross out any choices you know are wrong. Then, review the question and chart to choose between the remaining answers.

Five centuries is not a choice. A and D are the centuries when the discoveries were made. Because $20 - 16 = 4$, only four centuries passed between the discoveries. My choice is B.

Writing a Research Report

Have you heard about a snake that grows to be thirty feet long? Did you know that some gladiators in ancient Rome were women? When you find out an unusual fact, the first thing you want to do is tell someone else about it. Writers of research reports feel exactly the same way. They dig into subjects they are curious about, and then, through writing, they share what they have learned. In this workshop you will have the opportunity to exercise your curiosity about a topic that interests you and tell others about what you discover.

Choose and Narrow a Subject

What Grabs You? How did the Grand Canyon get there? Why do chipmunks hibernate? Asking questions like these can help you choose an interesting subject for your research report. Here are more strategies to help you brainstorm subjects.

- Take a survey of your classmates' hobbies (*in-line skating, coin collecting, building model boats . . .*)

- Make an "I wonder" log (*I wonder why cats purr . . . , how helicopters fly . . . , who discovered electricity . . .*)

Write to report. Write research papers. Choose a topic to write about.

- Browse a television guide or magazine or newspaper for interesting subjects (*people in the news, medical marvels, strange animals, space technology . . .*)

Pin It Down   Once you have listed several possible subjects, you can choose the most interesting one. **You will need to focus on a part of the subject small enough to cover in one report.** For example, suppose that volcanoes fascinate you. Can you imagine the amount of research it would take to cover everything there is to know about volcanoes? To make it easier on yourself, you need to narrow that subject down to a focused topic. Your focused topic might be an active volcano in Hawaii. Here are more examples of narrowing a broad subject to a focused topic:

KEY CONCEPT

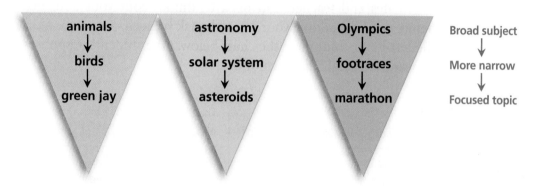

animals	astronomy	Olympics	Broad subject
↓	↓	↓	↓
birds	solar system	footraces	More narrow
↓	↓	↓	↓
green jay	asteroids	marathon	Focused topic

Here is how one writer narrowed a subject to a focused topic.

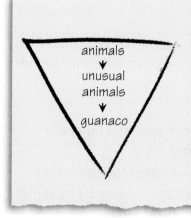

animals
↓
unusual animals
↓
guanaco

I like animals, but "animals" is too much to write about in a research report. I need to narrow this subject.

I want to write about an animal that most people have never heard of.

In an article about a wild animal ranch, I read about guanacos. I had never heard of a guanaco, and I doubt many other people have either.

TIP   Make a plan to be sure you have enough time to complete your report. Divide the total time you are given among these activities:

■ finding information (1/8 of total time)
■ taking notes (1/4)
■ organizing notes (1/8)
■ writing draft (1/4)
■ revising (1/8)
■ proofreading and publishing (1/8)

YOUR TURN 4   Choosing and Narrowing a Subject

Brainstorm some subjects that interest you, and choose one you want to research. Then, use an upside-down triangle to find a focused topic. Record your thoughts as you narrow your topic.

SKILLS FOCUS

Narrow the focus of the topic. Use graphic organizers to generate ideas.

Think About Purpose, Audience, and Voice

The *Why* of It   Your **purpose** is your reason for writing. You have two purposes for writing a research report: to discover information for yourself, and to share what you learn with others.

The *Who* of It   The **audience** for your report will be people who share your interest in the topic but do not already know a great deal about it. In most cases, that audience will include your classmates and teacher. You need to think about your audience before you begin doing your research. Ask yourself the questions in the left-hand column of the chart below. One student's responses appear in the right-hand column.

1. What does my audience already know about my topic?	They probably know nothing more about the guanaco than I do.
2. What does my audience need to know?	what it is, where it lives, what it looks like, what it does
3. What kind of information would my audience find interesting?	any unusual or surprising facts that I discover

The *How* of It   The sound of your writing is your **voice.** When your purpose is to inform, you should select a voice that sounds knowledgeable and interesting. Express your ideas in a clear, direct way, without using slang or clichés.

Confusing and slangy   I bet you never heard of a humpless camel-like thing.

Clear and interesting   Visitors to the Andes Mountains may spot a creature resembling a tiny camel without a hump.

YOUR TURN 5 Thinking About Purpose, Audience, and Voice

Your purpose is to discover information and share it with others. Answer the questions in the chart above to consider how you might communicate what you learn with your readers.

Ask Questions

The K-W-L Method When you think about your topic, you are probably full of questions such as: *What does it look like? Where does it come from? What does it do?* Research begins with questions like these. Of course, there are some things you already know about your topic.

You can use a K-W-L chart to list what you already **K**now about a topic, what you **W**ant to know about it, and what you **L**earned about it through research. Look at how one student organized his ideas about the topic of guanacos. As he finds answers to his questions, he will list them in the right-hand column.

TIP Another way to organize what you already know about a topic and what you would like to know is to create a cluster diagram. For more on **clustering,** see page 797 in the Quick Reference Handbook.

What I <u>K</u>now	What I <u>W</u>ant to Know	What I <u>L</u>earned
A guanaco is part of the camel family. It lives in South America.	What does a guanaco look like? What do guanacos do? Do humans and guanacos get along?	

TIP You might discover new questions once you begin doing research. Add them to your chart only if they really fit your topic. As one student researched his topic, he came up with and evaluated these questions:

Where do other members of the camel family live?	Other camels are not part of my topic. I won't add this question.
Why are there fewer guanacos now than there used to be?	This fits my topic. I'll add it to my K-W-L chart.

YOUR TURN 6 Asking Questions

Create a K-W-L chart like the one above on your own paper. In the left column, list everything that you already know about your topic. In the middle column, list the questions you have about your topic. Leave the right column of your chart blank. You will fill it out as you do your research.

SKILLS FOCUS

Organize prior knowledge about a topic. Cluster to generate ideas. Develop questions to guide research.

TIP Some sources are better than others for research. Look for non-fiction sources created by people or organizations likely to know a great deal about the topic. In other words, look for **authoritative** sources—ones that are credible, accurate, and unbiased. For example, you would get better information on African snakes from a *National Geographic* article than from a movie about the adventures of a fictional explorer.

| KEY CONCEPT

Reference Note

For more on using the **media center,** see page 728 in the Quick Reference Handbook.

| KEY CONCEPT

Find Sources

Who Has the Answers? The best place to start your research is in the library, but that is just the beginning. You will look in several places to find answers to your questions. Some of the resources you can use include

- **primary sources,** such as letters, diaries, journals, narratives, interviews, guest speakers, autobiographies, oral histories, and research notes
- **secondary sources,** such as encyclopedia articles, biographical sketches, and books, Web pages, and documentaries that compile researched information

Remember that information does not always have to come from print or online sources. You can also find answers to your questions by watching a documentary; listening to an informative radio program; or reading charts, maps, and other graphics. **You will not find all of the information you need in a single source.** You should plan to use at least three different kinds of sources in order to investigate all aspects of your topic, including various viewpoints on it. For example, you could find information on your topic in a book, in a magazine article, and on the Internet. Using a variety of sources will help you find complete answers to your research questions. If you have trouble finding sources **relevant,** or related, to your topic, go to the media center or ask your school's media specialist for help.

Make a List of Sources

Who Said That? When everyone talks at once, it is hard to remember who said what. You may have the same problem when you do research. When you find information about your topic in several different places, you may not remember where you found a particular fact. You will need to keep track of where you find the answers to your questions. **Make a numbered list of all of the sources you find that might be helpful in your research.** In your list, include information about each source. The chart on the next page tells you what information you need for each type of source you might use. The listings in the chart follow the style of the Modern Language Association (MLA).

Information on Sources

Books: Author. Title. City where book was published: Name of Publisher, copyright year.

Ricciuti, Edward R. <u>What on Earth Is a Guanaco?</u> Woodbridge: Blackbirch Press, 1994.

Magazine and Newspaper Articles: Author (if known). "Title of Article." <u>Name of Magazine or Newspaper</u> Date article was published: page numbers.

Lambeth, Ellen. "Here Comes Paco Guanaco: In the Hilly Grasslands of South America, a Camel Is Born." <u>Ranger Rick</u> Nov. 1996: 4-8.

Encyclopedia Articles: Author (if known). "Title of Article." <u>Encyclopedia Name</u>. Edition number (if known) and year published.

Goodwin, George G. "Guanaco." <u>Collier's Encyclopedia</u>. 1997 ed.

Television or Radio Programs: "Title of Episode." Title of Program. Name of host (if known). Network. Station Call Letters, City. Date of broadcast.

"In the Land of the Llamas." NOVA. PBS. WNPB, Morgantown. 20 Mar. 2008.

Movie or Video Recordings: <u>Title</u>. Name of Director or Producer (if known). Format (videocassette or DVD). Name of Distributor, year.

<u>The Living Edens: Patagonia</u>. Videocassette. PBS Home Video, 1997.

Internet Sources: Author. "Title." <u>Name of Web site</u>. Date of electronic publication. Name of Sponsoring Institution. Date you accessed information <Internet address>.

Note: Some sites may not list all of the above information. Include what the site does list and skip the items it does not list.

"Gwen the Guanaco." <u>Victory Ranch</u>. 26 Mar. 2008 <http://www.victoryranch.com/gwen.htm>.

Other Electronic Sources: Author (if known). "Title." <u>Title of Database or CD-ROM</u>. Medium (CD-ROM or Database). Copyright date.

Sentman, Everett. "Guanaco." <u>2003 Grolier Multimedia Encyclopedia</u>. CD-ROM. 2002.

 TIP Why should you keep track of your sources?

- You may need to find a source again if you come up with another interesting question later in your research.

- Your readers may want to go to your sources to learn more about your topic.

- Your teacher may expect you to include a list of sources to show the research you did.

 **SKILLS FOCUS**

Gather information and sources. Synthesize information from many sources. Use a variety of sources in writing. Document sources. Cite sources correctly.

Searching the World Wide Web for Information

The World Wide Web contains enormous amounts of information. One way you can find what you need is to use a *search engine*. A **search engine** is a Web site that allows you to hunt for information. By typing a **keyword**—a word related to your topic—into the search engine, you will get a list of possible sites.

Another way to find information from a search engine is to use a *directory*. A **directory** lists categories of information. Each category is divided into smaller and smaller subcategories that you can follow until you find a site that relates to your topic.

Below is a path a student took through categories and subcategories in a directory. The main menu, where he began his search, is on the left. The highlighted choice shows the category the student chose. His choice leads to the next list of subcategories and finally to a list of sites with information about guanacos and other mammals.

> **TIP** Remember, not all Web sites are equal. For your research report, choose sources such as universities, government sites, and major newspapers and broadcast networks. When you get a list of sites, look first at those that have URLs (addresses) ending in *.org* (nonprofit organizations), *.edu* (educational institutions), and *.gov* (U.S. government agencies). (For more on **evaluating Web sites,** see page 736.)

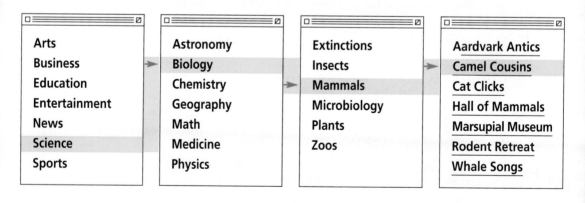

Arts	Astronomy	Extinctions	Aardvark Antics
Business	**Biology**	Insects	**Camel Cousins**
Education	Chemistry	**Mammals**	Cat Clicks
Entertainment	Geography	Microbiology	Hall of Mammals
News	Math	Plants	Marsupial Museum
Science	Medicine	Zoos	Rodent Retreat
Sports	Physics		Whale Songs

PRACTICE

Search the Internet two different ways for Web sites on the topic of your research report. In your first search, type a keyword into a search engine. In your second search, go through the categories and subcategories in a directory. Which search proved to be more successful? Compare your results with those of your classmates.

YOUR TURN 7   **Finding and Listing Sources**

Find at least five sources you might use for researching your focused topic. Follow the instructions on page 655 to list important information about these sources. Give each source a number to help you identify sources when you take notes later. For now, do not worry about the order of items in your list. You will alphabetize your source list later (by author's last name or by title, if no author is given).

COMPUTER TIP

Write down or bookmark the address of any Web site you come across that looks helpful, even if you are not using it right away. You will be able to find the site again quickly by calling up the exact address.

Take Notes

Getting the Facts   Now, begin looking for answers to your research questions. Remember, you are looking for answers to the questions in your K-W-L chart. **Your questions will guide your research process.** Record each fact, description, or expert opinion you find, along with information about where you found it. The guidelines below will help you take notes.

KEY CONCEPT

- Use a separate note card or a sheet of paper for each new note.

- At the top of each note card, write the question that the notes on the card answer.

- Write the number of the source at the top of each note, so you will always be able to tell exactly where you found the information.

- **Summarize** information explained in a long passage. Even with shorter passages, **paraphrase,** or write the ideas in your own words. If you copy exact words from a source, put them in quotation marks.

- If the information is from a printed book or article, put the page number at the end of your note.

Reference Note

For more on **paraphrasing** and **summarizing,** see pages 740 and 743 in the Quick Reference Handbook.

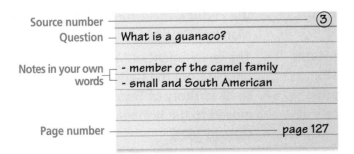

Source number ——————————————— ③
Question — What is a guanaco?

Notes in your own words — - member of the camel family
 - small and South American

Page number ——————————————— page 127

SKILLS FOCUS

Take notes from relevant and authoritative sources. Summarize sources. Paraphrase sources.
(page 656): Use technology to gather information.

Paraphrasing

Paraphrasing means putting information from a source into your own words. Copying an author's words and presenting them as your own is **plagiarizing.** Plagiarizing is the same as stealing another writer's work. If you want to use a writer's exact words, put them in quotation marks and identify the source.

The passages below show the difference between paraphrasing and plagiarizing. The paraphrase on the left tells the ideas of the source passage in different words. The plagiarized passage on the right copies long strings of words which are printed in boldface.

Source Passage: Guanacos, South American members of the camel family, lack the familiar humps of Asian and African camels. Slim and long-legged, guanacos move quickly and gracefully over the rugged terrain of their native Andes Mountains.

Paraphrase: Although it is part of the camel family, the South American guanaco does not have a hump like its cousins in Asia and Africa do. It is slim, has long legs, and can run fast in its habitat, the Andes Mountains.

Plagiarism: As **members of the camel family,** guanacos **lack the familiar humps of Asian and African camels.** They are able to **move quickly and gracefully over rugged terrain.** They live in the Andes Mountains.

PRACTICE

Read each source passage below, then the passage to its right. Tell whether the passage paraphrases or plagiarizes the source. Explain your answer in a sentence or two.

Source Passage

1. Manifest Destiny was the belief in the nineteenth century that the United States would eventually stretch across the entire continent, from the Atlantic Ocean to the Pacific Ocean.

2. The first settlers from the United States reached northeastern Texas in 1815, encouraged by the Mexican government, which controlled the territory at that time.

Paraphrase or Plagiarism?

1. People believed in the nineteenth century that the United States would eventually reach from the Atlantic Ocean to the Pacific Ocean. This belief was called Manifest Destiny.

2. The government of Mexico encouraged people from the United States to move to its territory of Texas. The first settlers moved to the northeast part of the state in 1815.

Researching Your Topic and Taking Notes

Using the sources you found earlier, locate answers for your research questions. Take notes from each source, being careful to put the information in your own words. Note the source of each piece of information you find by putting its source number on your note card.

TIP To make the most of your time, skim long passages looking for key words, ones that relate to your topic. Then, read only the sections that contain the key words.

Organize Your Information

Getting It Together   A pile of notes will be about as useful to your readers as a box full of bicycle parts. Both need to be put together in a logical way to be of any use. Once you have gathered information from your sources, organize those ideas into categories. The questions you wrote on the top of your note cards will help you. Group together note cards that answer the same question so you can compare your findings and get a complete picture. Each group of cards will become a paragraph in your report. If some note cards do not seem to belong to any group, set them aside for now.

Outline Your Report

Planning It Out   An **outline** is a plan for your report. It shows how you are grouping the information you have gathered and the order in which you will present the information in your report. One type of outline you can make is an *informal outline.* An **informal outline** lists a report's major **subtopics,** or categories of information related to your topic. It also lists the specific facts that make up each subtopic.

   To identify the subtopics for your informal outline, first change the questions from your K-W-L chart into headings. A **heading** is a phrase that covers all the items listed below it. For example, the question "Where do guanacos live?" could be turned into the heading "Where guanacos live." As you turn your questions into headings, write each heading on a piece of paper, leaving several lines after it blank. Then, under each heading, write facts from your note cards or jot down a few words that will remind you what to include when you write your report.

Reference Note

For more on **outlines,** both informal and formal, see page 799 in the Quick Reference Handbook.

SKILLS FOCUS

Organize writing by logical order. Organize information and ideas in paragraphs. Organize ideas from outlines. *(page 658):* Understand and know how to avoid plagiarism.

The partial informal outline below shows the information the student writing about guanacos will use in his research report.

TIP Review your outline to make sure you have at least two pieces of information under each body heading. If you don't, you may need to do a bit more research. You can also check any note cards you set aside to see if they fit under one of the headings. If not, you will not use those cards for this report.

Body:

Where guanacos live
  Andes Mountains of South America
  how guanacos handle their habitat
  protected reserves

What guanacos look like
  similarities to camels—legs, hoofs, neck, lips
  differences—ears, no hump, height, fur color

What guanacos do
  spit cud accurately
  run fast and early in life
  swim across streams and between islands

How guanacos get along with people
  carrying loads
  wool used for coats and robes
  hunted for meat

Reference Note

For help in making **graphic organizers** like conceptual maps and time lines, see pages 799 and 800 in the Quick Reference Handbook.

TIP Instead of an informal outline, you might create a **conceptual map** to organize your information. At the top of a conceptual map is a circle containing the topic. Extending out from the topic circle are circles containing subtopics. Circles containing facts and other information connect to the subtopics that they explain. Another useful tool for organizing information from various sources is a **time line.** You can use a time line to show the time order of events in history.

YOUR TURN 9  **Organizing Your Notes and Creating an Informal Outline**

Group your notes based on the questions they answer. Then, create an informal outline by following these steps:

- Turn questions into headings.

- List your headings on a sheet of paper, leaving several blank lines after each.

- Write notes under each heading telling which information you will include from your note cards. You do not need to use complete sentences.

SKILLS FOCUS

Organize ideas from conceptual maps. Organize ideas from time lines.

Creating Headings   To help readers see how your ideas are organized, include a descriptive heading before each section of your report. If you are writing on a computer, put your headings in boldface print or underline them using word-processing features. If you are typing or hand-writing your report, print the headings in capital letters or underline them.

Write a Main Idea Statement

Tell It Like It Is   To make sure your readers remember the major points you make about your topic, include a *main idea statement* in your introduction. A **main idea statement,** or **thesis,** tells readers the topic of a piece of writing and the main points the writer will make about the topic. Here is how you can develop a main idea statement for your report.

THINKING IT THROUGH
Writing a Main Idea Statement

▶ STEP 1 Identify the major points in your outline.

strange looking, unusual talents, useful to humans, threatened by hunting

▶ STEP 2 Combine the major points in a single sentence.

Guanacos are strange-looking animals with unusual talents, and they are useful to humans but threatened by hunting.

▶ STEP 3 If your step 2 sentence is long, condense the ideas into a more compact main idea statement.

Guanacos are unusual animals that are useful to humans but threatened by hunting.

YOUR TURN 10   Writing a Main Idea Statement

Use the Thinking It Through steps above to develop a clear and compact main idea statement for your research report.

SKILLS FOCUS

Design documents in preparation for publishing. Include a statement of thesis/main idea. *(page 664):* Format a Works Cited list.

Writing

Research Report

Framework	Think as a Reader/Writer

Introduction
- Attention-getting beginning
- Main idea statement

One way to grab your readers' attention is to begin with a colorful description of something related to your topic. Your **main idea statement** should clearly identify your topic and the major points in your report.

Body
- Heading 1 facts
- Heading 2 facts
  and so on

The headings in your informal outline represent subtopics. **Each subtopic will be covered in its own paragraph. Support** each subtopic with facts and explanations from your research, and **elaborate** on your support by explaining each fact or example. Clearly distinguish your own ideas from those of your sources' authors.

Conclusion
- Restatement of main idea

In addition to restating your main idea, your conclusion may be a good place to share information that did not fit in the body of your report. The Writer's Model, for example, tells what is being done to solve the problem discussed in the report.

List of Sources
- Alphabetized by author

A list of sources is also called a **Works Cited list** or **bibliography.** List only the sources you actually used for your report. See the chart on page 655 for how to list different kinds of sources.

YOUR TURN 11 Drafting Your Report

Write the first draft of your report. Use the framework above and the following Writer's Model to guide you.

A Writer's Model

The final draft below closely follows the framework for a research report on the previous page.

The South American Guanaco

Visitors to the Andes Mountains may spot a creature resembling a tiny camel without a hump. This animal is the guanaco, a South American member of the camel family. Guanacos are unusual animals that are useful to humans but threatened by hunting.

For thousands of years guanacos have grazed on tough grasses in the high plains and hills of the Andes Mountains. They can be found from southern Peru to the tip of South America. Their blood can handle the thin mountain air. Steep, rocky paths are no problem for guanacos because they are nimble like mountain goats and have thick, padded soles that protect their feet. Their only wild enemy is the mountain lion, but people have hunted the guanaco so much that the species is in danger. Some herds live in protected reserves in Argentina and Chile.

Like other camels, the guanaco has long legs, two-toed hoofs, a long neck, and floppy lips. It can survive without water for long periods of time, just like a desert camel. The guanaco looks different from the humped camel. It has pointed ears and a slender body, and it stands less than four feet high. In some ways it looks more like a deer or an antelope than a camel. It is reddish brown with a dark gray head and a pale belly.

The guanaco has some strange talents. Like other kinds of camels, the guanaco helps its stomach digest grass by chewing it up again after it has been in the stomach for a while. This rechewed grass, or cud, comes in handy when another animal bothers the guanaco. It can accurately hit whatever is annoying it with smelly green spit, with no warning at all. The guanaco

Attention grabber

Main idea statement

Heading 1:
Where guanacos live

Heading 2:
What guanacos look like

Heading 3:
What guanacos do

(continued)

(continued)

can also run fast and swim well. Almost as soon as they are born, guanacos can race to safety if their mothers spot danger. Adult guanacos can run as fast as thirty-five miles an hour. Guanacos swim almost as well as they run. They easily cross cold, fast-running mountain streams. Believe it or not, they even swim in the ocean. They have been seen swimming from island to island off the coast of Chile in the Pacific Ocean.

Heading 4: How guanacos get along with people

Guanacos are helpful to people and are in trouble because of them. People use guanacos to carry loads on the prairies and in the mountains of South America. Their wool is also used for making coats. Newborn guanacos are often killed so that their silky wool can be made into beautiful robes called *capas*. The number of guanacos has also been reduced by hunters, who kill them for their meat.

Restatement of main idea

To help the guanaco survive the threat of people hunting it for meat and hides, this unusual little camel will need to be protected. Some South American countries are already taking steps that may help guanacos to be plentiful again.

TIP A research report and its *List of Sources* are normally double-spaced. Because of limited space on these pages, A Writer's Model and A Student's Model are single-spaced. The *Elements of Language* Internet site provides a model of a research report in the double-spaced format. To see this interactive model, go to **go.hrw.com** and enter the keyword **EOLang 6-23**.

List of Sources

Burton, John A. The Collins Guide to the Rare
    Mammals of the World. Lexington: The Stephen
    Greene Press, 1987.
Goodwin, George G. "Guanaco." Collier's
    Encyclopedia. 1997 ed.
"Guanaco." Wildlife Gallery. Fota Wildlife Park.
    26 Mar. 2006 <http://www.zenith.ie/fota/
    wildlife/guanaco.html>.
Lambeth, Ellen. "Here Comes Paco Guanaco: In the
    Hilly Grasslands of South America, a Camel Is
    Born." Ranger Rick Nov. 1996: 4-8.

A Student's Model

Genna Offerman, a sixth-grader from Marshall Middle School in Beaumont, Texas, wrote about a game many people enjoy—billiards. Below is an excerpt of her research report.

Billiards

. . . Billiard games are played on a rectangular table. This table has rubber cushions around its inside upper edge and is covered with a felt cloth. A billiard table has six holes, called pockets, where the balls go. Many billiard games require fifteen numbered balls. Balls one through eight are all solid colors, and balls nine through fifteen are white with a colored stripe. Also, for some billiard games, a white cue ball is used. A player uses a cue stick, which is made of wood, to hit the white cue ball into a numbered ball. The goal is to get the numbered ball into a pocket.

Subtopic 1: Equipment needed to play billiards

The game of billiards has been around since the 1400s. It was developed in Europe from the game croquet, which is played on the lawn with mallets and balls. When croquet was moved indoors, people began playing it on a table that was made green to resemble grass. By the 1600s, the game of billiards had become so popular that Shakespeare mentioned it in the play *Antony and Cleopatra*.

Subtopic 2: History of billiards

No one knows when billiards came to the United States, but from an early date the game was popular. American woodworkers were producing billiard tables by the 1700s, and George Washington was said to have won a game in 1748. In 1850, Michael Phelan wrote the first American book on the game. . . .

Subtopic 3: History of billiards in the United States

List of Sources

Billiards: The Official Rules and Records Book.
  Guilford: Lyon's Press, 2005.
"Billiards." 2003 Grolier Multimedia Encyclopedia. CD-
  ROM. 2002.

Revising

Evaluate and Revise Content, Organization, and Style

Double Duty   To make the information in your research report as clear as possible for your readers, you will need to read it at least twice. First, evaluate the content and organization, using the guidelines below. Then, check your writing style using the guidelines on page 667.

▶ **First Reading: Content and Organization**   Use the following chart to evaluate the content and organization of your report. The tips in the middle column will help you decide how to answer the questions in the left column. If you answer *no* to any question, use the Revision Technique to improve that part of your writing.

Guidelines for Self-Evaluation and Peer Evaluation

Evaluation Questions	Tips	Revision Techniques
❶ Does the introduction contain a main idea statement that identifies the topic and major points of the report?	**Highlight** the main idea statement.	**Add** a main idea statement or **revise** the main idea statement to give complete information about the topic, if needed.
❷ Does each paragraph in the body explain only one part of the topic?	**Label** each body paragraph with the type of information it provides about the topic.	**Rearrange** ideas so each paragraph covers only one part of the topic, or **delete** ideas that do not belong.
❸ Does each paragraph contain facts that give clear information about the topic?	**Put a check mark** above each fact that explains the topic.	**Add** facts to any paragraph with fewer than two check marks.
❹ Does the conclusion restate the report's main idea?	**Circle** the sentence that puts the main idea statement in different words.	If needed, **add** a sentence that states the main idea in another way.
❺ Does the report include information from at least three sources?	**Number** the items on the list of sources.	**Elaborate** on the ideas in your report by using information from another source as needed.

ONE WRITER'S REVISIONS These are revisions of an early draft of the research report on pages 663–664.

The guanaco can also run fast and swim well. Almost as soon as they are born, guanacos can race to safety if their mothers spot danger. Adult guanacos can run as fast as thirty-five miles an hour. ~~This is another way that they are like antelopes and deer.~~ [delete] Guanacos swim almost as well as they run. They easily cross cold, fast-running mountain streams. Believe it or not, they even swim in the ocean. *They have been seen swimming from island to island off the coast of Chile in the Pacific Ocean.* [elaborate]

Think as a Reader/Writer

1. How did deleting a sentence improve the passage above?
2. Why was it important for the writer to add the final sentence?

▶ **Second Reading: Style**   When sharing information with others, you should communicate your ideas as clearly as possible. One way to do this is to use *precise nouns* in your writing. **Precise nouns** name a person, place, thing, or idea in a specific way. Look for places in your writing where you can be more precise by changing a vague noun to one that is more specific.

When you evaluate your research report for style, ask yourself whether your writing uses specific words to name people, places, things, and ideas. As you re-read your report, put an asterisk above each vague, non-specific noun (especially look for ones like *thing, stuff, animal,* and *person*). Then, replace vague nouns with more precise ones (for instance, *boulder, DVDs, giraffe,* and *landlord*). (You may find more specific nouns in your notes.) The Focus on Word Choice on the next page can help you learn more about using precise nouns.

PEER REVIEW

When you are reviewing another student's report, ask yourself these questions:

- Does this report explain information clearly enough for me to tell someone else about this topic?
- What part of this report caught my interest the most? Why?

SKILLS FOCUS

Evaluate others' writing. Develop writer's style. *(page 666):* Revise by adding or replacing text. Revise by rearranging text. Revise by deleting text. Revise by elaborating.

Focus on
Word Choice

TIP If you have trouble coming up with a precise noun, look up the vague noun in a **thesaurus**. Among the synonyms for the vague noun you will often find more specific ones that you might use to revise your writing.

SKILLS FOCUS

Use appropriate word choice and precise wording. Use reference materials for revising drafts. *(page 669):* Proofread one's own writing in preparation for publishing. Capitalize titles correctly. Punctuate titles correctly.

Using Precise Nouns

When you read the word *flower*, what image comes to mind? You might picture a daisy, while another reader might think of a buttercup or a daffodil. *Flower* is a vague noun because it lets the reader choose what to picture. When you write, give your readers the right picture by using *precise nouns* such as *honeysuckle* or *violet*. **Precise nouns** name people, places, things, or ideas in a specific way. Look at the sentences below. Which one tells you exactly what the writer had in mind?

Vague The author Luis Valdez created a *program* for *people.*

Precise The author Luis Valdez created a *theater company* for *farm workers.*

Replace vague nouns in your writing with more precise ones that will get your picture across. Precise nouns will help your readers learn about your topic.

ONE WRITER'S REVISIONS

For thousands of years, _∧the animals have grazed on *guanacos*

tough plants in the high plains and hills of the mountains. *grasses* *Andes*

Think as a Reader/Writer

How do you think the changes the writer made improve the sentence above?

YOUR TURN 12

Evaluating and Revising Content, Organization, and Style

Review the first draft of your report. Then, improve your report by using the Content and Organization Guidelines on page 666, the Focus on Word Choice above, and peer comments.

Proofread Your Report

Polish It   You want your readers to focus on learning about your topic, not on finding errors. Look over your report carefully and correct any mistakes. Use the following Grammar Link to make sure your sources are written correctly.

> **TIP** You can use other **resources** to help you proofread your report, such as a dictionary or a spellchecker.

Grammar Link

Capitalizing and Punctuating Titles

Sources of information for research reports are listed in a certain way. You may see the title of a source listed inside quotation marks, written in italics, or underlined. Some words are capitalized, and others are not. Here are three rules about how to write titles.

Titles of major works should be <u>underlined</u> or typed in *italics.* Major works include books, encyclopedias, magazines, newspapers, databases, Web sites, movies, and television series. <u>Underline</u> these titles when you type or hand-write your report. If you are using a computer, you can use the *italics* function.

Put titles of short works inside quotation marks. These include chapters of books; articles from encyclopedias, magazines, and newspapers; individual pages from Web sites; and titles of single episodes in a TV series.

Capitalize the important words in a title. The only words you will not capitalize in a title are articles (*a, an, the*), conjunctions (*and, but, or*), and prepositions

with fewer than five letters (*to, for, with, in,* and so on). However, capitalize the first and last words of a title, no matter what they are.

PRACTICE

Rewrite the following titles. Capitalize each correctly and place it inside quotation marks or underline it.

Example:
1. Newspaper article: students stop disaster on playground
1. "Students Stop Disaster on Playground"

1. Magazine article: with a song in his heart
2. Book: the giant guide to the internet
3. Movie: the iron giant
4. Whole Web site: the science of lightning
5. Episode in a TV program: the perfect pearl

For more information and practice on **punctuating titles,** see pages 336 and 343.

Publish Your Report

Share the Wealth   Now you can share what you have learned with an audience. Here are some ideas for presenting your findings in a variety of formats.

- With other students who wrote on similar topics, create and illustrate a book of research reports. This book might be kept in the classroom for independent reading or placed in the library for all students to enjoy.

- Make a display that includes your report and helpful illustrations. Place it in a hallway display case or the library, or share it with other classes.

- Try adapting your report into a children's book. Retell the most interesting facts and details in language children can understand. Work with a partner to illustrate your book.

PORTFOLIO

Reflect on Your Report

Building Your Portfolio   Take some time to think about how you researched your topic and wrote your report. Did you achieve your purpose? What would you do differently next time? Consider these questions:

- Where in your report do you think you did the best job of clearly answering a research question? Why do you think this was the best part?

- What kinds of information sources were useful? Would you use these types of sources for a future report?

 Proofreading, Publishing, and Reflecting on Your Report

- Correct any errors in spelling, punctuation, and sentence structure. Be particularly careful about writing titles of sources correctly.

- Publish your report for an audience of interested readers. You might use one of the suggestions above.

- Answer the Reflect on Your Report questions above. Record your responses in a learning log, or include them in your portfolio.

Writing an Informative Essay

In a research report you explain what you have learned about a topic. Some writing tests, though, will ask you to explain something about *yourself.* You may be asked to explain something that is important or enjoyable to you. Because these essays clarify, or make clear, your relationship to a topic, they are sometimes called **clarification essays.**

You can organize your ideas for a clarification essay just as you organized the information in your research report by using an informal outline. You will also elaborate on your ideas by using explanations. Read the following prompt, and think about how you would respond.

Everyone has a place that is important to him or her. It may be a place with special memories or a place that makes a person feel comfortable. Choose a place that is important to you, and write an essay about it. Explain three things that make this place special or tell three reasons why the place is special to you.

THINKING IT THROUGH — Responding to an Informative Prompt

STEP 1 Read the prompt to see what you must do. Identify the topic, audience, and format.

I'm going to write an essay that tells three reasons why a place is special to me. A specific audience was not named so I'll write to my teacher.

STEP 2 Choose a topic for your answer.

My grandfather's workshop is special to me.

STEP 3 Brainstorm ideas about your connection to the topic.

Things that make his workshop special:

1. good smells—oil, wood, sawdust
2. the furniture Grandpa makes
3. the jewelry box I made for Mom

STEP 4 Write your essay. In each body paragraph, elaborate on your connection to the topic.

1. smells—linseed oil & turpentine, fresh-cut pine, nose-tickling sawdust
2. furniture—high chair in progress, repairing Grandma's rocker, refinishing dresser
3. jewelry box—carved top, smooth finish

Creating Visuals to Share Information

Showing Them Think back to the time when you were first learning to read. Remember how the books had pictures? You used the pictures to figure out what was being said. **Visuals** help readers and listeners of all ages understand the topic better. In this section you will learn how you can boost your audience's understanding by creating or finding a visual to include in your report.

The most obvious kind of visual is a **photograph** or **drawing.** The writer of the research report on guanacos, for example, found this photograph in a book. He photocopied it and included it in his report.

Make a Choice Before you create a visual, you must first decide two things: what information you are going to show and how you are going to show it. To decide what information to show, read your report and find anything your audience may need help understanding. Then, decide how you can put that information in a visual. The chart on the next page gives you some examples.

Get the Picture Once you have made your decision about what kind of visual will be most helpful for your audience, you will need to create or find it. You might use one of the following ideas.

- Draw it freehand.
- Trace it, using tracing paper or a projector.
- Photocopy it if you have access to a copier.
- Cut it out of a magazine or newspaper if you have permission.
- Create it in a computer program.
- Download it from an Internet source if you have permission to do so.

When you create your own graphic, use color carefully. In general, use no more than three colors in a graph, chart, or time line. Color attracts attention, but too many colors distract the reader and make information hard to find. A map, however, may need more than three colors to contrast all adjoining states and countries.

TIP If you are using a computer and presentation software to show your visual, make sure the text and graphics are easy to read and understand even from across the room. Do some lines need to be bolder? Do some words need to be bigger? Would borders or colors help?

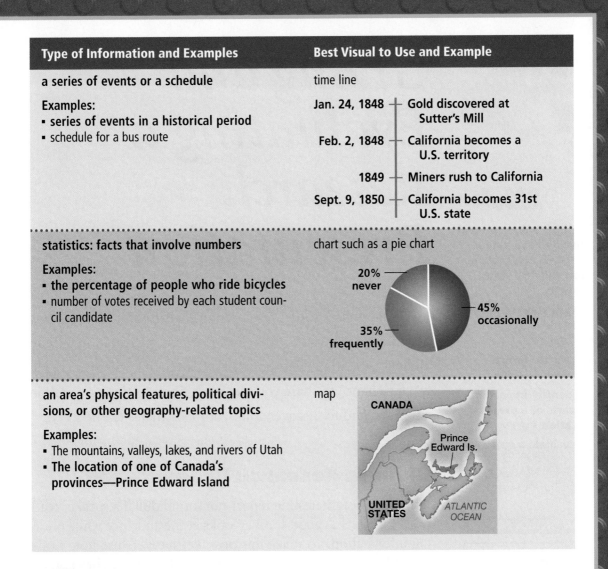

Type of Information and Examples	Best Visual to Use and Example
a series of events or a schedule Examples: • series of events in a historical period • schedule for a bus route	time line Jan. 24, 1848 — **Gold discovered at Sutter's Mill** Feb. 2, 1848 — **California becomes a U.S. territory** 1849 — **Miners rush to California** Sept. 9, 1850 — **California becomes 31st U.S. state**
statistics: facts that involve numbers Examples: • the percentage of people who ride bicycles • number of votes received by each student council candidate	chart such as a pie chart 20% never 45% occasionally 35% frequently
an area's physical features, political divisions, or other geography-related topics Examples: • The mountains, valleys, lakes, and rivers of Utah • The location of one of Canada's provinces—Prince Edward Island	map CANADA Prince Edward Is. UNITED STATES ATLANTIC OCEAN

YOUR TURN 14 Using Visuals

Use these steps to create a visual for your research report.

- Decide what information to show and the best visual to use.
- Create or find your visual, making sure it is large and clear.
- List the source if you have copied, cut out, or downloaded the visual. For a reminder about how to list sources, see page 655.

Talk   Listen

WHAT'S AHEAD?

In this section you will give and evaluate a research presentation. You will also learn how to

- turn your research report into notes for a speech

- practice formal speaking skills

- identify important parts of a presentation

- evaluate a speech

Giving and Evaluating a Research Presentation

Researchers sometimes present their findings in a formal presentation or speech. A research presentation tells an audience the important points a researcher has discovered. Here is your chance to share your research findings through oral presentations and to discover what your classmates learned.

Giving a Research Presentation

Even the most interesting report can sound dull if a speaker reads it word for word. A good speaker looks at the audience while presenting information. To make this possible, speakers use note cards to remind themselves of the points they want to make. They also practice their speeches until they are comfortable with what they are saying. To turn your research report into a research presentation, follow these guidelines.

- Look back at the informal outline you created for your research report. Each heading in your outline can be a separate note card.

- On each note card, neatly write words or phrases from your notes, outline, or report that will help you remember the points you want to share with your audience. Write major ideas only (including key evidence and examples), but plan to elaborate or clarify your ideas as you speak.

SKILLS FOCUS

Deliver informative presentations. Match purpose to audience. *(page 675):* Demonstrate effective verbal techniques when speaking. Demonstrate effective nonverbal techniques when speaking. Practice/rehearse before presenting oral messages. Evaluate and critique oral presentations and performances. Evaluate content when listening. Monitor your listening.

- Number the note cards in the order that you will present them.

- Practice your speech out loud. Because the occasion for giving your speech is fairly formal, use standard English and avoid using slang or clichés. Consider your volume and rate, speaking loudly and slowly. Everyone in your audience—including people at the back of the room—should be able to understand you.

- If you use a visual or prop, practice holding it up or pointing to it while facing the audience.

- Practice making eye contact by having a friend listen to you or by looking at yourself in a mirror.

- Refine your speech as you practice. Evaluate yourself, or collaborate or confer with a peer, using the criteria below.

TIP Have a partner help you practice by answering these questions about your presentation.

- Are there any points in the speech that are not clear?
- Does the visual (if one is used) help me better understand the information?

YOUR TURN 15 **Giving an Oral Research Presentation**

Follow the guidelines on page 674 and above to present the information in your research report to your class.

Reference Note

For more on **formal speaking,** see page 753 in the Quick Reference Handbook.

Evaluating a Research Presentation   When you evaluate a presentation, you will look at the content of the speech and the speaker's delivery. **Content** is the ideas a speaker presents. **Delivery** includes how the speaker talks, uses gestures, and makes eye contact with the audience.

Get the Message   To evaluate content, consider how clear and organized the speaker's information is. Here is how one student evaluated the content of a classmate's speech.

TIP Monitor your understanding as you listen to the speech. If you are confused about something the speaker said, wait until he or she is finished to raise your hand and ask a question for clarification.

Content	Comments
- Can you understand the main ideas in the speaker's verbal message?	- He says guanacos are unusual animals that are in trouble.
- Can you identify support for the speaker's main ideas?	- He describes what guanacos look like and what they do. He also talks about how they are being hunted.
- Does the speaker seem to understand the topic well?	- He really knows about guanacos. I wish he would explain how they swim. Overall content: great

Special Delivery   A speaker who mumbles or says "um" frequently draws attention to his or her delivery. When you listen to a speech, you may only notice a speaker's delivery if there are problems such as these. When a speaker's delivery is good, you can focus on the content of the speech. To identify good delivery, answer these questions as you listen.

Delivery	Comments
▪ Does the speaker talk loudly and clearly enough?	▪ He was easy to understand except when he turned to point at the map.
▪ Does the speaker look at the audience?	▪ He is mostly looking at his notes.
▪ Do the speaker's nonverbal signals (gestures or voice) emphasize important ideas in the verbal message?	▪ He emphasizes things with his voice, but not with gestures.
▪ If visuals are used, are they helpful?	▪ The map and picture both help me understand the topic better. Overall delivery: good

TIP   Many speakers use technology to incorporate visuals into their presentations. They might use a DVD, an overhead projector, or presentation software to present and enhance their ideas. To evaluate whether a presenter has used technology effectively, think about whether the technology helps the presenter achieve his or her purpose—to inform. Does the technology contribute to the presentation, or does it distract from the presenter's ideas?

Put It All Together   As you listen to a speech, use charts like the one on page 675 and the one above to make notes about content and delivery. Considering both the content and the delivery of a presentation takes concentration, so try to limit your distractions. You may want to sit closer to the speaker and put away everything except your evaluation charts and a pen or pencil.

SKILLS FOCUS

Evaluate delivery when listening: verbal techniques. Evaluate delivery when listening: nonverbal techniques. Limit distractions when listening.

YOUR TURN 16   **Evaluating an Oral Presentation**

Evaluate a research presentation by one or more of your classmates. Create charts like those on page 675 and this page to evaluate both the content and delivery of the speech.

23 *Choices*

Choose one of the following activities to complete.

▶ CAREERS

1. Expert Guidance When you see someone doing an exciting job on television, you might wonder how you might someday get that job. Choose a career that interests you. Then, ask classmates or adults you know to refer you to someone with that job. Interview this person, and ask what education and training are needed to get into that career. Present your findings by creating a **career guide** with other students who choose this activity.

▶ LISTENING

2. My Kind of Tune Do you enjoy hip-hop, country, or some other kind of music? Research the important elements of a particular style of music, and choose a recording of that style of music. Then, write a **review** that evaluates how well the recording uses the elements of its musical style. Give a **multimedia presentation** in which you share your review and play the recording.

▶ CROSSING THE CURRICULUM: PHYSICAL EDUCATION

3. Hall of Fame Make a **trading card** for a famous athlete of the past. Include a picture of the athlete, important dates, records, and other interesting facts you uncover in your research. You might consider choosing one of these athletes: Jim Thorpe, Jackie Joyner-Kersee, Sonja Henie, or Satchel Paige.

▶ CREATIVE WRITING

4. A Fresh Angle Try one of the following ideas to share information about your research topic: Write an entertaining **letter** about your topic to someone you think might be interested in it, or write a **short story** that uses the information you learned researching your topic. You could also write a **poem** about your topic, describing or explaining it in a creative way. Share your writing with others by mailing it, reading it aloud, or posting it on a bulletin board.

PORTFOLIO

SKILLS FOCUS

Adapt oral messages to occasion: interviews. Write a review. Integrate multimedia and technology into presentations. Use effective representing strategies. Write a letter. Write short stories or poems.

24

Making a Difference

Talk   Listen

Reading Workshop

Reading a Persuasive Essay

Writing Workshop

Writing a Persuasive Letter

Focus on Listening

Evaluating a Persuasive Speech

"Pleasepleasepleasepleaseplease?!" This may be how young children attempt to get their way, but by now you probably know that whining and repetition are not effective when you are older. You are more likely to get what you want through the art of **persuasion**—convincing others by giving reasons that make sense. Whether you are trying to persuade others or others are trying to persuade you, good reasons make all the difference.

Persuasion comes in many forms. A spoken request from a friend is usually casual and unplanned. The kind of persuasion you read or write is more carefully structured. It includes an opinion and specific reasons to support the opinion. The kind of persuasion you view, including TV ads and billboards, adds pictures and even jingles that appeal to your emotions as well as to your mind.

> **Informational Text**
>
> Persuasion

YOUR TURN 1 Discovering Persuasion

In a small group, discuss the following questions.

- What makes a spoken request convincing? a TV ad? a billboard?
- Is one of these types of persuasion usually more persuasive than the others? Which one? Why?

internetconnect

go.
hrw
.com
GO TO: go:hrw.com
KEYWORD: EOLang 6-24

Reading a Persuasive Essay

WHAT'S AHEAD?

In this section you will read a persuasive essay. You will also learn how to

■ identify facts and opinions

■ recognize the reasons and evidence writers use to persuade readers

You finish your lunch, and then you throw away the wrapper and bag. You pry a new computer game out of layers of plastic and cardboard, tossing the packaging away before you play the game. You even drag your broken desk chair out to the curb to be picked up on trash day. Think about the amount of stuff you throw away every day, and multiply that amount by 300 million, the estimated population of the United States. That is a lot of garbage! The author of the following essay will try to persuade you to change your ways. Will you be convinced?

Preparing to Read

READING SKILL → **Fact and Opinion** Strong *opinions* often inspire people to write persuasive essays. To be effective, though, a writer must support opinions with **facts,** or statements that can be proved true. As you read the following essay, watch out for statements of **opinion,** which cannot be proved.

READING FOCUS → **Reasons and Evidence** In the courtroom dramas you see in movies and on TV, do jurors accept a lawyer's argument without question? Of course not. Even TV lawyers provide *reasons* and *evidence* to convince juries of their cases. Writers have the same duty to their readers. They must support their opinions with enough reasons and evidence to persuade their readers. See if William Dudley, the writer of the following essay, has done a convincing job.

Read the following essay. In a notebook, jot down answers to the numbered active-reading questions in the shaded boxes. Underlined words will be used in the Vocabulary Mini-Lesson on page 687.

from The Environment:
Distinguishing Between Fact and Opinion

The U.S. Has a
GARBAGE CRISIS

BY WILLIAM DUDLEY

1   America is a "throwaway" society. Each year Americans throw away 16 billion disposable diapers, 1.6 billion pens, and 220 million tires. For the sake of convenience, we tend to throw these and other used goods away rather than repair or recycle them. The average American household generates 350 bags, or 4,550 gallons, of garbage per year. This comes out to a total of 160 million tons of garbage a year. We have to change our throwaway lifestyle before we are buried in it.

> **1. What opinion does the writer express in this paragraph?**

2   We are running out of places to put all the garbage we produce. About 80 percent of it is now buried in landfills. There are 6,000 landfills currently operating, but many of them are becoming full. The Environmental Protection Agency estimates that one-half of the remaining landfills will run out of space and close within the next five to ten years.

> **2. What reason does the writer give in this paragraph?**

3   Can we simply build new landfills to replace the old ones? The answer is no. For one thing, we are running out of space. We cannot afford to use up land that is needed for farms, parks, and homes.

4   In addition, many landfills contain toxic chemicals that can leak into and pollute underground water supplies. In New York City, over seventy-five wells had to be closed because of such toxic waste poisoning.

> **3. Which statements in paragraph 4 can be proved? How?**

5   One suggested alternative to landfills is to burn the trash. In some states, large incinerators are used to burn garbage, and the heat that is generated is used to produce electricity. But this solution

4. What evidence supports the writer's reason that there are problems with burning trash?

has drawbacks. Burning trash pollutes the air with dioxin and mercury, which are highly poisonous. Furthermore, burning does not completely solve the landfill problem. Leftover ash produced by burning is often highly toxic, and it still has to be buried somewhere.

6   The only real solution to the garbage crisis is for Americans to reduce the amount of trash they throw away. There are two methods of doing this. One is recycling—reusing garbage. Bottles can be washed and reused. Aluminum cans can be melted down and remade. Currently in the U.S., only 11 percent of solid waste is used again as something else. . . .

7   We must also reduce the amount of garbage we produce in the first place. We should use less plastic, which is hard to recycle and does not decompose in landfills. Much garbage is useless packaging. Consumers should buy foods and goods that use less packaging. We also should buy reusable products rather than things that are used once and thrown away. . . .

8   A woman in California was asked about garbage. She replied, "Why do we need to change anything? I put my garbage out on the sidewalk and they take it away." Attitudes like hers must be changed. We have to face the inevitable question posed by Ed Repa, manager of the solid waste disposal program at the National Solid Waste Management Association: "How do you throw something away when there is no 'away'?"

5. How does this example help the writer make his point?

Think as a Reader/Writer: First Thoughts

1. **What is the author trying to convince the reader to do?**

2. **Which parts of the essay were convincing to you? Why?**

Fact and Opinion

Is That a Fact?   Maybe you have seen a TV show in which a detective asks witnesses for "just the facts." *Facts,* not opinions, will help the detective solve the case. Facts also help writers persuade readers because **facts** are statements that can be proved true. Facts may include numbers, dates, or measurements.

Opinions, on the other hand, are impossible to prove. An **opinion** is a person's judgment. Phrases such as "I believe," "I feel," or "I think" indicate an opinion. Telling readers what *should* be done is another sure clue that an opinion is being expressed. Judgment words such as *best, worst, greatest,* and *prettiest* may be clues that a statement is an opinion. The following pairs of statements show the difference between facts and opinions.

Fact	The city council passed the proposal **five to one.**
Opinion	**I think** the city council made a **smart** decision.
Fact	Our school buses were made in **2002.**
Opinion	The school board **should** buy newer buses.
Fact	Jefferson was the **third** president.
Opinion	Jefferson was the country's **best** president.

Try identifying facts and opinions in the paragraph below. If you have trouble, follow the steps on the next page.

> The city should encourage people to ride bicycles for short trips. Bicycles do not pollute. Taking several short car trips can create more pollution than a longer drive. If people tried bicycling for these short trips, they would enjoy it. Cyclists travel at slower speeds, which allows them to take in nature's sights and sounds. I think an ad campaign could convince people to stop depending on cars for all of their transportation.

SKILLS FOCUS

Identify and understand the difference between fact and opinion.

▶ STEP 1 Read the paragraph. Look for clues, such as *should, good, bad,* or *I believe,* that signal an opinion.

Sentences with opinion clues: "The city <u>should</u> encourage people to ride bicycles for short trips." "If people tried bicycling for these short trips, they would <u>enjoy</u> it." "<u>I think</u> an ad campaign could convince people to stop depending on cars for all of their transportation."

▶ STEP 2 Read the paragraph again to identify facts. Look for numbers, measurements, or things that can be proved.

Sentences with fact clues: "Bicycles <u>do not pollute</u>." "Taking several short car trips can create <u>more pollution</u> than a longer drive." "Cyclists travel at <u>slower speeds.</u> . . ."

TIP Quiz a classmate by writing five sentences on your paper from the essay. Then, have your partner identify each sentence as either a fact or an opinion. Your partner should also explain his or her answers.

YOUR TURN 2 **Identifying Fact and Opinion**

Re-read the essay on pages 681–682, and look for fact and opinion clues. Identify three sentences that contain facts and three sentences that contain opinions, and explain how you can tell.

| READING FOCUS ▶

Reasons and Evidence

Building a Case Have you ever tried to build a human pyramid? The base of the pyramid needs to have more people, and stronger people, than the top does. Look at the following diagram of a persuasive essay. Notice how it looks like a pyramid.

Writer's opinion

Reason #1   Reason #2   Reason #3

Evidence for reason   Evidence for reason   Evidence for reason

The opinion in a persuasive essay is like the person at the top of a human pyramid. The *reasons* are like the people in the middle row who support the person on top. The *evidence* in a persuasive essay is like the group of people who form the base of a human pyramid. Persuasive writing must have support to be strong, just as a human pyramid needs strong supporters.

Reasons   A **reason** explains *why* the writer holds a particular opinion. In a persuasive essay the writer will usually write one or two paragraphs explaining each reason. For example, in the paragraph on page 683, the writer who wanted the city to encourage bike riding gave the reason that it would help reduce air pollution.

Evidence   Just saying that bicycling reduces air pollution is not convincing. The city council or mayor would need evidence before believing the reason. **Evidence** is the support for a reason, the specific *facts* and *examples* that illustrate the reason. You already know that a **fact** is a statement that can be proved true. An **example** is an event or illustration that shows one specific instance of a reason. Here is evidence a writer used to support a reason in an essay about creating more community bike trails. Would this reason be as convincing without the evidence?

> **Reason:** Many people enjoy bike riding.
>
> **Fact:** 80% of the students at my school own bicycles.
>
> **Example:** When I ride my bike in my neighborhood, I always see lots of other people riding bikes, too.

TIP   Using reasons and evidence to support an opinion is called making a *logical appeal*. A **logical appeal** persuades because it makes sense. There are two other ways persuasive writers appeal to readers. While logical appeals try to persuade your head, **emotional appeals** try to persuade your heart. Humane Society ads showing adorable puppies and kittens up for adoption are examples of emotional appeals. Finally, **ethical appeals** try to persuade you by making the presenter seem trustworthy. One example of an ethical appeal would be a public service announcement featuring a respected celebrity speaking sincerely about a serious issue.

See if you can spot the reasons and evidence in the paragraph on the next page. The graphic organizer below it will help you check your answers.

TIP   In paragraph 3 on page 681, the writer addresses a *counter-argument*. A **counter-argument** is a reader's **objection** to the writer's opinion. A writer can address a counterargument by presenting a reason that explains why the objection is either incorrect or unimportant.

SKILLS FOCUS

Identify an author's reasons for writing. Identify and evaluate the use of accurate supporting citations and evidence in a text. Evaluate facts used in a text. Evaluate examples used in a text. Identify and understand logical, emotional, and ethical appeals in a persuasive text.

People should donate supplies to the Helping Hands Community Assistance Program now. The supplies of clothing, shoes, and blankets are very low. There are only four coats, six blankets, and one pair of shoes now available. The director says that they need enough clothing for twenty adults and ten children. Also, winter is coming soon. Winter always brings a higher demand for warm clothing. Last winter some families left empty-handed because supplies were gone.

TIP The sentence that identifies the issue and the writer's opinion on the issue is called the **opinion statement.**

The writer of the paragraph above used reasons and evidence to be as persuasive as possible. Here is a graphic organizer showing how she built her case. Notice how the graphic organizer is shaped like a pyramid. The reasons and evidence hold up the opinion.

YOUR TURN 3 Identifying Reasons and Evidence

Re-read "The U.S. Has a Garbage Crisis" on pages 681–682. Then, create a graphic organizer like the one above. Fill in your boxes with the writer's opinion, his reasons for that opinion, and the evidence that supports each of his reasons. (Hint: You will find this information in paragraphs 1–5 of the reading selection.)

SKILLS FOCUS

(page 687): Use reference aids to clarify meanings and usage.
(page 688): Identify and understand the difference between fact and opinion.

Dictionary and Thesaurus

Persuasive writing asks you to take a side on an issue. To make an intelligent decision, you need to be sure you understand all of the words you read. You can use reference books to find an unfamiliar word's meaning. Here are two examples.

■ **Dictionary**   In a dictionary you will find the word's definition, its pronunciation, its part of speech, examples of how it is used, and its history.

■ **Thesaurus**   In a thesaurus you will find other words that are *synonyms* of the unfamiliar word. **Synonyms** are words that have almost the same meaning, such as *happy* and *glad*.

Dictionaries can sometimes be confusing when they list several definitions for one word. To find the right definition of a word, use the following steps.

THINKING IT THROUGH   Choosing the Right Definition

Here is an example based on the word *convenience* from the reading selection on page 681.

▶ **STEP 1** Look up the word in a dictionary. Read the entire definition.

Convenience means: 1. personal comfort 2. a favorable condition

▶ **STEP 2** Use each of the meanings in the context of the reading selection. Decide which meaning makes the most sense in the sentence.

"For the sake of personal comfort we tend to throw things away." That sounds good.

"For the sake of a favorable condition we tend to throw things away." That sounds strange. I think the first definition is correct in this context.

PRACTICE

Look up the words to the right in a dictionary. Use the steps above if the word has more than one definition. Write the correct definition of the word. Then, look the word up in a thesaurus and find a synonym that is familiar to you. Write that word next to the definition.

1. generates (page 681)
2. toxic (page 681)
3. incinerators (page 681)
4. decompose (page 682)
5. disposal (page 682)

Answering Questions About Fact and Opinion

When you take a reading test, you may be asked to identify statements of fact or opinion. Suppose the following paragraph and question were in a reading test. How would you approach them?

New equipment should be purchased for Esperanza Park. The existing playground equipment is old and dangerous. Three children have received serious cuts from the jagged metal edges of the swing set. The equipment is seventeen years old and cannot be repaired. The city should make Esperanza Park a fun, safe place to play for children and families in the city.

Which of the following is an OPINION expressed in this passage?

A. Children have gotten hurt on the playground.

B. The playground equipment should be repaired.

C. The playground equipment contains jagged metal edges.

D. Esperanza Park should be made safer for children.

THINKING IT THROUGH   Identifying Fact and Opinion

▶ **STEP 1** Determine what the question is asking you to do.

The question asks me to find an opinion in the passage. An opinion is a statement that makes a judgment and can't be proved.

▶ **STEP 2** Eliminate choices that do not answer the question. If the question asks for a fact, eliminate opinions. If it asks for an opinion, eliminate facts.

Choice A says "children have gotten hurt." This is a fact because you could ask parents whether their children have been hurt. C says the equipment has "jagged metal edges." This could be proved by looking at the equipment.

▶ **STEP 3** Look at the remaining choices to make sure that each is the kind of statement the question asks for. Then, choose the answer that is stated in the passage. (If the question asks you to identify an opinion, look for opinion clue words.)

The remaining choices are B and D. Choice B is an opinion because it uses the word should, but the passage says the equipment "cannot be repaired." Choice D also uses the word should, so it is an opinion, too. The last sentence of the passage says this in different words. I'll choose D.

Writing a Persuasive Letter

When you were younger, did you write letters to ask someone for a special toy? Maybe you wanted a certain doll or a new bicycle, so you described the toy and explained why you wanted it. Were you later thrilled to discover that your wish had been granted?

Now that you are older, you may know that letters can achieve results more important than toys. Here is your opportunity to use the power of persuasive writing to make a difference in the world around you. This workshop will teach you how to write a persuasive letter that will help make a positive change in your school, neighborhood, or town. The thrill of making a difference can be even more satisfying than receiving a new toy!

WHAT'S AHEAD?

In this workshop you will write a persuasive letter. You will also learn how to

- **develop reasons and evidence**
- **predict and answer objections**
- **choose and focus a call to action**
- **revise stringy sentences**
- **use possessives correctly**

Choose an Issue

Dare to Care   Given a choice between soup or sandwiches for lunch, you might answer, "I don't care." For you, the kind of food is not an issue. In persuasive writing, though, *issues* are important. An **issue** is a topic with at least two sides about which people disagree. **In a persuasive letter the writer tries to make the reader agree with his or her opinion on an issue.** Persuasive letters also may ask readers to take action on an issue.

◄ **KEY CONCEPT**

Take Your Pick   The issue you choose should be one that is important to you. If you do not feel strongly about an issue, how can you convince your readers to care about it? Ask yourself what issues most affect your world. Completing the following sentence starters will help you identify issues that matter to you.

> My school would be a better place if ____.
> I become upset when I see ____.

Little by Little   You should also choose an issue that is small enough for one person or group to have an effect. For example, one student chose the issue of littering. Although she also felt strongly about the issue of homelessness, she felt that by taking on a smaller issue, she would be better able to make a difference. She also knew that an anti-littering campaign for her soccer league would be an issue she could tackle in a letter.

Write Your Opinion Statement

Take a Stand   If you have chosen an issue that is important to you, you probably already know what your opinion on it is. You simply need to put that opinion into words. **An opinion statement should clearly state what the issue is and where the writer stands on it.** Here is how the writer who chose the issue of recycling came up with her opinion statement.

KEY CONCEPT

TIP An opinion statement may also be called a **thesis statement.**

---

issue: litter at soccer games
+ **how I feel about it:** soccer fields should be kept free of litter
_____

opinion statement: We need to start an anti-littering campaign to keep the soccer fields clean.

YOUR TURN 4

Choosing an Issue and Writing an Opinion Statement

Brainstorm issues that might make your community or the world a better place. Choose an issue that is both important to you and small enough to tackle in a letter. Write down your opinion about the issue. Then, put the issue and your opinion together into a single clear sentence—your opinion statement.

SKILLS FOCUS

Brainstorm to generate ideas. Choose a topic to write about. Include a statement of thesis/main idea. *(page 689)*: Write to persuade. Write a letter.

Consider Audience and Purpose

Dear Sir or Madam . . . You would not ask the President of the United States to shorten the school day. Yes, the President can do many things, but your request is likely to get lost in the shuffle of national issues. Because your **purpose** is to persuade your reader, it is important to write to someone who cares about the issue and can do something about it. **Contacting the right audience to consider your request is an important part of your letter's effectiveness.** Identify local people who have the power to do what you want. Your audience may be one person or a group of people. Notice how one student used the following questions to help identify her specific audience.

KEY CONCEPT

What part of your community does the issue involve?	Starting an anti-littering campaign at the soccer fields would involve my soccer league.
What is the specific name of the person or group you need to contact?	My league handbook says the president of the Eastside Soccer League is Jake Matsuo.
What do you know about this person or these people? (How old are they? What interests or concerns them? Why might they disagree with you, or object to your opinion?)	I know he's an adult, and he is interested in soccer. I think he is interested in keeping things running smoothly and in keeping fees low for players. He might object to my opinion if he thinks an anti-littering campaign would be time-consuming or expensive.

TIP In writing, **voice** reflects your tone and attitude. To persuade readers, you need to use a believable voice. In other words, you should sound as if you know what you are talking about and you take the issue seriously. You should also appeal to your audience by making it clear that you understand and care about their interests.

YOUR TURN 5 Considering Audience and Purpose

Your purpose is to persuade someone who has the power to grant your request. Use the questions above to figure out who that person or group of people is and think about what you know about them.

SKILLS FOCUS

Decide on a purpose for writing. Plan writing by targeting an audience. Plan writing by developing voice.

CRITICAL THINKING

Understanding Your Audience

Imagine sweltering under the hot summer sun at the beach when a vendor selling mugs of steaming hot chocolate comes along. Are you tempted to buy? Of course not. The vendor has forgotten the basic rule of persuasion: Appeal to your audience's interests. Once you know your audience's interests, you can predict their main **objection,** or reason why they might dis-

agree with you. Objections often revolve around how much time or effort a proposed change would take, or how much the change would cost. By appealing to your audience's interests, you can make objections such as these seem less important.

TIP An objection is also called a **counter-argument.**

THINKING IT THROUGH **Addressing Objections**

You want to persuade the city council to support a Latino cultural festival. Here's how to address their objection.

▶ **STEP 1** Identify the main reason your audience might disagree with you.

The city council might say that having a Latino cultural festival would be expensive.

▶ **STEP 2** Consider what is important to this audience.

■ saving money

■ bringing people together

▶ **STEP 3** Based on your audience's interests, identify a reason for your opinion that makes the audience's objection seem less important.

The festival can be a fun activity for the community, and it can be inexpensive. To save money, volunteers can organize the festival, and vendors can pay a fee to sell food and crafts.

PRACTICE

Suppose that you want to organize a tutoring program at your school. Older students would tutor younger students for one hour after school. Using the Thinking It Through steps above, identify a possible objection each of the audiences to the right might have. Then, list reasons that would address each audience's objection. Explain each reason.

1. the school principal
2. parents
3. students who would serve as tutors

Develop Reasons and Evidence

Answering the Big Question   Understanding your audience's interests will help you to answer their main question—"Why should I care?" **Your audience will want to know the reasons why they should accept your opinion.** You can begin developing solid reasons by asking why your opinion makes sense.

Your opinion needs more support than reasons alone, though. Evidence—from research and your experience—must support each reason for the reasons to be believable. **Facts,** which can be proved true, and **examples,** which illustrate a point, can provide support for reasons. See how the following reason is supported by a fact and an example.

> **Reason:** Volunteers help people.
>
> **Fact:** Since 1961, Peace Corps volunteers have helped people in 134 countries around the world.
>
> **Example:** My older sister volunteers by helping two fourth-graders with their math homework.

In the chart below, a student lists several reasons to begin an anti-littering campaign. In the middle column, the student gives facts and examples to support each of her reasons. In the right-hand column, she decides whether each reason and its supporting evidence will appeal to her audience.

KEY CONCEPT

TIP   The facts and examples should also provide **logical support** for your reasons. If they are not **relevant,** or clearly connected to the reason, your audience may become confused.

SKILLS FOCUS

Support, develop, and elaborate ideas in writing. Support ideas/theses with relevant evidence and details. Include appeals to logic. *(page 692):* Address potential objections.

Reasons	Supporting Evidence	Appealing to Audience?
An anti-littering campaign will make people aware of the trash problem.	My parents had to pick up trash left by others. That made them be more careful not to litter.	Yes. Most people want to enjoy the games and not worry about litter.
An anti-littering program will earn money.	By recycling, we can earn 32 cents for each pound of cans. This money can help pay for clinics to train new coaches.	Yes. If we pay for clinics with recycling money, the league won't have to raise fees to cover these things.
Participating in an anti-littering program helps players earn badges in Scouts.	I can earn 2 badges. Several players I know participate in Scouts.	No. This will help a few of us, but not the president of the soccer league.

From the chart on the previous page, you can tell that this student realized that the last reason might not appeal to her audience. The president of a soccer league is probably more interested in soccer than in scouting. The student thought about possible objections the president might have to the project. Then, she came up with a reason that would take his objection into account. See her revision in the chart below.

New Reason	Supporting Evidence	Appealing to Audience?
This project will not take very much time or effort.	Teams will make posters and rotate collecting the recycling containers. Parents and players do all the work.	Yes. He won't have to find people to do the work. This reason will also show that picking up trash and recycling is not too much trouble, which I think might be his objection.

TIP It is not enough just to give evidence. You also need to explain why your evidence is convincing. In the chart on page 693, the student explained in the Supporting Evidence column the meaning of each piece of evidence. ("This money can help pay for clinics to train new coaches.") This kind of explanation is called **elaboration**.

YOUR TURN 6 · Developing Reasons and Evidence

- Create a chart like the one on page 693, listing reasons and evidence to support your opinion. (Use the library to find facts to support your reasons.) Use the right-hand column to decide whether each reason will appeal to your audience.
- Replace any reasons that will not appeal to most of your audience. You should have at least two good reasons, each supported by facts or examples.

 **KEY CONCEPT**

Choose and Focus a Call to Action

911 Means Action! When you dial 911, the operator knows instantly that you are asking for help. In a way, your persuasive letter is also a 911 call because it includes a *call to action*. **A call to action tells readers how they can respond to your ideas.** To get your readers to take action, your call to action must be both *reasonable* and *specific*.

A **reasonable** request is financially possible and within the audience's power. There is no point in asking a local audience to spend billions of dollars to end all wars or to house all homeless people. Instead, your call to action should focus on smaller actions. Suggesting that your audience sign a petition or volunteer a few hours of time is not too much to ask.

A **specific** request is clear and tells exactly what you want readers to do about an issue. How can a reader tell whether "Please do more for our children" is a call for more sidewalks or for a new playground? The specific call to action, "Start a tutoring program for elementary students," would be more effective.

THINKING IT THROUGH   Writing a Call to Action

Here is how to write a reasonable and specific call to action.

▶ **STEP 1** Decide exactly what action you want to take place.

I want to see trash picked up and recycled at our soccer games.

▶ **STEP 2** State the call to action in concrete terms so there is no confusion about what you are asking.

Maybe my call to action is too vague. I can ask the league to get recycling containers and put them at the soccer fields.

▶ **STEP 3** Address your call to action directly to the audience.

"Please buy and place recycling bins for aluminum cans at the soccer fields. Then, ask teams to participate in the anti-littering campaign."

YOUR TURN 7   Choosing and Focusing a Call to Action

Decide what you want to ask your readers to do about the issue you have chosen. Then, use the steps above to write a **call to action** that is reasonable, clear, and specific. Be direct, but remember a call to action is a request. Therefore, be polite, too.

SKILLS FOCUS

Elaborate with explanations. Include a call to action.

Writing

Persuasive Letter

Framework	**Think as a Reader/Writer**

Introduction
- Attention-grabbing opening
- Opinion statement

Grab your readers' interest right away with an **interesting beginning.** For example, you could begin your letter with an anecdote (a brief story), or a question. Next, include a clear **opinion statement** that tells your audience exactly what you think about the issue you have chosen.

Body
- Reason #1
  Evidence supporting reason #1
- Reason #2
  Evidence supporting reason #2
  and so on

- Support your opinion with at least two good reasons. Write a **paragraph for each reason.** You can arrange your body paragraphs in **order of importance,** starting with the most important reason, or in **climactic order,** ending with the most important reason.

- Support each of your reasons with at least one specific **fact** or **example** each.

- **Elaborate** support by explaining the meaning of each fact or example or by summing up your point.

Conclusion
- Summary of reasons
- Call to action

Remind your audience why this issue is important by **summarizing** your reasons in a single sentence. Next, tell your audience what they should do about the issue with a reasonable and specific **call to action.**

 Drafting Your Persuasive Letter

Now, it is your chance to write a first draft of a persuasive letter. As you write, refer to the framework above and the Writer's Model on the next page.

A Writer's Model

The final draft below closely follows the framework for a persuasive letter on the previous page.

Dear Mr. Matsuo:

My soccer team won its game last Saturday. I was happy and excited until I started walking toward the parking lot. I passed cups and candy wrappers left in the stands and six trash cans overflowing with aluminum cans. Seeing all the trash that people did not throw away and the cans that could be recycled bothered me. With your help, we can improve the Eastside Soccer League. We need to start an anti-littering campaign to keep the soccer fields clean.

An anti-littering campaign would help people become aware of the trash problem. Since I talked to my family about the problem, they have noticed how bad the trash is, too. After last Saturday's game, they made sure they picked up their trash so that they were not contributing to the problem. Letting people know there is a problem is the first step to solving it.

If we make recycling part of the plan, the anti-littering campaign can earn money. By recycling aluminum cans, the Eastside Soccer League can earn 32 cents per pound. Since there are twelve trash cans at the soccer fields that each can hold about two pounds of cans, and there are fifteen games in the season, we could earn as much as $115.20. This money could be used to pay for clinics to train new coaches. That way, more people could get involved in the league because training would be available.

Finally, this project will take little time and effort. This can be a project for the parents and the players. Each team will make posters encouraging people to be responsible for their trash. Also, the two teams playing the last game on a field will pick up trash left in the stands and empty the two recycling containers on their field. Once all twelve

Attention-grabbing opening

Opinion statement

Reason #1: Help people become aware

Evidence (example)

Elaboration

Reason #2: Earn money

Evidence (facts)

Elaboration

Reason #3: Easy to do

Evidence (examples)

(continued)

(continued)

Elaboration

containers are emptied, one parent can drive the cans to the recycling center. This work will take just a few minutes of time. Since the teams already rotate playing times, no one team will be stuck with this chore every week.

Summary of reasons

An anti-littering campaign will help people become aware of the trash problem and earn money for the league without becoming a time-consuming or expensive project.

Call to action

Please buy and place recycling bins for aluminum cans at the soccer fields. Then, ask teams to participate in the anti-littering campaign.

Sincerely,

LaVonne Barton

LaVonne Barton

Designing Your Writing

Business Letter Format   To add to your persuasive letter's impact, use a business letter format like the one below.

Reference Note

For more on **business letters,** see page 792 in the Quick Reference Handbook.

your address

date

(audience) name and address

greeting

introduction

body

conclusion

(writing assignment)

closing

signature

typed or printed name

SKILLS FOCUS

Design documents in preparation for publishing. Use correct format in writing business documents.

A Student's Model

Concern for the global, rather than local, environment prompted sixth-grader Tyler Duckworth to write a letter to the President of the United States.

My name is Tyler Duckworth, and I am a sixth-grade student at Liberty Middle School in Morganton, North Carolina. I think the first thing you should do, Mr. President, is take specific action to protect our environment. As an avid reader of books about science, I am concerned about the natural wonders of our nation and of the world being preserved both for my generation and for future generations.

First of all, the pollution of our earth seems to be on the increase; factories, cars, and people continue to pollute. Statistics show that acid rain is on the increase, and the hole in the ozone layer is widening at an alarming rate. I feel action must be taken now, before it is too late. . . .

Also, the land in the rain forests is essential to our survival. Each year, more and more land in the rain forests is destroyed. If man continues to destroy the rain forests, the species present in them and the plant life present in them can never be replaced. The action taken must be firm and bound by law.

I believe that you, Mr. President, care about our country. You have stated in many speeches that I have listened to and in many articles that I have read that you care about our environment. It is essential that you, as our leader, do what is necessary to preserve the earth for future generations.

In my dad's office, he has a quote that reads, "We do not inherit the earth from our ancestors; we borrow it from our children." That, too, is my belief as a twelve-year-old citizen of the greatest country in the world. Mr. President, I ask you to please act now to save our country and our world.

Opinion statement

Reason #1: Increasing pollution

Evidence (facts)

Reason #2: Losing rain forests

Evidence (facts)

Reason #3: President's record

Evidence (facts)

Call to action

Revising

COMPUTER TIP

You can find many reference materials on CD-ROM, and you can use the Internet as a resource. For example, if you need additional support for a reason, you can look up facts on reliable Web sites or on a CD-ROM version of an encyclopedia.

Evaluate and Revise Content, Organization, and Style

Twice Is Nice Double the persuasive power of your letter by giving it at least two readings. In the first reading, focus on the content and organization of your first draft. The guidelines below can help. In the second reading, look at the individual sentences using the Focus on Sentences on page 702.

▶ **First Reading: Content and Organization** When you **edit** your letter, you evaluate what you have written and revise it to make it better. Use the following guidelines to make your letter more persuasive. First, answer the questions in the left-hand column. If you need help answering the questions, use the tips in the middle column. Then, use the revision techniques in the right-hand column to make necessary changes.

Guidelines for Self-Evaluation and Peer Evaluation		
Evaluation Questions	**Tips**	**Revision Techniques**
❶ Does the introduction have a clear opinion statement?	**Underline** the opinion statement.	**Add** an opinion statement, or **revise** a sentence to state your opinion clearly.
❷ Does the letter give at least two reasons to support the opinion?	**Put stars** next to the reasons that support the opinion.	If necessary, **add** reasons that support the opinion.
❸ Does at least one piece of evidence support each of the reasons?	**Circle** evidence that supports each reason. **Draw a line** to the reason each piece of evidence supports.	If necessary, **add** facts or examples to support each reason. **Rearrange** evidence so it is close to the reason it supports.
❹ Does the letter explain each fact and example?	**Put a check mark** next to each explanation.	**Elaborate** by adding explanations for each fact and example.
❺ Does the conclusion include a specific and reasonable call to action?	**Draw a wavy line** under the call to action.	**Add** a call to action, or **revise** the call to action to make it more specific and reasonable.

ONE WRITER'S REVISIONS This revision is an early draft of the letter on page 697.

> With your help, we can improve the Eastside Soccer
> *We need to start* ~~*to keep the soccer fields clean*~~
> League. An anti-littering campaign ~~would help~~.
>
> An anti-littering campaign would help people become
> aware of the trash problem. Since I talked to my family
> about the problem, they have noticed how bad the trash
> is, too. After last Saturday's game, they made sure they
> picked up their trash so that they were not contributing
> to the problem. *Letting people know there is a problem is*
> *the first step to solving it.*

revise

elaborate

Think as a Reader/Writer

1. Why did the writer revise the sentence at the end of the first paragraph?
2. Why did the writer add a sentence to the end of the second paragraph?

▶ **Second Reading: Style** You have taken a look at the big picture of your letter. In your second reading, you will look at the pieces of that picture by focusing on the sentences. One way to improve your writing is to make stringy sentences more compact.

When you evaluate your letter for style, ask yourself whether your writing avoids using long sentences made up of strings of ideas. As you re-read your letter, highlight long sentences that use *and, but,* or *so* to join two or more complete thoughts—ideas that can stand alone. Then, break one or more stringy sentences into two shorter sentences. The Focus on Sentences on the next page can help you learn more about eliminating stringy sentences.

PEER REVIEW

As you read a peer's persuasive letter, ask yourself these questions:

■ Who is the target audience for this letter? Does the writer appeal to their interests?

■ What is the strongest piece of support? What makes it stand out?

SKILLS FOCUS

Revise by adding or replacing text. Revise by rearranging text. Revise by elaborating. Revise for logical support of ideas. Use technology to revise texts. Evaluate others' writing. Develop writer's style.

Eliminating Stringy Sentences

When your purpose is to persuade, your style should also be persuasive. Avoid using stringy sentences. Reading long, stringy sentences is like listening to a person who goes on and on. They bore readers, and a bored reader is an unconvinced reader. To eliminate stringy sentences, follow these steps.

- First, find the conjunctions *and, but,* or *so* in a very long sentence. Put a slash mark before each conjunction.

- Then, see if each part has a subject and a verb. If each part of the sentence has both a subject and a verb and expresses a complete thought, then it can stand alone.

- Revise a stringy sentence by breaking it into two or more separate sentences. Each complete thought may have its own sentence.

Reference Note

For more on **parts of speech,** see Chapter 3.

TIP If part of the sentence does not express a complete thought, that part will not be able to stand alone in its own sentence.

ONE WRITER'S REVISIONS

> My soccer team won its game last Saturday. ̷s̷o̷ I was happy and excited until I started walking toward the parking lot. ̷a̷n̷d̷ I passed cups and candy wrappers left in the stands and six trash cans overflowing with aluminum cans.

Think as a Reader/Writer

How did breaking the sentence above into three sentences improve it?

SKILLS FOCUS

Demonstrate control of grammar and sentence structure. Use conjunctions to connect ideas meaningfully. *(page 703):* Use apostrophes correctly in possessives. Proofread one's own writing in preparation for publishing.

YOUR TURN 9 — Evaluating and Revising Your Persuasive Letter

Use the guidelines on page 700 and page 701 to evaluate and revise the content, organization, and style of your letter. If a peer read your letter, consider his or her comments as you revise.

Proofread Your Letter

Edit for Oomph   Careless mistakes decrease the persuasive power of your letter. Proofread your letter for mistakes in grammar, spelling, and punctuation.

Grammar Link

Punctuating Possessives Correctly

The **possessive** form of a noun or pronoun shows ownership. Using possessives helps writers make their points more concisely. Read the example below.

the playground equipment at our school
our school's playground equipment

   Here are four rules to remember about possessives.

To form the possessive case of a singular noun, add an apostrophe and an *s*.

girl's sweatshirt   car's bumper

To form the possessive case of a plural noun ending in *s*, add only the apostrophe.

books' pages   stores' signs

Do not use an apostrophe to make a noun plural. If you are not sure when to use an apostrophe, ask yourself, "Does the noun possess what follows?" If you answer *yes*, you need an apostrophe.

Do not use an apostrophe with possessive personal pronouns. These pronouns include

its, yours, theirs, his, hers, and *ours.*

The dog missed **its** owner.

PRACTICE

Write the following sentences on your own paper, adding apostrophes where they are needed. If a sentence is correct, write C next to the sentence on your paper.

Example:
1. In visitors eyes, our towns trash is its biggest problem.
1. *In visitors' eyes, our town's trash is its biggest problem.*

1. Recycling helps meet the citys goals as outlined in its long-range plan.
2. Other towns have recycling programs.
3. Theirs are successful. Ours still needs the councils approval.
4. The countys landfill is quickly filling up from the four towns trash.
5. Voters signatures filled page after page of one groups petition.

For more information and practice on **possessives,** see page 346.

Publish Your Letter

Post It!   Publishing a persuasive letter is simple. It requires an envelope, a correct address, and a stamp. Just mail it to the person or the individual people in your target audience. Here are two other ways to reach your readers.

- Even if you will not be mailing your letter, but handing it to someone you know well, use a business envelope to show that you mean business.

- If you have access to e-mail, you can send the letter electronically. Make sure you carefully type the message to avoid introducing mistakes. Be sure to confirm your readers' addresses before sending your letter.

PORTFOLIO

Reflect on Your Letter

Building Your Portfolio   The best way to judge your letter's effectiveness is to see what response you get. You may have to wait a while. Factors you may not know about may lead to a "No," a vague response such as "We will consider your request," or no response at all. However, you can judge your letter in the context of your entire portfolio by answering the following questions.

- What are my strengths as a writer? What did I do well in this piece and in other pieces in my portfolio? Which piece was my best or favorite? Why?

- What writing skills do I need to work on? If I had the chance, what would I do differently in this piece or in other pieces in my portfolio? Why?

- What are my goals as a writer now? What kinds of writing does my portfolio seem to be missing? What would I like to try next?

YOUR TURN 10
Proofreading, Publishing, and Reflecting on Your Persuasive Letter

- Correct mistakes in punctuation, spelling, capitalization, and grammar. Pay particular attention to possessives.

- Publish your letter to your target audience.

- Answer the Reflect on Your Letter questions above. Record your responses in a learning log, or include them in your portfolio.

Answering Questions That Ask You to Persuade

Some writing tests ask you to choose and support an opinion on an issue. Your response may be a persuasive letter or essay. If the following prompt were on a test, how would you approach it?

The city council has a limited budget for a new park. It is trying to decide between spending money for large shade trees or for an in-line skating path. Decide how you think the money should be spent. Then, write a letter convincing the city council to vote in favor of your decision. Give three reasons for your opinion.

THINKING IT THROUGH   Writing a Persuasive Essay

▶ **STEP 1** Identify the task the prompt is asking you to do.

The prompt asks me to decide how the council should spend the money. I have to write a letter stating my opinion and give three reasons to support it.

▶ **STEP 2** Decide on your opinion.

I like in-line skating, but I think trees are more important.

▶ **STEP 3** Develop three reasons to support your opinion.

1. More people will enjoy trees.

2. Trees give shade, which makes the park more comfortable.

3. Trees take time to grow, so we need to plant them now. A skating path can be added any time.

▶ **STEP 4** Develop evidence (facts and examples) to support your reasons.

1. All people appreciate trees. I only know people my age who skate.

2. Summer temperatures are in the 90s. Shade will keep the playground and picnic tables cool even in hot weather.

3. We planted a tree when I was six, and it is still not as tall as our house.

▶ **STEP 5** Write your essay. Include your opinion in the introduction, make each reason a paragraph—with support—and give a call to action in your conclusion.

▶ **STEP 6** Edit (evaluate, revise, proofread) your essay.

Writing a Humorous Advertisement

Is all persuasive writing serious? Not at all. Many people, in fact, find humor more persuasive than logic. Advertisers often rely on humor to persuade their audiences to buy their products. Humorous adver-tisements usually include these elements: a specific **product** being sold; a **reason** for buying the product, and funny **sounds** or **visuals**. Here is an example of a humorous print ad. Can you identify the elements?

Must be the
Grow Strong Vitamins
you gave her...

Grow Strong Vitamins give your children the boost they need to grow strong bones and healthy bodies. Who knows what your child could do with **Grow Strong Vitamins**? Try them and see!

A Little Imagination To come up with an idea for a humorous ad, begin by identifying a product you would like to advertise. Next, think of a brand name for your product. Brainstorm a list of reasons why people should buy your product. Then, choose a humorous way to get one of those reasons across to an audience. Consider these techniques.

- **Exaggeration** Exaggerate one of the claims of your product. This is the technique the ad on page 706 uses, exaggerating how strong and healthy children who use Grow Strong Vitamins become.

- **Irony** To create humor, say or show the opposite of what readers expect. You might show a family riding in a car. The dad says, "How much longer?" Then, the mom says, "Are we there yet?" The slogan would read, "Kids aren't the only ones who look forward to the fun at Giggles Amusement Park."

- **Silliness** Use silly sounds, voices, words, or visuals, or create a silly character to pitch your product. Talking animals, aliens, and cartoon characters are all used to sell products. For example, a cartoon version of a computer virus might complain about an antivirus software that keeps killing him off.

Sell It Once you have a good idea of what will be in your ad, you can produce it. Create one of these types of ads.

- **Radio Ad** You can turn your idea into a radio ad if the humor is in the words and sounds you include. To do this, you will need to write a script, create sound effects, and record the ad.

- **Print Ad** If the words and pictures are the funny parts of your idea, you can create a print ad like the one on page 706. You may create your ad by cutting and arranging pictures and words, or you might try creating it on a computer with copyright-free pictures.

- **Television Ad** If both sounds and visuals are important in your ad, turn your idea into a television commercial. You should write a script for the ad and find a good location to shoot, as well as any costumes or props that are important for your idea. Cast classmates to act in your ad if you wish, and record it using your school's video equipment.

(For information about **speaking,** see page 753. For information about **graphics,** see page 721. For information about **video production,** see page 531.)

YOUR TURN 11 Writing a Humorous Advertisement

Using the guidelines above, develop an idea for a humorous advertisement. Then, produce the ad as a radio ad, print ad, or television ad, and share it with your class.

Evaluating a Persuasive Speech

WHAT'S AHEAD?

In this section you will evaluate a persuasive speech. You will also learn how to

- **identify your purpose for listening**
- **develop criteria for evaluating persuasive messages**
- **analyze a speaker's delivery and persuasive techniques**

f you think you lack experience in evaluating persuasive speeches, think again. If you read magazines, watch TV commercials, or notice billboards, you are highly qualified. Any time you laugh at a clever advertisement or roll your eyes at a weak one, you are evaluating persuasion.

Listen with a Purpose

All persuasive messages, including advertisements, are created for the purpose of convincing people to do something or to believe something. When you listen to an ad or a persuasive speech, you may want to get information. However, your *main* purpose for listening will probably be to see whether you agree with the speaker's opinion. To do that, you must evaluate the speaker's message. Here are the elements to evaluate in a persuasive speech.

- **Content** is driven by the speaker's purpose. Since the speaker's purpose is to persuade, you can expect the content to include opinions, reasons, and evidence.
- **Delivery** refers to how the speaker delivers the message.
- **Believability** refers to whether or not you can believe the speaker.

Not all persuasive messages try to convince through solid evidence. Many persuasive speakers (and advertisers) also draw from a grab bag of *persuasive techniques*. **Persuasive techniques** rely on

Reference Note

For more on **evaluating a speech,** see page 764 in the Quick Reference Handbook.

SKILLS FOCUS

Listen to evaluate or form an opinion. Analyze and evaluate speaker's message.

emotional impact to "sell" an idea or product. Here are four of the most common persuasive techniques.

- **Bandwagon**   A speaker may use this method to make you feel that everyone else is doing something, so you should do it, too. The statement "Everyone agrees that recycling is important" is an example of the bandwagon approach.

- **Testimonial**   A speaker may try to persuade you with an example from his or her own experience, or a **testimonial.** For example, the speaker might say, "Volunteering at our local animal shelter has been a great experience for me."

- **"Plain Folks"**   A speaker may try to show that he or she shares the concerns of the audience members. "Like you, I'm concerned about the cost of school supplies. Getting the supplies we need can be difficult when prices keep going up."

- **Emotional Appeals**   This technique uses the audience's own emotions to get them on the speaker's side. An emotional appeal might tap into listeners' concern for others by telling sad stories about young refugees. Other appeals might spur the audience's school spirit or their anger about animal cruelty through words with positive or negative **connotations** (meanings beyond a dictionary definition).

Develop Criteria

Use the elements of a persuasive speech to develop **criteria** for evaluation. To develop criteria for a persuasive speech, first identify and interpret (or understand) these parts of each element.

- **Content**   Consider the **verbal elements:** major ideas and supporting reasons and evidence, facts and opinions, persuasive techniques.

- **Delivery**   Consider the **nonverbal elements:** posture, gestures, eye contact, voice, facial expressions.

- **Believability**   Consider the speaker's **perspective,** or attitude. For example, believable speakers are considerate of their audiences. They think about what their audiences will find persuasive. In contrast, speakers who try to force their opinions on their audiences without considering their audiences' views will be less believable.

Ask yourself what each item above would be like in a successful speech. The Thinking It Through steps on the next page can help.

> **TIP**   Persuasive techniques are sometimes called **propaganda** techniques. They are used not only to sell products, but also to convince others to share an opinion. Listeners should be careful not to be convinced by propaganda alone. They should demand that a persuasive speaker also give solid support for his or her opinions.

SKILLS FOCUS

Identify and evaluate persuasive/propaganda techniques when listening. Evaluate content when listening. Evaluate delivery when listening: verbal techniques. Evaluate delivery when listening: nonverbal techniques. Evaluate credibility when listening. Analyze speaker's perspective.
(page 710): Monitor your listening. Ask questions when listening.

▶ **STEP 1** Choose one item of a persuasive speech to evaluate, and ask yourself, "What should this be like in a persuasive speech?"

What should <u>eye contact</u> be like in a persuasive speech?

▶ **STEP 2** Brainstorm an answer to your question.

A speaker should try to look at various audience members, not just one or two people. This will make the speaker seem more honest and believable.

▶ **STEP 3** Turn your answer into a statement that says what a speaker should do when giving a persuasive speech. Then, develop criteria for the rest of the items listed on page 709.

A speaker should make eye contact with the audience often.

Reference Note

For more on **telling fact from opinion,** see page 683.

Evaluate a Speech

Once you have a list of criteria, you are ready to evaluate a persuasive speech. You may want to make a chart with your criteria in one column and space for notes in another. As you listen, remember your purpose. Do you agree with the speaker's opinion? To convince, speakers should support opinions with facts. Be sure you distinguish between facts and the speaker's opinions.

TIP As you listen to any speech, monitor your understanding, or make sure that everything the speaker is saying makes sense to you. Is anything confusing? If the situation allows, ask clarification questions to have any confusing points explained more clearly. After the speech, you might also look up in a dictionary or thesaurus any unfamiliar word the speaker uses.

YOUR TURN 12 **Evaluating a Persuasive Speech**

■ Follow the steps in the Thinking It Through above to develop criteria for evaluating a speech. Make sure your criteria cover content, delivery, and believability items.

■ Listen to a persuasive speech and make notes about how the speaker does or does not meet each of your criteria. Does the speaker convince through evidence or "sell" through emotion? Afterward, rewrite any illegible notes, and add explanations for any short or confusing notes.

■ Write a brief evaluation of the speech using the information in your notes. If other students evaluate the same speech, compare your impressions in a small group. Was the speaker effective? Why or why not?

Choices

Choose one of the following activities to complete.

▶ EDITORIAL CARTOONS

1. The Politics of Art An editorial cartoon is a humorous drawing that tries to persuade readers to believe something. Editorial cartoons are usually located on the opinion page of the newspaper. Find an editorial cartoon and analyze it. Answer questions such as these: What is the artist trying to convince readers to believe? How does the drawing help the cartoonist make his or her persuasive point? Were you persuaded by the cartoon? Why or why not? Create a **bulletin board display** that includes the cartoon and a one-paragraph analysis.

▶ CAREERS

2. Persuasion in Practice Lawyers, advertisers, and newspaper columnists use persuasion every day. Research one of these careers. How do people in these professions get others to think a certain way? Do they use logical, emotional, or ethical appeals? (See tip on page 685.) Summarize what you learn about the career in a short **essay.**

▶ CROSSING THE CURRICULUM: SOCIAL STUDIES

3. On the Go What place would you propose to visit as a class field trip? In a small group, create a petition with specific educational reasons for your selection. Your petition should begin with a short **letter** explaining where you want to go and why. The letter should be followed by a **form** with spaces for students to sign their names and list their grade level.

▶ SPEAKING

4. Talk Them into It Make a **persuasive speech** to your class, either on the issue you chose for your letter or on another issue that is important to you. Make sure your opinion and call to action are clear. Support your opinion with reasons and evidence, and organize them in a way that will make sense to your listeners.

PORTFOLIO

SKILLS FOCUS

Analyze and evaluate editorial and political cartoons. Use effective representing strategies. Identify and understand logical, emotional, and ethical appeals in a persuasive text. Write a letter. Adapt oral messages to occasion: persuasive presentations.

Quick Reference Handbook

The Dictionary

Types and Contents

Types of Dictionaries Different types of dictionaries provide different kinds of information. You should choose a dictionary that will have the kind of information you need. The following chart shows the types of dictionaries.

Types of Dictionaries

An **abridged** dictionary is the most common type of dictionary. The word *abridged* means shortened or condensed, so an abridged dictionary contains most of the words you are likely to use or encounter in your writing or reading.

Example

Merriam-Webster's Collegiate Dictionary, Tenth Edition

A **specialized** dictionary defines words or terms that are used in a particular profession, field, or area of interest.

Example

Stedman's Medical Dictionary

An **unabridged** dictionary contains nearly all the words in use in a language.

Example

Webster's Third International Unabridged Dictionary

Dictionary Entry

When you look up a word in the dictionary, the entry gives the word and other information about it. Look at the dictionary entry on the next page. The following explanations of the parts of the entry will help you get the most out of your dictionary.

1. **Entry word** The entry word is printed in boldface (thick) letters. It shows the way the word should be spelled and how to divide the word into syllables. It may also show whether a word should be capitalized or if the word can be spelled in other ways.

2. **Pronunciation** The pronunciation of a word is shown with symbols. These

① ② ③ ④

cloud (kloud) *n.* ⟦ME *cloude, clude,* orig., mass of rock, hence, mass of cloud < OE *clud,* mass of rock: for IE base see CLIMB⟧ **1** a visible mass of tiny, condensed water droplets or ice crystals suspended in the atmosphere: clouds are commonly classified in four groups: *A* (high clouds above 6,096 m or 20,000 ft.) CIRRUS, CIRROSTRATUS, CIRROCUMULUS; *B* (intermediate clouds 1,981 m to 6,096 or 6,500 ft. to 20,000 ft.) ALTOSTRATUS, ALTOCUMULUS; *C* (low clouds, below 1,981 m or 6,500 ft.) STRATUS, STRATOCUMULUS, NIMBOSTRATUS; *D* (clouds of great vertical continuity) CUMULUS, CUMULONIMBUS **2** a mass of smoke, dust, steam, etc. **3** a great number of things close together and in motion ⟦a *cloud* of locusts⟧ **4** an appearance of murkiness or dimness, as in a liquid **5** a dark marking, as in marble **6** anything that darkens, obscures, threatens, or makes gloomy —*vt.* **1** to cover or make dark as with clouds **2** to make muddy or foggy **3** to darken; obscure; threaten **4** to make gloomy or troubled **5** to cast slurs on; sully (a reputation, etc.) —*vi.* **1** to become cloudy **2** to become gloomy or troubled—**in the clouds 1** high up in the sky **2** fanciful; impractical **3** in a reverie or daydream —**under a cloud 1** under suspicion of wrongdoing **2** in a depressed or troubled state of mind

⑤ ⑥ ⑦

symbols help you pronounce the word correctly. In the sample entry, look at the *k* symbol. It shows you that the *c* in *cloud* sounds like the *c* in *can,* not like the *c* in *ice.* Special letters or markings that are used with letters to show a certain sound are called *phonetic symbols. Accent marks* show which syllables of the word are said more forcefully. Look in the front of a dictionary for an explanation of the symbols and marks it uses.

3. **Part-of-speech labels**   These labels are abbreviated and show how you may use the word in a sentence. Some words may be used as more than one part of speech. For each meaning of a word, the dictionary shows the part of speech. In the sample entry, *cloud* can be used as a noun or as a verb, depending on the meaning.

4. **Etymology**   The *etymology* tells how a word entered the English language. The etymology also shows how the word has changed over time. In the sample entry, the abbreviations *ME* and *OE* trace the history of the word *cloud* from Middle English back to Old English. The final abbreviation *IE* tells the word's parent language, which is Indo-European. (See also **History of English** on page 724.)

5. **Definitions**   If the word has more than one meaning, the different definitions are numbered. To help you understand the different meanings, dictionaries often include a sample phrase or sentence after a numbered definition. (See also **Examples** below.)

6. **Examples**   A dictionary may show how the entry word is used. The examples are often in the form of phrases or sentences using the word in context.

7. **Idioms**   A dictionary entry may sometimes give examples and definitions of *idioms* that include the word. An *idiom* is a phrase that means something different from the literal meanings of the words. Dictionaries provide definitions because you cannot always define idioms using the usual meanings of the words.

Document Design

Manuscript Style

Whether you write your paper by hand or use a word-processing program, you should always submit a paper that is neat and easy to read. The guidelines in the chart below can help. You should also ask your teacher for help. He or she may have additional guidelines for you to follow.

Guidelines for Manuscript Style

1. Use only one side of each sheet of paper.

2. Type your paper using a word processor, or write it neatly in blue or black ink.

3. For handwritten papers, ask your teacher if you should skip lines. For typed papers, many teachers prefer that you double-space your assignment.

4. Leave one-inch margins at the top, bottom, and sides of your paper.

5. The first line of every paragraph should be indented five spaces (letter lengths), or half an inch. You can set a **tab** on a word processor to indent five spaces automatically.

6. Number all pages in the top right-hand corner. Do not number the first page.

7. Make sure your pages look neat and clean. For handwritten papers, use correction fluid to correct your mistakes. However, if you have several mistakes on one page, write out the page again. For papers typed on a computer, you can make corrections and print out a clean copy.

8. Use the heading your teacher prefers for your name, your class, the date, and the title of your paper.

9. Include graphics if they will make your ideas clearer to the reader. (See also **Graphics** on page 721.)

Desktop Publishing

To produce professional-looking reports, newsletters, and other documents, writers use *desktop publishing*. **Desktop publishing** describes all of the techniques involved in using a computer to make attractive documents. A computer's desktop publishing program contains many features. These features help a writer create eye-catching documents that contain text (words) and graphics (images and pictures). You can also apply many of the following desktop publishing techniques to handwritten papers.

The following section explains how you can effectively arrange, or lay out, the text of your document. For information about how graphics can make your ideas clearer to readers, see page 721.

Page Layout

Page layout refers to the design, or appearance, of each page in a document. As you plan the design of your page, consider each of the following elements.

Alignment   The word *alignment* refers to how lines of text are arranged on the page. Aligning your text the right way can give your page a neat, attractive look.

■ **Center-aligned**   Text that is *center-aligned* is centered on an imaginary line that runs down the middle of the page or column. You may have used center-alignment for titles of papers or reports.

You might also find centered text on posters, advertisements, and invitations.

EXAMPLE

These lines are center-aligned.
The text is centered on
an imaginary line that runs down
the middle of this column.

■ **Left-aligned**   When text is *left-aligned,* each line begins on the left margin of the page or column. Because English is read from left to right, most blocks of text are left-aligned.

EXAMPLE

These lines of text are left-aligned. Each line in this column starts at the same place on the left margin.

■ **Right-aligned**   Text that is *right-aligned* is lined up on the right side of the page or column. Right alignment makes short, important bits of information stand out. For instance, when you write reports, you may right-align your name, the date, and the page numbers so that the teacher can find them.

EXAMPLE

These lines are right-aligned.
Each line in this column
ends at the same place
on the right margin.

■ **Justified**   Text that is *justified* forms a straight edge along the right and the left margins. Spaces may be added to the lines so that the lines are the same length. (The last line in justified text

QUICK REFERENCE HANDBOOK

may be shorter than the other lines if it contains only a few words.) You often see justified text in books, newspapers, and magazines.

EXAMPLE

This text is justified. The text forms a straight edge along the right and left margins of this column.

■ **Ragged**   Text that is *ragged* lines up along only one margin. Use ragged text for your reports.

EXAMPLE

This text is ragged. The text lines up along the left margin but not along the right.

Bullet   A *bullet* (•) is a large dot or other symbol used to separate items in a list. Bullets attract the reader's eyes and make information easier to read and remember. Consider these guidelines when using bullets.

■ A bulleted list should contain at least two items.

■ Each item in your list should begin with the same type of wording. For example, each item in this bulleted list begins with a declarative sentence, or a sentence that makes a statement.

Contrast   The balance of light and dark areas on a page is called *contrast.* Light areas have very little text and few, if any, pictures or graphics. Dark areas contain lots of text and perhaps pictures or graphics. Pages of high contrast—or a good mix of both light and dark areas—are easier to read than pages with low contrast.

Emphasis   *Emphasis* is a way of showing readers the most important information on a page. In a newspaper, a headline in large and heavy type can create emphasis. Color, graphics, and boxes around the text can also create emphasis.

EXAMPLE

Sunken Treasure Discovered
SUNNY SEA—Diving students made an amazing discovery Saturday one mile off the Texas coast. . . .

Gutter   A *gutter* is the inner margin of space from the printed area of a page to the binding.

Headers and Footers   A writer uses *headers* and *footers* to provide information about the document. Headers are lines of information that appear at the top of each page in a document. *Footers* are lines of information that appear at the bottom of each page in a document. Headers and footers frequently contain the following information.

■ author's name

■ name of magazine, newspaper, or document

■ publication date

■ chapter or section title

■ page numbers

Headings and Subheadings   Titles within a document are called *headings* and *subheadings* (also called *heads* and *subheads*). Headings and subheadings show readers how information in a document is organized.

- *Headings* tell readers the title or topic of a major section of text. A heading appears at the beginning of a section of text and is usually in bold or capital letters. (See also **Type** on this page.)

- *Subheadings* are more descriptive headings within a major section. Subheadings break a section into smaller sections. Subheadings help readers find the information they need. To separate the subhead from the main text, subheadings may be in a different size or style of type than that of the main text.

EXAMPLE

Keeping Our Parks ——(heading)
Clean

Weekend Cleanups Give ——(subheading)
Parks a Whole New Look

The biggest commitment Girl ——(text)
Scout Troop #912 is making
to the city this year is a program
called Weekend Cleanups. Every
Saturday, five girls from the troop
pick an area park and clean up
trash that people have left behind.

Indentation   When you *indent* a line, you move the first word a few spaces to the right of the left margin. Always indent five spaces or half an inch at the beginning of a new paragraph.

Margins   The *margin* on a page is the blank space that surrounds the text on the sides, top, and bottom. Some word-processing programs automatically set margins at 1.25 inches for the sides and 1 inch for the top and bottom. You can change the margins, however, to be larger or smaller. Changing the margins will allow you to fit more or less text on a page. Check with your teacher before changing your margins on an assignment.

Rules   *Rules* are vertical or horizontal lines in a document. Rules can be used to separate columns of text or to set off text from other elements, such as headlines or graphics.

Title and Subtitle   The *title* of a document is its name. A *subtitle* is a secondary, more descriptive title. Subtitles are sometimes joined to titles with a colon. However, if the subtitle is on its own line, no colon is needed. A title and subtitle appear on a separate page at the beginning of a book.

EXAMPLE

The 5 in 10 Pasta and
Noodle Cookbook   (title)
5 Ingredients in 10 Minutes or Less   (subtitle)

Type

Type refers to the characters (letters and other symbols) in a printed text. Thanks to computer programs, a writer can experiment with the size and design of type in a document until the right look is achieved. When you create a document, there are many different aspects of type that you should consider.

Fonts   A *font* is a set of characters (such as numbers, letters, and punctuation marks) of a certain size and design. For example, 12-point Courier is a font. The font size is 12 points (see below); the font design is called Courier. A computer program will let you use many different fonts. A font design is also called a *typeface*.

Font Size   The size of type in a document is called the **font size** or **point size.** The size of type is measured in points, which are $\frac{1}{72}$ of an inch. School assignments are usually printed in 10- or 12-point type. Captions for pictures are usually printed in smaller point sizes than the main text is. Titles may be printed in larger point sizes.

EXAMPLE

Title ———————— 24 point
Text text text text———————— 12 point
Caption caption caption ———————— 9 point

Font Style   The **font style** of type refers to the way the type is printed. You may use a font style, such as italic, to show that you are typing a book title. You may also use a different font style, such as boldface, to call attention to important words in your writing. Look at the examples of font styles below and in the next column.

■ **Boldface**   A **boldface** word is written in thick, heavy type. You can use boldface to show important information.

EXAMPLE

This entire sentence is written in boldface type.

■ **Capital letters**   A **capital** (or **uppercase**) **letter** usually signals a proper name, the beginning of a sentence, or a title. You can put titles and headings in all capital letters. To make an idea stand out, you can put a word or a sentence in text in all capital letters. However, if you put too many words in all capital letters, the idea may not stand out as much.

■ **Condensed**   When type is **condensed,** the letters in a word will have less space between them. A writer uses condensed type to save space.

EXAMPLE

This sentence is written in condensed type.

■ **Expanded**   When type is **expanded,** the letters in a word will have more space between them. Writers use expanded type to fill up space.

EXAMPLE

This sentence is written in expanded type.

■ **Italics**   Type that is **italic** has a slanted style. Like boldface, italic type can be used to call attention to information. Italic type is also used in text to signal titles. (See also page 336.)

EXAMPLE

This sentence is written in italic type.

■ **Lowercase letters**   A **lowercase letter** is not a capital or a small capital. (See **Small capitals** below.) Lowercase letters are the letters we use most often.

- **Shadow**   A word written in *shadow* style appears to cast shadows. Shadow style may be used for titles and headings.

  EXAMPLE
  This sentence is written in shadow style.

- **Small capitals**   Use *small capitals* when writing abbreviations referring to time. For example, when typing the time 5:45 P.M. and the year A.D. *1812*, you should use small capitals.

Leading   Another word for *line spacing* is *leading* (rhymes with *wedding*). **Leading** is the distance between each pair of lines of text. When a text is single-spaced, there is no extra space between lines. Books, magazines, and newspapers are usually single-spaced. Assignments for your teacher are usually double-spaced. Double-spacing your papers makes it easier for your teacher to read your assignment and make corrections or comments on the page.

Legibility   A document is *legible* when its text and graphics are clearly readable. A document with high legibility uses a simple, easy-to-read font size and design for the main text. Well-designed graphics are another key to legibility.

Typeface   See **Font** on page 719.

Graphics

Graphics can often communicate information more quickly and effectively than words. Graphics you can use in your document include *charts, graphs, tables, diagrams*, and *illustrations*. They can

- show information
- explain how to do something
- show how something looks, works, or is organized
- show what happens over a period of time

  The main purpose of a graphic is to support or explain the text of your document. Whether you create graphics by hand or by computer, make sure that they are informative and easy to read.

Arrangement and Design

Use the following ideas to create informative and effective graphics.

Accuracy   Make sure all of your graphics contain *accurate* information. In other words, the information in your graphics should be true and from reliable sources.

Color   Readers are attracted to colorful graphics, especially when colorful graphics appear on a page of black-and-white text. You can use *color* to do the following:

- get a reader's attention
- call attention to certain information
- group items on a page
- help organize a page or even an entire document

Keep these tips in mind when you choose colors for your graphics.

- **Use warm colors sparingly.** Red, orange, yellow, and other warm tones seem to jump off the page. Overusing warm tones will decrease their dramatic effect.
- **Use cool colors to create a calming effect.** Cool colors, such as blue and green, make readers feel calmer. Use them as background colors.

Labels, Captions, and Titles You can explain your graphics by adding *labels* and *captions*. **Labels** appear within the graphic or are connected to specific areas of the graphic by thin lines called *rules*. Labels identify different parts of graphics, charts, tables, and diagrams. **Captions** are phrases or sentences that describe a graphic. Many photographs and illustrations have captions. Captions appear directly beside, above, or under the graphic. If your graphic has no labels or captions, give it a descriptive *title*.

Types of Graphics

Use the definitions and examples below to help you decide which graphics to use in your document.

Chart A *chart* helps show how pieces of information relate to each other. Two of the most common types of charts are flowcharts and pie charts.

- **Flowcharts** show an order of events. The boxes in a flowchart contain text, and appear in order from left to right

or from top to bottom. Flowcharts usually contain arrows to direct readers from one box to the next.

EXAMPLE

How to Start a Flower Garden

Buy seeds of flowers that you like.

Prepare the soil for planting.

Plant seeds according to directions on the package.

Water your garden daily.

Enjoy the flowers!

- **Pie charts** show percentages, or how parts of a whole relate to each other. (See also **Charts** on page 745.)

Diagram A *diagram* uses symbols, such as arrows, to show how to do something or how something works. As with the other graphics in this section, diagrams can be drawn by hand or by using a computer program.

EXAMPLE

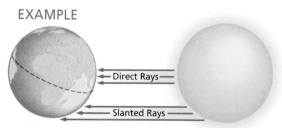

Direct Rays

Slanted Rays

Graph A *graph* can show changes over time in a way that allows readers to understand the changes at a glance. The horizontal axis (the line that runs across the page) of a line or bar graph usually shows periods or points in time. The vertical axis (the line that runs up and down) shows quantities. (See also **Line graphs** and **Bar graphs** on page 746.)

Illustration An *illustration* is a drawing or photograph that can show readers items or events that are unfamiliar, new, or hard to describe. It can also show how something works, how to do something, or what someone or something looks like. (See also **Diagrams** on page 746 and **Illustration** on page 782.)

Storyboard *Storyboards* illustrate the different moments, or scenes, of an event or story. Storyboards are frequently used to map out a story or to plan a video segment. Storyboards contain boxes that each represent one scene in the sequence. The boxes contain drawings and text to be spoken by a narrator or actors within the scene. Example storyboards appear below.

Table A *table* contains information such as numbers and statistics, but it does not show trends the way a graph does. While a reader of a graph can immediately see an increase or decrease, readers of tables must look at all of the information and draw their own conclusions. For example, after studying the following table, a reader could conclude that membership in the Park Hills Computer Club rose for three years in a row.

EXAMPLE

Number of Middle School Students in the Park Hills Computer Club	
Year	Number of Members
2006	10
2007	19
2008	21

Time Line A *time line* shows events that happen over a period of time. The points along a time line show years or groups of years. The events that happen during a given year or period of years are described above, below, or to the side of the time line. (See also **Time Lines** on page 747.)

EXAMPLE

Clarissa finds a nest of baby sea turtles on the beach. They head toward the ocean.

One of the turtles cannot walk to the ocean with its brothers and sisters. It struggles on its back.

Clarissa turns the baby sea turtle over so it can walk toward the ocean.

The History of English

Origins and Uses

A Changing Language

No one knows exactly when or how English got started. We do know that English and many other modern-day languages come from an early language that was spoken thousands of years ago. The related languages still resemble that parent language, just as you resemble your parents. For example, notice how similar the words for *mother* are in the following modern-day languages.

ENGLISH mother   FRENCH mère
SPANISH madre   ITALIAN madre
SWEDISH moder

Over 1,500 years ago, a few small tribes of people invaded the island that is now Britain. These tribes, called the Angles and Saxons, spoke the earliest known form of English, called **Old English.** Old English was very different from ours.

English continued to evolve through a form known as **Middle English.** While our language has always changed and grown, some of our most basic words have been around since the very beginning.

EARLY WORD
hand   dohtor   andswaru   hleapan
PRESENT-DAY WORD
hand   daughter   answer   leap

Changes in Meaning   It may be hard to believe that the word *bead* once meant "prayer." Many English words have changed meaning over time. Some of these changes have been slight. Others have been more obvious. Below are a few examples of words that have changed their meanings.

naughty—In the 1300s, *naughty* meant "poor or needy." In the 1600s, the meaning changed to "poorly behaved."

lunch—In the 1500s, a *lunch* was a large chunk of something, such as bread or meat.

caboose—*Caboose* entered the English language in the 1700s when it meant "the kitchen of a ship."

Even today the meanings of words may vary depending on where they are used. For example, in America a *boot* is a type of shoe, but in Great Britain, a *boot* may refer to the trunk of a car.

Changes in Pronunciation and Spelling

If you traveled back in time a few hundred years, you would probably have a hard time understanding spoken and written English.

■ **Changes in pronunciation** English words used to be pronounced differently from the way they are pronounced today. For example, in the 1200s, people pronounced *bite* like *beet* and *feet* like *fate*. They also pronounced the vowel sound in the word *load* like our word *awe*.

You may have wondered why English words are not always spelled as they sound. Changes in pronunciation help account for many strange spellings in English. For example, the *w* that starts the word *write* was not always silent. Even after the *w* sound that started the word *write* was dropped, the spelling stayed the same. The *g* in *gnat* and the *k* in *knee* were once part of the pronunciations of the words, too.

■ **Changes in spelling** The spellings of many words have changed over time. Some changes in spelling have been accidental. For example, *apron* used to be spelled *napron*. People mistakenly attached the *n* to the article *a*, and *a napron* became *an apron*. Here are some more examples of present-day English words and their early spellings.

EARLY SPELLING

| jaile | locian | slæp | tima |

PRESENT-DAY SPELLING

| jail | look | sleep | time |

■ **British vs. American spelling and pronunciation** Pronunciations and spellings still vary today. For instance, the English used in Great Britain differs from the English used in the United States. In Great Britain, people pronounce *bath* with the vowel sound of *father* instead of the vowel sound of *cat*. The British also tend to drop the *r* sound at the end of words like *copper*. In addition, the British spell some words differently from the way people in the United States do.

AMERICAN

| theater | pajamas | labor |

BRITISH

| theatre | pyjamas | labour |

Word Origins

English grows and changes along with the people who use it. New words must be created for new inventions, places, or ideas. Sometimes, people borrow words from other languages to create a new English word. Other times, people use the names of people or places as new words.

■ **Borrowed words** As English-speaking people came into contact with people from other cultures and lands, they began to borrow words. English has borrowed hundreds of thousands of words from French, Hindi, Spanish, African languages, and many other languages spoken around the world. In many cases, the borrowed words have taken new forms.

FRENCH ange	HINDI champo
ENGLISH angel	ENGLISH shampoo
AFRICAN banjo	SPANISH patata
ENGLISH banjo	ENGLISH potato

■ **Words from names**   Many things get their names from the names of people or places. For example, in the 1920s, someone in Bridgeport, Connecticut, discovered a new use for the pie plates from the Frisbie Bakery. He turned one upside down and sent it floating through the air. The new game sparked the idea for the flying plastic disk of today.

Dialects of American English

You probably know some people who speak English differently than you do. Different groups of people use different varieties of English. The kind of English you speak may sound unusual to someone else. The form of English a particular group of people speaks is called a *dialect*. Everyone uses a dialect, and no dialect is better or worse than another.

Ethnic Dialects   Your cultural background can make a difference in the way you speak. A dialect shared by people from the same cultural group is called an *ethnic dialect*. Because Americans come from many cultures, American English includes many ethnic dialects. One of the largest ethnic dialects is the English spoken by many African Americans (called African American Vernacular English). Another is the Hispanic English of many people whose families come from places such as Mexico, Central America, or Cuba.

Regional Dialects   Do you *make* the bed or *make up* the bed? Would you order a *sub* with the *woiks* or a *hero* with the *werks*? In the evening, do you eat *supper* or *dinner*? How you answer these questions is probably influenced by where you live. A dialect shared by people from the same area is called a *regional dialect*. Your regional dialect helps determine what words you use, how you pronounce words, and how you put words together.

Not everyone from a particular group speaks that group's dialect. Also, an ethnic or regional dialect may vary depending on the speaker's individual background and place of origin.

Standard American English

Every dialect is useful and helps keep the English language colorful and interesting. However, sometimes it is confusing to try to communicate using two different dialects. Therefore, it is important to be familiar with *standard American English*. Standard English is the most commonly understood variety of English. You can find some of the rules for using standard English in the **Grammar, Usage, and Mechanics** section of this textbook, beginning on page 46. Language that does not follow these rules and guidelines is called *nonstandard English*. Nonstandard English is inappropriate in situations where standard English is expected.

NONSTANDARD   I don't want *no* more spinach.

STANDARD   I don't want *any* more spinach.

NONSTANDARD   Jimmy was *fixing* to go hiking with us.

STANDARD   Jimmy was *about* to go hiking with us.

Formal and Informal   Read the following sentences.

Many of my friends are excited about the game.
A bunch of my friends are psyched about the game.

Both sentences mean the same thing, but they have different effects. The first sentence is an example of *formal English,* and the second sentence is an example of *informal English.*

Formal and informal English are each appropriate for different situations. For instance, you would probably use the formal example if you were talking to a teacher about the game. If you were talking to a friend, however, the second sentence would sound natural. Formal English is frequently used in news reports and in schools and businesses.

■ **Colloquialisms**   Informal English includes many words and expressions that are not appropriate in more formal situations. The most widely used informal expressions are *colloquialisms.* **Colloquialisms** are colorful words and phrases of everyday conversation. Many colloquialisms have meanings that are different from the basic meanings of words.

EXAMPLES

I wish Gerald would *get off my case.*
Don't get *all bent out of shape* about it.
We were about to *bust* with laughter.

■ **Slang**   *Slang* words are made-up words or old words used in new ways. Slang is highly informal language. It is usually created by a particular group of people, such as students or people who hold a particular job, like computer technicians or artists. Often, slang is familiar only to the groups that invent it.

Sometimes slang words become a lasting part of the English language. Usually, though, slang falls out of style quickly. The slang words in the sentences below will probably seem out of date to you.

That was a really *far-out flick.*
Those are some *groovy duds* you're wearing.
I don't have enough *dough* to buy a movie ticket.

The Library/ Media Center

Using Print and Electronic Sources

Libraries contain huge amounts of information. In a library you can read about your favorite celebrities in the latest magazine, research breeds of dogs to choose a family pet, or find tips to help you in a sport. Whatever information you are looking for, your library has the tools to help you find it. Knowing how to use the library can bring you hours of enjoyment.

The information in a library takes many forms. The resource you use depends on the type of information you need. The following chart shows ways that information is classified.

Print Sources	
Fiction	Stories (novels, short stories, and plays)
Nonfiction	Factual information about real people, events, and things; includes biographies and "how-to" books
Reference books	General information about many subjects
Magazines and newspapers	Current events, commentaries, and important discoveries
Maps, globes, atlases, and almanacs	Geographic information, facts, dates, and statistics
Pamphlets	Brief summaries of facts about specific subjects

Nonprint Sources	
Audio and video tapes, films, filmstrips, slides, DVDs, CD-ROMs	Stories (narrated, illustrated, or acted out), music, instructions and educational material, facts and information about many specific subjects
Computers	Information stored electronically, allowing for easy access and frequent updates

Books   Many books that you can use as sources are packed full of information. The specific information that you might need can sometimes be hard to find. You will find information more easily if you know how to use every part of a book. The following chart shows the types of information you will find in a book.

Information Found in Parts of a Book
The **title page** gives the full title, the name of the author (or authors), the publisher, and the place of publication.
The **copyright page** gives the date of the first publication of the book and the date of any revisions.
The **table of contents** lists titles of chapters or sections of the book and their starting page numbers.
The **appendix** provides additional information about subjects found in the book; it sometimes contains tables, maps, and charts.
The **glossary** defines, in alphabetical order, various difficult terms or important technical words used frequently in the book.
The **bibliography** lists sources used to write the book and provides names of books about related topics.
The **index** lists topics mentioned in the book, along with the page or pages on which they can be found; it sometimes lists the page where a certain illustration may be found.

Call Number   When you need to find a book in the library, first find its *call number.* A call number is a code using letters and numbers that is assigned to a source in a library. Call numbers indicate the category a book is in and where it is located. Books in school and community libraries use the *Dewey Decimal Classification system.* (See also **Card Catalog** below.)

The *Dewey Decimal Classification system* assigns a number to each nonfiction book. These numbers are assigned according to the book's subject. Using this system of arrangement, books that contain factual information about similar subjects are placed near each other on the library shelves. **Biographies** are arranged differently from other nonfiction books. Most libraries arrange biographies alphabetically by the name of the subject in a separate section. **Fiction** books are arranged alphabetically by author in their own section of the library.

Card Catalog   The easiest way to locate a book in the library is to look up the call number in the library's card catalog. There are two kinds of card catalogs: the traditional card catalog and the online catalog.

The traditional *card catalog* is a cabinet of small drawers. Each drawer holds many small file cards. There are cards in this file for every book in the library. The cards are arranged in alphabetical order by title, author, or subject. Each fiction book has a *title card* and an *author card.* A nonfiction book will also have a *subject card.* The graphic on the next page shows the information contained in the card catalog.

Information in the Card Catalog

① 790.1 [The Big Book of Games] Title Card
Stott

②

③ 790.1 [Stott, Dorothy M.] Author Card
Stott

④ 790.1 [Games—Juvenile Literature.] Subject Card
Stott

Stott, Dorothy M.
The Big Book of Games
⑤ New York: Dutton Children's Books, ©1998.
⑥ 64 p.: col. ill.; 29cm
ISBN 0525454543 :
1. Games—Juvenile Literature. 2. Games.
⑦ I. Title.

1. The **call number** assigned to a book by the Library of Congress or the Dewey Decimal Classification system
2. The full **title** of a book
3. The **author's full name,** last name first
4. The general **subject** of a book; a subject card may show specific headings
5. The place and date of **publication**
6. A **description** of the book, such as its size and number of pages, and whether it is illustrated
7. **Cross-references** to other headings or related topics under which you can find additional books

Many libraries now use electronic or online card catalogs instead of traditional card catalogs. (See also **Online Catalog** on page 732.)

CD-ROMs
CD-ROM stands for Compact Disc-Read Only Memory. A CD-ROM is a computer disc that holds visual and audio information. "Read Only" tells

you that you can get information from the disc, but you cannot make changes to the disc. In order to use a CD-ROM, you must have a computer with a CD-ROM disc drive. CD-ROMs are popular because they can hold as much as 100,000 pages of information per disc. CD-ROMs can also perform searches, provide interactive graphics, and supply sound. You might use an encyclopedia, dictionary, or other programs on CD-ROM.

Indexes
When researching a topic, you might start by consulting an *index,* which lists topics, sources, or authors. The *Readers' Guide to Periodical Literature,* for example, helps readers find articles, poems, and stories from more than two hundred magazines and journals. The guide lists articles alphabetically both by author and by subject. Each entry has a heading printed in boldface capital letters. In the front of the *Readers' Guide* is a guide to abbreviations that appear in the entries. Below is an example of an online *Readers' Guide* entry. The next page shows an example from the printed version.

Online

Result of Online Search of *Readers' Guide*

AUTHOR: Chadwick, Douglass H.
TITLE: Helping a great bear hang on (grizzlies; cover story)
SOURCE: National Wildlife v. 37 no1 (Dec. '98/ Jan '99) p. 22–31 il.
STANDARD NO: 0028-0402
DATE: 1998
RECORD TYPE: art
CONTENTS: feature article
SUBJECT: Endangered Species Act (1973) Bears. Wildlife conservation—Western States.

Printed *Readers' Guide*

(1) — **BEARS**
(2) —   *see also*
      Bear Attacks
(3) — The bears of summer [Grand Marais, Minn: condensed
      from Summers with the bears} J. Becklund. il por
(4) — *Reader's Digest* v 153 no918 p 186–93+ O '98
Grizzly fate [possible removal of Yellowstone Grizzlies
      from federal protection] T. Wilkinson. il *National Parks*
(5) — v72 no1 1–12 p30–3 N/D '98
Helping a great bear hang on [grizzlies; cover story]
      D.H. Chadwick. il *National Wildlife* v 37 no1 p22–31
(6) —
(7) — D '98/Ja '99
               Control
Barking dogs repel hungry park bears [Glacier National
      Park] il *National Parks* v72 no1 1–12 p13–14 N/D '98
(8) — **BEARY, THOMAS J.**
How to grow old [poem] *America* v180 no6 p17 F 27 '99
(9) —

1. **Subject entry heading**
2. **Subject cross-reference**
3. **Title of article**
4. **Author of article**
5. **Name of magazine**
6. **Volume number of magazine**
7. **Page reference**
8. **Author entry heading**
9. **Date of magazine**

Internet   The *Internet* does not exist in one place. Instead, it is a network, or web of connections, among computers all over the world. While the Internet was originally created to share science information, it has expanded today to include sites on virtually any topic. Many libraries have computers that you can use to connect to the Internet. The most popular way to view information on the Internet is through a World Wide Web browser. (See also **World Wide Web** on page 733.)

Microforms   *Microforms* are photographs of articles from newspapers and magazines that have been reduced to take up less space. Two types of microforms are **microfilm,** a continuous roll of film, and **microfiche,** small cards of film. To use microforms, you must also use machines that magnify the information and project it onto a screen for you to read.

Newspapers   Newspapers include different types of reading materials that are often contained in several separate sections. As a reader, you probably read the various parts of a newspaper for different reasons.

If you are reading to learn about differing viewpoints or opinions on an issue, read the editorial section. The editorial section is also a good place to get ideas for persuasive papers. As you read an editorial, identify points with which you agree or disagree. Also, try to identify the reasons and evidence the writer uses.

If you want to find information or gain knowledge, try reading the city, state, or national news sections. For each news story you read, ask yourself the *5W–How?* questions (see page 512). If you use the news story as a source for one of your papers, be sure to put the information into your own words.

If you want to be entertained, you might want to read the comics or the entertainment section.

Online Catalog

The *online catalog* is stored on a computer. To find the call number for a book, type in the title, the author, or the subject of the book. The computer will show the results of your search. The results are a little different in each library, but the search results that follow are typical.

```
┌─────────────────────────────────────────┐
│ ▢  ══════════════  Online  ══════════════ ▢ │
├─────────────────────────────────────────┤
│        Search Results from Online Catalog  ▲│
│  CALL NUMBER: 790.1/Stott                 │
│      AUTHOR: Stott, Dorothy M.            │
│       TITLE: The Big Book of Games        │
│     EDITION: 1st ed.                      │
│   PUBLISHER: New York: Dutton Children's  │
│             Books, ©1998                  │
│ DESCRIPTION: 64 p.: col. ill.; 29 cm.     │
│      NOTES : Includes index.              │
│    SUMMARY: Provides directions for playing │
│             a variety of indoor and out-  │
│             door games, party games, car  │
│             games, and singing games.     │
│    SUBJECTS: Games—Juvenile Literature.   │
│             Games                         │
│        ISBN: 0525454543                  ▼│
│                                    ▶      │
└─────────────────────────────────────────┘
```

Online Databases

Online databases are collections of information stored on a computer. You can use online databases to search for information. They are usually created for specific groups or organizations. Many databases require users to pay a fee, but other databases are free. You can use the World Wide Web to access some databases.

Once you have accessed a database, search for specific topics by typing in a *keyword* or key phrase. You can print out the information you find. The results of the search for articles about bears in the *Online Readers' Guide* on page 730 is an example of an online database.

Online Sources

An *online source* is a source of information that can be accessed only by computer. You can find and access online information through computer networks. A network is a group of computers connected by telephone lines, by fiber-optic cables, or via satellite. Computer networks make the Internet and the World Wide Web possible.

Radio, Television, Film, and Video

Some of the most common sources of information today are *radio* and *television.* You can find news broadcasts, newsmagazines, and documentaries on radio and television stations every day. Additional educational programs are available on *film* or *video.* To find shows that might have information you need, consult magazines or newspaper listings that contain descriptions of radio and television programs. If you want to rent or borrow a video, check out books that have descriptions of educational videos. You might find several books of video listings at your local library. Before using a film or video as a source of information, check the ratings to make sure it is appropriate. (See also **Critical Viewing** on page 780 and **Media Messages** on page 766.)

Reference Sources		
Type	**Description**	**Examples**
Encyclopedias	• many volumes • articles arranged alphabetically by subject • good source for general information	*Collier's Encyclopedia* *Compton's Encyclopedia* *The World Book Multimedia Encyclopedia™*
General Biographical References	• information about birth, nationality, and major accomplishments of outstanding people	*Current Biography* *Dictionary of American Biography* *The International Who's Who* *World Biographical Index on CD-ROM*
Atlases	• maps and geographical information	*Atlas of World Cultures* *National Geographic Atlas of the World*
Almanacs	• up-to-date information about current events, facts, statistics, and dates	*The Information Please Almanac, Atlas and Yearbook* *The World Almanac and Book of Facts*
Books of Synonyms	• lists of more interesting or more exact words to express ideas	*Roget's International Thesaurus* *Webster's New Dictionary of Synonyms*

Reference Sources   There are many different kinds of reference sources, print and nonprint, that you can use to find specific kinds of information. Most libraries devote an entire section to reference works. The chart above lists some of the reference sources you might use.

Vertical File   Many libraries have a *vertical file,* a filing cabinet containing up-to-date materials such as newspaper clippings, booklets, and pamphlets.

World Wide Web   (*WWW* or the *Web*) The **World Wide Web** is part of the Internet. It is a system of connected documents, called **Web pages** or **Web sites.** These pages or sites contain text, graphics, and multimedia presentations such as video and audio files. The documents on the Web are connected by *hyperlinks,* or *links.* By clicking on a link you can navigate from one Web site to another. The following terms will help you understand the workings of the World Wide Web.

■ **Blog** (or **Weblog**)　A *blog* or *Weblog* is an online journal frequently updated and maintained by an individual or group. Typically, readers can post responses to the original postings.

■ **Browser**　A *browser* is software that allows you to find and view Web pages. A browser also allows you to download software or files. (See also **Web site** on this page.)

■ **Hyperlink**　A *hyperlink* is a connection from one Web site to another. Hyperlinks, also known as *links,* might appear as words, images, or buttons. Text hyperlinks are usually a different color from the other text and underlined.

■ **Podcast**　A *podcast* is an online broadcast of audio or video content. Media files can be downloaded and accessed through mobile devices or personal computers.

■ **Search engine**　A search engine is a program used for searching for information on the World Wide Web. (See also **World Wide Web, Searching** on page 735.)

■ **URL**　(*U*niform *R*esource *L*ocator) A *URL* is the specific address of a Web page. URLs may include words, abbreviations, numbers, and punctuation. Below is a URL with its parts labeled.

1	2	3

http://www.go.hrw.com/language/eolang

1. The *protocol,* or how the site is accessed or retrieved.
2. The *domain name.* The domain name gives your computer information to help it find a Web site. In the example above, *.com* tells your computer that the Web site is part of a commercial network. Next, *hrw* is the company that manages the Web site. Last, *go* is the name of the computer at *hrw* that hosts the Web site.
    Here are the abbreviations of the most common domains.

Common Domains on the World Wide Web	
.com	commercial or individual
.edu	educational
.gov	governmental
.org	organizations, usually nonprofit

3. The path that leads to the requested page. Not all URLs contain this part.

■ **Web site** (or **Web page**) A Web site or Web page is a document or location on the World Wide Web. The *home page* is the first page on a Web site. A typical home page gives you an overview of the Web site's contents. It also contains hyperlinks to pages within the Web site and sometimes hyperlinks to other Web sites. (See also **Hyperlink** on this page.) Other information on a home page includes information about the site's author or sponsor as well as the date the site was last updated. The example Web site on the next page is for a girls' soccer team.

1. **Toolbar** The buttons on the toolbar let you move back to previous pages, move forward, print a page, search for information, or see or hide images.

2. **Location indicator** This box shows you the address (URL) of the site you are currently viewing.

3. **Content area** The area of the screen where the Web page appears.

4. **Hyperlink** Click on these buttons to find information and other Web sites available through the browser.

5. **Scroll bar** Clicking along the horizontal or vertical scroll bar (or on the arrows at either end) allows you to move left to right or up and down in the image area.

World Wide Web, Searching The World Wide Web is full of information, but you must find it before you can use it. Luckily, there are tools to help you find what you need. You can search the Internet by using a *search engine* or a *directory*.

■ **Search engines** When you use a search engine, you look for Web sites by doing a *keyword search*. A **keyword search** lets you look for Web sites that contain specific words or phrases. Type important words about your topic in the space provided on the search engine screen. Then press the Return key or click on the Search or Find button. The search engine will provide a list of sites that fit your search. Sites that contain all of your keywords will be at the top of the list.

Sometimes your keyword search will list too many Web sites to look at, or sometimes it may not find any sites at all. When this happens, you need to narrow your keyword search. Try the following strategies to narrow your searches, or consult the Help section of your search engine for other ideas.

Refining a Keyword Search	
Tip	**How It Works**
Use specific terms.	Words have many different, and sometimes unexpected, meanings. Using more specific words can help you get just the right results. EXAMPLE To find information on making videos, enter *video production* instead of *movies*.
Put words that go together as a phrase into quotation marks.	If you are searching for a phrase, type it in quotation marks. The search engine will find sites that use the words exactly as they are typed. EXAMPLE Type in "computer games" to find information on the latest gaming software instead of information on types of computers or board games.
Use "+" (plus) and "–" (minus) symbols.	Place a "+" between keywords to narrow your results to pages that contain all the keywords. Put a "–" between keywords to exclude sites with topics that are similar but unrelated. EXAMPLE Type in "Brooklyn Bridge" + "Golden Gate Bridge" to find sites on both the Brooklyn and Golden Gate bridges. To find sites about the human heart, but not romance, enter "heart – love."
Use OR.	Using *OR* can make your search broader. The results list will include sites that contain any of your important words. EXAMPLE Type in "Brooklyn Bridge" OR "Golden Gate Bridge" to find sites that discuss either the Brooklyn Bridge or Golden Gate Bridge.

■ **Directories**   A directory is an organized list of Web sites. Directories organize sites into categories, such as *sports*. Each category is broken down into smaller and smaller categories, helping you narrow your search. Most search engine sites include directories.

World Wide Web, Web Site Evaluation   The World Wide Web is full of information because anyone can post sites there. Since no one supervises the Web, you are much more likely to find false information there than you are in a newspaper or book. Follow the tips on the next page to **evaluate** Web sites you use.

Evaluating Web Sites

Questions to Ask	Why You Should Ask
Who created the Web site? Who is the Web site's sponsor?	The creator or sponsor of a Web site chooses its content. Look on the site's home page to find the author or sponsor. Make sure you use only Web sites that are sponsored by trustworthy organizations, such as government agencies, universities, and museums. To help identify these sites, look for URLs containing *edu, gov,* or *org.* National news organizations are also good sources of information.
When was the page first posted? Has it been updated?	Look for this information at the end of the home page. It sometimes includes the copyright notice, date last updated, and a link to the creator's e-mail. Make sure you use only up-to-date information.
What links to other Web pages does the site include?	The most trustworthy Web sites will usually provide links to other trusted sites. Look at the links provided to get hints about the quality of this site.
Is the Web site objective?	Objective sites present ideas from both sides and focus on facts rather than opinions. Avoid sites that appear to use fictional support for ideas or claims.
Is the Web site well designed?	Look for easy-to-read type, clear graphics, and working links. Well-designed and well-maintained Web sites are easy to read and navigate. Sites should also have correct spelling, punctuation, and grammar.

You can avoid spending a lot of time evaluating a Web site—not only for accuracy but also for relevance to your needs—if you learn to make **predictions.** When you see a list of search results, consider the title of each site to predict the content and the viewpoint of the Web site. If the title sounds appropriate, look at the home page. Professional-looking design, relevant photos, and clear organization may lead you to predict that the site will be useful to you. On the other hand, if you see misspelled words, cluttered graphics, or other unprofessional signs, you might instead try a different site from your list of search results.

Reading and Vocabulary

Reading

Skills and Strategies

You can become a better reader by using the following skills and strategies.

Author's Point of View, Determining
The opinion or attitude an author expresses is called *point of view,* or *bias.* Figuring out the author's point of view can help you evaluate what you are reading. (See also page 609.)

> EXAMPLE   Philately (fə •lat′′l•ē), or the study of postage stamps, is an interesting way to learn about the world. When you examine stamps from around the world, you learn about history, different cultures, and art all at the same time.
>
> Author's point of view: Collecting stamps is interesting and educational.

Author's Purpose, Determining
An author has a reason, or *purpose,* for writing. An author may write to inform, to persuade, to express feelings, or to entertain. Determining an author's purpose will help you decide if his or her conclusions are fair.

> EXAMPLE   Skateboarding is an exciting and athletic sport. It combines speed with control and is safe as long as it is done in a properly designed park with safety pads and helmets. If you want a fun way to stay fit, pick up your skateboard!
>
> Author's purpose: To persuade people that skateboarding is a good form of exercise.

Cause-and-Effect Relationships, Analyzing
A *cause* makes something happen, and an *effect* is what happens as a result of that cause. Ask "Why?" and "What are the effects?" as you read to examine causes and effects. (See also page 517.)

> EXAMPLE   Many traditional medicines of Asia use the bones and body parts of tigers. Local people can make a large amount of money by poaching, or illegally hunting, and selling parts of tigers. Because their parts are so valuable, tigers are close to extinction.
>
> Analysis: The *cause* is killing tigers to sell their parts for medicines. The *effect* is that tigers are threatened with extinction.

Clue Words, Using   Writers often use certain *clue words* to connect their ideas. The type of clue words a writer uses can help readers understand what type of organization the author is using. (See also **Text Structures** on page 743.)

Clue Words	
Cause-Effect Pattern	
as a result	since
because	so that
if . . . then	therefore
nevertheless	this led to
Chronological Order	
after	first, second
as	now
before	then
finally	when
Comparison-Contrast Pattern	
although	however
as well as	on the other hand
but	unless
either . . . or	yet
Listing Pattern	
also	most important
for example	to begin with
in fact	
Problem-Solution Pattern	
as a result	this led to
nevertheless	thus
therefore	

Conclusions, Drawing   You draw *conclusions* about a text by combining information that you read with information you already know. (See also page 644.)

EXAMPLE   The ancient Egyptian process of mummification was expensive and time-consuming. The entire process took seventy days and involved various ceremonies. Tombs where the mummies were laid to rest were sometimes crowded with furniture and models of other everyday items.

Conclusion: Most ancient Egyptians who were mummified were wealthy people in life.

Fact and Opinion, Distinguishing
A *fact* is a statement you can prove with an outside source. An *opinion* gives a personal belief or attitude, so it cannot be proved true or false. Writers often support their opinions with facts. Distinguishing facts from opinions can help you be a better reader. (See also page 683.)

EXAMPLE

Fact: The earliest armor of European knights of the Middle Ages was a short leather or cloth tunic known as a *hauberk*. [You could look this up in an encyclopedia or dictionary and find that it is true.]

Opinion: Knights of the Middle Ages were kindhearted soldiers. [This is what one writer thinks or believes. The statement cannot be proved true in every case.]

Generalizations, Forming
Generalizations are formed by gathering information as you read and connecting it to your own experiences to make a

judgment or statement about the world in general. (See also page 473.)

> EXAMPLE   Students at Jordan Middle School are now eating healthier meals at lunch. Inspired by student requests, cafeteria workers have stopped cooking fried, greasy foods and have created new recipes using fresh fruits and vegetables. While some school officials worried that students would not like the new menu, cafeteria sales have actually gone up. It seems that healthy food is the newest trend at Jordan Middle School.

> Generalization: Many young people prefer healthy choices for lunch to fatty, fried foods.

Implied Main Idea, Identifying

Sometimes the main idea of a piece of writing is not directly stated but only suggested or *implied.* To identify an implied main idea, read the text and think about the details in it. Then, create a statement that expresses the text's overall meaning. (See also page 505 and **Stated Main Idea** on page 743.)

> EXAMPLE   Many students sleep less than seven hours a night. In a school survey, sixty percent of the students complained of being tired during the school day. Fifteen percent of the students admitted that they had fallen asleep during class. This sleepiness makes it difficult to pay attention and learn at school.

> Implied main idea: Students should get more than seven hours of sleep.

Inferences, Making

Making an *inference* is making a guess based on what you read and what you already know about the topic. *Conclusions, generaliza-*tions, and *predictions* are types of inferences. Making inferences helps you to understand ideas about the situation in the text even though the author does not directly state them. (See also **Conclusions** and **Generalizations** on page 739 and **Predicting** on page 741.)

> EXAMPLE   Aruna sprang out of bed and quickly put on her soccer uniform, making sure she had her lucky socks. She ate a nutritious breakfast and tried not to be worried. As her dad drove her to the field she rehearsed the plays in her mind. When she met her team, each girl had an air of nervous determination about her.

> Inference: Aruna is about to play in an important soccer game.

Paraphrasing

To *paraphrase* is to express an author's ideas in your own words. Paraphrasing helps you understand complicated readings. *Plagiarism* is copying someone else's words and ideas and claiming that they are your own. Since a paraphrase is a rewording of another piece of writing, a paraphrased passage is usually around the same length as the original. A brief rewording that explains the key ideas of the original passage is called a *summary.* (See the chart on page 769 for **Paraphrasing Guidelines**.)

> EXAMPLE   A well-known French marine scientist and filmmaker, Jacques Cousteau spent much of his life exploring underwater. He contributed to the invention of the Aqua-Lung™, a breathing apparatus that allowed divers to stay underwater longer. Cousteau made films about his ocean explorations and won Academy Awards for *The Silent World* in 1956 and *World Without Sun* in 1966.

Paraphrase: Jacques Cousteau was a French filmmaker who explored the ocean as a diver and marine scientist. He contributed to the creation of the Aqua-Lung™, a breathing device for divers. Two of Cousteau's films about the ocean, *The Silent World* and *World Without Sun,* won Academy Awards.

Persuasive Techniques, Analyzing

When writers want to convince readers to think or act in a certain way, they may use *persuasive techniques.* Some persuasive techniques include using facts, reasons, and evidence. Other persuasive techniques use words and ideas that create an emotional reaction. Watch out for persuasive arguments that use only *emotional appeals.* (See also page 709.)

EXAMPLE   Homelessness is a problem that will not be solved until more people get involved in the solution. Many programs exist to help homeless citizens, including programs that build houses, distribute food, and give temporary shelter. The government recognized the importance of caring for the homeless with the passage of the McKinney Homeless Assistance Act in 1987. If you want to make a difference, you should get involved with solving the problem of homelessness. After all, not everyone is fortunate enough to have a place to call home.

Analysis: The second and third sentences use facts to support the opinion in the first sentence. The last sentence is an emotional appeal aimed at readers' sympathy. It may not be persuasive because it assumes that the readers probably have homes.

Predicting

Predicting is deciding what will happen next. To make predictions, read the passage and use your past experiences to help you guess what will happen next. The point of predicting is to get involved with what you are reading, not to be correct every time. Therefore, it is all right to make a wrong guess. (See also page 538.)

EXAMPLE   Jackie Joyner-Kersee approached the starting line at the 1992 Olympics in Barcelona. She had won track competitions since she was fourteen years old. At the 1984 Olympics, Joyner-Kersee won a silver medal in the heptathlon. She won two gold medals in the 1988 Olympics in Seoul, Korea. As Joyner-Kersee took her stance for this latest race, she was once again ready to run for gold.

Prediction: Jackie Joyner-Kersee is about to win another Olympic gold medal.

Problem-Solution Relationships, Analyzing

A *problem* is an unanswered question, while a *solution* is a suggested answer. Authors who write about problems often also write about one or two solutions and try to explain what effects the solutions will have. When you read, ask "What is the problem?" and "Who has the problem?" Then, identify the solutions that the writer suggests.

EXAMPLE   A vacant lot in the west side neighborhood of Journeyville had become a dumping area filled with trash. Tired of this eyesore, several neighbors approached the city council about creating a community center building. While the council was in favor of the proposal, they did not have the budget to build the center. Another group of neighbors got together on weekends and began to move the trash. As the land was cleared, they built swing sets and even started a community garden. Now the lot is a bustling center of the community.

Analysis: The problem was that the west Journeyville neighborhood had a vacant lot with too much trash in it. This problem disturbed the neighbors. One possible solution was to have the city create a community center there. Another solution was to create a community park and garden.

Reading Log, Using a When you write informally about what you read, you are keeping a *reading log.* In a reading log, you can write down questions, write about personal connections you make with the reading, or make note of important sections. In addition to writing down your thoughts during reading, you can use your reading log to write down ideas you have before reading (prereading), or after reading (postreading).

Reading Rate, Adjusting *Reading rate* is the speed at which you read something. Readers adjust their reading rates based on their purpose for reading, the difficulty of the reading material, and

their knowledge about the subject. The chart at the bottom of this page shows how you can adjust your reading rate for different purposes.

SQ3R *SQ3R* is a study strategy that you can use when you read. SQ3R is an abbreviation of the five steps in this process:

S *Survey* the passage. Look over the headings, titles, illustrations, charts, and any words in boldface or italics.

Q *Question* yourself about the passage. Make headings, subtitles, and boldface words into questions that you can answer after you read.

R *Read* the entire passage. Answer your questions as you read.

R *Recite,* or say out loud, the answers to your questions.

R *Review,* or look back over, the passage. Read it again quickly and quiz yourself with the questions.

Reading Rates According to Purpose		
Reading Rate	**Purpose**	**Example**
Scanning	Quickly reading for specific details	Finding the last name of a character in a novel
Skimming	Quickly reading for main points	Previewing a chapter from your science textbook by reading the headings before you read the text
Reading for mastery (reading to learn)	Reading to understand and remember	Reading and taking notes from a book for a research report
Reading at a comfortable speed	Reading for enjoyment	Reading a novel by your favorite writer

Stated Main Idea and Supporting Details, Identifying   The *main idea* of any piece of writing is its most important idea. Sometimes main ideas are found at the beginning of a paragraph in a topic sentence. Other times, the main idea may be found at the end of the passage, as a conclusion. Main ideas are backed up by *supporting details* that explain and give more information about the main idea. When a main idea is directly stated, it is called an *explicit main idea*. (See also page 505 and **Implied Main Idea** on page 740.)

EXAMPLE   Even though they are known as disease-causing organisms, today viruses are being used to fight illnesses. Scientists are using the organisms to produce proteins for research and industry. Also, since viruses carry genetic information, they are being used to carry correct genetic information to defective cells.

Stated main idea: Viruses are being used to combat illnesses.

Supporting details: Viruses are used to produce proteins for research and industry, and they carry correct genetic information to defective cells.

Summarizing   A *summary* is a brief restatement of the main points expressed in a piece of writing. Summarizing can help you understand a difficult reading passage. Summaries are similar to paraphrases since summaries restate someone else's ideas in your own words. Summaries, however, are usually much shorter than the original passage because they do not include every detail. (See also **Paraphrasing** on page 740. See the chart on page 770 for **Summarizing Guidelines**.)

EXAMPLE   Virtual reality lets even the most couch-bound television watcher feel like he or she is skiing in the Swiss Alps. Virtual reality combines computer-created worlds with a headset that enables a person to see images in three dimensions. By using data gloves that transmit hand motions, a person can seem to be inside the computer environment.

Summary: Virtual reality is a system combining computers, headsets, and data gloves to make a person feel that he or she is within a different setting.

Text Structures, Analyzing   *Text structures* are patterns of organization that a writer uses. There are five common patterns: *cause-effect, chronological order, comparison-contrast, listing,* and *problem-solution.* Sometimes a writer may use one pattern, and other times a writer may combine two or more patterns. By understanding the way a piece of writing is organized, you can better understand the information you are reading. These guidelines can help you analyze a text structure:

1. Look for clue words that might hint at a specific pattern of organization. (See also **Clue Words** on page 739.)

2. Look for important ideas and connections between those ideas. Is there an obvious pattern?

3. Draw a graphic organizer to help you understand the text structure. Your graphic organizer may look like one of the five common text structures illustrated on the next two pages.

- *Cause-effect pattern* focuses on the relationship between causes and their effects or results. (See also page 517.) The following chain shows how nutritional education can lead to health and energy.

Causal Chain

learning about nutrition

↓

identifying poor food choices

↓

making better eating choices

↓

feeling healthy and energetic

- *Chronological order* shows events or ideas in the order in which they happen. (See also page 475.) The sequence chain in the next column lists the steps for blowing up a balloon.

Sequence Chain

stretch the balloon

↓

blow air into the balloon

↓

repeat until balloon is full

↓

hold neck of balloon between finger and thumb

↓

use other hand to tie knot in balloon

- *Comparison-contrast pattern* focuses on how two or three ideas or events are alike or different. (See also page 576.) The Venn diagram at the bottom of the page compares a human brain and a computer.
- *Listing pattern* organizes information in a list form using classifications such

Venn Diagram

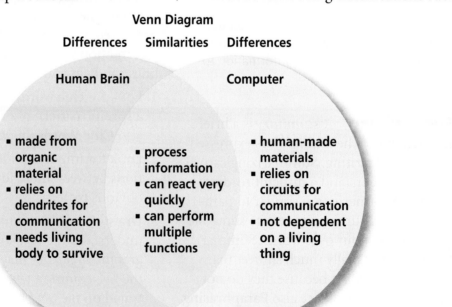

Differences   Similarities   Differences

Human Brain

- made from organic material
- relies on dendrites for communication
- needs living body to survive

- process information
- can react very quickly
- can perform multiple functions

Computer

- human-made materials
- relies on circuits for communication
- not dependent on a living thing

as importance, size, location, or other important criteria. The list below organizes dogs by size.

List

Dogs of Different Sizes

1. Chihuahua (small)
2. cocker spaniel (medium)
3. Saint Bernard (large)

■ *Problem-solution pattern* focuses on one or more problems and solutions to the problem. The pattern also explains the outcomes of each solution and the final results of the problem and solution. (See also page 526.) The following example shows a problem and some possible solutions.

Cluster

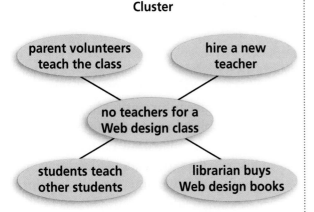

Transitional Words and Phrases, Identifying   *Transitions* are words and phrases writers use to connect ideas and to make writing read more smoothly. By identifying transitions, you can understand how the ideas in a piece of writing fit together. (See page 453 for a chart of **Transitional Words and Phrases.**)

Visuals and Graphics, Interpreting

Visuals and *graphics* communicate information with pictures or symbols. Visuals and graphics can communicate very complex information in a simple way. When you read writing that contains visuals or graphics, examine the information and draw your own conclusions.

■ **Elements**   Effective visuals and graphics contain the following elements. (See also page 721.)

1. A *title* identifies the subject or main idea of the graphic.
2. The *body* of the visual gives information in the form of a graph, chart, time line, diagram, or table.
3. *Labels* identify and explain the information shown in the visual or graphic.
4. A box called a *legend* may be included to identify symbols, colors, or scales to help the reader interpret the graphic.
5. The *source* tells where the information in the graphic was found; knowing the source helps readers evaluate the accuracy of the graphic.

■ **Types**   Several common types of visuals are *charts, diagrams, graphs, tables,* and *time lines.*

1. **Charts** show how the parts of something relate to the whole thing. In the *pie chart* on the next page, notice how all of the segments contribute to the whole picture. Pie charts often do not show specific numbers but focus on percentages instead.

Types of Volunteers

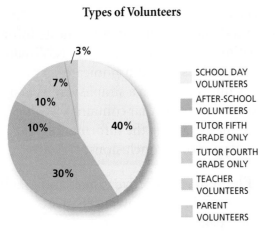

- SCHOOL DAY VOLUNTEERS
- AFTER-SCHOOL VOLUNTEERS
- TUTOR FIFTH GRADE ONLY
- TUTOR FOURTH GRADE ONLY
- TEACHER VOLUNTEERS
- PARENT VOLUNTEERS

Number of Students Tutored Through Volunteer Program

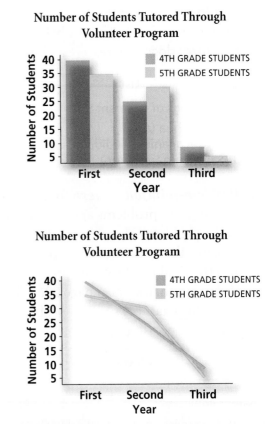

2. **Diagrams** use symbols (such as circles or arrows) or pictures to compare ideas, show a process, or show how an object is built. The following diagram shows how to make a "valley fold," a typical starting step in the Japanese art of origami.

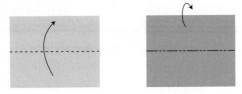

3. **Graphs,** including bar graphs and line graphs, show changes or trends over time. In a graph, the horizontal line, called an axis, represents points in time such as hours, days, or years. The vertical axis shows quantities or amounts. When you read graphs, check to see that the amounts on the axes are clearly marked. Also, look at the starting points of both axes to help you read the graph correctly. Notice that the same information is presented in the following bar graph and line graph.

4. **Tables** give information in a simple way. Tables do not include symbols or graphics that show patterns in the information. Instead, readers must think carefully about the information found in a table and draw their own conclusions. For example, a reader might conclude based on the following table that the number of volunteer tutors increases every year.

Number of Volunteers in the Peer Tutoring Program	
First year	8
Second year	10
Third year	15

5. Time lines place events in order as they take place over a period of time. In the example below, the events are identified below the time line, while segments of time are shown above it.

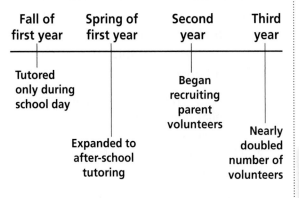

Development of the Tutoring Program

Fall of first year	Spring of first year	Second year	Third year
Tutored only during school day		Began recruiting parent volunteers	
	Expanded to after-school tutoring		Nearly doubled number of volunteers

■ **Viewing tips** When you come across graphics or visuals, stop and examine the information. Use the tips below to help you understand graphics.

1. Read the title, labels, and legend of a graphic before you try to analyze the information.

2. Draw your own conclusions from the graphic and compare them to the writer's conclusions.

3. Ask yourself if the graphic might be leaving out information. Sometimes, an author leaves out information that does not agree with his or her conclusions.

Vocabulary

Skills and Strategies

You can use the following skills and strategies to become a more effective reader.

Context Clues One way to figure out the meaning of an unfamiliar word is by finding clues in its *context,* the words and sentences surrounding it. This chart shows some of the most common types of context clues. (See also page 477.)

How to Use Context Clues
Type of Clue
Definitions and Restatements: Look for the meaning of the unfamiliar word restated in other words somewhere in the sentence.   *Dionne's little brother continued to* **aggravate** *her, doing all the things that bother her.* [*Aggravate* must mean "bother."]
Examples: Look for an example that gives you clues to the meaning of the unfamiliar word.   *Malik had many* **aspirations,** *such as his dream of being a doctor.* [*Aspirations* must be "dreams."]
Synonyms: Look for a word that has a similar meaning used in the context.   *The* **faculty** *of our school is well-educated. Most of the teachers have advanced degrees.* [*Faculty* must mean "teachers."]

(continued)

How to Use Context Clues
Type of Clue
Antonyms or Contrasts: Look for words that have an opposite meaning of the unfamiliar word. *My favorite aunt is eccentric. Her attitudes are anything but typical.* [*Eccentric* must mean "not typical."]
Cause and Effect: Look for clues that an unfamiliar word is related to the cause or is the result of a cause. *When Jaime ridiculed my hat, I felt embarrassed and took it off.* [*Ridicule* must mean "make fun of."]

Word Bank   You can create a ***word bank*** by making a list of unfamiliar words you encounter. Creating your own word bank can help you improve your vocabulary. When you add a word to your bank, look up its definition in the dictionary. You might keep your word bank in a notebook or in a computer file.

Word Meanings   The meanings of words change over time or in the situations in which they are used. You always want your words to say exactly what you mean. The following definitions and examples can help.

■ **Clichés and tired words**   A *cliché* is an overused expression. These expressions were once fresh and expressive, but their overuse has made them seem dull and tired. Clichés weaken your writing.

EXAMPLES   *fresh as a daisy, easy as pie, so hungry I could eat a horse*

A ***tired word*** has been used so often and so carelessly that it has become worn out and almost meaningless.

EXAMPLES   *nice, fine, pretty, terrific*

■ **Denotation and connotation**   A word's direct, "dictionary" definition is called its ***denotation.*** Words also have a ***connotation,*** the emotional meanings a word suggests. Connotations can have powerful effects on readers and listeners.

EXAMPLES   The words *firm* and *strict* have very similar denotations. However, *firm* has the positive connotation of being stable. *Strict* has more a negative connotation of being harsh and severe.

■ **Figurative language**   *Figurative language* is the imaginative use of words and phrases to describe one thing by comparing it to something else. Figurative language requires the reader to look beyond the literal, or usual, meaning of the words.

Type of Figurative Language	Example
A **metaphor** directly compares one thing to another.	*Daisies are little suns shining in a field.*
Personification uses human characteristics to describe non-human things.	*The plants stretched their arms toward the sun.*
A **simile** compares two different things using the words *like* or *as.*	*The dancers floated across the floor like leaves blowing in the wind.*

QUICK REFERENCE HANDBOOK

■ **Idioms** *Idioms* are phrases with a different meaning than each word's literal, or usual, meaning. Idioms are frequently common to a particular region, culture, or time period. They cannot be explained grammatically or translated word-for-word.

EXAMPLES

She was *sitting on pins and needles* as she waited.

Jim went *out on a limb* and asked another question.

Last night Sarah and Javier went out and *cut a rug.*

■ **Loaded words** *Loaded words* are terms that are used to have a strong positive or negative impact on the reader or listener. Loaded words can be very persuasive since they appeal to the reader's or listener's emotions.

EXAMPLES

Leah *frowned* at her dog's *misbehavior.*
Leah *scowled* at her dog's *disobedience.*

■ **Multiple meanings** Many words have several different meanings. To determine which meaning is being used, look at the word's context. If you still have difficulty figuring out the meaning, look up the word in the dictionary and read each meaning. Then, try each meaning in the sentence to pick the correct one. (See also page 508.)

EXAMPLE As we sailed out on the choppy waves of the lake, my brother looked *green.*
green (grēn) *adj.* **1.** relating to the color found in grass and plants; **2.** naive and inex-

perienced; **3.** sickly and nauseated [The third definition best fits the context.]

Word Origins See **The History of English** on page 724.

Word Parts Many words in English are made up of smaller *word parts.* These word parts are known as *roots, prefixes,* and *suffixes.* Knowing the meanings of word parts can help you understand the meanings of unfamiliar words.

■ **Roots** The *root* is the foundation on which a word is built. The root contains the word's basic meaning. Prefixes and suffixes are added to the root. (See also page 648.)

Commonly Used Roots		
Root	**Meaning**	**Example**
-audio-	hearing, sound	audience
–bibli–, –biblio–	book	bibliography
–log(ue) –, –logy–	study, word	geology
–magni–	large	magnificent
–micro–	small	microscope
–ped–	foot	pedestrian
–phon–	sound	telephone

■ **Prefixes** A *prefix* is a word part that is added before a root. When a prefix is added to a root, the word it forms is a combination of the prefix and the root meaning. (See also page 578.)

Commonly Used Prefixes

Prefix	Meaning	Example
anti–	against, opposing	antiwar
bi–	two	bicycle
dis–	away, opposing	disagree
mis–	wrong	mistake
non–	not	nonfat
over–	above, too much	overdone
pre–	before	preread
re–	again	replace
semi–	half	semicircle
sub–	under	submarine
un–	not	unhappy

Suffixes A *suffix* is a word part that is added after a root. Adding a suffix may change both a word's meaning and its part of speech, as in *joy/joyful*. (See also page 578.)

Commonly Used Suffixes

Suffix	Meaning	Example
–able	can, will	respectable
–dom	state, condition	kingdom
–en	make	weaken
–ful	full of	stressful
–hood	state, condition	neighborhood
–ish	suggesting, like	feverish
–less	without	penniless
–ly	characteristic of	quickly
–ment	result, act of	commitment
–ness	quality, state	goodness, sadness
–ous	characterized by	luxurious

Words to Learn You can study the 300 words below to improve your vocabulary this year. Try to learn as many unfamiliar words from this list as you can.

abdomen
absorb
abundant
acquire
adjust
amateur
ambitious
analyze
anthem
apologize
applaud
application
appreciate
appropriate
architect
arid
associate
assume
astonish
aviation

ballot
barrier
benefit
betray
biography
boast

bombard
Braille
bureau

campaign
candidate
captivity
career
caution
ceremony
characteristic
collapse
collide
commotion
competition
complaint
complex
compliment
conceal
conduct
conference
congratulate
conscience
consent
contrast
contribute
conviction

Quick Reference Handbook Reading and Vocabulary

cooperate
corporation
counterfeit
courteous
cultivate

dainty
debate
debt
decrease
definite
demonstration
deny
departure
descendant
descriptive
desirable
desperate
destination
detect
determination
disadvantage
disastrous
discomfort
discourage
disguise
disgust
dissolve
district
disturb
document
doubtful
doubtless
dramatic
dread
duplicate

earnest
eavesdrop
eliminate
employer
engage
entertain
envy

error
escort
essential
establish
eternal
exception
exclaim
exert
export
extraordinary

fatal
feat
flammable
flexible
flourish
foe
foul
foundation
fragrant
frantic
furious

gasp
generation
generous
genuine
glimpse
gorgeous
gossip
gratitude
guidance

hazard
hearty
heir
heroic
hesitate
hibernate
hoist
honorable

identical
ignite
imitate

impatience
import
impostor
inaccurate
incident
inexpensive
inform
inhale
innumerable
inspiration
instinct
interrupt
interview
intrusion
investment
inviting
involve
irregular
issue

jeopardy
journalism
justify
juvenile

keen
knapsack

legend
leisure
license
linger
locally
lunar
luscious
luxurious

majority
mammoth
management
marvel
maximum
merchandise
migrate
miraculous

mobile
mourning

navigator
nominate
notion
nuisance
numerous

oath
obvious
occasion
offense
offspring
omit
ordinary
ornamental

paralysis
particle
persuade
pharmacy
pierce
plead
plot
pollute
portion
possess
precipitation
predict
prehistoric
previous
prey
privacy
profession
prohibit
promotion
protest
portrait
provoke
pry
publicity

qualify
quantity

quarantine
quote

ransom
rash
reaction
realm
rebel
receipt
reckless
reduction
reference
regret
regulate
rehearsal
reign
relate
reliable
remedy
request
requirement
resemble

reservoir
resident
resign
respectable
responsibility
revolution
routine

sacrifice
satisfy
scheme
scholar
security
self-confidence
self-respect
separation
session
severe
simplify
solitary
specify
static

stray
suburbs
summarize
superior
surgery
survey
survival
suspicion
symbol
sympathy

temporary
tension
terminal
terrain
text
theme
thorough
threat
toll
toxic
tradition

tragedy
transparent
twilight

unexpectedly
unfavorable
unfortunate
unite
urge

vacuum
vault
vicinity
victim
victorious
villain
visual
vivid
vocal

wardrobe
widespread

yacht

Speaking and Listening

Speaking

You probably enjoy having conversations with your friends. You can build on the skills you use in conversations to develop new speaking skills for different situations. Use the strategies in this section to become a more effective speaker.

Formal Speaking

In formal speaking, a specific time and place are set aside for someone to give a presentation to a group. The purpose of this presentation may be to inform, to persuade, to discuss problems and solutions, or to entertain.

Content and Organization of a Presentation The following steps can help you create an effective presentation.

1. **Choose a topic.** Sometimes, your topic will be assigned. However, when you are free to choose your own topic, try one or more of these ideas.
   - Consider turning a piece you have written into a presentation.
   - Brainstorm a list of topics.
   - Re-read your journal to find ideas.
   - Ask friends, family members and teachers for ideas.
   - Look through magazines and newspapers.

2. **Identify the purpose and occasion of your presentation.** Your *purpose* is why you are speaking—what you want your presentation to accomplish. The purpose of your presentation will help you determine your word choice and usage (formal or informal). Here are some common purposes for presentations.

Purposes for Presentations	
Purpose	**Examples of Presentation Titles**
To inform give facts, explain how to do something, or present a problem and propose a solution	- Life Aboard a Covered Wagon - How to Choose a Bike Helmet - How We Can Protect Coral Reefs

(continued)

Purposes for Presentations	
Purpose	**Examples of Presentation Titles**
To persuade attempt to change opinions or get listeners to take action	• Where's Our School Spirit? • Hidden Dangers on the Playground
To entertain share a funny or interesting story or event	• A Birthday to Remember • My First Home Run

The **occasion** is the event or situation that prompts you to speak. Often, the occasion may be a class assignment. At other times it may be a meeting of a club you belong to or an awards ceremony. Reviewing what you know about the occasion will help you prepare a presentation. For example, think about the date, the time of day, the place, and how much time you will have.

3. **Think about your audience.** Knowing the occasion will give you a general idea of who your audience will be. Consider your listeners' needs and interests and use words they will understand. The questions in the following chart can help you. Your answers may also help you decide on your *point of view,* or the way you will approach your topic.

Analyzing Your Audience		
Question	**If your answer is . . .**	**Your presentation should . . .**
How much does the audience already know about the topic?	not much	provide background information about the topic
	some	connect information the audience may not know to what they already know
	a lot	share new and interesting information
How interested in the topic do you think the audience will be?	very interested	keep the audience interested by spacing out surprising ideas or information
	a little interested	get the audience more interested by beginning with a question or a surprising fact
	not interested	show the audience how the topic affects them personally

QUICK REFERENCE HANDBOOK

4. **Gather information.** For some topics, you can draw information from your own experience or papers you have already written. For others, you may need to do research. You can read newspapers and magazines, check the Internet, or talk to people who know the topic well. (See also **Library/Media Center** on page 728.)

5. **Organize your information.** Organizing your ideas for a presentation is like arranging information for a written paper. You will include an introduction that states your main idea, support your main idea with evidence, examples, and elaboration, and summarize your main points in a conclusion. Below is an example of a plan for a specific kind of presentation, one that explores a problem and a possible solution.
   - Define the problem.
   - Support your definition with evidence (reasons, facts, and the opinions of experts).
   - Present your ideas about the problem's causes (*Why is this happening?*) and effects (*What are the results?*).
   - Suggest a solution, and show how it is connected to the problem.
   - Present evidence showing why your solution is a good one.

   See the Writing Workshops in this book for ways to arrange information for other purposes.

6. **Make note cards.** Each note card for your speech should have notes on only one major point and include supporting details that elaborate on that point. Make a special note on the card to remind you when to show or refer to a visual in your speech. Number your note cards to help you keep them in order.

7. **Use media.** Consider including media such as visuals or sounds in your speech if they will make your ideas clearer or help listeners remember an important point. Media should be easy for you to use and easy for your audience to see, hear, and understand. Otherwise, you may lose your train of thought or confuse your listeners. Here are forms of media you might consider using.
   - electronic media, including Web pages
   - audio recordings such as music files or CDs
   - audiovisual recordings, including DVDs, videotapes, and short films
   - slides or filmstrips
   - traditional visuals such as charts, graphs, illustrations, and diagrams

   (See also **Creating Visuals to Share Information** on pages 672–673.)

Delivery of a Presentation These steps will help you give your presentation.

1. **Practice.** Practice your presentation until you are sure you know it well. Ask friends or family members to listen to your speech and suggest ways to make it better. If you plan to use visuals or other media, be sure to include them in your practice.

2. Deliver your presentation. Use these tips to help you deliver your presentation effectively.

- *Stay calm and confident.* Before you begin speaking, take a deep breath. Stand up straight, look alert, and pay attention to what you are saying.
- *Use body language.* The chart below lists nonverbal signals, or body language, that will add to your message.

Nonverbal Signals

Eye contact

Look into the eyes of your audience members

Purposes
- Shows that you are honest or sincere
- Keeps audience's attention

Facial expression

Smile, frown, raise an eyebrow

Purposes
- Shows your feelings
- Emphasizes parts of your message

Gestures

Give thumbs up, shrug, nod, or shake your head

Purposes
- Emphasizes your point
- Adds meaning to the speech

Posture

Stand tall and straight

Purpose
- Shows that you are sure of yourself

- *Use your voice effectively.* Here are verbal elements to consider as you practice and deliver your speech. You may adjust these elements depending on your **audience** and the **setting.** For example, you might use a soothing tone with children. If you are giving a morning talk, you might vary your pitch to capture your audience's attention.

Verbal Element	Definition
Diction	Pronounce words clearly, or *enunciate.* Speak carefully so that your listeners can understand you.
Mood (or tone)	Your speech or oral interpretation may make your listeners feel a certain emotion. Making listeners feel happy, angry, or sad about what you are saying can help them remember your points better.
Pitch	Your voice rises and falls naturally when you speak. If you are nervous, your voice may get higher. To control your pitch, take deep breaths and stay calm as you give your speech.
Rate (or tempo)	In conversations you may speak at a fast rate, or speed. When you make a speech, you should talk more slowly to help listeners understand you.
Volume	Even if you normally speak quietly, you will need to speak loudly in a formal speech. Listeners at the back of the room should be able to hear you clearly.

■ *Use standard English.* Pronounce words correctly, and use correct grammar. You should avoid using slang or jargon. If you use any technical terms in your speech, define them for your listeners.

Other Formal Speaking Situations

Here are two other types of formal speeches and strategies you might use to give each type of speech.

■ **Making an announcement**   An *announcement* is a short speech that provides information to a group of listeners. Often, it includes instructions about a current situation or an upcoming event. Write out your message ahead of time, and use the following tips.

How to Make an Announcement

1. Include all the important facts. Most announcements provide the following information:

- the kind of event or situation
- who is involved in the event or situation
- the time and location of the event or situation
- why the event is important
- any special information, such as the cost of admission

2. Add interesting details that will catch your listeners' attention.

3. Announce your message slowly, clearly, and briefly.

4. If necessary, repeat the most important facts.

■ **Introducing a speaker**   To introduce a speaker to an audience, identify the speaker and tell listeners a little about his or her background. Your introduction should also prepare the audience to hear what the speaker has to say. Make the speaker feel welcome, but keep your comments brief.

Informal Speaking

When you speak informally, you do not plan in advance what you will say. The guidelines that follow will help you to speak more effectively in discussions and in social situations.

Group Discussion   Group discussions are an important part of many clubs and classes. To get the most from such discussions, follow these tips.

1. **Set a purpose.** Setting a purpose will help your group identify what you need to accomplish in the time you have. This purpose may be
   - to connect ideas, insights, and experiences with others
   - to cooperate in gaining information
   - to solve a problem
   - to reach a decision or recommend a course of action

2. **Assign roles.** Each person in the group has a role to play. For example, your group may choose a chairperson, whose role is to keep the discussion moving smoothly. Another person may be named the recorder. This person's role is to take notes of what is said during

the discussion. No matter what your role is, use the guidelines below to contribute effectively to the discussion.

Guidelines for Group Discussions

1. Prepare for the discussion. If you know what topic your group will discuss, find out some information about the topic ahead of time.

2. Listen to what others say. Be willing to learn from the other members of your group. Do not interrupt when someone is speaking. Instead, listen and wait until it is your turn to speak.

3. Do your part. Contribute to the discussion by sharing your ideas and knowledge. Encourage other members of the group to do the same, and express your agreement or disagreement with their points in an appropriate way.

4. Stay on the discussion topic. If the discussion gives you other, related ideas, keep your group's purpose in mind. Make a note for yourself about an idea, but only discuss ideas that fit your group's topic and purpose.

5. Ask questions. If you are not sure you understand the point a member of your group is making, summarize it and ask him or her to explain it more clearly. Others in the group may also be confused.

Speaking Socially   In any social situation, remember to speak politely and clearly. The following strategies will help.

■ **Giving directions or instructions** When you need to give directions or explain how to do something, make sure your directions or instructions are clear and complete. Here are some pointers.

How to Give Directions or Instructions

1. Before you give information, plan what you want to say. Think of the information as a series of steps.

2. Explain the steps in order. Be sure you have not skipped any steps or left out important details.

3. If necessary, repeat all of the steps to be sure your listener understands them.

■ **Making introductions**   Use these tips to introduce people who do not know each other or to introduce yourself to someone new.

How to Make Introductions

1. You can use first names if you are introducing people your own age. ("Mirha, this is Josh.")

2. Speak first to the older person of the people you are introducing. ("Dad, this is my friend Keisha.")

3. Introduce yourself to others if no one introduces you first. Start a conversation by asking a question.

4. When you need to introduce someone to a large group of people, introduce him or her to just a few people at a time. ("Class, this is Gordon Delgado. Gordon, meet Letrice, Michael, and Bao.")

5. If someone you are meeting offers to shake your hand, do so. You may offer to shake hands with someone your own age.

6. Mention something the two people you are introducing to each other have in common. ("Trey, meet my cousin Li. Li runs as much as you do.")

■ **Speaking on the telephone** It is important to use the telephone courteously. Here are some suggestions.

Guidelines for Telephoning

1. Call at a time that is convenient for the person you are calling.

2. Be sure to dial the correct number. If you reach a wrong number, apologize for the error.

3. Speak clearly. Say who you are when the phone is answered. If the person you are calling is not there, you may want to leave your name, phone number, and a short message.

4. Do not stay on the telephone too long.

Oral Interpretation

An *oral interpretation* is a dramatic reading of a written piece. The purpose of the reading is to entertain.

1. Choose a selection. Poems, short stories, and plays can provide you with good material for an oral interpretation.

Type of Literature	Characteristics of a Good Selection
Poem	▪ tells a story (an epic or a narrative poem) ▪ has a speaker (uses the word *I*) or has dialogue (a conversation between characters) ▪ expresses a particular emotion
Short story	▪ has a beginning, middle, and end ▪ has characters whose words you can act out (a narrator who tells the story or characters who talk to one another)
Play	▪ has a beginning, middle, and end ▪ has one or more characters with dialogue

When you choose a selection, think about the occasion. Should you be serious, or can you have some fun? How much time will you have? Also, consider your audience. Will your listeners find the selection interesting? Will they understand its meaning?

2. Adapt the material. Sometimes, you may need to shorten a story, poem, or play to make it work as an oral interpretation. To make a shortened version, or *cutting,* follow these suggestions.

How to Make a Cutting

1. Decide where the part of the selection you want to use should begin and end. Follow that part of the story in time order.

2. Cut dialogue tags, such as *she said.*

3. Cut out parts that do not have anything to do with the part of the story you are telling.

3. **Present your interpretation.** Once you have chosen a selection, you can use the following guidelines to help you present it.

- *Prepare a reading script.* A *reading script* is a neatly typed or handwritten copy of the selection marked to show exactly how you will present it.

How to Mark a Reading Script

1. Underline words or phrases you plan to stress.

2. Use a slash (/) to show each pause.

3. Make notes in the margin about when you will raise or lower your voice, use gestures, or create a particular mood. Also, note where to use your voice to show juncture, or connect related ideas.

- *Write an introduction.* You may need to introduce your interpretation to your audience. In your introduction, you can tell what happened before your scene in the story, describe the characters involved, or tell listeners from whose point of view the story is being told (one of the characters, for example).
- *Practice.* Rehearse your selection carefully. Practice reading the material aloud, using voice tone, movements, and emphasis, or stress. Think about how you can make the meaning and mood of the selection clear to your audience. Practice in front of a friend or family member or in front of a mirror until you feel confident about your presentation.

Self-Evaluation

Evaluating means judging. Evaluating your formal speaking is a good way to improve your speaking skills. When you can judge what went well and what did not, you can focus on the areas that need work. After you give a speech or present an oral interpretation, take some time to review your performance. Coming up with a set of *evaluation criteria,* or standards, will help you cover all the bases. In general, evaluation criteria for speaking should look at

- content (what you say—"Did I state a main idea and support it with evidence? Were the media I used easy to see, hear, and understand? Did I handle them well?")
- organization (how you group and order your ideas—"Did I explain my ideas in a clear and logical way?")
- delivery (how you use language and present your ideas)

To come up with specific criteria for delivery, look at the charts on page 756. Ask a question about each of the important ideas covered. For the term *rate,* for example, you might ask "Did I speak at a steady rate?"

You can use these criteria during practice sessions as well as after you speak. They will help you to measure your progress during the year and judge for yourself just how far you have come as a speaker. (See also the **Points to Evaluate** chart on page 765.)

Listening

Active listening means making sense of the information you hear. Becoming an active listener will help you understand and evaluate a speaker's ideas.

Basics of the Listening Process

Like reading, listening is a process. Here are strategies you can use before, during, and after listening to get the most from a spoken message.

Before Listening Take these steps before you begin to listen.

1. **Know why you are listening.** You will be a more effective listener if you remember your purpose for listening. The amount of attention you give to a speaker depends on your purpose for listening. For example, you would probably pay closer attention to your teacher giving directions than to friends discussing a topic that does not interest you. Some common purposes for listening are
   - for enjoyment, entertainment, or appreciation
   - for information or explanation
   - for forming opinions or evaluating ideas

2. **Limit distractions.** Listening is not always easy. The room you are in may be too hot or too cold or too stuffy. You may have other things on your mind. These guidelines will help you make the best of the situation.

Eliminating Barriers to Effective Listening

Stay positive, and focus on the speaker. As you sit down, clear your mind to help you concentrate on what the speaker will say.

Adjust to your surroundings. Be sure to sit where you can see and hear the speaker well.

Prepare to think about the message. Focus on what the speaker is saying, not on how he or she looks, talks, stands, or moves.

Listening to a Speaker Follow these guidelines to be a courteous and effective listener.

- Look at the speaker, and pay attention.

- Do not interrupt the speaker. Do not whisper, fidget, or make distracting noises or movements.

- Respect the speaker's race, accent, clothing, customs, and religion.

- Try to understand the speaker's point of view. Remember that your own point of view or attitude toward the topic affects your judgment.

- Listen to the entire message before you form an opinion about it.

- Take notes. Do not try to write down every word. Instead, focus on the speaker's most important details. (See also **Notes** on page 768.)

Responding to a Speaker   Your role as a listener does not end when a presentation is over. Here are some ways to respond to the speaker and add to your understanding of the topic.

- Ask questions. If you did not understand something the speaker said, ask about it. The speaker's response to your question can clear up any confusion, which can help you and others.

- Give positive feedback. Point out one or two things the speaker did well. If you disagree with the speaker's message, find something else to praise, such as the use of media.

- Give constructive criticism. Politely point out something the speaker could do even better the next time.

- Use body language to give positive feedback. Listen to the questions and answers that follow the presentation. Stay seated until the speaker turns to leave.

- Compare your response to the presentation with the responses of others. You may gain a new insight or help someone else gain one.

Listening with a Purpose

Different strategies can help you achieve different purposes for listening. The strategies that follow will help you listen more effectively to appreciate (or be entertained), to comprehend (or understand), and to evaluate a speech.

Listening to Appreciate   When you listen to appreciate, you are listening to enjoy what you hear. Usually, you listen to literature or oral tradition for appreciation.

- **Listening to literature**   In a way, listening to literature is like reading it yourself. In both situations, you carry out a process, or series of steps.

Listening to Literature

Before you listen

- Preview the work by asking questions. What kind of literature is it—a story, a poem, a play? What is the title? Who wrote it? What is it about?

- Make **predictions** about what you will hear. (A prediction is a guess based on what you already know.) Do not worry about whether your predictions are correct. Making them is a way of sharpening your focus, not a test you must pass.

As you listen

- Picture the characters, actions, and scenes the writer describes.

- Identify the **tone** (the writer's attitude toward the topic) and the **mood** (the emotions, or feelings, the work creates in the listener).

- Connect the work with your own life. Which experiences or feelings seem similar to ones you have had?

- Jot down questions or comments the work brings to mind. Are there any parts you do not understand? What would you like to ask the writer?

Listening to Literature

After you listen

- Respond personally to the work. What did you like or dislike about it? How did it make you feel? What did you learn from it?

- Summarize the selection. What happened in the selection? What did you learn about life from listening to this work?

- Confirm or adjust your predictions. Which ones were right on target? Which ones did you need to change and in what ways?

- Identify how the writer uses elements of literature, such as rhyme, suspense, and imagery. How did these elements help shape the work?

■ **Listening to oral tradition** *Oral traditions* are messages that are passed down from older people to younger people through the spoken word. These messages often take the form of folk tales and songs that use stories to teach a moral—a lesson for living—or to pass down history or culture. The following tips will help you be an active listener when you have the chance to hear such stories.

Strategies for Listening to Oral Tradition

1. Compare the elements of literature in different stories. Many folk tales and folk songs have similar characters, settings, plots, and themes. As you listen, recall stories you know that have similar elements. How are the stories alike, and how are they different?

2. Compare how storytellers use language. A storyteller sometimes uses labels (names for objects or ideas) or sayings that reflect his or her culture or region. For example, depending on a storyteller's region, he or she might use the label *stoop* or *porch* to mean a covered entrance to a house. As you listen to a speaker from a different region or culture, compare his or her sayings and labels with your own.

3. Compare the way the story is told in different regions. Among Native Americans, for example, trickster tales appear widely. Depending on the region, though, the main character—the trickster—could be a raven, a coyote, a mink, a blue jay, a rabbit, a spider, or a human. Often, the geography, wildlife, or weather patterns mentioned are clues to where the story (or the storyteller) is originally from.

Listening to Comprehend Use the steps in the chart below and the strategies on the next page to help you get information from a message you hear.

How to Listen for Information

Find the major ideas.

Identify the most important points the speaker makes. Listen for clue words, such as *major* or *most important*.

Identify supporting evidence.

How does the speaker support the main idea? What details does the speaker emphasize with gestures, visuals, or verbal cues, like "for example"?

(continued)

(continued)

How to Listen for Information

Distinguish between facts and opinions.

A fact is a statement that can be proved to be true. An opinion is a belief or judgment about something. It cannot be proved to be true.

Listen for comparisons and contrasts.

The speaker may emphasize a point or explain an idea by comparing or contrasting it to something familiar to you.

Pay attention to causes and effects.

Does the speaker say or hint that some events cause others to happen? Does the speaker suggest that some events are the results of other events?

Predict outcomes and draw conclusions.

Connect the speaker's words and ideas to your own experiences. What conclusions can you draw about the topic? What might happen as a result of events the speaker discusses?

■ **LQ2R** The LQ2R study method is especially helpful when you are listening to a speaker who is giving information.

L *Listen* carefully to information as it is presented.

Q *Question* yourself as you listen. Make a list of your questions as you think of them.

R *Recite* to yourself, in your own words, the answers to your questions as the speaker presents them. Summarize the information in your mind, or jot down notes as you listen.

R *Relisten* as the speaker concludes the presentation. The speaker may repeat the major points of the speech.

■ *5W-How?* **questions** When you are listening for details, try to sort out information that answers the basic *5W-How?* questions: *Who? What? When? Where? Why?* and *How?* For example, when you are introduced to someone new, you may want to listen for the person's name (*Who?*) and their hometown (*Where?*).

■ **Listening to instructions and directions** Instructions and directions are usually made up of a series of steps. To understand the steps, follow these guidelines.

How to Listen to Instructions

1. Listen to each step. Listen for words that tell you when each step ends and the next one begins—for example, *first, second, next, then,* and *last.*

2. Listen for the number of steps required and the order you should follow. Take notes if necessary.

3. In your mind, make an outline of the steps you should follow. Then, picture yourself completing each step in order.

4. Make sure you have all the information you need and understand the instructions. Ask questions if you are not sure about a particular step.

5. If the situation allows, repeat the instructions back to the speaker. Listen to any further corrections or comments the speaker makes.

Listening to Interpret and Evaluate Evaluating a presentation involves judging its content, organization, delivery, and believability. The questions in the chart on the next page will help you.

Points to Interpret and Evaluate

Content and Organization

Interpret the speaker's message and purpose
- Can you sum up the main idea?
- Why is the speaker giving the presentation?

Evaluate how clearly the content was organized
- Does the speaker explain ideas in a clear and logical order?
- Can you list each of the main points?

Delivery

Evaluate the speaker's use of verbal and visual elements
- Did the speaker speak loudly and clearly?
- Did the speaker use visuals? If so, did the speaker handle them well? Were the visuals clear and easy to understand?

Evaluate the use of nonverbal elements
- Did the speaker use body language—posture, gestures, facial expressions?
- Did the nonverbal elements match the speaker's words? For example, did the speaker use hand gestures or a raised voice when making an important point?

Believability (Content + Delivery = Believability)

Interpret the speaker's perspective or point of view
- What is the speaker's attitude toward the topic?

Analyze the speaker's techniques
- Did the speaker try to *convince* by using reasons and evidence or *sell* his or her point by appealing to listeners' emotions? Did the speaker use propaganda? (See page 785.)

Special Listening Situations

Group Discussion See page 757.

Interviews An *interview* is a good way to gather firsthand information for a project or a report. The suggestions that follow can help when you interview.

How to Conduct an Interview

Before the interview
- Make an appointment with the person you would like to interview. Make sure you arrive on time.
- Decide what you want to know.
- Make a list of questions. Avoid questions that require only yes or no answers.

During the interview
- Listen carefully. Be respectful, even if you disagree with the person.
- Take notes. If you do not understand something, ask questions about it.
- Thank the person before you leave.

After the interview
- Make sure your notes are clear.
- Write a summary as soon as you can.

Media Messages   The *media* are communication forms that you read and hear. Media include newspapers, magazines, radio, television, and the Internet. They are sometimes called the *mass media* because they reach masses, or large numbers, of people. Much of the information we receive comes to us by listening to the media. For that reason, it is important to be a critical listener.

■ **Analyzing media messages**   *Analyzing* means identifying the parts of something and understanding how those parts work together. To analyze a media message, use the following questions.

Analyzing Media Messages

What is the purpose of the message? Many media messages have more than one purpose. For example, most news programs give information. To make money, though, a program will sell time to advertisers, who pay according to how many viewers will see their ads. Therefore, the program will also try to entertain so it can attract more viewers.

Is the information correct and up-to-date? What is the source of the information? If no sources are given, you have no way of knowing whether the information can be trusted.

How does the message use language? Does it include persuasive words, such as *you should*? Does it use persuasive techniques (see page 741)? Are you being given straight information, or are you being sold a product, service, or idea?

What ideas does the message take for granted? What is left out is as important as what is included. For example, a program on teens that tells only about the problems they cause presents a one-sided message.

What is your opinion of the message? Based on your answers to the questions in this chart, form your own opinion about the message. If you think the message may not be accurate, you may want to find more information on your own.

■ **Identifying lack of objectivity in the media**   The following chart lists some signs to watch for in media messages. Seeing any of these signs in a message is a clue that the message may be unfair or unbalanced.

Evaluating Media Messages

Bias—leaning toward one side of an issue. A biased speaker may not give opposing views equal time or may not mention them at all.

Misleading Information—bending facts or statistics to support an idea. A speaker may bend facts to move an audience to take action or to win over an undecided audience.

Prejudice—judging people or situations, most often in a negative way, before the facts are known. Prejudiced speakers may ignore facts that do not agree with their views.

Studying and Test Taking

Studying

Skills and Strategies

One purpose of studying is to learn information a little bit at a time so you can do well on tests and earn good grades. However, studying also helps you remember important information you may need later in life. (See also **Test Taking** on page 771.)

Making a Study Plan   Set up a study schedule that will help you succeed. Follow the suggestions below to make effective use of your study time.

1. **Know your assignments.** Write down your assignments for each class and the date when each one is due. Make sure you understand the instructions for each assignment.
2. **Plan to finish your work on time.** Break larger assignments into smaller steps. Use a calendar to set deadlines and keep track of when you should be finished with each step.

3. **Study.** Set aside a time and a place where you can work on your assignments without becoming distracted.

Organizing and Remembering Information   There are many different ways you can study because there are many different ways to handle information. The strategies listed on the following pages can help you organize and remember information as you study.

■ **Classifying**   When you *classify* items, you sort them into groups, or categories, with other items that are related to them. The name of the category describes the relationship between the items in the group. If you break your notes into categories, you will have an easier time learning the information.

EXAMPLE In what category do the following things fit?
dolphin, shark, whale, octopus

Answer: ocean animals

■ **Graphic organizers**   New information is sometimes easier to understand if you organize it visually. The process of classifying and organizing information in a *graphic organizer* will help you learn the information. Studying information in a **graphic organizer,** such as a map, chart, or diagram, is often more effective than studying the same information in a paragraph. (See also **Text Structures** on page 743.)

■ **Memorization**   Sometimes you need to *memorize* information. To develop memorization skills, follow the tips below. Information is easier to memorize if you practice in frequent, short, focused sessions. You may also find that working with another person who can quiz you helps you commit information to memory.

How to Memorize

Memorize only the most important information. Whenever possible, shorten the material you need to remember.

Practice the material in different ways. For example, write the material by hand onto a sheet of paper. Read the paper aloud. Put it away. Then, write out the material again from memory.

Invent memory games. Find words that have the same first letters as the important terms and string them together into a sentence, or make up poems or songs that help you remember facts and details.

■ **Notes on reading or lectures**   Taking accurate *notes* is worth the extra effort. As you read at home or listen in class, you should record detailed information in your notebook. Then, you will be ready to study for even the most challenging tests.

How to Take Study Notes

1. Identify and write down the main ideas presented in class or your reading. These main ideas should be headings in your notes. In class, listen for key words and phrases, such as *first, most important,* or *therefore.* These words often introduce main ideas and tell you how ideas are related. In a textbook, look for chapter headings and subheadings. They usually contain key ideas.

2. Keep your notes brief. Use abbreviations, and sum up source material in your own words.

3. Include brief examples or details from the source material. Important examples or details can help you recall the key ideas more easily.

4. Look over your notes as soon as you write them. Be sure you have included the most important information.

At the top of the next page is an example of careful study notes one student wrote after reading a passage about the Cherokee Nation. The notes show the main ideas as headings. Underneath each main heading, you will find a group of important details that relate to that heading. Notice that the notes are brief.

Background information
  Cherokee leaders wanted to
    modernize
  1827—formed a legislature, wrote a
    constitution, started a judicial
    system
  built a capital—New Echota in
    Georgia
Causes for removal
  New settlers of European descent
    did not want to share land in the
    Southeast with Indians
  1828—gold discovered on edge of
    Cherokee territory and Andrew
    Jackson was elected president.
    Jackson believed Indians should
    not have nations within the U.S.
Effects
  1830—Indian Removal Act passed
  Jackson gives the Five Civilized
    Tribes (Cherokee, Chickasaw,
    Choctaw, Creek, Seminole) land in
    Indian Territory (Oklahoma)
  Cherokees must leave their lands in
    Georgia and Tennessee

How to Paraphrase

1. Read the selection carefully before you begin.

2. Be sure you understand the main idea of the selection. Look up any unfamiliar words in a dictionary.

3. Determine the tone of the selection. (What is the attitude of the writer toward the subject of the selection?)

4. Identify the speaker in fictional material. (Is the poet or author speaking, or is a character speaking?)

5. Write your paraphrase in your own words. Shorten long sentences or stanzas. Use your own, familiar vocabulary, and keep the ideas in the same order as they are in the selection.

6. Be sure that the ideas in your paraphrase match the ideas expressed in the original text.

- **Outlines**   An *outline* can help you organize ideas. When you write an outline, you group ideas in a pattern that shows their relationship to one another. (See also **Prewriting Techniques** on page 795.)

- **Paraphrasing**   When you *paraphrase,* you explain someone else's idea in your own words. When you put an idea in your own words, you will understand it better and remember it longer. (See also **Paraphrasing** on page 740.)

- **SQ3R**   *SQ3R* stands for *Survey, Question, Read, Recite,* and *Review.* It is a reading strategy that helps you learn information from a book. (See also **SQ3R** on page 742.)

- **Summarizing**   A *summary* is a brief restatement of the main ideas expressed in a piece of writing. A summary is similar to a paraphrase because you express another person's ideas in your own words. However, a summary is usually shorter than a paraphrase because you only note the most important points. (See also **Summarizing** on page 743.)

How to Summarize

1. Skim the selection you wish to summarize.

2. Read the passage again closely. Look for main ideas and supporting details.

3. Write your summary in your own words. Include only the main ideas and the most important supporting points.

4. Evaluate and revise your summary. Check that you have covered the most important points. Make sure that the information is clearly expressed and that the reader can follow your ideas.

■ **Writing to learn** *Writing* is a valuable study tool. Writing helps you organize your thoughts, solve problems, make plans, and get your mind ready to learn. The chart below contains some kinds of writing that can help you learn about yourself and your world.

Types of *Writing to Learn*

Freewriting helps you focus your thoughts.

Example writing for five minutes to brainstorm everything you know about a subject you are studying

Autobiographies help you examine the meaning of important events in your life.

Example writing about a personal event that showed you the importance of learning

Diaries help you recall thoughts, express feelings, and clear your mind.

Example expressing the feelings you have about a subject about which you are learning

Journals help you record observations and descriptions or explore answers to questions.

Example recording questions that you develop about a topic, and exploring possible answers to them

Learning logs help you define or analyze information or propose a solution.

Example listing and defining words you learned in Spanish class

Test Taking

Studying for Tests

There are two common tests you are likely to take in school: essay tests and objective tests. The information in this section will help you prepare for both kinds of tests.

Essay Tests An *essay test* measures your understanding of the material you have learned in class by asking you to explain your answers. Essay answers are usually a paragraph or more in length.

How to Study for Essay Tests

1. Read the assigned material carefully.

2. Make an outline of the main points and important details.

3. Invent your own essay questions, and practice writing out the answers.

4. Evaluate and revise your practice answers by checking your work against your notes and textbook. You can also use the **Writing Workshops** in this book to help you write an essay answer.

Objective Tests *Objective tests* measure your ability to remember specific information, such as names, terms, dates, or definitions. Most objective test questions have only one correct answer.

How to Study for Objective Tests

1. Identify important terms or facts in your textbook and class notes.

2. Review the information in more than one way. For example, for a science test, you may need to learn the definitions for scientific terms. Make flashcards. Practice identifying the definition from the term, then the term from the definition.

3. Practice and repeat information to remember it. Go over difficult information more than once.

4. If possible, briefly review all the information shortly before the actual test.

Types of Test Questions

The following section describes the different types of questions you may find on tests you take in school. Read about these questions to find tips and strategies for answering them.

- **Essay questions** To answer an *essay question,* you usually write a paragraph or several paragraphs. Your essay should have a topic sentence, supporting details, and a conclusion. The following steps can help you answer essay questions. (See also the **Key Verbs That Appear in Essay Questions** chart on page 772.)

1. **Scan the directions on the test.** How many questions are you required to answer? Select the ones you think you can answer best. Plan how much time you can afford to spend on each answer. Then, stick with your plan.

2. **Read each question carefully.** Be sure you understand exactly what the question is asking before you plan your response. If a question contains several parts, your answer should contain several parts as well.

3. **Pay attention to important terms in the question.** Identify the task that the essay question asks you to complete. You can tell what the task is by looking at the key verb that appears in the essay question. Refer to the chart below.

Key Verbs That Appear in Essay Questions		
Key Verb	**Task**	**Sample Question**
analyze	Take something apart to see how each part works.	Analyze the effects that a balanced diet has on a growing body.
compare	Point out ways that things are alike.	Compare cross-country skiing to water skiing.
contrast	Point out ways that things are different.	Contrast the schools in Japan and the United States.
define	Give specific details that make something unique.	Define the term *personification*.
demonstrate	Give examples to support a point.	Demonstrate how the Internet helps people communicate.
describe	Give a picture in words.	Describe the appearance of a test tube of water after another substance is added.
explain	Give reasons.	Explain why the moon looks different at various times each month.
identify	Point out specific characteristics.	Identify the types of figurative language.
list	Give all steps in order or all details about a subject.	List the countries that make up the United Kingdom.
persuade	Give your opinion on an issue and provide reasons to support it.	Persuade your science teacher that your science class should or should not start a vegetable garden.
summarize	Give a brief overview of the main points.	Summarize the story told in "Raymond's Run."

4. Use prewriting strategies. After you identify the key verbs in the question, make notes and an outline to help you decide what you want to say. Write your notes or a rough outline on a piece of scratch paper.

5. Evaluate and revise as you write. You may not have time to write your whole essay over, but you can edit your essay to strengthen it. Correct any spelling, punctuation, or grammatical errors, and make sure you have answered every part of the question.

Qualities of a Good Essay Answer
The essay is well organized.
The main ideas and supporting points are clearly presented.
The sentences are complete and well written.
There are no distracting errors in spelling, punctuation, or grammar.

■ **Matching questions** *Matching questions* ask you to match the items in one list to items in another list.

EXAMPLE

Directions: Match the animals in the left-hand column to the correct kind of animal in the right-hand column.

B	1. Greyhound	**A.**	Amphibian
D	2. Sparrow	**B.**	Mammal
A	3. Bullfrog	**C.**	Reptile
C	4. Crocodile	**D.**	Bird
E	5. Sea Bass	**E.**	Fish

How to Answer Matching Questions

1. Read the directions carefully. Some items may be used more than once. Others might not be used at all.

2. Scan the columns. Match the items you know first. That way you can spend more time thinking about more difficult items you are less sure about.

3. Complete the rest of the matching. Make your best guess on the remaining items.

■ **Multiple-choice questions** A *multiple-choice question* provides a number of possible answers and asks you to select the one that is correct.

EXAMPLE

1. Which of the following items is *not* a characteristic of poison ivy?
   - **A.** Its oil causes people to itch.
   - **B.** Each leaf has three leaflets.
   - **C.** It produces white berries.
   - **D.** It grows into a tall tree.

How to Answer Multiple-Choice Questions

1. Read the question or statement carefully. Before you look at answer choices, make sure you understand the question or statement. Watch for words such as *not* and *only.* These words limit your choice of possible answers.

2. Read all the choices before answering. If you know an answer choice is incorrect, rule it out. Think carefully about the remaining choices, and select the one that makes the most sense.

On-demand reading questions

On-demand questions are ones you cannot study in advance. *On-demand reading questions* ask you about a reading passage. In some cases, you will find answers to the questions in the passage. Other times, you may need to draw from your own experiences or understanding of the passage.

EXAMPLE

Directions: Read the passage below, and answer the question that follows.

Julia threw her roller skates down on the sofa. She plopped down next to them and pouted. Didn't anyone remember that it was her birthday? No one in her family had said "Happy birthday" to her before she went skating this morning. She walked into the kitchen to get lunch, and her face brightened. Her family was there and so were all her friends! On the table, there was a cake with twelve candles. It was surrounded by presents.

1. Why does Julia pout?
- **A.** She thinks her family has forgotten that it is her birthday.
- **B.** She fell while roller-skating.
- **C.** Her friends did not come to her birthday party.
- **D.** Her family forgot her presents.

How to Answer On-Demand Reading Questions

1. Read the passage carefully. Make sure you know the main idea and important details.

---

2. Read the questions that follow the reading passage. Usually the questions are multiple-choice. (See also **Multiple-Choice Questions** on page 773.) Sometimes you will be asked to write short, precise answers to questions. (See also **Short-Answer Questions** on page 776.)

3. Notice which words from the passage are repeated in the questions. In the example above, the question includes the word *pout,* which is part of the word *pouted* from the second sentence of the reading passage. That clue tells you that the answer is in the second sentence of the reading passage or somewhere near it.

4. If the language of the passage does not appear in the question, you must draw your own conclusions. Your conclusion may be based on your own experiences and knowledge.

On-demand writing questions

On-demand writing questions are the core of many state writing tests. They are essay questions that ask you to write a persuasive, informative, narrative, or descriptive essay. Since these questions are broad and related to your experience, you cannot study for the content of an on-demand writing question. However, you can prepare by writing a practice essay and asking for feedback from your teacher or classmates.

EXAMPLE

Your principal is thinking about requiring all students to take a class about career selection. Persuade your principal that such a class is or is not a good idea.

How to Answer On-Demand Writing Questions

1. Read the question and decide what it is asking. Look for the key verbs in the question. These verbs will tell you whether your answer should be persuasive, informative, narrative, or descriptive. (See also the **Key Verbs That Appear in Essay Questions** chart on page 772.)

2. Plan your answer. Use prewriting strategies to help you plan before you begin writing. (See also **Prewriting Techniques** on page 795.)

3. Evaluate and revise your answer as you write. Make sure your answer has a clear topic sentence, supporting details, transitions between ideas, and a conclusion.

■ Reasoning or logic questions

Reasoning or *logic questions* test your reasoning skills rather than your knowledge of a specific subject. Reasoning or logic questions may ask you to identify the relationship among several items, to identify a pattern in a sequence of numbers, or to predict the next item in a sequence.

EXAMPLE

What comes next?

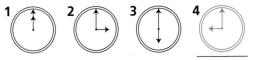

In this sequence of drawings, the hour hand on the clock starts at noon and moves three hours forward in each picture. In the fourth position, the hour hand will have reached the nine o'clock position.

How to Answer Reasoning or Logic Questions

1. Make sure you understand the instructions. Reasoning or logic questions are often multiple-choice. On some tests, however, you may need to write a word or phrase, complete a number sequence, or draw a picture for your answer.

2. Analyze the relationship implied in the question. Look carefully at the question to gather information about the relationship of the items.

3. Draw reasonable conclusions. Evaluate the relationship of the items to decide your answer.

■ Sentence-completion questions

Sentence-completion questions test your knowledge of vocabulary words. These types of questions ask you to choose an answer that correctly completes the meaning of a sentence.

EXAMPLE

1. On stage the two performers seemed like good friends. In reality, however, the two were _____ who were always competing for the same roles.
   A. cousins
   B. pals
   C. rivals
   D. equals

How to Answer Sentence-Completion Questions

1. Read the sentence carefully. Make sure you understand the words in the sentence. Some sentences may contain

(continued)

QUICK REFERENCE HANDBOOK

How to Answer Sentence-Completion Questions

clues to the meaning of the word or words that go in the blanks. In the example on the previous page, *however* is a clue that the two performers were not friends offstage. Therefore, the correct answer is *rivals*.

2. Rule out incorrect answer choices. If you can immediately rule out an answer choice, mark through it.

3. Fill in the blank with the remaining choices, and choose the best answer. If you are not sure which choice is correct, use each one in the blank of the sentence and choose the answer that makes the most sense.

■ **Short-answer questions** *Short-answer questions* ask you to write brief, precise responses. Short-answer questions vary in length. You may be asked to fill in a blank, label a map, or write one or two sentences.

EXAMPLE Why do whales frequently rise to the surface of the sea?

Answer: Whales cannot breathe underwater. They come up to the surface to get air through their blowholes.

How to Answer Short-Answer Questions

1. Read the question carefully. Some questions have more than one part. Be sure to answer the entire question.

2. Plan your answer. Briefly decide what ideas and details you need to include in the answer.

3. Be as specific as possible. Write a full, exact answer.

4. Budget your time. Answer the questions you know first. Save time for more difficult questions.

■ **True-false questions** *True-false questions* ask you to determine whether the statement you are given is a true statement or a false statement.

EXAMPLE

1. T (F) Cockroaches never fly.

How to Answer True-False Questions

1. Read the statement carefully. If any part of the statement is false, then the whole statement is false. A statement is true only if it is entirely and always true.

2. Look for word clues. Words such as *always* or *never* limit a statement's meaning.

QUICK REFERENCE HANDBOOK

Viewing and Representing

Understanding Media Terms

People who work in and write about the media often use special terms. Learning some of those terms will help you evaluate or judge the media messages you see and hear. It will also help you create your own media messages.

The terms in this section are divided into three lists: **Electronic Media Terms, General Media Terms,** and **Print Media Terms.** If a term is used in both print media and electronic media, it is defined under **Print Media Terms** only. For information on the Internet and the World Wide Web, see the **Library/Media Center** section beginning on page 728. For more on using type and graphics, see **Document Design** beginning on page 716.

Electronic Media Terms

Advertising See **Advertising** on page 785.

Animation *Animation* is a way of making photographs of drawings appear to move. Each drawing in an animated film is only slightly different from the ones before and after it. When the photographs of these drawings are projected very quickly (at 24 images per second), the figures in them seem to move.

Broadcasting *Broadcasting* is the use of electronic media to send audio and video content over a wide area. *Commercial broadcasting* is done for profit. Advertisers pay to include commercials along with commercial broadcasters' programming. *Public broadcasting* refers to nonprofit media, such as the Public Broadcasting Service (PBS) and National Public Radio (NPR), that transmit over radio and television signals and through cable and the Internet. The federal government, companies, and individual viewers and listeners pay most of the cost of public broadcasting.

Cable Television   *Cable television* uses powerful antennas to pick up television signals and then delivers the signals to homes and businesses through cables. Some cable companies only provide the signals to viewers. Others create original programs as well. (See also **Broadcasting** on page 777.)

Camera Angle   The *camera angle* is the angle at which a camera points toward a subject. Placing the camera at a high angle above the subject makes the subject look small. Placing the camera at a low angle makes the subject look tall and powerful. Tilting the camera makes the subject seem off-balance.

Camera Shot   A *camera shot* is the way an image in a film or video is presented to viewers. The following are the three most common shots used in film production.

- **Close-up shot**   a shot made from very close to the subject, for example, a shot of a person's eyes
- **Medium shot**   a shot made from a midrange distance, for example, a shot of a person from the waist up
- **Long shot**   a shot made from far away, for example, a shot of a football field from a blimp

Commercial Broadcasting   See **Broadcasting** on page 777.

Copy   See **Copy** on page 785.

Credits   *Credits* list the people who worked on a presentation. Credits are usually listed at the end of a television program, film, or video.

Documentary   A *documentary* is a film or television program that explores the meaning of an actual event. Most documentaries include a combination of interviews and footage of actual events. Some documentaries include reenactments of events by actors and an offscreen narrator. A documentary's main purpose may be to inform, to persuade, or to entertain. In addition, some documentaries are intended to make money for their producers. A documentary may have more than one purpose. For example, a filmmaker might create a documentary that both informs viewers about the problem of pet overpopulation and tries to persuade them to take actions to help solve that problem.

Editor   See **Editor** on page 785.

Feature News   See **Feature News** on page 786.

Film   *Film* is a medium for recording sounds and images. Message makers who need sounds and images to be crisp and clear, to last a long time, or to be presented on a large screen will film their messages. Filmed images can appear more sophisticated than images recorded on videotape, but film is more expensive to buy and develop than videotape is. (See also **Videotape** on page 780.)

Hard News   See **Hard News** on page 786.

Internet   The *Internet* is a network of computers that lets users communicate with each other. Using the Internet requires a computer or other Internet-capable device, such as a cell phone or personal digital assistant (PDA). For a monthly fee, Internet service providers (ISPs) provide access to the Internet. (See also **World Wide Web** on page 733.)

Lead   See **Lead** on page 786.

Medium   See **Medium** on page 786.

Message   See **Message** on page 784.

News   See **News** on page 787.

Newsmagazine   See **Newsmagazine** on page 787.

Photography   See **Photography** on page 787.

Producer   A *producer* is the person who oversees the production of a movie or a radio or TV program. He or she decides what overall message to present. The producer also gathers a crew or staff, raises and manages the money needed to create the film or program, and keeps the production on schedule. (See also **Production** on page 787.)

Public Broadcasting   See **Broadcasting** on page 777.

Reporter   See **Reporter** on page 788.

Script   A *script* is the words to be spoken during a play, a film, or a TV or radio program. TV, film, and play scripts also include notes about the images to be shown and the movements or emotions that actors will perform. The script for a news broadcast is called *copy*. (See also **Copy** on page 785.)

Soft News   See **Soft News** on page 788.

Sound   In film and video, sound is all of the recorded material that you hear, including dialogue, music, sound effects, and so on. In addition to getting the spoken words across to viewers, producers and filmmakers use sound to achieve the following goals.

- **Create an illusion**   You might see two actors in a film rushing to get farm animals into a barn. Sound effects, such as wind noise and thunder, can signal to you as a viewer that these characters want to protect their livestock from an approaching storm. It is unlikely that the scene was shot on a stormy day, though.

- **Create a mood**   The music that a producer chooses to play while certain images are on screen can guide the audience to feel a certain way about those images. For example, music with a strong rhythm played during a chase scene can make viewers feel tense, as if they are moving quickly, too.

Source See **Source** on page 788.

Storyboard A *storyboard* is a set of drawings that show the order of shots and scenes in a script. A storyboard may also include dialogue, narration, and audio and visual cues. For an example of a storyboard, see page 723.

Target Audience See **Target Audience** on page 788.

Text See **Text** on page 788. (See also **Script** on page 779.)

Video *Video* is a medium used to record sounds and images. Video comes in two formats: *digital video* (DVDs, MPEGs) and *analog videotape* (VHS). When compared with film, video is a relatively inexpensive medium. The equipment needed to record video is often more accessible and easier to use than film equipment. However, images and sounds recorded on video generally have less resolution, or clarity, than those on film. While digital video has better resolution than analog videotape, film is still far superior. Also, videotape does not last as long as digital video or film. (See also **Film** on page 778.)

General Media Terms

Audience An *audience* is a group of people who see or hear a media message. Advertisers aim their messages at the audiences they think will buy their products or services. (See also **Advertising**

on page 785 and **Target Audience** on page 788.)

Authority The term *authority* means how well the source of a message seems to know the subject. If a message appears to come from an expert source, you will think it has authority.

Bias A *bias* is a slanted point of view, either in favor of an issue or against it. A biased message maker may not even mention information that supports views other than his or her own. (See also **Point of View** on page 785.)

Context *Context* is the material that surrounds a media message. For example, the context of an ad on a children's TV program is the other ads on the program and the program itself. Context may affect the way people respond to a message.

Credibility *Credibility* means being believable. Whether or not a speaker or writer seems believable is up to the audience to decide. (See also **Message** on page 784.)

Critical Viewing *Critical viewing* means analyzing visual messages to understand them and evaluate or judge them. Visual messages include photographs, editorial cartoons, films, and television programs, to name just a few.

Keeping the five key ideas on the next page in mind as you view messages will help you become a more critical viewer.

Key Ideas for Critical Viewing

Key Idea 1: All messages are put together by people.

People who create visual messages must make many choices. They must decide which elements (words, images, sounds) to include and how to arrange them. One of the most important decisions the creator of a visual message makes is what to leave out. When you understand that visual messages are constructed, you can analyze how the elements work together. You can also recognize the skill that went into creating the message.

Key Idea 2: Messages are one person's version of reality.

When you see something in a visual message, remember that the reality may be quite different. For a TV ad for a theme park, for example, everything from the actors to the camera angles to the background music is carefully chosen and arranged to make the park seem even more fun than it is. When you understand that a visual message is a version of reality, you can evaluate how authentic (true-to-life) the message seems.

Key Idea 3: People make their own meanings from messages.

The meaning you draw from a visual message depends on your prior knowledge (what you already know) and on your experience. Everyone's prior knowledge and experience are different, so different viewers may draw different meanings from the same message. When you connect the message to your own knowledge and experience, you can form your own ideas about what the message means.

Key Idea 4: Messages have a wide range of purposes.

Every message has a purpose. Usually, that purpose is to inform, to persuade, to entertain, or to express thoughts and feelings. Most mass-media messages also have another purpose: to make money for the message makers and for the people who own and run the media. Knowing that a visual message might be presented to make money can help you decide for yourself whether you will let it influence you.

Key Idea 5: The medium shapes the message.

Different visual media have different strengths and weaknesses. For example, a still photograph shows just one moment in time, but it can be studied over and over. Film has movement and sound, but the images flash by quickly. The people who create visual messages must choose the medium that will best help them achieve their purpose. Understanding how the medium shapes the message can help you see why a message affects you in a certain way.

Evaluating Media Messages   The following questions will help you analyze and evaluate media messages.

- Who created the message?
- What elements (words, images, or sounds) does the message include?
- How are the elements arranged?

- How well are the elements used?
- What may have been left out of the message?
- How is this version of reality similar to and different from what I know from my own experience or from other sources?
- How authentic (true-to-life) does the message seem? Why?
- Of what does the message make me think? How does it make me feel about the world? about myself? about other people?
- What seems to be the main purpose of the message? Is there also another purpose? If so, what is it?
- What medium carries the message?
- How do the characteristics of the medium (image, sound, motion) shape the message?

Formula   A *formula* is a set way of doing something. In television and film, it refers to a common way of presenting material or combining characters. For example, situation comedies often use this formula: A character gets into an uncomfortable situation, which is usually caused by a misunderstanding or by one of the character's own faults. The situation gets sillier and sillier until finally, someone or something comes along and solves the character's problem. By the end of the show, the character is out of trouble and everything is back to normal.

Genre   A *genre* is a category of art forms or media products that share certain common ways of doing things. Genres found on television include

- children's programming
- documentary
- drama
- game show
- infomercial
- music video
- news broadcast
- sitcom (situation comedy)
- soap opera
- talk show

Illustration   An *illustration* is a picture created as a decoration or to explain something. Drawings, paintings, photographs, and computer-generated artwork can all be illustrations. The following are some elements of illustration.

- **Color**   Color creates a certain mood or draws attention to a certain part of an illustration.
- **Form**   Form refers to the three-dimensional look of an illustration. Depth and weight make an illustration more effective. Illustrators can create shadows and bright spots to make an illustration look three-dimensional.
- **Line**   Everything you see around you has some sort of line. Some lines are obvious, like the vertical line made by walls meeting in a corner. However, you might not notice other lines, for example, the lines made by the fur of a cat. Illustrators use line to show depth in

a drawing and to show viewers where the horizon in a drawing is.

- **Shape** Shape is the two-dimensional outline of something. Lines come together to make a shape, and all of the shapes in an illustration are connected.

Images An *image* is a visual representation of something. It may be a painting, a photograph, a sculpture, or a moving picture, among other things. An image may be *still* or *moving.*

- A *still image,* such as a photograph, allows viewers to notice detail and spend time considering the meaning of the image. Still images may also be easier than moving images for message makers to manipulate through cropping or using computer programs.

- A *moving image* is a series of still images projected quickly onto a television or film screen. A moving image may show an actual event (called *documentary footage*), or it may show an event arranged by the message maker (a *dramatization*). Documentary footage includes scenes shown on the evening news; dramatizations include fictional movies. Both kinds of moving images are the message maker's version of an event and may be incomplete or altered in some way.

To analyze how message makers create certain effects using images, consider the points in the chart below.

Creating Effects with Images	
Technique	**Definition/Effects**
Color	Color can emphasize certain parts of an image or guide viewers to feel a certain way about an image. When a spot of color suddenly appears in a black-and-white movie, the director wants viewers to pay special attention to that part of the image. Photographing an image through a yellow filter can create a happy mood in the image.
Juxtaposition	This technique involves putting two or more images next to each other to create meaning. For example, a comedy show that cuts between images of a person happily walking down a city street and a piano dangling from an apartment window tells its viewers that the person's walk will be rudely interrupted by the piano. Editing moving images together or placing still images side by side can sometimes communicate more meaning than an individual image.
Slow or Fast Motion	A message maker may speed up or slow down a moving image to create a certain effect. Making an image move faster than normal can create a comic effect, while slowing an image down can create a tense, dramatic effect.

Media Law The First Amendment of the U.S. Constitution states that Congress shall pass no law that limits the freedom of the press. One effect of this amendment is that, except during wartime, the United States government seldom uses *censorship.* *Censorship* is any attempt by a government or other group to limit the amount or type of information people receive. However, there are laws that regulate, or control, the media. The Federal Communications Commission (FCC) enforces U.S. laws dealing with electronic media, including radio, television, and the Internet. A person whose reputation has been hurt by lies that were printed or broadcast about him or her may sue the people responsible for the false statements. The creator of a media message may *copyright* that message to stop anyone from *plagiarizing,* or stealing his or her work.

Media Literacy *Media literacy* is the ability to find, analyze, evaluate, and communicate messages in many different forms. (See also **Critical Viewing** on page 780.)

Message A *message* is an idea communicated using symbols (things that stand for ideas). Symbols may be language, gestures, images, or sounds. The *content* of a message is the information it presents. (See also **Credibility** on page 780, **Realism** on page 785, and **Source** on page 788.)

Multimedia Presentation A *multimedia presentation* is any presentation that uses two or more forms of media. For example, when you give an oral presentation including visuals (such as slides, transparencies, or posters), you are giving a multimedia presentation. One medium is your voice, and the other is the visuals you use to support your presentation. A multimedia presentation that involves the use of presentation software or Web sites is sometimes called a **technology presentation.**

Newsworthiness *Newsworthiness* is the quality that makes a news event seem worth reporting. An event may be considered newsworthy if it meets any of the following criteria, or standards.

Criteria	Definitions
Timeliness	events or issues that are happening now or that people are interested in right now
Impact	events or issues that have a direct effect on people's lives
Human Interest	stories about people's basic needs or stories that affect the audience's emotions
Celebrity Angle	stories about famous people

Persuasion See **Propaganda** on page 785.

Point of View   A message maker's *point of view* is the way he or she approaches a topic. The message maker's background and beliefs often affect his or her point of view. For example, in a newspaper story about a local zoo, one reporter might focus on how the zookeepers are helping save endangered species. Another reporter with different experiences might focus on what the animals are missing by not being in the wild. (See also **Bias** on page 780 and **Propaganda** below.)

In photography, point of view refers to the photographer's approach to his or her subject. Choices that affect the photographer's point of view include selecting the subject and the camera angle. (See also **Photography** on page 787.)

Propaganda   *Propaganda* is the use of certain techniques to make a message as persuasive as possible. The word *propaganda* has a negative connotation as it originally referred to messages that lied or distorted the truth in order to influence public opinion. However, the practice of using some propaganda techniques—such as the celebrity testimonial—is widely accepted in the field of advertising. Many of these techniques work by leading you to make a generalization about the ad. Suppose, for example, a company uses a basketball star to advertise its shoes. The company wants you to generalize that anyone who wears those shoes will play as well as the basketball star does. (See also **Advertising** on this page, **Bias** on page 780, and **Point of View** above.)

Realism   *Realism* means showing people and events just the way they appear, without making them seem better or worse in any way.

Stereotypes   *Stereotypes* are beliefs (usually negative ones) about a whole group of people. For example, some adults do not trust teenagers even though relatively few teenagers ever cause problems. Such beliefs are usually based on too little evidence or on false or misleading information.

Visual Literacy   *Visual literacy* is the ability to understand how the visual media communicate meaning. (See also **Critical Viewing** on page 780.)

Print Media Terms

Advertising   *Advertising* is using images or words to persuade an audience to buy, use, or accept a product, service, or idea. Advertisers pay the media for time or space in which to run their ads.

Byline   A *byline* lists the name of the reporter or writer of a print article or a broadcast presentation.

Copy   *Copy* is the text in a media message. (See also **Script** on page 779.)

Editor   An *editor* oversees the work of reporters. Editors decide what news stories will appear, check facts, and correct mistakes.

Editorial Cartoon An *editorial cartoon* is a cartoon, usually found in the editorial section of a newspaper, that shows the cartoonist's opinion about a current event or issue. An editorial cartoonist may make his or her point in the following ways.

- exaggerating the impact of an event or issue
- drawing people involved in the event as *caricatures,* or giving them exaggerated features that make it obvious to readers who is being represented
- connecting the event to another event or story with which readers will be more familiar

Feature News The primary purpose of *feature news* (or soft news) is to entertain. These stories may or may not be timely. They may be about ordinary people or celebrities or about animals, events, places, or products. A profile of a neighborhood volunteer who brings food to homeless people is an example of a feature-news story. (See also **Hard News** below and **Soft News** on page 788.)

Font A *font* is a style of lettering used for printing. (See also **Font** on page 719.)

Hard News *Hard news* is reporting based on facts. It covers important current events and issues such as politics. Usually, it answers the basic *5W-How?* questions. A hard-news story might provide information about a flood that occurred today or about the problem of overcrowded classrooms in local schools. (See also **Feature News** on this page and **Soft News** on page 788.)

Headline A *headline* is the title of a newspaper article. Headlines are usually set in large, bold type. They have two purposes: to hook the reader's attention and to tell the reader the topic of the article.

EXAMPLE: **Fido Fetches Family from Flames**

Lead A *lead* is the first few words or the first paragraph of a news story. It answers some or all of the *5W-How?* questions and tries to hook the audience's attention with a surprising fact or idea.

EXAMPLE: (HOBBS, NM) A family pet proved himself a hero early yesterday when he alerted the sleeping occupants of a burning home here. Even though he could have easily escaped through his doggie door, Fido the terrier chose to stay and bark until the Yellowbird family had all woken up and fled the house.

Medium The *medium* of a message is the means by which it is sent. *(Medium is the singular form of media.)* **Print media** include newspapers and magazines. **Electronic media** include radio and television, audio and video recordings, film, and the Internet. The **mass media** are the media that reach a very large audience.

Message See **Message** on page 784.

News *News* is the presentation of current information. The people who own and run *media outlets,* such as newspapers or television stations, decide which stories to cover. They try to choose stories that will interest or affect their audience. Local news outlets present stories about their region of the country. National news outlets cover national and world issues and events.

Newsmagazine A *newsmagazine* is a publication that discusses recent events and issues. Most print newsmagazines appear once a week. In television the term refers to a news program that airs one or more times a week. Such programs usually analyze and explore the meanings of events.

Photography *Photography* is the process of recording a still image on film with a camera. Like any other visual message, a photograph records only the parts of an image that the message maker chooses to include. The choices a photographer can make about an image include the following.

■ **Camera angle** By placing the camera at different angles relative to the subject, a photographer can guide viewers to feel a certain way about the subject. (See also **Camera Angle** on page 778.)

■ **Film type** A photographer may choose color or black-and-white film depending on what he or she wants viewers to get from the image. Black-and-white film can emphasize shapes

or create a dramatic effect, while color images appear more realistic.

■ **Lighting** A photographer may have control over the light available when the photo is taken. If so, he or she can use just a few lights set at dramatic angles for effect, or use full light for a more natural-looking image.

■ **Subject** When taking a photo of a scene, a photographer may position the camera to get only the most important part of the scene or to eliminate images that take away from his or her message. Even after the photo has been taken, *cropping* can be used to cut out an unwanted part of the scene. Message makers can also add *captions* that guide viewers to draw a conclusion about the photo. (See also **Message** on page 784.)

Political Cartoon See **Editorial Cartoon** on page 786.

Production *Production* is the process of creating a publication, a film, a video, or a radio or television program. Production takes place in three stages.

■ **Preproduction** Copy or scripts are gathered and fine-tuned. Money is raised, and plans are made for how it will be spent. Staff and crew are hired, and schedules are planned.

■ **Production** The work is filmed, recorded, or printed.

■ **Postproduction** Finishing touches are added. Books and newspapers are bound or gathered. Films and tapes are edited, soundtracks are recorded, and sound and special effects are added.

Reporter   A *reporter* is a journalist who gathers information. Reporters work with editors to create print or electronic reports.

Soft News   *Soft news* is general-interest material, such as information on fashion trends, presented in a news format. The purpose of soft news is to entertain. For example, a soft-news story might explain how the special effects for a new science fiction movie were created. (See also **Feature News** and **Hard News** on page 786.)

Source   A *source* is a person or publication that gives a journalist information or ideas. Journalists try to use sources that have authority and seem credible. (See also **Authority** and **Credibility** on page 780, and **Message** on page 784.)

Target Audience   A *target audience* is a group of people for whom a message or product is designed. For example, the target audience of advertisements for acne medications is teenagers.

Text   The term *text* refers to the words, printed or spoken, that are used to create a message. (See also **Message** on page 784.)

Writing

Skills, Structures, and Techniques

Good writing does not just happen. A writer must work at his or her writing. You can use the following ideas and information to become a more effective writer.

Applications   See **Forms** on page 791.

Composition   A *composition* is a piece of writing that has several paragraphs. Compositions have three main parts: *introduction*, *body*, and *conclusion*. All three parts work together to communicate the author's main idea or point.

- **Introduction**   The *introduction* is the first paragraph of your composition. An introduction should do two things: Get your readers' attention and tell them the main idea of the composition.

  1. **Grab the readers' attention.** Your introduction should make your readers want to read more. The chart in the next column gives some strategies for drawing in your reader.

How to Catch Your Readers' Attention

Begin by asking a question.
Do you wonder what to do with all of your free time after school and on the weekends?

Begin with an anecdote or a funny story.
House painting has always been something I do well, so when I showed up at the volunteer building site, I was ready to paint. Little did I know that my friend Joaquin was ready to paint me.

Begin with a startling fact.
You may not think that you can help to build a house, but with the teamwork of young people and adults, a house can be quickly built, painted, landscaped, and prepared for a family to move in.

2. **Present the main idea statement, or thesis.** The *main idea statement,* or *thesis,* is a sentence or two that tells your topic and your main idea about it. Use your main idea as a guide as you plan, write, and revise your paper. Here are some strategies for writing a main idea statement.

> ### How to Write a Main Idea Statement
>
> **1. Ask yourself, "What is my topic?"**
> *volunteering*
>
> **2. Review your prewriting notes.** Think about how the facts and details fit together. Identify the idea that connects the details to one another.
> *Volunteering is good, hard work.*
>
> **3. Use specific details to make the main idea clear.** Zooming in on specific details will make the main idea more focused.
> *Volunteering to build homes taught me to respect all kinds of people, to work hard, and to challenge myself.*

■ **Body** The main idea is supported and developed in the *body* of the composition. The body usually contains several paragraphs with supporting statements, facts, and details. Each paragraph has its own main idea, called a *topic sentence,* and all of the topic sentences support the main idea statement. As you write the body of a composition, keep the following tips in mind.

1. Make sure that you arrange the information in your composition in a way that will make sense to your reader. (See also page 449.)
2. Do not include details that distract from your main idea.
3. Show how your ideas are connected by using *transitional words and phrases.* (See also page 453.)

■ **Conclusion** The *conclusion* of your paper sums up your information and makes your final points. Your conclusion should do the following things.

1. **Give the readers a sense of completion.** Good conclusions leave the readers feeling satisfied, not as if they have been left hanging.
2. **Restate the main idea.** The conclusion is your last chance to make your point. In addition to summing up your main points, restate your main idea in different words.

> ### How to Write a Conclusion
>
> **Refer to your introduction.**
>
> *When I thought that I was in for an easy day of fun and painting, I was only partly right. I had fun with my friends. We even had a paint fight. However, I also learned how to work with others to help others.*
>
> **Restate your main idea.**
>
> *I now know that by giving up a Saturday, I did not miss out on fun. I had a great time and felt that my day was spent in an important way.*

Close with a final idea or example.

I enjoyed my Saturday of painting so much that I have decided to spend one day each month volunteering in some way.

E-mail Electronic mail, or *e-mail,* is a way of sending messages over the Internet rather than through the post office. E-mail is used for both personal and business correspondence. Since e-mail messages are instant, people sometimes write casually. Casual messages are fine for informal e-mail with friends. When e-mailing teachers or businesses, however, you should follow the guidelines below.

E-Mail Guidelines

- Keep your message short, since reading through long e-mails can be difficult and confusing.

- When you have several questions or points, use a bulleted list or indentations to make your e-mail easier to read.

- Use correct spelling, grammar, punctuation, and standard English.

- Include salutations (or greetings) and closings, especially if you are writing to someone for the first time.

- Do not send angry or rude messages. E-mail is easily forwarded. Therefore, someone other than the person you originally wrote to may end up receiving your message.

- Avoid using all capital letters in your messages. Writing in capitals in e-mail is similar to shouting. If you need to emphasize a word or phrase, place an asterisk (*) before and after it.

- Double-check the address in the address line of your message to make sure you are sending your message to the right person.

- Fill in the subject line in your message. Giving your readers an idea of the topic of your message allows them to read the most important messages first.

- Do not forward e-mails to others unless you have the original author's permission.

Forms You will be called upon to fill out forms many times throughout your life. You fill out forms or applications for library cards, savings accounts, even school club memberships. Below is an example of a simple information form.

Information Form

Date ___7/26/09___

Name ___Bliss Winston___

Address ___705 E. Oak St.___

City ___Oakland___ State ___CA___ ZIP ___90821___

Home Phone ___555-0141___

Date of Birth ___12/21/97___

Parent or Guardian ___Joseph Winston___

The following tips will help you fill out forms correctly.

1. Read all instructions before you begin. Look for special instructions to see whether you should use a pen or pencil.
2. Read each item carefully.
3. Print neatly all the information that is requested.
4. Proofread the form to make sure you did not leave anything blank. Also, check for errors and correct them neatly.
5. Mail the form to the correct address or give it to the correct person.

Letters   Most people like to receive mail. To get letters, though, you need to write letters. That is why it is important to develop good writing skills for social and business letters. There are several different kinds of letters. All of them have a purpose and an audience. The chart at the bottom of this page lists some common types, purposes, and audiences for letters.

Letters, Business   *Business letters* have specific purposes. People write business letters to apply for a job or communicate about a business. Make sure your business letters look professional. Type or use your best handwriting, and use standard, formal English.

■ **Envelopes**   To make sure that your letter goes where you want it to go, address the envelope neatly and correctly. Follow these tips.

1. Place your return address in the top left-hand corner of the envelope.
2. Write the name and address of the person to whom the letter is being sent in the center of the envelope.
3. Use the standard two-letter postal abbreviation for the state name, followed by the ZIP Code.

Return address

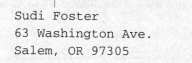

Sudi Foster
63 Washington Ave.
Salem, OR 97305

Aola Washington
2119 Brushcreek Ave. #302
Independence, MO 64055

Mailing address

Letters		
Type of Letter	**Purpose for Writing**	**Probable Audience**
Business	to inform a business about a service you need or how a service was performed	a business or organization
Informal or Personal	to tell about your ideas or feelings, to be polite, to thank someone, or to tell someone about a planned event	close friends, relatives, or social acquaintances

- **Forms for business letters**   The six parts of a business letter are usually arranged in one of the two following styles.

1. **Block form**   In the block form, every part of the letter begins at the left margin of the page. A blank line is left between paragraphs, which are not indented.

2. **Modified block form**   In the modified block form, the heading, the closing, and your signature are placed to the right of an imaginary line down the center of the page. The middle parts of the letter begin at the left margin. Paragraphs are indented.

Block Style

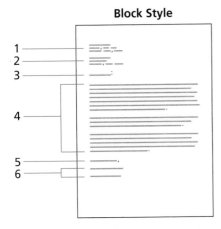

Modified Block Style

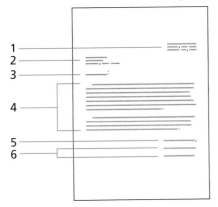

- **Parts of a business letter**   There are six parts to a business letter.

1. The **heading** of a business letter has three lines: your street address; your city, state, and ZIP Code; and the date you are writing the letter.

2. The **inside address** gives the name and address of the person to whom you are writing. If you are directing your letter to someone by name, use a courtesy title (such as *Mr., Ms., Mrs.,* or *Miss*) or a professional title (such as *Dr.* or *Professor*) in front of the person's name. After the person's name, include the person's business title (such as *Principal* or *Business Manager*). If you do not have a person's name, use a business title or position title (such as *Refunds Department* or *Editor in Chief*).

3. Your **salutation** is your greeting to the person to whom you are writing. In a business letter, the salutation usually ends with a colon (such as in *Dear Professor García:*).
   If you are writing to a specific person, you can use the person's name (such as *Dear Ms. Lyon*). If you do not have a specific name, use a general greeting (such as *Dear Sir or Madam:* or *Ladies and Gentlemen:*). You can also use a business or position title instead (*Dear Committee Leader:*).

4. The **body** contains the message of your letter. Leave a blank line between paragraphs in the body of the letter.

5. Conclude your letter politely. The **closing** of a business letter often uses one of several common phrases (such as *Sincerely, Yours truly,* or *Respectfully*

yours). Capitalize only the first word. End the closing with a comma.

6. Your *signature* should be written in ink directly below the closing. Your name should be typed or printed neatly just below your signature.

- **Types of business letters** Types of business letters include the following.

1. **Adjustment or complaint letters** When you write an *adjustment* or *complaint letter,* you state a problem and explain how you think it should be solved. For example, if you are unhappy with a product you bought, you might write a letter like the one below.

```
5208 Range Drive
St. Louis, MO 63117
June 15, 2008

Gadgets Mail Order
1992 Highland Road
Albany, NY 12212

Dear Sir or Madam:

I am returning science kit #609 that
was delivered yesterday. It arrived
with a broken microscope.

Please replace the kit or refund my
purchase price of $69.95 plus $4.30
that I paid for postage and han-
dling.

Sincerely,
Ramiro Sanchez
Ramiro Sanchez
```

2. **Appreciation letters** When you write an *appreciation letter,* you tell people in a business or organization that they did a good job. Give details about what they did that you liked. For example, perhaps you want to tell the manager of a restaurant that you appreciate the good service you received there.

3. **Request or order letters** In a *request letter,* you ask for specific information about a product service. An *order letter* tells a business about a product or service you want such as a free brochure (an excerpt is shown below). Be sure to include all important information, such as the item number, size, color, brand name, and price.

```
I would like to order three back
issues of Zip! magazine. Please
send the issues from March, April,
and May 2008. In the magazine, you
state that back issues are $3 each,
including postage. I have enclosed
a money order for $9. Thank you for
sending the issues as soon as pos-
sible.
```

Letters, Informal or Personal An *informal* or *personal letter* is a good way to communicate with a friend or relative. A personal letter is like a conversation, only much better. Conversations may be interrupted or forgotten, but a letter is often treasured and read many times.

A personal letter is a token of friendship. It usually contains a personal message from you, the sender, to the person you are writing to, the receiver. For example, you might write a friend to congratulate him or her for receiving a school award. You might write to tell a friend about the new school you attend.

When you are sending a personal letter, remember to write about a subject that interests you and the person you are writing.

■ **Types of informal or personal letters**
There are three common types of informal or personal letters. Each of these types is meant for a particular purpose.

1. **Invitations** You write an invitation to ask someone to an event. Include specific information about the occasion, such as the type of event, time, and place, and any other information your guests might need to know (such as how to dress and what to bring, if anything).

2. **Letters of regret** You will need to write a letter of regret when you receive an invitation to an event that you will not be able to attend. You should always respond in writing to invitations that include the letters *RSVP.* (These letters are an abbreviation for the French words that mean "please reply.")

3. **Thank-you letters** When you receive a gift or a favor, you should write a thank-you letter. The purpose of a thank-you letter is to express your appreciation when someone has spent time, trouble, or money to do something for your benefit. In addition to thanking the person, you might include a paragraph or so of personal news or friendly, chatty information. Try to think of something about the person's effort or gift that made it special to you. In the following exam-

ple, the writer explains why she enjoys a gift from her grandfather.

9300 Leon St.
Burlington, VT 05401
October 6, 2009

Dear Grandpa,
   Thank you so much for the wonderful beagle puppy you brought down from the farm. She must have been the smartest one in the litter. She already knows her name after only two days. We named her Waggles because her tail wags all the time. She's the greatest gift. Thanks!

Love,

Rita

Prewriting Techniques One of the hardest parts of writing is getting started. The following prewriting techniques can help you find topics for writing. They can also help you gather information and ideas about a topic. As you try the different techniques, you may find some are more helpful to you than others. You might even use more than one technique when writing a composition.

Prewriting techniques often include the use of a *graphic organizer*. A **graphic organizer** is a visual way of representing thoughts or ideas. Graphic organizers can help you "see" what you are thinking. You can use graphic organizers to find a subject to write about, to gather information, and to organize your information.

1. Finding ideas   Use the following techniques to find ideas for writing.

■ **Asking *5W-How?* questions**   To gather information, news reporters often ask the ***5W-How? questions: Who? What? Where? When? Why?*** and *How?* You can do the same for any topic. Some questions may not apply to your topic. For other topics, there may be many answers to one question. Here are some *5W-How?* questions about Native American cliff dwellings.

WHO?	*Who* lived in cliff dwellings?
WHAT?	*What* was their daily life like?
WHERE?	*Where* are cliff dwellings found?
WHEN?	*When* did people live in cliff dwellings? *When* did they leave them?
WHY?	*Why* did they build their villages on or into cliffs? *Why* did they leave their villages?
HOW?	*How* did they get food and water?

■ **Asking "What if?" questions**   ***"What if?" questions*** can help you think creatively. Let your imagination wander to find as many answers as you can.

What if I could change one thing in my life? (What if I could make myself invisible? What if I had a car and a driver's license?)

What if some everyday thing did not exist? (What if the earth had no moon? What if radios had not been invented?)

What if I could change one thing about the world? (What if everyone in the world had enough food and a home? What if animals could talk with people?)

■ **Brainstorming**   When you ***brainstorm,*** your thoughts fly in all directions. Start with a broad subject, then quickly list everything you can think of about the subject. You can brainstorm alone or with a group.

Guidelines for Brainstorming

Write any subject at the top of a piece of paper or on a chalkboard.

Write down every idea that occurs to you. If you are brainstorming in a group, one person should record all the ideas.

Do not stop to judge what is listed.

Do not stop until you run out of ideas.

Here are some brainstorming notes on the subject *astronauts.* When you are brainstorming, it is fine to list unusual ideas. Unusual ideas may lead to the perfect topic.

<u>Astronauts</u>

Sally Ride	space explorers
Neil Armstrong walking on the moon	floating without gravity
space shuttle	cramped space, food in tubes
spacesuits	man in the moon
diving suits	woman in the moon
lunar rover	Astrodome

■ **Clustering** *Clustering* is sometimes called *mapping* or *webbing*. It is a visual kind of brainstorming.

Guidelines for Clustering

Write your subject in the center of your paper and then circle it.

Around the subject, write related ideas that come to you. Circle these, and draw lines to connect them with the subject or with other ideas.

Keep going. Write new ideas, circle them, and draw lines to show connections.

The following is a cluster diagram on the topic of Hispanic grocery stores, or *bodegas*.

■ **Freewriting** *Freewriting* means just that—writing freely. Begin with a word or phrase, and then write whatever comes to mind.

Guidelines for Freewriting

Time yourself for three to five minutes, and keep writing until the time is up.

Write your topic first. Then, write down the ideas your topic gives you.

Do not stop or pause. If you can't think of anything to write, keep writing the same word or phrase until something else pops into your head.

Do not worry about spelling, punctuation, or complete sentences.

EXAMPLE

Bicycling. I like pedaling pedaling pedaling. Aching muscles, biking in the rain. Ride everywhere—school, soccer, down to lake. Never without my helmet, remember Travis's accident. Dangerous at night—reflectors, headlight, reflective tape on jacket. Safety, safety rules—driver's license for bike riders?

In *focused freewriting* (or *looping*), you begin with a word or phrase from freewriting you have already done. You might choose "biking in the rain" and do three minutes of freewriting on this limited topic.

■ **Writer's notebook or journal**
Fill your *writer's journal* with experiences, feelings, and thoughts. You can put in cartoons, quotations, song lyrics, and poems that have special meaning for you. When you need a writing topic, look through your journal to find an idea you want to expand. You can also have a section called a *learning log,* where you write about things you learn. Keep your journal in a notebook, file folder, or computer file.

Writer's Notebook Guidelines
Write every day, and date your entries.
Write as much or as little as you want. Do not worry about spelling, punctuation, or grammar.
Give your imagination some space. Write about dreams, daydreams, and far-out fantasies.

EXAMPLE

July 12, 2008. Saw people doing strange exercise in the park Sat. morning. They moved SO slowly like in a dream. A slow-motion dance. Seven people following movements of an old Chinese woman, few old, mostly young, all moving together. We watched a long time. They call it tai chi—it made me feel good.

2. **Gathering information**   When you run out of ideas from your imagination or you need facts, you can turn to other sources. Use the following strategies to find more information on a topic.

■ **Listening with a focus**   You can find information by listening to radio and TV programs and tapes or by interviewing someone who knows something about your topic. Before you listen, write out some questions about your topic. Then, listen for answers and take notes. (See also **Listening** on page 761.)

■ **Reading with a focus**   When you look for information in print, follow the guidelines in the chart below.

Reading Guidelines
Find your topic in a book's table of contents or index. Turn to the pages listed.
Do not read every word. Skim pages quickly, looking for your topic.
When you find information on your topic, slow down and read carefully.
Note main ideas and key details.

3. **Arranging ideas**   The following strategies will help you to organize and summarize your ideas. These strategies can be especially helpful for organizing ideas from a number of different sources.

■ **Charts**   A *chart* is a way of classifying information. Charts help you begin to gather and organize your facts and details before you write. One type of chart is a table like the one below made by a student who is researching types of armor worn by knights in the Middle Ages.

Armor in the Middle Ages	
Type of Armor	Description
hauberk	a tunic made from chain mail with a hood
surcoat	a coat worn over the chain mail suits to protect them from the sun; the coats are decorated with identifying emblems
plate armor	plates of solid metal designed to deflect arrows

■ **Conceptual mapping** *Mapping,* or *conceptual mapping,* is similar to clustering. The difference is that it is used to organize information that you have gathered rather than to find ideas. You can use conceptual mapping to group your main ideas and supporting details before you write your paragraphs. An example of a conceptual map is shown at the bottom of the page.

■ **Outlines** An *outline* is another way to organize important information. When you make an outline, you arrange the ideas to show the main ideas and the supporting details. You can use the outline as a guide to writing.

You may need to use different types of outlines. For a report, your teacher might require you to write a *formal outline,* like the one at the top of the next page, with Roman numerals for headings and capital letters for subheadings.

Conceptual Map

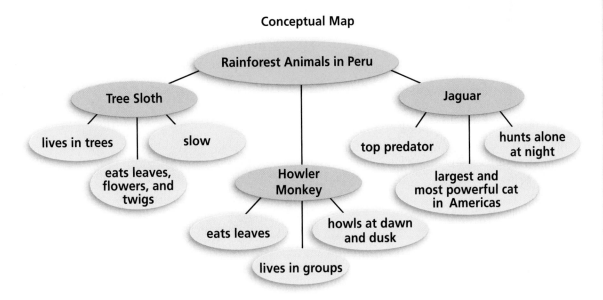

Formal Outline

```
Title: Kids About Town
Main Idea: After-school activi-
ties are good, but you should
limit how many you do.
I. Benefits
   A. Group Activities (soccer
      team)
      1. learn teamwork
      2. make friends
      3. physical fitness
   B. Individual Activities
      (violin lessons)
      1. develop self-discipline
      2. learn a skill
II. Drawbacks
   A. Less Study Time
   B. Stress
```

To organize your writing quickly, you can use an *informal outline* like the one below.

Informal Outline

Topic: After-School Activities

Benefits	Drawbacks
group activities (soccer): learn teamwork	sometimes too busy to study
make friends	stress caused by worrying about my grades and when I will have time for everything
physical fitness	
individual activities (violin lessons): develop self-discipline	
learn a skill	

■ **Sequence chain**   See **Text Structures, Analyzing** on page 743.

■ **Time line**   A *time line* organizes information by the date it happened. The time line below shows one student's progress in learning to use a personal computer.

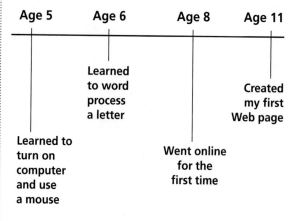

Age 5	Age 6	Age 8	Age 11
	Learned to word process a letter		Created my first Web page
Learned to turn on computer and use a mouse		Went online for the first time	

■ **Venn diagram**   A *Venn diagram* uses circles to show how two subjects are alike and different. Each subject has its own circle, but the circles overlap. In the overlapping part, you write details that are the same for both subjects. In the parts that do not overlap, you write details that make these subjects different. (See also page 584.)

Differences   Similarities   Differences

QUICK REFERENCE HANDBOOK

Symbols for Revising and Proofreading

Symbol	Example	Meaning of Symbol
≡	I will see you on saturday morning.	Capitalize a lowercase letter.
/	My Dog's name is Spot.	Lowercase a capital letter.
∧	Do not walk ^away^ from me.	Insert a missing word, letter, or punctuation mark.
ℓ	After you go go home, give me a call.	Leave out a word, letter, or punctuation mark.
∩	peice	Change the order of letters.
¶	¶ After you finish the first steps, continue on to the next.	Begin a new paragraph.
⊙	Dr Chavez	Add a period.
⋏	Yes I like strawberry smoothies.	Add a comma.

Revising and Proofreading Symbols   When you are revising and proofreading, indicate any changes by using the symbols in the chart above.

Style   When you act a certain way or dress a certain way, you are creating your personal style. When you write, you decide what words you are going to use and how you are going to arrange those words in sentences. The choices you make create your *style* of writing. Your writing style is personal because you are the one who created it.

Transitions   *Transitions,* or *transitional expressions,* are words and phrases that show the connections between ideas in a piece of writing. Transitions make your writing *coherent,* or smooth and easy to read. (See page 453 for a chart of **Transitional Words and Phrases.**)

Voice   The way a piece of writing "sounds" is its *voice.* As you write, try to express your ideas clearly and naturally. Although some writing requires a formal voice because of its audience and purpose, the writing should still sound like you. Your writing voice also reveals your attitude about your topic and your audience. Treat both with respect by choosing your words carefully.

Grammar at a Glance

A

abbreviation An abbreviation is a shortened form of a word or a phrase.

■ **capitalization of** (See page 296.)

TITLES USED WITH NAMES	**M**r.	**D**r.	**J**r.	**Ph.D.**
KINDS OF ORGANIZATIONS	**C**o.	**I**nc.	**D**ept.	**C**orp.
PARTS OF ADDRESSES	**B**lvd.	**A**ve.	**S**t.	**P.O. B**ox
NAMES OF STATES	[without ZIP Codes]		**K**y.	**W**yo.
			Wis.	**N.J.**
	[with ZIP Codes]		**KY**	**WY**
			WI	**NJ**
TIMES	**A.M.**	**P.M.**	**B.C.**	**A.D.**

■ **punctuation of** (See page 311.)

WITH PERIODS	(See preceding examples.)
WITHOUT PERIODS	DVD UN PBS NASA
	DC (**D.C.** without ZIP Code)
	kg ft lb yd cm
	[Exception: in.]

action verb An action verb expresses physical or mental activity. (See page 98.)

EXAMPLES   Stefan **rode** the bike over the bridge.

Teresa **trimmed** the hedge and **raked** the leaves.

I **thought** about the problem.

adjective An adjective modifies a noun or a pronoun. (See page 84.)

EXAMPLE   **The** Nobles live in **a beautiful, old** house.

adjective clause An adjective clause is a subordinate clause that modifies a noun or a pronoun. (See page 137.)

EXAMPLE   The woman **who directs the City Ballet** is from Romania.

adjective phrase A prepositional phrase that modifies a noun or a pronoun is called an adjective phrase. (See page 125.)

EXAMPLE   Fruit **from Mr. Park's market** always seem fresher than the produce **in the grocery store.**

adverb An adverb modifies a verb, an adjective, or another adverb. (See page 105.)

EXAMPLE   **Occasionally,** when he's feeling **especially** energetic, Dino goes ice-skating.

adverb clause An adverb clause is a subordinate clause that modifies a verb, an adjective, or an adverb. (See page 139.)

EXAMPLE   **Before I watch TV,** I have to do my homework.

adverb phrase A prepositional phrase that modifies a verb, an adjective, or an adverb is called an adverb phrase. (See page 129.)

EXAMPLE   **At the shore,** Trish and Sandy played volleyball.

agreement Agreement is the correspondence, or match, between grammatical forms. Grammatical forms agree when they have the same number and gender.

■ **of pronouns and antecedents** (See page 183.)

SINGULAR   **Marcie** could not check out the book because **she** did not have **her** library card with **her.**

PLURAL	**Readers** who do not have **their** library cards with **them** cannot check out books.
SINGULAR	Every afternoon, **each** of the students is given time to write in **his or her** journal.
PLURAL	Every afternoon, **all** of the students are given time to write in **their** journals.

■ **of subjects and verbs** (See page 170.)

SINGULAR	That **box** of blankets **is** for the homeless shelter.
PLURAL	The **blankets** in that box **are** for the homeless shelter.
SINGULAR	**Mixed vegetables, roasted potatoes, or rice pilaf comes** with any seafood entree.
PLURAL	**Rice pilaf, mixed vegetables, or roasted potatoes come** with any seafood entree.
SINGULAR	**Each** of these books **was written** by Amy Tan.
PLURAL	**All** of these books **were written** by Amy Tan.
SINGULAR	**Neither Eli nor Leo wants** to go skateboarding.
PLURAL	**Both Eli and Leo want** to go skateboarding.
SINGULAR	Here **is** my **collection** of baseball cards.
PLURAL	Here **are** the most valuable baseball **cards** in my collection.
SINGULAR	Where **is** my **wallet?**
PLURAL	Where **are** the **tickets?**
SINGULAR	**He doesn't** know how to play jai alai.
PLURAL	**They don't** know how to play jai alai.

antecedent An antecedent is the word or word group that a pronoun stands for. (See page 76.)

EXAMPLE	**Patricia** told **Aunt Sally** and **Uncle Ted** that **she** was thinking of **them.** [*Patricia* is the antecedent of *she. Aunt Sally* and *Uncle Ted* are the antecedents of *them.*]

apostrophe

- **to form contractions** (See page 350. See also **contractions.**)

  EXAMPLES hasn°t   you°ll   let°s   o°clock   °01

- **to form plurals of letters, numerals, symbols, and words used as words** (See page 353.)

  EXAMPLES *a*°s, *e*°s, *i*°s, *o*°s, and *u*°s

             A°s, *I*°s, and *U*°s

             v°s and *w*°s

             1900°s

             UFO°s

             +°s and −°s

             using *and*°s instead of *&*°s

- **to show possession** (See page 346.)

  EXAMPLES the astronaut°s spacesuit

             the astronauts° spacesuits

             someone°s book bag

             Kim°s and Mariah°s math projects

             Kim and Mariah°s math project

appositive An appositive is a noun or a pronoun placed beside another noun or pronoun to identify or describe it. (See page 318.)

EXAMPLE   The manager, **Max,** always brought his lunch to work.

appositive phrase An appositive phrase consists of an appositive and its modifiers. (See page 318.)

EXAMPLE   Claude Baker, **the manager of our local branch,** has been in banking for ten years.

article The articles, *a*, *an*, and *the*, are the most frequently used adjectives. (See page 268.)

EXAMPLE   **The** jetliner, **a** new model, had **an** eventful voyage.

bad, badly (See page 269.)

NONSTANDARD	This tuna salad smells badly.
STANDARD	This tuna salad smells **bad.**

base form The base form, or infinitive, is one of the four principal parts of a verb. (See page 193.)

EXAMPLE   Lee helped me **lift** the heavy box.

capitalization

- **of abbreviations** (See page 296. See also **abbreviation.**)
- **of first words** (See page 285.)

EXAMPLES   **I**n Norse mythology, Thor is the god of thunder.

His sister asked him, "**H**ave you already fed our goldfish today?"

Dear Mrs. Yellowfeather:

Yours truly,

- **of proper nouns and proper adjectives** (See pages 287 and 296.)

Proper Noun	Common Noun
Col. **C**urtis **L. B**rown, **J**r.	astronaut
Charles the **W**ise	leader
North **A**merica	continent
Argentina	country
Elk **P**oint, **S**outh **D**akota	city and state
Kodiak **I**sland	island
Yukon **R**iver	body of water
Guadalupe **P**eak	mountain
Cheyenne **M**ountain **Z**oological **P**ark	park
Siuslaw **N**ational **F**orest	forest
Luray **C**averns	caves
the **S**outhwest	region
Twenty-**f**ourth **S**treet	street

Proper Noun	Common Noun
World **H**ealth **O**rganization (**WHO**)	organization
Federal **A**viation **A**dministration (**FAA**)	government body
North **C**arolina **S**tate **U**niversity (**NCSU**)	institution
Klondike **G**old **R**ush	historical event
Ice **A**ge	historical period
Little **L**eague **W**orld **S**eries	special event
Hana **M**atsuri, or **F**lower **F**estival	holiday
February, **M**ay, **A**ugust, **N**ovember	calendar items
winter, **s**pring, **s**ummer, **f**all (**a**utumn)	seasons
Nez **P**erce	people
Islam	religion
Protestant	religious follower
God (*but* the Greek **g**od **A**pollo)	deity
Rosh **H**ashanah	holy days
Koran	sacred writing
Joshua **T**ree **N**ational **M**onument	monument
Metropolitan **M**useum of **A**rt	building
Caldecott **M**edal	award
Uranus	planet
Canopus	star
Delphinus, or **D**olphin	constellation
HMS *Leopard*	ship
Lunar Prospector	spacecraft
Physical **S**cience **I** (*but* **p**hysical **s**cience)	school subject
Cherokee	people or language

■ **of titles** (See page 300.)

    EXAMPLES   **M**ayor Maria Sanchez [preceding a name]

                  Maria Sanchez, the city's **m**ayor [following a name]

                  Welcome, **M**ayor. [direct address]

                  Uncle Darnell [*but* our **u**ncle Darnell]

                  The **C**all *of the* **W**ild [book]

*S*aved by the *B*ell [television series]

*A*mahl and the *N*ight *V*isitors [musical composition]

"*O*ver the *R*ainbow" [song]

"*T*he *S*mallest *D*ragonboy" [short story]

"*I* *A*m of the *E*arth" [poem]

*R*eader's *D*igest [magazine]

*T*he *W*ashington *P*ost [newspaper]

*R*ose *I*s *R*ose [comic strip]

case of pronouns Case is the form a pronoun takes to show how it is used in a sentence. (See page 223.)

NOMINATIVE   Louis and **she** were the finalists in the spelling bee. [part of the compound subject of the verb *were*]

The only sixth-graders in the contest were Felicia and **he.** [part of the compound predicate nominative referring to the subject *sixth-graders*]

We volunteers spent Saturday afternoon making piñatas for the fiesta. [subject followed by the noun appositive *volunteers*]

Who painted *Cow's Skull: Red, White and Blue*? [subject of the verb *painted*]

Who is the author of *Yolanda's Genius*? [predicate nominative referring to the subject *author*]

OBJECTIVE   On Friday, Ms. Yabuuchi took **them** on a field trip to the planetarium. [direct object of the verb *took*]

Gwen sent **me** an invitation to her family's Kwanzaa party. [indirect object of the verb *sent*]

I went with Carla and **her** to a Japanese tea ceremony. [part of the compound object of the preposition *with*]

The judge awarded each of **us** contestants a certificate of achievement. [object of the preposition *of*, followed by the noun appositive *contestants*]

Whom did the coach select as the captain of the team? [direct object of the verb *did select*]

In the last line of the poem, to **whom** is the speaker referring? [object of the preposition *to*]

POSSESSIVE   **Your** birthday is the same day as **mine** is. [*Your* is used as an adjective before the subject *birthday*; *mine* is used as the subject of the verb *is*.]

clause A clause is a group of words that contains a subject and a verb and that is used as part of a sentence. (See page 135. See also **independent clause** and **subordinate clause**.)

INDEPENDENT CLAUSE   she stripped the walls of the living room

SUBORDINATE CLAUSE   before I painted them

colon (See page 327.)

■ before lists

EXAMPLES   Amber's favorite fables by Aesop are as follows: "Belling the Cat," "The Fox and the Grapes," and "The Frogs Who Wished for a King."

I need to get a few items at the pet shop: a bag of colored gravel for the aquarium, a small mirror for the birdcage, and a new collar for my pet Chihuahua.

■ in conventional situations

EXAMPLES   9:15 A.M.

Genesis 4:1–16

State Names, Seals, Flags and Symbols: A Historical Guide

Dear Dr. Kawabata:

comma (See page 314.)

■ in a series

EXAMPLES   Dad made chicken quesadillas and topped them with a relish of diced tomatoes, onions, and chilies.

The book is a collection of stories that tell about the daring exploits of Heracles, King Arthur, Gilgamesh, and fourteen other heroes of ancient times.

in compound sentences

EXAMPLES My neighbor Mr. Kim owns a hardware store, and occasionally he hires me to restock the shelves.

We should leave now, or we may not get home before curfew.

with introductory elements

EXAMPLES Well, were you able to get the pitcher's autograph after the ballgame?

Yes, here's the baseball that he autographed!

with interrupters

EXAMPLES The Jaw-Dropper, the world's tallest and fastest roller coaster, is at the amusement park near my house.

On Saturday afternoon, Tyrone, let's play miniature golf after we finish our chores.

in conventional situations

EXAMPLES San Antonio, Texas, is the home of the Alamo.

I was born on July 17, 1998, in Des Moines, Iowa.

Is 483 Cottonwood Way, Columbia, SC 29250-3840, your current address?

comparison of modifiers (See page 245.)

comparison of adjectives and adverbs

Positive	Comparative	Superlative
sharp	sharper	sharpest
friendly	friendlier	friendliest
loyal	more loyal	most loyal
cheerfully	less cheerfully	least cheerfully
good/well	better	best

comparing two

EXAMPLES These red grapes are **sweeter** than those.

Jiro speaks the language **more fluently** than Anzu does.

■ **comparing more than two**

EXAMPLES Of all the planets, Mercury is **nearest** the sun.

Of a gazelle, a cheetah, and an ostrich, which animal can run **most swiftly**?

Alaska is the **largest** of all the U.S. states.

complement A complement is a word or word group that completes the meaning of a verb. (See page 151. See also **direct object, indirect object, predicate nominative** and **predicate adjective.**)

EXAMPLES Ed gave **Martha** a **nod.**

Rei is the **leader** because he is so **organized.**

complex sentence A complex sentence has one independent clause and at least one subordinate clause. (See page 145.)

EXAMPLES Two of my favorite writers are Katherine Paterson, who wrote *Bridge to Terabithia,* and Beverly Cleary, who wrote *Dear Mr. Henshaw.* [one independent clause and two subordinate clauses]

When Jason and I were stargazing last night, we clearly saw the planets Venus, Mars, Jupiter, and Saturn. [one subordinate clause and one independent clause]

compound-complex sentence A compound-complex sentence has two or more independent clauses and at least one subordinate clause. (See page 146.)

EXAMPLES Most people think of dolphins as gentle, playful creatures, but as the documentary film shows, they can become fiercely aggressive predators in the wild. [one subordinate clause between two independent clauses]

When we were in Boston last summer, we visited The Computer Museum; we were especially impressed by the exhibit called The Giant Walk-Through Computer. [one subordinate clause followed by two independent clauses]

compound sentence A compound sentence has two or more independent clauses and no subordinate clauses. (See page 143.)

EXAMPLE   This Saturday, the Library Club at our school will hold a book fair; the price of each hardcover book will be one dollar, and the price of each paperback will be fifty cents. [three independent clauses]

conjunction A conjunction joins words or groups of words. (See page 112.)

EXAMPLE   **Both** Sy **and** Ben went to the Chinese restaurant, **but** they had to wait before being served, **for** the power was out.

contraction A contraction is a shortened form of a word, a numeral, or a group of words. Apostrophes in contractions indicate where letters or numerals have been omitted. (See page 350. See also **apostrophe.**)

EXAMPLES   we'd [we had *or* we would]   it's [it is *or* it has]

who's [who is *or* who has]   won't [will not]

'08 [a year ending in *08*]   o'clock [of the clock]

declarative sentence A declarative sentence makes a statement and is followed by a period. (See page 64.)

EXAMPLE   Birmingham is the second-largest city in the United Kingdom.

direct object A direct object is a word or word group that receives the action of the verb or shows the result of the action. A direct object answers the question *Whom?* or *What?* after a transitive verb. (See page 153.)

EXAMPLE   Ms. Echavarría saw **John** and **Peter.**

double comparison A double comparison is the nonstandard use of two comparative forms (usually *more* and *–er*) or two superlative forms (usually *most* and *–est*) to express comparison. In standard usage, the single comparative form is correct. (See page 252.)

NONSTANDARD	King's Holly, a shrub growing in Tasmania, is considered the world's most oldest living plant.
STANDARD	King's Holly, a shrub growing in Tasmania, is considered the world's **oldest** living plant.

double negative A double negative is the nonstandard use of two or more negative words to express a single negative idea. (See page 255.)

NONSTANDARD	Without her eyeglasses, Ally couldn't hardly read the letters in the bottom line of the eye chart.
STANDARD	Without her eyeglasses, Ally **could hardly** read the letters in the bottom line of the eye chart.

end marks (See page 309.)

■ **with sentences**

EXAMPLES At the state fair, we rode in a hot-air balloon. [declarative sentence]

Have you ever ridden in a hot-air balloon? [interrogative sentence]

Wow! [interjection] What a thrilling adventure that was! [exclamatory sentence]

Don't be afraid to look down. [imperative sentence]

■ **with abbreviations** (See **abbreviation.**)

EXAMPLES Your tae kwon do class begins at 7:00 P.M.

Doesn't your tae kwon do class begin at 7:00 P.M.?

exclamation point (See **end marks.**)

exclamatory sentence An exclamatory sentence expresses strong feeling and is followed by an exclamation point. (See page 65.)

EXAMPLE How kind you are!

fragment (See **sentence fragment.**)

QUICK REFERENCE HANDBOOK

E

F

good, well (See page 250.)

EXAMPLES   Doreen is a **good** saxophone player.

            Doreen plays the saxophone **well** [not *good*].

hyphen (See page 354.)

■ **to divide words**

EXAMPLE   The bright star Sirius is part of the constellation Canis Major.

■ **in compound numbers**

EXAMPLE   In a leap year, February has twenty-nine days.

imperative sentence An imperative sentence gives a command or makes a request and is followed by either a period or an exclamation point. (See page 64.)

EXAMPLES   Please close the window. [request]

            Close the window! [command]

independent clause An independent clause (also called a *main clause*) expresses a complete thought and can stand by itself as a sentence. (See page 135.)

EXAMPLE   After you get home, **don't forget to water the plants.**

indirect object An indirect object is a word or word group that often comes between a transitive verb and its direct object and that tells to whom or to what or for whom or for what the action of the verb is done. (See page 155.)

EXAMPLE   Give the **dog** a bath.

interjection An interjection expresses emotion and has no grammatical relation to the rest of the sentence. (See page 114.)

EXAMPLE   **Wow,** look at that sunset!

interrogative sentence An interrogative sentence asks a question and is followed by a question mark. (See page 64.)

EXAMPLE   Is Clay Regazzoni still racing?

intransitive verb An intransitive verb is a verb that does not take an object. (See page 101.)

EXAMPLE   The crowd **laughed,** but Bob only **smiled.**

irregular verb An irregular verb is a verb that forms its past and past participle in some way other than by adding *–d* or *–ed* to the base form. (See page 196. See also **regular verb.**)

Base Form	Present Participle	Past	Past Participle
be	[is] being	was, were	[have] been
begin	[is] beginning	began	[have] begun
bring	[is] bringing	brought	[have] brought
burst	[is] bursting	burst	[have] burst
fall	[is] falling	fell	[have] fallen
go	[is] going	went	[have] gone
make	[is] making	made	[have] made

italics (See **underlining.**)

its, it's (See page 274.)

EXAMPLES   **Its** [the snow leopard's] scientific name is *Panthera uncia.*

It's [It is] considered an endangered species.

It's [It has] been overhunted for **its** fur.

lie, lay (See page 214.)

EXAMPLES   Anxious about his first day at a new school, Harry **lay** awake most of the night. [past tense of *lie*]

Aunt Una **laid** the map on the table and showed us the route we would travel. [past tense of *lay*]

linking verb A linking verb connects the subject with a word that identifies or describes the subject. (See page 99.)

EXAMPLE   Cousin Marty **became** a clarinetist.

L

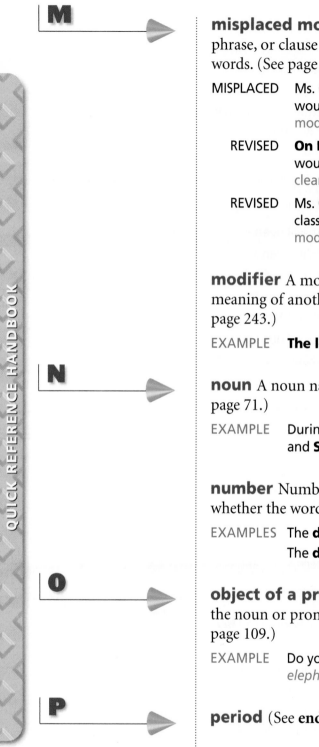

misplaced modifier A misplaced modifier is a word, phrase, or clause that seems to modify the wrong word or words. (See page 257.)

MISPLACED   Ms. Osaka said on Friday the sixth-grade students would elect class officers. [Does the phrase *on Friday* modify the verb *said* or the verb phrase *would elect*?]

REVISED   **On Friday,** Ms. Osaka said the sixth-grade students would elect class officers. [The phrase *On Friday* clearly modifies the verb *said*.]

REVISED   Ms. Osaka said the sixth-grade students would elect class officers **on Friday.** [The phrase *on Friday* clearly modifies the verb phrase *would elect*.]

modifier A modifier is a word or word group that makes the meaning of another word or word group more specific. (See page 243.)

EXAMPLE   **The loud** chirping **of sparrows** filled **the** air.

noun A noun names a person, place, thing, or idea. (See page 71.)

EXAMPLE   During the **drive, Ms. Washington** asked **Tommy** and **Sarah** to sing their **version** of the **song.**

number Number is the form a word takes to indicate whether the word is singular or plural. (See page 170.)

EXAMPLES   The **dove** dipped **its head** as **it** drank.
The **doves** dipped **their heads** as **they** drank.

object of a preposition An object of a preposition is the noun or pronoun that ends a prepositional phrase. (See page 109.)

EXAMPLE   Do you have any books about **elephants**? [*About elephants* is a prepositional phrase.]

period (See **end marks.**)

phrase A phrase is a group of related words that does not contain both a verb and its subject and that is used as a single part of speech. (See page 122.)

EXAMPLE Marcia **is designing** a dress **for her cousin Francine's wedding.** [*Is designing* is a verb phrase. *For her cousin Francine's wedding* is a prepositional phrase.]

predicate The predicate is the part of a sentence that says something about the subject. (See page 55.)

EXAMPLES She **is waiting for the bus.**

Does Walter **know Rebecca?**

predicate adjective A predicate adjective is an adjective that completes the meaning of a linking verb and that modifies the subject of the verb. (See page 160.)

EXAMPLE At the farm, the cows looked **sleek** and **healthy.**

predicate nominative A predicate nominative is a noun or pronoun that completes the meaning of a linking verb and identifies or refers to the subject of the verb. (See page 158.)

EXAMPLE The first passengers to exit were **Ron** and **Dee.**

prefix A prefix is a word part that is added before a base word or root. (See page 364.)

EXAMPLES un + solved = **un**solved

im + mature = **im**mature

dis + satisfied = **dis**satisfied

preposition A preposition shows the relationship of a noun or a pronoun to some other word in a sentence. (See page 108.)

EXAMPLE **At** the market, Tancredo bought green peppers, cheese, and tomatoes **for** the meal he was planning.

prepositional phrase A prepositional phrase is a group of words that includes a preposition, an object of the preposition, and any modifiers of that object. (See page 109.)

EXAMPLE   A book **of swashbuckling adventure** is *Treasure Island,* **by Robert Louis Stevenson.**

pronoun A pronoun is used in place of one or more nouns or pronouns. (See page 76.)

EXAMPLE   Julie told Mom and Dad **she** would be happy to drive **them** to the airport.

question mark (See **end marks.**)

quotation marks (See page 338.)

■ **for direct quotations**
EXAMPLE   **"**On our vacation in Mexico,**"** said Mrs. Tamayo, **"**we visited Chichén Itzá, where we saw the ruins of pyramids and temples that the Maya had built.**"**

■ **with other marks of punctuation** (See also preceding example.)
EXAMPLES   **"**In what year was the first Earth Day celebration held**?"** asked Megan.

Who is the main character in Gary Soto's story **"**The No-Guitar Blues**"?**

The teacher asked, **"**What do you think Benjamin Franklin meant when he wrote the proverb **'**Hunger is the best pickle**'?"**

■ **for titles**
EXAMPLES   **"**Amigo Brothers**"** [short story]

"Madam and the Rent Man**"** [short poem]

"Under the Sea**"** [song]

regular verb A regular verb is a verb that forms its past and past participle by adding *–d* or *–ed* to the base form. (See page 194. See also **irregular verb.**)

Base Form	Present Participle	Past	Past Participle
ask	[is] asking	asked	[have] asked
drown	[is] drowning	drowned	[have] drowned
move	[is] moving	moved	[have] moved
risk	[is] risking	risked	[have] risked
suppose	[is] supposing	supposed	[have] supposed
use	[is] using	used	[have] used

rise, raise (See page 212.)

EXAMPLES When the sun **rose,** the restless scouts were still awake. [past tense of *rise*]

The orchestra conductor **raised** the baton to begin the concert. [past tense of *raise*]

run-on sentence A run-on sentence is two or more complete sentences run together as one. (See page 431.)

RUN-ON Nishi and I have been computer pen pals for two years she lives in Tokyo, Japan I live in Omaha, Nebraska.

REVISED Nishi and I have been computer pen pals for two years; she lives in Tokyo, Japan, **and** I live in Omaha, Nebraska.

REVISED Nishi and I have been computer pen pals for two years. She lives in Tokyo, Japan, **and** I live in Omaha, Nebraska.

semicolon (See page 325.)

EXAMPLE In 1993, Ramon Blanco from Spain became the oldest person to scale Mount Everest; he was sixty years old at the time.

sentence A sentence is a group of words that contains a subject and a verb and that expresses a complete thought. (See page 50.)

         S   **V**
EXAMPLE The fish swam lazily in the clear water.

sentence fragment A sentence fragment is a group of words that is punctuated as if it were a complete sentence but that does not contain both a subject and a verb or that does not express a complete thought. (See pages 428 and 50.)

FRAGMENTS   Hera, the queen of the Greek gods, casting a spell on Hercules. Because she was jealous of him.

SENTENCE   Hera, the queen of the Greek gods, cast a spell on Hercules because she was jealous of him.

simple sentence A simple sentence has one independent clause and no subordinate clauses. (See page 142.)

EXAMPLE   On the Internet, Milo and I accessed a search page and searched for information about King Tutankhamen. [one independent clause with a compound subject and a compound verb]

sit, set (See page 211.)

EXAMPLES   Carmen **sat** on the bench, anxiously waiting for Coach Engle to send her back into the game. [past tense of *sit*]

Anthony **set** the box of dominoes on the table, hoping that someone in his family would play the game with him. [past tense of *set*]

stringy sentence A stringy sentence is a sentence that has too many independent clauses. Usually, the clauses are strung together with coordinating conjunctions like *and* or *but*. (See page 432.)

STRINGY   One day, the gods Jupiter and Mercury decided to come down to the earth to test the people of Phrygia for their hospitality, so the gods disguised themselves as peasants who were in desperate need of food and shelter, and they stopped at hundreds of houses, and at each one the "peasants" were turned away, but finally, they came to the very small house of a poor, elderly couple named Baucis and Philemon.

REVISED   One day, the gods Jupiter and Mercury decided to come down to the earth to test the people of Phrygia for their hospitality. The gods disguised themselves as peasants who were in desperate need of food and shelter. They stopped at hundreds of houses, and at each one the "peasants" were turned away. Finally, they came to the very small house of a poor, elderly couple named Baucis and Philemon.

subject The subject tells whom or what a sentence is about. (See page 53.)

EXAMPLE   The **geraniums** bloomed early this year.

subject complement A subject complement is a word or word group that completes the meaning of a linking verb and identifies or describes the subject. (See page 158. See also **predicate adjective** and **predicate nominative.**)

EXAMPLES   My cousin Brian is a **software technician.**

The art room was **messy.**

subordinate clause A subordinate clause (also called a *dependent clause*) does not express a complete thought and cannot stand alone as a sentence. (See page 136. See also **adjective clause** and **adverb clause.**)

EXAMPLE   **After I read that article,** I changed my opinion.

suffix A suffix is a word part that is added after a base word or root. (See page 365.)

EXAMPLES   steady + ly = steadi**ly**
forgive + ness = forgive**ness**
obey + ing = obey**ing**
adore + able = ador**able**
shop + ing = shop**ping**

tense of verbs The tense of verbs indicates the time of the action or of the state of being that is expressed by the verb. (See page 206.)

T

Present Tense

I do	we do
you do	you do
he, she, it does	they do

Past Tense

I did	we did
you did	you did
he, she, it did	they did

Future Tense

I will (shall) do	we will (shall) do
you will (shall) do	you will (shall) do
he, she, it will (shall) do	they will (shall) do

Present Perfect Tense

I have done	we have done
you have done	you have done
he, she, it has done	they have done

Past Perfect Tense

I had done	we had done
you had done	you had done
he, she, it had done	they had done

Future Perfect Tense

I will (shall) have done	we will (shall) have done
you will (shall) have done	you will (shall) have done
he, she, it will (shall) have done	they will (shall) have done

transitive verb A transitive verb is an action verb that takes an object. (See page 101.)

EXAMPLE   Their dog **chased** our cat.

underlining (italics) (See page 336.)

■ **for titles**

EXAMPLES   *The Way to Rainy Mountain* [book]

           National Geographic World [magazine]

           Sleeping Gypsy [work of art]

           Duke Bluebeard's Castle [long musical composition]

■ **for names of vehicles**

EXAMPLES   *Orient Express* [train]

           Spruce Goose [aircraft]

verb A verb expresses an action or a state of being. (See page 95.)

EXAMPLE   Evelyn **wore** a blue blazer.

          Is the desert nearby?

verb phrase A verb phrase consists of a main verb and at least one helping verb. (See page 96.)

EXAMPLES   The helicopter **should have been** here by now.

           I **have** never **heard** Marcus Hearn sing.

well (See *good, well.*)

who, whom (See page 234.)

EXAMPLES   **Who** was the first astronaut to walk in space?
[nominative form used as the predicate nominative referring to the subject *astronaut*]

          Whom have you invited to your bat mitzvah party?
[objective form used as the direct object of the verb phrase *have invited*]

U

V

W

QUICK REFERENCE HANDBOOK

Diagramming Appendix

Diagramming Sentences

A *sentence diagram* is a picture of how the parts of a sentence fit together. It shows how the words in the sentence are related.

Subjects and Verbs

Reference Note

For more about **subjects** and **verbs,** see page 53.

To diagram a sentence, first find the simple subject and the simple predicate, or verb, and write them on a horizontal line. Then, separate the subject and verb with a vertical line. Keep any capital letters, but leave out sentence punctuation.

EXAMPLES   Dogs bark.

Dogs	bark

Children were singing.

Children	were singing

The preceding examples are easy because each sentence contains only a simple subject and a verb. Now, look at a longer sentence.

EXAMPLE   My older brother is studying Arabic in school.

To diagram the simple subject and the verb of this sentence, follow these three steps:

Step 1:   Separate the complete subject from the complete predicate.

complete subject | complete predicate
My older brother | is studying Arabic in school.

Step 2:   Find the simple subject and the verb.

simple subject | verb
brother | is studying

Step 3:   Draw the diagram.

brother | is studying

Exercise 1 **Diagramming Simple Subjects and Verbs**

Diagram the simple subject and verb in each of the following sentences.

EXAMPLES   **1.** Aunt Carmen is teaching me to cook.

1.   Aunt Carmen | is teaching

2. The dog sleeps in the garage.

2.   dog | sleeps

1. My family goes to the store together every Saturday.
2. We shop at the grocery store at the corner of our street.
3. I select the red beans, rice, meat, and cheese.
4. Grandma López must have written the shopping list.
5. Rosita is buying the chile peppers and cilantro.

┌HELP┐

Remember
that simple subjects and verbs may consist of more than one word.

Compound Subjects

Reference Note

For more about **compound subjects,** see page 59.

To diagram a compound subject, put the subjects on parallel lines. Then, put the connecting word (the conjunction, such as *and, but,* or *or*) on a dotted line between the subject lines.

EXAMPLE   **Koalas** and **kangaroos** are found in Australia.

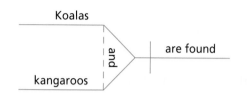

Compound Verbs

Reference Note

For more about **compound verbs,** see page 60.

To diagram a compound verb, put the two verbs on parallel lines. Then, put the conjunction on a dotted line between the verbs.

EXAMPLE   Callie **washes** and **dries** the dishes after dinner.

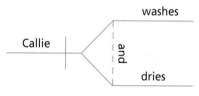

Compound Subjects and Compound Verbs

A sentence with both a compound subject and a compound verb combines the two patterns you just learned.

EXAMPLE   The **cat** and her **kittens ate** and then **slept.**

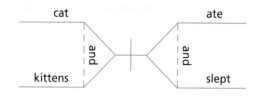

┌HELP┐

Sentences in Exercise 2 may contain compound subjects, compound verbs, or both.

Exercise 2 **Diagramming Compound Subjects and Compound Verbs**

Diagram the simple subjects and verbs in the following sentences.

EXAMPLE   **1.** Spike Lee and Denzel Washington made and
            released movies recently.

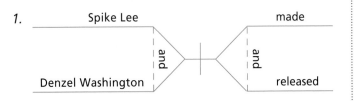

1. Ursula LeGuin and Nicholasa Mohr are my favorite
   authors.
2. Ms. Sanchez and Mr. Charles teach Spanish.
3. Bill Russell first played and later coached in the NBA.
4. My friends and I hurried home and told our parents the
   good news.
5. The students and the teacher visited the museum but did
   not have time for a complete tour.

Questions

To diagram a question, first make the question into a
statement without changing or dropping any words.
Then, diagram the sentence.

EXAMPLE   Can all insects fly? [question]
          All insects can fly. [statement]

          insects | Can fly

Notice that the diagram uses the capitalization of the original
sentence.

Understood Subjects

In an imperative sentence (a request or command) the subject
is always understood to be *you*. Place the understood subject
you in parentheses on the horizontal line.

EXAMPLE   Look over there.

          (you) | Look

Reference Note

For more information
about **questions,** see
page 64.

─HELP─

Remember
that in a diagram, the
subject always comes first,
even if it does not come
first in the sentence.

Reference Note

For information about
imperative sentences
and **understood sub-
jects,** see page 64.

Exercise 3 Diagramming Questions and Commands

Diagram the simple subjects and verbs in the following sentences.

EXAMPLE **1.** Please wash the dishes.

1.
(you)	wash

1. Eat the rest of your jambalaya.
2. Do you know much about the Jewish holidays?
3. Where is the driver going?
4. Please help me with these cartons.
5. Why are they standing in line?

Adjectives and Adverbs

Reference Note

For more information about **adjectives,** see page 84.

Adjectives and adverbs are written on slanted lines connected to the words they modify. Notice that possessive pronouns are diagrammed in the same way adjectives are. Also notice that the articles *a, an,* and *the* are included as adjectives.

Adjectives

EXAMPLES **yellow** bird   **her best** blouse   **a playful** puppy

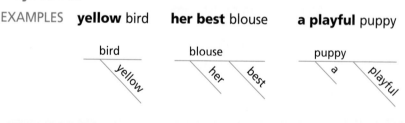

Exercise 4 Diagramming Sentences with Adjectives

Diagram the subjects, verbs, and adjectives in the following sentences.

EXAMPLE **1.** A strong, cold wind blew all night.

1. My favorite singer is coming to town.
2. The long, grueling hike tired us.
3. Red, ripe tomatoes grow there.
4. The two brave astronauts stepped into space.
5. Is a funny movie playing downtown?

Adverbs

When an adverb modifies a verb, the adverb is placed on a slanted line below the verb.

Reference Note

For more about **adverbs,** see page 105.

EXAMPLES   wrote **quickly**   walked **there slowly**

When an adverb modifies an adjective or another adverb, it is placed on a slanted line connected to the word it modifies.

EXAMPLES   **incredibly** large poster   **runs** very fast

Exercise 5   **Diagramming Sentences with Adverbs**

Diagram the subjects, verbs, adjectives, and adverbs in the following sentences.

EXAMPLE   **1.** We almost always recycle newspapers.

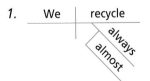

1. Nathan Wayne recently won the cooking contest.
2. That new band plays very loudly.

3. Her two brothers visited Chinatown yesterday.

4. The busy librarian almost never rests.

5. An extremely unusual program will be broadcast tonight.

Prepositional Phrases

Reference Note

For more information about **prepositional phrases,** see page 109.

Prepositional phrases are diagrammed below the words they modify. Write the preposition on a slanting line. Then, write the object of the preposition on a horizontal line connected to the slanting line. Notice that the slanting line extends a little beyond the horizontal line.

Adjective Phrases

Reference Note

For more about **adjective phrases,** see page 125.

EXAMPLES   time **of day**   several **in a row**

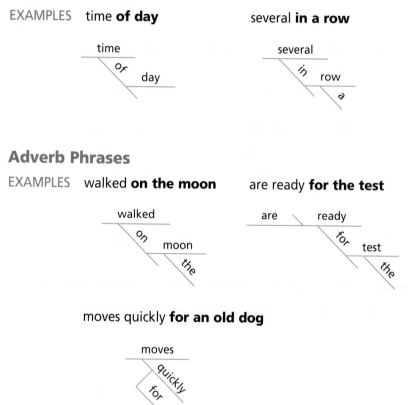

Adverb Phrases

Reference Note

For more about **adverb phrases,** see page 129.

EXAMPLES   walked **on the moon**   are ready **for the test**

moves quickly **for an old dog**

Diagramming Sentences with Prepositional Phrases

Diagram the following sentences.

EXAMPLE   **1.** The freighter slowed for the first lock.

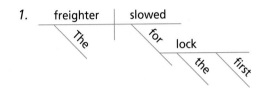

1. Tamales are wrapped in corn husks.
2. The soccer team from Brazil ran onto the field.
3. My friend from India skis very well.
4. The students in his class went to the library.
5. Catherine Zeta-Jones and Will Smith may star in that new movie.

Direct and Indirect Objects

Direct Objects

A direct object is diagrammed on the horizontal line with the subject and verb. A short vertical line separates the direct object from the verb.

Reference Note

For more about **direct objects,** see page 153.

EXAMPLE   We have been playing **music**.

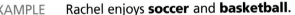

Compound Direct Objects

EXAMPLE   Rachel enjoys **soccer** and **basketball**.

Reference Note

For more information about **compound direct objects,** see page 153.

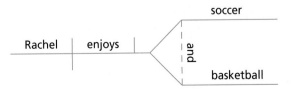

Reference Note

For more about **indirect objects,** see page 155.

Indirect Objects

The indirect object is diagrammed on a horizontal line beneath the verb. The verb and the indirect object are joined by a slanting line.

EXAMPLE   Dad fixed **us** some spaghetti.

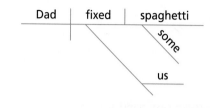

Compound Indirect Objects

Reference Note

For more information about **compound indirect objects,** see page 156.

EXAMPLE   Marisa gave her **brother** and **me** some grapes.

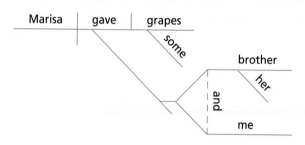

┌HELP┐

Not every sentence in Exercise 7 contains an indirect object.

Exercise 7 **Diagramming Direct Objects and Indirect Objects**

Diagram the following sentences.

EXAMPLE   **1.** He handed her the report.

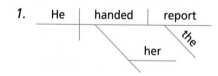

1. Amy Tan wrote that book.
2. Marcus made a touchdown.

3. My grandmother knitted me a sweater.
4. Marilyn won a bronze medal in the Special Olympics.
5. I bought Jolene and her sister a present.

Subject Complements

A subject complement is diagrammed on the horizontal line with the subject and the verb. The complement comes after the verb. A line slanting toward the subject separates the subject complement from the verb.

Predicate Nominatives

EXAMPLE   Mickey Leland was a famous **congressman** from Texas.

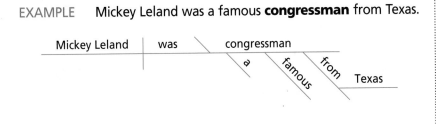

Reference Note

For more information about **predicate nominatives,** see page 158.

Compound Predicate Nominatives

EXAMPLE   Maddie is a **singer** and a **dancer.**

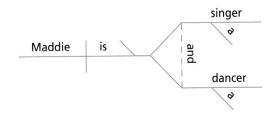

Reference Note

For more information on **compound predicate nominatives,** see page 159.

Predicate Adjectives

EXAMPLE   The guitarist was very **skillful.**

Reference Note

For more information on **predicate adjectives,** see page 160.

Compound Predicate Adjectives

Reference Note

For more about **compound predicate adjectives,** see page 161.

EXAMPLE   They were **weary** but **patient**.

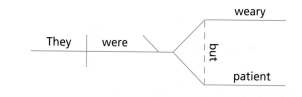

Exercise 8 Diagramming Sentences with Subject Complements

Diagram the following sentences.

EXAMPLE   **1.** Ms. Chang is an excellent teacher and a fine lawyer.

1.

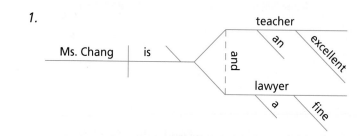

1. Your little brother looks quite sleepy.
2. Ossie Davis was an actor and a playwright.
3. These CDs are oldies but goodies.
4. Coyote is a trickster in American Indian mythology.
5. The library is full of interesting books.

Subordinate Clauses

Adjective Clauses

Reference Note

For more information about **independent clauses,** see page 135. For more about **adjective clauses** and **relative pronouns,** see page 137.

Diagram an adjective clause by connecting it with a broken line to the word it modifies. Draw the broken line between the relative pronoun and the word to which it relates. The adjective clause is diagrammed below the independent clause.

EXAMPLE   Certain land crabs **that are found in Cuba** can
           run fast.

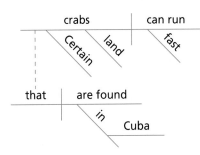

HELP

The words
who, whom, whose, which,
and *that* are often used as
relative pronouns.

Adverb Clauses

Diagram an adverb clause by using a broken line to connect
the adverb clause to the word it modifies. Place the subordinating conjunction that introduces the adverb clause on the
broken line. The adverb clause is diagrammed below the
independent clause.

EXAMPLE   **When Halley's Comet returns,** I will be a very
           old man.

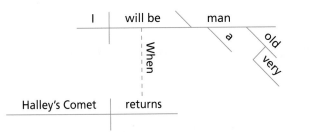

Reference Note

For more information
about **adverb clauses,**
see page 139. For a list of
**subordinating conjunc-
tions,** see page 136.

HELP

The words
*after, because, if, since,
unless, when,* and *while*
are often used as subordinating conjunctions.

PEANUTS reprinted by permission
of United Feature Syndicate, Inc.

Diagram the following sentences.

EXAMPLE 1. If you go to the library, will you return this book for me?

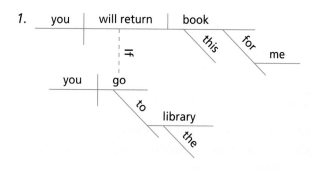

1. Mark Twain wrote books that people of all ages enjoy.
2. When you visit, the park will be open.
3. After Dawn saw the pandas, she wrote a report about them.
4. The people who were invited will see the performance.
5. Replace the scissors where you found them.

The Kinds of Sentence Structure

Simple Sentences

Reference Note

For more about **simple sentences,** see page 142.

A simple sentence contains one independent clause.

EXAMPLE The coach gave Alfonso a pat on the back. [one independent clause]

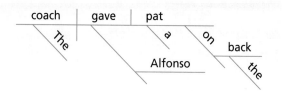

Compound Sentences

A compound sentence contains at least two independent clauses. The second independent clause in a compound sentence is diagrammed below the first and is joined to it by a coordinating conjunction.

EXAMPLE   Ostriches walk in a funny way, but they can run fast.
[two independent clauses]

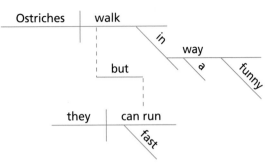

NOTE   The coordinating conjunctions are *and, but, for, nor, or,* *so,* and *yet.*

Reference Note

For more information about **compound sentences,** see page 143. For more about **coordinating conjunctions,** see page 112.

Exercise 10   Diagramming Compound Sentences

Diagram the following compound sentences.

EXAMPLE   **1.** Genna went to the mall, but I stayed home.

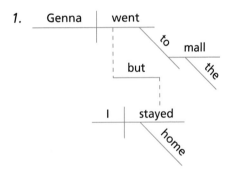

1. Lisa likes soccer, but I prefer basketball.
2. Gabriela Mistral is a poet, but she has also written essays.
3. Cactuses are desert plants, yet they can grow in milder climates.
4. I can give Jewel the news tonight, or you can call her now.
5. Chinese immigrants worked on the railroad in the West, but Irish immigrants built the railroad in the East.

Reference Note

For more about **complex sentences,** see page 145.

Complex Sentences

A complex sentence contains one independent clause and at least one subordinate clause.

EXAMPLE   Leon received a letter that was mailed from Germany. [one independent clause and one subordinate clause]

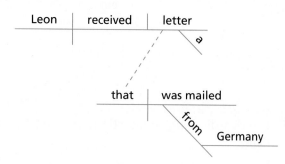

Compound-Complex Sentences

Reference Note

For more about **compound-complex sentences,** see page 146.

A compound-complex sentence contains two or more independent clauses and at least one subordinate clause.

EXAMPLE   After we rehearse this scene, we will move to another room, and the stage crew will work on the set. [two independent clauses and one subordinate clause]

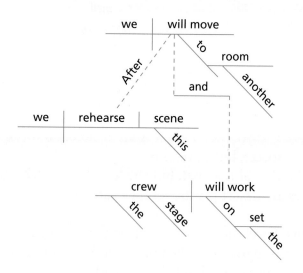

Exercise 11 **Diagramming Complex and Compound-Complex Sentences**

Diagram the following complex and compound-complex sentences.

EXAMPLE   **1.** If the Bulldogs win their last two games, they will finish in first place.

1.

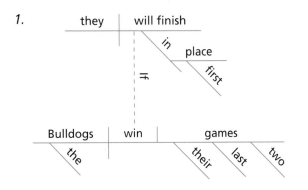

1. Hector walked to school because his bicycle had a flat tire.
2. Rosa was the contestant who knew the correct answer.
3. Unless the rain stops soon, the umpire will cancel the game.
4. As the lights dimmed, the audience grew quiet.
5. The student that designs the best cover receives a free yearbook, so many students will be entering designs.

INDEX

Selling, in persuasive speech, 708–710, 765
Semicolons, 325, 820
    between parts of a compound sentence, 325
Send, principal parts of, 201
Sensory details, 482, 561
    definition of, 447
    in short story, 629
    in storytelling, 498
Sentence(s). *See also* Sentence fragments.
    adjective placement in, 258
    adverb placement in, 258
    capitalization of direct quotations, 339
    classified by purpose, 64–65
    classified by structure, 142–146
    clincher sentences, 445, 448
    combining sentences, 435–441, 593
    complete sentences, 428–429
    compound-complex sentences, 146
    compound sentences, 143, 316–317,
        325, 440–441
    declarative sentences, 64, 309
    definition of, 50, 819
    diagrams of, 836–838
    exclamatory sentences, 65, 309
    fragments, 428–429
    imperative sentences, 64, 310
    interrogative sentences, 64, 309
    joining two related sentences, 440–441
    prepositional phrase placement in, 258–259
    run-on sentences, 431, 524
    simple sentences, 142–143, 317
    stringy sentences, 432–433, 702
    supporting sentences, 445, 447
    topic sentences, 445
    transitional words in, 556, 557
    varying for interest, 69, 523
Sentence-completion questions, 775–776
Sentence fragments, 428–429
    definition of, 50, 820
    identification of, 50
    in speech, 51
    subordinate clause as, 136
    use by professional writers, 51
Sentence parts
    predicate, 55–58
    subject, 53–54
Sentence punctuation. *See* End marks.
Sentence structure
    complex sentences, 145
    compound-complex sentences, 146
    compound sentences, 143
    simple sentences, 142–143
    stringy sentences, 432–433
Sequence chain. *See* Text structures.
Sequential order. *See* Chronological order;
    Organization.
Series

commas with, 314, 558
    semicolons with, 315, 325
Set, sit, 211–212, 820
Setting, 614, 615
    for novel, 608
    for short story, 628
    and verbal elements of speech, 756
Shadow style, 721
Shah, Idries, 342
Ships
    capitalization of names of, 293
    underlining (italicizing) names of, 337
Short-answer questions, 776
Short stories, 535, 628–629
    about research topic, 677
Should of. See Could of.
Show and tell, in storytelling, 498
Shrink, principal parts of, 201
Signature, of business letter, 794
Silent *e,* suffixes with, 365–366
Silliness, in humorous advertisement, 707
Similarities, 581, 583, 597. *See also* Comparing and
    contrasting.
Simile, 494, 561, 603, 748
Simple predicate, 57
    compared with complete predicate, 57
Simple sentences, 142–143
    with compound verb, 317
    diagram of, 836
Simple subjects, 54
Sing, principal parts of, 201
Single-spaced text, 721
Singular nouns, possessive case of, 346
Singular pronouns
    indefinite pronouns, 175, 176
    pronoun-antecedent agreement and, 184
Singular subjects, 170, 178
Singular words, 170
Sink, principal parts of, 201
Sit, set, 211, 212, 820
Skimming, 614, 742
    key words in, 659
Slang, 497, 727
Slow motion, creating effects with images, 783
Small capitals, 721
Social situations, speaking in, 758–759
Social studies, letters and forms for field trips, 711
Soft news, 788. *See also* Feature news.
Software. *See* Computer software.
Somewheres, 269
Sort of, kind of, 274
Sound
    in film and video, 779–780
    in humorous advertisement, 706
Sound effects, in poems, 630, 632
Sources, reference, 733. *See also* Authority; Credibility;
    Dictionary; Information; Messages; Reference

Unabridged dictionary, 714
Underlining (italics), 336–337, 338, 720
    for names of trains, ships, aircraft, spacecraft, 337
    with titles of works, 336–337, 343, 669
Understanding
    monitoring, 676, 710
Units of measure, abbreviations for, 312
Unity, in paragraphs, 454
Uppercase letters. *See* Capital letters.
URL, 734
Usage. *See also* English language; Modifiers; Pronoun(s); Verb(s).
    common problems in, 267–278
    double negatives, 255
    formal English, 267, 283
    informal English, 267, 350
Use, **principal parts of,** 194
Use to, used to, 277
"U.S. Has a Garbage Crisis, The" (Dudley), 681–682

Venn diagram, 584
    prewriting and, 800
    tools for writers, TV producers, and filmmakers, 635
Verb(s)
    action verbs, 98
    agreement with subjects, 170–171, 180
    compound verbs, 60, 439
    definition of, 95
    diagrams of, 824–826
    in essay questions, 772
    exact, 489, 490
    helping verbs, 95–96
    intransitive verbs, 101–102
    irregular verbs, 194, 196–198
    lie, lay, 214
    linking verbs, 99–100
    main verbs, 95–96
    objects of verbs, 153–154, 155–156
    principal parts of, 193–201
    progressive forms of, 207–209
    regular verbs, 194
    rise, raise, 212
    sit, set, 211, 212
    tenses of, 206–210
    transitive verbs, 101–102
Verbal elements, in speech delivery, 756

Verb phrases, 96
    definition of, 57
Vertical file, 733
Video. *See also* Documentaries; Films.
    in electronic media, 780
    "how-to" videos, 564
    producing a television news segment, 531–534
    as sources, 654–655, 732
    for television advertisements, 707
    television and, 567–568
Viewing and listening to learn, about charts and graphics, 564–568
Viewing and representing, 777–788
    analyzing an editorial cartoon, 711
    analyzing visual media, 564–568, 598, 600, 601–602, 635–636
    assessing language, medium, and presentation of TV news segment, 534
    comparing documentaries, 598
    comparing film, TV, and literature, 633–636
    comparing ideas in photographs, 599–602
    creating a graphic showing a process, 569
    creating a humorous advertisement, 706–707
    creating an editorial cartoon, 535
    creating charts comparing folk tales, 637
    creating illustrations, 486, 603
    evaluating how various media influence or inform, 602, 781–782
    giving a multimedia presentation, 603, 677
    interpreting and evaluating visual media, 568, 598, 599, 602, 633–636, 676
    interpreting visuals and graphics, 745–747
    key ideas for critical viewing, 781
    making a trading card, 677
    newspaper production, 528–530
    predicting while viewing, 737
    producing a TV news segment, 531–534
    producing visual media, 486, 528–530, 531–534, 553, 672
    sharing information through visuals, 672–673
    summarizing information, 568
    using visuals to complement meaning, 486, 553, 672
    viewing to learn, 564–568
Visualizing, 543
Visual literacy, 785
Visuals, 673. *See also* Graphic(s); Illustrations; Photographs and photography.
    creating, 672–673
    elements of effective visuals, 745
    in humorous advertisement, 706
    interpreting, 745–747
    types of, 745–747
    using visuals to complement meaning, 486, 553, 672
Vocabulary. *See also* English language; Mini-lesson (vocabulary); Word(s).

ACKNOWLEDGMENTS

For permission to reproduce copyrighted material, grateful acknowledgment is made to the following sources:

Quote by **Neil Armstrong** from Apollo 11 on January 23, 1969. Reproduced by permission of the author.

From review of *Catherine, Called Birdy* by Karen Cushman from *Great Books for Girls: More Than 600 Books to Inspire Today's Girls and Tomorrow's Women* by Kathleen Odean. Copyright © 1997 by Kathleen Odean. Reproduced by permission of **Ballantine Books, a division of Random House, Inc., www.randomhouse.com.**

From "Making a Flying Fish" by Paula Morrow from *FACES': Happy Holidays*, vol. 7, no. 4, December 1990. Copyright © 1990 Cobblestone Publishing, 30 Grove Street, Suite C, Peterborough, NH 03458. All rights reserved. Reproduced by permission of **Carus Publishing Company.**

From "You're Under Arrest" from *Rosa Parks: My Story* by Rosa Parks with Jim Haskins. Copyright © 1992 by Rosa Parks. All rights reserved. Reproduced by permission of **Dial Books for Young Readers, an imprint of Penguin Putnam Books for Young Readers, a division of Penguin Group (USA) Inc.** and electronic format by permission of **Betsy Nolan Literary Agency.**

From "Let's Clean Up the Planet for Future Generations" by Tyler Duckworth from *Time for Kids Archive*, February 1, 1997. Copyright © 1997 by **Tyler Duckworth.** Reproduced by permission of the author.

From *Tuck Everlasting* by Natalie Babbitt. Copyright © 1975, renewed 2003 by Natalie Babbitt. Reproduced by permission of **Farrar, Straus and Giroux, LLC.**

From "Side View of Complex" from *Friends of Volunteers* Web site, at http://www.fov.org. Copyright © 1999 by **Friends of Volunteers, Inc.** Reproduced by permission of the publisher.

From "Volunteering - It's So Easy, a Kid Can Do It" by Liv Learner from *Girl Zone* Web site, at http://www.girlzone.com. Copyright © 1998 by **Girl Zone.** Reproduced by permission of the publisher.

From "The U.S. has a garbage crisis" from *The Environment: Distinguishing Between Fact and Opinion* by William Dudley. Copyright © 1990 by **Greenhaven Press, Inc.** Reproduced by permission of the publisher.

From "Picky-picky" from *Ramona Forever* by Beverly Cleary. Copyright © 1984 by Beverly Cleary. Reproduced by permission of **HarperCollins Publishers, Inc.**

From "Last Night I Dreamed of Chickens" from *Something Big Has Been Here* by Jack Prelutsky. Copyright © 1990 by Jack Prelutsky. Reproduced by permission of **HarperCollins Publishers, Inc.**

From *How TV Changed America's Mind* by Edward Wakin. Copyright © 1996 by Edward Wakin. Reproduced by permission of **HarperCollins Publishers, Inc.**

"April Rain Song" from *The Collected Poems of Langston Hughes* by Langston Hughes, edited by Arnold Rampersad with David Roessel, Associate Editor. Copyright © 1994 by The Estate of Langston Hughes. Reproduced by permission of **Alfred A. Knopf, Inc., a division of Random House, Inc.** and electronic format by permission by **Harold Ober Associates Incorporated.**

From "Whale Watch: Kids Use Internet to Track Progress of Newly Freed J. J." by Lisa Richardson from *Los Angeles Times: Orange County Edition*, April 3, 1998, Metro, p. 1. Copyright © 1998 by **Los Angeles Times.** Reproduced by permission of the publisher.

"Do Animals Think?" by Ellen Lambeth from *Ranger Rick*, vol. 31, issue 3, March 1997. Copyright © 1997 by **National Wildlife Federation.** Reproduced by permission of the publisher.

"Critter Crew" by Anna Mearns from *Ranger Rick*, vol. 27, no. 9, September 1993. Copyright © 1993 by **National Wildlife Federation.** Reproduced by permission of the publisher.

"Camel Fodder" from *The Subtleties of the Inimitable Mulla Nasrudin* by Idries Shah. Copyright © 1983 by **The Octagon Press, Ltd., London.** Reproduced by permission of the publisher.

From *DK Nature Encyclopedia*. Copyright © 1998 by Dorling Kindersley Ltd. All rights reserved. Reproduced by permission of **Penguin Books Ltd.**

From "The California Gold Rush" by Kathy Wilmore from *Junior Scholastic,* vol. 100, no. 8, December 1, 1997. Copyright © 1997 by **Scholastic Inc.** Reproduced by permission of the publisher.

From "Ta-Na-E-Ka" by Mary Whitebird from *Scholastic Voice,* December 13, 1973. Copyright © 1973 by **Scholastic Inc.** Reproduced by permission of the publisher.

"Foul Shot" by Edwin A. Hoey from *Read®.* Copyright © 1962 and renewed © 1989 by **Weekly Reader Corporation.** All rights reserved. Reproduced by permission of the publisher.

Entry for "cloud" from *Webster's New World™ College Dictionary, Fourth Edition.* Copyright © 1999, 2000 by Wiley Publishing, Inc., Reproduced by permission of **John Wiley & Sons, Inc.**

Entry for "Bears" from *Reader's Guide to Periodical Literature.* Copyright © 1999 by **The H. W. Wilson Company.** Reproduced by permission of the publisher.

SOURCES CITED:

Screen shot for "Grizzly fate" from *FirstSearch®* database at http://firstsearch.oclc.org. FirstSearch and WorldCat are registered trademarks of OCLC Online Computer Library Center, Incorporated.

From *The Pride of Puerto Rico: The Life of Roberto Clemente* by Paul Robert Walker. Published by Harcourt Brace & Company, Orlando, 1988.

From *Women Who Made America Great* by Harry Gersh. Published by HarperCollins Publishers, New York, 1962.

From "The Wild Plains Buffalo" from *The Buffalo Book* by David A. Dary. Published by Swallow Press/Ohio University Press, Athens, OH, 1989.

PHOTO CREDITS

TABLE OF CONTENTS: Page viii, SuperStock; ix, Rod Planck/Photo Researchers, Inc.; x, Image Copyright ©2001 PhotoDisc, Inc.; xi, H. Knaus/SuperStock; xii, Photograph by Franko Khoury, National Museum of African Art, Eliot Elisofon Photographic Archives, Smithsonian Institution; xiii, Mike Okoniewski/The Image Works; xv(t), Fred Bavendam/Peter Arnold, Inc.; xv(b), Egyptian National Museum, Cairo, Egypt/SuperStock; xvi, Carl Purcell/Photo Researchers, Inc.; xvii, Image Copyright ©2001 PhotoDisc, Inc.; xviii, M. K. Denny/Photo Edit.

PART OPENERS: Kazu Nitta/The Stock Illustration Source, Inc.

TAKING TESTS: Page 2, Rob Gage/Getty Images/Taxi; 4, Steve Kaufman/CORBIS; 7, Theo Allofs/CORBIS.

CHAPTER 1: Page 51, SuperStock; 55, Russel Dian/HRW Photo; 56, Comstock; 61, David Allen/CORBIS; 66, Spencer Swager/Tom Stack & Associates.

CHAPTER 2: Page 73, Orion Press, Japan; 75, Image Copyright ©2001 PhotoDisc, Inc.; 76, Bob Daugharty, AP/Wide World Photos; 82, Photograph by Franko Khoury, National Museum of African Art, Eliot Elisofon Photographic Archives, Smithsonian Institution; 85, China Tourism Press/The Image Bank/Getty Images; 88, Image Copyright ©2001 PhotoDisc, Inc.; 89, SuperStock; 93, Forrest J. Ackerman Collection/CORBIS.

CHAPTER 3: Page 98, Jerry Jacka Photography/Courtesy: The Heard Museum, Phoenix, Arizona; 101, Johnson Publishing Company, Inc.; 103, Bananastock/Jupiter Images; 104 (l), Sam Dudgeon/HRW; 104 (br), Dr. Ronald H. Cohn/The Gorilla Foundation/Koko.org; 107, Lionel Delvigne/Stock Boston; 119, Jonathan Nourak/Photo Edit.

CHAPTER 4: Page 131, Michael Newman/Photo Edit; 133 (c), Lowell Georgia/Photo Researchers, Inc.; 133 (br), Katherine Feng/Viesti Collection; 144, J. Lotter Gurling/Tom Stack & Associates; 145, Michele Burgess/Stock Boston; 149, Ellen Senisi/Photo Researchers, Inc.

CHAPTER 5: Page 163, H. Knaus/SuperStock; 167, Dana White/Photo Edit.

CHAPTER 6: Page 172 (bc), Bruce Davidson/Animals Animals; 174, CORBIS/W. Perry Conway; 180, Joe Viesti/Viesti Collection; 183, Bob Couey/Seaworld Inc. ©1998. All rights reserved. Reproduced by permission; 188, Image Copyright ©2001 PhotoDisc, Inc.; 191, Michael Pole/CORBIS.

CHAPTER 7: Page 196, Hampton University Museum, Hampton, Virginia; 203, Bettmann/CORBIS; 217, ©1997 Radlund & Associates for Artville; 221, AP/Wide World Photos/The Argus Press.

CHAPTER 8: Page 225, National Museum of American Art, Washington, D.C./Art Resource, New York; 229 (cr), Joe Jaworski/HRW; 229 (br), Mike Okoniewski /The Image Works; 236, Image Copyright ©2001 PhotoDisc, Inc.; 241, Spencer Grant/Photo Edit.

CHAPTER 9: Page 254 (bc), Giraudon/Art Resource, New York; 254 (br), Gianni Dagli Orti/CORBIS; 265, Bill Aron/Photo Edit.

CHAPTER 10: Page 274, Image Copyright ©2001 PhotoDisc, Inc.; 280 (br), Photo Image Technologies; 283, Mug Shots/CORBIS.

CHAPTER 11: Page 295, SuperStock; 304, Margaret Sulanowska/Woods Hole Oceanographic Institution; 307, Michelle Chaplow/CORBIS.

CHAPTER 12: Page 311 (tr), Carl Purcell/Photo Researchers, Inc.; 313, Michael Newman/Photo Edit; 319, Giraudon/Art Resource, New York; 324, Eastcott/Momatiuk/Animals Animals.

CHAPTER 13: Page 341 (tr), Clementine Hunter, (c.1945). Photo from the Mildred Bailey Collection, Mildred H. Bailey, Natchitoches, Louisiana; 347, Keystone/Sygma; 348, (cl), Rod Planck/Photo Researchers, Inc.; 348 (tr), Gordon and Cathy Illg/Animals Animals/Earth Scenes; 359, Digital Image copyright ©2004 PhotoDisc.

CHAPTER 14: Page 363, Aaron Horowitz/CORBIS; 368, Chris Brown/SIPA Press; 371, A. Ramey/Photo Edit; 376 (tl), T. Harmon Parkhurst/Courtesy Museum of New Mexico. #55189; 376 (br), Photo Edit; 380 (tl) (tr), Aaron Haupt/Photo Researchers, Inc.; 384 (cl), Werner Forman Archive/Museum für Völkerkunde, Berlin/Art Resource, New York; 387, AFP/CORBIS.

CHAPTER 15: Page 394, Richard Weiss/HRW; 401, News Office, Woods Hole Oceanographic Institution; 407, Fred Bavendam/Peter Arnold, Inc.; 413, Courtesy of Joe Rosenberg; 416, Robert Trippett/SIPA Press.

CHAPTER 16: Page 428, Jim Corwin/Stock Boston; 433, Image Copyright ©2001 PhotoDisc, Inc.; 434 (bl), Patti Murray/Animals Animals/Earth Scenes; 434 (bc), SuperStock; 434 (br), Toni Angermayer/Photo Researchers, Inc.; 436, Huntington Library/SuperStock; 437, Bettmann/CORBIS; 440, Zigmund Leszczynski/Animals Animals/Earth Scenes; 443, David Madison Sports Images, Inc.

CHAPTER 17: Page 446, Herb Scharfman/Sports Illustrated; 448, Corbis Images; 450, Hubertus Kanus/Photo Researchers, Inc.; 454, Allsport/Getty; 456, E. R. Degginger/Earth Scenes; 459 (tr), Image Copyright ©2001 PhotoDisc, Inc.; 459 (br), M. K. Denny/Photo Edit; 461, Robert & Linda Mitchell.